EDWARD B

THE BROWNING CYCLOPÆDIA

A GUIDE TO THE STUDY OF THE WORKS

OF

ROBERT BROWNING

WITH

COPIOUS EXPLANATORY NOTES AND REFERENCES
ON ALL DIFFICULT SUBJECTS

Elibron Classics
www.elibron.com

Elibron Classics series.

ISBN 0-543-94689-4 (paperback)
ISBN 0-543-94688-6 (hardcover)

This Elibron Classics Replica Edition is an unabridged facsimile
of the edition published in 1912 by George Allen & Company, Ltd., London;
the Macmillan Company, New York.

"The Browning Cyclopædia."

SOME OPINIONS OF THE PRESS ON THE FIRST EDITION.

"Conscientious and painstaking."—*The Times.*

"Obviously a most painstaking work, and in many ways it is very well done."—*Pall Mall Gazette.*

"In many ways a serviceable book, and deserves to be widely bought."—*The Speaker.*

"A book of far-reaching research and careful industry . . . will make his poet clearer, nearer, and dearer to every reader who systematically uses his book."—*Scotsman.*

"Dr. Berdoe is a safe and thoughtful guide; his work has evidently been a labour of love, and bears many marks of patient research."—*Echo.*

"Students of Browning will find it an invaluable aid."—*Graphic.*

"A work suggestive of immense industry."—*Morning Post.*

"Erudite and comprehensive."—*Glasgow Herald.*

"As a companion to Browning's works the Cyclopædia will be most valuable; it is a laborious, if necessary, piece of work, conscientiously performed, for which present and future readers and students of Browning ought to be really grateful."—*Nottingham Daily Guardian.*

"A monumental labour, and fitting company for the great compositions he elucidates."—*Rock.*

"It is very well that so patient and ubiquitous a reader as Dr. Berdoe should have written this useful cyclopædia, and cleared the meaning of many a dark and doubtful passage of the poet."—*Black and White.*

"It is not too much to say that Dr. Berdoe has earned the gratitude of every reader of Browning, and has materially aided the study of English literature in one of its ripest developments."—*British Weekly.*

"Dr. Berdoe's Cyclopædia should make all other handbooks unnecessary."—*Star.*

"We are happy to commend the volume to Browning students as the most ambitious and useful in its class yet executed."—*Notes and Queries.*

"A most learned and creditable piece of work. Not a difficulty is shirked."—*Vanity Fair.*

OPINIONS OF THE PRESS

(*Continued*).

"A monument of industry and devotion. It has really faced difficulties, it is conveniently arranged, and is well printed and bound."—*Bookman.*

"A wonderful help."—*Gentlewoman.*

"Can be strongly recommended as one for a favourite corner in one's library."—*Whitehall Review.*

"Exceedingly well done; its interest and usefulness, we think, may pass without question."—*Publishers' Circular.*

"In a singularly industrious and exhaustive manner he has set himself to make clear the obscure and to accentuate the beautiful in Robert Browning's poem . . . must have involved infinite labour and research. It cannot be doubted that the book will be widely sought for and warmly appreciated."—*Daily Telegraph.*

"Dr. Berdoe tackles every allusion, every proper name, every phase of thought, besides giving a most elaborate analysis of each poem. He has produced what we might almost call a monumental work."—*Literary Opinion.*

"This cyclopædia may certainly claim to be by a long way the most efficient aid to the study of Browning that has been published, or is likely to be published . . . Lovers of Browning will prize it highly, and all who wish to understand him will consult it with advantage."—*Baptist Magazine.*

"The work has evidently been one of love, and we doubt whether any one could have been found better qualified to undertake it."—*Cambridge Review.*

"All readers of Browning will feel indebted to Dr. Berdoe for his interesting accounts of the historical facts on which many of the dramas are based, and also for his learned dissertations on 'The Ring and the Book' and 'Sordello.'"—*British Medical Journal.*

"The work is so well done that no one is likely to think of doing it over again."—*The Critic* (New York).

"This work reflects the greatest credit on Dr. Berdoe and on the Browning Society, of which he is so distinguished a member,—it is simply invaluable."—*The Hawk.*

"The Cyclopædia has at any rate brought his (Browning's) best work well within the compass of all serious readers of intelligence—Browning made easy."—*The Month.*

THE BROWNING CYCLOPÆDIA.

By the Same Author.

BROWNING'S MESSAGE TO HIS TIME. His Religion, Philosophy, and Science. With Portrait and Facsimile Letters. Fifth edition, price *2s. 6d.*

OPINIONS OF THE PRESS.

"Full of admiration and sympathy."—*Saturday Review.*

"Much that is helpful and suggestive."—*Scotsman.*

"Should have a wide circulation, it is interesting and stimulative."—*Literary World.*

"It is the work of one who, having gained good himself, has made it his endeavour to bring the same good within the reach of others, and, as such, it deserves success."—*Cambridge Review.*

"We have no hesitation in strongly recommending this little volume to any who desire to understand the moral and mental attitude of Robert Browning. . . . We are much obliged to Dr. Berdoe for his volume."—*Oxford University Herald.*

"Cannot fail to be of assistance to new readers."—*Morning Post.*

"The work of a faithful and enthusiastic student is here."—*Nation.*

THE

BROWNING CYCLOPÆDIA

A GUIDE TO THE STUDY OF THE WORKS

OF

ROBERT BROWNING

WITH

Copious Explanatory Notes and References on all Difficult Passages

BY

EDWARD BERDOE

LICENTIATE OF THE ROYAL COLLEGE OF PHYSICIANS, EDINBURGH; MEMBER OF THE ROYAL COLLEGE OF SURGEONS, ENGLAND, ETC., ETC.

Author of "Browning's Message to his Time," "Browning as a Scientific Poet," etc., etc.

LONDON

GEORGE ALLEN & COMPANY, LTD.

RUSKIN HOUSE

44 & 45 RATHBONE PLACE

NEW YORK: THE MACMILLAN COMPANY

1912

First Edition, *December*, 1891; Second Edition, *September*, 1897; Third Edition, *July*, 1898; Fourth Edition, *March*, 1902. Fifth Edition, 1906; Sixth Edition, 1909; Seventh Edition, 1912.

I gratefully Dedicate these pages

TO

DR. F. J. FURNIVALL

AND

MISS E. H. HICKEY,

THE FOUNDERS OF

THE BROWNING SOCIETY.

PREFACE TO THE SECOND EDITION.

THE demand for a second edition of this work within three months of its publication is a sufficient proof that such a book meets a want, notwithstanding the many previous attempts of a more or less partial character which have been made to explain Browning to "the general." With the exception of certain superfine reviewers, to whom nothing is obscure—except such things as they are asked to explain without previous notice—every one admits that Browning requires more or less elucidation. It is said by some that I have explained too much, but this might be said of most commentaries, and certainly of every dictionary. It is difficult to know precisely where to draw the line. If I am not to explain (say for lady readers) what is meant by the phrase "*De te fabula narratur*," I know not why any of the classical quotations should be translated. If Browning is hard to understand, it must be on account of the obscurity of his language, of his thought, or the purport of his verses; very often the objection is made that the difficulty applies to all these. I have not written for the "learned," but for the people at large. *The Manchester Guardian*, in a kindly notice of my book, says "the error and marvel of his book is the supposition that any cripple who can only be crutched by it into an understanding of Browning will ever understand Browning at all." There are many readers, however, who understand Browning a little, and I hope that this book will enable them to understand him a great deal more: though all cripples cannot be turned into athletes, some undeveloped persons may be helped to achieve feats of strength.

A word concerning my critics. No one can do me a greater service than by pointing out mistakes and omissions in this work. I cannot hope to please everybody, but I will do my best to make future editions as perfect as possible.

E. B.

March 1892.

PREFACE.

I MAKE no apology for the publication of this work because some such book has long been a necessity to any one who seriously proposes to study Browning Up to its appearance there was no single book to which the reader could turn, which gave an exposition of the leading ideas of every poem, its key-note, the sources—historical, legendary, or fanciful—to which the poem was due, and a glossary of every difficult word or allusion which might obscure the sense to such readers as had short memories or scanty reading. It would be affectation to pretend to believe that every educated person ought to know, without the aid of such a work as this, what Browning means by phrases and allusions which may be found by hundreds in his works. The wisest reader cannot be expected to remember, even if he has ever learned, a host of remote incidents in Italian history, for example, to say nothing of classical terms which "every schoolboy" ought to know, but rarely does. Browning is obscure, undoubtedly, if a poem is read for the first time without any hint as to its main purport: the meaning in almost every case lies more or less below the surface;

the superficial idea which a careless perusal of the poem would afford is pretty sure to be the wrong one. Browning's poetry is intended to make people think, and without thought the fullest commentary will not help the reader much. "I can have little doubt," said the poet, in his preface to the First Series of *Selections* from his works, "that my writing has been in the main too hard for many I should have been pleased to communicate with; but I never designedly tried to puzzle people, as some of my critics have supposed. On the other hand, I never pretended to offer such literature as should be a substitute for a cigar or a game at dominoes to an idle man. So, perhaps, on the whole, I get my deserts, and something over—not a crowd, but a few I value more." As for my own qualifications for the task I have undertaken, I can only say that I have attended nearly every meeting of the Browning Society from its inauguration; I have read every book, paper, and article upon Browning on which I could lay my hands, have gone over every line of the poet's works again and again, have asked the assistance of literary friends in every difficulty, and have pegged away at the obscurities till they *seemed* (at any rate) to vanish. It is possible that a scientific education in some considerable degree assists a man who addresses himself to a task of this sort: a medical man does not like to be beaten by any difficulty which common perseverance can conquer; when one has spent days in tracing a nerve thread through the body to its origin, and through all its ramifications, a few visits to the library of the British Museum, or a few hours' puzzling over the meaning of a difficult passage in a poem, do not deter him from solving a mystery,—and this is all I can claim. I have not shirked any obscurities; unlike some commentators of the old-fashioned sort, who in dealing with the Bible carefully told us that a score meant twenty, but said nothing as to the meaning of the verse in Ezekiel's dream about the women who wept for Tammuz—but have honestly tried to help my readers in every case where they have a right to ask such aid. Probably I have overlooked many things which I ought to have explained. It is not less certain that some will say I have explained much that they already knew. I can only ask for a merciful judgment in either case. I am quite anxious to be set right in every particular in which I may be wrong, and shall be grateful for hints and suggestions concerning anything which is not clear. I have to thank Professor Sonnenschein for permission to publish his valuable Notes to *Sordello*, with several articles on the history of the Guelf and Ghibelline leaders: these are all indicated by the initial [S.] at the end of each note or article. I am grateful also to Mr. A. J. Campbell for permission to use his notes on Rabbi Ben Ezra. I have also to thank Dr. Furnivall, Miss Frances Power Cobbe, and the Very Rev. Canon Akers, M.A., for their kindness in helping me on certain difficult points which came within their lines of study. It would be impossible to read the works of commentators on Browning for the years which I have devoted to the task without imbibing the opinions and often insensibly adopting the phraseology of the authors: if in any case I have used the ideas and language of other writers without acknowledging them, I hope it will be credited to the infirmity of human nature, and not attributed to any wilful appropriation of other men's and women's literary valuables. As for the poet himself, I have largely used his actual words and phrases in putting his ideas into plain prose; it has not always been possible, for reasons which every one will understand, to put quotation marks to every few words or portions of lines where this has occurred. When, therefore, a beautiful thought is expressed in appropriate language, it is most certainly not mine, but Browning's. My only aim has been to bring the Author of the vast body of literature to which this book is an introduction a little nearer to the English and American reading public; my own opinions and criticisms I have endeavoured as much as possible to suppress. In the words of Dr. Furnivall, "This is a business book," and simply as such I offer it to the public.

EDWARD BERDOE.

LONDON, *November 28th*, 1891.

BOOKS, ESSAYS, ETC., WHICH ARE ESPECIALLY USEFUL TO THE BROWNING STUDENT.

BIOGRAPHICAL WORKS.

Life of Robert Browning. By MRS. SUTHERLAND ORR. London: 1891.

Life of Robert Browning. By WILLIAM SHARP. London: 1890.

On the whole, Mr. Sharp's Biography will be found the more useful for the student. It contains an excellent Bibliography by Mr. John P. Anderson of the British Museum, and a Chronological List of the Poet's Works.

Robert Browning: Chief Poet of the Age. By W. G. KINGSLAND. London: 1890. Excellent for beginners.

Robert Browning: Personalia. By EDMUND GOSSE. Boston: 1890.

WORKS OF CRITICISM AND EXPOSITION.

Robert Browning: Essays and Thoughts. By JOHN T. NETTLESHIP. London: 1868. Artistic and suggestive.

Stories from Robert Browning. By F. M. HOLLAND; with Introduction by MRS. SUTHERLAND ORR. London: 1882.

A Handbook to the Works of Robert Browning. By MRS. SUTHERLAND ORR. London: 1885.

An Introduction to the Study of Browning. By ARTHUR SYMONS. London: 1886. Intensely sympathetic and appreciative.

A Bibliography of Robert Browning, from 1833 to 1881. By DR. F. J. FURNIVALL. 1881.

An Introduction to the Study of Robert Browning's Poetry. By HIRAM CORSON. Boston: 1888.

Studies in the Poetry of Robert Browning. By JAMES FOTHERINGHAM. London: 1887.

Browning Guide Book. By GEORGE WILLIS COOKE. Boston: 1891.

Strafford: a Tragedy. With Notes and Preface, by E. H. HICKEY, and Introduction by S. R. GARDINER. London: 1884.

Browning and the Christian Faith. The Evidences of Christianity from Browning's Point of View. By EDWARD BERDOE. London: 1896.

Browning as a Philosophical Religious Teacher. By Prof. HENRY JONES. Glasgow: 1891.

Browning's Message to His Time: His Religion, Philosophy and Science. By EDWARD BERDOE. London: 1890.

THE BROWNING SOCIETY'S PUBLICATIONS.

The Browning Society's Papers, Part I. Vol. I., 1881-4, pp. 1-116 (*presented by Dr. Furnivall*). [1881-2.

1. A Reprint of BROWNING's Introductory Essay to the 25 spurious *Letters of Percy Bysshe Shelley*, 1852: On the Objective and Subjective Poet, on the Relation of the Poet's Life to his Work; on Shelley, his Nature, Art, and Character.
2. A Bibliography of ROBERT BROWNING, 1833-81: Alphabetical and Chronological Lists of his Works, with Reprints of discontinued Prefaces, of *Ben Karshook's Wisdom*, partial collations of *Sordello* 1840, 1863, and *Paracelsus* 1835, 1863, etc., and with Trial-Lists of the Criticisms on BROWNING, Personal Notices of him, etc., by F. J. FURNIVALL.

The Browning Society's Papers, Part II. Vol. I., 1881-4, pp. 117-258. [1881-2.

3. Additions to the Bibliography of R. BROWNING, by F. J. FURNIVALL. 1. Browning's Acted Plays. 2. Fresh Entries of Criticisms on Browning's Works. 3. Fresh Personal Notices of Browning. 4. Notes on Browning's Poems and my Bibliography. 5. Short Index.
4. Mr. KIRKMAN's Address at the Inaugural Meeting of the Society, October 28th, 1881.
5. Mr. SHARPE's Paper on "*Pietro of Abano*," *and* "*Dramatic Idyls*, Series II."
6. Mr. NETTLESHIP's *Analysis and Sketch of* "*Fifine at the Fair.*"
7. Mr. NETTLESHIP's Classification of Browning's Poems.
8. Mrs. ORR's Classification of Browning's Poems.
9. Mr. JAMES THOMSON's Notes on *The Genius of Robert Browning.*
10. Mr. ERNEST RADFORD on *The Moorish Front to the Duomo of Florence, in* "*Luria,*" I., pp. 122-132.

11. Mr. ERNEST RADFORD on *The Original of "Ned Bratt's" Dramatic Lyrics*, I., pp. 107-43.
12. Mr. SHARPE'S Analysis and Summary of *Fifine at the Fair.*

The Browning Society's Papers, Part III. Vol. I., 1881-4, pp. 259-380, with *Abstract*, pp. 1*-48*. [1882-3.

13. Mr. BURY on *Browning's Philosophy.*
14. Prof. JOHNSON on *Bishop Blougram.*
15. Prof. CORSON on *Personality, and Art as its Vice-agent, as treated by Browning.*
16. Miss BEALE on *The Religious Teaching of Browning.*
17. *A Short Account of the Abbé Vogler ("Abt Vogler").* By Miss E. MARX.
18. Prof. JOHNSON on *Science and Art in Browning.*

The *Monthly Abstract* of such papers as have not been printed in full, and of the Discussions on all that have been discussed. Nos. I.—X.

Illustrations to Browning's Poems. Part I.: Photographs of (*a*) Andrea del Sarto's Picture of Himself and his Wife, in the Pitti Palace, Florence, which suggested Browning's poem *Andrea del Sarto;* (*b*) Fra Lippo Lippi's 'Coronation of the Virgin,' in the Accademia delle belle Arti, Florence (the painting described at the end of Browning's *Fra Lippo*); and (*c*) Guercino's 'Angel and Child,' at Fano (for *The Guardian Angel*); with an Introduction by ERNEST RADFORD. [1882-3.

Illustrations to Browning's Poems. Part II.* (*d*) A photo-engraving of Mr. C. Fairfax Murray's drawing of Andrea del Sarto's Picture named above. (*e*) A Woodburytype copy of Fredelle's Cabinet Photograph of ROBERT BROWNING in three sizes, to bind with the Society's *Illustrations*, and *Papers*, and Browning's *Poems:* presented by Mrs. Sutherland Orr. (*f*) Reductions in fcap. 8vo, to bind with Browning's *Poems*, of *d, b, c,* above, and of (*g*) the engraving of Guercino's First Sketch for his "Angel and Child." [1882-3.

The Browning Society's Papers, Part IV. Vol. I., 1881-4, pp. 381-476, with *Abstract*, pp. 49*-84* and *Reports*, i-xvi. [1883-4.

* Out of print at present.

19. Mr. NETTLESHIP on *Browning's Intuition, specially in regard to Music and the Plastic Arts.*
20. Prof. B. F. WESTCOTT on *Some Points in Browning's View of Life.*
21. Miss E. D. WEST on *One Aspect of Browning's Villains.*
22. Mr. REVELL on *Browning's Poems on God and Immortality as bearing on Life here.*
23. The Rev. H. J. BULKELEY on *"James Lee's Wife."*
24. Mrs. TURNBULL on *"Abt Vogler."*

The *Monthly Abstract* of the Proceedings of Meetings Eleven to Eighteen.

First and Second Reports of the Committee (1881-2 and 1882-3).

The Browning Society's Papers, Part V. Vol. I., 1881-4, pp. 477-502, with *Abstract* and *Notes and Queries*, pp. 85*-153*, and *Report*, pp. xvii-xxiii. [1884-5,

25. Mr. W. A. RALEIGH on *Some Prominent Points in Browning's Teaching.*
26. Mr. J. COTTER MORISON on *"Caliban on Setebos," with some Notes on Browning's Subtlety and Humour.*
27. Mrs. TURNBULL on *"In a Balcony."*

The *Monthly Abstract* of the Proceedings of Meetings Nineteen to Twenty-six, including "Scraps" contributed by Members.

Third Report of the Committee, 1883-4.

Illustration, Part III. Presented by Sir F. Leighton, P.R.A., etc., Vice-President of the Browning Society. A Woodburytype Engraving of Sir Frederick Leighton's picture (in the possession of Sir Bernhard Samuelson, Bart., M.P.) of "Hercules contending with Death for the Body of Alkestis" (*Balaustion's Adventure*).

[**Part VI.** of the Browning Society's Papers, a Second Supplement to Parts I. and II., with illustrations, is in the press.]

The Browning Society's Papers, Part VII. Vol. II., 1885-90, (being Part I. of Vol. II.), pp. 1-54, with *Abstract* and *Notes and Queries*, 1*-88*, i.-viii., and Appendix, 1-16. [1885-6.

28. Mr. ARTHUR SYMONS' Paper, *Is Browning Dramatic?*
29. Prof. E. JOHNSON on *"Mr. Sludge the Medium."*
30. Dr. BERDOE on *Browning as a Scientific Poet.*

* Out of print at present.

The *Monthly Abstract* of Proceedings of Meetings Twenty-seven to Thirty-three; *Notes and Queries, etc.; Fourth Annual Report;* Programme of the Annual Entertainment at Prince's Hall, etc.

The Browning Society's Papers, Part VIII. Vol. II., 1885-90, pp. 55-146, with *Abstract* and *Notes and Queries*, 89*-164*, and Report i-vii. [1886-7.

31. Mr. J. T. NETTLESHIP on *The Development of Browning's Genius in his Capacity as Poet or Maker.*
32. Mr. J. B. BURY on "*Aristophanes' Apology.*"
33. Mr. OUTRAM on *The Avowal of Valence* (*Colombe's Birthday*).
34. Mr. ALBERT FLEMING on "*Andrea del Sarto.*"
35. Mr. HOWARD S. PEARSON on *Browning as a Landscape Painter.*
36. Rev. H. J. BULKELEY on *The Reasonable Rhythm of some of Mr. Browning's Poems.*
37. Prof. C. H. HERFORD on "*Hohenstiel-Schwangau.*"

Abstracts of all Meetings held, *Notes and Queries, Fifth Annual Report, etc.*

Reprint of the First Edition of Browning's *Pauline.* [1886-7.

The Browning Society's Papers, Part IX. (being Part III. of Vol. II.). [1887-8.

38. Dr. TODHUNTER on *The Performance of* "*Strafford.*"
39. Mrs. GLAZEBROOK on "*A Death in the Desert.*"
40. Dr. FURNIVALL on *A Grammatical Analysis of* "*O Lyric Love.*"
41. Mr. ARTHUR SYMONS on "*Parleyings with Certain People.*"
42. Miss HELEN ORMEROD on *The Musical Poems of Browning.*

Abstracts of all Meetings held, *Notes and Queries, Sixth Annual Report, etc.*

The Browning Society's Papers, Part X. (being Part IV. of Vol. II.). [1888-9.

43. Mr. REVELL on *Browning's Views of Life.*
44. Dr. BERDOE on *Browning's Estimate of Life.*
45. Prof. BARNETT on *Browning's Jews and Shakespeare's Jew.*
46. Miss HELEN ORMEROD on *Abt Vogler, the Man.*
47. Miss C. M. WHITEHEAD on *Browning as a Teacher of the Nineteenth Century.*
48. Miss STODDART on "*Saul.*"

Abstracts of all Meetings held, *Notes and Queries, Seventh Annual Report, etc.*

* Out of print at present.

The Browning Society's Papers, Part XI. (being Part V. of Vol. II.). [1889-90.

49. Dr. BERDOE on *Paracelsus: the Reformer of Medicine.*
50. Miss HELEN ORMEROD on *Andrea del Sarto and Abt Vogler.*
51. Rev. W. ROBERTSON on "*La Saisiaz.*"
52. Mr. J. B. OLDHAM on *The Difficulties and Obscurities encountered in a Study of Browning's Poems.*
53. Mr. J. KING, Jun., on "*Prince Hohenstiel-Schwangau.*"
54. Mrs. ALEXANDER IRELAND on "*A Toccata of Galuppi's.*"
55. Mrs. GLAZEBROOK on "*Numpholeptos and Browning's Women.*"
56. Rev. J. J. G. GRAHAM on *The Wife-love and Friend-love of Robert Browning.*

Abstracts of all Meetings held, *Notes and Queries, Eighth Annual Report, etc.*

The Browning Society's Papers, Part XII. (being Part I. of Vol. III.). [1890-91.

57. Prof. ALEXANDER'S *Analysis of* "*Sordello.*"
58. Dr. FURNIVALL on *Robert Browning's Ancestors.*
59. Mrs. IRELAND on *Browning's Treatment of Parenthood.*
60. Mr. SAGAR on *The Line-numbering, etc., in* "*The Ring and th Book.*"
61. Mr. REVELL on *The Value of Browning's Work* (Part I.).
62. Mr. W. M. ROSSETTI on "*Taurello Salinguerra.*"

List of Some of the Periodicals in which Notices of Robert Browning have appeared since his Death.

Abstracts of all Meetings held, *Notes and Queries, Ninth Annual Report, etc.*

The Browning Society's Papers, Part XIII. (being Part II. of Vol. III., 1890-93). [1891-92.

63. Mrs. A. IRELAND on "*Christina and Monaldeschi.*"
64. JÓN STEFÁNSSON, M.A., on *How Browning Strikes a Scandinavian.*
65. W. F. REVELL, Esq., on *Browning's Work in Relation to Life* (Part II.).
66. J. B. OLDHAM, B.A., on *Browning's Dramatic Method in Narrative.*
67. R. G. MOULTON, M.A., on *Browning's* "*Balaustion*" *a beautiful Perversion of Euripides'* "*Alcestis.*"

Abstracts of all Meetings held, *Notes and Queries, Tenth Annual Report, etc.*

CHRONOLOGICAL LIST OF WORKS, Etc.

1812. Robert Browning born at Camberwell on May 7th. He "went to the Rev. Thos. Ready's school at Peckham till he was near fourteen, then had a private tutor at home, and attended some lectures at the London University, now University College, London" (Dr. Furnivall).

1833. *Pauline* published.

1834. Browning travelled in Russia.

1835. *Paracelsus* published.

1836. *Porphyria*, *Johannes Agricola*, *The King*, and the lines "Still ailing wind" in *James Lee* published by Mr. W. J. Fox in his magazine *The Monthly Repository*.

1837. *Strafford* published.

1840. *Sordello* published.

1841-6. *Bells and Pomegranates* appeared.

1841. *Pippa Passes* published.

1842. *King Victor and King Charles* published.
Dramatic Lyrics published.

1843. *The Return of the Druses* published.
A Blot in the 'Scutcheon published.

1844. *Colombe's Birthday* published.

1845. *The Tomb at St. Praxed's* published in *Hood's Magazine*, March.
The Flight of the Duchess published.
Dramatic Romances and Lyrics published.

1846. *Lucia* published.
A Soul's Tragedy published.
Robert Browning married (34), Sept. 12th, at St. Mary-le-bone parish church our greatest poetess, Elizabeth Barrett, aged 37 (Dr. Furnivall).

1847. The Brownings resident in Florence.

1849. March 9th, Robert Wiedemann Barrett Browning born.
Browning's Poems published in two vols.

1850. *Christmas-Eve and Easter-Day* published.

1852. Browning writes the Introductory Essay to the Shelley (spurious) Letters.

1855. *Men and Women* published.
The Brownings travel to Normandy.

1861. June 28th, Mrs. Browning died at Casa Guidi.

1863. *The Poetical Works* of Robert Browning published in three vols.

1864. *Dramatis Personæ* published.

1868. *The Poetical Works* published in six vols.

1868-9. *The Ring and the Book* published.

1871. *Hervé Riel* published in the *Cornhill Magazine*.
Balaustion's Adventure published.
Prince Hohenstiel-Schwangau published.

1872. *Fifine at the Fair* published.

1873. *Red Cotton Night-Cap Country* published.

1875. *Aristophanes' Apology* published.
The Inn Album published.

1876. *Pacchiarotto* published.

1877. *The Agamemnon of Æschylus* published.

1878. *La Saisiaz* published.
The Two Poets of Croisic published.

1879. *Dramatic Idyls* published.

1880. *Dramatic Idyls* (*Second Series*) published.

1881. The Browning Society inaugurated, Oct. 28th.

1883. *Jocoseria* published.

1884. *Ferishtah's Fancies* published.

1887. *Parleyings with Certain People of Importance in their Day* published.

1889. *Asolando: Fancies and Facts*, published.
Robert Browning died in Venice, December 12th; buried in Westminster Abbey, December 31st.

BROWNING CYCLOPÆDIA.

Abano, a town of Northern Italy, 6 miles S.W. of Padua, the birthplace of PIETRO D'ABANO *(q.v.)*.

Abate, Paolo (or Paul), brother of Count Guido Franceschini. He was a priest residing in Rome. (*Ring and the Book.*)

Abbas I., surnamed THE GREAT. *See* SHAH ABBAS.

Abd-el-Kader, a celebrated Algerian warrior, born in 1807, who in 1831 led the combined tribes in their attempt to resist the progress of the French in Algeria. He surrendered to the French in 1847, and was set at liberty by Louis Napoleon in 1852. (*Through the Metidja to Abd-el-Kader.*)

Abt Vogler. [THE MAN.] (*Dramatis Personæ*, 1864.) George Joseph Vogler, usually known as Abbé Vogler, or, as Mr. Browning has called him, Abt Vogler, was an organist and composer, and was born at Würzburg, June 15th, 1749. He was educated for the Church from his very early years, as is the custom with Catholics; but every opportunity was taken to develop his musical talents, which were so marked that at ten years old he could play the organ and the violin well. In 1769 he studied at Bamberg, removing thence in 1771 to Mannheim. In 1773 he was ordained priest in Rome, and was admitted to the famous Academy of Arcadia, was made a Knight of the Golden Spur, and was appointed protonotary and chamberlain to the Pope. He returned to Mannheim in 1775, and opened a School of Music. He published several works on music, composition, and the art of forming the voice. He was made chaplain and *Kapellmeister* at Mannheim, and about this time composed a *Miserere*. In 1779 Vogler went to Munich. In 1780 he composed an opera, *The Merchant of Smyrna*, a ballet, and a melodrama. In 1781 his opera *Albert III.* was produced at the Court Theatre of Munich. As it was not very favourably received, he resigned his posts of chaplain and choirmaster. He was severely criticised by German musical critics, and Mozart spoke of him with much bitterness. Having thus failed in his own country, he went to Paris, and in 1783 brought out his comic opera, *La Kermesse*. It was so great a failure that it was not possible to conclude the performance. He then travelled in Spain, Greece, and the East. In 1786 he returned to Europe, and went to Sweden, and was appointed *Kapellmeister* to the King. At Stockholm he founded his second School of Music, and became famous by his performances on an instrument which he had invented, called the "Orchestrion." This is described by Mr. G. Grove as a very compact organ, in which four keyboards of five octaves each, and a pedal board of thirty-six keys, with swell complete, were packed into a cube of nine feet. In 1789 Vogler performed without success at Amsterdam. He then went with his organ to London, and gave a series of concerts at the Pantheon in January 1790. These proved eminently successful: Vogler realised over £1200, and made a name as an organist. He seems to have excelled in pedal playing, but it is not true that pedals were unknown in England until the Abbé introduced them. "His most popular pieces," says the *Encyclopædia Britannica*, "were a fugue on themes from the 'Hallelujah Chorus,' composed after a visit to the Handel festival at Westminster Abbey, and on 'A Musical Picture for the Organ,' by Knecht, containing the imitation of a storm. In 1790 Vogler returned to Germany, and met with the most brilliant receptions at Coblentz and Frankfort, and at Esslingen was presented with the 'wine of honour' reserved usually for royal personages. At Mannheim, in 1791, his opera *Castor and Pollux* was performed, and became very popular. We find him henceforward travelling all over Europe. At Berlin he performed in 1800, at Vienna in 1804, and at Munich in 1806. Next year we find him at Darmstadt, accepting by the invitation of the Grand Duke Louis I. the post of *Kapellmeister*. He opened his third school of music at Darmstadt, one of his pupils being Weber, another Meyerbeer, a third Gänsbacher. The affection of these three young students for their master was 'unbounded.' He was indefatigable in the pursuit of his art to the last, genial, kind and pleasant to all; he lived for music, and died in harness, of apoplexy, at Darmstadt, May 6th, 1814."

[THE POEM.] The musician has been extemporising on his organ, and as the performance in its beauty and completeness impresses his mind with wonderful and mysterious imagery, he wishes it could be permanent. He has created something, but it has vanished. He compares it to a palace built of sweet sounds, such a structure as angels or demons might have reared for Solomon, a magic building wherein to lodge some loved princess, a palace more beautiful than anything which human architect could plan or power of man construct. His music structure has been real to him, it took shape in his brain, it was his creation: surely, somewhere, somehow, it might be permanent. It was too beautiful, too perfect to be lost. Only the evil perishes, only good is permanent; and this music was so true, so good, so beautiful, it could not be that it was lost, as false, bad, ugly things are lost! But Vogler was but an extemporiser, and such musicians cannot give permanence to their performances. He has reached a state almost of ecstasy, and the spiritual has asserted its power over the material, raising the soul to heaven and bringing down heaven to earth. In the words of Milton, he had become—

> "All ear,
> And took in strains that might create a soul
> Under the ribs of death,"

and in this heavenly rapture he saw strange presences, the forms of the better to come, or "the wonderful Dead who have passed through the body and gone." The other arts are inferior to music, they are more human, more material than music,—"here is the finger of God." And this was all to go—"Never to be again!" This reflection starts the poet on a familiar train of thought—the permanence of good, the impermanence, the nullity of evil. The Cabbalists taught that evil was only the shadow of the Light; Maimonides, Spinoza, Hegel and Emerson taught the doctrine which Mr. Browning here inculcates. Leibnitz speaks of "evil as a mere set-off to the good in the world, which it increases by contrast, and at other times reduces moral to metaphysical evil by giving it a merely negative existence." "God," argued Aquinas (*Sum. Theol.*, i., § 49), "created everything that exists, but Sin was *nothing*; so God was not the Author of it." So, Augustine and Peter Lombard maintained likewise the negative nature of moral evil:—

> "Evil is more frail than nonentity."
>
> (Proclus, *De Prov.*, in Cory's *Fragm.*)

"Let no one therefore say that there are precedaneous productive principles of evil in the nature of intellectual paradigms of evil in the same manner as there are of good, or that there is a malefic soul or an evil-producing cause in the gods, nor let him introduce sedition or eternal war against the First God" (Proclus, *Six Books*, trans. Thomas Taylor, B. i., c. 27). In heaven, then, we are to find "the perfect round," "the broken arcs" are all we can discover here. Rising in the tenth stanza to the highest stature of the philosophical truth, the poet proclaims his faith in the existence of a home of pure ideals. The harmony of a few bars of music on earth suggests the eternal harmonies of the Author of order; the rays of goodness which brighten our path here suggest a Sun of Righteousness from which they emanate. The lover and the bard send up to God their feeble aspirations after the beautiful and the true, and these aspirations are stored in His treasury. Failure? It is but the pause in the music, the discords that set off the harmony. To the musician this is not something to be reasoned about mathematically; it is knowledge, it is a revelation which, however informing and consoling while it lasts, must not too long divert a man from the common things of life; patient to bear and suffer because strengthened by the beautiful vision of the Mount of Transfiguration, proud that he has been permitted to have part and lot with such high matters, he can solemnly acquiesce in the common round and daily task. He feels for the common chord, descends the mount, gliding by semitones, glancing back at the heights he is leaving, till at last, finding his true resting-place in the C Major of this life, soothed and sweetly lulled by the heavenly harmonies, he falls asleep. The Esoteric system of the Cabbalah was largely the outcome of Neo-Platonism and Gnosticism, and from these have sprung the theosophy of Meister Eckhart and Jacob Boehme. It is certain that Mr. Browning was a student of the latter "theosophist" *par excellence*. In his poem *Transcendentalism* he refers to the philosopher by name, and there are evidences that the poet's mind was deeply tinctured with his ideas. The influence of Paracelsus on Boehme's mind is conspicuous in his works, and the sympathy with that great medical reformer which the poem of *Paracelsus* betrays on every page was no doubt largely due to Boehme's teaching. The curious blending of theosophy and science which is found in the poem of *Paracelsus* is not a less faithful picture of Mr. Browning's philosophical system than of that of his hero. Professor Andrew Seth, in the article on theosophy in the *Encyclopædia Britannica*, thus expounds Boehme's speculation on evil: it turns "upon the necessity of reconciling the existence and the might of evil with the existence of an all-embracing and all-powerful God. . . . He faces the difficulty boldly—he insists on the necessity of the Nay to the Yea, of the negative to the positive." Eckhart seems to have largely influenced Boehme. We have in this poem what has been aptly called "the richest, deepest, fullest poem on music in the language." (Symons.) Mr. Browning was a thorough musician himself, and no poet ever wrote what the musician felt till he penned the wonderful music-poems *Abt Vogler*, *Master Hugues of Saxe Gotha* and *A Toccata of Galuppi's*. The comparison between music and architecture is as old as it is beautiful. Amphion built the walls of Thebes to the sound of his lyre —fitting the stones together by the power of his music, and "Ilion's towers," they say, "rose with life to Apollo's song." The "Keeley Motor" was an attempt in this direction. Coleridge, too, in *Kubla Khan*, with "music loud and long would build that dome in air." In the May 1891 number of the *Century Magazine* there is a very curious and a very interesting account by Mrs. Watts Hughes of certain "Voice-figures" which have lately excited so much interest in scientific and musical circles. "By a simple method figures of sounds are produced which remain permanent. On a thin indiarubber membrane, stretched across the bottom of a tube of sufficient diameter for the purpose, is poured a small quantity of water or some denser liquid, such as glycerine; and into this liquid are sprinkled a few grains of some ordinary solid pigment. A note of music is then sung down the tube by Mrs. Watts Hughes, and immediately the atoms of suspended pigment arrange themselves in a definite form, many of the forms bearing a curious resemblance to some of the most beautiful objects in Nature—flowers, shells, or trees. After the note has ceased to sound the forms remain, and the pictorial representations given in the *Century* show how wonderfully accurate is the lovely mimicry of the image-making music." (*Spectator*, May 16th, 1891.) The thought of some soul of permanence behind the transience of music, provided the motive of Adelaide Procter's *Lost Chord.* In the *Idylls of the King* Lord Tennyson says—

"The city is built
To music, therefore never built at all,
And therefore built for ever."

Cardinal Newman, too, as the writer in the *Spectator* points out, expresses the same thought in his Oxford sermon, "The Theory of Development in Christian Doctrine." The preacher said: "Take another example of an outward and earthly form of economy, under which great wonders unknown seem to be typified—I mean musical sounds, as they are exhibited most perfectly in instrumental harmony. There are seven notes in the scale: make them fourteen; yet what a slender outfit for so vast an enterprise! What science brings so much out of so little? Out of what poor elements does some great master create his new world! Shall we say that all this exuberant inventiveness is a mere ingenuity or trick of art, like some fashion of the day, without reality, without meaning? . . . Is it possible that inexhaustible evolution and disposition of notes, so rich yet so simple, so intricate yet so regulated, so various yet so majestic, should be a mere sound which is gone and perishes? Can it be that those mysterious stirrings of heart, and keen emotions, and strange yearnings after we know not what, and awful impressions from we know not whence, should be wrought in us by what is unsubstantial, and comes and goes, and begins and ends in itself? It is not so! It cannot be."

NOTES.—STANZA I. "*Solomon willed.*" Jewish legend gave Solomon sovereignty over the demons and a lordship over the powers of Nature. In the Moslem East these fables have found a resting-place in much of its literature, from the Koran onwards. Solomon was thought to have owed his power over the spiritual world to the possession of a seal on which the "most great name of God was engraved" (see Lane, *Arabian Nights*, Introd., note 21, and chap. i., note 15). In Eastern philosophy, the "Upādana" or the intense desire produces WILL, and it is the *will* which develops *force*, and the latter generates *matter*, or an object having form" (see *Isis Unveiled*, Blavatsky, vol. ii., p. 320). "*Pile him a palace.*" Goethe called architecture "petrified music." "*The ineffable Name*": the unspeakable name of God. Jehovah is the European transcription of the sacred tetragrammaton יהוה. The later Jews substituted the word Adonai in reading the ineffable Name in their law and prayers. Mysterious names of the Deity are common in other religions than the Jewish. In the Egyptian *Funeral Ritual*, and in a hymn of the Soul, the Word and the Name are referred to in connection with hidden secrets. The Jewish enemies of Christ said that the miracles were wrought by the power of the ineffable Name, which had been stolen from the Sanctuary. (See *Isis Unveiled*, vol. ii., p. 387.)—STANZA III. *Rampired*: an old form of ramparted. "*The Illumination of Rome's Dome.*" One of the great sights of Rome used to be the illumination of the dome of St. Peter's on great festivals, such as that of Easter. Since the occupation of Rome by the Italian Government such spectacles, if not wholly discontinued, have been shorn of most of their splendour.—STANZA IV. "*No more near nor far.*" Hegel says that "Music frees us from the phenomena of time and space," and shows that they are not essentials, but accidents of our condition here.—STANZA V. "*Protoplast.*" The thing first formed, as a copy to be imitated.—STANZA VII. "*That out of three sounds he frame, not a fourth sound, but a star.*' "A star is perfect and beautiful, and rays of light come from it." STANZA XII. "*Common chord.*" A chord consisting of the fundamental tone with its third and fifth. "*Blunt it into a ninth.*" A ninth is (*a*) An interval containing an octave and a second; (*b*) a chord consisting of the common chord, with the eighth advanced one note. "*C Major of this life.*" Miss Helen Ormerod, in a paper read to the Browning Society of London, November 30th, 1888, has explained these musical terms and expressions. "C Major is what may be called the natural scale, having no sharps or flats in its signature. A Minor, with A (a third below C) for its keynote, has the same signature, but sharps are introduced for the formation of correct intervals. Pauer says that minor keys are chosen for expressing 'intense seriousness, soft melancholy, longing, sadness, and passionate grief'; whilst major keys with sharps and flats in their signatures are said to have distinctive qualities;—perhaps Browning chose C major for the key, as the one most allied to matters of every-day life, including rest and sleep. The common chord, as it is called, the keynote with its third and fifth, contains the rudiments of all music"

Adam, Lilith, and Eve (*Jocoseria*, 1883). The Talmudists, in their fanciful commentaries on the Old Testament, say that Adam had a wife before he married Eve, who was called Lilith; she was the mother of demons, and flew away from Adam, and the Lord then created Eve from one of his ribs. Lilith had been formed of clay, and was sensual and disobedient; the more spiritual Eve became his saviour from the snares of his first wife. Mr. Browning in this poem merely uses the names, and makes no reference to the Talmudic or Gnostic legends connected with them. Under the terror inspired by a thunder-storm, two women begin a confession of which they make light when the danger has passed away. The man says he saw through the joke, and the episode was over. It is a powerful and suggestive story of falsehood, fear, and a forgiveness too readily accorded by a man who makes a joke of guilt when he has lost nothing by it.

Adelaide, The Tuscan (*Sordello*), was the second wife of Eccelino da Romano, of the party of the Ghibellines.

Admetus (*Balaustion's Adventure*). King of Pheræ, in Thessaly. Apollo tended his flocks for one year, and obtained the favour that Admetus should never die if another person could be found to lay down his life for him: his wife, Alcestis, in consequence cheerfully devoted herself to death for him.

Æschylus. The Greek tragic poet who wrote the *Agamemnon* translated by Mr. Browning. Æschylus was born in the year 525 before Christ, at Eleusis, a town of Attica opposite the island of Salamis. When thirty-five years old Æschylus not only fought at Marathon, but distinguished himself for his valour. He was fifty-three years old when he gained the prize at Athens, B.C. 472, for his trilogy or set of three connected plays. He wrote some seventy pieces, but only seven have come down to our times: they are *Prometheus Chained*, *The Suppliants*, *The Seven Chiefs against Thebes*, *Agamemnon*, *The Choëphoræ*, *The Furies*, and *The Persians*. The *Agamemnon*, which Mr. Browning has translated, is one of the plays of the Oresteia, the *Choëphoræ* and the *Eumenides* or Furies completing the trilogy. The poet died at Gela, in Sicily, B.C. 456. Æschylus both in order of time and power was the first of the three great tragic poets of ancient Greece. Euripides and Sophocles were the other two.

After. See BEFORE and AFTER.

Agamemnon of Æschylus, The. A translation published in London, 1877. The scene of the play is laid by Æschylus at Argos, before the palace of Agamemnon, Mycenæ, however, really being his seat. Agamemnon was a son of Atreus according to Homer, and was the brother of Menelaus. In a later account he is described as the son of Pleisthenes, who was the son of Atreus. He was king over Argolis, Corinth, Achaia, and many islands. He married Clytemnestra, daughter of Tyndarus, king of Sparta, by whom he had three daughters Chrysothemis, Iphigenia and Electra, and one son Orestes. When Helen was carried off by Paris, Agamemnon was chosen to be commander-in-chief of the expedition sent against Troy by the Greeks, as he was the mightiest prince in Greece. He contributed one hundred ships manned with warriors, besides lending sixty more to the Arcadians. The fleet being detained at Aulis by a storm, it was declared that Agamemnon had offended Diana by slaying a deer sacred to her, and by boasting that he was a better hunter than the goddess; and he was compelled to sacrifice his daughter Iphigenia to appease her anger. Diana is said by some to have accepted a stag in her place. Homer describes Agamemnon as one of the bravest warriors before Troy, but having received Chryseis, the daughter of Chryses, priest of Apollo, as a prize of war, he arrogantly refused to allow her father to ransom her. This brought a plague on the Grecian host, and their ruin was almost completed by his carrying off Briseis, who was the prize of Achilles—who refused in consequence to fight, remaining sulking in his tent. After the fall of Troy the beautiful princess Cassandra fell to Agamemnon as his share of the spoils. She was endowed with the gift of prophecy, and warned him not to return home. The warning, however, was disregarded, although he was assured that his wife would put him to death. During the absence of Agamemnon Clytemnestra had formed an adulterous connection with Ægisthus, the son of Thyestes and Pelopia; and when he returned, the watchman having announced his approach to his palace, Clytemnestra killed Cassandra, and her lover murdered Agamemnon and his comrades. The tragic poets, however, make Clytemnestra throw a net over her husband while he was in his bath, and kill him with the assistance of Ægisthus, in revenge for the sacrifice of her daughter Iphigenia. In the introduction to the translation of the Agamemnon in *Morley's Universal Library* we have an excellent description of the great play. "In this tragedy the reader will find the strongest traces of the genius of Æschylus, and the most distinguishing proofs of his skill. Great in his conceptions, bold and daring in his metaphors, strong in his passion, he here touches the heart with uncommon emotions. The odes are particularly sublime, and the oracular spirit that breathes through them adds a wonderful elevation and dignity to them. Short as the part of Agamemnon is, the poet has the address to throw such an amiable dignity around him that we soon become interested in his favour, and are predisposed to lament his fate. The character of Clytemnestra is finely marked —a high-spirited, artful, close, determined, dangerous woman. But the poet has nowhere exerted such efforts of his genius as in the scene where Cassandra appears: as a prophetess, she gives every mark of the divine inspiration, from the dark and distant hint, through all the noble imagery of the prophetic enthusiasm; till, as the catastrophe advances, she more and more plainly declares it; as a suffering princess, her grief is plaintive, lively, and piercing; yet she goes to meet her death, which she clearly foretells, with a firmness worthy the daughter of Priam and the sister of Hector; nothing can be more animated or more interesting than this scene. The conduct of the poet through this play is exquisitely judicious: every scene gives us some obscure hint or ominous presage, enough to keep our attention always raised, and to prepare us for the event; even the studied caution of Clytemnestra is finely managed to produce that effect; whilst the secrecy with which she conducts her design keeps us in suspense, and prevents a discovery till we hear the dying groans of her murdered husband." As Mr. Browning announces in his preface to his translation of the tragedy, he has aimed at being literal at every cost, and has everywhere reproduced the peculiarities of the original. He has also made an attempt to reproduce the Greek spelling in English, which has made the poem more difficult than some other translations to the non-classical reader. We have ample recompense for this peculiarity by the way in which he has imbibed the spirit of his author, and so faithfully reproduced, not alone his phraseology, but his mind. It required a rugged poet to interpret for us correctly the ruggedness of an Æschylus.

Line for line and word for word we have the tragedy in English as the Greeks had it in their own tongue. If there are obscurities, we must not in the present instance blame Mr. Browning: a reference to the original, so authorities tell us, will prove that Greek poets were at times obscure. The *Agamemnon* is part of the Oresteian Trilogy or group of three plays; this trilogy of Æschylus is our only example extant, and it is necessary to say something of the other parts. Atreus, the son of Pelops, was king of Mycenæ. By his wife Ærope were born to him Pleisthenes, Menelaus, and Agamemnon. Thyestes, the brother of Atreus, had followed him to Argos, and there seduced his wife, by whom he had two, or according to some, three children. Thyestes was banished from court on account of this, but was soon afterwards recalled by his brother that he might be revenged upon him. He prepared a banquet where Thyestes was served with the flesh of the children who were the offspring of his incestuous connection with his sister-in-law the queen. When the feast was concluded, the heads of the murdered children were produced, that Thyestes might see of what he had been partaking. It was fabled that the sun in horror shrank back in his course at the horrible sight. Thyestes fled. The crime brought the most terrible evils upon the family of which Agamemnon was a member. When this hero was murdered by his wife and her paramour, young Orestes was saved from his mother's dagger by his sister Electra. When he reached the years of manhood, he visited his ancestral home, and assassinated both his mother and her lover Ægisthus. In consequence of this he was tormented by the Furies, and he exiled himself to Athens, where Apollo purified him. The murder of Clytemnestra by her son is described in the second play of the Trilogy, called the *Choëphoræ or the Libation Pourers*. *The Furies* is the title of the third and concluding play of the Trilogy. (For an account of Æschylus see p. 8.)

NOTES.—[N.B. The references here are to the pages of the poem in the last edition of the complete works in sixteen vols.]—P. 269, *Atreidai*, a patronymic given by Homer to Agamemnon and Menelaus, as being the sons of Atreus; *Troia*, the capital of Troas = Troy. p. 270, *Ilion*, a citadel of Troy; *Menelaos*, a king of Sparta, brother of Agamemnon. p. 271, *Argives*, the inhabitants of Argos and surrounding country; *Alexandros*, the name of Paris in the Iliad; *Atreus*, son of

Pelops, was king of Mycenæ; *Danaoi*, a name given to the people of Argos and to all the Greeks; *Troes* = Trojans. p. 272, *Tundareus*, king of Lacedæmon, who married Leda; *Klutaimnestra* = Clytemnestra, daughter of Tyndarus by Leda. p. 273, *Teukris land*, the land of the Trojans — from Teucer, their king; "*Achaians' two-throned empery*": the brother kings Agamemnon and Menelaos. p. 274, *Linos*, the personification of a dirge or lamentation; *Priamos*, the last king of Troy, made prisoner by Hercules when he took the city. p. 275, *Ieïos Paian*, an epithet of Apollo; *Kalchas*, a soothsayer who accompanied the Greeks to Troy. p. 277, *Kalchis*, the chief city of Eubœa, founded by an Athenian colony; *Aulis*, a town of Bœotia, near Kalchis: *Strumon*, a river which separates Thrace from Macedonia. p. 282, *Hephaistos*, the god of fire, according to Homer the son of Zeus and Hera. The Romans called the Greek Hephaistos Vulcan, though Vulcan was an Italian deity. The news of the fall of Troy was brought to Mycenæ by means of beacon fires, so fire was the messenger. *Ide* = Mount Ida; *of Lemnos*, an island in the Ægean Sea. p. 283, *Athoan*, of Mount Athos; *Makistos* = Macistos, a city of Tryphylia; *Euripos*, a narrow strait separating Eubœa from Bœotia; *Messapios*, a name of Bœotia; *Asopos*, a river of Thessaly; *Mount Kitharion*, sacred to the Muses and Jupiter. Hercules killed the great lion there: *Mount Aigiplanktos* was in Megaris; *Strait Saronic*: Saronicus Sinus was a bay of the Ægean Sea; *Mount Arachnaios*, in Argolis. p. 286, *Ate*, the goddess of revenge; *Ares*, the Greek name of the war-god Mars. p. 288, *Aphrodite*, a name of Venus. p. 290, *Erinues* = the Furies. p. 292, *Puthian* = Delphic; *Skamandros*, a river of Troas. p. 293, *Priamidai*, the patronymic of the descendants of Priam. p. 300, *Threkian breezes* — Thracian breezes; *Aigaian Sea*, the Ægean Sea; *Achaian*, pertaining to Achaia, in Greece. p. 301, *Meneleos*, son of Atreus, brother to Agamemnon and husband of Helen; *water-Haides*, the engulfing sea. p. 302, *Zephuros*, the west wind; *Simois*, a river in Troas which rises in Mount Ida and falls into the Xanthus. p. 304, *Erinus*, an avenging deity. p. 307, *the Argeian monster* = the company of Argives concealed in the wooden horse; *Pleiads*, a name given to seven of the daughters of Atlas by Pleione, one of the Oceanides. They became a constellation in the heavens after death. p. 309, "*triple-bodied Geruon the Second*," Geryon, king of the Balearic Isles, fabled to have three bodies and three heads: Hercules slew him; *Strophios the Phokian*, at whose house Orestes was brought up with Pylades son of Strophios. p. 316, *Kassandra*, daughter of Priam, slain by Clytemnestra. p. 317, "*Alkmene's child*"—Hercules was the son of Alkmene. p. 319, *Ototoi*—alas! *Loxias*, a surname of Apollo. p. 322, *papai, papai* = O strange! wonderful! p. 324, *Itus*, or *Itys*, son of Tereus, killed by his mother. p. 325, "*Orthian style*," in a shrill tone. p. 332, *Lukeion Apollon*—Lyceus was a surname of Apollo. p. 335, *Surian* = Syrian. p. 343, *Chruseïds*, the patronymic of the descendants of Astynome, the daughter of Chryses. p. 348, *Iphigeneia*, daughter of Agamemnon and Clytemnestra; her father offered to sacrifice her to appease the wrath of Diana. p. 350, *The Daimon of the Pleisthenidai*, the genius of Agamemnon's family. p. 351, *Thuestes*, son of Pelops, brother of Atreus; *Pelopidai*, descendants of Pelops, son of Tantalus.

Agricola, Johannes, (*Johannes Agricola in Meditation*,) was one of the foremost of the German Reformers. He was born at Eisleben, April 20th, 1492. He met Luther whilst a student at Wittenberg, and became attached to him, accompanying him to the Leipsic Assembly of Divines, where he acted as recording secretary. He established the reformed religion at Frankfort. In 1536 he was called to fill a professorial chair at Wittenberg. Here he first taught the views which Luther termed *Antinomian*. He held that Christians were entirely free from the Divine law, being under the Gospel alone. He denied that Christians were under any obligations to keep the ten commandments. Mr. Browning has quite accurately, though unsparingly, exposed his impious teaching in his poem *Johannes Agricola in Meditation* (*q.v.*).

Agrippa, Henry Cornelius, the mediæval doctor and magician, was born at Cologne in 1486, and was educated at the university of that city. He was denounced in 1509 by the monks, who called him an "impious cabalist"; in 1531 he published his treatise *De Occulta Philosophia*, written by the advice and with the assistance of the Abbot Trithemius of Wurzburg, the preceptor of Paracelsus. In 1510 he came to London on a diplomatic mission, and was the guest of Dean Colet at Stepney. He afterwards fought at the battle of Ravenna. In 1511 he attended the schismatic council of Pisa as a theologian. In 1515 he lectured at the university of Pavia. We afterwards find him at Metz, Geneva, and Freiburg, where he practised as a physician. In 1529 he was appointed historiographer to Charles V. He died at Grenoble in 1535. A man of such vast and varied learning could hardly in those days have avoided being accused of diabolical practices and heretical opinions; the only wonder is that he was not burned alive for his scientific attainments, which were looked upon as dangerous in the highest degree. (*Pauline* in the Latin prefatory note.)

"A King lived long ago." Song in *Pippa Passes*, which is sung by the girl as she passes the house of Luigi. Mr. Browning first published the song in the *Monthly Repository*, in 1835 (vol. ix., N.S., pp. 707-8), it was reprinted with added lines, and was revised throughout, in *Pippa Passes* 1841.

Alberic (*Sordello*). Son of Eccelino the monk, described in the poem as "many-muscled, big-boned Alberic."

Alcestis (*Balaustion's Adventure*), the daughter of Pelias, was the wife of Admetus, son of Pheres, who was king of Pheræ in Thessaly. Apollo, when—for an offence against Jupiter—he was banished from heaven, had been kindly received by Pheres, and had obtained from the Fates a promise that his benefactor should never die if he could find another person willing to lay down his life for him. The story how this promise was obtained is set forth with great dramatic force in Mr. Browning's *Apollo and the Fates* (*q.v.*). Alcestis volunteered to die in the place of her husband when he lay sick unto death. Her sacrifice was accepted, and she died. But Hercules, who had been hospitably entertained by Pheres, hearing of the tragic circumstance, brought Alcestis from Hades out of gratitude to his host, and presented her to her grief-stricken husband. Euripides has used these circumstances as the basis of his tragedy of *Alcestis*.

"All Service ranks the same with God." A song in *Pippa Passes*.

Amphibian. The Prologue to *Fifine at the Fair* is headed "Amphibian," under which title it is included in the *Selections*.

Anael. A Druse girl who loves Djabal and believes him to be divine (*The Return of the Druses*).

Andrea del Sarto [the MAN], *Men and Women*, 1855, called "the faultless painter," also Andrea senza Errori (Andrew the Unerring) was a great painter of the Florentine School. His father was a tailor (*sarto*), so the Italians, with their passion for nicknames, dubbed him "The Tailor's Andrew." He was born in Gualfonda, Florence, in 1487. It is not certain what was his real name: Vannuchi has been constantly given, but without authority. He was at first put to work with a goldsmith, but he disliked the business, and preferred drawing his master's models. He was next placed with a wood-carver and painter, one Gian Barill, with whom he remained till 1498. He then went to the draughtsman and colourist, Piero di Cosimo, under whom he studied the cartoons of Leonardo da Vinci and Michelangelo. We next find him opening a shop in partnership with his friend Francia Bigio, but the arrangement did not last long. The brotherhood of the Servi employed Andrea from 1509 to 1514 in adorning their church of the Annunziata at Florence. Mrs. Jameson, in her *Legends of the Monastic Orders*, thus describes the church and cloisters identified with the work of this painter at Florence: "Every one who has been at Florence must remember the Church of the 'Annunziata'; every one who remembers that glorious church, who has lingered in the cloisters and the cortile where Andrea del Sarto put forth all his power—where the *Madonna del Sacco* and the *Birth of the Virgin* attest what he could *do* and *be* as a painter—will feel interested in the Order of the SERVI. Among the extraordinary outbreaks of religious enthusiasm in the thirteenth century, this was in its origin one of the most singular. Seven Florentines, rich, noble, and in the prime of life, whom a similarity of taste and feeling had drawn together, used to meet every day in a chapel dedicated to the Annunciation of the Blessed Virgin (then outside the walls of Florence), there to sing the *Ave* or evening service in honour of the Madonna, for whom they had an especial love and veneration. They became known and remarked in their neighbourhood for those acts of piety, so that the women and children used to point at them as they passed through the streets and exclaim, *Guardate i Servi di Maria* (Behold the *Servants* of the Virgin!) Hence the title afterwards assumed by the Order." These seven gentlemen at length forsook the world, sold all their possessions and distributed their money to the poor, and retired to a solitary spot in the mountains about six miles out of Florence; here they built themselves huts of boughs and stones, and devoted themselves to the service of the Virgin. It was for the cloisters of the church of the Servi at Florence that Andrea del Sarto painted the *Riposo*. His *Nativity of the B.V. Mary* is a grand fresco, the characters are noble and dignified, and "draped in the magnificent taste which distinguished Andrea." The following account of the artist's life is summarised from the article on Del Sarto by Mr. W. M. Rossetti in the *Encyc. Brit.* He was an easy-going plebeian, to whom a modest position in life and scanty gains were no grievances. As an artist he must have known his own value; but he probably rested content in the sense of his superlative powers as an executant, and did not aspire to the rank of a great inventor or leader, for which, indeed, he had no vocation. He led a social sort of life among his compeers of the art. He fell in love with Lucrezia del Fede, wife of a hatter named Carlo Recanati; the latter dying opportunely, the tailor's son married her on December 26th, 1512. She was a very handsome woman, and has come down to us treated with great suavity in many a picture of her lover-husband, who constantly painted her as a Madonna or otherwise; and even in painting other women he made them resemble Lucrezia in general type. Vasari, who was at one time a pupil of Andrea, describes her as faithless, jealous, overbearing, and vixenish with the apprentices. She lived to a great age, surviving her second husband forty years. Before the end of 1516, a Pietà of his composition, and afterwards a Madonna, were sent to the French Court. These were received with applause; and the art-loving monarch Francis I. suggested in 1518 that Andrea should come to Paris. He left his wife in Florence and went accordingly, and was very cordially received, and moreover for the first time in his life handsomely remunerated. His wife urged him to return to Italy. The king assented, on the understanding that his absence was to be short; and he entrusted Andrea with a sum of money to be expended in purchasing works of art for the king. Andrea could not resist temptation, and spent the king's money and some of his own in building a house for himself in Florence. He fell into disgrace with the king, but no serious punishment followed. In 1520 he resumed work in Florence, and painted many pictures for the cloisters of Lo Scalzo. He dwelt in Florence throughout the memorable siege, which was followed by an infectious pestilence. He caught the malady, struggled against it with little or no tending from his wife, who held aloof, and died, no one knowing much about it at the moment, on January 22nd, 1531, at the early age of forty-three. He was buried unceremoniously in the church of the Servi. Mr. Rossetti gives the following criticisms on his work as an artist. "Andrea had true pictorial style, a very high standard of correctness, and an enviable balance of executive endowments. The point of technique in which he excelled least was perhaps that of discriminating the varying textures of different objects and surfaces. There is not much elevation or ideality in his works—much more of reality." He lacked invention notwithstanding his great technical skill. He had no inward impulse toward the high and noble; he was a man without fervour, and had no enthusiasm for the true and good. It is said that Michelangelo once remarked that if he had attempted greater things he might have rivalled Rafael, but Andrea was not a man for the mountain-top—the plains sufficed for him.

[The Poem.] On the bare historical facts, as recorded by Vasari in his life of Andrea del Sarto, Mr. Browning has framed this wonderful art-poem. He has taken Vasari's "notes" and framed "not another sound but a star," as he says in his *Abt Vogler*. Given the Vasari life, he has mixed it with his thought, and has transfigured it so that the sad, infinitely pathetic soul, in its stunted growth and wasted form, lives before us in Mr. Browning's lines. As *Abt Vogler* is his greatest music-poem, so this is his greatest art-poem, and both are unique. No poet has ever given us such utterances on music and painting as we possess in these works: if all the poet's work were to perish save these, they would suffice to insure immortality for their author. It is said that the poem was suggested by a picture in the Pitti Palace at Florence. "Faultless but soulless" is the verdict of art critics on Andrea's works Why is this? Mr. Browning's poem tells us in no hesitating phrase that the secret lay in the fact that Andrea was an immoral man, an infatuated man, passionately demanding love from a woman who had neither heart nor intellect, a wife for whom he sacrificed his soul and the highest interests of his art. He knew and loved Lucrezia while she was another man's wife; he was content that she should also love other men when she was his. He robbed King Francis, his generous patron, that he might give the money to his unworthy spouse. He neglected his parents in their poverty and old age. Is there not in these facts the secret of his failure? To Mr. Browning there is, and his poem tells us why. But, it will be objected, many great geniuses have been immoral men. This is so, but we cannot argue the point here; the poet's purpose is to show how in this particular case the evil seed bore fruit after its kind. The poem opens with the artist's attempts to bribe his wife by money to accord him a little semblance of love: he promises to paint that he may win gold for her. The keynote of the poem is struck in these opening words. It is evening, and Andrea is weary with his work, but never weary of praising Lucrezia's beauty; sadly he owns that he is at best only a shareholder in his wife's affections, that even her pride in him is gone, that she neither understands nor cares to understand his art. He tells her that he can do easily and perfectly what at the bottom of his heart he wishes for, deep as that might be; he could do what others agonise to do all their lives and fail in doing, yet he knows for all that there burns a truer light of God in them than in him. Their works drop groundward, though their souls have glimpses of heaven that are denied to him. He could have beaten Rafael had he possessed Rafael's soul; for the Urbinate's technical skill, as he half hesitatingly shows, is inferior to his own; and had his Lucrezia urged him, inspired him, to claim a seat by the side of Michelangelo and Rafael, he might for her sake have done it. He sees he is but a half-man working in an atmosphere of silver-grey. He had his chance at Fontainebleau; there he sometimes seemed to leave the ground, but he had a chain which dragged him down. Lucrezia called him. Not only for her did he forsake the higher art ambitions, but the common ground of honesty; he descended to cement his walls with the gold of King Francis which he had stolen, and for her. From dishonesty to connivance at his wife's infidelity is an easy step; and so, while in the act of expressing his remorse at his ingratitude to the king, we find him asking Lucrezia quite naturally, as a matter of ordinary occurrence—

> "Must you go?
> That cousin here again? he waits outside?
> Must see you—you, and not with me?"

Here we discover the secret of the soullessness: the fellow has the tailor in his blood, even though the artist is supreme at the fingers' ends. He is but the craftsman after all. Think of Fra Angelico painting his saints and angels on his knees, straining his eyes to catch the faintest glimpse of the heavenly radiance of Our Lady's purity and holiness, feeling that he failed, too dazzled by the brightness of Divine light, to catch more than its shadow, and we shall know why there is soul in the great Dominican painter, and why there is none in the Sarto. Lucrezia, despicable as she was, was not the cause of her husband's failure. His marriage, his treatment of Francis, his allowing his parents to starve, to die of want, while he paid gaming debts for his wife's lover,—all these things tell us what the man was. No woman ruined his soul; he had no soul to ruin!

NOTES.—*Fiesole*, a small but famous episcopal city of Italy, on the crown of a hill above the Arno, about three miles to the west of Florence. *Morello*, a mountain of the Apennines. *The Urbinate:* Rafael was born at Urbino. *George Vasari*, painter and author of the "Lives of the Most Excellent Italian Painters, Sculptors and Architects." *Rafael*, Raphael Sanzio of Urbino. *Agnolo:* Michel Agnolo is the more correct form of Michael Angelo. *Francis*, King Francis I. of France, the royal patron of Andrea. *Fontainebleau*, a town of France 37 miles S.E. of Paris; its palace is one of the most sumptuous in France. "*The Roman's is the better when you pray.*" Catholics, however, do not use the works of the great masters for devotional purposes nearly so much as might be supposed. No "miraculous" picture is by this class. *Cue-owls:* The Scops Owl: Scops Giû (Scopoli). Its cry is a ringing "ki-ou"—whence Italian "chiù" or "ciù." "*Walls in the New Jerusalem.*" Revelation xxi. 15-17. *Leonard*, Leonardo da Vinci.

Andromeda. In *Pauline*, Mr. Browning has commemorated the fascination for his youthful mind which was exercised by an engraving of a picture by Caravaggio of Andromeda and Perseus. This picture was always before him as a boy, and he loved the story of the divine deliverer and the innocent victim which it presented. The lines begin

"Andromeda!
And she is with me,—years roll, I shall change,
But change can touch her not."

Another Way of Love. See *One Way of Love*, this poem being its sequel.

Any Wife to Any Husband. A dying wife finds the bitterest thing in death to be the certainty that her husband's love for her, which, would life but last, she could retain, will fade and wither when she is no longer present to tend it:

> "Man's love is of man's life a thing apart,
> 'Tis woman's whole existence."

The great pure love of a wife is a reign of love. Woman's love is more durable and purer than man's, and few men are entirely worthy of being the objects of that which they can so imperfectly understand. Mr. Nettleship, commenting on this poem, very truly says, "The real love of the man is never born until the love of the woman supplements it." The wife of the poem feels that there would be no difficulty in her case about being faithful to the memory of her husband; but she foresees that his love will not long survive the loss of her personal presence. This will be to depreciate the value of his life to him; his love will come back to her again at last, back to the heart's place kept for him, but with a stain upon it. The old love will be re-coined, re-issued from the mint, and given to others to spend, alas! with some alloy as well as with a new image and superscription. She foresees that he will dissipate his soul in the love of other women, he will excuse himself by the assurance that the light loves will make no impression on the deep-set memory of the woman who is immortally his bride; he will have a Titian's Venus to desecrate his wall rather than leave it bare and cold,—but the flesh-loves will not impair the soul-love.

Apollo and the Fates. (See Prologue to *Parleyings*.) Apollo (the Sun God), having offended Jupiter by slaying the Cyclopes, who forged his thunderbolts by which he had killed Æsculapius for bringing dead men to life, had been banished from heaven. He became servant to Admetus, king of Thessaly, in whose employment he remained nine years as one of his shepherds. He was treated with great kindness by his master, and they became true lovers of each other. When Apollo, restored to the favour of heaven, had left the service of Admetus and resumed his god-like offices, he heard that his old master and friend was sick unto death, and he determined to save his life. Accordingly he descended on Mount Parnassus, and penetrated to the abode of the Fates, in the dark regions below the roots of the mountains, and there he found the three who preside over the destinies of mankind—Clotho with her distaff, Lachesis with her spindle, and Atropos with a pair of scissors about to cut the thread of Admetus' life—and begins to plead for the life of his friend Admetus, whom Atropos has just doomed to death. The Fates bid Apollo go back to earth and wake it from dreams. Apollo demands a truce to their doleful amusement, and requests them to extend the years of Admetus to threescore and ten. The Fates ask him if he thinks it would add to his friend's joy to have his life lengthened, seeing that life is only illusion? Infancy is but ignorance and mischief, youth becomes foolishness, and age churlishness. Apollo should ask for life for one whom he hates, not for the friend he loves. The Sun's beams produce such semblance of good as exists by simply gilding the evil. Apollo objects that if it were happier to die, men's greeting would not be "Long life!" but "Death to you!" Man loves his life, and he ought to know best. The Fates say this is all the glamour shed by Apollo's rays. Apollo concedes that man desponds when debarred of illusion: "suppose he has in himself some compensative law?" and the God then produces a bowl of wine, man's invention, of which he invites them to taste. The Fates, after some objection, drink and get tipsy and merry, Atropos even declaring she could live at a pinch! Apollo delivers them a lecture; he tells them Bacchus invented the wine; as he was the youngest of the gods, he had to discover some new gift whereby to claim the homage of man. He tampered with nothing already arranged, yet would introduce change without shock. As the sunbeams and Apollo had transformed the Fates' cavern without displacing a splinter, so has the gift of Bacchus turned the adverse things of life to a kindlier aspect; man accepts the good with the bad, and acquiesces in his fate; this is the work of Zeus. He demands of the Fates if, after all, Life be so devoid of good? "Quashed be our quarrel!" they exclaim, and they dance till an explosion from the earth's centre brings them to their senses once more, and the pact is dissolved. They learn that the powers above them are not to be cajoled into interfering with the laws of life and the inevitable decrees of which the Fates are but the ministers. At last they agree to lengthen the life of Admetus if any mortal can be found to forgo the fulfilment of his own life on his account. Apollo protests that the king's subjects will strive with one another for the glory of dying that their king may survive. First in all Pheræ will his father offer himself as his son's substitute. "Bah!" says Clotho. "Then his mother," suggests Apollo; "or, spurning the exchange, the king may choose to die." With the jeers of the three the scene closes. Mr. Browning's lovely poem *Balaustion's Adventure* should be read next after this, as the Prologue to the *Parleyings* has little or no relation to the rest of the volume.

NOTES.—*Parnassus*, a mountain of Greece, sacred to the Muses and Apollo and Bacchus. *Dire ones*, the Fates, Clotho, Lachesis and Atropos. *Admetus*, the husband of Alcestis, whose wife died to save his life. *The Fates*, the Destinies, the goddesses supposed to preside over human life: *Clotho*, who spins the thread of life; *Lachesis*, who determines the length of the thread; *Atropos*, who cuts it off. *Woe-purfled*, embroidered with woe. *Weal-prankt*, decked out with prosperity. *Moirai*, the Parcæ, the Fates. *Zeus*, Jupiter, the Supreme Being. *Eld*, old age. *Sweet Trine*, the Three, the Trinity of Fates. *Bacchus*, the Wine-God. *Semele's Son*: Semele was the daughter of Cadmus and Harmonia; when Zeus appeared to her in his Divine splendour she was consumed by the flames and gave birth to Bacchus, whom Zeus saved from the fire and hid in his thigh. Bacchus, when made a god, raised her to heaven under the name of Thyone. *Swound*, a swoon. *Cummers*, gossips, female acquaintances. *Collyrium*, eye-wash. *Pheræ*, a town in Thessaly, where King Pheres reigned, who was the father of Admetus.

Apparent Failure. (*Dramatis Personæ*, 1864.) Mr. Ruskin has laboured hard to save St. Mark's, Venice, from the destroying hand of the restorer. Mr. Browning wrote this poem to save from complete destruction a much less important, though a celebrated building, the Paris Morgue, the deadhouse wherein are exposed the bodies of persons found dead, that they may be claimed by their friends. The Doric little Morgue is close to Notre Dame, on the banks of the Seine, and is one of the sights of Paris—repulsive as it is—which everybody makes a point of seeing. The poet entered the building and saw behind the great screen of glass three bodies exposed for identification on the copper couch fronting him. They were three men who had killed themselves, and the poet mentally questions them why they abhorred their lives so much. You "poor boy" wanted to be an emperor, forsooth; you "old one" were a red socialist, and this next one fell a prey to misdirected love. The three deadly sins of Pride, Covetousness, and Lust had each its victim. And before them stands the poet of optimism, not staggered in his doctrine even by this sad sight. Not for a moment does his faith fail that "what God blessed once can never prove accurst." His optimism in this poem is at high-water mark; where some weak-kneed believers in humanity would have found a breaking link in the chain, Mr. Browning sees but "apparent failure," and declines to believe the doom of these poor wrecks of souls to be final.

Apparitions. (Introduction to *The Two Poets of Croisic*, 1878.) This exquisite poem is a tribute to the charm exercised by a human face, from which looks out God's own smile, gladdening a cold and scowling prospect as a burst of May soon dispels the lingering chills of winter.

Appearances. (*Pacchiarotto, with other Poems*, 1876.) Metaphysicians would explain this poem by an essay on the association of ideas; strong as imagination is, it can never exceed experience which has come to us through sight. Feelings are associated with one another according as they have been operant in more or less frequent succession. Reasoning may associate ideas, but for force and permanence our actual sight, and contact are the wonder-workers in this department of soul-life. Nothing can beautify the place where we have in the past suffered some great mental distress or wrong; so no place can ever be unbeautiful where the true lover wins his life's prize. When the upholsterer's art does more for a room than the memory of a first love, that love is not of the eternal sort our poet sings.

Aprile. The Italian poet who sought to love, as Paracelsus sought to know. He represents the Renaissance spirit in its emotional aspect, as Paracelsus represents the spirit of the Reformation in its passion for knowledge. As Mr. Browning says, they were the "two halves of a dissevered world." (*Paracelsus.*)

Arcades Ambo. (*Asolando*, 1889.) If a man runs away in battle when the balls begin to fly, we call him a coward. He may excuse himself by the argument that man must at all risks shun death. This is the excuse made by the vivisector: he is often a kind and amiable man in every other relation of life than in that aspect of his profession which demands, as he holds, the torture of living animals for the advancement of the healing art Health of the body must be preserved at all costs; the moral health is of little or no consequence in comparison with that of the body; above all we must not die, death is the one thing to be avoided, hide therefore from the darts of the King of Terrors behind the whole creation of lower animals. Mr. Browning says this is cowardice exactly parallel with that of the soldier who runs away in battle; the principle being that at all costs life is the one thing to be preserved. The Anti-Vivisectionist principles of Mr. Browning were very pronounced. He was for many years associated with Miss F. P. Cobbe in her efforts to suppress the practice of torturing animals for scientific purposes, and was a Vice-President of the Victoria Street Society for the Protection of Animals from Vivisection at the time of his death. See my *Browning's Message to his Time* (chapter on "Browning and Vivisection").

Aristophanes, the celebrated comic poet of Athens, was born probably about the year 448 B.C. His first comedy was brought out in 427 B.C. Plato in his *Symposium* gives Aristophanes a position at the side of Socrates. The festivals of Dionysus greatly promoted the production of tragedies, comedies and satiric dramas. The greater Dionysia were held in the city of Athens in the month of March, and were connected with the natural feeling of joy at the approach of summer. These Bacchanalian festivals were scenes of gross licentiousness, and the coarseness which pervades much of the work of the great Greek comedian was due to the fact that the popular taste demanded grossness of allusion on occasions like these. The Athenian dramatist of the old school was entirely unrestrained. He could satirise even the Eleusinian mysteries, could deal abundantly in personalities, burlesque the most sacred subjects, and ridicule the most prominent persons in the republic. Professor Jebb, in his article on Aristophanes in the *Encyclopedia Britannica*, says: "It is neither in the denunciation nor in the mockery that he is most individual. His truest and highest faculty is revealed by those wonderful bits of lyric writing in which he soars above everything that can move to laughter or tears, and makes the clear air thrill with the notes of a song as free, as musical and as wild as that of the nightingale invoked by his own chorus in the *Birds*. The speech of Dikaios Logos in the *Clouds*, the praises of country life in the *Peace*, the serenade in the *Eccleziazusæ*, the songs of the Spartan and Athenian maidens in the *Lysistrata*; above all, perhaps, the chorus in the *Frogs*, the beautiful chant of the Initiated,—these passages, and such as these, are the true glories of Aristophanes. They are the strains, not of an artist, but of one who warbles for pure gladness of heart in some place made bright by the presence of a god. Nothing else in Greek poetry has quite this wild sweetness of the woods. Of modern poets Shakespeare alone, perhaps, has it in combination with a like richness and fertility of fancy." Fifty-four comedies were ascribed to Aristophanes. We possess only eleven: these deal with Athenian life during a period of thirty-six years. The political satires of the poet, therefore, cannot be understood without a knowledge of Athenian history, and an acquaintance with its life during the period in which the poet wrote. "Aristophanes was a natural conservative," says Professor Jebb; "his ideal was the Athens of the Persian wars. He detested the vulgarity and the violence of mob-rule; he clove to the old worship of the gods; he regarded the new ideas of education as a tissue of imposture and impiety. As a mocker he is incomparable for the union of subtlety with wit of the comic imagination. As a poet he is immortal." The momentous period in the history of Greece during which Aristophanes began to write, forms the groundwork, more or less, of so many of his comedies, that it is impossible to understand them, far less to appreciate their point, without some acquaintance with its leading events. All men's thoughts were occupied by the great contest for supremacy between the rival states of Athens and Sparta, known as the Peloponnesian War. It is not necessary here to enter into details; but the position of the Athenians during the earlier years of the struggle must be briefly described. Their strength lay chiefly in their fleet; in the other arms of war they were confessedly no match for Sparta and her confederate allies. The heavy-armed Spartan infantry, like the black Spanish bands of the fifteenth century, was almost irresistible in the field. Year after year the invaders marched through the Isthmus into Attica, or were landed in strong detachments on different points of the coast, while the powerful Bœotian cavalry swept all the champaign, burning the towns and villages, cutting down the crops, destroying vines and olive-groves,—carrying this work of devastation almost up to the very walls of Athens. For no serious attempt was made to resist these periodical invasions. The strategy of the Athenians was much the same as it had been when the Persian hosts swept down upon them fifty years before. Again they withdrew themselves and all their movable property within the city walls, and allowed the invaders to overrun the country with impunity Their flocks and herds were removed into the islands on the coasts, where, so long as Athens was mistress of the sea, they would be in comparative safety. It was a heavy demand upon their patriotism; but, as before, they submitted to it, trusting that the trial would be but brief, and nerved to it by the stirring words of their great leader Pericles. The ruinous sacrifice, and even the personal suffering, involved in this forced migration of a rural population into a city wholly inadequate to accommodate them, may easily be imagined, even if it had not been forcibly described by the great historian of those times. Some carried with them the timber framework of their homes, and set it up in such vacant spaces as they could find. Others built for themselves little "chambers on the wall," or occupied the outer courts of the temples, or were content with booths and tents set up under the Long Walls, which connected the city with the harbour of Piræus. Some—if our comic satirist is to be trusted—were even fain to sleep in tubs and hen-coops. Provisions grew dear and scarce. Pestilence broke out in the overcrowded city; and in the second and third years of the war the great plague carried off, out of their comparatively small population, about 10,000 of all ranks. But it needed a pressure of calamity far greater than the present to keep a good citizen of Athens away from the theatre. If the times were gloomy, so much the more need of a little honest diversion. The comic drama was to the Athenians what a free press is to modern commonwealths. It is probable that Aristophanes was himself earnestly opposed to the continuance of the war, and spoke his own sentiments on this point by the mouth of his characters; but the prevalent disgust at the hardships of this long-continued siege—for such it practically was—would in any case be a tempting subject for the professed writer of burlesques; and the caricature of a leading politician, if cleverly drawn, is always a success for the author. The *Thesmophoriazusæ* is a comedy about the fair sex, whose whole point—like that also of the comedy of the *Frogs*—lies in a satire upon Euripides. Aristophanes never wearied of holding this poet up to ridicule. Why this was so is not to be discovered: it may have been that the conservative principles of Aristophanes were offended by some new-fashioned ideas of his brother poet. The *Thesmophoria* was a festival of women only, in honour of Ceres and Proserpine. Euripides was reputed to be a woman-hater: in one of his tragedies he says,

> "O thou most vile! thou—*woman!*—for what word
> That lips could frame, could carry more reproach?"

He can hardly, however, have been a woman-hater who created the beautiful characters of Iphigenia and Alcestis. In this comedy the Athenian ladies have resolved to punish Euripides, and the poet is in dismay in consequence, and takes measures to defend himself. He offers terms of peace to the offended fair sex, and promises never to abuse them in future.

Aristophanes' Apology; including a Transcript from Euripides, being the last adventure of Balaustion. London, 1875.—As Aristophanes' Apology is the last adventure of Balaustion, it is necessary to read *Balaustion's Adventure* (*q.v.*) before commencing this poem. Balaustion has married Euthukles, the young man whom she met at Syracuse. She has met the great poet Euripides, paid her homage to his genius, and has received from his own hands his tragedy of *Hercules*. The poet is dead, and Athens fallen. She returns to the city after its capture by the Spartans, but she can no longer remain therein. Athens will live in her heart, but never again can she behold the place where ghastly mirth mocked its overthrow and death and hell celebrated their triumph. She has left the doomed city, now that it is no longer the free Athens of happier times, and has set sail with her husband for Rhodes. The glory of the material Athens has departed. But Athens will live as a glorious spiritual entity—

> "That shall be better and more beautiful,
> And too august for Spartè's foot to spurn!"

She and Euthukles are exiles from the dead Athens, not the living: 'That's in the cloud there, with the new-born star!" As they voyage, for her consolation she will record her recollections of her Euripides in Athens, and she bids her husband set down her words as she speaks. She must "speak to the infinite intelligence, sing to the everlasting sympathy." There are dead things that are triumphant still; the walls of intellectual construction can never be overthrown; there are air-castles more real and permanent than the work of men's hands. She will tell of Euripides and his undying work. She recalls the night when Athens was still herself, when they heard the news that Euripides was dead—"gone with his Attic ivy home to feast." Dead and triumphant still! She reflected how the Athenian multitude had ever reproached him: "All thine aim thine art, the idle poet only." It was not enough in those times that thought should be "the soul of art." The Greek world demanded activity as well as contemplation. The poet must leave his study to command troops, forsake the world of ideas for that of action, otherwise he was a "hater of his kind." The world is content with you if you do nothing for it; if you do aught you must do all. But when Euripides was at rest, censorious tongues ceased to wag, and the next thing to do was to build a monument for him! But for the hearts of Balaustion and her husband no statue is required: he stood within their hearts. The pure-souled woman says, "What better monument can be than the poem he gave me? Let him speak to me now in his own words; have out the Herakles and re-sing the song; hear him tell of the last labour of the god, worst of all the twelve." And lovingly and reverently the precious gift of the poet was taken from its shrine and opened for the reading. Suddenly torchlight, knocking at the door, a cry "Open, open! Bacchos bids!" and a sound of revelry and the drunken voices of girl dancers and players, led by Aristophanes, the comic poet of Greece. A splendid presence, "all his head one brow," drunk, but in him sensuality had become a rite. Mind was here, passions, but grasped by the strong hand of intellect. Balaustion rose and greeted him. "Hail house," he said, "friendly to Euripides!" and he spoke flatteringly, but in a slightly mocking tone, as men who are sensual defer to spiritual women whom they rather affect to pity while they admire. Balaustion loves genius; to her mind it is the noblest gift of heaven: she can bow to Aristophanes though he is drunk. (Greek intoxication was doubtless a very different thing from Saxon!) The comic poet had just achieved a great triumph: his comedy had been crowned. The "Women's Festival" (the *Thesmophoriazusæ* as it was called in Greek) was a play in which the fair sex had the chief part. It was written against Euripides' dislike of women, for which the women who are celebrating the great feast of Ceres and Proserpine (the Thesmophoria) drag him to justice. And so, with all his chorus troop, he comes to the home of Balaustion, as representing the Euripides whom he disliked and satirised, to celebrate his success. The presence of Balaustion has stripped the proper Aristophanes of his "accidents," and under her searching gaze he stands undisguised to be questioned. She puts him on his defence, and hence the "Apology." He recognises the divine in her, and she in him. The discussion, therefore, will be on the principles underlying the works of Euripides, the man of advance, the pioneer of the newer and better age to come, and those of the conservative apologist of prescription, Aristophanes the aristocrat. He defends his first *Thesmophoriazusæ*, which failed; his *Grasshopper*, which followed and failed also. There was reason why he wrote both: he painted the world as it was, mankind as they lived and walked, not human nature as seen though the medium of the student's closet. "Old wine's the wine; new poetry drinks raw." The friend of Socrates might weave his fancies, but flesh and blood like that of Aristophanes needs stronger meat. "Curds and whey" might suit Euripides, the Apologist must have marrowy wine. The author of the *Alkestis*, which Balaustion raved about, was but a prig: he wrote of wicked kings. Aristophanes came nearer home, and attacked infamous abuses of the time, and scourged too with tougher thong than leek-and-onion plait. He wrote *The Birds*, *The Clouds*, and *The Wasps*. The poison-drama of Euripides has mortified the flesh of the men of Athens, so nothing but warfare can purge it. The play that failed last year he has rearranged; he added men to match the women there already, and had a hit at a new-fangled plan by which women should rule affairs. It succeeded, and so they all flocked merrily to feast, and merrily they supped till something happened,—he will confess its influence upon him. Towards the end of the feast there was a sudden knock: in came an old pale-swathed majesty, who addressed the priest, "Since Euripides is dead to-day, my choros, at the Greater Feast next month, shall, clothed in black, appear ungarlanded!" Sophocles (for it was he) mutely passed outwards and left them stupefied. Soon they found their tongues and began to make satiric comment, but Aristophanes swore that at the moment death to him seemed life and life seemed death. The play of which he had made a laughing-stock had meaning he had never seen till now. The question who was the greater poet, once so large, now became so small. He remembers his last discussion with the dead poet, two years since, when he said, "Aristophanes, you know what kind's the nobler—what makes grave or what makes grin!" He pointed out why his Ploutos failed: he had tried, alas! but with force which had been spent on base things, to paint the life of Man. The strength demanded for the race had been wasted ere the race began. Such thoughts as these, long to relate, but floating through the mind as solemn convictions are wont to do, occupied him till the Archon, the Feast-Master, divining what was passing in his mind, thought best to close the feast. He gave "To the good genius, then!" as a parting cup. Young Strattis cried, "Ay, the Comic Muse"; but Aristophanes, stopping the applause, said, "Stay! the Tragic Muse" (in honour of the dead Tragic Poet), and then he told of all the work of the man who had gone from them. But he had mocked at him so often that his audience would not believe him to be serious now, and burst into laughter, exclaiming, "The unrivalled one! He turns the Tragic on its Comic side!" He felt that he was growing ridiculous, and had to repair matters; so he thanked them for laughing with him, and also those who wept rather with the Lord of Tears, and bade the priest—president alike over the Tragic and Comic function of the god,—

"Help with libation to the blended twain!"

praising complex poetry operant for body as for soul, able to move to laughter and to tears, supreme in heaven and earth. The soul should not be unbodied; he would defend man's double nature. But, even as he spoke, he turned to the memory of "Cold Euripides," and declared that he would not abate attack if he were to encounter him again, because of his principle—"Raise soul, sink sense, Evirate Hermes!" And so, as they left the feast, he asked his friends to accompany him to Balaustion's home, to the lady and her husband who, passionate admirers of Euripides, had not been present on his triumph-day. When they heard the night's news, neither, he knew, would sleep, but watch; by right of his crown of triumph he would pay them a visit. Balaustion said, "Commemorate, as we, Euripides!" "What?" cried the comic poet, "profane the temple of your deity!—for deity he was, though as for himself he only figured on men's drinking mugs. And then, as his glance fell on the table, he saw the Herakles which the Tragic Poet had given to Balaustion. "Give me the sheet," he asks. She interrupted, "You enter fresh from your worst infamy, last instance of a long outrage—throw off hate's celestiality, show me a mere man's hand ignobly clenched against the supreme calmness of the dead poet." Scarcely noticing her, he said, "Dead and therefore safe; only after death begins immunity of faultiness from punishment. Hear Art's defence. Comedy is coeval with the birth of freedom, its growth matches the greatness of the Republic. He found the Comic Art a club, a means of inflicting pnnishment without downright slaying: was he to thrash only the crass fool and the clownish knave, or strike at malpractice that affects the State? His was not the game to change the customs of Athens, lead age or youth astray, play the demagogue at the Assembly or the sophist at the Debating Club, or (worst and widest mischief) preach innovation from the theatre, bring contempt on oaths, and adorn licentiousness. And so he new-tipped with steel his cudgel, he had demagogues in coat-of-mail and cased about with impudence to chastise; he was spiteless, for his attack went through the mere man to reach the principle worth purging from Athens. He did not attack Lamachos, but war's representative; not Cleon, but flattery of the populace; not Socrates, but the pernicious seed of sophistry, whereby youth was perverted to chop logic and worship whirligig. His first feud with Euripides was when he maintained that we should enjoy life as we find it instead of magnifying our miseries. Euripides would talk about the empty name, while the thing's self lay neglected beneath his nose. Aristophanes represented the whole Republic,—gods, heroes, priests, legislators, poets—all these would have been in the dust, pummelled into insignificance, had Euripides had his way. To him heroes were no more, hardly so much, as men. Men were ragged, sick, lame, halt, and blind, their speech but street terms; and so, having drawn sky earthwards, he must next lift earth to sky. Women, once mere puppets, must match the male in thinking, saying, doing. The very slave he recognised as man's mate. There are no gods. Man has no master, owns neither right nor wrong, does what he likes, himself his sole law. As there are no gods, there is only "Necessity" above us. No longer to Euripides is there one plain positive enunciation, incontestable, of what is good, right, decent here on earth. And so Euripides triumphed, though he rarely gained a prize. And Aristophanes, wielding the comic weapon, closed with the enemy in good honest hate, called Euripides one name and fifty epithets. He hates "sneaks whose art is mere desertion of a trust." And so he doses each culprit with comedy, doctors the word-monger with words. Socrates he nicknames chief quack, necromancer; Euripides—well, he acknowledges every word is false if you look at it too close, but at a distance all is indubitable truth behind the lies. Aristophanes declares the essence of his teaching to be, Accept the old, contest the strange, misdoubt every man whose work is yet to do, acknowledge the work already done. Religion, laws, are old—that is, so much achieved and victorious truth, wrung from adverse circumstance by heroic men who beat the world and left their work in evidence. It was Euripides who caused the fight, and Aristophanes has beaten him; if, however. Balaustion can adduce anything to contravene this, let her say on." Balaustion replies that she is but a mere mouse confronting the forest monarch, a woman with no quality, but the love of all things lovable. How should she dare deny the results he says his songs are pregnant with? She is a foreigner too. Many perhaps view things too severely, as dwellers in some distant isles,—the Cassiterides, for example,—ignorant and lonely, who seeing some statue of Phidias or picture of Teuxis, might feebly judge that hair and hands and fashion of garb, not being like their own, must needs be wrong. So her criticism of art may be equally in fault as theirs, nevertheless she will proceed if she may. "Comedy, you say, is prescription and a rite; it rose with Attic liberty, and will fall with freedom; but your games, Olympian, Pythian and the others, the gods gave you these; and Comedy, did it come so late that your grandsires can remember its beginning? And you were first to change buffoonery for wit, and filth for cleanly sense. You advocate peace, support religion, lash irreverence, yet rebuke superstition with a laugh. Innovation and all change you attack:

with you the oldest always is the best; litigation, mob rule and mob favourites you attack; you are hard on sophists and poets who assist them: snobs, scamps, and gluttons you do not spare,—all these noble aims originated with you! Yet Euripides in Cresphontes sang Peace before you! Play after play of his troops tumultuously to confute your boast. No virtue but he praised, no vice but he condemned ere you were boy! As for your love of peace, you did not show your audience that war was wrong, but Lamachos absurd, not that democracy was blind, but Cleon a sham, not superstition vile but Nicias crazy. You gave the concrete for the abstract, you pretended to be earnest while you were only indifferent. You tickled the mob with the idea that peace meant plenty of good things to eat, while in camp the fare is hard and stinted. Peace gives your audience flute girls and gaiety. War freezes the campaigners in the snow. And so, with all the rest you advocate; do not go to law: beware of the Wasps! but as for curing love of lawsuits, you exhibit cheating, brawling, fighting, cursing as capital fun! And when the writer of the new school attacks the vile abuses of the day, straightway to conserve the good old way, you say the rascal cannot read or write, is extravagant, gets somebody to help his sluggish mind, and lets him court his wife; his uncle deals in crockery, and himself—a stranger! And so the poet-rival is chased out of court. And this is Comedy, our sacred song, censor of vice and virtue's safeguard! You are indignant with sophistry, and say there is but a single side to man and thing; but the sophists at least wish their pupils to believe what they teach, and to practise what they believe; can you wish that? Assume I am mistaken: have you made them end the war? Has your antagonist Euripides succeeded better? He spoke to a dim future, and I trust truth's inherent kingliness. 'Arise and go: both have done honour to Euripides!'" But Aristophanes demands direct defence, and not oblique by admonishment of himself. Balaustion tells him that last year Sophocles was declared by his son to be of unsound mind, and for defence his father just recited a chorus chant of his last play. The one adventure of her life that made Euripides her friend was the story of Hercules and Alcestis. When she met the author last, he said, "I sang another Hercules; it gained no prize, but take it—your love the prize! And so the papyrus, with the pendent style, and the psalterion besides, he gave her: by this should she remember the friend who loved Balaustion once. May I read it as defence? I read." [The HERAKLES, or Raging Hercules of Euripides, is translated literally by Mr. Browning on the principles which he laid down in the preface to the Agamemnon. In Potter's *Translation of the Tragedies of Euripides* we have the following from the introduction to the play: "The first scenes of this tragedy are very affecting; Euripides knew the way to the heart, and as often as his subject leads him to it, he never fails to excite the tenderest pity. We are relieved from this distress by the unexpected appearance of Hercules, who is here drawn in his private character as the most amiable of men: the pious son, the affectionate hnsband, and the tender father win our esteem as much as the unconquered hero raises our admiration. Here the feeling reader will perhaps wish that the drama had ended, for the next scenes are dreadful indeed, and it must be confessed that the poet has done his subject terrible justice, but without any of that absurd extravagance which, in Seneca becomes *un tintamarre horrible qui se passe dans le tête de ce Héros devenu fou.* From the violent agitation into which we are thrown by these deeds of honour, we are suffered by degrees to subside into the tenderest grief, in which we are prepared before to sympathise with the unhappy Hercules by that esteem which his amiable disposition had raised in us; and this perhaps is the most affecting scene of sorrow that ever was produced in any theatre. Upon the whole, though this tragedy may not be deemed the most agreeable by the generality of readers, on account of the too dreadful effects of the madness of Hercules, yet the various turns of fortune are finely managed, the scenes of distress highly wrought, and the passions of pity, terror and grief strongly touched. The scene is at Thebes before the palace of Hercules. The persons of the Drama—Amphitryon, Megara, Lycus, Hercules, Iris, Lyssa (the goddess of madness), Theseus, Messenger; Chorus of aged Thebans.]" They were silent after the reading for a long time. "Our best friend—lost, our best friend!" mused Aristophanes, "and who is our best friend?" He then instances in reply a famous Greek game, known as *kottabos*, played in various ways, but the latest with a sphere pierced with holes. When the orb is set rolling, and wine is adroitly thrown a figure suspended in a certain position can be struck by the fluid; but its only chance of being so hit is when it fronts just that one outlet. So with Euripides: he gets his knowledge merely from one single aperture—that of the High and Right; till he fronts this he writes no play. When the hole and his head happen to correspond, in drops the knowledge that Aristophanes can make respond to every opening—Low, Wrong, Weak; all the apertures bring him knowledge; he gets his wine at every turn; why not? Evil and Little are just as natural as Good and Great, and he demands to know them, and not one phase of life alone. So that he is the "best friend of man." No doubt, if in one man the High and Low could be reconciled, in tragi-comic verse he would be superior to both when born in the Tin Islands (as he eventually was in the person of Shakespeare). He will sing them a song of Thamyris, the Thracian bard, who boasted that he could rival the Muses, and was punished by them by being deprived of sight and voice and the power of playing the lute. Before he had finished the song, however, he laughed, "Tell the rest who may!" He had not tried to match the muse and sing for gods; he sang for men, and of the things of common life. He bids this couple farewell till the following year, and departs. In a year many things had happened. Aristophanes had produced his play, *The Frogs*. It had been rapturously applauded, and the author had been crowned; he is now the people's "best friend." He had satirised Euripides more vindictively than before; he had satirised even the gods and the Eleusinian Mysteries; and, in the midst of the "frog merriment," Lysander, the Spartan, had captured Athens, and his first word to the people was, "Pull down your long walls: the place needs none!" He gave them three days to wreck their proud bulwarks, and the people stood stupefied, stonier than their walls. The time expired, and when Lysander saw they had done nothing, he ordered all Athens to be levelled in the dust. Then stood forth Euthukles, Balaustion's husband, and "flung that choice flower," a snatch of a tragedy of Euripides, the *Electra*; then—

> "Because Greeks are Greeks, though Sparté's brood,
> And hearts are hearts, though in Lusandros' breast,
> And poetry is power, and Euthukles
> Had faith therein to, full face, fling the same—
> Sudden, the ice thaw!"

And the assembled foe cried, "Reverence Elektra! Let stand Athenai!" and so, as Euripides had saved the Athenian exiles in Syracuse harbour, now he saved Athens herself. But her brave long walls were destroyed, destroyed to sound of flute and lyre, wrecked to the kordax step, and laid in the dust to the mocking laughter of a Comedy-chorus. And so no longer would Balaustion remain to see the shame of the beloved city. "Back to Rhodes!" she cried. "There are no gods, no gods! Glory to God—who saves Euripides!" [The long walls of Athens consisted of the wall to Phalerum on the east, about four miles long, and of the wall to the harbour of Piraeus on the west, about four and a half miles long; between these two, at a short distance from the latter and parallel to it, another wall was erected, thus making two walls leading to the Piraeus, with a narrow passage between them. The entire circuit of the walls was nearly twenty-two miles, of which about five and a half miles belonged to the city, nine and a half to the long walls, and seven miles to Piraeus, Munychia, and Phalerum.]

Plutarch, in his life of Lysander, tells how Euripides saved Athens from destruction and the Athenians from slavery:—"After Lysander had taken from the Athenians all their ships except twelve, and their fortifications were delivered up to him, he entered their city on the sixteenth of the month Munychon (April), the very day they had overthrown the barbarians in the naval fight at Salamis. He presently set himself to change their form of government; and finding that the people resented his proposal, he told them 'that they had violated the terms of their capitulation, for their walls were still standing after the time fixed for the demolishing of them was passed; and that, since they had broken the first articles, they must expect new ones from the council.' Some say he really did propose, in the council of the allies, to reduce the Athenians to slavery; and that Erianthis, a Theban officer, gave it as his opinion that the city should be levelled with the ground, and the spot on which it stood turned to pasturage. Afterwards, however, when the general officers met at an entertainment, a musician of Phocis happened to begin a chorus in the *Electra* of Euripides, the first lines of which are these—

> 'Unhappy daughter of the great Atrides,
> Thy straw-crowned palace I approach.'

The whole company were greatly moved at this incident, and could not help reflecting how barbarous a thing it would be to raze that noble city, which had produced so many great and illustrious men. Lysander, however, finding the Athenians entirely in his power, collected the musicians of the city, and having joined to them the band belonging to the camp, pulled down the walls, and burned the ships, to the sound of their instruments."

NOTES. [The pages are those of the complete edition, in 16 vols.]—P. 3, *Euthukles*, the husband of Balaustion, whom she met first at Syracuse. p. 4, *Koré*, the daughter of Ceres, the same as Proserpine. p. 6, *Peiraios*, the principal harbour of Athens, with which it was connected by the long walls; "*walls, long double-range Themistoklean*": after Themistocles, the Athenian general, who planned the fortifications of Athens; *Dikast* and *heliast*: the Dikast was the judge (*dike*, a suit, was the term for a civil process); the heliasts were jurors, and in the flourishing period of the democracy numbered six thousand. p. 7, *Kordax-step*, a lascivious comic dance: to perform it off the stage was regarded as a sign of intoxication or profligacy; *Propulaia*, a court or vestibule of the Acropolis at Athens; *Pnux*, a place at Athens set apart for holding assemblies: it was built on a rock; *Bema*, the elevated position occupied by those who addressed the assembly. p. 8, *Dionusia*, the great festivals of Bacchus, held three times a year, when alone dramatic representations at Athens took place; "*Hermippos to pelt Perikles*": Hermippos was a poet who accused Aspasia, the mistress of Pericles, of impiety; "*Kratinos to swear Pheidias robbed a shrine*": Kratinos was a comic poet of Athens, a contemporary of Aristophanes; *Eruxis*, the name of a small satirist. (Compare "*The Frogs*" ll. 933-934.) *Momos*, the god of pleasantry: he satirised the gods; *Makaria*, one of the characters in the *Heraclidæ* of Euripides: she devoted herself to death to enable the Athenians to win a victory. p. 9, "*Furies in the Oresteian song*"—Alecto, Tisiphone, and Megæra: they haunted Orestes after he murdered his mother Clytemnestra: "*As the Three*," etc., the three tragic poets, Æschylus, Sophocles and Euripides. *Klutaimnestra*, wife of Agamemnon and mother of Orestes, Iphigenia, and Electra: she murdered her husband on his return from Troy; *Iocasté*, Iocasta, wife of Laius and mother of Œdipus; *Medeia*, daughter of Aetes: when Jason repudiated her she killed their children; *Choros:* the function of the chorus, represented by its leader, was to act as an ideal public: it might consist of old men and women or maidens; dances and gestures were introduced, to illustrate the drama. p. 10, *peplosed and kothorned*, robed and buskined. *Phrunicos*, a tragic poet of Athens: he was heavily fined by the government for exhibiting the sufferings of a kindred people in a drama. (Herod., vi., 21.) "*Milesian smart-place*," the Persian conquest of Miletus. p. 11, *Lenaia*, a festival of Bacchus, with poetical contentions, etc.; *Baccheion*, a temple of Bacchus; *Andromedé*, rescued from a sea-monster by Perseus; *Kresphontes*, one of the tragedies of Euripides; *Phokis*, a country of northern Greece, whence came the husband of Balaustion, who saved Athens by a song from Euripides; *Bacchai*, a play by Euripides, not acted till after his death. p. 12, *Amphitheos*, a priest of Ceres at Athens, ridiculed by Aristophanes to annoy Euripides. p. 14, *stade*, a single course for foot-races at Olympia—about a furlong; *diaulos*, the double track of the racecourse for the return. p. 15, *Hupsipule*, queen of Lemnos, who entertained Jason in his voyage to Colchis: "*Phoinissai*" (*The Phœnician Women*), title of one of the plays of Euripides; "*Zethos against Amphion*": Zethos was a son of Jupiter by Antiope, and brother to Amphion; *Macedonian Archelaos*, a king of Macedonia who patronised Euripides. p. 16, *Phorminx*, a harp or guitar; "*Alkaion*," a play of Euripides; *Pentheus*, king of Thebes, who refused to acknowledge Bacchus as a god; "*Iphigenia in Aulis*," a play by Euripides; *Mounuchia*, a port of Attica between the Piræus and the promontory of Sunium; "*City of Gapers*," Athens—so called on account of the curiosity of the people; *Kopaic eel:* the eels of Lake Copais, in Bœotia, were very celebrated, and to this day maintain their reputation. p. 17, *Arginousai*, three islands near the shores of Asia Minor; *Lais*, a celebrated courtesan, the mistress of Alcibiades; *Leogoras*, an Athenian debauchee; *Koppa-marked*, branded as high bred; *choinix*, a liquid measure; *Mendesian wine:* Wine from Mende, a city of Thrace, famous for its wines; *Thesmophoria*, a women's festival in honour of Ceres, made sport of by Aristophanes. p. 18, *Krateros*, probably an imaginary character.

Arridaios and *Krateues*, local poets in royal favour; *Protagoras*, a Greek atheistic philosopher, banished from Athens, died about 400 B.C.; "*Comic Platon*," a Greek poet, called "the prince of the middle comedy," flourished 445 B.C.; *Archelaos*, king of Macedonia. p. 19, "*Lusistraté*," a play by Aristophanes, in which the women demand a peace; *Kleon*: Cleon was an Athenian tanner and a great popular demagogue, 411 B.C., distinguished afterwards as a general; he was a great enemy of Aristophanes. p. 20, *Phuromachos*, a military leader; *Phaidra*, fell in love with Hippolytus, her son-in-law, who refused her love, which proved fatal to him p. 21, *Salabaccho*, a performer in Aristophanes' play, *The Lysistrata*, acting the part of "Peace", *Aristeides*, an Athenian general, surnamed the Just, banished 484 B.C.; *Miltiades*, the Athenian general who routed the armies of Darius, died 489 B.C.; "*A golden tettix in his hair*" (a grasshopper), an Athenian badge of honour worn as indicative that the bearer had "sprung from the soil"; *Kleophon*, a demagogue of Athens. p. 22, *Thesmophoriazousai*, a play by Aristophanes satirising women and Euripides, B.C. 411. p. 23, *Peiraios*, the seaport of Athens; *Alkamenes*, a statuary who lived 448 B.C., distinguished for his beautiful statues of Venus and Vulcan; *Thoukudides* (Thucydides), the Greek historian, died at Athens 391 B.C. p. 24, *Herakles* (Hercules), who had brought Alcestis back to life: the subject of a play by Euripides. p. 25, *Eurustheus*, king of Argos, who enjoined Hercules the most hazardous undertakings, hoping he would perish in one of them; *King Lukos*, the son of an elder Lukos said to have been the husband of Dirke; *Megara*, daughter of Creon, king of Thebes, and wife of Hercules; *Thebai—i.e.*, of Creon of Thebes; *Heracleian House*, the house of Hercules. p. 26, *Amphitruon*, a Theban prince, foster-father of Herakles, *i.e.*, the husband of Alkmene the mother of Herakles by Zeus; *Komos-cry*, a "Komos" was a revel; *Dionusos*, *Bacchos*, *Phales*, *Iacchos* (all names of Bacchus): the goat was sacrificed to Bacchus on account of the propensity that animal has to destroy the vine. p. 27, *Mnesilochos*, the father-in-law of Euripides, a character in the *Thesmophoriazousai*; *Toxotes*, an archer in the same play; *Elaphion*, leader of the chorus of females or flute-players. p. 30, *Helios*, the God of the Sun; *Pindaros*, the greatest lyric poet of Greece, born 552 B.C.; "*Idle cheek band*" refers to a support for the cheeks worn by trumpeters; *Cuckoo-apple*, the highly poisonous tongue-burning Cuckoo-pint (*Arum maculatum*); *Thasian*, Thasus, an island in the Ægean Sea famous for its wine; *threttanelo* and *neblaretai*, imitative noises; *Chrusomelolonthion-Phaps*, a dancing girl's name. p. 31, *Artamouxia*, a character in the *Thesmophoriazousai* of Aristophanes; *Hermes* = Mercury; *Goats-breakfast*, improper allusions, connected with Bacchus; *Archon*, a chief magistrate of Athens; "*Three days' salt fish slice*": each soldier was required to take with him on the march three days' rations. p. 32, *Archinos*, a rhetorician of Athens (Schol. in Aristoph. *Ran.*); *Agurrhios*, an Athenian general in B.C. 389: he was a demagogue; "*Bald-head Bard*": this describes Aristophanes, and the two following words indicate his native place; *Kudathenaian*, native of the Deme Cydathenê; *Pandionid*, of the tribe of Pandionis; "*son of Philippos*": Aristophanes here gives the names of his father and of his birthplace; *anapæsts*, feet in verse, whereof the first syllables are short and the last long; *Phrunichos* (see on p. 10); *Choirilos*, a tragic poet of Athens, who wrote a hundred and fifty tragedies. p. 33, *Kratinos*, a severe and drunken satirist of Athens, 431 B.C.; "*Willow-wicker-flask*," *i.e.*, "Flagon," the name of a comedy by Kratinos which took the first prize, 423 B.C.; *Mendesian*, from Mende in Thrace. p. 36, "*Lyric shell or tragic barbiton*," instruments of music: the barbiton was a lyre; shells were used as the bodies of lyres; *Tuphon*, a famous giant chained under Mount Etna. p. 38, *Sousarion*, a Greek poet of Megara, said to have been the inventor of comedy; *Chionides*, an Athenian poet, by some alleged to have been the inventor of comedy. p. 39, "*Grasshoppers*," a play of Aristophanes?; "*Little-in-the-Fields*," suburban or village feasts of Bacchus. p. 40, *Ameipsias*, a comic poet ridiculed by Aristophanes for his insipidity; *Salaminian*, of Salamis, an island on the coast of Attica. p. 41, *Archelaos*, king of Macedonia, patron of Euripides. p. 42, *Iostephanos* (violet-crowned), a title applied to Athens; *Dekeleia*, a village of Attica north of Athens; *Kleonumos*, an Athenian often ridiculed by Aristophanes; *Melanthios*, a tragic poet, a son of Philocles; *Parabasis*, an address in the old comedy, where the author speaks through the mouth of the chorus; "*The Wasps*," one of the famous plays of Aristophanes. p. 43, *Telekleides*, an Athenian comic poet of the age of Pericles; *Murtilos*, a comic poet; *Hermippos*, a poet, an elder contemporary of Aristophanes; *Eupolis:* is coupled with Aristophanes as a chief representative of the old comedy (born 446 B.C.); *Kratinos*, a contemporary comic poet, who died a few years after Aristophanes began to write for the stage; *Mullos* and *Euetes*, comic poets of Athens; *Megara*, a small country of Greece. p. 44, *Morucheides*, an archon of Athens, in whose time it was ordered that no one should be ridiculed on the stage by name; *Sourakosios*, an Athenian lawyer ridiculed by the poets for his garrulity; *Tragic Trilogy*, a series of three dramas, which, though complete each in itself, bear a certain relation to each other, and form one historical and poetical picture—*e.g.*, the three plays of the *Oresteia*, the *Agamemnon*, the *Choëphoræ*, and the *Eumenides*, by Æschylus. p. 45, "*The Birds*," the title of one of Aristophanes' plays. p. 46, *Triphales*, a three-plumed helmet-wearer; *Trilophos*, a three-crested helmet-wearer; *Tettix* (the grasshopper), a sign of honour worn as a golden ornament; "*Autochthon-brood*": the Athenians so called themselves, boasting that they were as old as the country they inhabited; *Taügetan*, a mountain near Sparta. p. 47, *Ruppapai*, a sailor's cry; *Mitulenê*, the capital of Lesbos, a famous seat of learning, and the birthplace of many great men; *Oidipous*, son of Laius, king of Thebes, and Jocasta: he murdered his own father; *Phaidra*, who fell in love with her son Hippolytus; *Augê*, the mother of Telephus by Hercules; *Kanakê*, a daughter of Æolus, who bore a child to her brother Macareus; *antistrophê*, a part of the Greek choral ode. p. 48, *Aigina*, an island opposite Athens. p. 49, *Prutaneion*, the large hall at Athens where the magistrates feasted with those who had rendered great services to the country; *Ariphrades*, a person ridiculed by Aristophanes for his filthiness; *Karkinos* and his sons were Athenian dancers: supposed here to have been performing in a play of Ameipsias. p. 50, *Parachoregema*, the subordinate chorus; *Aristullos*, an infamous poet; "*Bald Bard's hetairai*," Aristophanes' female companions. p. 51, *Murrhinê* and *Akalanthis*, chorus girls representing "good-humour" and "indulgence"; *Kalligenia*, a name of Ceres: here it means her festival celebrated by the woman chorus of the *Thesmophoriazousai; Lusandros* = Lysander, a celebrated Spartan general; *Euboia*, a large island in the Ægean Sea; "*The Great King's Eye*," the nickname of the

Persian ambassador in the play of *The Acharnians; Kompolakuthes*, a puffed-up braggadocio. p. 52, *Strattis*, a comic poet; *klepsudra*, a water clock; *Sphettian vinegar* = vinegar from the village of Sphettus; *silphion*, a herb by some called masterwort, by some benzoin, by others pellitory; *Kleonclapper*, *i.e.*, a scourge of Cleon; *Agathon*, an Athenian poet, very lady-like in appearance, a character in *The Women's Festival* of Aristophanes; "*Babaiax!*" interjection of admiration. p. 54, "*Told him in a dream*" (see Cicero, *Divinatione*, xxv); *Euphorion*, a son of Æschylus, who published four of his father's plays after his death, and defeated Euripides with one of them; *Trugaios*, a character in the comedy of *Peace*: he is a distressed Athenian who soars to the sky on a beetle's back; *Philonides*, a Greek comic poet of Athens; *Simonides*, a celebrated poet of Cos, 529 B.C.: he was the first poet who wrote for money: he bore the character of an avaricious man; *Kallistratos*, a comic poet, rival of Aristophanes; *Asklepios* = Æsculapius; *Iophon*, a son of Sophocles, who tried to make out that his father was an imbecile. p. 58, *Maketis*, capital of Macedonia; *Pentelikos*, a mountain of Attica, celebrated for its marble. p. 60, *Lamachos*: the "Great Captain" of the day was the brave son of Xenophanes, killed before Syracuse B.C. 414: satirised by Aristophanes in *The Acharnians*; *Pisthetairos*, a character in Aristophanes' *Birds*; *Strepsiades*, a character in *The Clouds* of Aristophanes; *Ariphrades* (see under p. 49). p. 63, "*Nikias, ninny-like*," the Athenian general who ruined Athens at Syracuse—was very superstitious. p. 64, *Hermai*, statues of Mercury in the streets of Athens: we have one in the British Museum. p. 67, *Sophroniskos*, was the father of Socrates. p. 75, *Kephisophon*, a friend of Euripides, said to have afforded him literary assistance. p. 79, *Palaistra*, the boy's school for physical culture. p. 82, *San*, the letter S, used as a horse-brand. p. 81, *Aias* = Ajax. p. 82, *Pisthetairos*, an enterprising Athenian in the comedy of the *Birds*. p. 83, "*Rocky-ones*" = Athenians; *Peparethian*, famous wine of Peparethus, on the coast of Macedonia. p. 85, *Promachos*, a defender or champion, name of a statue: the bronze statue of *Athene Promachos* is here referred to, which was erected from the spoils taken at Marathon, and stood between the Propylæa and the Erechtheum: the proportions of this statue were so gigantic that the gleaming point of the lance and the crest of the helmet were visible to seamen on approaching the Piræus from Sunium (Seyffert, *Dict. Class. Ant.*); *Oresteia*, the trilogy or three tragedies of Æschylus—the *Agamemnon*, the *Chöephoræ*, and the *Eumenides*. p. 86, *Kimon*, son of Miltiades: he was a famous Athenian general, and was banished by the *Boulé*, or council of state; *Prodikos*, a Sophist put to death by the Athenians about 396 B.C., satirised by Aristophanes. p. 87, *Kottabos*, a kind of game in which liquid is thrown up so as to make a loud noise in falling: it was variously played (*see* Seyffert's *Dict. Class. Ant.*, p. 165); *Choes*, an Athenian festival; *Theoros*, a comic poet of infamous character. p. 88, *Brilesian*, Brilessus, a mountain of Attica. p. 89, "*Plataian help*," prompt assistance: the Platæans furnished a thousand soldiers to help the Athenians at Marathon; *Saperdion*, a term of endearment; *Empousa*, a hobgoblin or horrible sceptre: "Apollonius of Tyana saw in a desert near the Indus an empousa or ghûl taking many forms" (*Philostratus*, ii., 4); *Kimberic*, name of a species of vestment. p. 93, "*Kuthereia's self*," a surname of Venus. p. 94, *plethron square*, 100 square feet; *chiton*, the chief and indispensible article of female dress, or an undergarment worn by both sexes. p. 95, *Ion*, a tragic poet of Chios; *Iophon*, son of Sophocles, a poor poet; *Aristullos*, an infamous poet. p. 98, *Cloudcuckooburg*, in Aristophanes' play *The Birds* these animals are persuaded to build a city in the air, so as to cut off the gods from men; *Tereus*, a king of Thrace, who offered violence to his sister-in-law Philomela; *Hoopoe triple-crest*: Tereus was said to have been changed into a hoopoe (*The Birds*); *Palaistra tool*, *i.e.*, one highly developed; *Amphiktuon*, a council of the wisest and best men of Greece: *Phrixos*, son of Athamas, king of Thebes, persecuted by his stepmother was fabled to have taken flight to Colchis on a ram. p 99, *Priapos*, the god of orchards, gardens, and licentiousness; *Phales Iacchos*, indecent figure of Bacchus. p. 102, *Kallikratidas*, a Spartan who routed the Athenian fleet about 400 B.C.; *Theramenes*, an Athenian philosopher and general of the time of Alcibiades. p. 103, *chaunoprockt*, a catamite. p. 113, *Aristonumos* a comic poet contemporary with Aristophanes; *Ameipsias*, a comic poet satirised by Aristophanes; *Sannurion*, a comic poet of Athens: *Neblaretai! Rattei!* exclamations of joy. p. 117, *Sousarion*, a Greek poet of Megara, who introduced comedy at Athens on a movable stage,

562 B.C.: he was unfriendly to the ladies. p. 118, *Lemnians*, *The Hours*, *Female Playhouse*, etc., these are all lost plays of Aristophanes. p. 119, *Kassiterides*, "the tin islands": the Scilly Islands, Land's End, and Lizard Point. p. 121, "*Your games*": *Olympian*, in honour of Zeus at Olympia; *Pythian*, held near Delphi; *Isthmian*, held in the Isthmus of Corinth; *Nemeian*, celebrated in the valley of Nemea. p. 126, *Phoibos*, name of Apollo or the sun; *Kunthia* = Cynthia, a surname of Diana, from Mount Cynthus, where she was born. p. 128, *skiadeion*, the umbel or umbrella-like head of plants like fennel or anise—hence a parasol or umbrella; *Huperbolos*, an Athenian demagogue. p. 129, *Theoria*, festival at Athens in honour of Apollo — character in *The Peace*; *Opôra*, a character in *The Peace*. p. 133, "*Philokleon turns Bdelukleon*," an admirer of Cleon, turned detester of Cleon: character in Aristophanes' comedy *The Wasps*. p. 135, *Logeion*, the stage where the actors perform—properly "the speaking place." p. 137, *Lamia-shape*, as of the monsters with face of a woman and body of a serpent; *Kukloboros*, roaring—a noise as of the torrent of the river in Attica of that name; *Platon* = Plato. p. 140, *Konnos*, the play of Ameipsias which beat the *Clouds* of Aristophanes in the award of the judges; *Moruchides*, a magistrate of Athens, in whose time it was decided that no one should be ridiculed on the stage by name; *Euthumenes*, *Argurrhios*, *Surakosios*, *Kinesias*, Athenian rulers who endeavoured to restrain the gross attacks of the comic poets. p. 141, *Acharnes*, Aristophanes' play *The Acharnians*: it is the most ancient specimen of comedy which has reached us. p. 143, *Poseidon*, the Sea = Neptune. p. 144, *Triballos*, a vulgar deity. p. 145, *Kolonos*, an eminence near Athens; *stulos*, a style or pen to write with on wax tablets; *psalterion*, a musical instrument like a harp, a psaltery. p. 146, *Pentheus*, king of Thebes, who resisted the worship of Bacchus, and was driven mad by the god and torn to pieces by his own mother and her two sisters in their Bacchic frenzy. p. 147, *Herakles* = Hercules; *Argive Amphitruon*, son of Alkaios and husband of Alcmene; *Alkaios*, father of Amphitruon and grandfather of Hercules; *Perseus*, son of Jupiter and Danae; *Thebai*, capital of Bœotia, founded by Cadmus; *Sownones*, the armed men who rose from the dragons' teeth sown by Cadmus; *Ares*, Greek name of Mars; *Kadmos*, founder of Bœotian

Thebes; *Kreon*, king of Thebes, father of Megara slain by Lukos; *Menoikeus*, father of the Kreon above referred to. p. 148, *Kuklopian city*: Argos, according to Euripides, was built by the seven Cyclopes: "These were architects who attended Prœtus when he returned out of Asia; among other works with which they adorned Greece were the walls of Mycenæ and Tiryns, which were built of unhewn stones, so large that two mules yoked could not move the smallest of them" (Potter); *Argos*, an ancient city, capital of Argolis in Peloponnesus; *Elektruon* a son of Perseus; *Herê* = Juno; *Tainaros*, a promontory of Laconia, where was the cavern whence Hercules dragged Cerberus; *Dirkê*, wife of the Theban prince Lukos; *Amphion*: "His skill in music was so great that the very stones were said to have been wrought upon by his lyre, and of themselves to have built the walls of Thebes" —*Carey* (*see* ABT VOGLER); *Zethos*, brother of Amphion; *Euboia*, the largest island in the Ægean Sea, now Negroponte. p. 149, *Minuai*, the Argonauts, companions of Jason. p. 150, *Taphian town*, Taphiæ, islands in the Ionian Sea. p. 153, *peplos*, a robe. p. 154, *Hellas* = Greece; *Nemeian monster*, the lion slain by Hercules. p. 156, *Kentaur race*, a people of Thessaly represented as half men and half horses; *Pholoé*, a mountain in Arcadia; *Dirphus*, a mountain of Eubœa which Hercules laid waste; *Abantid*: Abantis was an ancient name of Eubœa. p. 158, *Parnasos*, a mountain of Phocis. p. 165, *Peneios*, a river of Thessaly; *Mount Pelion*, a celebrated mountain of Thessaly; *Homole*, a mountain of Thessaly; *Oinoe* = Œne, a small town of Argolis; *Diomede*, a king of Thrace who fed his horses on human flesh, and was himself destroyed by Hercules. p. 166, *Hebros*, the principal river of Thrace; *Mukenaian tyrant*, Eurystheus, king of Mycenæ; *Amauros*, Amaurus, a river of Thessaly near the foot of Pelion; *Kuknos*, a son of Mars by Pelopea, killed by Hercules; *Amphanaia*, a Dorian city; *Hesperian*, west, towards Spain; *Maiotis*, Lake Mæotis, *i.e.*, the Sea of Azov. p. 167, *Lernaian snake*, the hydra slain by Hercules, who then drained the marsh of Lerna; *Erutheia*, an island near Cadiz, where Hercules drove the oxen of Geryon. p. 169, *Pelasgia* = Greece; *Daidalos*, mythical personage, father of Icarus; *Oichalia*, a town of Laconia, destroyed by Hercules. p. 177, *Ismenos*, a river of Bœotia flowing through

Thebes. p. 180, *Orgies*, festivals of Bacchus; *Chthonia*, a surname of Ceres; *Hermion*, a town of Argolis where Ceres had a famous temple; *Theseus*, king of Athens, conqueror of the Minotaur. p. 182, *Aitna* = Etna. p. 183, *Mnemosuné*, the mother of the Muses; *Bromios*, a surname of Bacchus; *Delian girls*, of Delos, one of the Cyclades islands; *Latona*, mother of Apollo and Diana. p. 188, *Acherontian harbour:* Acheron was one of the rivers of hell. p. 189, *Asopiad sisters*, daughters of the god of the river Asopus; *Puthios*, surname of the Delphian Apollo. *Helikonian muses:* Mount Helicon, in Bœotia, was sacred to Apollo and the Muses. p. 190, *Plouton* = Pluto, god of hell; *Paian*, name of Apollo, the healer; *Iris*, the swift-footed messenger of the gods. p. 193, *Keres*, the daughters of Night and personified necessity of Death. p. 194, *Ototoloi*, woe! alas! p. 195, *Tartaros* = Hades; *Pallas*, *i.e.*, Minerva. p. 198, *Niso's city*, port town of Megara; *Isthmos*, the isthmus of Corinth. p. 201, *Argolis*, a country of Peloponnesus, now Romania; *Danaos*, son of Belus, king of Egypt: he had fifty daughters, who murdered the fifty sons of Egyptus; *Prokné*, daughter of Pandion, king of Athens, wife of Tereus, king of Thrace. p. 202, *Itus*, son of Prokné. p. 206, *Taphioi*, the Taphians, who made war against Electryon, and killed all his sons; *Erinues* = the Furies. p. 213, *Erechtheidai's town* = Athens. p. 215, *Hundredheaded Hydra*, a dreadful monster slain by Hercules. p. 216, *Phlegruia*, a place of Macedonia, where Hercules defeated the giants. p. 234, *Iostephanos*, violet-crowned, a name of Athens. p. 235, *Thamuris*, an ancient Thracian bard; *Poikilé*, a celebrated portico of Athens, adorned with pictures of gods and benefactors; *Rhesus* was king of Thrace and ally of the Trojans; *Blind Bard* = Thamuris. p. 236, *Eurutos*, a king of Œchalia, who offered his daughter to a better shot than himself: Hercules won, but was denied the prize; *Dorion*, a town of Messenia, where Thamyris challenged the Muses to a trial of skill; *Balura*, a river of Peloponnesus. p. 241, *Dekeleia*, a village of Attica north of Athens, celebrated in the Peloponnesian war; *spinks*, chaffinches. p. 242, *Amphion*, son of Jupiter and inventor of Music: he built the walls of Thebes to the sound of his lyre. p. 245, *Castalian dew*, the fountain of Castalia, near Phocis, at the foot of Parnassus. p. 247, *Pheidippides*, the celebrated runner, a character also in *The Clouds*. p. 248, *Aigispotamoi*, Ægospotamos was the river where the Athenians were defeated by Lysander, B.C. 405; *Elaphebolion month*, stag-hunting time, when the poetical contests took place; *Lusandros*, the celebrated Spartan general Lysander; *triremes*, galleys with three banks of oars one above another. p. 249, *Bakis-prophecy*. Bacis was a famous soothsayer of Bœotia. p. 253, *Elektra*, daughter of Agamemnon, king of Argos; *Orestes* brother of Elektra, who saved his life p 254, *Klutaimnestra*, murdered her husband Agamemnon. p. 255, *Kommos*, a great wailing; *elelelelelen*, a loud crying; *Lakonians*, the Lacedemonians = the Spartans. p. 258, *Young Philemon*, a Greek comic poet; there was an old Philemon, contemporary with Menander.—Mr. Fotheringham, in his "Studies in the Poetry of Robert Browning," says: "Browning's *preference for Euripides* among Greek dramatists, and his defence of that poet in the person of Balaustion against Aristophanes, shows how distinctly he has considered the principles raised by the later drama of Greece, and how deliberately he prefers Euripidean art and aims to Aristophanic naturalism. He likes the human and ethical standpoint, the serious and truth-loving spirit of the tragic rather than the pure Hellenism of the comic poet; while the *Apology* suggests a broader spirit and a larger view, an art that unites the realism of the one with the higher interests of the other—delight in and free study of the world with ideal aims and spiritual truth" (p. 356).

Arezzo. A city of Tuscany, the residence of Count Guido Franceschini, the husband of Pompilia and her murderer. It is now a clean, well-built, well-paved, and flourishing town of ten thousand inhabitants. It is celebrated in connection with many remarkable men, as Mæcenas, Guido the musician, Guittone the poet, Cesalpini the botanist, Vasari, the author of the "Lives of the Painters," and many others. (*The Ring and the Book.*)

Art Poems. The great poems dealing with painting are "Fra Lippo Lippi," "Andrea del Sarto," "Old Pictures in Florence," "Pictor Ignotus," and "The Guardian Angel."

Artemis Prologizes. (*Dramatic Lyrics*, in *Bells and Pomegranates*, No. III. 1842.) Theseus became enamoured of Hippolyta when he attended Hercules in his expedition against the Amazons. Before she accepted him as her lover, he had to vanquish her in single combat, which difficult and dangerous task he accomplished. She accompanied him to Athens, and bore him a son, Hippolytus. The young prince excelled in every manly virtue, but he was averse to the female sex, and grievously offended Venus by neglecting her and devoting himself entirely to the worship of Diana, called by the Greeks Artemis. Venus was enraged, and determined to ruin him. Hippolyta in process of time died, and Theseus married Phædra, the daughter of Minos, the king of Crete. Unhappily, as soon as Phædra saw the young and accomplished Hippolytus, she conceived for him a guilty passion—which, however, she did her utmost to conceal. It was Venus who inspired her with this insane love, out of revenge to Hippolytus, whom she intended to ruin by this means. Phædra's nurse discovered the secret, and told it to the youth, notwithstanding the commands of her mistress to conceal it. The chaste young man was horrified at the declaration, and indignantly resented it. The disgraced and betrayed Phædra determined to take her own life; but dying with a letter in her hand which accused Hippolytus of attempts upon her virtue, the angry father, without asking his son for explanations, banished him from the kingdom, having first claimed the performance from Neptune of his promise to grant three of his requests. As Hippolytus fled from Athens, his horses were terrified by a sea monster sent on shore by Neptune. The frightened horses upset the chariot, and the young man was dragged over rocks and precipices and mangled by the wheels of his chariot. In the tragedy, as left by Euripides, Diana appears by the young man's dying bed and comforts him, telling him also that to perish thus was his fate:—

> "But now
> Farewell: to see the dying or the dead
> Is not permitted me: it would pollute
> Mine eyes; and thou art near this fatal ill."

The tragedy ends with the dying words of Hippolytus:—

> "No longer I retain my strength: I die;
> But veil my face, now veil it with my vests."

So far Euripides. Mr. Browning, however, carries the idea further, and makes Diana try to save the life of her worshipper, by handing him over to the care of Æsculapius, to restore to life and health by the wisest pharmacies of the god of healing. Mr. Browning's poem closes with the chaste goddess watching and waiting for the result of the attempt to save his life. The poet has adopted the Greek spelling in place of that to which we are more accustomed. The Greek names require their Latin equivalents for non-classical scholars. *Artemis* is the Greek name for *Diana; Asclepios* is *Æsculapius*; *Aphrodite*, the Greek name of *Venus*; *Poseidon* is *Neptune*; and *Phoibus* or *Phœbus* is *Apollo*, the Sun. *Heré* = Hera or Juno, Queen of Heaven. *Athenai* = Minerva. *Phaidra*, daughter of Minos and Pasiphae, who married Theseus. *Theseus*, king of Athens. *Hippolutos*, son of Theseus and Hippolyte. *Henetian horses*, or *Enetian*, of a district near Paphlagonia.

Artemisia Genteleschi (Beatrice Signorini, *Asolando*), "the consummate Artemisia" of the poem, was a celebrated artist (1590—1642). *See* BEATRICE SIGNORINI.

"Ask not the least word of praise," the first line of the lyric at the end of "A Pillar at Sebzevah," No. 11 of *Ferishtah's Fancies*.

Asolando: Fancies and Facts. Published in London, December 12th, 1889, on the day on which Mr. Browning died in Venice. *Contents:* Prologue; Rosny; Dubiety; Now; Humility; Poetics; Summum Bonum; A Pearl, A Girl; Speculative; White Witchcraft; Bad Dreams, I., II., III., IV.; Inapprehensiveness; Which? The Cardinal and the Dog; The Pope and the Net; The Bean-Feast; Muckle-mouth Meg; Arcades Ambo; The Lady and the Painter; Ponte dell' Angelo, Venice; Beatrice Signorini; Flute Music, with an Accompaniment; "Imperante Augusto, Natus est ——"; Development; Rephan; Reverie; Epilogue. The volume is dedicated to the poet's friend, Mrs. Arthur Bronson. In the dedication the poet explains the title Asolando: it was a "*title-name popularly ascribed to the inventiveness of the ancient secretary of Queen Cornaro, whose palace-tower still overlooks us.*" Asolare—"to disport in the open air, amuse oneself at random." "The objection that such a word nowhere occurs in the works of the Cardinal is hardly important. Bembo was too thorough a purist to conserve in print a term which in talk he might possibly toy with; but the word is more likely derived from a Spanish source. I use it for love of the place, and in requital of your pleasant assurance that an early poem of mine first attracted you thither; where and elsewhere, at La Mura as Cà Alvisi, may all happiness attend you!—Gratefully and affectionately yours, R. B."—Asolo, *Oct. 5th*, 1889.

Asolo (*Pippa Passes—Sordello—Asolando*), the ancient

Acelum: a very picturesque mediæval fortified town, in the province of Treviso, in Venetia, Italy, 5500 inhabitants, at the foot of a hill surmounted by the ruins of a castle, from which one of the most extensive panoramas of the great plain of the Brenta and the Piave, with the encircling Alps, and the distant insulated group of the Euganean hills, opens before the traveller. On a fine summer evening the two silver lines of the Piave and the Brenta may be followed from their Alpine valleys to the sea, in the midst of the green alluvial plain in which Treviso, Vicenza and Padua are easily recognised. Venice, with its cupolas and steeples, is seen near the extreme east horizon, which is terminated by the blue line of the Adriatic; whilst behind, to the north, the snow-capped peaks of the Alps rise in majestic grandeur. The village of Asolo is surrounded by a wall with mediæval turrets, and several of its houses present curiously sculptured façades.—The castle, a quadrangular building with a high tower, is an interesting monument of the thirteenth century. It was the residence of the beautiful Caterina Cornaro, the last queen of Cyprus, after the forced resignation of her kingdom to the Venetians in 1489. Here this lady of elegant tastes and refined education closed her days in comparative obscurity, in the enjoyment of an empty title and a splendid income, and surrounded by a small court and several literary characters. Of these, one of the most celebrated was Pietro Bembo, the historian of Venice, afterwards Cardinal, whose celebrated philosophical dialogues on the nature of love, the *Asolani*, have derived their name from this locality. Mr. Browning visited Asolo first when a young man; it was here that he gathered ideas for *Pippa Passes* and *Sordello*, and in the last year of his life his loving footsteps found their way to the little hill-town of that Italy whose name was graven on his heart. Here, as Mr. Sharp reminds us in his *Life of Browning*, the poet heard again the echo of Pippa's song—

"God's in His heaven, All's right with the world!"

He heard it as a young man, he hears it as he nears the dark river, the conviction had never left his soul for a moment in all the length of intervening years. Asolo will be a pilgrim spot for Browning lovers. The Catherine Cornaro referred to was the wife of King James II., of Cyprus; his marriage with this

Venetian lady of rank was designed to secure the support of the Republic of Venice. After his death, and that of his son James III., Queen Catherine felt she was unable to withstand the attacks of the Turks, and was induced to abdicate in favour of the Republic of Venice, which in 1487 took possession of the island. Catherine was assigned a palace and court at Asolo, as already mentioned. Her palace was the resort of the learned and accomplished men and women of Venice, famous amongst whom was her secretary, Cardinal Pietro Bembo, the celebrated author of the *History of Venice*, from 1487 to 1513, and a number of essays, dialogues, and poems. His dialogue on Platonic love is entitled *Gli Asolani*. He died in 1547. When Queen Catherine settled in her beautiful castle of Asolo, she could have found little cause to regret the circumstances which led her from her troubled kingdom of Cyprus to the idyllic sweetness of her later life. Surrounded by her twelve maids of honour and her eighty serving-men, her favourite negress, her parrots, apes, peacocks, and hounds, her peaceful life passed in ideal pleasantness. But the wealth and luxury of her surroundings did not make her selfish, or unconcerned for the welfare of her little kingdom. In all that concerned the happiness and well-being of her people she was as deeply interested as the monarchs of more important states. She opened a pawnbroking bank for the poor, imported corn from Cyprus and distributed it, and appointed competent officials to settle the complaints and difficulties of her subjects. She lived for her people's welfare, and wo their affections by her goodness and grace. For twenty years she lived at Asolo, leaving it on only three occasions: to visit her brother in Brescia; to walk to Venice across the frozen lagoon; and once when troops occupied her little town. She died then, at Venice, on July 10th, 1510, and was buried by the republic of the city in the sea, with its utmost magnificence. The fate could scarcely have been called cruel which gave a royal residence amid scenery such as Asolo can boast, under such conditions as blessed the later years of good Queen Catherine.

At the Mermaid. The Mermaid Tavern, in Cheapside, was the favourite resort of the great Elizabethan dramatists and poets. Raleigh's Club at the Mermaid was the meeting-place of Shakespeare's contemporaries, where he feasted with Raleigh, Ben Jonson, Beaumont and Fletcher, Ford, Massinger, Donne,

Drayton, Camden, Selden, and the rest. "At this meeting-place of the gods," says Heywood, in his *Hierarchy of Angels*:—

> "Mellifluous Shakespeare, whose enchanting quill
> Commanded mirth or passion, was but *Will*,
> And famous Jonson, tho' his learned pen
> Be dipt in Castaly, is still but *Ben*."

Mr. Browning introduces us to Shakespeare protesting that he makes no claim and has no desire to be the leader of a new school of poetry. In the person of Shakespeare Mr. Browning tells the world that if they want to know anything about him they must take his ideas as they are expressed in his works, not seek to pry into his life and opinions behind them. His works are the world's, his rest is his own. He protests, too, that when he utters opinions and expresses ideas dramatically they are not to be snatched at by leaders of sects and parties, and bottled as specimens for their museums, or used to give authority to their own pet principles. He does not set open the door of his bard's breast: on the contrary, he bars his portal, and leaves his work and his inquisitive visitors alike "outside." Notwithstanding this emphatic declaration, it is probable that few great poets have opened their hearts to the world more completely than Mr. Browning: it is as easy to construct his personality from his works as it is to reconstruct an old Greek temple from the sculptured stones which are scattered on its site. All Mr. Browning's characters talk the Browning tongue, and are as little given to barring their portals as he to closing the door of his breast. This fact must not, of course, be unduly pressed. The utterances of Caliban are not to be put on the same level as the thoughts, expressed a hundred times, which justify the ways of God to man. Having declared himself as determined to let the public have no glimpse inside his breast, in Stanza 10 he proceeds to admit us to his innermost soul, in its joy of life and golden optimism. It is as perfect a picture of the poet's healthy mind as he could possibly have given us, and is an earnest deprecation of the idea that a poet must necessarily be more or less insane. NOTES.—*Oreichalch* (7), a mixed metal resembling brass—bronze. "*Threw Venus*" (15): in dice the best cast (three sixes) was called "Venus." Ben Jonson tells us that his own wife was "a shrew, yet honest."

Austin Tresham. Gwendolen Tresham's betrothed, in *A Blot in the 'Scutcheon.* He is next heir to the earldom.

Azoth (*Paracelsus*). The universal remedy of Paracelsus, in alchemy. The term was applied to mercury, which was supposed to exist in every metallic body, and constitute its basis. The Azoth of Paracelsus, according to Mr. Browning, was simply the laudanum which he had discovered. The alchemists by Azoth sometimes meant to express the creative principle of nature. As "he was commonly believed to possess the double tincture, the power of curing diseases and transmuting metals," as Mr. Browning explains in a note to the poem, the expression is often difficult to define precisely, as indeed are many of the terms used by alchemists.

Azzo. Lords of Este (*Sordello*): Guelf leaders. The poem is concerned with Azzo VI. (1170—1212), who became the head of the Guelf party. During the whole lifetime of Azzo VI. a civil war raged almost without interruption in the streets of Ferrara, each party, it is said, being ten times driven from the city. Azzo VII. (1205-64) was constantly at war with Eccelino III. da Romano, who leagued himself with Salinguerra. Azzo married Adelaide, niece of Eccelino, and died 1264. (*Encyc. Brit.*)

Bad Dreams. (*Asolando.*) I. In the first dream the lover sees that the face of the loved one has changed: love has died out of the eyes, and the charm of the look has gone. Love is estranged, for faith has gone. With a breaking heart the lover can say love is still the same for him. II. A weird dream of a strange ball, a dance of death and hell, where, notwithstanding harmony of feet and hands, "man's sneer met woman's curse." The dreamer creeps to the wall side, avoiding the dance of haters, and steps into a chapel where is performed a strange worship by a priest unknown. The dreamer sees a worshipper—his wife—enter, to palliate or expurgate her soul of some ugly stain How contracted? "A mere dream" is an insufficient excuse. The soul in sleep, free from the disguises of the day, wanders at will. Perhaps it may indeed be that our suppressed evil thoughts—thoughts that, kept down by custom, conventionality, and respect for public opinion, never become incarnate in act—walk at night and revel in unfettered freedom, as foul gases rise from vaults and basements when the house is closed at night, and the purifying influences of the light and air are excluded. III. Is a dream of a primeval forest: giant trees, impenetrable tangle of enormous undergrowths, where lurks some brute-type. A lucid city of bright marbles, domes and spires, pure streets too fine for smirch of human foot, its solitary traverser the soul of the dreamer; and all at once appears a hideous sight: the beautiful city is devoured by the forest, the trees by the pavements turned to teeth. Nature is represented by the forest, Art by the city and its palaces. Each in its place is seen to be good and worthy, but when each devours the other both are accurst. The man seems to think that his wife conceals some part of her life from him; her nature is good and true, but he fears her art (or perhaps arts, we should say) destroys it. IV. A dream of infinite pathos. The wife's tomb, its slab weather-stained, its inscription overgrown with herbage, its name all but obliterated. Her husband comes to visit the grave. Was he her lover?—rather the cold critic of her life. She had felt her poverty in all that he demanded, and she had resigned him and life too; and as she moulders under the herbage, she sees in spirit her husband's strength and sternness gone, and he broken and praying that she were his again, with all her foibles, her faults: aye, crowned as queen of folly, he would be happy if her foot made a stepping-stone of his forehead. What had worked the miracle? Was the date on the stone the record of the day when his chance stab of scorn had killed her? There are cruel deeds and still more cruel words that no veiling herbage of balm and mint shall keep from haunting us in the time when repentance has come too late.

Badman, Mr. *The Life and Death of Mr. Badman*, as told by John Bunyan, contains the story of "Old Tod," which suggested to Mr. Browning the poem of *Ned Bratts* (*q.v.*).

Balaustion. The name of the Greek girl of Rhodes, who, when the Athenians were defeated at Syracuse and her countrymen had determined to side with the enemies of Athens, refused to forsake Athens, the light and life of the world. She saved her companions in the ship by which she fled from Rhodes by reciting to the people of Syracuse the *Alcestis* of Euripides. Her story is told in *Balaustion's Adventure*, and *Aristophanes'*

Apology, which is its sequel. Her name means "wild pomegranate flower."

Balaustion's Adventure, including a transcript from Euripides. London, 1871.—The adventure of Balaustion in the harbour of Syracuse came about as follows. Nicias (or Nikias as he is called in the poem), the Athenian general, was appointed, much against his inclination, to conduct the expedition against Sicily. After a long series of ill-successes he was completely surrounded by the enemy and was compelled to surrender with all his army. He was put to death, and all his troops were sent to the great stone quarries, there to perish of disease, hard labour and privation. At Syracuse Athens was shamed, and lost her ships and men, gaining a "death without a grave." After the disgraceful news had reached Greece the people of Rhodes rose in tumult, and, casting off their allegiance to Athens, they determined to side with Sparta. Balaustion, though only a girl, was so patriotic that she cried to all who would hear, begging them not to throw Athens off for Sparta's sake, nor be disloyal to all that was worth calling the world at all. She begged that all who agreed with her would take ship for Athens at once; a few heard and accompanied her. They were by adverse winds driven out of their course, and, being pursued by pirates, made for the island of Crete. Balaustion, to encourage the rowers, sprang upon the altar by the mast, crying to the sons of Greeks to free their wives, their children, and the temples of the gods; so the oars "churned the black waters white," and soon they saw to their dismay Sicily and the city of Syracuse,—they had run upon the lion from the wolf. A galley came out, demanding "if they were friends or foes?" "Kaunians," replied the captain. "We heard all Athens in one ode just now. Back you must go, though ten pirates blocked the bay." It was explained to the exiles that they wanted no Athenians there to spirit up the captives in the quarries. The captain prayed them by the gods they should not thrust suppliants back, but save the innocent who were not bent on traffic. In vain! And as they were about to turn and face the foe, one cried, "Wait! that was a song of Æschylus: how about Euripides? Might you know any of his verses too?" The captain shouted, "Praise the god. Here she stands—Balaustion. Strangers, greet the lyric girl!" And Balaustion said, "Save us, and I will recite hat strangest, saddest, sweetest song of his

—ALKESTIS. Take me to Herakles' temple you have here. I come a suppliant to him; put me upon his temple steps, to tell you his achievement as I may!" And so they rowed them in to Syracuse, crying, "We bring more of Euripides!" The whole city came out to hear, came rushing to the superb temple, on the topmost step of which they placed the girl; and plainly she told the play, just as she had seen it acted in Rhodes. A wealthy Syracusan brought a whole talent, and bade her take it for herself; she offered it to the god—

"For had not Herakles a second time
Wrestled with death and saved devoted ones?"

The poor captives in the quarries, when they heard the tale, sent her a crown of wild pomegranate flower—the name (Balaustion in Greek) she always henceforth bore. But there was a young man who every day, as she recited on the temple steps, stood at the foot; and, when liberated, they set sail again for Athens. There in the ship was he: he had a hunger to see Athens, and soon they were to marry. She visited Euripides, kissed his sacred hand, and paid her homage. The Athenians loved him not, neither did they love his friend Socrates; but they were fellows, and Socrates often went to hear him read.—Such was her adventure; and the beautiful Alcestis' story which she told is transcribed from the well-known play of Euripides in the succeeding pages of Mr. Browning's book. Whether the story has undergone transformation in the process we must leave to the decision of authorities on the subject. A comparison between the Greek original and Mr. Browning's translation or "transcript" certainly shows some important divergences from the classic story. We have only to compare the excellent translation of Potter in Morley's "Universal Library," vol. 54 (Routledge, 1*s*.), to discern this fact at once. As the question is one of considerable literary importance, it is necessary to call attention to it in this work. For those of my readers who may have forgotten the *Alkestis* tragedy, it may be well to recall its principal points. Potter, in his translation of the *Alkestis* of Euripides, gives the following prefatory note of the plot:—"Admetus and Alcestis were nearly related before their marriage. Æolus, the third in descent from Prometheus, was the father of Cretheus and Salmoneus; Æson, the father of

Jason, and Pheres, the father of Admetus, were sons of Cretheus; Tyro, the daughter of Salmoneus, was by Neptune mother to Pelias, whose eldest daughter Alcestis was. The historian, who relates the arts by which Medea induced the daughters of Pelias to cut their father in pieces in expectation of seeing him restored to youth, tells us that Alcestis alone, through the tenderness of her filial piety, concurred not with her sisters in that fatal deed (Diodor. Sic.). Pheres, now grown old, had resigned his kingdom to his son, and retired to his paternal estate, as was usual in those states where the sceptre was a spear. Admetus, on his first accession to the regal power, had kindly received Apollo, who was banished from heaven, and compelled for the space of a year to be a slave to a mortal; and the god, after he was restored to his celestial honours, did not forget that friendly house, but, when Admetus lay ill of a disease from which there was no recovery, prevailed upon the Fates to spare his life, on condition that some near relation should consent to die for him. But neither his father nor his mother, nor any of his friends, was willing to pay the ransom. Alcestis, hearing this, generously devoted her own life to save her husband's.—The design of this tragedy is to recommend the virtue of hospitality, so sacred among the Grecians, and encouraged on political grounds, as well as to keep alive a generous and social benevolence. The scene is in the vestibule of the house of Admetus. Palæphatus has given this explanation of the fable: After the death of Pelias, Acastus pursued the unhappy daughters to punish them for destroying their father. Alcestis fled to Pheræ; Acastus demanded her of Admetus, who refused to give her up; he therefore advanced towards Pheræ with a great army, laying the country waste with fire and sword. Admetus marched out of the city to check these devastations, fell into an ambush, and was taken prisoner. Acastus threatened to put him to death. When Alcestis understood that the life of Admetus was in this danger on her account, she went voluntarily and surrendered herself to Acastus, who discharged Admetus and detained her in custody. At this critical time Hercules, on his expedition to Thrace, arrives at Pheræ, is hospitably entertained by Admetus, and being informed of the distress and danger of Alcestis, immediately attacks Acastus, defeats his army, rescues the lady, and restores her to Admetus."—At the eighty-fourth meeting of the

London Browning Society (June 26th, 1891), Mr. R. G. Moulton, M.A. Camb., read a paper on *Balaustion's Adventure*, which he described as "a beautiful misrepresentation of the original." In this he said: "To those who are willing to decide literary questions upon detailed evidence, I submit that analysis shows the widest divergence between the Admetus of Euripides and the Admetus sung by Balaustion. And, in answer to those who are influenced only by authority, I claim that I have on my side of the question an authority who on this matter must rank higher than even Browning himself; and the name of my authority is Euripides." The following extracts from Mr. Moulton's able and scholarly criticism will explain his chief points. (The whole paper is published in the Transactions of the Browning Society, 1890-1.) Mr. Moulton says: "My position is that Browning, in common with the greater part of modern readers, has entirely misread and misrepresented Euripides' play of *Alcestis*. If any one wishes to pronounce "Balaustion's Adventure" a more beautiful poem than the Greek original, I have no wish to gainsay his estimate; but I maintain, nevertheless, that the one gives a distorted view of the other. The English poem is no mere translation of the Greek, but an interpretation with comments freely interpolated. And the poet having caught a wrong impression as to one of the main elements of the Greek story, has unconsciously let this impression colour his interpretations of words and sentences, and has used his right of commenting to present his mistaken conception with all the poetic force of a great master, until I fear that the Euripidean setting of the story is for English readers almost hopelessly lost. The point at issue is the character of Admetus. Taken in the rough, the general situation has been understood by modern readers thus: A husband having obtained from Fate the right to die by substitute, when no other substitute was forthcoming his wife Alcestis came forward, and by dying saved Admetus. And the first thought of every honest heart has been, "Oh, the selfishness of that husband to accept the sacrifice!" But my contention is, that if Euripides' play be examined with open and unbiassed mind, it will be found that not only Admetus is not selfish, but, on the contrary, he is as eminent for unselfishness in his sphere of life as Alcestis proves in her own. If this be so, the modern readers, with Browning at their head, have been introducing into the play a disturbing element that has no place there. And they have further, I submit, missed another conception—to my thinking a much more worthy conception—which really does underlie and unify the whole play. If Admetus is in fact selfish, how comes it that no personage in the whole play catches this idea?—no one, that is, except Pheres, whose words go for nothing, since he never discovers this selfishness of Admetus until he is impelled to fasten on another the accusation which has been hurled at himself. Except Pheres, all regard Admetus as the sublime type of generosity. Apollo, as representing the gods, uses the unexpected word "holy" to describe the demeanour with which his human protector cherished him during the trouble that drove him to earth in human shape. The Chorus, who, it is well known, represent in a Greek play public opinion, and are a channel by which the author insinuates the lesson of the story, cannot restrain their admiration at one point of the action, and devote an ode to the lofty character of their king. And Hercules, so grandly represented by Browning himself as the unselfish toiler for others, feels at one moment that he has been outdone in generosity by Admetus. There can be no question, then, what Euripides thought about the character of Admetus. And will the objector seriously contend that Euripides has, without intending it, presented a character which must in fact be pronounced selfish? The suggestion that the poet who created Alcestis did not know selfishness when he saw it, seems to me an improbability far greater than the improbability that Browning and the English readers should go wrong. Browning's suggestion of Pheres as Admetus "push'd to completion" seems to me grossly unfair: it ignores all Admetus' connection with Apollo and Hercules, and all his world-wide fame for hospitality. There is nothing in the legend or in the play to suggest that Pheres is anything more than an ordinary Greek: certainly the gods never came down from heaven to wonder at Pheres, nor did Hercules ever recognise him as generous beyond himself. In no view can the scene be other than a painful one. But it is intelligible only when we see in it, not the son rebuking his father, but the head of the State pouring out indignation on the officer whose self-preserving instinct has shirked at once a duty and an honourable opportunity to sacrifice, and thereby lost a life more valuable than his own. In this light the situation before us wears a different aspect. It is no case of a wife dying for a husband, but it is a subject dying to save the head of the State. And nothing can be clearer than that such a sacrifice is *taken for granted* by the personages who appear before us in Euripides' play. For I must warn the reader of *Balaustion* that there is not the shadow of a shade of foundation in the original for the scornful words of the English poet telling how the idea of a substitute for their king nowhere appears unnatural to the personages of the play; the sole surprise they express is that the substitute should be the youthful Alcestis and not the aged parents. The situation may fairly be paralleled in this respect with the crisis that arises in Sir Walter Scott's *Fair Maid of Perth*, when the seven sons of Torquil go successively to certain death to shield their chief; and, while they cover themselves with glory, no one accuses Hector of selfishness for allowing the sacrifice: the sentiment of clan institutions makes it a matter of course. The hospitality of Admetus is the foundation of the story; for it is this which has led Apollo (as he tells us in the prologue) to wring out of Fate the sparing to earth of the generous king on condition of a substitute being found."

The stone quarries of ancient Syracuse are now called Latomia, the largest and most picturesque of which is named Latomia de' Cappuccini. It is a vast pit, from eighty to a hundred feet in depth, and is several acres in extent. Murray, describing these vast quarries, says: "It is certain that they existed before the celebrated siege by the Athenians, 415 B.C.; and that some one of them was then deep enough to serve for a prison, and extensive enough to hold the unhappy seven thousand, the relics of the great Athenian host who were captured at the Asinarus. There is every probability that that of the Capuchins is the one described by Thucydides, who gives a touching picture of the misery the Athenians were made to endure from close confinement, hunger, thirst, filth, exposure and disease. Certain holes in the angles of the rocks are still pointed out by tradition as the spots where some of the Athenians were chained. The greater part of them perished here, but Plutarch tells us that some among them who could recite the verses of Euripides were liberated from captivity." Lord Byron's lines in *Childe Harold* may be quoted in this connection—

> "When Athens' armies fell at Syracuse,
> And fettered thousands bore the yoke of war,

Redemption rose up in the Attic Muse—
Her voice the only ransom from afar.
See! as they chaunt the tragic hymn, the car
Of the o'ermastered victor stops; the reins
Fall from his hands; his idle scimitar
Starts from his belt: he rends his captive's chains,
And bids him thank the bard for freedom and his strains."

"Some there were who owed their preservation to Euripides. Of all the Grecians, his was the muse whom the Sicilians were most in love with. From every stranger that landed in their island, they gleaned every small specimen or portion of his works, and communicated it with pleasure to each other. It is said that on this occasion a number of Athenians, upon their return home, went to Euripides, and thanked him in the most respectful manner for their obligations to his pen; some having been enfranchised for teaching their masters what they remembered of his poems, and others having got refreshments, when they were wandering about after the battle, for singing a few of his verses. Nor is this to be wondered at, since they tell us that when a ship from Caunus, which happened to be pursued by pirates, was going to take shelter in one of their ports, the Sicilians at first refused to admit her; but upon asking the crew whether they knew any of the verses of Euripides, and being answered in the affirmative, they received both them and their vessel." (Plutarch's life of Nicias.)

NOTES. [The numbers refer to the pages in the complete edition of the Works.]—P. 5, *Kameiros*, a Dorian town on the west coast of Rhodes, and the principal town before the foundation of Rhodes itself; *The League*, the Spartan league against the domination of Athens. p. 6, *Knidos,* city famous for the statue of Venus by Praxiteles, in one of her temples there; *Ilissian*, Trojan; *gate of Diomedes*, the Diomæan gate, leading to a grove and gymnasium; *Hippadai*, the gate of Hippadas, leading to the suburb of Cerameicus; *Lakonia* or *Laconica* or *Lacedæmon:* Sparta was the only town of importance—in this connection it means Sparta; *Choës* (the Pitchers) an Athenian festival of Dionysus or Bacchus; *Chutroi*, a Bacchic festival at Athens—the feast of pots; *Agora*, the Athenian market and chief public place; *Dikasteria*, tribunals; *Pnux* = the Pnyx, the place of public assembly for the people of Athens;

Keramikos, two suburban places at Athens were thus called: the one a market and public walk, the other a cemetery; *Salamis*, an island on the west coast of Attica, memorable for the battle in which the Greeks defeated the fleet of Xerxes, 480 B.C.; *Psuttalia*, a small island near Salamis; *Marathon:* the plain of Marathon was twenty-two miles from Athens, and the famous battle there was fought 490 B.C.; *Dionusiac Theatre*, the great theatre of Athens on the Acropolis. p. 7, *Kaunos*, one of the chief cities of Caria, which was founded by the Cretans. p. 8, *Ortugia*, the island close to Syracuse, and practically part of the city. p. 9, *Aischulos* = the song was from Æschylus, the great tragic poet of Greece; *pint of corn:* the wretched captives in the quarries were kept alive by half the allowance of food given to slaves. Thucydides says (vii. 87): "They were tormented with hunger and thirst; for during eight months they gave each of them daily only a *cotyle* (the *cotyle* was a little more than half an English pint) of water, and two of corn." p. 10, *salpinx*, a trumpet. p. 11, *rhesis*, a proverb; *monostich*, a poem of a single verse; *region of the steed:* horses were supposed by the Greeks to have originated in their land. p. 12, *Euoi*, *Oöp*, *Babai*, exclamations of wonder. p. 13, *Rosy Isle*, Rhodes, the Greek word meaning rose. p. 16, *Anthesterion month* = February-March; *Peiraieus*, the chief harbour of Athens, about five miles distant; *Agathon*, a tragic poet of Athens, born 448 B.C.—a friend of Euripides and Plato; *Iophon*, son of Sophocles: he was a distinguished tragic poet; *Kephisophon*, a contemporary poet; *Baccheion*, the Dionysiac temple. p. 17, *The mask of the actor:* it should be remembered that the Greek actors were all masked. p. 20, *Phoibos*, the *bright* or *pure*—a name of Apollo; *Asklepios* = Æsculapius, the god of medicine; *Moirai*, the Fates—Clotho, Lachesis, and Atropos, the divinities of human life. p. 25, *Eurustheus*, king of Mycenæ, who imposed the "twelve labours" on Hercules. p. 26, *Pelias' child:* Alcestis was the daughter of Pelias, son of Poseidon and of Tyro; *Paian*, a surname of Apollo, derived from *pæan*, a hymn which was sung in his honour. p. 27, *Lukia* = Lycia, a country of Asia Minor; *Ammon*, a god of Libya and Upper Egypt: Jupiter Ammon with the horns of a ram. p. 32, *pharos*, a veil or cloak covering the eyes. p. 35, *Iolkos*, a town in Thessaly. p. 41, *Koré*, the Maiden, a name by which Proserpine is often called. p. 47, *Achcrontian lake:* Acheron was one of the rivers of hell; *Karneian month* = August-September, when the Carnean festival was celebrated in honour of Apollo Carneus, protector of flocks. p. 48, *Kokutos' stream*, a river in the lower world: the river Cocytus is in Epirus. p. 51, *Thrakian Diomedes*, a king of Thrace who fed his horses on human flesh: it was one of the labours of Hercules to destroy him; *Bistones* = Thracians. p. 53, *Ares*, Greek name of Mars; *Lukaon*, a mythical king of Arcadia; *Kuknos*, son of Mars and Pelopia = Cycnus. p 60, *Lyric Puthian:* musical contentions in honour of Apollo at Delphi were called the Pythian modes: so Apollo, worshipped with music, was called the lyric Pythian, in commemoration of his victory over the Python, the great serpent; *Othrus' dell*, in the mountains of Othrys, in Thessaly, the residence of the Centaurs. p. 61, *Boibian lake*, in Thessaly, near Mount Ossa; *Molossoi*, a people of Epirus, in Greece. p. 68, *Ludian* = Lydian; *Phrugian* = Phrygian. p. 73, *Akastos*, the son of Peleus, king of Iolchis; he made war against Admetus. p. 74, *Hermes the infernal:* he was the son of Zeus and Maia, and was herald of the gods and guide of the d ad in Hades—hence the epithet "infernal." p. 78, *Turranos*, Tyrant or King. p. 79, *Ai, ai! Pheu! pheu! e, papai* = woe! alas, alas! oh, strange! p. 81, *The Helper* = Hercules. p. 83, *Kupris*, Venus, the goddess of Cyprus. p. 87, "*Daughter of Elektruon, Tiruns' child*": Electryon was the father of Alcmene, Tiryns was an ancient town in Argolis. p. 88, *Larissa*, a city in Thessaly. p. 94, *Thrakian tablets*, the name of Orpheus is associated with Thrace: the Orphic literature contained treatises on medicine, plants, etc., originally written on tablets, and preserved in the temple; *Orphic voice*, of Orpheus, which charmed all Nature; *Phoibos*, Apollo was the god of medicine, and taught the art to Æsculapius; *Asklepiadai*, who received from Phoibos or Apollo the medical remedies. p. 95, *Chaluboi*, a people of Asia Minor, near Pontus. p. 96, *Alkmenê* was the daughter of Electryon: she was the mother of Hercules, conceived by Jupiter. p. 99, *Pheraioi*, the belongings of Admetus as a native of Pheræ. p. 110, "*The Human with his droppings of warm tears*," a quotation from a poem by Mrs. Browning, entitled *Wine of Cyprus.* p. 111, *Mainad*, a name of the priestesses of Bacchus. p. 119, "*Straying among the flowers in Sicily*":

Proserpine, daughter of Ceres, one day gathering flowers in the meadows of Enna, was carried away by Pluto into the infernal regions, of which she became queen. p. 121, "*a great Kaunian painter*": Protogenes, a native of Caunus in Caria, a city subject to the Rhodians, flourished 332-300 B.C., and was one of the most celebrated of Greek painters. "The story of his friendly rivalry with Apelles, who was the first to recognise his genius, is familiar to all."—*Browning Notes and Queries* (Pt. vii. 25): the description of the picture refers to Sir Frederick Leighton's noble work on this subject. p. 122, *Poikilé*, the celebrated portico at Athens, which received its name from the variety of the paintings which it contained. It was adorned with pictures of the gods and of public benefactors.

Balkis ("Solomon and Balkis," *Jocoseria* 1883). The Queen of Sheba who came to visit Solomon. See SOLOMON AND BALKIS.

Bean Feast, The (*Asolando*). Pope Sixtus the Fifth (Felice Peretti) was pope from 1585 to 1590. He was born in 1521, and certainly in humble circumstances, but there seems no proof that he was the son of a swineherd, as described in the poem (see *Encyc. Brit.*, vol. xxii., p. 104). He was a great preacher, and one of the most vigorous and able of the popes that ever filled the papal chair. Within two years of his election he issued seventy-two bulls for the reform of the religious orders alone. When anything required to be done, he did it himself, and was evidently of the same opinion as Mr. Spurgeon, who holds that a committee should never consist of more than one person. He reformed the condition of the papal finances, and expended large sums in public works; he completed the dome of St. Peter's, and erected four Egyptian obelisks in Rome. Ever anxious to reform abuses, he made it his business to examine into the condition of the people and see with his own eyes their mode of life. Mr. Browning's poem relates how, going about the city in disguise, he one day turned into a tumbledown house where a man and wife sat at supper with their children. He inquired if they knew of any wrongs which wanted righting; bade them not stop eating, but speak freely of their grievances, if any. He bade them have no fear when he threw his hood back and let them see it was the Pope. The poor people were filled with a joyful wonder, the more so as the Pope begged a plate of their tempting beans. He sat down on the doorstep, and having eaten, thanked God that he had appetite and digestion.

Bean-Stripe, A: also Apple Eating. (*Ferishtah's Fancies*, No. 12.) One of Ferishtah's scholars demanded to know if on the whole Life were a good or an evil thing. He is asked if beans are taken from a bushelful, what colour predominates? Make the beans typical of our days. What is Life's true colour,—black or white? The scholar agrees with Sakya Muni, the Indian sage who declared that Life, past, present and future, was black only—existence simply a curse. Memory is a plague, evil's shadow is cast over present pleasure. Ferishtah strews beans, blackish and whitish, figuring man's sum of moments good and bad; in companionship the black grow less black and the white less white: both are modified—grey prevails. So joys are embittered by sorrows gone before and sobered by a sense of sorrow that may come; thus deepest in black means white most imminent. Pain's shade enhances the shine of pleasure, the blacks and whites of a lifetime whirl into a white. But to the objector the world is so black, no speck of white will unblacken it. Ferishtah bids his pupil contemplate the insect on a palm frond: what knows he of the uses of a palm tree? It has other uses than such as strike the aphis. It may be so with us: our place in the world may, in the eye of God, be no greater than is to us the inch of green which is cradle, pasture and grave of the palm insect. The aphis feeds quite unconcerned, even if lightning sear the moss beneath his home. The philosopher sees a world of woe all round him; his own life is white, his fellows' black. God's care be God's: for his own part the sorrows of his kind serve to sober with shade his own shining life. There is no sort of black which white has not power to disintensify. His philosophy, he admits, may be wrecked to-morrow, but he speaks from past experience. He cannot live the life of his fellow, yet he knows of those who are not so blessed as to live in Persia, yet it would not be wise to say: "No sun, no grapes,—then no subsistence!" There are lands where snow falls; he will not trouble about cold till it comes to Persia. But the Indian sage, the Buddha, concluded that the best thing of Life was that it led to Death! The dervish replied that though Sakya Muni said so he did not believe it, as he lived out his seventy years and liked his dinner to the last—he lied, in fact. The pupil demands truth at any cost, and is told to take this: God is all-good, all-wise, all-powerful. What is man? Not God, yet he is a creature, with a creature's qualities. You cannot make these two conceptions agree: God, that only can, does not; man, that would, cannot. A carpet web may illustrate the meaning: the sage has asked the weaver how it is that apart the fiery-coloured silk, and the other of watery dimness, when combined, produce a medium profitable to the sight. The artificer replies that the medium was what he aimed at. So the quality of man blended with the quality of God assists the human sight to understand Life's mystery. Man can only know *of* and think *about*, he cannot understand, earth's least atom. He cannot know fire thoroughly, still less the mystery of gravitation. But, it is objected, force has not mind; man does not thank gravitation when an apple drops, nor summer for the apple: why thank God for teeth to bite it? Forces are the slaves of supreme power. The sense that we owe a debt to somebody behind these forces assures us there is somebody to take it. We eat an apple without thanking it. We thank Him but for whose work orchards might grow gall-nuts.

Ferishtah in the Lyric asks no praise for his work on behalf of mankind. He who works for the world's approval, or even for its love, must not be surprised if both are withheld. He has sought, found and done his duty. For the rest he looks beyond.

Beatrice Signorini (*Asolando*, 1889) was a noble Roman lady who married Francesco Romanelli, a painter, a native of Viterbo, in the time of Pope Urban VIII. He was a favourite of the Barberini family. Soon after his marriage he became attached to Artemisia Gentileschi, a celebrated lady painter. One day he proposed to her that she should paint him a picture filled with fruit, except a space in the centre for her own portrait, which he would himself insert. He kept this work amongst his treasures; and one day, wishing to make his wife jealous, he unveiled it in her presence, dilating on the graces and beauty of the original. His wife was a very beautiful woman also, and was not inclined to tolerate this rivalry for her husband's affections; she therefore destroyed the face of the fair artist in the picture, so that it could not be recognised. Her husband was not angry at this, but admired and loved his wife all the more for this outburst of natural wrath, and soon ceased to think further of his quondam love. Artemisia

Gentileschi, daughter of Orazio Gentileschi, lived 1590—1642. She was a pupil of Guido, and acquired great fame as a portrait painter. She was a beautiful woman; her portrait painted by herself is in Hampton Court. Her greatest work is the picture of Judith and Holofernes, in the Pitti Palace, Florence. She came to England with her father in the reign of Charles I., and painted for him David with the head of Goliath. She soon returned to Italy, and passed the remainder of her life at Naples. Baldinucci tells the story of Romanelli.

Beer. See NATIONALITY IN DRINKS (*Dramatic Lyrics*).

"Before and After." (*Men and Women*, 1855; *Lyrics*, 1863; *Dramatic Lyrics*, 1868.) Two men have quarrelled, and a duel is proposed. It is urged that the injured man should forgive his enemy, but a philosophical adviser considers that Christianity is hardly equal to this particular matter: "Things have gone too far." Forgiveness is all very well in good books, but these men are sunk in a slough where they must not be left to "stick and stink." As the offender never pardons, and the offended in this case will not, there is nothing for it but to fight. Besides, "while God's champion lives" (the just man), "wrong shall be resisted" and the wrong-doer punished. These two men have quarrelled, and it is impossible to say which of them is the injured and which the injurer. Wrong has been done—this much is certain; beyond that human judgment is at fault, and the Divine must be invoked. Let them fight it out, then! Of course the poet is speaking dramatically, and not laying down the principle that where we see evil done, especially in our own concerns, we are bound to avenge the wrong. This sentiment is that of the philosophical observer of the feud, though there are phrases here and there quite in accord with Mr. Browning's axioms: "Better sin the whole sin"; "Go, live his life out"; "Life will try his nerves." [This teaching is much in the way of that in the concluding verses of *The Statue and the Bust* (*q.v.*)] For the culprit there, the speaker says, it is better he should add daring courage to face the consequences of his crime, than by running away from them be coward as well as criminal, He may come off victor, but his future life, his garden of pleasure, will have a warder, a leopard-dog thing (his sin), ever at his side. This leering presence, this "sly, mutething," crouching under every "rose wall" and "grape-tree," will exact the penalty of past sin, and mayhap sting the sinner to repentance. "So much for the culprit." The injured, "the martyred man," has borne so much, he can at least bear another stroke—"give his blood and get his heaven." If death end it, well for him—"he forgives"; if he be victor he has punished sin as God's minister of justice. In "After," what is not said is more powerful than any words which could have filled the intervening space between these two poems. The imagination here is all-sufficient. The chill presence of death has altered the aspect of everything. The rush of thought, the casuistry, the intensity of the preceding poem, is all hushed and silent here. Death makes things so real in its presence, masks drop off from souls' faces, and truth can make her voice heard above the contentions of sophistry. The victor speaks—he has no desire to masquerade here as God's avenging angel; he recognises that even his foe has the rights of a man, and as the spirit of the dead man wanders, absorbed in his new life, he heeds not his wrongs nor the vengeance of his slayer; the great realities of the other world make those of this world trivial, and the victor estimates at its true value the worthlessness of his conquest. If they could be as they were of old! So forgiveness would have been better and Christ's command is vindicated—"I say unto you that ye resist not evil." There are some victories which are always the worst of defeats.

"**Bells and Pomegranates.**" Under this title Mr. Browning published a cheap edition, in serial form, of his poems in 1841. The following works appeared in this manner:—*Pippa Passes; King Victor and King Charles; Dramatic Lyrics; The Return of the Druses; A Blot in the 'Scutcheon; Colombe's Birthday; Dramatic Romances and Lyrics; Luria;* and *A Soul's Tragedy.* ("A golden bell and a pomegranate, a golden bell and a pomegranate, upon the hem of the robe round about."—Exod. xxviii. 34, 35.) "The reason supposed in the Targum for the directions given to the priest is that the priest's approach should be *cautious* to the innermost 'Holy of Holies,' or Sanctuary of the Tabernacle. The sound of the small bells upon his robe was intended to announce his approach before his actual appearance." Philo says the bells were to denote the harmony of the universe. St. Jerome says they also indicated that every movement of the priest should be for edification. Mr. Browning, however, intimated that he had no such symbolical intention in the choice of his title. In the preface to the last number of the series, he said: "Here ends my first series of 'Bells and Pomegranates,' and I take the opportunity of explaining, in reply to inquiries, that I only meant by that title to indicate an endeavour towards something like an alternation or mixture of music with discoursing, sound with sense, poetry with thought; which looks too ambitious, thus expressed, so the symbol was preferred. It is little to the purpose that such is actually one of the most familiar of the many Rabbinical (and Patristic) acceptations of the phrase; because I confess that, letting authority alone, I supposed the bare words, in such juxtaposition, would sufficiently convey the desired meaning. 'Faith and good works' is another fancy, for instance, and, perhaps, no easier to arrive at; yet Giotto placed a pomegranate fruit in the hand of Dante, and Raffaelo crowned his theology (in the *Camera della Segnatura*) with blossoms of the same; as if the Bellari and Vasari would be sure to come after, and explain that it was merely '*simbolo delle buone opere—il qual Pomogranato, fu però usato nelle vesti del Pontefice appresso gli Ebrei.*'—R. B."

"**Ben Karshook's Wisdom.**" Mr. Sharp says, in his *Life of Browning*, "In the late spring (April 27th, 1854), also, he wrote the short dactylic lyric, "Ben Karshook's Wisdom." This little poem was given to a friend for appearance in one of the then popular *keepsakes*—literally given, for Browning never contributed to magazines. As "Ben Karshook's Wisdom," though it has been reprinted in several quarters, will not be found in any volume of Browning's works, and was omitted from *Men and Women* by accident, and from further collections by forgetfulness, it may be fitly quoted here. *Karshook*, it may be added, is the Hebraic word for a thistle.

"'Would a man 'scape the rod? —
Rabbi Ben Karshook saith,
'See that he turns to God,
The day before his death.'

'Ay, could a man inquire,
When it shall come!' I say,
The Rabbi's eye shoots fire—
'Then let him turn to-day!'

Quoth a young Sadducee,—
  'Reader of many rolls,
Is it so certain we
  Have, as they tell us, souls?'—

'Son, there is no reply!'
  The Rabbi bit his beard;
'Certain, a soul have *I*,—
  We may have none,' he sneered.

Thus Karshook, the Hiram's-Hammer,
  The Right-hand Temple column,
Taught babes in grace their grammar,
  And struck the simple, solemn."

(ROME, *April 27th*, 1854.)

The reference in the last verse is to 1 Kings vii. 13-22. Hiram was a Phœnician king, and a skilful builder of temples. The Temple columns referred to were called Jachin and Boaz, and were made of brass and set up at the entrance; Boaz (*strength*) on the left hand, and Jachin (*stability*) on the right. The Freemasons have adopted the names of these pillars in their ceremonial and symbolism.

Bernard de Mandeville [THE MAN] (1670—1733) was a native of Rotterdam, and the son of a physician who practised in that city. He studied medicine at Leyden, and came to England "to learn the language." He did this with such effect that it was doubted if he were a foreigner. He practised medicine in London, and is known to fame by his celebrated book *The Fable of the Bees*, a miscellaneous work which includes "*The Grumbling Hive, or Knaves Turned Honest; An Inquiry into the Origin of Moral Virtue; An Essay on Charity Schools;* and *A Search into the Origin of Society.*" When, in 1705, the country was agitated by the question as to the continuance of Marlborough's war with France, Mandeville published his *Grumbling Hive.* All sorts of charges were being made against public officials; every form of corruption and dishonesty was freely charged on these persons, and it was in the midst of this agitation that Mandeville humorously maintained that "private vices are public benefits,"—that self-seeking, luxury, ambition, and greed are all necessary to the greatness and prosperity of a nation. "Fools only strive to make a great and honest hive."

"The bees of his fable," says Professor Minto, "grumbled, as many Englishmen were disposed to do,—cursed politicians, armies, fleets, whenever there came a reverse, and cried, 'Had we but honesty!'" Jove, at last, in a passion, swore that he would "rid the canting hive of fraud," and filled the hearts of the bees with honesty and all the virtues, strict justice, frugal living, contentment with little, acquiescence in the insults of enemies. Straightway the flourishing hive declined, till in time only a small remnant was left; this took refuge in a hollow tree, "blest with content and honesty," but "destitute of arts and manufactures." "He gives the name of virtue to every performance by which man, contrary to the impulse of nature, should endeavour the benefit of others, or the conquest of his own passions, out of a rational ambition of being good"; while everything which, without regard to the public, man should commit to gratify any of his appetites, is vice." He finds self-love (a vice by the definition) masquerading in many virtuous disguises, lying at the root of asceticism, heroism, public spirit, decorous conduct,—at the root, in short, of all the actions that pass current as virtuous." He taught that "the moral virtues are the political offspring which flattery begot upon pride." Politicians and moralists have worked upon man to make him believe he is a sublime creature, and that self-indulgence makes him more akin to the brutes. In 1723 Mandeville applied his analysis of virtue in respect to the then fashionable institution of charity schools, and a great outcry was raised against his doctrines. His book was presented to the justices, the grand jury of Middlesex, and a copy was ordered to be burned by the common hangman. It is probable that Mandeville was not serious in all he wrote; much of his writings must be considered merely as a political *jeu d'esprit.* His was an age of speculation upon ethical questions, and a humorous foreigner could not but be moved to satirise English methods, which are frequently peculiarly open to this kind of attack.

[THE POEM.] (*Parleyings with Certain People of Importance in their Day:* London, 1887.) The sketch of Mandeville's opinion given above will afford a key to the drift of Mr. Browning's poem. His aim is to point out the great truths which, on a careful examination, will be found to underlie much of the old philosopher's paradoxical teaching; not as understood by fools, he says, but by those who let down their sounding line below the turbid surface to the still depths where evil harmoniously combines with good, Mandeville's teaching is worthy of examination. We must take life as we find it, ever remembering that law deals the same with soul and body; life's rule is short, infancy's probation is necessary to bodily development; and we might as well expect a new-born infant to start up strong, as the soul to stand in its full-statured magnificence without the necessary faculty of growth. Law deals with body as with soul. Both, stung to strength through weakness, strive for good through evil. And all the while the process lasts men complain that "no sign, no stirring of God's finger," indicates His preference for either. Never promptly and beyond mistake has God interposed between oppression and its victim. But suppose the Gardener of mankind has a definite purpose in view when he plants evil side by side with good? How do we know that every growth of good is not consequent on evil's neighbourhood? As it is certain that the garden was planted by intelligence, would not the sudden and complete eradication of evil repeal a primal law of the all-understanding Gardener? "But," retorts the objector, "suppose these ill weeds were interspersed by an enemy?" Man's faculty avails not to see the whole sight. When we examine the plan of an estate, we do not ask where is the roof of the house—where the door, the window. We do not seek a thing's solid self in its symbol: looking at Orion on a starry night, who asks to see the man's flesh in the star-points? If it be objected that we have no need of symbols, and that we should be better taught by facts, it is answered that a myth may teach. The rising sun thrills earth to the very heart of things; creation acknowledges its life-giving impulse and murmurs not, but, unquestioning, uses the invigorating beams. Is man alone to wait till he comprehends the sun's self to realise the energy that floods the universe? Prometheus drew the sun's rays into a focus, and made fire do man service. Thus to utilise the sun's influence was better than striving to follow beam and beam upon their way, till we faint in our endeavour to guess their infinitude of action. The teaching of the poem is, that to make the best use of the world as we find it, is wiser than torturing our brains to comprehend mysteries which by their nature and our own weakness are insoluble.

Bifurcation. (*Pacchiarotto and other Poems*: London, 1876.) A woman loves a man, but "prefers duty to love"—enters a convent, perhaps, or adopts some life for reasons which she considers imperative, and so cannot marry. Rejecting love, she thinks she rejects the tempter's bribe when the paths before her diverge. It is a sacrifice, she feels, and a great one; but her heart tells her, probably because it has been suggested by those whose influence over her was very great, that heaven will repair the wrongs of earth. She chooses the darkling half of life, and waits her reward in the world "where light and darkness fuse." The man loved the woman. Love was a hard path for him, but duty was a pleasant road. When the ways parted, and his love forsook him to abide by duty, she told him their roads would converge again at the end, and bade him be constant to his path, as she would be to hers, that they might meet once more. But, when the guiding star is gone, man's footsteps are apt to stray, and every stumbling-block brought him to confusion. And after his falls and flint-piercings he would rise and cry "All's well!" and struggle on, since he must be content with one of the halves that make the whole. He would have the story of each inscribed on their tomb, and he demands to know which tomb holds sinner and which holds saint! If love be all—if earth and its best be our highest aim—then the woman was the sinner for not marrying her lover, and settling down in a suburban villa, and surrounding herself with children and domestic pleasures. But if the ideal life—if a love infinitely higher and purer than any earthly affection—be taken into account; if in her soul she had heard the call, "Leave all and follow Me," and she obeyed with breaking heart, in a perfect spirit of self-sacrifice, then was she no sinner, but saint indeed. Surely there are higher paths in life than even the holy one of wedded love. Mr. Browning's own married life was so ideally perfect that he has been led into some exaggeration of its advantages to the mass of mankind.

Bishop Blougram's Apology. (*Men and Women*, vol. i., 1855.) Bishop Blougram is a *bon vivant*, a man of letters, of fastidious taste and of courtly manners—a typical Renaissance prince of the Church, in fact. He has been successful in life, as he understands it, and there seems no reason why he should make any apology for an existence so in every way congenial to his nature. Mr. Gigadibs is a young literary man, smart at "articles" for the magazines, but possessing no knowledge outside the world of books, and incapable of deep thought on the great problems of life and mind. He can settle everything offhand in his flippant, free-thinking style, and he has arrived at the conclusion that a man of Blougram's ability cannot really believe in the doctrines which he pretends to defend, and that he is only acting a part; as such a life cannot be "ideal," he considers his host more or less of an impostor. By some means he finds himself dining with the Bishop, and after dinner he is treated to his lordship's "Apology." The ecclesiastic has taken the measure of his man, and good-humouredly puts the case thus: "You say the thing is my trade, that I am above the humbug in my heart, and sceptical withal at times, and so you despise me—to be plain. For your own part you must be free and speak your mind. You would not choose my position if you could you would be great, but not in my way. The problem of life is not to fancy what were fair it only it could be, but, taking life as it is, to make it fair so far as we can. For a simile, we mortals make our life-voyage each in his cabin. Suppose you attempt to furnish it after a landsman's idea. You bring an Indian screen, a piano, fifty volumes of Balzac's novels and a library of the classics, a marble bath, and an "old master" or two; but the ship folk tell you you have only six feet square to deal with, and because they refuse to take on board your piano, your marble bath, and your old masters, you set sail in a bare cabin. You peep into a neighbouring berth, snug and well-appointed, and you envy the man who is enjoying his suitable sea furniture; you have proved your artist nature, but you have no furniture. Imagine we are two college friends preparing for a voyage; my outfit is a bishop's, why won't you be a bishop too? In the first place, you don't and can't believe in a Divine revelation; you object to dogmas, so overhaul theology; you think I am by no means a fool, so that I must find believing every whit as hard as you do, and if I do not say so, possibly I am an impostor. Grant that I do not believe in the fixed and absolute sense—to meet you on your own premise—overboard go my dogmas, and we both are unbelievers. Does that fix us unbelievers for ever? Not so: all we have gained is, that as unbelief disturbed us by fits in our believing days, so belief will ever and again disturb our unbelief, for how can we guard our unbelief and make it bear fruit to us? Just when we think we are safest a flower, a friend's death, or a beautiful snatch of song, and lo! there stends before us the grand Perhaps! The old misgivings and crooked questions all are there—all demanding solution, as before. All we have gained by our unbelief is a life of doubt diversified by faith, in place of one of faith diversified by doubt. "But," says Gigadibs, "if I drop faith and you drop doubt, I am as right as you!" Blougram will not allow this: "the points are not indifferent; belief or unbelief bears upon life, and determines its whole course; positive belief brings out the best of me, and bears fruit in pleasantness and peace. Unbelief would do nothing of the sort for me: you say it does for you? We'll try! I say faith is my waking life; we sleep and dream, but, after all, waking is our real existence—all day I study and make friends; at night I sleep. What's midnight doubt before the faith of day? You are a philosopher; you disbelieve, you give to dreams at night the weight I give to the work of active day; to be consistent, you should keep your bed, for you live to sleep as I to wake—to unbelieve, as I to still believe. Common-sense terms you bed-ridden: common-sense brings its good things to me; so it's best believing if we can, is it not? Again, if we are to believe at all, we cannot be too decisive in our faith; we must be consistent in all our choice—succeed, or go hang in worldly matters. In love we wed the woman we love most or need most, and as a man cannot wed twice, so neither can he twice lose his soul. I happened to be born in one great form of Christianity, the most pronounced and absolute form of faith in the world, and so one of the most potent forms of influencing the world. External forces have been allowed to act upon me by my own consent, and they have made me very comfortable. I take what men offer with a grace; folks kneel and kiss my hand, and thus is life best for me; my choice, you will admit, is a success. Had I nobler instincts, like you, I should hardly count this success; grant I am a beast, beasts must lead beasts' lives; it is my business to make the absolute best of what God has made. At the same time, I do not acknowledge I am so much your inferior, though you do say I pine among my million fools instead of living for the dozen men of sense who observe me, and even they do not know whether I am fool or knave. Be a Napoleon, and if you disbelieve, where's the good of it? Then concede there is just a chance: doubt may be wrong—just a chance of judgment and a life to come. Fit up your cabin another way. Shall we be Shakespeare? What did Shakespeare do? Why, left his towers and gorgeous palaces to build himself a trim house in Stratford. He owned the worth of things; he enjoyed the show and respected the puppets too. Shakespeare and myself want the same things, and what I want I have. He aimed at a house in Stratford—he got it; I aim at higher things, and receive heaven's incense in my nose. Believe and get enthusiasm, that's the thing. I can achieve nothing on the denying side—ice makes no conflagration." Gigadibs says, "But as you really lack faith, you run the same risk by your indifference as does the bold unbeliever; an imperfect faith like that is not worth having; give me whole faith or none!" Blougram fixes him here. "Own the use of faith, I find you faith!" he replies. "Christianity may be false, but do you wish it true? If you desire faith, then you've faith enough. We could not tolerate pure faith, naked belief in Omnipotence; it would be like viewing the sun with a lidless eye. The use of evil is to hide God. I would rather die than deny a Church miracle." Gigadibs says, "Have faith if you will, but you might purify it." Blougram objects that "if you first cut the Church miracle, the next thing is to cut God Himself and be an atheist, so much does humanity find the cutting process to its taste." If Gigadibs says, "All this is a narrow and gross view of life," Blougram answers, "I live for this world now; my best pledge for observing the new laws of a new life to come is my obedience to the present world's requirements. This life may be intended to make the next more intense. Man ever tries to be beforehand in his evolution, as when a traveller throws off his furs in Russia because he will not want them in France; in France spurns flannel because in Spain it will not be required; in Spain drops cloth too cumbrous for Algiers; linen goes next, and last the skin itself, a superfluity in Timbuctoo. The poor fool was never at ease a minute in his whole journey. I am at ease now, friend, worldly in this world, as I have a right to be. You meet me," continues Blougram, "at this issue: you think it better, if we doubt, to say so; act up to truth perceived, however feebly. Put natural religion to the test with which you have just demolished the revealed, abolish the moral law, let people lie, kill, and thieve, but there are certain instincts, unreasoned out and blind, which you dare not set aside; you can't tell why, but there they are, and there you let them rule, so you are just as much a slave, liar, hypocrite, as I—a conscious coward to boot, and without promise of reward. I but follow my instincts, as you yours. I want a God—must have a God—ere I can be aught, must be in direct relation with Him, and so live my life; yours, you dare not live. Something we may see, all we cannot see. I say, I see all: I am obliged to be emphatic, or men would doubt there is anything to see at all." Then the Bishop turns upon his opponent and presses him: "Confess, don't you want my bishopric, my influence and state? Why, you will brag of dining with me to the last day of your life! There are men who beat me,—the zealot with his mad ideal, the poet with all his life in his ode, the statesman with his scheme, the artist whose religion is his art—such men carry their fire within them; but you, you Gigadibs, poor scribbler,—but not so poor but we almost thought an article of yours might have been written by Dickens,—here's my card, its mere production, in proof of acquaintance with me, will double your remuneration in the reviews at sight. Go, write,—detest, defame me, but at least you cannot despise me!" The average superficial reasoner is in the constant habit of setting down as insincere such learned persons as make a profession of faith in the dogmas of Christianity. The ordinary man of the world considers the mass of Christian people as bound to their faith by the fetters of ignorance. Such men, however, as it is impossible to term ignorant, who profess to hold the dogmas of Christianity in their integrity, are actuated, they say, by unworthy motives, self-interest, the desire to make the best of both worlds, unwillingness to cast in their lot with those who put themselves to the pain and discredit of thinking for themselves, and casting off the fetters of superstition. So, say these cynics, the dignified clergy of the Established Church repeat creeds which they no longer believe, that they may live in splendour and enjoy the best things of life, while the poorer clergy retain their positions as a decent means of gaining a livelihood. When such flippant thinkers and impulsive talkers contemplate the lives of such men as Cardinal Wiseman or Cardinal Newman, who were acknowledged to be learned and highly cultivated men, they say it is impossible such men can be sincere when they profess to believe the teachings of the Catholic Church, which they hold to be contemptible superstition; they must be actuated by unworthy motives, love of power over men's minds, craving for worldly dignities and the adulation of men and the like. That a man like Newman should give up his intellectual life at Oxford "to perform mummeries at a Catholic altar" in Birmingham, was plainly termed insanity, intellectual suicide, or sheer knavery. The late Cardinal Wiseman was an exceedingly learned man, of great scientific ability, and such admirable *bonhomie* that this class of critic had no difficulty whatever in relegating his Eminence to what was considered his precise moral position. Mr. Browning in this monologue accurately postulates the popular conception of the Cardinal's character in the utterances of one Gigadibs, a young man of thirty who has rashly expressed his opinions of the great churchman's religious character. The poet, though completely failing to do justice to the Bishop's side of the question, has presented us with a character perfectly natural, but which in every aspect seems more the picture of an eighteenth-century fox-hunting ecclesiastic than that of a bishop of the Roman Church, who would have had a good deal more to say on the subject of faith as understood by his Church than the poet has put into the mouth of his Bishop Blougram. As it is impossible to see in the description given of the Bishop anybody but the late Cardinal Wiseman, it is necessary to say that the description is to the last degree untrue, as must have been obvious to any one personally acquainted with him. A review of the poem appeared in the magazine known as the *Rambler*, for January 1856, which is credibly supposed to have been written by the Cardinal himself. "The picture drawn in the poem," says the article in question, "is that of an arch hypocrite, and the frankest of fools." The writer says that Mr. Browning "is utterly mistaken in the very groundwork of religion, though starting from the most unworthy notions of the work of a Catholic bishop, and defending a self-indulgence which every honest man must feel to be disgraceful, is yet in its way triumphant."

NOTES.—"*Brother Pugin*," a celebrated Catholic architect, who built many Gothic churches for Catholic congregations in England. "*Corpus Christi Day*," the Feast of the Sacrament of the Altar, literally the Body of Christ; it occurs on the Thursday after Trinity

Sunday. *Che, che,* what, what! *Count D'Orsay* (1798—1852), a French savant, and an intellectual dandy. "*Parma's pride—the Jerome,*" the St. Jerome by Correggio, one of the most important paintings in the Ducal Academy at Parma. There is a curious story of the picture in Murray's Guide to North Italy. *Marvellous Modenese*—the celebrated painter Correggio was born in the territory of Modena, Italy. "*Peter's Creed, or rather, Hildebrand's,*" Pope Hildebrand (Gregory VII., 1073-85). The temporal power of the popes, and the authority of the Papacy over sovereigns, were claimed by this pope. *Verdi and Rossini.* Verdi wrote a poor opera, which pleased the audience on the first night, and they loudly applauded. Verdi nervously glanced at Rossini, sitting quietly in his box, and read the verdict in his face. *Schelling,* Frederick William Joseph von, a distinguished German philosopher (1775-1854). *Strauss*, David Friedrich (1808-74), who wrote the Rationalistic *Life of Jesus,* one of the Tūbingen philosophers. *King Bomba,* a soubriquet given to Ferdinand II. (1810-59), late king of the Two Sicilies; it means King Puff-cheek, King Liar, King Knave. *lazzaroni,* Naples beggars—so called from Lazarus. *Antonelli,* Cardinal, secretary of Pope Pius IX., a most astute politician, if not a very devout churchman. "*Naples' liquefaction.*" The supposed miracle of the liquefaction of the blood of St. Januarius the Martyr. A small quantity of the saint's blood in a solid state is preserved in a crystal reliquary; when brought into the presence of the head of the saint it melts, bubbles up, and, when moved, flows on one side. It is preserved in the great church at Naples. On certain occasions, as on the feast of St. Januarius, September 19th, the miracle is publicly performed. See Butler's *Lives of the Saints* for September 19th. The matter has been much discussed, but no reasonable theory has been set up to account for it. Mr. Browning is quite wrong in suggesting that belief in this, or any other of this class of miracles, is obligatory on the Catholic conscience. A man may be a good Catholic and believe none of them. He could not, of course, be a Catholic and deny the miracles of the Bible, because he is bound to believe them on the authority of the Church as well as that of the Holy Scriptures. Modern miracles stand on no such basis. *Fichte,* Johann Gottlieb (1762-1814). An eminent German metaphysician. He defined God as the *moral order* of the universe. "*Pastor est tui Dominus,*" the Lord is thy Shepherd. *In partibus, Episcopus.* A bishop *in partibu. infidelium.* In countries where the Roman Catholic faith is not regularly established, as it was not in England before the time of Cardinal Wiseman, there were no bishops of sees in the kingdom itself, but they took their titles from heathen lands; so that an English bishop would perhaps be called Bishop of Mesopotamia when he was actually appointed to London. This is now altered, so far as this country is concerned.

"**Bishop orders his Tomb at St. Praxed's Church, The**" (Rome, 15—. *Dramatic Romances and Lyrics—Bells and Pomegranates* No. VII., 1845).—First published in *Hood's Magazine*, 1845, and the same year in *Dramatic Romances and Lyrics;* in 1863 it appeared under *Men and Women*: St. Praxed or Praxedes. An old *title* or parish church in Rome bears the name of this saint. It was mentioned in the life of Pope Symmachus (A.D. 498-514). It was repaired by Adrian I. and Paschal I., and lastly by St. Charles Borromeo, who took from it his title of cardinal. He died 1584; there is a small monument to his memory now in the church. St. Praxedes, Virgin, was the daughter of Pudens, a Roman senator, and sister of St. Pudentiana. She lived in the reign of the Emperor Antoninus Pius. She employed all her riches in relieving the poor and the necessities of the Church. The poem is a monologue of a bishop of the art-loving, luxurious, and licentious Renaissance, who lies dying, and, instead of preparing his soul for death, is engaged in giving directions about a grand tomb he wishes his relatives to erect in his church. He has secured his niche, the position is good, and he desires the monument shall be worthy of it. Mr. Ruskin, in *Modern Painters*, vol. iv., pp. 377-79, says of this poem: "Robert Browning is unerring in every sentence he writes of the Middle Ages—always vital, right, and profound; so that in the matter of art, with which we are specially concerned, there is hardly a principle connected with the mediæval temper that he has not struck upon in these seemingly careless and too rugged lines of his" (here the writer quotes from the poem, "As here I lie, In this state chamber dying by degrees," to "Ulpian serves his need!"). "I know no other piece of modern English prose or poetry in which there is so much told, as in these lines, of the Renaissance spirit—its worldliness, inconsistency, pride, hypocrisy, ignorance of itself, love of art, of luxury, and of good Latin. It is nearly all that I have said of the central Renaissance, in thirty pages of the *Stones oj Venice*, put into as many lines, Browning's also being the antecedent work." It was inevitable that the great period of the Renaissance should produce men of the type of the Bishop of St. Praxed's; it would be grossly unfair to set him down as the type of the churchmen of his time. As a matter of fact, the Catholic church was undergoing its Renaissance also. The Council of Trent is better known by some historians for its condemnation of heresies than for the great work it did in reforming the morals of Catholic nations. The regulations which it established for this end were fruitful in raising up in different countries some of the noblest and most beautiful characters in the history of Christianity. St. Charles Borromeo, archbishop of Milan, whose connection with St. Praxed's Church is noticed above, was the founder of Sunday-schools, the great restorer of ecclesiastical discipline and the model of charity. St. Theresa rendered the splendour of the monastic life conspicuous, leading a life wholly angelical, and reviving the fervour of a great number of religious communities. The congregation of the Ursulines and many religious orders established for the relief of corporeal miseries—such as the Brothers Hospitallers, devoted to nursing the sick; the splendid missionary works of St. Ignatius Loyola, St. Francis Xavier—all these, and many other evidences of the awakening life of the Catholic Church, were the products of an age which is as often misrepresented as it is imperfectly understood. There were bishops of St. Praxed's such as the poet has so inimitably sketched for us; but had there been no others of a more Christian type, religion in southern Europe would have died out instead of starting up as a giant refreshed to win, as it did, the world for Christ. The worldly bishop of the poem is an "art for art's sake" ecclesiastic, who is not at all anxious to leave a life which he has found very satisfactory for a future state about which he has neither anxiety nor concern. What he is concerned for is his tomb. His old rival Gandolf has deprived him of the position in the church which he longed for as a resting-place, but he hopes to make up for the loss by a more tasteful and costly monument, with a more classical inscription than his. The old fellow is as much Pagan as Christian, and his ornaments have as much to do with the gods and goddesses of old Rome as with the Church of which he is a minister. In all this Mr. Browning finely satirises the Renaissance spirit, which, though it did good service to humanity in a thousand ways, was much more concerned with flesh than spirit.

NOTES.—*Basalt*, trap rock of a black, bluish, or leaden-grey colour; *peach-blossom marble*, an Italian marble used in decorations; *olive-frail* = a rush basket of olives; *lapis lazuli*, a mineral, usually of a rich blue colour, used in decorations *Frascati* is a beautiful spot on the Alban hills, near Rome; *antique-black* = Nero antico, a beautiful black stone; *thyrsus*, a Bacchanalian staff wrapped with ivy, or a spear stuck into a pine-cone; *travertine*, a cellular calc-tufa, abundant near Tivoli; *Tully's Latin* = Cicero's, the purest classic style; *Ulpian*, a Roman writer on law, chiefly engaged in literary work (A.D. 211-22). "*Blessed mutter of the mass.*" To devout Catholics the low monotone of the priest saying a low mass, in which there is no music and only simple ceremonies, is more devotional than the high mass, where there is much music and ritual to divert the attention from the most solemn act of Christian worship; *mortcloth*, a funeral pall; *elucescebat*, he was distinguished; *vizor*, that part of a helmet which defends the face; *term*, a bust terminating in a square block of stone, similar to those of the god Terminus; *onion-stone* = cippolino, cipoline, an Italian marble, white, with pale-green shadings.

Blot in the 'Scutcheon, A (Part V. of *Bells and Pomegranates*, 1843.) *A Tragedy.* Time, 17—. The story is exceedingly dramatic, though simple. Thorold, Earl Tresham, is a monomaniac to family pride and conventional morality: his ancestry and his own reputation absorb his whole attention, and the wreck of all things were a less evil to him than a stain on the family honour. He is the only protector of his motherless sister, Mildred Tresham, who has in her innocence allowed herself to be seduced by Henry, Earl Mertoun, whose estates are contiguous to those of the Treshams. He, too, has a noble name, and he could have lawfully possessed the girl he loved if he had not been deterred by a mysterious feeling of awe for Lord Tresham, and had asked her in marriage. But he is anxious to repair the wrong he has done, and the play opens with his visit to Thorold to formally present himself as the girl's lover. Naturally the Earl, seeing no objection to the match, makes none. The difficulty seems at an end; but, unfortunately,

Gerard, an old and faithful retainer, has seen a man, night after night, climb to the lady's chamber, and has watched him leave. He has no idea who the visitor might be, and, after some struggles with contending emotions, decides to acquaint his master with the things which he has seen. Thorold is in the utmost mental distress and perturbation, and questions his sister in a manner that is as painful to him as to her. She does not deny the circumstances alleged against her. Her brother is overwhelmed with distress at the sudden disgrace brought upon his noble line, and confounded at the idea of the attempt which has been made to involve in his own disgrace the nobleman who has sought an alliance with his family. Mildred refuses to say who her lover is, and weakly—as it appears to her brother—determines to let things take the proposed course. Naturally Thorold looks upon his sister as a degraded being who is dead to shame and honour, and he rushes from her presence to wander in the grounds in the neighbourhood of the house, till at midnight he sees the lover Mertoun preparing to mount to his sister's room. They fight, and the Earl falls mortally wounded. In the chamber above the signal-light in the window has been placed as usual by Mildred, who awaits Thorold in her room. He does not appear, and her heart tells her that her happiness is at an end. Now she sees all her guilt, and the consequences of her degradation to her family. In the midst of these agonising reflections her brother bursts into her room. She sees at once that he has killed Mertoun, sees also that he himself is dying of poison which he has swallowed. Her heart is broken, and she dies. Mildred's cousin Gwendolen, betrothed to the next heir to the earldom, Austin Tresham, is a quick, intelligent woman, who saw how matters stood, and would have rectified them had it not been rendered impossible by the adventure in the grounds, when the unhappy young lover allowed Thorold to kill him. Mr. Forster, in his *Life of Charles Dickens* (Book iv. 1), says: "This was the date [1842], too, of Mr. Browning's tragedy of the *Blot in the 'Scutcheon*, which I took upon myself, after reading it in the manuscript, privately to impart to Dickens; and I was not mistaken in the belief that it would profoundly touch him. 'Browning's play,' he wrote (November 25th), 'has thrown me into a perfect passion of sorrow. To say that there is anything in its subject save what is lovely, true, deeply affecting, full of the best emotion, the most earnest feeling, and the most true and tender source of interest, is to say that there is no light in the sun and no heat in blood. It is full of genius, natural and great thoughts, profound and yet simple and beautiful in its vigour. I know nothing that is so affecting—nothing in any book I have ever read—as Mildred's recurrence to that "I was so young—I had no mother!" I know no love like it, no passion like it, no moulding of a splendid thing after its conception like it. And I swear it is a tragedy that MUST be played; and must be played, moreover, by Macready. There are some things I would have changed if I could (they are very slight, mostly broken lines); and I assuredly would have the old servant *begin his tale upon the scene*, and be taken by the throat, or drawn upon, by his master in its commencement. But the tragedy I never shall forget, or less vividly remember, than I do now. And if you tell Browning that I have seen it, tell him that I believe from my soul there is no man living (and not many dead) who could produce such a work.'" Mr. Browning wrote the play in five days, at the suggestion of Macready, who read it with delight. The poet had been led to expect that Macready would play in it himself, but was annoyed to hear that he had given the part he had intended to take to Mr. Phelps, then an actor quite unknown. Evidently Macready expected that Mr. Browning would withdraw the play. On the contrary, he accepted Phelps, who, however, was taken seriously ill before the rehearsal began. The consequence was (though there was clearly some shuffling on Macready's part) that the great tragedian himself consented to take the part at the last moment. It is evident that Macready had changed his mind. He had, however, done more: he had changed the title to *The Sisters*, and had changed a good deal of the play, even to the extent of inserting some lines of his own. Meanwhile, Phelps having recovered, and being anxious to take his part, Mr. Browning insisted that he should do so; and, to Macready's annoyance, the old arrangement had to stand. The play was vociferously applauded, and Mr. Phelps was again and again called before the curtain. Mr. Browning was much displeased at the treatment he had received, but his play continued to be performed to crowded houses. It was a great success also when Phelps revived it at Sadlers Wells. Miss Helen Faucit (who afterwards became Lady Martin) played the part of Mildred Tresham on the first appearance of *The Blot* in 1843. The Browning Society brought it out at St. George's Hall on May 2nd, 1885; and again at the Olympic Theatre on March 15th, 1888, when Miss Alma Murray played Mildred Tresham in an ideally perfect manner. It was, as the *Era* said, "a thing to be remembered. From every point of view it was admirable. Its passion was highly pitched, its elocution pure and finished, and its expression, by feature and gesture, of a quality akin to genius. The agonising emotions which in turn thrill the girl's sensitive frame were depicted with intense truth and keen and delicate art, and an excellent discretion defeated any temptation to extravagance." It cannot be seriously held by any unprejudiced person that *A Blot in the 'Scutcheon* has within it the elements of success as an acting play. The subject is unpleasant, the conduct of Thorold monomaniacal and improbable, the wholesale dying in the last scene "transpontine." The characters philosophise too much, and dissect themselves even as they die. They come to life again under the stimulation of the process, only to perish still more, and to make us speculate on the nature of the poison which permitted such self-analysis, and on the nature of the heart disease which was so subservient to the patient's necessities. An analytic poet, we feel, is for the study, not for the boards.

Bluphocks. (*Pippa Passes.*) The vagabond Englishman of the poem. "The name means *Blue-Fox*, and is a skit on the *Edinburgh Review*, which is bound in a cover of blue and fox." (Dr. Furnivall.)

Bombast. The proper name of *Paracelsus*; "probably acquired," says Mr. Browning in a note to *Paracelsus*, "from the characteristic phraseology of his lectures, that unlucky signification which it has ever since retained." This is not correct. Bombast, in German *bombast*, cognate with Latin *bombyx* in the sense of cotton. "Bombast, the cotton-plant growing in Asia" (Phillips, *The New World of Words*). It was applied also to the cotton wadding with which garments were lined and stuffed in Elizabeth's time; hence inflated speech, fustian. (See Stubbes, *The Anatomy of Abuses*, p. 23; Trench, *Encyc. Dict.*, etc.)

Boot and Saddle. No. III. of the "Cavalier Songs," published in *Bells and Pomegranates* in 1842, under the title "Cavalier Tunes."

Bottinius. (*The Ring and the Book.*) Juris Doctor Johannes-Baptista Bottinius was the Fisc or Public Prosecutor and Advocate of the Apostolic Chamber at Rome. The ninth book of the poem contains his speech as prosecutor of Count Guido.

Boy and the Angel, The. (*Hood's Magazine*, vol. ii., 1844, pp. 140-42.) Reprinted, revised, and with five fresh couplets, in "Dramatic Romances and Lyrics" (1845), No. VII. *Bells and Pomegranates.* Theocrite was a poor Italian boy who, morning, evening, noon and night, ever sang "Praise God!" As he prayed well and loved God, so he worked well and served his master faithfully and cheerfully. Blaise, the monk, heard him sing his *Laudate*, and said: "I doubt not thou art heard, my son, as well as if thou wert the Pope, praising God from Peter's dome this Easter day"; but Theocrite said: "Would God I might praise Him that great way and die!" That night there was no more Theocrite, and God missed the boy's innocent praise. Gabriel the archangel came to the earth, took Theocrite's humble place, and praised God as did the boy, only with angelic song,—playing well, moreover, the craftsman's part, content at his poor work, doing God's will on earth as he had done it in heaven. But God said: "There is neither doubt nor fear in this praise; it is perfect as the song of my new-born worlds; I miss my little human praise." Then the flesh disguise fell from the angel, and his wings sprang forth again. He flew to Rome: it was Easter Day, and the new pope Theocrite, once the poor work-lad, stood in the tiring room by the great gallery from which the popes are wont to bless the people on Easter morning, and he saw the angel before him, who told him he had made a mistake in bringing him from his trade to set him in that high place; he had done wrong, too, in leaving his angel-sphere: the stopping of that infant praise marred creation's chorus; he must go back, and once more that early way praise God—"back to the cell and poor employ"; and so Theocrite grew to old age at his former home, and Rome had a new pope, and the angel's error was rectified. Legends and stories of saints, angels, and our Lord Himself, are common in all Catholic countries, where these heavenly beings are far more real to the minds of the people than they are to the colder intelligence of Protestant and more logical lands. In southern Europe, hosts of such stories as these cluster round our Lady and the Saints. The Holy Virgin does not disdain to take her needle and sew buttons on the clothing of her worshippers, and the angels and saints think nothing of a little domestic or trade employment if it will assist their devout clients.

In *Notes and Queries*, 3rd Series, xii. 6, July 6, 1867, there appeared two queries on this poem by "John Addis, Jun.": "1. What is the precise inner meaning? 2. On what legend is it founded? With regard to my first question, I see dimly in the poem a comparison of three kinds of praise—viz., human, ceremonial, and angelic. Further, I see dimly a contrasting of Gabriel's humility with Theocrite's ambition. . . . The poem . . . has been recalled to me by reading 'Kyng Roberd of Cysillé' (Hazlitt's *Early Popular Poetry*, vol. i., p. 264). There is a general analogy (by contrast perhaps rather than likeness) between the two poems, which points, I think, to the existence of a legend kindred to 'Kyng Roberd' as the prototype of Browning's poem, rather than to 'Kyng Roberd' itself as that prototype. . . . To 'Sir Gowghter' and the Jovinianus story of *Gesta Romanorum*, I have not present access; but both I fancy (while akin to 'Kyng Roberd of Cysillé') have nothing in common with 'The Boy and the Angel.'" At page 55 another correspondent says that according to Warton (ii. 22), "'Sir Gowghter' is only another version of 'Robert the Devil,' and therefore of 'King Roberd of Cysillé.' He goes on to say that Longfellow has closely followed the old poem in 'King Robert of Sicily' printed in *Tales of a Wayside Inn*; but no answer is given to Mr. Addis' queries about 'The Boy and the Angel'" (*Browning Notes and Queries*, No. 13, Pt. I., vol. ii.) Leigh Hunt, in his *Jar of Honey*, chap. vi., gives the story of King Robert of Sicily. We can only include the following abbreviation here of the beautiful legend told so delightfully by the great essayist.

One day, when King Robert of Sicily was hearing vespers on St. John's Eve, he was struck by the words of the *Magnificat*—"Deposuit potentes de sede, et exaltavit humiles" ("He hath put down the mighty from their seat, and hath exalted the humble"). He asked a chaplain near him what the words meant; and when they were explained to him, scoffingly replied that men like himself were not so easily put down, much less supplanted by those contemptible poor folk. The chaplain was horrified, and made no reply, and the king relieved his annoyance by going to sleep. After some time the king awoke and found himself in the church with no creature present except an old deaf woman who was dusting it. When the old lady saw the man who was trying to make her hear, she cried "Thieves!" and scuttled off to the door, closing it behind her. King Robert looked at the door, then at the empty church, then at himself. His ermine robe was gone, his coronet, his jewels, all the insignia of his royalty had disappeared. Raging at the door, he demanded that it should be opened; but they only mocked him through the keyhole and threatened him with the constable; but as the sexton mocked the captive king the great door was burst open in his face, for the king was a powerful man and had dashed it down with his foot. He strode towards his palace, but they would not admit him, and to all his raving replied "Madman!" Then the king caught sight of his face in a glass, which he tore from the hands of one of his captains who was admiring himself, and saw that he was changed: it was not his own face. Fear came upon him: he knew it was witchcraft, and his violence was increased when the bystanders laughed to hear him declare he was his majesty changed. Next the attendants came from the palace to say the king wanted to see the madman they had caught; and so he was taken to the presence chamber, where he found himself face to face with another King Robert, whom the changed king called "hideous impostor," which made the court laugh consumedly, because the king on the throne was very handsome, and the man who fell asleep in the church was very coarse and vulgar. And now the latter could see that it was an angel who had taken his place, and hated him accordingly. He was still more disgusted when the king told him he would make him his court fool, because he was so amusing in his violence; and he had to submit while they cut his hair and crowned the king of fools with the cap and bells. King Robert then gave way, for he felt he was in the power of the devil and it was no use to resist; and so went out to sup with the dogs, as he was ordered. Matters went on in this way for two years. The new king was good and kind to everybody except the degraded monarch, whom he never tired of humiliating in every possible way. At the end of two years the king went to visit his brother the Pope and his brother the Emperor, and he dressed all his court magnificently, except the fool, whom he arrayed in fox-tails and placed beside an ape. The crowds of people who came out to see the grand procession laughed heartily at the sorry figure cut by the poor fool. He, however, was glad he was going to see the Pope, as he trusted the meeting would dispel the magic by which he was enchained; but he was disappointed, for neither Pope nor Emperor took the slightest notice of him. Now, it happened that day it was again St. John's Eve, and again they were all at vespers singing: "He hath put down the mighty from their seat, and exalted the humble." And now with what different feelings he heard those words! The crowded church was astonished to see the poor fool in his ridiculous disguise bathed in tears, meekly kneeling in prayer, his head bowed in penitence and sorrow. Somehow every one felt a little holier that day: Pope and Emperor wished to be kinder and more sympathetic to their people, and the sermon went to every one's heart, for it was all about charity and humility. After service they told the angel-king of the singular behaviour of the fool. Of course he knew all about it, though he did not say so; but he sent for the fool, and, when he had him in private (except that the ape was there, to whom the fool had become much attached), he asked him, "Art thou still a king?" "I am a fool, and no king." "What wouldst thou, Robert?" asked the angel gently. "What thou wouldst," replied poor King Robert. Then the angel touched him, and he felt an inexpressible calm diffuse itself through his whole being. He knelt, and began to thank the angel. "Not to me," the heavenly being said—"not to me! Let us pray." They knelt in prayer; and when the King rose from his knees the angel was gone, the ermine was once more on the King's shoulder and the crown upon his brow; his humiliation was over, but his pride never returned. He lived long and reigned nobly, and died in the odour of sanctity. Mr. Browning may have drawn upon some Italian legend for his story of Theocrite: it may even have been suggested by the legend of King Robert; but he must have been so familiar with the Catholic idea of the interest in human affairs taken by angels and saints, that he might readily have invented the story. Nothing can be easier to understand than its lesson. With God there is no great or small, no lofty or mean, nothing common or unclean. To do the will of God in the work lying nearest us, to praise God in our daily task and the common things of life as they arise, this is better for us and more acceptable service to Him than doing some great thing, as we, with our false estimates of things, may be led to apprise it.

By the Fireside. (First published in vol. i. of *Men and Women*, 1855.) A man of middle life and very learned is addressing his wife. He looks forward to his old age, and prophesies how it will be passed. He will pursue his studies; but, deep as he will be in Greek, his soul will have no difficulty in finding its way back to youth and Italy, and he will delight to reconstruct the scene in his imagination where he first made all his own the heart of the woman who blessed him with her love and became his wife. Once more he will be found on that mountain path, again he will conjure from the past the Alpine scene by the ruined chapel in the gorge, the poor little building where on feast days the priest comes to minister to the few folk who live on the mountain-side. The bit of fresco over the porch, the date of its erection, the bird which sings there, and the stray sheep which drinks at the pond, the very midges dancing over the water, and the lichens clinging to the walls,—all will be present, for it was there heart was fused with heart, and two souls were blent in one. "With whom else," he asks his wife, "dare he look backward or dare pursue the path grey heads abhor?" Old age is dreaded by the young and middle-aged, none care to think of it; but the speaker dreads it not, he has a soul-companion from whom not even death can separate him, and with the memory of this moment of irrevocable union he can face the bounds of life undaunted. "The moment one and infinite," to which both their lives had tended, had wrought this happiness for him that it could never cease to bear fruit, never cease to hallow and bless his spirit; the mountain stream had sought the lake below, and had lost itself in its bosom; two lives were joined in one without a scar. "How the world is made for each of us!" everything tending to a moment's product, with its infinite consequences—the completion, in this case, of his own small life, whereby Nature won her best from him in fitting him to love his wife. The

"great brow
And the spirit small hand propping it,"

refer to Mrs. Browning, and the whole poem, though the incidents are imaginary, is without doubt a confession of his love for her, and its influence on his own spiritual development.

Caliban upon Setebos; or, Natural Theology in the Island. (*Dramatis Personæ*, 1864.) The original of Caliban is the savage and deformed slave of Shakespeare's *Tempest.* The island may be identified with the Utopia (ουτοπος, the nowhere) of Hythloday. Setebos was the Patagonian god (Settaboth in Pigafetta), which was by 1611 familiar to the hearers of *The Tempest.* Patagonia was discovered by Magellan in 1520. The new worlds which Columbus, Amerigo Vespucci, Gomara, Lane, Harriott and Raleigh described, should, according to the popular fancy of the time, be peopled by just such beings of bestial type as the Caliban of *The Tempest.* The ancients thought the inhabitants of strange and distant lands were half human, half brutal, and monstrous creatures, ogres, and "anthropophagi, men who each other eat." The famous traveller Sir John Mandeville, in the fourteenth century, describes "the land of Bacharie, where be full evil folk and full cruel. In that country been many Ipotaynes, that dwell sometimes in the water and sometimes on the land; half-man and half-horse, and they eat men when they may take them." Marco Polo (1254-1324) represents the Andaman Islanders as a most brutish savage race, having heads, eyes and teeth resembling the canine species, who ate human flesh raw and devoured every one on whom they could lay their hands. The islander as monster was therefore familiar enough to English readers in Shakespeare's time, and the date of the old book of travels "Purchas his Pilgrimage," very nearly corresponding with the probable date of the production of *The Tempest*, affords reasonable proof that the poet has embodied the story given in that work of the pongo, the huge brute-man seen by Andrew Battle in the kingdom of Congo, where he lived some nine months. This pongo slept in the trees, building a roof to shelter himself from the rain, and living wholly on nuts and fruits. Mr. Browning has taken the Caliban of Shakespeare, "the strange fish legged like a man, and his fins like arms," yet "no fish, but an islander that hath lately suffered by a thunderbolt," and has evolved him into "a savage with the introspective powers of a Hamlet and the theology of an evangelical churchman." Shakespeare's monster did not speculate at all; he liked his dinner, liked to be stroked and made much of, and was willing to be taught how to name the bigger light and how the less. He could curse, and he could worship the man in the moon; he could work for those who were kind to him, and had a doglike attachment to Prospero. Mr. Browning's Caliban has become a metaphysician; he talks Browningese, and reasons high

> "Of providence, foreknowledge, will, and fate,
> Fixed fate, free will, foreknowledge absolute."

He has studied Calvin's *Institutes of Theology*, and knows enough of St. Augustine to caricature his teaching. Considered from the anthropologist's point of view, the poem is not a scientific success; Caliban is a degradation from a higher type, not a brute becoming slowly developed into a man. Mr. Browning's early training amongst the Nonconformists of the Calvinistic type had familiarised him with a theology which, up to fifty years ago, was that of a very large proportion of the Independents, the Baptists, and a considerable part of the Evangelical school in the Church of England. Without some acquaintance with this theological system it is impossible to understand the poem. At the head is a quotation from Psalm l. 21, where God says to the wicked, "thou thoughtest that I was altogether such an one as thyself," and the object of the poem is to rebuke the anthropomorphic idea of God as it exists in minds of a narrow and unloving type. It is not a satire upon Christianity, as has been sometimes declared, but is an attempt to trace the evolution of the concrete idea of God in a coarse and brutal type of mind. Man from his advent on the earth has everywhere occupied himself in creating God in his own image and likeness:

> "Make us a god, said man:
> Power first the voice obeyed;
> And soon a monstrous form
> Its worshippers dismayed."

The motto of the poem shows us how much nobler was the Hebrew conception of God than that of the nations who knew Him not. The poem opens with Caliban talking to himself in the third person, while he sprawls in the mire and is cheating Prospero and Miranda, who think he is at work for them. He begins to speculate on the Supreme Being—Setebos: he thinks His dwelling-place is the moon, thinks He made the sun and moon, but not the stars—the clouds and the island on which he dwells; he has no idea of any land beyond that which is bounded by the sea. He thinks creation was the result of God being ill at ease. The cold which He hated and which He was powerless to change impelled Him. So He made the trees, the birds and beasts and creeping things, and made everything in spite. He could not make a second self to be His mate, but made in envy, listlessness or sport all the things which filled the island as playthings. If Caliban could make a live bird out of clay, he would laugh if the creature broke his brittle clay leg; he would play with him, being his and merely clay. So he (Setebos). It would neither be right nor wrong in him, neither kind nor cruel —merely an act of the Divine Sovereignty. If Caliban saw a procession of crabs marching to the sea, in mere indifferent playfulness he might feel inclined to let twenty pass and then stone the twenty-first, pull off a claw from one with purple spots, give a worm to a third fellow, and two to another whose nippers end in red, all the while "Loving not, hating not, just choosing so!" [Apart from revelation, mankind has not reached the conception of the Fatherhood of God, whose tender mercies are over all His works. The gods of the heathen are gods of caprice, of malice and purposeless interference with creatures who are not the sheep of their pastures, but the playthings of unloving Lords.] But he will suppose God is good in the main; He has even made things which are better than Himself, and is envious that they are so, but consoles Himself that they can do nothing without Him. If the pipe which, blown through, makes a scream like a bird, were to boast that it caught the birds, and made the cry the maker could not make, he would smash it with his foot. That is just what God Setebos does; so Caliban must be humble, or pretend to be. But why is Setebos cold and ill at ease? Well, Caliban thinks there may be a something over Setebos, that made Him, something quiet, impassible—call it The Quiet. Beyond the stars he imagines The Quiet to reside, but is not much concerned about It. He plays at being simple in his way—makes believe: so does Setebos. His mother, Sycorax, thought The Quiet made all things, and Setebos only troubled what The Quiet made. Caliban does not agree with that. If things were made weak and subject to pain they were made by a devil, not by a good or indifferent being. No! weakness and pain meant sport to Him who created creatures subject to them. Setebos makes things to amuse himself, just as Caliban does; makes a pile of turfs and knocks it over again. So Setebos. But He is a terrible as well as a malicious being; His hurricanes, His high waves, His lightnings are destructive, and Caliban cannot contend with His force, neither can he tell that what pleases Him to-day will do so to-morrow. We must all live in fear of Him therefore, till haply The Quiet may conquer Him. All at once a storm comes, and Caliban feels that he was a fool to gibe at Setebos. He will lie flat and love Him, will do penance, will eat no whelks for a month to appease Him.

There are, few, if any, systems of theology which escape one or other of the arrows of this satire. Anthropomorphism in greater or less degree is inseparable from our conceptions of the Supreme. The abstract idea of God is impossible to us, the concrete conception is certain to err in making God to be like ourselves. That the Almighty must in Himself include all that is highest and noblest in the soul of man is a right conception, when we attribute to Him our weaknesses and failings we are but as Caliban. The doctrine of election, and the hideous doctrine of reprobation, are most certainly aimed at in the line—

"Loving not, hating not, just choosing so."

The doctrine of reprobation is thus stated in the Westminster Confession of Faith, iii. 7. "The rest of mankind [*i.e.* all but the elect] God was pleased, according to the unsearchable counsel of His own will, whereby He extendeth or withholdeth mercy as He pleaseth, for the glory of His sovereign power over His creatures to pass by, and to ordain them to dishonour and wrath for their sin, to the praise of His glorious grace." Calvin, in his *Institutes of the Christian Religion*, taught that "God has predestinated some to eternal life, while the rest of mankind are predestinated to condemnation and eternal death" (*Encyc. Brit.* iv., art. "Calvin," p. 720).

Camel Driver, A. (Punishment by Man and by God: *Ferishtah's Fancies*, 7.) A murderer had been executed, the criminal acknowledging the justice of his punishment, but lamenting that the man who prompted him to evil had escaped; the murderer reflected with satisfaction that God had reserved a hell for him. But punishment is only man's trick to teach; if he could see true repentance in the sinner's soul, the fault would not be repeated.

God's process in teaching or punishing nowise resembles man's. Man lumps his kind in the mass, God deals with each individual soul as though they two were alone in the universe, "Ask thy lone soul what laws are plain to thee," said Ferishtah, "then stand or fall by them!" Ignorance that sins is safe,—our greatest punishment is knowledge. No other hell will be needed for any man than the reflection that he deliberately spurned the steps which would have raised him to the regard of the Supreme. In the Lyric it is complained that mankind is over-severe with mere imperfections, which it magnifies into crimes; but the greater faults, which should have been crushed in the egg, are either not suspected at all or actually praised as virtues.

Caponsacchi (*The Ring and the Book*), the chivalrous priest, Canon of Arezzo, who aided Pompilia in her flight to Rome from the tyranny of Count Guido.

Cardinal and the Dog, The. (*Asolando*, 1889.) The Papal Legate, at the later sessions of the Council of Trent in 1551 and 1552, was Marcel Crescenzio, who came of a noble Roman family. At the fifteenth session of the Council (March 20th, 1552) he was writing to the Pope nearly the whole night, although he was ill at the time; and as he rose from his seat he saw a black dog of great size, with flaming eyes and ears hanging down to the ground, which sprang into the chamber, making straight for him, and then stretched himself under the table where Crescenzio wrote. He called his servants and ordered them to turn out the beast, but they found none. Then the Cardinal fell melancholy, took to his bed and died. As he lay on his death-bed at Verona he cried aloud to every one to drive away the dog that leapt on his bed, and so passed away in horror. The poem was written at the request of William Macready, the eldest son of the great actor. He asked the poet to write something which he might illustrate. This was in 1840, but the work was only published in the *Asolando* volume in 1889. Howling dogs have from remote times been connected with death. In Ossian we have: "The mother of Culmin remains in the hall—his dogs are howling in their place—'Art thou fallen, my fair-haired son, in Erin's dismal war?'" There is no doubt that the howling of the wind suggested the idea of a great dog of death. The wind itself was a magnified dog, heard but not seen. Burton, in *The Anatomy of Melancholy*, says (Part I., sect. ii., mem. 1, subs. 2): "Spirits often foretell men's death by several signs, as knockings, groanings, etc., though Rich. Argentine, c. 18, *De præstigiis dæmonum*, will ascribe these predictions to good angels, out of the authority of Ficinus and others; prodigies frequently occur at the deaths of illustrious men, as in the Lateran Church in Rome the popes' deaths are foretold by Sylvester's tomb. Many families in Europe are so put in mind of their last by such predictions; and many men are forewarned (if we may believe Paracelsus) by familiar spirits in divers shapes—as cocks, crows, owls—which often hover about sick men's chambers." The dog is such a faithful friend of man that we are unwilling to believe him, even in spirit-form, the harbinger of evil to any one. Cardinal Crescenzio, had he been a vivisector, would have been very appropriately summoned to his doom in the manner described in the poem. If the men who, like Professor Rutherford of Edinburgh University, boast of their ruthless torturing of dogs by hundreds, should ever find themselves in Cardinal Crescenzio's plight, there would be a fitness in things we could readily appreciate. The devil in the form of a great black dog is a familiar subject with mediæval historians. Not all black dogs were evil, though—for example, the black dog which St. Dominic's mother saw before the birth of the saint. Some of the animals called dogs were probably wolves; but even these appeared not entirely past redemption, such as the one of which we read in the *Golden Legend*, who was converted by the preaching of St. Francis, and shed tears of repentance, and became as meek as a lamb, following the saint to every town where he preached! Such is the power of love. In May 1551 the eleventh session of the Council of Trent was held, under the presidency of Cardinal Crescenzio, sole legate in title, but with two nuncios—Pighini and Lippomani. It was merely formal, as was also the twelfth session, in September 1551. It was Crescenzio who refused all concession, even going so far as to abstract the Conciliar seal, lest the safe-conduct to the Protestant theologians should be granted. He was, however, forced to yield to pressure, and had to receive the Protestant envoys in a private session at his own house. The legate in April 1552 was compelled to suspend the Council for two years, in consequence of the perils of war. There was a general stampede from Trent at once, and the legate Crescenzio, then very ill, had just strength to reach

Verona, where he died three days after his arrival (*Encyc. Brit.*, art. "Trent," vol. xxiii.). Moreri (*Dict. Hist.*) tells the story in almost the same way as Mr. Browning has given it, and adds: "It could have been invented only by ill-meaning people, who lacked respect for the Council."

Carlisle, Lady. (*Strafford.*) Mr. Browning says: "The character of Lady Carlisle in the play is wholly imaginary," but history points clearly enough to the truth of Mr. Browning's conception.

Cavalier Tunes. (Published first in *Bells and Pomegranates* in 1842.) Their titles are: "Marching Along," "Give a Rouse," and "Boot and Saddle." Villiers Stanford set them to music.

Cenciaja. (*Pacchiarotto, with other Poems*, London, 1876.)

"Ogni cencio vuol entrare in bucato."

The explanation of the title of this poem, as also of the Italian motto which stands at its head, is given in the following letter written by the poet to Mr. Buxton Forman:—

"19, Warwick Crescent, W., *July 27th*, '76.

"Dear Mr. Buxton Forman,—There can be no objection to such a simple statement as you have inserted, if it seems worth inserting. 'Fact,' it is. Next: 'Aia' is generally an accumulative yet depreciative termination. 'Cenciaja,' a bundle of rags—a trifle. The proverb means 'every poor creature will be pressing into the company of his betters,' and I used it to deprecate the notion that I intended anything of the kind. Is it any contribution to 'all connected with Shelley,' if I mention that my 'Book' (*The Ring and the Book*) [rather the 'old square yellow book,' from which the details were taken] has a reference to the reason given by Farinacci, the advocate of the Cenci, of his failure in the defence of Beatrice? 'Fuisse punitam Beatricem' (he declares) 'pœnâ ultimi supplicii, non quia ex intervallo occidi mandavit insidiantem suo honori, sed quia ejus exceptionem non probavi tibi. Prout, et idem firmiter sperabatur de sorore Beatrice si propositam excusationem probasset, prout non probavit.' That is, she expected to avow the main outrage, and did not; in conformity with her words, 'That which I ought to confess, that will I confess; that to which I ought to assent, to that I assent; and that which I ought to deny, that will I deny.' Here is another Cenciaja!

"Yours very sincerely, Robert Browning."

The opening lines of the poem refer to Shelley's terrible tragedy, *The Cenci*, in the preface to which the story on which the work is founded, is briefly told as follows: "A manuscript was communicated to me during my travels in Italy, which was copied from the archives of the Cenci Palace at Rome, and contains a detailed account of the horrors which ended in the extinction of one of the noblest and richest families of that city, during the pontificate of Clement VIII., in the year 1599. The story is, that an old man, having spent his life in debauchery and wickedness, conceived at length an implacable hatred towards his children; which showed itself towards one daughter under the form of an incestuous passion, aggravated by every circumstance of cruelty and violence. This daughter, after long and vain attempts to escape from what she considered a perpetual contamination both of body and mind, at length plotted with her mother-in-law and brother to murder their common tyrant. The young maiden, who was urged to this tremendous deed by an impulse which overpowered its horror, was evidently a most gentle and amiable being; a creature formed to adorn and be admired, and thus violently thwarted from her nature by the necessity of circumstances and opinion. The deed was quickly discovered; and, in spite of the most earnest prayers made to the Pope by the highest persons in Rome, the criminals were put to death. The old man had, during his life, repeatedly bought his pardon from the Pope for capital crimes of the most enormous and unspeakable kind, at the price of a hundred thousand crowns; the death, therefore, of his victims can scarcely be accounted for by the love of justice. The Pope, among other motives for severity, probably felt that whosoever killed the Count Cenci deprived his treasury of a certain and copious source of revenue." This explanation is exactly what might be expected from a priest-hater and religion-despiser like Shelley. The *Encyclopædia Britannica*, in the article on Clement VIII., says: "Clement was an able ruler and a sagacious statesman. He died in March 1605, leaving a high character for prudence, munificence, and capacity for business." Mr. Browning's contribution to the Cenci literature affords a more reasonable motive for refusing to spare the lives of the Cenci. Sir John Simeon lent the poet a copy of an old chronicle, of which he made liberal use in the poem we are considering. According to this account, the Pope would probably have pardoned Beatrice had not a case of matricide occurred in Rome at the time, which determined him to make an example of the Cenci. The Marchesa dell' Oriolo, a widow, had just been murdered by her younger son, Paolo Santa Croce. He had quarrelled with his mother about the family rights of his elder brother, and killed her because she refused to aid him in an act of injustice. Having made his escape, he endeavoured to involve his brother in the crime, and the unfortunate young man was beheaded, although he was perfectly innocent. In *Cenciaja* Mr. Browning throws light on the tragic events of the Cenci story. When Clement was petitioned on behalf of the family, he said: "She must die. Paolo Santa Croce murdered his mother, and he is fled; she shall not flee at least!"

Charles Avison. [THE MAN.] (*Parleyings with Certain People of Importance in their Day.* 1887. No. VII.) "Charles Avison, a musician, was born in Newcastle about 1710, and died in the same town in 1770. He studied in Italy, and on his return to England became a pupil of Geminiani. He was appointed organist of St. Nicholas' Church, Newcastle, in 1736. In 1752 appeared his celebrated *Essay on Musical Expression*, which startled the world by the boldness with which it put the French and Italian schools of music above the German, headed by Handel himself. This book led to a controversy with Dr. Hayes, in which, according to the *Dictionary of National Biography*, from which we take the facts, 'Hayes had the best of the argument, though Avison was superior from a literary point of view. Avison, who is reported to have been a man of great culture and polish, published several sets of sonatas and concertos, but there are probably few persons at the present day who have ever heard any of his music." (*Pall Mall Gazette*, Jan. 18th, 1887.)

[THE POEM.] This is a criticism of the province and office of music in its influence on the mind of man.

> "There is no truer truth obtainable
> By man, than comes of music,"

says Mr. Browning. Underneath Mind rolls the unsounded sea —the Soul. Feeling from out its deeps emerges in flower and foam.

> "Who tells of, tracks to source the founts of Soul?"

Music essays to solve how we feel, to match feeling with knowledge. Manifest Soul's work on Mind's work, how and whence come the hates, loves, joys, hopes and fears that rise and sink ceaselessly within us? Of these things Music seeks to tell. Art may arrest some of the transient moods of Soul; Poetry discerns, Painting is aware of the seething within the gulf, but Music outdoes both: dredging deeper yet, it drags into day the abysmal bottom growths of Soul's deep sea.

NOTES.—ii., "*March*": Avison's *Grand March* was possessed in MS. by Browning's father. The music of the march is added to the poem. iv., "*Great John Relfe*": Browning's music master—a celebrated contrapuntist. *Buononcini, Giovanni Battista*, Italian musician. He was a gifted composer, declared by his clique to be infinitely superior to Handel, with whom he wrote at one time in conjunction. *Geminiani, Francesco*, Italian violinist (1680-1762). He came to London under the protection of the Earl of Essex in 1714. His musical opinions are said to have had no foundation in truth or principle. *Pepusch, John Christopher*, an eminent theoretical musician, born at Berlin about 1667. He performed at Drury Lane in about 1700. He took the degree of Mus. Doc. at Oxford at the same time with Croft, 1713. He was organist at the Charter-House, and died in 1752. v., *Hesperus*. The song to the Evening Star in *Tannhauser*, "O Du mein holder Abendstern," is referred to here (Mr. A. Symons). viii., "*Radamista*," the name of an opera by Handel, first performed at the Haymarket in 1720. "*Rinaldo*," the name of the opera composed by Handel, and performed under his direction at the Haymarket for the first time on Feb. 24th, 1711. xv., "*Little Ease*," an uncomfortable punishment similar to the stocks or the pillory.

Charles I. (*Strafford.*) The character of this king, who basely sacrifices his best friend Strafford, is founded in fact, but his weakness and meanness are doubtless exaggerated by the poet—to show his meaning, as the artists say.

Cherries. (*Ferishtah's Fancies*, 9.) "On Praise and Thanksgiving." All things are great and small in their degree. A disciple objects to Ferishtah that man is too weak to praise worthily the All-mighty One; he is too mean to offer fit praise to Heaven,—let the stars do that! The dervish tells a little story of a subject of the Shah who came from a distant part of the realm, and wandered about the palace wonderingly, till all at once he was surprised to find a nest-like little chamber with his own name on the entry, and everything arranged exactly to his own peculiar taste. Yet to him it was as nothing: he had not faith enough to enter into the good things provided for him. He tells another story. Two beggars owed a great sum to the Shah. This one brought a few berries from his currant-bush, some heads of garlic, and five pippins from a seedling tree. This was his whole wealth; he offered that in payment of his debt. It was graciously received; teaching us that if we offer God all the love and thanks we can, it will gratify the Giver of all good none the less because our offering is small, and lessened by admixture with lower human motives. For the grateful flavour of the cherry let us lift up our thankful hearts to Him who made that, the stars, and us. We know why He made the cherry,—why He made Jupiter we do not know. The Lyric compares verse-making with love-making. Verse-making is praising God by the stars, too great a task for man's short life; but love-making has no depths to explore, no heights to ascend; love now will be love evermore: let us give thanks for love, if we cannot offer praise the poet's own great way.

Chiappino. (*A Soul's Tragedy.*) The bragging friend of Luitolfo, who was compelled to be noble against his inclination, and who became "the twenty-fourth leader of a revolt" ridiculed by the legate.

"Childe Roland to the Dark Tower came." (*Men and Women*, 1855; *Romances*, 1863; *Dramatic Romances*, 1868.) The story of a knight who has undertaken a pilgrimage to a certain dark tower, the way to which was full of difficulties and dangers, and the right road quite unknown to the seeker. Those who had preceded him on the path had all failed, and he himself is no sooner fairly engaged in the quest than he is filled with despair, but is impelled to go on. At the stage of his journey which is described in the poem he meets a hoary cripple, who gives him directions which he consents to follow, though with misgivings. The day was drawing to a close, the road by which he entered on the path to the tower was gone; when he looked back, nothing remained but to proceed. Nature all around was starved and ignoble: flowers there were none; some weeds that seemed to thrive in the wilderness only added to its desolation; dock leaves with holes and rents, grass as hair in leprosy; and wandering on the gloomy plain, one stiff, blind horse, all starved and stupefied, looking as if he were thrust out of the devil's stud. The pilgrim tried to think of earlier, happier sights: of his friend Cuthbert—alas! one night's disgrace left him without that friend; of Giles, the soul of honour, who became a traitor, spit upon and curst. The present horror was better than these reflections on the past. And now he approached a petty, yet spiteful river, over which black scrubby alders hung, with willows that seemed suicidal. He forded the stream, fearing to set his foot on some dead man's cheek; the cry of the water-rat sounded as the shriek of a baby. And as he toiled on he saw that ugly heights (mountains seemed too good a name to give such hideous heaps) had given place to the plain, and two hills in particular, couched like two bulls in fight, seemed to indicate the place of the tower. Yes! in their midst was the round, squat turret, without a counterpart in the whole world. The sight was as that of the rock which the sailor sees too late to avoid the crash that wrecks his ship. The very hills seemed watching him; he seemed to hear them cry, "Stab and end the creature!" A noise was everywhere, tolling like a bell; he could hear the names of the lost adventurers who had preceded him. There they stood to see the last of him. He saw and knew them all, yet dauntless set the horn to his lips and blew, "*Childe Roland to the Dark Tower came.*"

NOTES.—At the head of the poem is a note: "See Edgar's song in *Lear.*" In Act III., scene iv., Edgar, disguised as a madman, says, while the storm rages: "Who gives anything to poor Tom? whom the foul fiend hath led through fire and through flame, through ford and whirlpool, over bog and quagmire; that hath laid knives under his pillow and halters in his pew; set ratsbane by his porridge; made him proud of heart to ride on a bay trotting-horse over four-inched bridges, to course his own shadow for a traitor.—Bless thy five wits! Tom's a-cold.—O do de, do de, do, de.——Bless thee from whirlwinds, star-blasting, and taking! Do poor Tom some charity, whom the foul fiend vexes." At the end of the scene Edgar sings:—

"Childe Rowland to the dark tower came,
His word was still,—Fie, foh, and fum
I smell the blood of a British man."

"Childe Roland was the youngest brother of Helen. Under the guidance of Merlin he undertook to bring back his sister from elf-land, whither the fairies had carried her, and he succeeded in his perilous exploit."—Dr. Brewer. (See the ancient Ballade of *Burd Helen.*) *Childe* was a term specially applied to the scions of knightly families before their admission to the degree of knighthood, as "Chyld Waweyn, Loty's Sone" (*Robert of Gloucester*).

This wonderful poem, one of the grandest pieces of word-painting in our language, has exercised the ingenuity of Browning students more than any other of the poet's works. *Sordello* is difficult to understand, but it was intended by the poet to convey a definite meaning and important lessons, but *Childe Roland*, we have been warned again and again, was written without any moral purpose whatever. "We may see in it," says Mrs. Orr, "a poetic vision of life. . . . The thing we may not do is to imagine that we are meant to recognise it." A paper was read at the Browning Society on this poem by Mr. Kirkman (*Browning Society Papers*, Part iii., p. 21) suggesting an interpretation of the allegory. In the discussion which followed, Dr. Furnivall said "he had asked Browning if it was an allegory, and in answer had, on three separate occasions, received an emphatic 'no'; that it was simply a dramatic creation called forth by a line of Shakespeare's. Browning had written it one day in Paris, as a vivid picture suggested by Edgar's line; the horse was suggested by the figure of a red horse in a piece of tapestry in Browning's house. . . . Still, Dr. Furnivall thought, it was quite justifiable that any one should use the poem to signify whatever image it called up in his own mind. But he must not confuse the poet's mind with his. The poem was *not* an allegory, and was never meant to be one." The Hon. Roden Noel, who was in the chair on this occasion, said "he himself had never regarded *Childe Roland* as having any hidden meaning; nor had cared so to regard it. But words are mystic symbols: they mean more, very often, than the utterer of them, poet or puppet, intended." When some one asked Mendelssohn what he meant by his *Lieder ohne Worte*, the musician replied that "they meant what they said." A poem so consistent as a whole, with a narrative in which every detail follows in a perfectly regular and natural sequence, must inevitably convey to the thinking mind some great and powerful idea, suiting itself to his view of life considered as a journey or pilgrimage. The wanderings of the children of Israel from Egypt to the Promised Land may be considered simply as a historical event, like the migrations of the Tartars or the Northmen; or they may be viewed as an allegory of the Christian life, like Bunyan's immortal dream. The historian of the Exodus could never have had in his mind all the interpretations put upon the incidents which he recorded; yet we have the warrant of St. Paul for allegorising the story. Any narrative of a journey through a desert to a definite end held in view throughout the way, is certain to be pounced upon as an allegory; and it is impossible but that Mr. Browning must have had some notion of a "central purpose" in his poem. Indeed, when the Rev. John W. Chadwick visited the poet, and asked him if constancy to an ideal—"He that endureth to the end shall be saved"—was not a sufficient understanding of the central purpose of the poem, he said, "Yes, just about that." Mr. Kirkman, in the paper already referred to, says, "There are overwhelming reasons for concluding that this poem describes, after the manner of an allegory, the sensations of a sick man very near to death—*Rabbi Ben Ezra* and *Prospice*—are the two angels that lead on to *Childe Roland*." Mr. Nettleship, in his well-known essay on the poem, says the central idea is this: "Take some great end which men have proposed to themselves in life, which seemed to have truth in it, and power to spread freedom and happiness on others; but as it comes in sight, it falls strangely short of preconceived ideas, and stands up in hideous prosaicness." Mrs. James L. Bagg, in the *Interpretation of Childe Roland*, read to the Syracuse (U.S.) Browning Club, gives the following on the lesson of the poem:—"The secrets of the universe are not to be discovered by exercise of reason, nor are they to be reached by flights of fancy, nor are duties loyally done to be recompensed by revealment. A life of *becoming*, *being*, and *doing*, is not loss, nor failure, nor discomfiture, though the dark tower for ever tantalise and for ever withhold." Some have seen in the poem an allegory of *Love*, others of *the Search after Truth*. Others, again, understand the Dark Tower to represent Unfaith, and the obscure land that of Doubt—Doubting Castle and the By-Path Meadow of John Bunyan, in short. For my own part, I see in the allegory—for I can consider it no other—a picture of the Age of Materialistic

Science, a "science falsely so called," which aims at the destruction of all our noblest ideals of religion and faith in the unseen. The pilgrim is a truth-seeker, misdirected by the lying spirit—the hoary cripple, unable to be or do anything good or noble himself; in him I see the cynical, destructive critic, who sits at our universities and colleges, our medical schools and our firesides, to point our youth to the desolate path of Atheistic Science, a science which strews the ghastly landscape with wreck and ruthless ruin, with the blanching bones of animals tortured to death by its "engines and wheels, with rusty teeth of steel"—a science which has invaded the healing art, and is sending students of medicine daily down the road where surgeons become cancer-grafters (as the Paris and Berlin medical scandals have revealed), and where physicians gloat over their animal victims—

"Toads in a poisoned tank,
Or wild cats in a red-hot iron cage,"

in their passion to reach the dark tower of Knowledge, which to them has neither door nor window. The lost adventurers are the men who, having followed this false path, have failed, and who look eagerly for the next fool who comes to join the band of the lost ones. "In the Paris School of Medicine," says Mr. Lilly in his *Right and Wrong*, "it has lately been prophesied that, 'when the rest of the world has risen to the intellectual level of France, the present crude and vulgar notions regarding morality, religion, Divine providence, and so forth, will be swept entirely away, and the dicta of science will remain the sole guide of sane and educated men.'" Had Mr. Browning intended to write for us an allegory in aid of our crusade, a sort of medical Pilgrim's Progress, he could scarcely have given the world a more faithful picture of the spiritual ruin and desolation which await the student of medicine who sets forth on the fatal course of an experimental torturer. I have good authority for saying that, had Mr. Browning seen this interpretation of his poem, he would have cordially accepted it as at least one legitimate explanation. Most of the commentators agree that when Childe Roland "dauntless set the slug horn to his lips and blew '*Childe Roland to the Dark Tower came*,'" he did so as a warning to others that he had failed in his quest, and that the way of the Dark Tower was the way of destruction and death.

Christmas Eve. (*Christmas Eve and Easter Day:* London, 1850.) Two poems on the same subject from different points of view. The scene is a country chapel, a barnlike structure, from which ornament has been rigorously excluded, not so much on account of want of funds as horror of anything which should detract from "Gospel simplicity." The night is stormy, and Christmas Day must have fallen on a Monday that year, or surely no worshippers in that building would have troubled themselves about keeping the vigil of such a "Popish feast" as Christmas. It must have been Sunday night as well as Christmas Eve, that year of '49. The congregation eyed the stranger "much as some wild beast," for "not many wise" were called to worship in their particular way, and the stranger was evidently not of their faith or class. In came the flock: the fat woman with a wreck of an umbrella; the little old-faced, battered woman with the baby, wringing the ends of her poor shawl soaking with the rain; then a "female something" in dingy satins; next a tall, yellow man, like the Penitent Thief; and from him, as from all, the interloper got the same surprised glance. "What, you, Gallio, here!" it expressed. And so, after a shoemaker's lad, with a wet apron round his body and a bad cough inside it, had passed in, the interloper followed and took his place, waiting for his portion of New Testament meat, like the rest of them. What with the hot smell of greasy coats and frowsy gowns, combined with the preacher's stupidity, the visitor soon had enough of it, and he "flung out of the little chapel" in disgust. As he passed out he found there was a lull in the rain and wind. The moon was up, and he walked on, glad to be in the open air, his mind full of the scene he had left. After all, why should he be hard on this case? In many modes the same thing was going on everywhere—the endeavour to make you believe—and with much about the same effect. He had his own church; Nature had early led him to its door; he had found God visibly present in the immensities, and with the power had recognised his love too as the nobler dower. Quite true was it that God stood apart from man—apart, that he might have room to act and use his gifts of brain and heart. Man was not perfect, not a machine, not unaware of his fitness to pray and praise. He looked up to God, recognised how infinitely He surpassed man in power and wisdom, and was convinced He would never in His love bestow less than man requires. In this great way *he* would seek to press towards God; let men seek Him in a narrow shrine if they would. And as he mused thus, suddenly the rain ceased and the moon shone out, the black clouds falling beneath her feet; a moon rainbow, vast and perfect, rose in its chorded colours. Then from out the world of men the worshipper of God in Nature was called, and at once and with terror he saw Him with His human air, the back of Him—no more. He had been present in the poor chapel—He, with His sweeping garment, vast and white, whose hem could just be recognised by the awed beholder, He who had promised to be where two or three should meet to pray—and He had been present as the friend of these poor folk! He was leaving him who had despised the friends of the Human-Divine. Then he clung to the salvation of His vesture, and told Him how he had thought it best He should be worshipped in spirit and becoming beauty; the uncouth worship he had just left was scarcely fitted for Him. Then the Lord turned His whole face upon him, and he was caught up in the whirl of the vestment, and was up-borne through the darkness and the cold, and held awful converse with his God; and then he came to know who registers the cup of cold water given for His sake, and who disdains not to slake His Divine thirst for love at the poorest love ever offered—came to know it was for this he was permitted to cling to the vesture himself. And so they crossed the world till they stopped at the miraculous dome of God, St. Peter's Church at Rome, with its colonnade like outstretched arms, as if desiring to embrace all mankind. The whole interior of the vast basilica is alive with worshippers this Christmas Eve. It is the midnight mass of the Feast of the Nativity under Rome's great dome. The incense rises in clouds; the organ holds its breath and grovels latent, as if hushed by the touch of God's finger. The silence is broken only by the shrill tinkling of a silver bell. Very man and Very God upon the altar lies, and Christ has entered, and the man whom He brought clinging to His garment's fold is left outside the door, for He must be within, where so much of love remains, though the man without is to wait till He return:

> "He will not bid me enter too,
> But rather sit as I now do."

He muses as he remains in the night air, shut out from the glory and the worship within, and he desires to enter. He thinks he can see the error of the worshippers; but he is sure also that he can see the love, the power of the Crucified One, which swept away the poetry, rhetoric and art of old Rome and Greece, "till filthy saints rebuked the gust" which gave them the glimpse of a naked Aphrodite. Love shut the world's eyes, and love sufficed. Again he is caught up in the vesture's fold, and transferred this time to a lecture-hall in a university town in Germany, where a hawk-nosed, high-cheek-boned professor, with a hacking cough, is giving a Christmas Eve discourse on the Christ myth. He was just discussing the point whether there ever was a Christ or not, and the Saviour had entered here also; but He would not bid His companion enter "the exhausted air-bell of the critic." Where Papist with Dissenter struggles the air may become mephitic; but the German left no air to poison at all. He rejects Christ as known to Christians; yet he retains somewhat. Is it His intellect that we must reverence? But Christ taught nothing which other sages had not taught before, and who did not damage their claim by assuming to be one with the Creator. Are we to worship Christ, then, for His goodness? But goodness is due from man to man, still more to God, and does not confer on its possessor the right to rule the race. Besides, the goodness of Christ was either self-gained or inspired by God. On neither ground could it substantiate His claim to put Himself above us. We praise Nature, not Harvey, for the circulation of the blood; so we look from the gift to the Giver—from man's dust to God's divinity. What is the point of stress in Christ's teaching? "Believe in goodness and truth, now understood for the first time"? or "Believe in Me, who lived and died, yet am Lord of Life"? And all the time Christ remains inside this lecture-room. Could it be that there was anything which a Christian could be in accord with there? The professor has pounded the pearl of price to dust and ashes, yet he does not bid his hearers sweep the dust away. No; he actually gives it back to his hearers, and bids them carefully treasure the precious remains, venerate the myth, adore the man as before! And so the listener resolved to value religion for itself, be very careless as to its sects, and thus cultivate a mild indifferentism; when, lo! the storm began afresh, and the black night caught him and whirled him up and flung him prone on the college-step. Christ was gone, and the vesture fast receding. It is borne in upon him then that there must be one best way of worship. This he will strive to find and make other men share, for man is linked with man, and no gain of his must remain unshared by the race. He caught at the vanishing robe, and, once more lapped in its fold, was seated in the little chapel again, as if he had never left it, never seen St. Peter's successor nor the professor's laboratory. The poor folk were all there as before—a disagreeable company, and the sermon had just reached its "tenthly and lastly." The English was ungrammatical; in a word, the water of life was being dispensed with a strong taint of the soil in a poor earthen vessel. This, he thinks, is his place; here, to his mind, is "Gospel simplicity"; he will criticise no more.

NOTES.—Sect. ii., "*a carer for none of it, a Gallio*": "And Gallio cared for none of these things" (Acts xviii. 17). "*A Saint John's candlestick*" (see Rev. i. 20). "*Christmas Eve of 'Forty-nine*": Dissenters do not keep Christmas Eve, nor Christmas Day itself; they would not, therefore, have been found at chapel unless Christmas happened to fall on a Sunday. In 1849 Christmas Eve fell on a Monday. Sect. x., *the baldachin*: the canopy over the high altar of St. Peter's at Rome is supported by magnificent twisted brazen columns, from designs by Bernini. It is 95 feet in height, and weighs about 93 tons. The high altar stands immediately over the tomb of St. Peter. Sect. xiv., "*Göttingen, most likely*": a celebrated university of Germany, which has produced many eminent Biblical critics. Neander and Ewald were natives of Göttingen. Sect. xvi.,—

> "*When A got leave an Ox to be,*
> *No Camel (quoth the Jews) like G.*"

The letter Aleph, in Hebrew, was suggested by an ox's head and horns. Gimel, the Hebrew letter G, means camel. Sect. xviii., "*anapæsts in comic-trimeter*": in prosody an *anapæst* is a foot consisting of three syllables; the first two short, and the third long. A *trimeter* is a division of verse consisting of three measures of two feet each. "*The halt and maimed 'Iketides'*": *The Suppliants*, an incomplete play of Æschylus, called "maimed" because we have only a portion of it extant. Sect. xxii., *breccia*, a kind of marble.

Christopher Smart. (*Parleyings with Certain People of*

Importance in their Day. 1887.) [THE MAN.] (1722-1771.) It has only recently been discovered that Smart was anything more than a writer of second-rate eighteenth-century poetry. He was born at Shipbourne, in Kent, in 1722. He was a clever youth, and the Duchess of Cleveland sent him to Cambridge, and allowed him £40 a year till her death in 1742. He did well at college, and became a fellow of Pembroke, gaining the Seaton prize five times. When he came to London he mixed in the literary society adorned by Dr. Johnson, Garrick, Dr. James, and Dr. Burney—all of whom helped him in his constant difficulties. He married a daughter of Mr. Newbery, the publisher. He became a Bohemian man of letters, but the only work by which he will be remembered is the *Song to David*, the history of which is sufficiently remarkable. It was written while he was in confinement as a person of unsound mind, and was—it is said, though we know not if the fact be precisely as usually stated—written with a nail on the wall of the cell in which he was detained. The poem bears no evidence of the melancholy circumstances under which it was composed: it is powerful and healthy in every line, and is evidently the work of a sincerely religious mind. He was unfortunately a man of dissipated habits, and his insanity was probably largely due to intemperance. He died in 1771 from the effects of poverty and disease. His *Song to David* was published in 1763, and is quite unlike any other production of the century. The poem in full consists of eighty-six verses, of which Mr. Palgrave, in the *Golden Treasury*, gives the following:—

"He sang of God—the mighty Source
Of all things, the stupendous force
On which all strength depends;
From Whose right arm, beneath Whose eyes,
All period, power, and enterprise
Commences, reigns, and ends.

"The world,—the clustering spheres, He made,
The glorious light, the soothing shade,
Dale, champaign, grove, and hill:
The multitudinous abyss.
Where Secrecy remains in bliss,
And Wisdom hides her skill.

"Tell them, I AM, Jehovah said
To Moses, while earth heard in dread,
And, smitten to the heart,
At once above, beneath, around,
All Nature, without voice or sound,
Replied, O LORD, THOU ART."

[THE POEM.] "How did this happen?" asks Mr. Browning. He imagined that he was exploring a large house, had gone through the decently-furnished rooms, which exhibited in their arrangement good taste without extravagance, till, on pushing open a door, he found himself in a chapel which was

"From floor to roof one evidence
Of how far earth may rival heaven."

Prisoned glory in every niche, it glowed with colour and gleamed with carving: it was "Art's response to earth's despair." He leaves the chapel big with expectation of what might be in store for him in other rooms in the mansion, but there was nothing but the same dead level of indifferent work everywhere, just as in the rooms which he had passed through on his way to the exquisite chapel: nothing anywhere but calm Common-Place. Browning says this is a diagnosis of Smart's case: he was sound and sure at starting, then caught up in a fireball. Heaven let earth understand how heaven at need can operate; then the flame fell, and the untransfigured man resumed his wonted sobriety. But what Browning wants to know is, How was it this happened but once? Here was a poet who always could but never did but once! Once he saw Nature naked; once only Truth found vent in words from him. Once the veil was pulled back, then the world darkened into the repository of show and hide.

Clara de Millefleurs. (*Red Cotton Night-Cap Country.*) The mistress of Miranda, the jeweller of Paris.

Claret. See "Nationality in Drinks" (*Dramatic Lyrics*).

Classification. Mr. Nettleship's classification of Browning is the best I know. It is no easy matter to table the poet's works: they do not readily accommodate themselves to classification. Such poems as the great Art and Music works, the Dramas Love, and Religious poems are to be found in this book under the respective subjects.

Cleon. (*Men and Women*, 1855.) The speculation of this poem may be compared with a picture in a magic lantern slowly dissolving into another view, and losing itself in that which is succeeding it. We have the latest utterances of the beautiful Greek thought, saddened as they were by the despairing note of the sense of hopelessness which marred the highest effort of man, and which was never so acutely felt as at the period when the Sun of Christianity was rising and about to fill the world with the Spirit of Eternal Hope. The old heathenism is dissolving away, the first faint outlines of the gospel glory are detected by the philosopher who has heard of the fame of Paul, and is not sure he is not the same as the Christ preached by some slaves whose doctrine "could be held by no sane man." The quotation with which the poem is headed is from Acts of the Apostles, chap. xvii. 28: "As certain also of your own poets have said, 'For we are also his offspring.'" The quotation is from the *Phænomena* of Aratus, a poet of *Tarsus*, in Cilicia, St. Paul's own city. There is also a very similar passage in a hymn of the Stoic Cleanthes: "Zeus, thou crown of creation, Hail!—We are thy offspring." The persons of the poem are not historical, though the thought expressed is highly characteristic of that of the Greek philosophers of the time. As the old national creeds disappeared under the advancing tide of Roman conquest, and as philosophers calmly discussed the truth or falsity of their dying religions, an easy tolerance arose, all religions were permitted because "indiffererence had eaten the heart out of them." Four hundred years before our era Eastern philosophy, through the Greek conquests in Asia, had begun to influence European thinkers by its strange and subtle attempts to solve the mystery of existence. A spirit of inquiry, and a restless craving for some undefined faith which should take the place of that which was everywhere dying out, prepared the way for the progress of the simple, love-compelling religion of Christ, and made every one's heart more or less suitable soil for the good seed. Cleon is a poet from the isles of Greece who has received a letter from his royal patron and many costly gifts, which crowd his court and portico. He writes to thank his king for his munificence, and in his reply says it is true that he has written that epic on the hundred plates of gold; true that he composed the chant which the mariners will learn to sing as they haul their nets; true that the image of the sun-god on the lighthouse is his also; that the Pœcile—the portico at Athens painted with battle pictures by Polygnotus the Thasian, has been adorned, too, with his own works. He knows the plastic anatomy of man and woman and their proportions, not observed before; he has moreover

> "Written three books on the soul,
> Proving absurd all written hitherto,
> And putting us to ignorance again."

He has combined the moods for music, and invented one:—

> "In brief, all arts are mine."

All this is known; it is not so marvellous either, because men's minds in these latter days are greater than those of olden time because more composite. Life, he finds reason to believe, is intended to be viewed eventually as a great whole, not analysed to parts, but each having reference to all: the true judge of man's life must see the whole, not merely one way of it at once; the artist who designed the chequered pavement did not superimpose the figures, putting the last design over the old and blotting it out,—he made a picture and used every stone, whatever its figure, in the composition of his work. So he conceives that perfect, separate forms which make the portions of mankind were created at first, afterwards these were combined, and so came progress. Mankind is a synthesis—a putting together of all the single men. Zeus had a plan in all, and our souls know this, and cry to him—

> "To vindicate his purpose in our life."

As for himself, he is not a poet like Homer, such a musician as Terpander, nor a sculptor like Phidias; point by point he fails to reach their height, but in sympathy he is the equal of them all. So much for the first part of the king's letter: it is all true which has been reported of him. Next he addresses himself to the questions asked by the king: "has he not attained the very crown and proper end of life?" and having so abundantly succeeded, does he fear death as do lower men? Cleon replies that if his questioner could have been present on the earth before the advent of man, and seen all its tenantry, from worm to bird, he would have seen them perfect. Had Zeus asked him if he should do more for creatures than he had done, he would have replied, "Yes, make each grow conscious in himself"; he chooses then for man, his last premeditated work, that a quality may arise within his soul which may view itself and so be happy. "Let him learn how he lives." Cleon would, however, tell the king it would have been better had man made no step beyond the better beast. Man is the only creature in whom there is failure; it is called advance that man should climb to a height which overlooks lower forms of creation simply that he may perish there. Our vast capabilities for joy, our craving souls, our struggles, only serve to show us that man is inadequate to joy, as the soul sees joy. "Man can use but a man's joy while he sees God's." He agrees with the king in his profound discouragement: most progress is most failure. As to the next question which the letter asks: "Does he, the poet, artist, musician, fear death as common men? Will it not comfort him to know that his works will live, though he may perish?" Not at all, he protests—he, sleeping in his urn while men sing his songs and tell his praise! "It is so horrible." And so he sometimes imagines Zeus may intend for us some future state where the capability for joy is as unlimited as is our present desire for joy. But no: "Zeus has not yet revealed it. He would have done so were it possible!" Nothing can more faithfully portray the desolation of the soul "without God," the sense of loss in man, whose soul, emanating from the Divine, refuses to be satisfied with anything short of God Himself. Art, wealth, learning, honours, serve not to dissipate for a moment the infinite sadness of this soul "without God and without hope in the world." And, as he wrote, Paul, the Apostle of the Gentiles, had turned to the Pagan world with the Gospel which the Jews had rejected. To the very island in the Grecian sea whence arose this sad wail of despair the echo of the angel-song of Bethlehem had been borne, "Peace on earth, good-will towards men." Round the coasts of the Ægean Sea, through Philippi, Troas, Mitylene, Chios, and Miletus, "the mere barbarian Jew Paulus" had sown the seeds of a faith which should grow up and shelter under its branches the weary truth-seekers who knew too well what was the utter hopelessness of "art for art's sake" for satisfying the infinite yearning of the human heart. In the crypt of the church of San Marziano at Syracuse is the primitive church of Sicily, constructed on the spot where St. Paul is said to have preached during his three days' sojourn on the island. Here is shown the rude stone altar where St. Paul broke the bread of life; and as we stand on this sacred spot and recall the past in this strange city of a hundred memorials of antiquity—the temples of the gods, the amphitheatre, the vast altar, the Greek theatre, the walls of Epipolæ, the aqueducts, the forts, the harbour, the quarries, the Ear of Dionysius, the tombs, the streams and fountains famed in classic story and sung by poets—all fade into insignificance before the hallowed spot whence issued the fertilising influences of the Gospel preached by this same Paulus to a few poor slaves. The time would come, and not so far distant either, when the doctrines of Christ and Paul would be rejected "by no sane man."

Clive. (*Dramatic Idylls*, Series II., 1880.) The poem deals with a well-known incident in the life of Lord Clive, who founded the empire of British India and created for it a pure and strong administration. Robert Clive was born in 1725 at Styche, near Market Drayton, Shropshire. The Clives formed one of the oldest families in the county. Young Clive was negligent of his books, and devoted to boyish adventures of the wildest sort. However, he managed to acquire a good education, though probably by means which schoolmasters considered irregular. He was a born leader, and held death as nothing in comparison with loss of honour. He often suffered, even in youth, from fits of depression, and twice attempted his own life. He went out to Madras as a "writer" in the East India Company's civil service. Always in some trouble or other with his companions, he one day fought the duel which forms the subject of Mr. Browning's poem. In 1746 he became disgusted with a civilian's life, and obtained an ensign's commission. At this time a crisis in Indian affairs opened up to a man of high courage, daring and administrative ability, like Clive, a brilliant path to fortune. Clive seized his opportunity, and won India for us. His bold attack upon the city of Arcot terminated in a complete victory for our arms; and in 1753, when he sailed to England for the recovery of his health, his services were suitably rewarded by the East India Company. He won the battle of Plassey in 1757. Notwithstanding his great services to his country, his conduct in India was severely criticised, and he was impeached in consequence, but was acquitted in 1773. He committed suicide in 1774, his mind having been unhinged by the charges brought against him after the great things he had done for an ungrateful country. He was addicted to the use of opium; this is referred to in the poem in the line "noticed how the furtive fingers went where a drug-box skulked behind the honest liquor." Lord Macaulay in his Essay on Clive, says he had a "restless and intrepid spirit. His personal courage, of which he had, while still a writer, given signal proof by a desperate duel with a military bully who was the terror of Fort St. David, speedily made him conspicuous even among hundreds of brave men." The duel took place under the following circumstances. He lost money at cards to an officer who was proved to have cheated. Other losers were so in terror of this cheating bully that they paid. Clive refused to pay, and was challenged. They went out with pistols; no seconds were employed, and Clive missed his opponent, who, coming close up to him, held his pistol to his head and told him he would spare his life if he were asked to do so. Clive complied. He was next required to retract his charge of cheating. This demand being refused, his antagonist threatened to fire. "Fire, and be damned!" replied Clive. "I said you cheated; I say so still, and will never pay you!" The officer was so amazed at his bravery that he threw away his pistol. Chatting, with a friend, a week before he committed suicide, he tells the story of this duel as the one occasion when he felt fear, and that not of death, but lest his adversary should contemptuously permit him to keep his life. Under such circumstances he could have done nothing but use his weapon on himself. This part of the story is, of course, imaginary.

Colombe of Ravenstein. (*Colombe's Birthday.*) Duchess of Juliers and Cleves. When in danger of losing her sovereignty by the operation of the Salic Law, she has an offer of marriage from Prince Berthold, who could have dispossessed her. Colombe loves Valence, an advocate, and he loves her. The prince does not even pretend that love has prompted his offer, and so Colombe sacrifices power at the shrine of love.

Comparini, The. (*The Ring and the Book.*) Violatne and Pietro Comparini were the foster-parents of Pompilia, who, with her, were murdered by Count Guido Franceschini.

Confessional, The. (*Dramatic Romances* in *Bells and Pomegranates*, 1845.) The scene is in Spain, in the time of the Inquisition. A girl has confessed to an aged priest some sinful conduct with her lover Bertram; as a penance, she has been desired to extract from him some secrets relating to matters of which he has been suspected. As a proof of his love, he tells the girl things which, if known, would imperil his life. The confidant, as requested, carries the story to the priest. She sees her lover no more till she beholds him under the executioner's hands on the scaffold. Passionately denouncing Church and priests, she is herself at the mercy of the Inquisition, and the poem opens with her exclamations against the system which has killed her lover and ruined her life.

Confessions. (*Dramatis Personæ*, 1864.) A man lies dying. A clergyman asks him if he has not found the world "a vale of tears"?—a suggestion which is indignantly repudiated. As the man looks at the row of medicine bottles ranged before him, he sees in his fancy the lane where lived the girl he loved, and where, in the June weather, she stood watching for him at that farther bottle labelled "Ether"—

> "How sad and bad and mad it was!—
> But then, how it was sweet!"

Constance (*In a Balcony*), a relative of the Queen in this dramatic fragment. She is loved by Norbert, and returns his love. The queen, however, loves the handsome young courtier herself, and her jealousy is the ruin of the young couple's happiness.

Corregidor, The. (*How it strikes a Contemporary.*) In Spain the corregidor is the chief magistrate of a town; the name is derived from *corregir*, to correct—one who corrects. He is represented as going about the city, observing everything that takes place, and is consequently suspected as a spy in the employment of the Government. He is, in fact, but a harmless poet of very observant habits, and is exceedingly poor.

Count Gismond. Aix in Provence. Published in *Dramatic Lyrics* under the title "*France*," in 1842. An orphan maiden is to be queen of the tourney to-day. She lives at her uncle's home with her two girl cousins, each a queen by her beauty, not needing to be crowned. The maiden thought they loved her. They brought her to the canopy and complimented her as she took her place. The time came when she was to present the victor's crown. All eyes were bent upon her, when at that proud moment Count Gauthier thundered "Stay! Bring no crown! bring torches and a penance sheet; let her shun the chaste!" He accuses her of licentious behaviour with himself; and as the girl hears the horrible lie, paralysed at the baseness of the accusation, she never dreams that answer is possible to make. Then out strode Count Gismond. Never had she met him before, but in his face she saw God preparing to do battle with Satan. He strode to Gauthier, gave him the lie, and struck his mouth with his mailed hand: the lie was damned, truth upstanding in its place. They fought. Gismond flew at him, clove out the truth from his breast with his sword, then dragging him dying to the maiden's feet, said "Here die, but first say that thou hast lied." And the liar said, "To God and her I have lied," and gave up the ghost. Gismond knelt to the maiden and whispered in her ear; then rose, flung his arm over her head, and led her from the crowd. Soon they were married, and the happy bride cried:

> "Christ God who savest man, save most
> Of men Count Gismond who saved me!"

Count Guido Franceschini. (*The Ring and the Book.*) The wicked nobleman of Arezzo who marries Pompilia for her dowry, and treats her so cruelly that she flies from his home to Rome, in company with Caponsacchi, who chivalrously and innocently devotes himself to her assistance. While they rest on the way they are overtaken by the Count, who eventually kills Pompilia and her foster-parents.

Courts of Love (*Sordello*) "were judicial courts for deciding affairs of the heart, established in Provence during the palmy days of the Troubadours. The following is a case submitted to their judgment: A lady listened to one admirer, squeezed the hand of another, and touched with her toe the foot of a third. Query, Which of these three was the favoured suitor?" (*Dr. Brewer's Dictionary of Phrase and Fable.*) It was at a Court of Love at which Palma presided, that Sordello outdid Eglamour in song, and received the prize from the lady's hand. At these courts, Sismondi tells us, *tensons* or *jeux partis* were sung, which were dialogues between the speakers in which each interlocutor recited successively a stanza with the same rhymes. Sismondi introduces a translation of a *tenson* between Sordello and Bertrand, adding that this "may, perhaps, give an idea of those poetical contests which were the great ornament of all festivals. When the haughty baron invited to his court the neighbouring lords and the knights his vassals, three days were devoted to jousts and tourneys, the mimicry of war. The youthful gentlemen, who, under the name of pages, exercised themselves in the profession of arms, combated the first day; the second was set apart for the newly-dubbed knights; and the third, for the old warriors. The lady of the castle, surrounded by youthful beauties, distributed crowns to those who were declared by the judges of the combat to be the conquerors. She then, in her turn, opened her court, constituted in imitation of the seignorial tribunals, and as her baron collected his peers around him when he dispensed justice, so did she form her Court of Love, consisting of young, beautiful, and lively women. A new career was opened to those who dared the combat—not of arms, but of verse; and the name of *tenson*, which was given to these dramatic skirmishes, in fact signified a contest. It frequently happened that the knights who had gained the prize of valour became candidates for the poetical honours. One of the two, with his harp upon his arm, after a prelude, proposed the subject of the dispute. The other then advancing, and singing to the same air, answered him in a stanza of the same measure, and very frequently having the same rhymes. This extempore composition was usually comprised in five stanzas. The Court of Love then entered upon a grave deliberation, and discussed not only the claims of the two poets, but the merits of the question; and a judgment or *arrêt d'amour* was given, frequently in verse, by which the dispute was supposed to be decided. At the present day we feel inclined to believe that these dialogues, though little resembling those of Tityrus and Melibæus, were yet, like those, the production of the poet sitting at ease in his closet. But, besides the historical evidence which we possess of the troubadours having been gifted with those improvisatorial talents which the Italians have preserved to the present time, many of the *tensons* extant bear evident traces of the rivalry and animosity of the two interlocutors. The mutual respect with which the refinements of civilisation have taught us to regard one another, was at this time little known. There existed not the same delicacy upon questions of honour, and injury returned for injury was supposed to cancel all insults. We have a *tenson* extant between the Marquis Albert Malespina and Rambaud de Vaqueiras, two of the most powerful lords and valiant captains at the commencement of the thirteenth century, in which they mutually accuse one another of having robbed on the highway and deceived their allies by false oaths. We must charitably suppose that the perplexities of versification and the heat of their poetical inspiration compelled them to overlook sarcasms which they could never have suffered to pass in plain prose. Many of the ladies who sat in the Courts of Love were able to reply to the verses which they inspired. A few of their compositions only remain, but they have always the advantage over those of the Troubadours. Poetry, at that time, aspired neither to creative energy nor to sublimity of thought, nor to variety. Those powerful conceptions of genius which, at a later period, have given birth to the drama and the epic, were yet unknown; and, in the expression of sentiment, a tenderer and more delicate inspiration naturally endowed the productions of these poetesses with a more lyrical character." (Sismondi, *Lit. Mod. Europe*, vol. i., pp. 106-7.)

Cristina (or **Christina**). *Dramatic Lyrics* (*Bells and Pomegranates* No. III.), 1842.—Maria Christina of Naples is the lady of the poem. She was born in 1806, and in 1829 became the fourth wife of Ferdinand VII., King of Spain. She became Regent of Spain on the death of her husband, in 1833. Her daughter was Queen Isabella II. She was the dissolute mother of a still more dissolute daughter. Lord Malmesbury's *Memoirs of an Ex-Minister*, 1884, vol. i., p. 30, have the following reference to the Christina of the poem: "Mr. Hill presented me at Court before I left Naples [in 1829]. . . . The Queen [Maria Isabella, second wife of Francis I., King of the Two Sicilies] and the young and handsome Princess Christina, afterwards Queen of Spain, were present. The latter was said at the time to be the cause of more than one inflammable victim languishing in prison for having too openly admired this royal coquette, whose manners with men foretold her future life after her marriage to old Ferdinand [VII., King of Spain]. When she came up to me in the circle, walking behind her mother, she stopped, and took hold of one of the buttons of my uniform—to see, as she said, the inscription upon it, the Queen indignantly calling to her to come on." The passion of love, throughout Mr. Browning's works, is treated as the most sacred thing in the human soul. We are here for the chance of loving and of being loved; nothing on earth is dearer than this; to trifle with love is, in Browning's eyes, the sin against that Divine Emanation which sanctifies the heart of man. The man or woman who dissipates the capacity for love is the destroyer of his or her own soul; the flirt and the coquette are the losers,—the forsaken one has saved his own soul and gained the other's as well.

Cristina and Monaldeschi. (*Jocoseria*, 1883.)—I am indebted to the valuable paper which Mrs. Alexander Ireland contributed to the Browning Society on Feb. 27th, 1891, for the facts relating to the subject of this poem. Queen Cristina of Sweden was the daughter of Gustavus Adolphus. She was born in 1626, and came to the throne on the death of her father, in 1632. She was highly educated and brilliantly accomplished. She was perfectly acquainted with Greek, Latin, French, German, English, Italian, and Spanish. In due time she had batches of royal suitors, but she refused to bind herself by the marriage tie; rather than marry, she decided to abdicate, choosing as her successor her cousin Charles Gustavus. The formal and unusual ceremony of abdication took place in the cathedral of Upsala, in June 1654. Proceeding to Rome, she renounced the Protestant religion, and publicly embraced that of the Catholic Church. The officers of her household were exclusively Italian. Among these was the Marquis Monaldeschi, nominated "Master of the Horse," described by Cristina in her own memoirs as "a gentleman of most handsome person and fine manners, who from the first moment reigned exclusively over my heart." Cristina abandoned herself to this man, who proved a traitor and a scoundrel. He took every advantage of his position as favourite, and having reaped honour and riches, Monaldeschi wearied of his royal mistress and sought new attractions. The closing scene of Queen Cristina's *liaison* with the Grand Equerry inspired Mr. Browning's poem. He has chosen the moment when all the treachery of Monaldeschi has revealed itself to the Queen. The scene is at Fontainebleau, whither Cristina has removed from Rome; here the letters came into her hands which broke her life. A Cardinal Azzolino had obtained possession of a wretched and dangerous correspondence. The packet included the Queen's own letters to her lover—letters written in the fulness of perfect trust, telling much that the unhappy lady could have told to no other living being. Monaldeschi's letters to his young Roman beauty made a jest, a mockery of the Queen's exceeding fondness for him. They were letters of unsparing and wounding ridicule; and, while acting thus, Monaldeschi had steadily adhered to the show of unaltered attachment to the Queen and deep respect for his royal mistress. Cristina's emotions on seeing the whole hateful, cowardly treachery laid bare were doubtless maddening. She arranged an interview with the Marquis in the picture gallery in the Palace of Fontainebleau. She was accompanied by an official of her Court, and had at hand a priest from the neighbouring convent of the Maturins, armed with copies of the letters which were to serve as the death-warrant of the Marquis. They had been placed by Cardinal Azzolino in Cristina's hands through the medium of her "Major-Domo," with the knowledge that the Cardinal had already seen their infamous contents. The *originals* she had on her own person. Added to this, she had in the background her Captain of the Guard, Sentinelli, with two other officers. In the Galerie des Cerfs hung a picture of François I. and Diane de Poictiers. To this picture the Queen now led the Marquis, pointing out the motto on the frame—"Quis separabit?" The Queen reminds her lover how they were vowed to each other. The Marquis had vowed, at a tomb in the park of Fontainebleau, that, as the grave kept a silence over the corpse beneath, so would his love and trust hold fast the secret of Cristina's love to all eternity. Now the woman's spirit was wounded to death. She was scorned, her pride outraged; but she was a queen, and the man a subject, and she felt she must assert her dignity at least once more. The Marquis doubtless tottered as he stood. "Kneel," she says. This was the final scene of the tragedy. Cristina now calls forth the priest and the assassins, having granted herself the bitter pleasure of such personal revenge as was possible for her, poor woman!

"Friends, my four! You, Priest, confess him!
I have judged the culprit there:
Execute my sentence! Care
For no mail such cowards wear!
Done, Priest? Then, absolve and bless him!
Now—you three, stab thick and fast,
Deep and deeper! Dead at last?"

In October 1657 Cristina already felt suspicious of Monaldeschi. Keenly watching his actions, she had found him guilty of a double perfidy, and had led him on to a conversation touching a similar unfaithfulness. "What," the Queen had said, "does the man deserve who should so have betrayed a woman?" "Instant death," said Monaldeschi; "'twould be an act of justice." "It is well," said she; "I will remember your words." As to the right of the Queen to execute Monaldeschi, it must be remembered that, by a special clause in the Act of Abdication, she retained absolute and sovereign jurisdiction over her servants of all kinds. The only objection made by the French Court was, that she ought not to have permitted the murder to take place at Fontainebleau. After this crime Cristina was compelled to leave France, and finally retired to Rome, giving herself up to her artistic tastes, science, chemistry and idleness. She died on April 19th, 1689; her epitaph on her tomb in St. Peter's at Rome was chosen by herself—"Cristina lived sixty-three years."

NOTES.—"*Quis separabit?*" who shall separate? *King Francis*—François I. The gallery of this king is the most striking one in the palace. *Diane*, the gallery of Diana, the goddess. *Primatice* = Primaticcio, who designed some of the decorations of the *Galerie de François I*. *Salamander sign*: the emblem of Francis I., often repeated in the decorations. *Florentine Le Roux* = Rossi, the Florentine artist. *Fontainebleau*: its Château Royal is very famous. "*Juno strikes Ixion*," who attempted to seduce her. *Avon*, a village near Fontainebleau.

Croisic. The scene of the *Two Poets of Croisic*. Le Croisic is a seaport on the southern coast of Brittany, with about 2500 inhabitants, and is a fashionable watering-place. It has a considerable industry in sardine fishing.

Cunizza, called Palma in *Sordello*, till, at the close of the poem the heroine's historical name is given. She was the sister of Ezzelino III. Dante places her in *Paradise* (ix. 32). Longfellow, in his translation of the *Divine Comedy*, has the following note concerning her: "Cunizza was the sister of Azzolino di Romano. Her story is told by Rolandino, *Liber Chronicorum*, in Muratori (*Rer. Ital. Script.*, viii. 173). He says that she was first married to Richard of St. Boniface; and soon after had an intrigue with Sordello—as already mentioned (*Purg.* vi., Note 74). Afterwards she wandered about the world with a soldier of Treviso, named Bonius, 'taking much solace,' says the old chronicler, 'and spending much money' (*multa habendo solatia, et maximas faciendo expensas*). After the death of Bonius, she was married to a nobleman of Braganza; and finally, and for a third time, to a gentleman of Verona. The *Ottimo* alone among the commentators takes up the defence of Cunizza, and says: 'This lady lived lovingly in dress, song, and sport; but consented not to any impropriety or unlawful act; and she passed her life in enjoyment, as Solomon says in Ecclesiastes," alluding probably to the first verse of the second chapter—"I said in my heart, Go to now, I will prove thee with mirth; therefore enjoy pleasure; and behold, this is also vanity."

"Dance, Yellows and Whites and Reds." A beautiful lyric at the end of "Gerard de Lairesse," in *Parleyings with Certain People of Importance in their Day*, begins with this line. It originally appeared in a little book published for the Edinburgh University Union Fancy Fair, in 1886.

Daniel Bartoli. *Parleyings with Certain People of Importance in their Day*: 1887. [The Man.] "Born at Ferrara in 1608, died at Rome in 1685. He was a learned Jesuit, and his great work was a history of his Order, in six volumes, published at various times. It is enriched with facts drawn from the Vatican records, from English colleges, and from memoirs sent him by friends in England; and is crowded with stories of miracles which are difficult of digestion by ordinary readers. His style is highly esteemed by Italians for its purity and precision, and his life was perfectly correct and virtuous" (*Pall Mall Gazette*, Jan. 18th, 1887). "His eloquence was wonderful, and his renown as a sacred orator became universal. He wrote many essays on scientific subjects; and although some of his theories have been refuted by Galileo, they are still cited as models of the didactic style, in which he excelled. His works on moral science and philology are numerous. Died 1684." (*Imp. Dict. Biog.*)

[The Poem.] The poet tells the narrator of saintly legends that he has a saint worth worshipping whose history is not legendary at all, but very plain fact. It is her story which is told in the poem, and not that of Bartoli. The minister of a certain king had managed to induce a certain duke to yield two of his dukedoms to the king at his death. The promise was a verbal one, but the duke was to sign the deed of gift which deprived him of his rights when it was duly prepared by the lawyers. While this was in progress the duke met at his sister's house a good and beautiful girl, the daughter of an apothecary. He proposed to marry her, and was accepted, notwithstanding the opposition of his family. The banns were duly published, and the marriage ceremony was soon to follow. Meanwhile this turn in the duke's affairs came to the ear of the crafty minister of the king, who promptly informed his royal master that the assignment of the dukedoms might not proceed so smoothly under the altered circumstances. "I bar the abomination—nuptial me no such nuptials!" exclaimed the king. The minister hinted that caution must be used, lest by offending the duke the dukedoms might be lost. The next day the preliminary banquet, at which all the lady's friends were present, took place; when lo—a thunderclap! —the king's minister was announced, and the lady was requested to meet him at a private interview. She was informed that the duke must at once sign the paper which the minister held in his hand, ceding to the king the promised estates, or the king would withhold his consent to the marriage and the lady would be placed in strict seclusion. Should he, however, sign the deed of gift without delay, the king would give his consent to the marriage, and accord the bride a high place at court; and the druggist's daughter would become not only the duke's wife but the king's favourite. They returned to the dining-room, and the lady, addressing the duke, who sat in mute bewilderment at the head of the table, made known the king's commands. She told him that she knew he loved her for herself alone, and was conscious that her own love was equal to his. She bade him read the shameful document which the king had sent, and begged him to bid her destroy it. She implored him not to part with his dukedoms, which had been given him by God, though by doing so he might make her his wife: if, however, he could so far forget his duty as to yield to these demands, he would, in doing so, forfeit her love. The duke was furious, but could not be brought to yield to the lady's request, and she left the place never to meet again. Next day she sent him back the jewellery he had given her. This story was told to a fervid, noble-hearted lord, who forthwith in a boyish way loved the lady. When he grew to be a man he married her, dropped from camp and court into obscurity, but was happy, till ere long his lady died. He would gladly have followed, but had to be content with turning saint, like those of whom Bartoli wrote. The poet next philosophises on the life which the duke might have led after this crisis in his history. He would sooner or later reflect sadly on the beautiful luminary which had once illumined his path: he could fancy her mocking him as false to Love; he would reflect how, with all his lineage and his bravery, he had failed at the test, but would recognise that it was not the true man who failed, not the ducal self which quailed before the monarch's frown while the more royal Love stood near him to inspire him;—some day that true self would, by the strength of that good woman's love, be raised from the grave of shame which covered it, and he would be hers once more.

NOTES.—vi., *Pari passu:* with equal pace, together. xv., "*Saint Scholastica . . . in Paynimrie*": she lived about the year 543. She was sister to St. Benedict, and consecrated herself to God from her earliest youth. The legend referred to is not given, either in Butler's *Lives of the Saints*, or Mrs. Jameson's *Legends of the Monastic Orders*. *Paynimrie* means the land of the infidel. xvi., *Trogalia:* sweetmeats and candies.

Dante is magnificently described in *Sordello* (Book I., lines 374-80):—

> "Dante, pacer of the shore
> Where glutted hell disgorgeth filthiest gloom,
> Unbitten by its whirring sulphur-spume—
> Or whence the grieved and obscure waters slope
> Into a darkness quieted by hope;
> Plucker of amaranths grown beneath God's eye
> In gracious twilights where His chosen lie."

Date et Dabitur. "Give, and it shall be given unto you." (See *The Twins.*)

David. (See *Saul*, and Epilogue to *Dramatis Personæ:* First Speaker).

Deaf and Dumb. A group by Woolner (1862). How a glory may arise from a defect is the keynote of this poem. A prism interposed in the course of a ray of sunlight breaks it into the glory of the seven colours of the spectrum; the prism is an obstruction to the white light, but the rainbow tints which are seen in consequence of the obstacle reveal to us the secret of the sunbeam. So the obstruction of deafness or dumbness often greatly enhances the beauty of the features, as in the group of statuary which forms the subject of the poem, and which was exhibited at the International Exhibition of 1862. The children were Constance and Arthur, the son and daughter of Sir Thomas Fairbairn.

Death in the Desert, A. (*Dramatis Personæ*, 1864.) John, the disciple whom Jesus loved, who lay on His breast at the last sad paschal supper, who stood by the cross, and received from the lips of his Lord His only earthly possession—His mother; John, the writer of the Gospel which bears his name, and of the letters which breathe the spirit of the incarnated love which was to transform a world lying in wickedness; the seer of the awful visions of Patmos—the tremendous Apocalypse which closes the Christian revelation—lay dying in the desert; recalled from exile after the death of Domitian from the isle of the Sporades, the volcanic formation of which, with its daily scenes of smoke, brimstone, fire, and streams of molten lava, had aided the apostle to imagine the day of doom, when the angel should cry, "Time shall be no longer." The beloved disciple, who had borne the message of Divine love through the cities of Asia Minor, had founded churches, established bishoprics, and had laboured by spoken and written word, and even more effectually by his beautiful and gentle life, to extend the kingdom of God and of His Christ, now worn out with incessant labours, and bent with the weight of well-nigh a hundred years, the last of the men who had seen the Lord, the final link which bound the youthful Church to its apostolic days, lies dying in a cave, hiding from the bloody hands of those who breathed out threatenings and slaughter against the followers of Christ. Companioned by five converts who tenderly nursed the dying saint, he had been brought from the secret recess in the rock where they had hidden him from the pursuers into the midmost grotto, where the light of noon just reached a little, and enabled them to watch

"The last of what might happen on his face."

And at the entrance of the cave there kept faithful watch the Bactrian convert, pretending to graze a goat, so that if thief or soldier passed they might have booty without prying into the cave. The dying man lies unconscious, but his attendants think it possible to rouse him that he may speak to them before he departs: they wet his lips with wine, cool his forehead with water, chafe his hands, diffuse the aromatic odour of the spikenard through the cave, and pray; but still he sleeps. Then the boy, inspired by a happy thought, brings the plate of graven lead on which are the words of John's gospel, "I am the Resurrection and the Life," and having found the place, he presses the aged man's finger on the line, and repeats it in his ear. Then he opened his eyes, sat up, and looked at them; and no one spoke, save the watcher without, signalling from time to time that they were safe. And first, the beloved one said, "If one told me there were James and Peter, I could believe! So is my soul withdrawn into its depths."—"Let be awhile!"—And then—

> "It is long
> Since James and Peter had release by death,
> And I am only he, yonr brother John,
> Who saw and heard, and could remember all."

He reminds them how in Patmos isle he had seen the Lord in His awful splendour; how in his early life he saw and handled with his hands the Word of Life. Soon it will be that none will say "I saw." And already—for the years were long—men had disputed, murmured and misbelieved, or had set up antichrists; and remembering what had happened to the faith in his own days, he could well foresee that unborn people in strange lands would one day ask—

> "Was John at all, and did he say he saw?"

"What can I say to assure them?" he asks; the story of Christ's life and death was not mere history to him: "*It is*," he cries,—"*is, here and now.*" Not only are the events of the gospel history present before his eyes, so that he apprehends nought else; but not less plainly, not less firmly printed on his soul, are the more mysterious truths of God's eternal presence in the world visibly contending with wrong and sin; and, as the wrong and sin are manifest to his soul-sight, so equally does he see the need, yet transiency of both. But matters, which to his spiritualised vision were clear, must be placed before his followers through some medium which shall, like an optic glass, segregate them, diminish them into clearness; and so he bids them stand before that fact, that Life and Death of Jesus Christ, till it spreads apart like a star, growing and opening out on all sides till it becomes their only world, as it is his. "For all of life," he says, "is summed up in the prize of learning love, and having learnt it, to hold it and truth, despite the world in arms against the holder. We can need no second proof of God's love for man. Man having once learned the use of fire, would not part with the gift for purple or for gold. Were the worth of Christ as plain, he could not give up Christ. To test man, the proofs of Christianity shift; he cannot grasp that fact as he grasps the fact of fire and its worth." He asks his disciples "why they say it was easier to believe in Christ once than now—easier when He walked the earth with those He loved? "But," says John, who had seen all, —the transfiguration, the walking on the sea, the raising of the dead to life,—"could it be possible the man who had seen these things should ever part from them? Yes, it was! The torchlight, the noise, the sudden inrush of the Roman soldiers, on the night of the betrayal, caused even him, John, the beloved disciple, to forsake Him and fly. Yet he had gained the truth, and the truth grew in his soul, so that he was enabled to impress it so indelibly on others, that children and women who had never seen the least of the sights he had seen would clasp their cross with a light laugh, and wrap the burning robe of martyrdom round them, giving thanks to God the while. But in the mind of man the laws of development are ever at work, and questioners of the truth arose, and it was necessary that he should re-state the Lord's life and work in various ways, to rectify mistakes. God has operated in the way of Power, later in the way of Love, and last of all in Influence on Soul: men do not ask now, "Where is the promise of His coming?" but—

"Was He revealed in any of His lives,
As Power, as Love, as Influencing Soul?"

"Miracles, to prove doctrine," John says, "go for nought, but love remains." Then men ask, "Did not we ourselves imagine and make this love?" (That is to say, love having been discovered by mankind to be the noblest thing on earth, have not men created a God of Infinite Love, out of their own passionate imagining of what man's love would be if perfectly developed?)

9

"The mind of man can only receive what it holds—no more.' Man projects his own love heavenward, it falls back upon him in another shape—with another name and story added; this, he straightway says, is a gift from heaven. Man of old peopled heaven with gods, all of whom possessed man's attributes; horses drew the sun from east to west. Now, we say the sun rises and sets as if impelled by a hand and will, and it is only thought of as so impelled because we ourselves have hands and wills. But the sun must be driven by some force which we do not understand; will and love we do understand. As man grows wiser the passions and faculties with which he adorned his deities are taken away: Jove of old had a brow, Juno had eyes; gradually there remained only Jove's wrath and Juno's pride; in process of time these went also, till now we recognise will and power and love alone. All these are at bottom the same—mere projections from the mind of the man himself. Having then stated the objections brought against the faith of Christ, St. John proceeds to meet them. "Man," he says, "was made to grow, not stop; the help he needed in the earlier stages, being no longer required, is withdrawn; his new needs require new helps. When we plant seed in the ground we place twigs to show the spots whree the germs lie hidden, so that they may not be trodden upon by careless steps. When the plants spring up we take the twigs away; they no longer have any use. It was thus with the growth of the gospel seed: miracles were required at first, but, when the plant had sprung up and borne fruit, had produced martyrs and heroes of the faith, what was the use of miracles any more? The fruit itself was surely sufficient testimony to the vitality of the seed. Minds at first must be spoon-fed with truth, as babes with milk; a boy we bid feed himself, or starve. So, at first, I wrought miracles that men might believe in Christ, because no faith were otherwise possible; miracles now would compel, not help. I say the way to solve all questions is to accept by the reason the Christ of God; the sole death is when a man's loss comes to him from his gain, when—from the light given to him—he extracts darkness; from the knowledge poured upon him he produces ignorance; and from the manifestation of love elaborates the lack of love. Too much oil is the lamp's death; it chokes with what would otherwise feed the flame. An overcharged stomach starves. The man who rejects Christ because he thinks the love of Christ is only a projection of his own is like a lamp that overswims with oil, a stomach overloaded with nurture; that man's soul dies. "But," the objector may say, "You told your Christ-story incorrectly: what is the good of giving knowledge at all if you give it in a manner which will not stop the after-doubt? Why breed in us perplexity? why not tell the whole truth in proper words?" To this St. John replies, "Man of necessity must pass from mistake to fact; he is not perfect as God is, nor as is the beast; lower than God, he is higher than the beast, and higher because he progresses,—he yearns to gain truth, catching at mistake. The statuary has the idea in his mind, aspires to produce it, and so calls his shape from out the clay:

> "Cries ever, 'Now I have the thing I see':
> Yet all the while goes changing what was wrought,
> From falsehood like the truth, to truth itself."

Suppose he had complained, 'I see no face, no breast, no feet'? It is only God who makes the live shape at a jet. Striving to reach his ideals, man grows; ceasing to strive, he forfeits his highest privileges, and entails the certainty of destruction. Progress is the essential law of man's being, and progress by mistake, by failure, by unceasing effort, will lead him,

> "Where law, life, joy, impulse are one thing!"

Such is the difficulty of the latest time; so does the aged saint answer it. He would remain on earth another hundred years, he says, to lend his struggling brothers his help to save them from the abyss. But even as he utters the loving desire, he is dead,

> "Breast to breast with God, as once he lay."

They buried him that night, and the teller of the story returned, disguised, to Ephesus. St. John is said to have been banished into the Isle of Patmos, A.D. 97, by the order of Domitian. After this emperor had reigned fifteen years Nerva succeeded him (A.D. 99), and historians of the period wrote that "the Roman senate decreed that the honours paid to Domitian should cease, and such as were injuriously exiled should return to their native land and receive their substance again. It is also among the ancient traditions, that then John the Apostle returned from banishment and dwelt again at Ephesus." Eusebius, quoting from Irenæus, says that John after his return from Patmos governed the churches in Asia, and remained with them in the time of Trajan. Irenæus also says that the Apostle carried on at Ephesus the work begun by Paul; Clement of Alexandria records the same thing. It is said that St. John died in peace at Ephesus in the third year of Trajan—that is, the hundredth of the Christian era, or the sixty-sixth from our Lord's crucifixion, the saint being then about ninety-four years old; he was buried on a mountain without the town. A stately church stood formerly over this tomb, which is at present a Turkish mosque. The sojourn of the Apostle in Asia, a country governed by Magi and imbued with Zoroastrian ideas, and in those days full of Buddhist missionaries, may account for many things found in the Book of Revelation. Mr. Browning refers to this in the bracketed portion of the poem, commencing:—

> "This is the doctrine he was wont to teach,
> How divers persons witness in each man,
> Three souls which make up one soul."

They are described by Theosophists as (1) The fluidic perisoul or astral body; (2) The soul or individual; and (3) The spirit, or Divine Father and life of his system." (See *The Perfect Way*, Lecture I., 9.) These three souls make up, with the material body, the fourfold nature of man.

NOTES.—*Pamphylax the Antiochene*, an imaginary person. *Epsilon*, *Mu*, *Xi*, letters of the Greek alphabet—e, m, and ch respectively. *Xanthus* and *Valens*, disciples of St. John. *Bactrian*, of Bactria, a province in Persia. "*A ball of nard*," an unguent of spikenard, odorous and highly aromatic and restorative. *Glossa*, a commentary. *Theotypas*, a fictitious character. *Prometheus*, son of the Titan Iapetus and the Ocean-nymph Clymene, brother of Atlas, Menœtius, and Epimetheus, and father of Deucalion. When Zeus refused to mortals the use of fire, Prometheus stole it from Olympus, and brought it to men in a hollow reed. Zeus bound him to a pillar, with an eagle to consume in the daytime his liver, which grew again in the night. *Æschylus*, the earliest of the three great tragic poets of Greece, born at Eleusis, near Athens, B.C. 525. He wrote the *Prometheus Bound*. *Ebion*, the founder of the early sect of heretics called

Ebionites. They held that the Mosaic law was binding on Christians, and believed Jesus to have been a mere man, though an ambassador from God and possessed of Divine power (*Encyc. Dict.*). *Cerinthus* raised great disturbances in obstinately defending an obligation of circumcision, and of abstaining from unclean meats in the New Law, and in extolling the angels as the authors of nature: this was before St. Paul wrote his Epistle to the Colossians, etc. He pretended that the God of the Jews was only an angel; that Jesus was born of Joseph and Mary, like other men. He taught that Christ flew away at the time of the crucifixion, and that Jesus in the human part of His nature alone suffered and rose again, Christ continuing always immortal and impassible. St. Irenæus relates that on one occasion, when St. John went to the public baths, he found that this heretic was within, and he refused to remain lest the bath which contained Cerinthus should fall upon his head.

"De Gustibus——" [*De Gustibus non disputandum*—"there is no accounting for tastes."] (*Men and Women*, 1855; *Lyrics*, 1863; *Dramatic Lyrics*, 1868.) Every lover of Nature finds some particular kind of scenery which most appeals to his heart, and to which his thoughts revert in moments of reflection and meditation. The poet tells the lover of trees that after death (if loves persist) his ghost will be found wandering in an English lane by a hazel coppice in beanflower and blackbird time. For his own part, he loves best in all the world the scenery of his beloved Italy—a castle on a precipice in "the wind-grieved Apennine"; and if ever he gets his head out of the grave and his spirit soars free, he will be away to the sunny South, by the cypress guarding the seaside home, where scorpions sprawl on frescoed walls; in "Italy, my Italy,"—which beloved name he declares will be found graven on his heart.

De Lorge. (*The Glove.*) Sir de Lorge was the knight who recovered his lady's glove from the lions, amongst which she had cast it to test his courage, and then threw it in her face.

Development. (*Asolando*, 1889.) Mr. Sharp, in his admirable *Life of Browning*, says that the poet's father was a man of exceptional powers. He was a poet both in sentiment and expression; and he understood, as well as enjoyed, the excellent in art. He was a scholar, too, in a reputable fashion; not indifferent to what he had learnt in his youth, nor heedless of the high opinion generally entertained for the greatest writers of antiquity, but with a particular care himself for Horace and Anacreon. As his son once told a friend, "The old gentleman's brain was a storehouse of literary and philosophical antiquities. He was completely versed in mediæval legend, and seemed to have known Paracelsus, Faustus, and even Talmudic personages, personally." Development, indeed! That the embryonic mediæval lore of the banker's clerk should have potentially contained the treasures of *Paracelsus*, *Sordello*, and *Rabbi Ben Hakkadosh*, is as wonderful as that the primary cell should contain the force which gathers to itself the man.

NOTES.—*Philip Karl Buttmann* was a distinguished German philologist, born at Frankfort-on-the-Main, 1764, and died at Berlin, 1829. He studied at Göttingen, and in 1796 was appointed secretary of the Royal Library at Berlin. His fame rests on his *Griechische Grammatik*, the *Ausführliche Griechische Sprachlehre*, and the *Lexilogus oder Beiträge zur Griechischen Worterklärung*. These works are ranked highly for their exact criticism. He brought out valuable editions of Plato's *Dialogues* and the *Meidias* of Demosthenes. *Friedrich August Wolf*, the great critic, was born at Haynrode, near Nordhausen, in 1759; he died in 1824. He studied philology at Göttingen, and published an edition of Shakespeare's *Macbeth*, with notes, in 1778. He filled the chair of philology and pedagogial science at Halle for twenty-three years. In 1806 he repaired to Berlin. His fame chiefly rests on his *Prolegomena in Homerum*, which was devoted to the argument that the *Iliad* and the *Odyssey* are not the work of one single and individual Homer, but a much later compilation of *hymns* sung and handed down by oral tradition. Its effect was overwhelming. *Stagirite* = Aristotle. "*The Ethics*" = the *Nicomachean Ethics*, the great work of Aristotle. "*Battle of the Frogs and Mice*," a mock epic attributed to Homer. "*The Margites*," a humorous poem, which kept its ground down to the time of Aristotle as the work of Homer; it began with the words, "There came to Colophon an old man, a divine singer, servant of the Muses and Apollo."

Dîs Aliter Visum; or, Le Byron de Nos Jours. "Dîs aliter visum" is from Virgil, *Æn.* ii. 428, and means "Heaven thought not so." (*Dramatis Personæ*, 1864.) The poem describes a meeting of two friends after a parting of ten years.

They should have been more than friends: they were made for each other's love; but love came in a guise which was not acceptable, and the heart which the man might have won, and the love which would have blessed him and ennobled his life, was for reasons of prudence disregarded, and both lovers went their way, having missed their life's chance. It is the woman who speaks—the "poor, pretty, thoughtful thing" of other days; a woman who tried to love and understand ar and literature—to love all, at any rate, that was great and good and beautiful. She wonders if he—the man who might have completed his partial life with a great love—ever for a moment valued her rightly, and determined that "love found, gained and kept," was for him beyond art and sense and fame? She was young and inexperienced in the world's ways; he was old and full of wisdom: too wise, perhaps, to see where his best interests lay. It would never do, he thought—a match "'twixt one bent, wigged and lamed—— and this young beauty, round and sound as a mountain apple." And so they parted. He chose a lower ideal, she married where she could not love; so the devil laughed in his sleeve, for not two only, but four souls were in jeopardy.

The poem is a good example of the poet's way of drawing from a half-serious, half-bantering and indifferent confession of thoughts and feelings one of his great moral lessons. It has been compared to what is termed *vers de société*, and as such, up to stanza xxiii., it may be fitly described; then comes Mr. Browning's sudden uprising to his highest power. It is as though he had lightly touched on the ways of men, and discussed them half-playfully with some light-hearted, not to say frivolous, audience in a drawing-room. The listeners stand smiling, and speculating as to his real meaning, when all at once he rises from his chair and brings in a moment before the thoughtless group of listeners the great and awful import of life, and the real meaning of the things which men call trifles, but which in God's sight are big with the interests of Eternity. So, in this poem he leads us from pretty talk of "Heine for songs and kisses," "gout, glory, and love freaks, love's dues, and consols," to one of his grandest life-lessons—the necessary incompleteness of all human existence here, because heaven must finish what earth can never complete,—the supreme evolution of the soul of man. Earth completes her star-fishes; Heaven itself could make no more perfect or more beautiful star-fish:

> "He, whole in body and soul, outstrips
> Man, found with either in default."

The star-fish is whole. What is whole can increase no more. It has nothing to do but waste and die, and there is an end of it.

> "Leave Now for dogs and apes!
> Man has Forever."

On the side of the man in the poem it could be fairly argued that a more unreasonable match could hardly be imagined than one between a "bent, wigged and lame" old gentleman and a "poor, pretty, thoughtful" young beauty, notwithstanding her offer of body and soul.

NOTES.—viii., *Robert Schumann*, musical critic and composer: was born 1810, died 1856. *Jean August Dominique Ingres* (born 1780, died 1867). "The modern man that paints," a celebrated historical painter, a pupil of David. He was opposed to the Romantic School, and depended for success on form and line. "His paintings, with all their cleverness, appear to English eyes deficient in originality of conception, coarse, hard and artificial in manner, and untrue in colour" (*Imp. Dict. Biog.*). xii., "*The Fortieth spare Arm-chair.*" This refers to the French Academy, founded by Richelieu in 1635. When one of the forty members dies a new one is elected to fill his place.

Djabal. (*Return of the Druses.*) The son of the Emir, who seeks revenge for the murder of his family, and declares himself to be the Hakim—who is to set the Druse people free. He loves the maiden Anael, and when she dies stabs himself on her dead body.

Doctor ——. (*Dramatic Idyls*, Second Series, 1880.) A Rabbinical story: Satan, as in the opening scene of Job, stands with the angels before God to make his complaints. Asked "What is the fault now?" he declares that he has found something on earth which interferes with his prerogatives:—

> "Death is the strongest-born of Hell, and yet
> Stronger than Death is a Bad Wife, we know."

Satan protests that this robs him of his rights, as he claims to be Strongest. He is commanded to descend to earth in mortal shape and get married, and so try for himself the bitter draught. It was Solomon who said that "a woman whose heart is snares and nets is more bitter than death" (Ecclesiastes vii. 27), and some commentators on the poem have thought the Rabbinical legend was suggested by this verse. Satan, married, in due time has a son who arrives at maturity, and then the question arises of a profession for him: "I needs must teach my son a trade." Shall he be a soldier? That is too cowardly. A lawyer would be better, but there is too much hard work for the sluggard. There's divinity, but that is Satan's own special line, and that be far from his poor offspring! At last he thinks of the profession of medicine. Physic is the very thing! So *Medicus* he is appointed; and it is arranged that a special power shall be given to the young doctor's eyes, so that when on his rounds he shall behold the spirit-person of his father at his side. Doctor once dubbed, ignorance shall be no barrier to his success; cash shall follow, whatever the treatment, and fees shall pour in. Satan tells his son that the reason he has endowed him with power to recognise his spirit-form is that he may judge by Death's position in the sick room what are the prospects of the patient's recovery. If he perceive his father lingering by the door, whatever the nature of the illness recovery will be speedy; if higher up the room, death will not be the sufferer's doom; but if he is discovered standing by the head of the bed's the patient's doom is sealed. It happened that of a sudden the emperor himself was smitten with sore disease. Of course Dr. —— was called in and promised large rewards if he saved the imperial life. As he entered the room he saw at once that all was lost: there stood his father Death as sentry at the bed's head. Gold was offered in abundance; the doctor begged his father to go away and let him win his fee. "No inch I budge!" is the response. Then honours are offered him whom apparently wealth failed to tempt. The result is the same. Then Love: "Take my daughter as thy bride—save me for this reward!" The Doctor again implores a respite from his father, who is obdurate as ever. A thought strikes the physician: "Reverse the bed, so that Death no longer stands at the head;" but "the Antic passed from couch-foot back to pillow," and is master of the situation again. The son now curses his father, and declares that he will go over to the other side. He sends to his home for the mystic Jacob's-staff—a knobstick of proved efficacy in such cases. "Go, bid my mother (Satan's wife, be it remembered) bring the stick herself." The servant rushes off to do his errand, and all the anxious while the emperor sink's lower and lower, as the icy breath of Death freezes him to the marrow. All at once the door of the sick room opens, and there enters to Satan "Who but his Wife the Bad?" The devil goes off through the ceiling, leaving a sulphury smell behind; and, "Hail to the Doctor!" the imperial patient straightway recovers. In gratitude he offers him the promised daughter and her dowry; but the Doctor refuses the fee—"No dowry, no bad wife!" If this Talmudic legend has any relation to Solomon, it is well to bear in mind that his bitter experience, as St. Jerome says, was due to the fact that no one ever fell a victim to impurer loves than he. He married strange women, was deluded by them, and erected temples to their respective idols. His opinion, therefore, on marriage as we understand it is of little importance to us.

Dominus Hyacinthus De Archangelis. (*The Ring and the Book.*) The procurator or counsel for the poor, who defends Count Guido in the eighth book of the poem.

Domizia (*Luria*), a noble lady of Florence. She is loved by the Moorish captain Luria, who commanded the army of the Florentines. Domizia was greatly embittered against the republic for its ingratitude to her two brothers—Porzio and Berto—and hoped to be revenged for their deaths.

Don Juan. (*Fifine at the Fair.*) The husband of the poem is a philosophical study of the Don Juan of Molière. He is full of sophistries, and an adept in the art of making the worse appear the better reason. In Molière's play Juan's valet thus describes his master: "You see in Don Juan the greatest scoundrel the earth has ever borne—a madman, a dog, a demon, a Turk, a heretic—who believes neither in heaven, hell, nor devil, who passes his life simply as a brute beast, a pig of an epicure, a true Sardanapalus; who closes his ear to every remonstrance which can be made to him, and treats as idle talk all that we hold sacred."

Donald. (*Jocoseria*, 1883.) The story of the poem is a true one, and is told by Sir Walter Scott, in *The Keepsake* for 1832, pp. 283-6. The following abridgement of the account is from the Browning Society's *Notes and Queries*, No. 209, p. 328: "... The story is an old but not an ancient one: the actor and sufferer was not a very aged man, when I heard the anecdote in my early youth. Duncan (for so I shall call him) had been engaged in the affair of 1746, with others of his clan; ... on the one side of his body he retained the proportions and firmness of an active mountaineer; on the other he was a disabled cripple, scarce able to limp along the streets. The cause which reduced him to this state of infirmity was singular. Twenty years or more before I knew Duncan he assisted his brothers in farming a large grazing in the Highlands. ... It chanced that a sheep or goat was missed from the flock, and Duncan ... went himself in quest of the fugitive. In the course of his researches he was induced to ascend a small and narrow path, leading to the top of a high precipice. ... It was not much more than two feet broad, so rugged and difficult, and at the same time so terrible, that it would have been impracticable to any but the light step and steady brain of the Highlander. The precipice on the right rose like a wall, and on the left sank to a depth which it was giddy to look down upon. ... He had more than half ascended the precipice, when in midway ... he encountered a buck of the red-deer species coming down the cliff by the same path in an opposite direction. ... Neither party had the power of retreating, for the stag had not room to turn himself in the narrow path, and if Duncan had turned his back to go down, he knew enough of the creature's habits to be certain that he would rush upon him while engaged in the difficulties of the retreat. They stood therefore perfectly still, and looked at each other in mutual embarrassment for some space. At length the deer, which was of the largest size, began to lower his formidable antlers, as they do when they are brought to bay. ... Duncan saw the danger ... and, as a last resource, stretched himself on the little ledge of rock ... not making the least motion, for fear of alarming the animal. They remained in this posture for three or four hours. ... At length the buck ... approached towards Duncan very slowly ... he came close to the Highlander ... when the devil, or the untameable love of sport, ... began to overcome Duncan's fears. Seeing the animal proceed so gently, he totally forgot not only the dangers of his position, but the implicit compact which certainly might have been inferred from the circumstances of the situation. With one hand Duncan seized the deer's horn, whilst with the other he drew his dirk. But in the same instant the buck bounded over the precipice, carrying the Highlander along with him. . . . Fortune . . . ordered that the deer should fall undermost, and be killed on the spot, while Duncan escaped with life, but with the fracture of a leg, an arm, and three ribs. . . . I never could approve of Duncan's conduct towards the deer in a moral point of view, . . . but the temptation of a hart of grease offering, as it were, his throat to the knife, would have subdued the virtue of almost any deer stalker. . . . I have given you the story exactly as I recollect it." As the practice of medicine does not necessarily make a man merciful, so neither does sport necessarily imply manliness and nobility of soul. In both cases there is a strong tendency for the professional to be considered the right view. In the story we have the stag, after four hours' consideration, offering terms of agreement which Donald accepted and then treacherously broke. The animal broke Donald's fall, yet he has no gratitude for its having thus saved his life. As one of the poems covered by the question in the prologue, "*Wanting is —— What?*" we should reply, Honour and humanity.

D'Ormea. (*King Victor and King Charles.*) He was the unscrupulous minister of King Victor. He became necessary to King Charles when he received the crown on his father's abdication, and was active in defeating the attempt of the latter to recover his crown.

Dramas. For the Stage: *A Blot in the 'Scutcheon, Colombe's Birthday, Strafford, Luria, In a Balcony, The Return of the Druses.* For the Study: *Pippa Passes, King Victor and King Charles, A Soul's Tragedy,* and *Paracelsus. A Blot in the 'Scutcheon, Strafford, Colombe's Birthday,* and *In a Balcony,* have all been recently performed in London, under the direction of the Browning Society, greatly to the gratification of the spectators who were privileged to attend these special performances. Whether such dramas would be likely to attract audiences from the general public for any length of time is, however, extremely problematical. Mr. Browning's poetry is of too subjective and psychological a character to be popular on the stage.

Dramatic Idyls (1879-80). *Series I.:* Martin Relph, Pheidippides, Halbert and Hob, Ivan Ivânovitch, Tray, Ned Bratts;

Series II.: Proem, Echetlos, Clive, Muleykeh, Pietro of Abano, Doctor ——, Pan and Luna, Epilogue.

Dramatic Lyrics. (*Bells and Pomegranates*, No. III., 1842.) Cavalier Tunes: i., Marching Along; ii., Give a Rouse; iii., My Wife Gertrude. Italy and France: i., Italy; ii., France. Camp and Cloister: i., Camp (French); ii., Cloister (Spanish); In a Gondola, Artemis Prologizes, Waring. Queen Worship: i., Rudel and the Lady of Tripoli; ii., Cristina. Madhouse Cells: i., Johannes Agricola; ii., Porphyria. Through the Metidja, The Pied Piper of Hamelin.

Dramatic Monologue. Mr. Browning has so excelled in this particular kind of poetry that it may be fitly called a novelty of his invention. The dramatic monologue is quite different from the soliloquy. In the latter case the speaker delivers his own thoughts, uninterrupted by objections or the propositions of other persons. "In the dramatic monologue the presence of a silent second person is supposed, to whom the arguments of the speaker are addressed. It is obvious that the dramatic monologue gains over the soliloquy, in that it allows the artist greater room in which to work out his conceptions of character. The thoughts of a man in self-communion are apt to run in a certain circle, and to assume a monotony" (Professor Johnson, M.A.). This supposed second person serves to "draw out" the speaker and to stimulate the imagination of the reader. *Bishop Blougram's Apology* is an admirable example of this form of literature, where Mr. Gigadibs, the critic of Bishop Blougram, is the silent second person above referred to.

Dramatic Romances and Lyrics. (*Bells and Pomegranates*, No. VII.: 1845.) How they Brought the Good News, Pictor Ignotus, Italy in England, England in Italy, The Lost Leader, The Lost Mistress, Home Thoughts from Abroad, The Tomb at St. Praxed's; Garden Fancies: i. The Flower's Name; ii. Sibrandus Schafnaburgensis. France and Spain: i. The Laboratory; ii. The Confessional. The Flight of the Duchess, Earth's Immortalities, Song, The Boy and the Angel, Night and Morning, Claret and Tokay, Saul, Time's Revenges, The Glove.

Dramatis Personæ (1864). James Lee, Gold Hair, The Worst of it, Dîs Aliter Visum, Too Late, Abt Vogler, Rabbi Ben Ezra, A Death in the Desert, Caliban upon Setebos, Confessions,

May and Death, Prospice, Youth and Art, A Face, A Likeness, Mr. Sludge, Apparent Failure, Epilogue.

Dubiety. (*Asolando*, 1889.) Richardson said that "a state of dubiety and suspense is ever accompanied with uneasiness. Sleep, if sound, is restful; but the poet asks for comfort, and to be comfortable implies a certain amount of consciousness—a dreamy, hazy sense of being in "luxury's sofa-lap." An English lady once asked a British tar in the Bay of Malaga, one lovely November day, if he were not happy to think he was out of foggy England—at least in autumn? The sailor protested there was nothing he disliked so much as "the everlasting blue sky" of the Mediterranean, and there was nothing he longed for so much as "a good Thames fog." So the poet here demands,

> "Just a cloud,
> Suffusing day too clear and bright."

He does not wish to be shrouded, as the sailor did, but his idea of comfort is that the world's busy thrust should be shaded by a "gauziness" at least. Vivid impressions are always more or less painful: they strike the senses too acutely, as "the eternal blue sky" of the south is too trying for English eyes. As such a light is sometimes too stimulating, so even too much intellectual light may be painful; a "gauziness," a "dreaming's vapour wreath" is to the overwrought brain of the thinker happiness "just for once." In the dim musings, neither dream nor vision, but just a memory, comes the face of the woman he had loved and lost, the memory of her kiss, the impress of the lips of Truth, "for love is Truth."

Eagle, The. (*Ferishtah's Fancies*: I. "On Divine Providence.") The story is taken from the fable of Pilpai (or Bidpai, as is the more correct form), called *The Dervish, the Falcon and the Raven.* A father told a young man that all effects have their causes, and he who relies upon Providence without considering these had need to be instructed by the following fable:—

"A certain dervish used to relate that, in his youth, once passing through a wood and admiring the works of the great Author of Nature, he spied a falcon that held a piece of flesh in his beak; and hovering about a tree, tore the flesh into bits, and gave it to a young raven that lay bald and featherless in its nest.

The dervish, admiring the bounty of Providence, in a rapture of admiration cried out, 'Behold, this poor bird, that is not able to seek out sustenance for himself, is not, however, forsaken of its Creator, who spreads the whole world like a table, where all creatures have their food ready provided for them! He extends His liberality so far, that the serpent finds wherewith to live upon the mountain of Gahen. Why, then, am I so greedy? wherefore do I run to the ends of the earth, and plough up the ocean for bread? Is it not better that I should henceforward confine myself in repose to some little corner, and abandon myself to fortune?' Upon this he retired to his cell, where, without putting himself to any further trouble for anything in the world, he remained three days and three nights without victuals. At last, 'Servant of mine,' said the Creator to him in a dream, 'know thou that all things in this world have their causes; and though my providence can never be limited, my wisdom requires that men shall make use of the means that I have ordained them. If thou wouldst imitate any one of the birds thou hast seen to my glory, use the talents I have given thee, and imitate the falcon that feeds the raven, and not the raven that lies a sluggard in his nest, and expects his food from another.' This example shows us that we are not to lead idle and lazy lives upon the pretence of depending upon Providence."—*Fables of Pilpay* (Chandos Classics), p. 53.

Ferishtah is in training for a dervish, and is anxious to feed hungry souls. Mr. Browning makes his charitable bird an eagle, and the moral is that man is not to play the helpless weakling, but to save the perishing by his helpful strength. The dervish, duly admonished, asks which lacks in him food the more—body or soul? He reflects that, as he starves in soul, so may mankind, wherefore he will go forth to help them; and this Mr. Browning proposes to do by the series of moral and philosophical lessons to be drawn from *Ferishtah's Fancies.* The lyric teaches that, though a life with nature is good for meditation and for lovers of solitude, we are human souls and our proper place is "up and down amid men," for God is soul, and it is the poet's business to speak to the divine principle existing under every squalid exterior and harsh and hateful personality.

Earth's Immortalities. (First published in *Dramatic Romances and Lyrics—Bells and Pomegranates* No. VII.) The poet was famous, and not so very long since; but the gravestones above him are sinking, and the lichens are softening out his very name and date. So fades away his fame. And the lover who could be satisfied with nothing less than "for ever" has the fever of passion quenched in the snows that cover the tomb beside the poet's. One demanded to be remembered, the other to be loved, for ever. Thus do "Earth's immortalities" perish either under lichens or snows.

Easter-Day. (*Christmas Eve and Easter Day:* Florence, 1850.) The poem is a dialogue. The first speaker exclaims, "How very hard it is to be a Christian!" and says the difficulty does not so much consist in living up to the Christ-ideal,—hard enough, by the very terms, but hard to realise it with the moderate success with which we realise the ordinary aims of life. Of course the aim is greater, consequently the required effort harder: may it not be God's intention that the difficulty of being a Christian should seem unduly great? "Of course the chief difficulty is belief," says the second speaker: "once thoroughly believe, the rest is simple. Prove to me that the least command of God is really and truly God's command, and martyrdom itself is easy." Joint the finite into the infinite life, and fix yourself safely inside, no doubt all external things you would safely despise. The second speaker says, "But faith may be God's touchstone: God does not reward us with heaven because we see the sun shining, nor crown a man victor because he draws his breath duly. If you would have faith exist at all, there must perforce be some uncertainty with it. We love or hate people because either they do or do not believe in us. But the Creator's reign, we are apt to think, should be based on exacter laws: we desire God should geometrise." The first speaker says, "You would grow as a tree, stand as a rock, soar up like fire, be above faith. But creation groans, and out of its pains we have to make our music." The second speaker replies, "I confess a scientific faith is absurd; the end which it was meant to serve would be lost if faith were certainty. We may grant that, but may we not require at least probability? We do not hang a curtain flat along a wall; we prefer it to hang in folds from point to point. We would not mind the gaps and intervals, if at point and point we could pin our life upon God. It would be no hardship then to renounce the world. There are men who live merely to collect beetles, giving up all the pleasures of life to make a completer collection than has been hitherto formed. Another set lives to collect snuff-boxes, or in learning to play chess blindfold. It would not be hard to renounce the world if we had as much *certainty* as these hermits obtain in their pleasures to inspire them in renouncing the vanities of life. Of course, as some will say, there is evidence enough of a sort: as is your turn of mind, so is your search—you will find just what you look for, and so you get your Christian evidences in a sense; you may comfort yourself in having found a scrap of papyrus in a mummy-case which declares there really was a living Moses, and you may even get over the difficulty of Jonah and the whale by turning the whale into an island or a rock and set your faith to clap her wings and crow accordingly. You may do better: you may make the human heart the minister of truth, and prove by its wants and needs and hopes and fears how aptly the creeds meet these:

> "You wanted to believe; your pains
> Are crowned—you do!"

If once in the believing mood, the renunciation of pleasures adds a spice to life. Do you say that the Eternal became incarnate—

> "Only to give our joys a zest,
> And prove our sorrows for the best?"

The believing man is convinced that to be a Christian the world's gain is to be accounted loss, and he asks the sceptic what he counsels in that case? The answer is, he would take the safe side—deny himself. The believer does not relish the idea of renouncing life for the sake of death. The collectors of curiosities at least had something for their pains, and the believer gets—well, hope! The sceptic claims that he lives in trusting ease. "Yes," says the believer, "blind hopes wherewith to flavour life—that is all; and he proceeds to relate an incident which happened in his life one Easter night, three years ago. He was crossing the common near the chapel (spoken of in *Christmas Eve*), when he fell to musing on what was his personal relationship to Christianity, how it would be with him were he to fall dead that moment—would he lie faithful or faithless? It was always so with him from childhood; he always desired to know the worst of everything. "Common-sense" told him he had nothing to fear: if he were not a Christian, who was? All at once he had this vision.

" Burn it ! " was written in lines of fire across the sky ; the dome of heaven was one vast rack of ripples, infinite and black ; the whole earth was lit with the flames of the Judgment Day. In a moment he realised that he stood before the seat of Judgment, choosing the world—his naked choice, with all the disguises of old and all his trifling with conscience stripped away. A Voice beside him spoke :—

" Life is done,
Time ends, Eternity's begun,
And thou art judged for evermore."

The Christ stood before him, told him that, as he had deliberately chosen the world, the finite life in opposition to God, it should be his :—

" 'T is thine
For ever—take it ! "

For the world he had lived, for the things of time and sense he had fought and sighed ; the ideal life, the truth of God, the best and noblest things, had interested him noway. His sentence, his awful doom—which at first he was so far from realising that he was thrilled with pleasure at the words—was that he should take and for ever keep the partial beauty for which he had struggled. Wedded for ever to the gross material life, in that he imagined he saw his highest happiness ! " Mine—the World ? " he cried, in transport. " Yes," said the awful Judge : " if you are satisfied with one rose, thrown to you over the Eden-barrier which excludes you from its glory—take it ! " Our greatest punishment would be the gratification of our lowest aims. " All the world ! " and the sense of infinite possession of all the beauty of earth, from fern leaf to Alpine heights, brought the warmth to the man's heart and extinguished the terror inspired by the Judgment-seat of God. And the great Judge saw the thought, told him he was welcome so to rate the mere hangings of the vestibule of the Palace of the Supreme ; and in the scorn of the awful gift the man read his error, and asked for Art in place of Nature. And that, too, was conceded : he should obtain the one form the sculptors laboured to abstract, the one face the painters tried to draw, the perfection in their soul which these only hinted at. But " very good " as God pronounced earth to be, earth can only serve earth's ends; its completeness transferred to a future state would be the dreariest deficiency. The good, tried once, were bad retried. Then the judged man, seeing the World and the World of Art insufficient to satisfy his new condition, cried in anguish, "Mind is best—I will seize mind—forego the rest!" And again it was answered to him that all the best of mind on earth—the intuition, the grasps of guess, the efforts of the finite to comprehend the infinite, the gleams of heaven which come to sting with hunger for the full light of God, the inspiration of poetry, the truth hidden in fable,—all these were God's part, and in no wise to be considered as inherent to the mind of man. Losing God, he loses His inspirations; bereft of them in the world he had chosen, mind would not avail to light the cloud he had entered. And the bleeding spirit of the humbled man prays for love alone. And God said, "Is this thy final choice: Love is best? 'Tis somewhat late! Love was all about thee, curled in its mightiness around all thou hadst to do with. Take the show of love for the name's sake; but remember Who created thee to love, died for love of thee, and thou didst refuse to believe the story, on the ground that the love was too much." Cowering deprecatingly, the man, who now saw the whole truth of God, cried, "Thou Love of God! Let me not know that all is lost! Let me go on hoping to reach one eve the Better Land!" And the man awoke, and rejoiced that he was not left apart in God's contempt; thanking God that it is hard to be a Christian, and that he is not condemned to earth and ease for ever.

NOTES.—Stanza iv., "*In all Gods acts (as Plato cries He doth) He should geometrise*": see Plutarch, *Symposiacs*, viii. 2. "Diogenianas began and said, 'Let us admit Plato to the conference, and inquire upon what account he says—supposing it to be his sentence—that *God always plays the geometer.*' I said: 'This sentence was not plainly set down in any of his books; yet there are good arguments that it is his, and it is very much like his expression.' Tyndares presently subjoined: 'He praises geometry as a science that takes off men from sensible objects, and makes them apply themselves to the intelligible and Eternal Nature, the contemplation of which is the end of philosophy, as a view of the mysteries of initiation into holy rites.'" vi., "*My list of coleoptera*": in entomology, an order of insects having four wings—the beetle tribe. "*A Grignon with the Regent's crest*",

Grignon was a famous snuff-box maker, and his name was used for the fashionable boxes. vii., "*Jonah's whale*": The latest theory is that the great deity of Nineveh was a "fish-god." Mr. Tylor considers the story to be a solar myth. Madame Blavatsky says (*Isis Unveiled*, vol. ii., p. 258), "'Big Fish' is Cetus, the latinised form of Keto—κητω, and Keto is Dagon, Poseidon." She suggests that Jonah simply went into the cell within the body of Dagon, the fish-god. *Orpheus*, the mythical poet, whose mother was the Muse Calliope. His song could move the rocks and tame wild beasts (see EURYDICE TO ORPHEUS). *Dionysius Zagrias.* Zagreus was a name given to Dionysus by the Orphic poets. The conception of the Winter-Dionysus originated in Crete: sacrifice was offered to him at Delphi on the shortest day. This is quite evidently one of the myths of winter. xii., *Æschylus*: "*the giving men blind hopes.*" In the *Prometheus Chained* of Æschylus the chorus of ocean nymphs ask Prometheus—

"*Chor.* But had th' offence no further aggravation?
Pro. I hid from men the foresight of their fate.
Chor. What couldst thou find to remedy that ill?
Pro. I sent blind Hope t' inhabit in their hearts.
Chor. A blessing hast thou given to mortal man."

Morley's *Plays of Æschylus*, p. 18.

xiv., "*The kingcraft of the Lucomons*": Heads of ancient Etruscan families, and combining both priest and patriarch. The kings were drawn from them. (Dr. Furnivall.) *Fourier's scheme*: Fourierism was the system of Charles Fourier, a Frenchman, who recommended the reorganisation of society into small communities living in common. xx., "*Flesh refine to nerve*": this is a remarkable instance of the poet's scientific apprehension of the process of nerve formation five years before Herbert Spencer speculated on the evolution of the nervous system. (See my *Browning's Message to his Time*: "Browning as a Scientific Poet.") xxvi., *Buonarrotti* = Michael Angelo.

Eccelino da Romano III. (*Sordello.*) Known as Eccelin the Monk, or Ezzelin III. He was the Emperor Frederick's chief in North Italy, and was a powerful noble. He was termed "the Monk" because of his religious austerity. He is described by Mr. Browning in the poem as "the thin, grey, wizened, dwarfish devil Ecelin." He was the most prominent of Ghibelline leaders, was tyrant of Padua, and nicknamed "the Son of the Devil." Ariosto, *Orlando Furioso*, iii. 33, describes him as

> "Fierce Ezelin, that most inhuman lord,
> Who shall be deemed by men a child of hell."

"His story," says Longfellow, in his notes to Dante's *Inferno*, may be found in Sismondi's *Histoire des Républiques Italiennes*, chap. xix. He so outraged the religious sense of the people by his cruelties that a crusade was preached against him, and he died a prisoner in 1259, tearing the bandages from his wounds, and fierce and defiant to the last. 'Ezzelino was small of stature,' says Sismondi, 'but the whole aspect of his person, all his movements, indicated the soldier. His language was bitter, his countenance proud, and by a single look he made the boldest tremble. His soul, so greedy of all crimes, felt no attraction for sensual pleasures. Never had Ezzelino loved women; and this, perhaps, is the reason why in his punishments he was as pitiless against them as men. He was in his sixty-sixth year when he died; and his reign of blood had lasted thirty-four years.'"

Eccelino IV. was the elder of the two sons of Eccelino III., surnamed the Monk, who divided his little principality between them in 1223, and died in 1235. In 1226, at the head of the Ghibellines, he got possession of Verona, and was appointed Podesta. He became one of the most faithful servants of the Emperor Frederick II. In 1236 he invited Frederick to enter Italy to his assistance, and in August met him at Trent. Eccelino was soon after besieged in Verona by the Guelfs, and the siege was raised by the Emperor. Vicenza was next stormed and the government given to Eccelino. In 1237 he marched against Padua, which capitulated, when he behaved towards the people with great cruelty. He then besieged Mantua, and mastered the Trevisa. In 1239 he was excommunicated by the Pope and deprived of his estates. He behaved with such terrible cruelty that the Emperor would have gladly been rid of him. Dante, in the *Divina Commedia*, Inferno xii., places Eccelino in the lake of blood in the seventh circle of hell.

Echetlos. (*Dramatic Idyls*, Second Series: 1880.) A Greek legend (of which there are many) about the battle of Marathon, in which the Athenians and Platæans, under Miltiades, defeated the Persians, 490 B.C. Wherever the Greeks were hardest pressed in the fight a figure driving a ploughshare was seen mowing down the enemy's ranks. After the battle was over the Greeks were anxious to learn who was the man in the clown's dress who had done them this great service. They demanded of the oracles his name. But the oracles declined to tell: "Call him Echetlos, the Ploughshare-wielder," they said. "Let his deed be his name:

"The great deed ne'er grows small."

NOTES.—"*Not so the great name—Woe for Miltiades, woe for Themistokles!*" After the victory of Marathon, Miltiades sullied his honour by employing the fleet in an attempt to wreak a private grudge on the island of Paros. He was sentenced to a heavy fine, which he was unable to pay, and died in debt and dishonour. Themistocles was accused of having entered into a traitorous communication with the Persians in his own interest. He was banished from Greece, and died at Magnesia.

Elcorte (*Sordello*, Book ii.) was a poor archer who perished in saving a child of Eccelin's. He was supposed to be Sordello's father, but the poet discovered that he was not.

Eglamour. (*Sordello.*) The minstrel defeated by Sordello at the contest of song in the Court of Love. He was the chief troubadour of Count Richard of St. Bonifacio. He died of grief at his discomfiture in the art of song by Sordello. "He was a typical troubadour, who loved art for its own sake; thought more of his songs than of the things about which he sang, or of the soul whose passion song should express" (Fotheringham, *Studies in Browning*, p. 116). Mrs. James L. Bagg, in a comparative study of Eglamour and Sordello, gives the following as the chief characteristics of this poet:—"He was a poet not without effort and often faltering; he exhibits the beautiful as the natural outburst of a heart full of a sense of beauty that possesses it. He loses himself in his song,—it absorbs his life; his art ends with his art, and is its own reward. He understands and loves nature; they are bound up together. He loves all beauty for its own sake, asking no reward. He craves nothing, takes no thought for the morrow. He lacks character, and is dreamy, inactive; and, attempting little, fails in little. His life is barren of results as men reckon; he lives and loves, and sings and dies. His life is almost one unbroken strain of harmony—he is pleased to please and to serve. His nature is simple and easily understood; Eglamour is born and dies a creature of perceptions, never conscious that beyond these there lies a world of thought. His life goes out in tragic giving up of love, hope and heart."

Elvire. (*Fifine at the Fair.*) The wife of Don Juan, who discusses with her husband the nature of conjugal love, after he has been fascinated by the gipsy girl at Pornic fair. She is the Donna Elvira of Molière's *Don Juan*, and the part she plays in this poem of *Fifine* is suggested by her speech in Act i., Scene 3:—

> "Why don't you arm your brow
> With noble impudence?
> Why don't you swear and vow
> No sort of change is come to any sentiment
> You ever had for me?"

Englishman in Italy, The: Piano di Sorrento (the Plain of Sorrento). (*Dramatic Romances*, published in *Bells and Pomegranates*, VII. 1845.)—Sorrento, in the province of Naples, is situated on the north side of the peninsula that separates the Bay of Naples from the Bay of Salerno. In the time of Augustus it was a finer city than Naples itself. The neighbourhood of this delightful summer resort is the realm of the olive tree, and its plain is clothed with orange and lemon groves. A deep blue sky above and a deep blue sea below, coast scenery unequalled for loveliness even in Italy, and an atmosphere breathing perfume and intoxicating the senses with the soft delights of a land of romance and gaiety, combine to make a residence in this earthly paradise almost too luxurious for a phlegmatic Englishman. It has a drawback in the form of the Scirocco—a hot, oppressive and most relaxing wind, crossing from North Africa over the Mediterranean, and the "long, hot, dry autumn" referred to in the poem. The Englishman is seated by the side of a dark-complexioned tarantella-dancing girl, whom he is sheltering from the approaching storm, and who is timidly saying her rosary, and to whom he is describing the incidents of Italian life which have most interested him—the ripening grapes, the quails and the curious nets arranged to catch them, the pomegranates splitting with ripeness on the trees, the yellow rock-flower on the road side, all the landscape parched with the fierce Southern heat, which the sudden rain-storm was about to cool and moisten. The quail nets are rapidly taken down, for protection; on the flat roofs, where the split figs lie in sieves drying in the sun, the girls are busy putting them under cover; the blue sea has changed to black with the coming storm; the fishing boat from Amalfi—loveliest spot in all the lovely landscape—sends ashore its harvest of the sea, to the delight of the naked brown children awaiting it. The grape harvest has begun, and in the great vats they are treading the grapes, dancing madly to keep the bunches under, while the rich juice runs from beneath; and still the laden girls pour basket after basket of fresh vine plunder into the vat, and still the red stream flows on. And under the hedges of aloe, where the tomatoes lie, the children are picking up the snails tempted out by the rain, which will be cooked and eaten for supper, when the grape gleaners will feast on great ropes of macaroni and slices of purple gourds. And as he dwells on all the Southern wealth of the land, he tempts the timid little maid with grape bunches, whose heavy blue bloom entices the wasps, which follow the spoil to the very lips of the eater; with cheese-balls, white wine, and the red flesh of the prickly pear. Now the Scirocco is loose—down come the olives like hail; fig trees snap under the power of the storm; they must keep under shelter till the tempest is over: and now he amuses the girl by telling her how in a few days they will have stripped all the vines of their leaves to feed the cattle, and the vineyards will look so bare. He rode over the mountains the previous night with her brother the guide, who feasted on the fruit-balls of the myrtles and sorbs, and while he ate the mule plodded on, now and then neighing as he recognised his mates, laden with faggots and with barrels, on the paths below. Higher they ascended till the woods ceased; as they mounted the path grew wilder, the chasms and piles of loose stones showed but the growth of grey fume reed, the ever-dying rosemary, and the lentisks, till they reached the summit of Calvano; then he says—

"God's own profound
Was above me, and round me the mountains, and under, the sea."

The crystal of heaven and its blue solitudes; the "infinite movement" of the mountains, which seem, as they overlook the sensual landscape, to enslave it—filled him with a grave and solemn fear.

And now he turns to the sea, wherein slumber the three isles of the siren, looking as they did in the days of Ulysses; he will sail among them, and visit with his companion their strangely coloured caves, and hear the secret sung to Ulysses ages ago. The sun breaks out over Calvano, the storm has passed; the gipsy tinker ventures out with his bellows and forge, and is hammering away there under the wall; the children watch him mischievously. He rouses his sleepy maiden, and bids her come with him to see the preparations at the church for the Feast of the Rosary; for the morrow is Rosary Sunday, and it was on that day the Catholic powers of Europe destroyed the Turkish fleet at the battle of Lepanto, and in every Catholic church the victory is annually commemorated by devotions to Our Lady of the Rosary, whose prayers, they say, won the contest for the Christian arms. The Dominican brother is to preach the sermon, and all the gay banners and decorations are being put up in the church. The altar will be ablaze with lights, the music is to be supplemented by a band, and the statue of the Virgin is to be borne in solemn procession through the plain. Bonfires, fireworks, and much trumpet-blowing will wind up the day; and the Englishman anticipates as great pleasure from the festival as any child, and more—for, "Such trifles!" says the girl. "Trifles!" he replies; "why, in England they are gravely debating if it be righteous to abolish the Corn Laws!"

Epilogue to "Asolando" (1889). The words of this poem have a peculiar significance: they are the last which the poet addressed to the world, and the volume in which they appeared was published in London on the very day on which he died in Venice. Had he known when he wrote them that these were the last lines of his message to the world—that he who had for so many years urged men to "strive and thrive—fight on!" would pass away as they were given to the world, would he have wished to close his life's work with braver, better, nobler words than these? All Browning is here. From *Pauline* to this epilogue the message was ever the same, and the confidence in the ultimate and eternal triumph of right uniform throughout. In the *Pall Mall Gazette* of February 1st, 1890, there appeared the following reference to this poem: "One evening, just before his death illness, the poet was reading this (the third verse) from a proof to his daughter-in-law and sister. He said. 'It almost looks like bragging to say this, and as if I ought to cancel it; but it's the simple truth; and as it's true, it shall stand.' His faith knew no doubting. In all trouble, against all evil, he stood firm."

Epilogue to "Dramatic Idyls" (Second Series). This poem combats the notion that a quick-receptive soil, on which no feather seed can fall without awakening vitalising virtue, is the hot-bed for a poet; rather must we hold that the real song-soil is the rock, hard and bare, exposed to sun and wind-storm, there in the clefts where few flowers awaken grows the pine tree—a nation's heritage. (Compare on this Emerson's *Woodnotes* II.)

Epilogue to "Dramatis Personæ."—First Speaker, as *David*. At the Feast of the Dedication of Solomon's Temple, when Priests and Levites in sacrificial robes attended with the multitude praising the Lord as a single man; when singers and trumpets sound and say, "Rejoice in God, whose mercy endureth for ever," then the presence of the Lord filled the house with the glory of His cloud. This is the highest point reached by the purest Theism of the Hebrew people.

Second Speaker, as *Renan*. A star had beamed from heaven's vault upon our world, then sharpened to a point in the dark, and died. We had loved and worshipped, and slowly we discovered it was vanishing from us. A face had looked from out the centuries upon our souls, had seemed to look upon and love us. We vainly searched the darkling sky for the dwindling star, faded from us now and gone from keenest sight. And so the face—the Christ-face—we had seen in the old records, the Gospels which had seemed to dower us with the Divine-human Friend, and which warmed our souls with love, has faded out, and we search the records and sadly fail to find the face at all, and our hope is vanished and the Friend is gone. The record searchers tell us we shall never more know ourselves are seen, never more speak and know that we are heard, never more hear response to our aspirations and our love. The searcher finds no god but himself, none higher than his own nature, no love but the reflection of his own, and realises that he is an orphan, and turning to his brethren cries, with Jean Paul, "There is no God! We are all orphans!"

Third Speaker is Mr. Browning himself, who offers us consolation in our bereavement; he asks us to see through his eyes. In head and heart every man differs utterly from his fellows; he asks how and why this difference arises; he bids us watch how even the heart of mankind may have some mysterious power of attracting Nature's influences round himself as a centre. In Arctic seas the water gathers round some rock-point as though the waste of waves sought this centre alone; for a minute this rock-point is king of this whirlpool current, then the waves oversweep and destroy it, hastening off to choose another peak to find, and flatter, and finish in the same way. Thus does Nature dance about each man of us, acting as if she meant to enhance his worth; then, when her display of simulated homage is done with, rolls elsewhere for the same performance. Nature leaves him when she has gained from him his product, his contribution to the active life of the time. The time forces have utilised the man as their pivot, he has served for the axis round which have whirled the energies which Nature employed at the moment. His quota has been contributed; he has not been a force, but the central point of the forces' revolution; as the play of waves demanded for their activity the rock-centre, so the mind forces required for their gyrations the passive man-centre; the rock stood still in the dance of the waves, but their dance could not have existed without its mysterious influence on their motion. The man was necessary to the mind-waves; the play of forces could not have been secured without just that soul-point standing idly as the centre of the dance of influences. The waves, having obtained the whirl they demanded, submerge the rock—the mind forces having gained such direction, such quality of rotation, dispense with the man; the force lives, however, and his contribution to its direction is not lost, but husbanded. Now, there is no longer any use for the old Temple service of David, neither is the particular aspect of the Christ-face required as at first beheld. The face itself does not vanish, or but decomposes to recompose. The face grows; the Christ of to-day is a greater conception than that which Renan thinks he has decomposed. It is not the Christ of an idea that sufficed for old-world conception, but one which expands with the age and grows with the sentient universe.

Epilogue to "Ferishtah's Fancies" (VENICE, *December 1st*, 1884). This poem brings into a focus the rays of the fancies which compose the volume: the famous ones of old, the heroes whose deeds are celebrated in the different poems, were not actors merely, but soldiers, and fought God's battle; they were not cowards, because they had confidence in the supremacy of good, and fighting for the right knew they could leave results to the Leader. But a chill at the heart even in its supremest joy induces the question: What if all be error?—if love itself were responsible for a fallacy of vision?

Epilogue to "Pacchiaratto and other Poems" (1876). In this poem the author deals with his critics. "The poets pour us wine," and as they pour we demand the impracticable feat of producing for us wine that shall be sweet, yet strong and pure. One poet gives the world his potent man's draught; it is admitted to be strong and invigorating, yet is swallowed at a gulp, as evidently unpleasant to the taste. Another dispenses luscious sweetness, fragrant as a flower distillation; and men say contemptuously it is only fit for boys—is useless for nerving men to work. Now, it is easy to label a bottle as possessing body and bouquet both, but labels are not always absolute guarantees of that which they cover. Still there is wine to be had, by judicious blending, which combines these qualities of body and bouquet. How do we value such vintage when we do possess it? Go down to the vaults where stand the vats of Shakespeare and Milton wine: there in the cellar are forty barrels with Shakespeare's brand—some five or six of his works are duly appreciated, the rest neglected; there are four big butts of Milton's brew, and out of them we take a few drops, pretending that we highly esteem him the while! The fact is we hate our bard, or we should not leave him in the cellar. The critics say Browning brews stiff drink without any flavour of grape: would the public take more kindly to his wine if he gave it all the cowslip fragrance and bouquet of his meadow and hill side? The treatment received by Shakespeare and Milton proves that the public taste is vitiated, notwithstanding all the pretence of admiration of them. It is our furred tongue that is at fault; it is nettle-broth the world requires. Browning has some Thirty-four Port for those who can appreciate it; as for the multitude, let them stick to their nettle-broth till their taste improves.

NOTES.—Verse i., "*The Poets pour in wine*": the quotation is from Mrs. Browning's "Wine of Cyprus." V. 20, "*Let them 'lay, pray, bray'*": this in ridicule of Byron's grammar in verse clxxx.

of Canto IV. of *Childe Harold's Pilgrimage*:—"And dashest him again to earth;—there let him lay."

Epilogue to the "Two Poets of Croisic" (1878). (Published in the *Selections*, vol. ii., as A TALE). A bard had to sing for a prize before the judges, and to accompany his song on the lute. His listeners were so pleased with his melody that it seemed as though they would hasten to bestow the award even before the end of the song; when, just as the poet was at the climax of his trial, a string broke, and all would have been lost, had not a cricket "with its little heart on fire" alighted on the instrument, and flung its heart forth, sounding the missing note; and there the insect rested, ever at the right instant shrilling forth its F-sharp even more perfectly than the string could have done. The judges with one consent said, "Take the prize—we took your lyre for harp!" Did the conqueror despise the little creature who had helped him with all he had to offer? No: he had a statue of himself made in marble, life-size; on the lyre was "perched his partner in the prize." The author of the volume of poems of which this story forms the epilogue, says that he tells it to acknowledge the love which played the cricket's part, and gave the missing music; a girl's love coming aptly in when his singing became gruff. Love is ever waiting to supply the missing notes in the arrested harmony of our lives.

NOTES.—"*Music's Son*": Goethe. "*Lotte*," of the *Sorrows of Werther*, was Charlotte Buff, who married Kestner, Goethe's friend, the Albert of the novel. Goethe was in love with Charlotte Buff, and her marriage with Kestner roused the temper of his over-sensitive mind." (See *Dr. Brewer's Reader's Handbook.*)

Epistle, An, Containing the Strange Medical Experience of Karshish, the Arab Physician. (*Men and Women*, vol. i., 1855.) [The subject of the poem is the raising of Lazarus from the dead.] Karshish, a wandering scholar-physician, writing to the sage Abib, from whom he has learned his art, gives him an account of certain matters of medical interest which he has discovered in the course of his travels, and which, like a good student, he communicates to his venerable teacher. After informing him that he has sent him some samples of rare pharmaceutical substances, he says that his journeyings brought him to Jericho, on the dangerous road from which city to Jerusalem he had met with sundry misadventures, and noted several cases of clinical interest, all of which he reports in the matter-of-fact way which betokens the scientific practitioner of the period. Amongst his plague, ague, epileptic, scalp-disease, and leprosy cures, he particularly describes "a case of mania subinduced by epilepsy," which especially interested him. The disorder seemed to him of quite easy diagnosis: "'Tis but a case of mania," complicated by trance and epilepsy, but well within his powers as a physician to account for, except in the after circumstances and the means of cure. "Some spell, exorcisation or trick of art" had evidently been employed by a Nazarene physician of his tribe, who bade him, when he seemed dead, "Rise!" and he did rise He was "one Lazarus, a Jew"—of good habit of body, and indeed quite beyond ordinary men in point of health; and his three days' sleep had so brightened his body and soul that it would be a great thing if the medical art could always ensure such a result from the use of any drug. He has undergone such change of mental vision that he eyes the world now like a child, and puts all his old joys in the dust. He has lost his sense of the proportion of things: a great armament or a mule load of gourds are all the same to him, while some trifle will appear of infinite import; yet he is stupefied because his fellow-men do not view things with his opened eyes. He is so perplexed with impulses that his heart and brain seem occupied with another world while his feet stay here. He desires only perfectly to please God; he is entirely apathetic when told that Rome is on the march to destroy his town and tribe, yet he loves all things old and young, strong and weak, the flowers and birds, and is harmless as a lamb: only at ignorance and sin he is impatient, but promptly curbs himself. The physician would have sought out the Nazarene who worked the cure, and would have held a consultation with him on the case, but discovered that he perished in a tumult many years ago, accused of wizardry, rebellion, and of holding a prodigious creed. Lazarus—it is well, says the physician, to keep nothing back in writing to a brother in the craft—regards the curer as God the Creator and sustainer of the world, that dwelt in flesh amongst us for a while; but why write of trivial matters? He has more important things to tell.

> "I noticed on the margin of a pool,
> Blue-flowering borage, the Aleppo sort
> Aboundeth, very nitrous. It is strange!"

He begs the sage's pardon for troubling him with this man's tedious case, but it has touched him with awe, it may be partly the effect of his weariness. But he cannot close his letter without returning to the tremendous suggestion once more. "Think, Abib! The very God!"—

"So the All-Great, were the All-Loving too,—
It is strange."

Professor Corson says this poem "is one of Browning's most remarkable psychological studies. It may be said to polarise the idea, so often presented in his poetry, that doubt is a condition of the vitality of faith. It is a subtle representation of a soul conceived with absolute spiritual standards, while obliged to live in a world where all standards are relative and determined by the circumstances and limitations of its situation." Lazarus has seen things as they are. "This show of things," so far as he is concerned, is done with. He now leads the *actual* life; his wonder and his sorrow are drawn from the reflection that his fellow-men remain in the region of phantasm. He lives really in the world to come. How infinitely little he found the things of time and sense in the presence of the eternal verities is grandly shown in the poem. The attitude of Lazarus under his altered conditions affords an answer to those who demand that an All-Wise Being should not leave men to struggle in a region of phenomena but exhibit the actual to us in the present life. Under such conditions our probation would be impossible. As Browning shows in *La Saisiaz*, a condition of certainty would destroy the school-time value of life; the highest truths are insusceptible of scientific demonstration. Lazarus is the hero of the poem, not Karshish. As the Bishop of Durham says in his paper "On Browning's View of Life," Lazarus "is not a man, but a sign: he stands among men as a patient witness of the overwhelming reality of the divine—a witness whose authority is confessed, even against his inclination, by the student of nature, who turns again and again to the phenomena which he affects to disparage. In this crucial example Browning shows how the exclusive dominance of the spirit destroys the fulness of human life, its uses and powers, while it leaves a passive life, crowned with an unearthly beauty." The professional attitude of Karshish is drawn with marvellous fidelity. A paper in the *Lancet* on such a "case" would be precisely on the same lines to-day, though the wandering off into side details would not be quite so obvious, and there would be an entire absence of any trifling with the idea that "the All-Great were the All-Loving too." This is "emotional," and modern science has nothing but contempt for that.

NOTES.—*Snake-stone*, a name applied to any substance used as a remedy for snake-bites. Professor Faraday once analysed several which had been used for this purpose in Ceylon. One turned out to be a piece of animal charcoal, another was chalk, and a third a vegetable substance like a bezoar. The animal charcoal might possibly have been useful if applied immediately. The others were valueless for the purpose. (Tennant, *Ceylon*, third ed., i., 200.) "*A spider that weaves no web.*" Dr. H. McCook, a specialist in spider lore, has explained this passage in *Poet-Lore*, vol. i., p. 518. He says the spider referred to belongs to the Wandering group: they stalk their prey in the open field, or in divers lurking places, and are quite different in their habits from the web-spinners. The spider sprinkled with mottles he thinks is the Zebra spider (*Epiblemum scenicum*). It belongs to the Saltigrade tribe. The use of spiders in medicine is very ancient. Pliny describes many diseases for which they were used. Spiders were boiled in water and distilled for wounds by Sir Walter Raleigh. *Greek-fire* was the precursor of gunpowder; it was the *oleum incendiarum* of the Romans. Probably petroleum, tar, sulphur, and nitre were its chief ingredients. *Blue flowering borage* (*Borago officinalis*). The ancients deemed this plant one of the four "cordial flowers" for cheering the spirits, the others being the rose, violet, and alkanet. Pliny says it produces very exhilarating effects. The stem contains nitre, and the whole plant readily gives its flavour even to cold water. (See Anne Pratt's *Flowering Plants*, vol. iv., p. 75.)

Este. (*Sordello.*) A town of Lombardy, in the delegation of Padua, situated at the southern extremity of the Euganean hills. The Rocca or castle is a donjon tower occupying the site of the original fortress of Este.

Este, The House of. (*Sordello.*) One of the oldest princely houses of Italy, called Este after the name of the town above mentioned. Albert Azzo II. first bore the title of Marquis of

Este; he married a sister of Guelph III., who was duke of Carinthia. The Italian title and estates were inherited by Fulco I. (1060-1135), son of Albert Azzo II. In the twelfth, thirteenth, and fourteenth centuries the history of the house of Este is mixed up with that of the other noble houses of Italy in the struggles of the Guelphs and Ghibellines. The Estena were the head of the Guelph party, and at different times were princes of Ferrara, Modena and Reggio. "Obizzo I., son of Folco I., entered into a league against Frederick Barbarossa, and was comprehended in the Venetian treaty of 1177, by which municipal podestas (chief magistrates of great cities) were instituted" (*Encyc. Brit.*). Strife existed between this house and that of the Torelli, which raged for two centuries, in consequence of Obizzo I. carrying off Marchesella, heiress of the Adelardi family, of Ferrara, and marrying her to his son Azzo V.

Eulalia. (*A Soul's Tragedy.*) The shrewd woman who was betrothed to Luitolfo.

Euripides. The Greek tragiepoet, who was born of Athenian parents in 480 B.C. He brought out his first play—*The Peliades*—at the age of twenty-five. At thirty-nine he gained the first prize, which honour he received only five times in his long career of fifty years. He was the mediator between the ancient and modern drama, and was regarded at Athens as an innovator. Aristophanes was an exceedingly hostile and witty critic of Euripides, and from his point of view his conduct was justified, taking as he did the standard of Æschylus and Sophocles as the only right model of tragedy. He is variously said to have written seventy-five, seventy-eight and ninety-two tragedies. Eighteen only have come down to us: *The Alcestis*, *Andromache*, *Bacchæ*, *Hecuba*, *Helena*, *Electra*, *Heraclidæ*, *Heracles in Madness*, *The Suppliants*, *Hippolytus*, *Iphigenia at Aulis*, *Iphigenia among the Tauri*, *Ion*, *Medea*, *Orestes*, *Rhesus*, the *Troades*, the *Phœnissæ*, and a satiric play, the *Cyclops*. "Aristophanes calls Euripides 'meteoric,' because he was always rising into the air; he was famous for allusions to the stars, the sea and the elements. Aristophanes uses the epithet sneeringly: Browning, praisingly" (*Br. P.* iii 43).

Eurydice to Orpheus. A Picture by Leighton. (Published for the first time in the Royal Academy Catalogue, 1864. It was reprinted in the first volume of the *Selections* in 1865.) Orpheus was a famous mythical poet, who was so powerful in song that he could move trees and rocks and tame wild beasts by the charms of his voice. His wife (the nymph Eurydice) died from the bite of a serpent, and Orpheus descended to the lower regions in search of her. He so influenced Persephone by his music that she gave him permission to take back his wife on the condition that he should not look round during his passage from the nether world to the regions above. In his impatience he disregarded the condition, and having turned his head to gaze back, Eurydice had to return for ever to Hades (Vergil, *Geor.* iv., v. 457, etc.). The poet has represented Eurydice speaking to Orpheus the passionate words of love which made him forget the commands of Pluto and Persephone not to look back on pain of losing his wife again.

Euthukles. (*Balaustion's Adventure; Aristophanes' Apology.*) He was the man of Phokis who heard Balaustion recite *Alcestis* at Syracuse, and who followed her when she returned to Athens, and married her. On their voyage to Rhodes, after the fall of Athens, Balaustion dictated to him the *Apology* of Aristophanes, which he wrote down on board the vessel. It was Euthukles, according to Browning, who saved Athens from destruction by reciting at a critical moment the lines from Euripides' *Electra* and *Agamemnon*.

Evelyn Hope. (*Men and Women*, 1855; *Lyrics*, 1863; *Dramatic Lyrics*, 1868.) The lament of a man who loved a young girl who died before she was old enough to appreciate his love. The maiden was sixteen, the man "thrice as old." He contemplates her as she lies in the beauty of death, and asks: "Is it too late then? Because you were so young and I so old, were we fellow-mortals and nought beside? Not so: God creates the love to reward the love," and he will claim her not in the next life alone, but, if need be, through lives and worlds many yet to come. His love will not be lost, for his gains of the ages and the climes will not satisfy him without his Evelyn Hope. He can wait. He will be more worthy of her in the worlds to come. Modern science has taught us that no atom of matter can ever be lost to the world, no infinitesimal measure of energy but is conserved, and the poet holds that there shall never be one lost good. The eternal atoms, the vibrations that cease not through the eternal years, shall not mock at the evanescence of human love.

Face, A. (*Dramatis Personæ*, 1864.) A portrait of a beautiful girl painted in words by a poet who had all the sympathies of an artist.

Family, The. (*Ferishtah's Fancies*, 4: "On the Lawfulness of Prayer.") Ferishtah has prayed for a dying man that he might recover. An objector asks why he does this: if God is all-wise and good, what He does must be right: "Two best wills cannot be." Man has only to acquiesce and be thankful. The dervish tells a tale. A man had three sons, and a wife who was bitten by a serpent. The husband called in a doctor, who said he must amputate the injured part. The husband assented. The eldest son said, "Pause, take a gentler way." The next in age said, "The doctor must and should save the limb." The youngest said, "The doctor knows best: let him operate!" He agreed with the doctor. Let God be the doctor; let us call the husband's acquiescence wise understanding, call the first son's opinion a wise humanity. In the second son we see rash but kind humanity; in the youngest one who apes wisdom above his years. "Let us be man and nothing more," says Ferishtah.—man hoping, fearing, loving and bidding God help him till he dies. The lyric bids us while on earth be content to be men. The wider sense of the angel cannot be expected while we remain under human conditions.

Fancy and Reason, in *La Saisiaz*, discuss the *pros* and *cons* of the probabilities of the existence of God, the soul, and future life, etc.

Fears and Scruples. (*Pacchiarotto and Other Poems*, 1876: "The Spiritual Uses of Uncertainty.") "Why does God never speak?" asks the doubter. The analogy of the poem compares this silence of the Divine Being with that of a man's friend, who wrote him many valued letters, but otherwise kept aloof from him It is suggested by experts that the letters are forgeries. The man loves on. It is then suggested that his friend is acting as a spy upon him, sees him readily enough and knows all he does, and some day will show himself to punish him. But this is to make the friend a monster! Hush!—"What if this friend happen to be—God?" In explanation of this poem, Mr.

Kingsland received from the poet the following letter :—"I think that the point I wanted to illustrate in the poem you mention was this : Where there is a genuine love of the 'letters' and 'actions' of the invisible 'friend,' however these may be disadvantaged by an inability to meet the objections to their authenticity or historical value urged by 'experts' who assume the privilege of learning over ignorance, it would indeed be a wrong to the wisdom and goodness of the 'friend' if he were supposed capable of overlooking the actual 'love' and only considering the 'ignorance" which, failing to in any degree affect 'love,' is really the highest evidence that 'love' exists. So I *meant*, whether the result be clear or no."

Ferishtah's Fancies. A criticism of Life : Browning's mellow wisdom. Published in 1884, with the following quotations as mottoes on the page facing the title:—

"His genius was jocular, but, when disposed, he could be very serious."—Article *Shakespeare*, Jeremy Collier's *Historical, etc., Dictionary*, 2nd edition, 1701. "You, sir, I entertain you for one of my Hundred ; only, I do not like the fashion of your garments : you will say, they are Persian ; but let them be changed."—*King Lear*, Act III., sc. vi.

The work embraces the following collection of poems :—Prologue. 1. "The Eagle." 2. "The Melon-seller." 3. "Shah Abbas." 4. "The Family." 5 "The Sun." 6. "Mihrab Shah." 7. "A Camel-driver." 8. "Two Camels." 9. "Cherries." 10. "Plot Culture." 11. "A Pillar at Sebzevah." 12. "A Bean Stripe : also Apple Eating." Epilogue. There was a real personage named Ferishtah, a celebrated Persian historian, born about 1570. He is one of the most trustworthy of the Oriental historians. Several portions of his work have been translated into English. He has, however, no connection with the subject-matter of Mr. Browning's book, but it is probable that his name suggested itself to the poet as a good one for his work. We have here Mr. Browning in a dervish's robe, philosophising in a Persian atmosphere, yet talking the most perfect Browningese, just as do the Pope in the *Ring and the Book* and the rabbis in the Jewish poems. Age, experience, and the calm philosophy of a religious mind, are required for the poet's highest teaching. It matters little, these being given, whether the philosophers wear the tiara of the pope, the robe of the dervish, or the gaberdine of the Jew: the philosophy is the same. The aim is "to justify the ways of God to men," and to make reasonable an exalted Christian Theism. Three great Eastern classics—*The Fables of Bidpai*, Firdausi's *Sháh-Námeh*, and the Book of Job—are the sources of the inspiration of the pages of *Ferishtah's Fancies.* Both the *Sháh-Náhmeh* and the *Fables of Bidpai*, or *Pilpay* as they are commonly termed, are published in the *Chandos Classics.* Bidpai is supposed to be the author of a famous collection of Hindū fables. The name Bidpai occurs in their Arabic version. Their origin was doubtless the *Pantcha Tantra*, or "Five Sections," a great collection of fables. The *Hitopadesa* is another such collection. The fables were translated into Pehlvi in the sixth century. Then the Persian fables were translated into Arabic, and were transmitted to Europe. They were translated into Greek in the eleventh century, then into Hebrew and Latin, afterwards into nearly every European tongue. We must go to Firdausi, the Persian author of that "standing wonder in poetic literature," the *Sháh Námeh*, for an explanation of several allusions in the poem. This great chronicle, the Persian Book of Kings, is a history of Persia in sixty thousand verses. The poem is as familiar to every Persian as our own great epics to us, and the use Mr. Browning makes of it in this work is managed in the most natural manner. This we shall notice more particularly in dealing with the separate poems which compose the volume. In a letter to a friend, Browning wrote:—"I hope and believe that one or two careful readings of the poem will make its sense clear enough. Above all, pray allow for the poet's inventiveness in any case, and do not suppose there is more than a thin disguise of a few Persian names and allusions. There was no such poet as Ferishtah—the stories are all inventions. . . . The Hebrew quotations are put in for a purpose, as a direct acknowledgment that certain doctrines may be found in the Old Book, which the concocters of novel schools of morality put forth as discoveries of their own."

Festus. (*Paracelsus.*) The old and faithful friend of Paracelsus, who believes in him from the first. He is the husband of Michal, and both influence the mind of the hero of medicine for good at various stages of his career.

Fifine at the Fair. (1872.) The key-note of the work is given in the quotation before the Prologue, which is the motto of the poem, from Molière's *Don Juan*, Act I., Sc. 3. There is a certain historic basis for the character of the Don Juan of European legend. In Seville, in the time of Peter the Cruel, lived Don Juan Tenorio, the prince of libertines. He attempted to abduct Giralda, daughter of the governor of Seville: the consequence was a duel, in which the lady's father was killed. The sensual excesses of Don Juan had destroyed his faith, and he defied the spirit-world so far as to visit the tomb of the murdered man and challenge his statue to follow him to supper The statue accepted the invitation, and appeared amongst the guests at the meal, and carried the blaspheming sceptic to hell. "As a dramatic type," says the author of the article "Don Juan," in the *Encyclopædia Britannica*, "Don Juan is essentially the impersonation of the scepticism that results from sensuality, and is thus the complement of Faust, whose scepticism is the result of speculation." The Prologue describes a swimmer far out at sea, disporting himself under the noon-sun; as he floats, a beautiful butterfly hovers above him, a creature of the sky, as he for the time a creature of the water; neither can unite with the other, for neither can exchange elements; still, if we cannot fly, the next best thing is to swim,—a half-way house, as it were, between the world of spirit and that of grosser earth. Poetry is in this sense, a substitute for heaven: whatever the heaven-dwellers are, the poets seem; what deeds they do, the poets dream. Does the soul of his departed wife hover over him in this way, and look with pity on the mimicry of her airy flight? he wonders. (Mrs. Browning died eleven years before *Fifine* was published.)—The scenery of the poem is that of the neighbourhood of Pornic, a seaside town in the department of the Loire, in Brittany, the little town being twenty-seven miles distant from Nantes. It is noted for its sea bathing and mineral waters, and, like many other places in Brittany, possesses some curious Druidical and other architectural remains. Mr. Browning, while staying at Pornic with his family, saw the gipsy woman who suggested to him the idea of Fifine. He selected her as a type of the sensual woman, in contrast to the spiritual type of womanhood. The poem deals with incidents connected with Pornic fair. Don Juan, addressing his wife Elvire, says: "Let us see the strolling players and the fun of the fair! Who would have supposed that the night could effect such a change? Yesterday all was rough and raw—mere tubs, poles and hoarding; now this morning all is gay as a butterfly, the scaffolding has burst out in colour like a flower-bed in full bloom. Nobody saw them enter the village, but that is the way of these tumblers, they like to steal a march and exhibit their spectacle only when the show is ready. Had any one wandered about the place at night he would have seen the sober caravan which was the bud that blossomed to-day into all this gaiety. An airy structure pitched beneath the tower appeared in the morning surmounted by a red pennon fluttering in the air, and frantic to be free. To be free!—the fever of the flag finds a response in my soul, my heart fires up for liberty from the restraints of law, I would lead the bohemian life these players lead. Why is it that disgraced people, those who have burst the bonds of conventional life, always seem to enjoy their existence more than others? They seem conscious of possessing a secret which sets them out of reach of our praise or blame; now and again they return to us because they must have our money, just as a bird must bear off a bit of rag filched from mankind to work up into his nest. But why need they do that? We think much of our reputation and family honour, but these people for a penny or two will display themselves undraped to any visitor. You may tell the showman that his six-legged sheep is an imposition,—he does not care, he values his good name at nothing. But offer to make these mountebanks respectable, promise them any reward you like to forsake their ways, to work and live as the rest of the world, and your offer will not tempt them. What is the compensatory unknown joy which turns dross to gold in their case? You sigh," says the speaker to his wife, "you shake your head: what have I said to distress you? Fifine, the gipsy beauty of the show, will illustrate my meaning: this woman is to me a queen, a sexless, bloodless sprite; yet she has conquered me. I want to understand how. There is a honeyed intoxication in the Eastern lily, which lures insects to their death for its own nourishment: is that a flaw in the flower? Wiser are we not to be tempted by such dangerous delights; we may admire and keep clear of them · not poison lilies, but the rose, the daisy, or the violet, for me,—it is Elvire, not Fifine, I love. You ask how does this woman explain my thought? When Louis the Eleventh lay dying he had a procession of the famous women of all time made to pass before him: Helen of Troy, who magically brought men to acquiesce in their own destruction; next was Cleopatra, all the wonder of her body dominated by her high and haughty soul, and trampling on her lovers; then the saint of Pornic church who saves the shipwrecked sailors, and who thinks in her innocence that Cleopatra has given away her clothes to the poor; then comes my gipsy beauty Fifine, with her tambourine. Suppose you, Elvire, in spirit join this procession; then you confront yourself, and I will show you how you beat each personage there—even this Fifine, whom I will reward with a franc that you may study her. You draw back your skirts from such filth as you consider her to be; though, born perhaps as pure and sensitive as any other woman, she can afford to bear your scorn possibly,—we know such people often thus minister to age and the wants of sick parents. Her ogre husband, with his brute-beast face, takes the money she has earned by her exhibiting herself to us as she passes into the tent. I want to make you see the beauty of the mind underlying the form in all these women. No creature is made so mean but boasts an inward worth: this Fifine, a mere sand-grain on the shore, reflects some ray of sunshine. Say that there was no worst of degradation spared this woman, yet she makes no pretence—she is absolutely truthful, she assumes not to be Helen or the Pornic Saint, she only offers to exhibit herself to you for money." The wife is not deceived by all this sophistry; Fifine's attraction for the man lies in the fact, not that she possesses some hidden beauty of soul, but some unconcealed physical charms which awaken desire in him because they are not his own. What is one's own is safe, and so despised; any waif which is a neighbour's is for the time more desirable,—"Give you the sun to keep, you would want to steal a boor's rushlight or a child's squib." He explains that this is always women's way about such matters—they cannot be made to comprehend mental analysis. He reminds her how at great cost and a year's anxiety he had purchased a Rafael; he gloated over his prize for a week, and then had more relish in turning over leaf by leaf Doré's last picture-book. Suppose the picture reproached him with inconstancy, he would reply that he knew the picture was his own: anxiety had given place to confidence, and were the house on fire, he would risk his life to save it, though he were knee deep in Doré's engravings. He tells his wife she is to him as the Rafael, the Fifines are as Doré's wood engravings. Elvire is the precious wife, her face fits into the cleft in the heart of him, to him she is perfection; but is she perfect to her mirror? He thinks not. Where, then, is her beauty? In his soul. He cannot explain the reason, any more than naming the notes will explain a symphony or describing lines will call up the idea of a picture. Still there is reason in our choice of each other. It is principally the effort of one soul to seeks its own completion—that which shall aid its development—in another's. As the artist's soul sees the form he is about to create in the marble block, so does the lover see in his choice that which will draw out his soul-picture into concrete perfection. The world of sense has no real value for any of us, save in so far as our souls can detect and appropriate it. It is the idea which gives worth to that on which it is exercised. The value of all externals to the soul is just in proportion to its own power of transmuting them into food for its own growth. The soul flame is maintained not only by gums and spices, but straw and rottenness may feed it; if the soul has power to extract from evil things that which supports its life, what matters the straw so long as the ash is left behind? and so of the conquests of the soul, its power to evoke the good from the ungainly and the partial, gives us courage to ignore the failures and the slips of our lives. The pupil does not all at once evoke the masterpiece from the marble—he puts his idea in plaster by the side of the Master's statue. If the scholar at last evoke Eidotheé, the Master is to thank. "To love" in its intensest form means to yearn to invest another soul with the accumulated treasures of our own. The chemic force exerted by one soul in transmuting coarse things to beautiful is aided by another's flame. Each may continue to supplement the other, till the red, green, blue and yellow imperfections may be fused into achromatic white, the perfect light-ray. Soul is discernible by soul, and soul is evoked by soul—Elvire by Don Juan. The wife objects that he abdicates soul's empire and accepts the rule of sense: man has left the monarch's throne, and lies in the kennel a brute. Searching for soul through all womankind, you find no face so vile but sense may extract from it some good for soul. This fine-spun theory, this elaborate sophistry, she declares, is merely an ingenious excuse for sensuality:—

"Be frank—who is it you deceive—
Yourself, or me, or God?"

Don Juan would reply by an illustration from music, which can penetrate more subtly than words: he would show how we may rise out of the false into the true, out of the dark into the brightness above the dense and dim regions where doubt is bred. Bathing in the sea that morning, out in mid-channel, he was standing in the water with head back, chin up, body and limbs below—he kept himself alive by breath in the nostrils, high and dry; ever and again a wavelet or a ripple would threaten life, then back went the head, and all was safe. But did he try to ascend breast high, wave arms free of tether, to be in the air and leave the water, under he went again; before he had mastered his lesson he had plenty of water in mouth and eyes. "I compare this," he says, "to the spirit's efforts to rise out of the medium which sustains it." He was upborne by that which he beat against, too gross an element to live in, were it not for the dose of life-breath in the soul. Our business is with the sea, not with the air, so we must endure the false below while we bathe in this life. It is by practice with the false that we reach the true. We gain confidence, and learn the trick of doing what we will—sink or rise. His senses do not reel when a billow breaks over him; he grasps at a wave that will not be grasped at all, but glides through the fingers—still the failure to grasp the water sends the head above, far beyond the wave he tried to hold:—

"So with this work o' the world,"

we try to grasp a soul, catch at it, think we have a prize; it eludes us, yet the soul helped ours to mount. He seizes Elvire by grasping at Fifine. Not even this specious reasoning deceives the wife. It is an ugly fact that the wave grasped at is a woman. He replies that a woman can be absorbed into the man: women *grow* you, men at best *depend* upon you. A rill that empties itself into the sea can never be separated from it. That is woman. Man takes all and gives nought. To raise men you must stoop to teach them, learn their ignorance, stifle your soul in their mediocrities; but to govern women you must abandon stratagem, cast away disguise, and reveal your best self at your uttermost. When the music of Arion attracted the dolphins to the doomed man, one of them bore him on its back to the coast, and so saved his life; revealing his best to this "true woman-creature," he was saved from the men who would have killed him for gain. A man never puts out his whole self in love—this is reserved for hate. You do not get the best out of a man by nourishing his root, but by pruning his branch; as wine came through goats, which, browsing on the tendrils of the grape, "stung the stock to fertility," and so gained "the indignant wine—wrath of the red press." Mites of men are sore that God made mites at all; love avails not from such men-animalculæ to coax a virile thought, but touch the elf with hate, and the insect swells to thrice its bulk "and cuckoo spits some rose!" Nothing is to be gained from ruling men; women take nothing, and give all. Elvire and Fifine, in their degree, are alike in this respect. "To have secured a woman's faith in me is to have centred my soul on a fact. Falseness and change I see all around me; I expect truth because Fifine knows me much more than Elvire does." To this his wife replies, "Why not only she? There can be for each but one Best, which abolishes the simply Good and Better. Why not be content with the Elvire, who substitutes belief in truth, in your own soul, for the falseness which you fear? By toil and effort the boatman may do with pole and oars what by waiting a few hours the rising water would do for him without his labour; but men affect unusual ways,—Elvire could do far better for you all that you expect from Fifine." To this he replies that "a voyage may be too safe; there is no excitement, no experiment when wind and tide do all the needful work. Then may not our hate of falsehood be that which charms us in these actors who confess 'A lie is all we do or say'? Everything has a false outside, stage-play is honest cheating. The poet never dreams; prose-folk always do." Then he tells how his thought had recently sought expression in music rather than in words—as he played Schumann's *Carnival*, and reflected that in the masque of life and banquet of the world we have ever the same things in a new guise, the difficulty was ever to conquer commonplace and spice the same old viands and games. His fancies bore him to a pinnacle above St. Mark's at Venice, in Carnival time; he gazed down on a prodigious Fair, the men and women were disguised as beasts, birds, and fishes.

Descending into the crowd, disgust gave way to pity; the people were not so beast-like, but much more human, than when he viewed them from the height, and he began to contemplate them with a delight akin to that which animates the chemist when he untwines the composite substance, traces effect back to cause, and then constructs from its elements the complex and complete. So did he get to know the thing he was, while contemplating in that Carnival the thing he was not. Thus Venice Square became the world, the masquerade was life, the disgust at the pageant was due to the distance from which it was contemplated, when he learned that the proper goal for wisdom is the ground and not the sky, he discovered how *wisely balanced are our hates and loves*, and how peace and good come from strife and evil. It is no business of ours to fret about what should be, but we should accept and welcome what is—*is*, that is to say, for the hour, for change is the law even of the religions by which man approaches God. His temples fade to recompose into other fanes. And not only temples, but the domes of learning and the seats of science are subject to the same law. Yet Religion has always her true temple-type; Truth, though founded in a rock, builds on sands; churches and colleges that grow to nothing always reappear as something; some building, round or square or polygonal, we shall always have. But leave the buildings, and let us look at the booths in the Fair. History keeps a stall, Morality and Art set up their shops. They acquiesce in law, and adapt themselves to the times; and so, as from a distance the scene is contemplated as a whole, the multiform subsides in haze, the buildings, distinct in the broad light of day, merge and lose their individuality in a common shape. See this Druid monument: how does its construction strike you? How came this cross here? Learning cannot enlighten us. It meant something when it was erected which is lost now, yet the people of the place respect it and are persuaded that what a thing meant once it must still mean. They thought it had some reference to the Creator of the world, and was there to remind them that the world came not of itself. And so, with all the change in religions, there is an imperial chord which subsists and underlies the mists of music. In all the change there is permanence as a substratum. Truth inside and truth outside, but falsehood is between each; it is the falsehood which is change, the truth is the permanence.

There is an unchanging truth to which man in all his waverings is constant. This Druid monument said what it had to say to its own age; it never promised to help our dream. Don Juan and his wife having now completed their walk, he proposes to return home to end where they began; as we were nursed into life, death's bosom receives us at last, and that is final, for death is defeat. Our limbs came with our need of them, our souls grew by mastering the lessons of life; but when death comes, the soul, which ruled by right while the bodily powers remained, loses its right to rule. And so the soul has run its round. Love ends too where love began, and goes back to permanence; each step aside (from Elvire to Fifine, for example) proves divergency in vain:

> "Inconstancy means raw, 'tis faith alone means ripe."

And as they reach their villa, he resolves to live and die a quiet married man, earning the approbation of the mayor, and unoccupied with soul problems, especially those of women. At that moment a letter is put into his hand: there has been some mistake, Fifine thinks—he has given her gold instead of silver; he will go and see about it, and is off. Five minutes was all the time he asked. He is absent much longer, and on his return Elvire has vanished.

The Epilogue describes the householder sitting desolate in his melancholy home, weary and stupid; he is suddenly surprised by the appearance of his lost wife, whose spirit has returned to claim him; he tells her how the time has dragged without her, "And was I so much better off up there?" quoth she. For decency, arrangements are made that the reunion may be in order; and so, the powers above and those below having been duly conciliated, husband and wife are once more united: "Love is all, and death is nought"—the final lesson of life.

The means whereby we may rise from the false to the true are never wanting to the earnest and faithful striver, this is the esoteric truth of *Fifine at the Fair.* The exoteric meaning may be "an apologia for the revolt of passion against social rules and fetters." "Frenetic to be free," like the pennon, is in this sense the concentration of its meaning. What was Browning's object in this difficult and remarkable work? The question is not so difficult to answer as it appears at first sight. The poet is a soul analyst first, and a teacher next. He teaches admirably in scores of passages in *Fifine*, but his main idea has been to interpret the mental processes which he supposed might underlie the actions of such a selfish and heartless voluptuary as Don Juan. Not, of course, was there any idea of rehabilitating the character of the historic personage; but, as Browning held that every soul has something to say for itself, every man some ideal soul-advance at which he aims, however mistaken may be his methods, so he imagined that even this selfish libertine had his golden ideal, however deeply bedded in mire. He has not—like the great dramatists—sunk himself in his character, and striven thus to present the real man on his stage, but he has lent Don Juan his Browning soul for a while, that he may make his Apologia to the wife, whom he finds it very hard to deceive. Dr. Furnivall once asked the poet what his idea really was in the poem. The poet replied that his "fancy was to show morally how a Don Juan might justify himself partly by truth, somewhat by sophistry." (*Browning Society Papers*, vol. ii., p. 242*.) See also vol. i., pp. 377, 379, pp. 18*, 61*, vol. ii., p. 240*. Mr. Nettleship's exhaustive analysis leaves nothing to be desired. (*Essays*, p. 221.)

NOTES.—Verse ii., "*bateleurs and baladines*," conjurors and mountebanks. Verse iv., "*Gawain to gaze upon the Grail*": Gawain was the son of King Lot and Margause, in the Arthurian legend of the Holy Grail. Verse xv., *almandines*, a variety of garnet. Verse xix., *sick Louis*: King Louis XI. of France. Verse xxv., *tricot*: a knitted vest. Verse xxvii., *Helen*: she was declared by some of the Greeks never to have been really present at Troy, and that Paris only carried off a phantom created by Hera: the real Helen, they said, was wafted by Hermes to Proteus in Egypt, whence she was taken home by Menelaus. Verse xxxvi., *pochade*, a rough sketch. Verse xlii., *Razzi*, a corruption of Bazzi, or properly Il Sodona, the Italian painter (1479-1549). Verse xlvii., *Gerôme*, a French painter (born 1824): he exhibited a great picture at the Exposition of 1859, called "The Gladiators." Verse lii., *Eidotheé*: a sea-goddess, daughter of Proteus, the old man of the sea. Verse lix., *Glumdalclich*, in *Gulliver's Travels*, was a girl nine years old, and "only forty feet high." "*Theosutos e broteios eper kekramene*," Greek for "God, man, or both together mixed," from the *Prometheus Bound* of Æschylus. Verse lx., *Chrysopras*: a precious stone, a variety of chalcedony, or perhaps beryl. Verse lxvii. cannot be understood without reference to the fourth canto of Byron's *Childe Harold*: the lines and words between inverted commas are taken from verse clxxx., and the argument is directed against Byron's teaching as therein expressed: this verse was particularly obnoxious to Mr. Browning, both on account of its sentiments and grammar (see under LA SAISIAZ, p. 247). Verse lxix., *Thalassia*: sea-nymph, from the Greek word for the sea: *Triton*, a sea deity, a son of Neptune. Verse lxxviii., *Arion*: a Greek poet and musician: he was rescued from drowning on the back of a dolphin; his song to his lyre drew the creatures round the vessel, and one of them bore him to the shore. *Periander*, the tyrant of Corinth. "*Methymnæan hand*": Arion was born at Methymna, in Lesbos. *Orthian*, of Orthia: this was a surname of Diana. *Tænarus*, the point of land to which the dolphin carried Arion, whence he travelled to the court of Periander. Verse lxxxii., "*See Horace to the boat*": the ode is the third of the First Book of Horace's Odes. Verse lxxxiii., "*The long walls of Athens*" (see under ARISTOPHANES' APOLOGY, p. 36). *Iostephanos*, violet crowned—a name of Athens. Verse xcviii., *Simulacra*, images or likenesses. Verse cxxiv., *protoplast*, the original, the thing first formed. Verse cxxv., *Moirai Trimorphoi*, the Tri-form Fates.

Filippo Baldinucci on the Privilege of Burial: A Reminiscence of A.D. 1676. (*Pacchiarotto and other Poems*, 1876.) Filippo Baldinucci was a distinguished Italian writer on the history of the arts. He was born at Florence in 1624, and died in 1696. His chief work is entitled *Notizie de Professori del Disegno da Cimabue in quà*" (*dal* 1260 *sino al* 1670), and was first published, in six vols. 4to, 1681-1728. The *Encyclopædia Britannica* says: "The capital defect of this work is the attempt to derive all Italian art from the schools of Florence." The incidents of the poem are historical, and are related in the account which Baldinucci gives of the painter Buti. Its subject is that of the persecution to which the Jews were subjected in Italy, as in other countries of Europe, and unhappily down to the present time in Russia. We have the story as told by a frank persecutor, who regrets that the altered state of the law no longer permits the actual pelting of the Jews. The good old times had departed, but in his youth they could play some capital tricks with "the crew," as he will narrate. There was a Jews' burying-place hard by San Frediano, in Florence. Just below the Blessed Olivet, and adjoining this cemetery, was "a good farmer's Christian field." The Jews hedged their ground round with bushes, to conceal their rites from Christian gaze, for the public road ran by one corner of it. The farmer, partly from devotion, partly to annoy the Jews, built a shrine in his vineyard, and employed the painter Buti to depict thereon the Virgin Mary, fixing the picture just where it would be most annoying to the Jews. They tried to bribe the owner of the shrine to turn the picture the other way, to remove its disturbing presence from spectators to whom it could do no good, and let it face the public road, frequented by a class of Christians evidently much in need of religious supervision and restraint. The farmer agreed to remove the offending fresco in consideration of the bag of golden ducats offered; and he at once called the painter to cause Our Lady to face the other way. Buti covers up the shrine with a hoarding, and sets to work. Meanwhile the Chief Rabbi's wife died, and was taken for burial to the cemetery. In passing the shrine in the farmer's field the mourners became aware of a scurvy trick played upon them by the Christians; for the Virgin was removed according to the bargain, but a Crucifixion had been substituted, and now confronted them. The cheated Jews protested, but in vain: there was nothing for them but to suffer. Next day, as the farmer and his artist friend sat laughing over the trick, the athletic young son of the Rabbi entered the studio, desiring to purchase the original oil painting of the Madonna from which the fresco of the shrine was painted. The artist was so frightened at his stalwart form, and so amazed at the request, that, taken unaware, he asked no more than the proper price! and Mary was borne in triumph to deck a Hebrew household. They thought a miracle had happened, and that the Jew had been converted; but the Israelite explained that the only miracle wrought was that which had restrained him from throttling the painter. The truth was, he had changed his views about art, and had reflected that, since cardinals hung up heathen gods and goddesses in their palaces, there was no reason why his picture of Mary should not be hung with Ledas and what not, and be judged on its merits, or, more probably, on its flaws! And he walked off with his picture..

Fire is in the Flint. (*Ferishtah's Fancies*—opening words of the fifth lyric.)

Flight of the Duchess, The. (*Dramatic Romances and Lyrics*, 1845—in *Bells and Pomegranates*, VII.). When Mr Browning was little more than a child, he heard a woman one Guy Fawkes' Day sing in the street a strange song, whose burden was, "Following the Queen of the Gipsies, O!" The singular refrain haunted his memory for many years, and out of it was ultimately born this poem. There is a strange fascination in the mysterious story, which is told by an old huntsman, who has spent his life in the service of a Duke and his mother at their castle in a land of the North which is an appanage of the German Kaiser. The young Duke's father died when he was a child, and his mother took him in early life to Paris, where they remained till the youth grew to manhood. Returning to the old castle with his head full of mediæval fancies, the Duke upset everybody by his revivals of outlandish customs and feudal fashions, and this in a manner which irritated every one concerned. In course of time the Duchess found a wife for her son—a young, warm-hearted girl from a convent, who won the affection of the servants of the castle, but was treated with coldness and severity by its lord and his "hell-cat" of a mother. Chilled by the want of affection, and neglected by those whose care it should have been to make her happy, the girl sickened, and was visibly pining away. It occurred to the Duke to revive, amongst other old customs, those connected with the hunting of the stag, and a great hunting party on mediæval lines was arranged. In the course of his researches into the customs of mediæval hunting, he discovered that the lady of the castle had a special office to perform when the stag was killed. The authorities said the dame must prick forth on her jennet and preside at the disembowelling. But the poor, mewed-up little duchess, secluded from all the pleasures of life, did not care to be brought out just to play a part in a ceremony for which she had no heart, and thanking the Duke for the intended honour, begged to be excused on account of her ill-health; and so the Duke had to give way, but he sent his mother to scold her. When the hunt began the Duke was sulky and disheartened; as he rode down the valley he met a troop of gipsies on their march, and from the company an old witch came forth to greet the huntsmen. Sidling up to the Duke.

she began to whine and make her appeal for the usual gifts. She said she desired to pay her duty to the beautiful new Duchess, at which the Duke was struck by the idea that he might use the old crone as a means to frighten his wife and make her more submissive, so he bade the huntsman who tells the story conduct the gipsy to the young Duchess. The old hag promised to engage in the project with hearty goodwill, and, quickened by the sight of a purse as the sign of a forthcoming reward, she hobbled off to the castle, and the Duke rejoined his party. The huntsman had a sweetheart at the castle named Jacynth, who conducted the crone to the lady's chamber while he waited without. And now began the mysteries of that eventful day. The maid protested she never could tell what it was that made her fall asleep of a sudden as soon as the gipsy was introduced to her mistress. The huntsman had waited on the balcony for some considerable time, when his attention was arrested by a low musical sound in the chamber of his lady; then he pushed aside the lattice, pulled the curtain, and saw Jacynth asleep along the floor. In the midst of the room, on a chair of state, was the gipsy, transformed to a queen, with her face bent over the lady's head, who was seated at her knees, her face intent on that of the crone. Wondering whether the old woman was banning or blessing the Duchess, he was about to spring in to the rescue, when he was stopped by the strange expression on her face. She was drinking in "Life's pure fire" from the old woman, was becoming transformed by some powerful influence that seemed to stream from the elder to the younger woman; her very tresses shared in the pleasure, her cheeks burned and her eyes glistened. The influence reached the soul of the retainer, and he fell under the potent spell as he listened to the gipsy's words as she told the Duchess she had discovered she was of their race by infallible signs. At last he came to know that his mistress was being bewitched, and he ran to the portal, where he met her, so altered and so beautiful that he felt that whatever had happened was for the best and he had nothing to do but take her commands. He was hers to live or to die, and he preceded his mistress, followed by the gipsy, who had shrunk again to her proper stature. They went to the courtyard, where, as he was desired, he saddled the Duchess's palfrey, which his mistress mounted with the crone behind her; then, putting a little plait of hair into the servant's hand, the Duchess rode off, and they lost her. As the old retainer tells the tale, thirty years have passed since the flight took place. No search was made for the lady; the Duke's pride was wounded, and he would not seek her, and made small inquiry about her. The man says he must see his master through this life, and then he will scrape together his earnings and travel to the land of the gipsies, to find his lady or hear the last of her. Has all this an allegorical meaning? Many have tried to find such in this remarkable poem. But Browning does not teach by allegory: he rather prefers to let events as they actually happen tell their own lessons to minds awakened to receive them. It is not at all difficult, without resorting to allegorical interpretation, to discover what the poem teaches. And in the first place we are taught that a human soul cannot thrive without the living sympathy of its kind. The Duchess was withering under the chill neglect of the hateful mother-in-law and her contemptible son. The bewitchment of the gipsy was the charm of love—the strong, passionate love of a great human heart, enshrined though it was in a witch-like and decrepit frame. The outpouring of the old woman's sympathy on this friendless girl sufficed to transfigure the crone till she became to the huntsman a young and a beautiful queen herself. In the supreme act of perfectly loving, the woman herself became lovely; for there is no rejuvenescence like that which comes from loving others and helping the weak. Then we learn that, as the Duchess seemed to be imbibing new life from the gipsy queen, virtue goes forth from every true lover of his kind, and degrees of rank, education, and station, are no barriers to the magnetism which streams forth from a human heart, however humble, towards another human heart, however highly placed. Life without love is a living death, and the Duchess no more did wrong when she rode off with the gipsy who saw the signs of her people in the marks on her forehead than the flowers do wrong when they bloom at the invitation of the Spring. The sign which the gipsy saw was that of a soul capable of responding to a heart yearning to help it. The girl had a right to human love; she had a right to seek it in a gipsy heart when she could find it nowhere else. In the sermon by Canon Wilberforce preached before the British Medical Association, at their meeting at Bournemouth in 1891, speaking of the power of Jesus over human diseases, the preacher said, "The secret of this power was His perfect sympathy. He violated or suspended no natural laws. . . . His healings were an influential outpouring of that inherent divine life which is latent and in some degree operative in every man, but which existed in fulness and perfection of operation only in Him. Is not this the force of the word " compassion " used of Him? The verb σπλαγχνίζομαι is not found in any former Greek author. It indicates, so far as language can express it, a forceful movement of the whole inward nature towards its object, and personal identification with it. It indicates that compassion and love are not superficial emotions, but dynamic forces." Mrs. Owen, of Cheltenham, read a paper at the meeting of the Browning Society, Nov. 24th, 1882, entitled " What is 'The Flight of the Duchess?' " in which it was suggested that the Duke represents our gross self; the huntsman represents the simple human nature that may either rise with the Duchess or sink with the Duke,—the better man. The Duchess represents the soul, the highest part of our complex nature. The huntsman aids the Duchess (the soul) to free herself from the coarse, low, earth-nature, the Duke. So that the 'Flight of the Duchess' is "the supreme moment when the soul shakes off the bondage of self and finds its true freedom in others." The paper is published in the *Browning Society's Transactions* (Part iv., p. 49*), and is well worthy of study by those who seek a deeper spiritual meaning in " this mystic study of redeemed womanhood " than its primary sense conveys.

NOTES.—Stanza iii., *merlin*, a species of hawk anciently much used in falconry; *falcon-lanner*, a species of long-tailed hawk. vi., *urochs*, wild bulls; *buffle*, buffalo. x., *St. Hubert*, before his conversion, was passionately devoted to hunting: he is the patron saint of hunters; *venerers, prickers, and verderers*, huntsmen, light horsemen, and preservers of the venison. xi., *wind a mort*, to sound a horn at the death of the stag; *a fifty-part canon:* Mr. Browning explained that " a canon, in music, is a piece wherein the subject is repeated in various keys, and, being strictly obeyed in the repetition, becomes the "canon"—the imperative law to what follows. Fifty of such parts would be indeed a notable peal; to manage three is enough of an achievement for a good musician." xiii., *hernshaw*, a heron; *fernshaw*, a fern-thicket; *helicat*, a hag; "*imps the wing of the hawk*": to "imp" means to insert a feather in the broken wing of a bird.

xiv., *tomans*, Persian gold coins. xv., *gor-crow*, the carrion crow. xvii., *morion*, a kind of open helmet. *Orson the wood-knight:* twin-brother of Valentine; born in a wood near Orleans, and carried off by a bear, which suckled him with its cubs. He became the terror of France, and was called "the wild man of the forest."

Flower's Name, The. (*Garden Fancies*, I.—*Dramatic Lyrics.*) [Published in *Hood's Magazine*, July 1844.] With very few exceptions, Browning did not contribute to magazines. At the request of Mr. Monckton Milnes (afterwards Lord Houghton), he sent *The Flower's Name*, *Tokay* and *Sibrandus Schafnaburgensis* to "help in making up some magazine numbers for poor Hood, then at the point of death from hæmorrhage of the lungs, occasioned by the enlargement of the heart, which had been brought on by the wearing excitement of ceaseless and excessive literary toil." A lover visits a garden, and recalls a previous walk therein with the woman he loved; he remembers the flowers which she noticed, especially one whose name—"a soft, meandering Spanish name"—she gave him; he must learn Spanish "only for that slow, sweet name's sake." The very roses are only beautiful so far as they tell her footsteps.

Flower Songs, Italian. (*Fra Lippo Lippi.*) The flower songs in this poem are of the description known as the *stornello*. This is not to be confounded with the *rispetto*, which consists of a stanza of inter-rhyming lines, ranging from six to ten in number. "The Luccan and Umbrian *stornello* is much shorter, consisting indeed of a hemistich having some natural object which suggests the motive of the little poem. The nearest approach to the Italian *stornello* appears to be, not the *rispetto*, but the Welsh *triban*" (*Encyc. Brit.*, xix. 272). See also notes to *Fra Lippo Lippi*.

Flute-music with an Accompaniment. (*Asolando*, 1889.) "Is not outside seeming real as substance inside?" A man hears a bird-like fluting; he wonders what sweet thoughts find expression in such sweet notes. Passion must give birth to such expression. Love, no doubt! Assurance, contentment, sorrow and hope—he detects all these moods in the music, softened and mellowed by the interposing trees. His lady companion brushes away all his fancy-spun notions by telling the prosy fact that the music proceeds from a desk-drudge, who spends the hour of his luncheon with the *Youth's Complete Instructor how to Play the*

Flute, the plain truth being that his hoarse and husky tootlings have not the remotest relation to the romantic ideas with which her male companion has associated them. Distance has altered the sharps to flats; the missing bar was not due to "kissing interruption," but to a blunder in the playing. The man philosophises on this to the effect that, if fancy does everything for us, it matters little what may be the facts. If appearance produces the effect of reality, seeming is as good as being.

Forgiveness, A. (*Pacchiarotto, and other Poems*, 1876.) A man kneels in confession before a monk in a church. He tells the story of a life destroyed by an insane jealousy of his wife, who was innocent of any fault in the matter but some slight deception The penitent was a statesman, happy in the love of wife and home, but neglectful of his duties to both in his absorption in the affairs of his sovereign. Returning home one night, he enters by the private garden way, and sees the veiled figure of a man flying from the house. Before him, as he turns to enter his door, he sees his wife, "stone-still, stone-white." "Kill me!" she cried. "The man is innocent; the fault is mine alone. I love him as I hate you. Strike!" But he refrains from this speedy vengeance: henceforth they act a part before strangers—all goes on as though nothing had happened; alone, they never meet, never speak. Three years of this life pass, when one night the wife demands that the acting shall end; she will explain. "Follow me to my study," he replies. The wife begins, "Since I could die now . . ." and then tells him she had loved him and had lost him through a lie. She had thought he gave away his soul in statecraft; she strung herself therefore, to teach him that the first fool she threw a fond look upon would prize beyond life the treasure which he neglected. It was contempt for the woman which filled his mind now. At this avowal his feeling rose to hate. He made her write her confession in words which he dictated, and with her own blood, drawn by the point of a poisoned poniard. The monk was the woman's lover; the husband killed him also.

Founder of the Feast, The. This was the title of some inedited lines by Browning, written in the album presented to Mr. Arthur Chappell (of the St. James's Hall Saturday and Monday Popular Concerts), April 5th, 1884. They are printed in the Browning Society's *Notes and Queries*, vol. ii., p. 18*.

Fra Lippo Lippi. (*Men and Women*, 1855; Rome, 1853-54.) [THE MAN.] Fra Filippo Lippi (1412-69), the painter, was the son of a butcher in Florence. His mother died while he was a baby, and his father two years later than his mother. His aunt, Monna Lapaccia, took him to her home, but in 1420, when the boy was but eight years old, placed him in the community of the Carmelites of the Carmine in Florence. He stayed at the monastery till 1432, and there became a painter. He seems to have ultimately received a more or less complete dispensation from his religious vows. In 1452 he was appointed chaplain to the convent of S. Giovannino in Florence, and in 1457 he was made rector of S. Quirico at Legnaia. At this time he made a large income; but ever and again fell into poverty, probably on account of the numerous love affairs in which he was constantly indulging. Lippi died at Spoleto on or about Oct. 8th, 1469. Vasari, in his *Lives of the Painters*, tells the whole romantic story of his life.

[THE POEM.] Brother Lippo the painter, working for the munificent House of the Medici, has been mewed up in the Palace, painting saints for Cosimo dei Medici. Unable longer to tolerate the restraint (for he was a dissolute friar, with no vocation for the religious life), he has tied his sheets and counterpane together and let himself out of the window for a night's frolic with the girls whom he heard singing and skipping in the street below. He has been arrested by the watchmen of the city, who noticed his monastic garb, and did not consider it in accord with his present occupation. He is making his defence and bribing them to let him go. He tells them his history: how he was a baby when his mother and father died, and he was left starving in the street, picking up fig skins and melon parings, refuse and rubbish as his only food. One day he was taken to the monastery, and while munching his first bread that month was induced to "renounce the pomps and vanities of this wicked world," and so became a monk at eight years old. They tried him with books, and taught him some Latin; as his hard life had given him abundant opportunity for reading peoples' faces, he found he could draw them in his copybooks, and so began to make pictures everywhere. The Prior noticed this, and thought he detected genius, and would not hear of turning the boy out: he might become a great painter and "do our church up fine," he said. So the lad prospered; he began to draw the monks—the fat, the lean, the black, the white; then the folks at church. But he was too realistic in his work: his faces, arms and legs were too true to nature, and the Prior shook his head—

> "And stopped all that in no time."

He told him his business was to paint men's souls and forget there was such a thing as flesh:

> "Paint the soul, never mind the legs and arms!"

And so they made him rub all out. The painter asks if this was sense:

> "A fine way to paint soul, by painting body
> So ill, the eye can't stop there, must go further
> And can't fare worse!"

He maintained that if we get beauty we get the best thing God invents. But he rubs out his picture and paints what they like, clenching his teeth with rage the while; but sometimes, when a warm evening finds him painting saints, the revolt is complete, and he plays the fooleries they have caught him at. He knows he is a beast, but he can appreciate the beauty, the wonder and the power in the shapes of things which God has made to make us thankful for them. They are not to be passed over and despised, but dwelt upon and wondered at, and painted too, for we must count it crime to let a truth slip. We are so made that we love things first when we see them painted, though we have passed them over unnoticed a hundred times before—

> "And so they are better, painted—better to us.
> Art was given for that."

"The world is no blot for us, nor blank; it means intensely, and means good." "Ah, but," says the Prior, "your work does not make people pray!" "But a skull and cross-bones are sufficient for that; you don't need art at all." . . . . And then the poor monk begs the guard not to report him: he will make amends for the offence done to the Church; give him six months' time, he will paint such a picture for a convent! It will please the nuns. "So six months hence. Good-bye! No lights: I know my way back!"

NOTES.—"*The Carmine's my cloister*," the monastery of the friars Del Carmine, where Fra LIPPO was brought up. "*Cosimo of the Medici"* (1389-1464), the great Florentine statesman, who was called the "Father of his country." *Saint Laurence* = San Lorenzo at Florence, the church which contains the Medici tombs and several of Michael Angelo's pictures. "*Droppings of the wax to sell again*": in Catholic countries, where many wax torches are used, the wax drippings are carefully gathered by the poor boys to sell; in Spain they pick up even the ends of the wax vestas used by smokers at the bull fights for the same purpose. *The Eight*, the magistrates who governed Florence. *Antiphonary*, the Roman Service-Book, containing all that is sung in the choir—the antiphons, responses, etc.; it was compiled by Gregory the Great. *Carmelites*, monks of the Order of Mount Carmel in Syria; established in the twelfth century. *Camaldolese*, an order of monks founded by St. Romualdo in 1027; the name is derived from the family who owned the land on which the first monastery was built—the *Campo Maldoli*. "*Preaching Friars*": the Dominicans, established by St. Dominic; the name of the "Brothers Preachers" or "Friars Preachers" was given them by Pope Innocent III. in 1215. *Giotto*, a great architect and painter (1266-1337); he was a friend of Dante. *Brother Angelico* = Fra Angelico; his real name was Giovanni da Fiesole; he was the famous religious painter, painting the soul and disregarding the flesh; he was said to paint some of his devotional pictures on his knees. *Brother Lorenzo*, Don Lorenzo *Monaco* = the monk; he was a great painter, of the Order of the Camaldolese. *Guidi* = Tommaso Guidi or Masaccio, nicknamed *Hulking Tom*, was a painter, born 1401; he "laboured," says the chronicler, in "nakeds." "*A St. Laurence at Prato*," near Florence, where are frescoes by Lippi: St. Laurence suffered martyrdom by being burned upon a gridiron; he bore it with such fortitude, says the legend, that he cried to his tormentors to turn him over, as he "was done on one side." *Chianti wine*, a famous wine of Tuscany. *Sant' Ambrogio's* = Saint Ambrose's at Florence. "*I shall paint God in the midst, Madonna and her babe*": the beautiful picture of the Coronation of the Virgin in the Accademia delle Belle Arti at Florence is the one referred to in these lines. The Browning Society in 1882 published a very fine photograph of this great work, by Alinari Brothers of Florence. The flower songs in the poem are of the variety known as the *stornelli*; the peasants of Tuscany sing these songs at their work, "and as one ends a song another caps it with a fresh one, and so they go on vying with each other. These *stornelli* consist of three lines. The first usually contains the name of a flower, which sets the rhyme, and is five syllables long. Then the love theme is told in two lines of eleven syllables each, agreeing by rhyme, assonance, or repetition with the first." [See *Poet Lore*, vol. ii., p. 262. Miss R. H. Busk's "Folk Songs of Italy," and Miss Strettel's "Spanish and Italian Folk Songs."]

Francesco Romanelli (*Beatrice Signorini*), the artist who paints Artemisia's portrait, which his wife destroys in a fit of jealousy.

Francis Furini, Parleyings with. (*Parleyings with Certain People of Importance in their Day*: 1887.) [THE MAN.] "Francis Furini was born in 1600 at Florence, and has been styled the 'Albani' and the 'Guido' of the Florentine school. At the age of forty he took orders, and until his death in 1649 remained an exemplary parish priest. In his earlier days he was especially famous for his painting of the nude figure; his drawing is remarkably graceful, but the colour is defective. One of his French biographers complains that he paints the nude too well to be quite proper, and points to the 'Adam and Eve,' in the Pitti Palace as a proof of this statement. Perhaps the painter thought so too, for there is a tradition that on his death-bed he desired all his undraped pictures to be collected and destroyed. His wishes were not carried out, and few private galleries at Florence are without pictures by him." (*Pall Mall Gazette*, January 18th, 1887.)

[THE POEM.] In the opening lines we are introduced to the good pastor, the painter-priest who lived two hundred and fifty years ago at Florence, and fed his flock with spiritual food while he helped their bodily necessities. The picture is a pleasant one, but the poet deals not with the pastor but the artist; and this painter of the nude has been selected by Browning as a text on which to express the sentiments of artists on the subject of,—

"The dear
Fleshly perfection of the human shape,"

as a gospel for mankind. When Mr. Browning writes on and

we have, as Mr. Symons expresses it, "painting refined into song." The lines in the seventh canto beginning—

> "Bounteous God,
> Deviser and dispenser of all gifts
> To soul through sense,—in art the soul uplifts
> Man's best of thanks!"

aptly define the poet's position in the passionate defence of the nude as his art-gospel. As we are intended to admire God's handiwork in the "naked star," so is "the naked female form' declared to be—

> "God's best of bounteous and magnificent,
> Revealed to earth."

Should any object that "the naked female form," however beautiful, is not perhaps the best thing to display in the shop windows of the Rue de Rivoli or Regent Street, he is set down as "a grubber for pig-nuts," like Filippo Baldinucci, who praises the painter-priest for ordering his pictures of the nude to be destroyed. Mr. Browning deals very severely with those who think that pictures of the nude have a deleterious influence on the public character, and who endeavour to prevent their exhibition. It is instructive, however, to notice the fact that the Paris police are adopting even severer measures than our own against shopkeepers and others who exhibit pictures of the nude. Where the governing bodies of the two greatest cities of the world take the same view of this serious moral question, we must take leave to hold that if "the gospel of art" has no better means whereby to elevate the race than those of familiarising our youth of both sexes with—

> "The dear
> Fleshly perfection of the human shape,"

we can very well afford to dispense with it. "Omnia non omnibus," concludes the poet. What is perfectly innocent for the artist is not expedient for the general public, just as the dissecting room, though an excellent school for doctors, is not a suitable place for the people in the street below.

NOTES.—*Baldinucci*, author of the Italian *History of Art*,—he was a friend of Furini, and it is from his biography that Browning has derived the facts recorded in his poem. *Quicherat, J.*, edited the *Procès de condamnation et de réhabilitation de Jeanne d'Arc*, in five vols., 1841-9. *D'Alençon—Percival de Cagny*, a retainer of the Duke D'Alençon, who wrote an account of Joan of Arc, which is to be found in the fourth volume of Quicherat.

Fuseli. See MARY WOLLSTONECRAFT AND FUSELI.

Fust and his Friends (The Epilogue *to Parleyings*.) The scene is laid "*Inside the home of Fust, Mayence*, 1457." Johann Fust is often considered the inventor, or at least one of the inventors of printing. He was born at Mayence, in Germany, in the early part of the fifteenth century (date uncertain). The name ultimately became Faust. It has been said that Fust was a goldsmith, but there is no evidence of this. He was a money-lender or speculator, and was connected with Gutenberg, who is now considered to have been the real inventor of printing. Some however, say that Fust invented typography, and was the partner of Gutenberg, to whom he advanced the means to carry out his invention. On Fust first showing his printed books he was suspected of magic, as he appears to have concealed the method by which he turned them out. There is no proof that the monks were hostile to printing, or that they resented the new process of multiplying books on the ground of interference with their business as copyists. Fust and Gutenberg were on good terms with several monasteries, and the early printers often set up their presses in religious houses of various orders. It is exceedingly probable that the whole magic story arose from the similarity between the names Fust and Faust, the pupil of the devil. Browning in this poem accepts the Fust story of the invention of printing. Fust is visited by some monks, who, having heard confused accounts of his work, have come to the conclusion that he has made a compact with Satan, and is in danger of losing his soul; they prepare to exorcise the demon, but cannot remember the proper formula, and make amusing mistakes in their repeated attempts to capture the appropriate Latin terms of the exorcism. They find the inventor melancholy and depressed: he has not succeeded in perfecting his machinery; but while they argue with him the right process suddenly dawns upon him, and invoking the aid of Archimedes (thought by the monks to be a devil of some sort), he runs to his printing room, and in five minutes returns with the psalm which they could not remember accurately printed on slips of paper, one of which he hands to each of the friars. Fust then shows them the printing press, and explains the use of the types and blocks, bursting out into a noble hymn of praise to God for having enabled him to bless mankind with his invention. The monks find it exceedingly simple, and perceive there is no miracle at all. They doubt whether the invention will prove an unmixed blessing for the Church, and dread the trash which will come flying from Jew, Moor and Turk. Huss declared in dying that a swan would succeed the goose they were burning. Fust says he foresees such a man. (*Huss* means goose in the dialect he spoke. The swan of whom he prophesied was Luther.)

NOTES.—*Faust* and *Fust:* these names were often confounded, when people thought printing a diabolical art. *Palinodes*, songs repeated a second time. "*Barnabites and Dominican experts*": The Barnabites as a religious order were inferior in learning and theological attainments to the Dominicans, who were experts in matters of heresy. *Famulus*, a servant, an attendant. "*Ne pulvis et ignis*": Latin words misquoted from some monastic exorcism which the monks have half forgotten. "*Asmodeus inside of a Hussite*," the devil animating the heretic Hussite or follower of Huss. "*Pou sto*," *point d'appui:* Archimedes said, "Give me *pou sto* ('a place to stand on'), and I could move the world."

Future State, A. Mr. Browning's belief in the doctrine of a future state of reward and punishment is expressed at great length and with much force in *La Saisiaz*.

Garden Fancies. (Published in *Hood's Magazine*, July 1844.) I. *The Flower's Name.* The poem describes a garden wherein to a lover's fancy every shrub and flower is hallowed by the looks and touch of the woman he loves. One flower in particular she named by its "soft meandering Spanish name." He bids the buds she touched to stay as they are, never to open, but to be loved for ever. Even the roses are not so fair after all, compared with the "shut pink mouth" her fingers have touched. In II., *Sibrandus Schafnaburgensis*, we have a garden without romance. A student takes amongst the flowers a pedantic old volume, a treatise as dry and crabbed as its title. He read it; then, for his revenge, threw the book into the crevice of a plum tree, amongst the fungi, the moss, and creeping things. Solacing himself with bread and cheese and wine, he read the jolly Rabelais to rid his brain of cobwebs. In process of time the student came to think he had been too severe with the old author, so he fished him up with a rake and put him in an appropriate place on the library shelves, there to dry-rot at ease.

Galuppi, Baldassarre. A musical composer (1706-85). See TOCCATA OF GALUPPI'S, A.

George Bubb Dodington, Parleyings with. (*Parleyings with Certain People of Importance in their Day*, 1887.) THE MAN.] "George Bubb Dodington (born 1691, died 1762) was the son of a gentleman of good fortune named Bubb. He was educated at Oxford, elected member of Parliament for Winchelsea in 1715, and soon after sent as envoy to Madrid. In 1720 he inherited the estate of Eastbury, in Dorsetshire, and took the name of Dodington. On his entrance into public life he connected himself with Sir Robert Walpole, to whom he addressed a poetic epistle, which later on he made, by changing the name, to serve for Lord Bute. His career was full of political vicissitudes of the most discreditable kind, by which he managed to obtain a considerable share of the prizes of politics. He held various offices, chiefly in connection with the navy, to which he was more than once treasurer. It was from Lord Bute, with whom he was a great favourite, that he received the title of Lord Melcombe. He loved to surround himself with the distinguished men of the day, whom he entertained at his country seat; and his interesting diary is a storehouse of information about the political intrigues and cabals of the time. Pope and Churchill both wrote in abuse of him, and Hogarth immortalised his wig in his *Orders of Periwigs*." (*Pall Mall Gazette*, Jan. 18th, 1887.)

[THE POEM.] Mr. Symons describes this as "a piece of sardonic irony long drawn out," and as a "Superior Rogues' Guide or Instructions for Knaves." Browning satirically tells Dodington that he went the wrong way to work in his attempts to impose upon the world. Admitting the right of the statesman to "feather his own nest" while pretending to care only for the public weal, because even the birds build the kind of nests that suit their own convenience, without regard to other species, he yet declares there is a right and a wrong way even in deceiving people. "You say, my Lord, that the rabble will not believe and follow you unless you lie boldly, and pretend to be animated only by the desire to serve them; but the rabble tell lies for their own purposes daily, and understand the art as well as you do, and as no man obeys his equal, you must produce something which outdoes in this respect anything with which they are familiar." Browning offers him a hint: wit has replaced force, now intelligence in its turn must go. "You must have a touch of the supernatural, you must awe men—not by miracles, they will not be accepted—but still, you must pretend to some secret and mysterious power, pretend that, though you know you have fools to deal with, there are some wise men amongst them who are not to be deceived, and each man will flatter himself that he is one of these. . . . Persuade the people that your real character was merely an assumed one. Pretend to despise, not them, but yourself. That will make men think you obey some law, 'quite above man's—nay, God's!' Missing this secret, your name is greeted with scorn."

NOTE.—*The Bower-bird:* the name given to certain birds of the genera Ptilorhynchus and Chlamydera, which are ranked under the starling family. They are found in Australia. They are called bower-birds because they build bowers as well as nests.

Gerard. (*A Blot in the 'Scutcheon.*) Lord Tresham's faithful and trusted man-servant.

Gerard de Lairesse, Parleyings with. (*Parleyings with Certain People of Importance in their Day:* 1877, No. VI.) [THE MAN.] "Gerard de Lairesse, a Flemish painter, was born at Liége in 1640. He early began his career, and produced portraits and historical pictures at the age of fifteen. He was of dissipated life, extravagant, and fond of dress, notwithstanding that he was of deformed figure. The Dutch admired him very much, and modestly called him their 'second Raphael,' Heemskirk being the first. He painted for many years at Amsterdam, and towards the close of his life was much troubled by his eyesight, which several times left him. He died in 1711. Very fond of teaching, he was always ready to communicate his method to students, and his name is associated with a *Treatise on the Art of Painting*, which it is not, however, thought that he wrote. His execution was very rapid, and there is a story told that he made a wager that he would paint, in one day, a large picture of Apollo and the Muses, and that he not only gained the wager, but painted into the picture a capital portrait of a curious bystander. His method of work was eccentric: he would prepare his canvas, and, sitting down before it, take up his violin and play for some time; then, putting down the instrument, he would rapidly sketch in the picture, and again resuming the fiddle, would derive fresh inspiration from the music." (*Pall Mall Gazette*, Jan. 18th, 1887.)

[The Poem.] Browning rejoices that, though Gerard had lost his sight, his mouth was unsealed and "talked all brain's yearning into birth." He prizes his saying that the artist should discern abundant worth in commonplace, and not despise the vulgar things of town and country as unworthy of his art. Beyond the actual, he taught there was ever "Imagination's limitless domain": even dull Holland to him became Dreamland. And so in that great "Walk" of his, written after his blindness, he could evolve greater things than we with all our sight. Perhaps his sealed sight-sense left his mind free from obstruction to indulge fancies "worth all facts denied by fate." But though we cannot see what the poets of old saw in nature when they invested trees with human attributes, and yet lost no gain of the tree, "we see deeper." "You," says Browning, "saw the body,—'tis the soul we see." We can fancy, too, though fact unseen has taken the place of fancy somehow. Poets never go back at all: if the past become more precious than the present, then blame the Creator! But it can never be so. He invites Gerard to 'walk with him and see what a poet of the present time discerns in the face of Nature, in her varying moods from daybreak till the shades of night. Then follows a series of magnificent descriptions of a thunderstorm in the mountains, the defiant pine tree daring all the outrage of the lightning. Then the laugh of morning, the baffled tempest, the trees shaking off the night stupor from their strangled branches. Diana, with her bow and unerring shaft; for gentle creatures, even on a morn so blithe, must writhe in pain—so pitiless is Nature still! And then the conquering noon: the mist ascends to heaven, and the filmy haze soothes the sun's sharp glare till tyrannous noon reigns supreme. And when at last the long day dies, clouds like hosts confronting each other for battle come trooping silent. Two shapes from out the mass show prominent, as if the Macedonian flung his purple mantle on the dead

Darius. And now the darkness gathers, the human heroes tread the world of cloud no longer. 'Tis a ghost appears on earth:

> "There he stands,
> Voiceless, scarce strives with deprecating hands."

But, says Browning, though we to-day could paint Nature in thi manner in the colours of the Past, we rather prefer "the all including, the all-reconciling Future:

> 'Let things be—not seem,
> Do, and nowise dream.'

Sad school was Hades! Let it be granted that death is the last and worst of man's calamities: come what come will—what once lives never dies."

NOTES.—2. "*The Walk*": this was the title of a part of Gerard's work entitled *The Art of Painting*, by Gerard de Lairesse, translated by J. S. Fritsch, 1778. 5. *Dryope:* the fable of Dryope turned into a tree is told in Ovid's *Metamorphoses*, book ix. 9. *Artemis*, Diana, the huntress goddess. 10. *Lyda*, a nymph beloved by Pan, but who disdained his uncouth pathos. 11. *Macedonian:* Alexander, king of Macedonia, invaded Persia, and was met by Darius with an army of 600,000 men. Alexander defeated them, and Darius was slain by the traitor Bessus. Alexander covered the dead body with his own royal mantle, and honoured it with a magnificent funeral.

Gigadibs, Mr. (*Bishop Blougram's Apology.*) He is a young man of thirty—immature, desultory, and impulsive—who criticises Bishop Blougram's life, and serves to draw out his ideas on his religion and the honesty of his religious conduct.

Give a Rouse. (*Cavalier Tunes*, No. II.)

"Give her but the least excuse to love me." (*Pippa Passes.*) The song which Pippa sings as she passes the house of Jules.

Glove, The. [PETER RONSARD *loquitur.*] (*Dramatic Romances and Lyrics* in *Bells and Pomegranates*, VII., 1845.) This is an old French story of the time of Francis I. It is familiar in various forms to students of literature, and may be found in Schiller, Leigh Hunt, and St. Foix. Mr. Browning, as is his wont, does not tell the story for the sake of telling it, but that he may give a new turn to it and point out something which has been overlooked, but which, on reflection, will always prove to be the precise truth to be conveyed by the narration. The Peter Ronsard who tells the tale was born in 1524, and was called the 'prince of poets" by his own generation. He was educated at the Collége de Navarre at Paris, and was page to the Duke of Orleans. He was afterwards attached to the suite of Cardinal du Bellay-Langey. He became deaf, and in consequence gave up diplomacy for literature. He published his *Amours* and some odes in 1552. Charles IX. gave him rooms in his palace. He died in 1585. The story of the poem is as follows. King Francis I. was one day amusing himself by viewing the lions in his courtyard, in company with the lords and ladies of the palace. The king bade his keeper make sport with an old lion, which was let out of his den to fight in the pit, the spectators being secured by a barrier. The king said, "Faith, gentlemen, we are better here than there." De Lorge's lady-love overheard this, and she thought it a good opportunity to test the courage of her lover, so she dropped her glove over the barrier amongst the lions, at the same time smiling to De Lorge the command to jump down and recover it. This was speedily done, but the lover threw the glove in the lady's face. The king approved this course, and said, "So should I: 'twas mere vanity, not love, which set that task to humanity!" Mr. Browning brings his analysis to bear on this exploit, and shows that the test was not the outcome of mere idle trifling with a man's life to flatter a woman's vanity. She desired to try as in a crucible the real meaning of the protestations made by De Lorge; it was necessary for her to know if her lover was going to serve her alone or many. He had offered to brave endless descriptions of death for her sake. When she saw the lions, for whose capture many poor men had dared death with no spectators to applaud, she felt justified in asking this of her lover before she trusted herself in his hands for life. A youth led her away from the scene. She carried her shame from the court, and married the man who protected her from further mockery. Of course De Lorge was at once the favourite both of women and men. He married a beauty. The Clement Marot referred to in the poem was a famous poet of France (1496-1544), and greatly distinguished in her literary history.

God. Browning's noblest utterances on God are to be found in

Christmas Eve, *Easter Day*, "The Pope" in *The Ring and the Book*, and *Paracelsus.*

Goito Castle (*Sordello*), near Mantua, where Sordello was brought up by Adelaide, wife of Ecelin, with Palma, daughter of Ecelin by a former wife. Sordello lived at Goito in seclusion and boyish pleasures till he was nearly twenty years old.

Gold Hair: A Legend of Pornic. (*Dramatis Personæ*, 1864.) The poem is said by Mr. Orr to be founded on facts well known at Pornic, a seaside town in Brittany. A young girl well connected died with a great reputation for holiness. She had beautiful golden hair, of which she was very proud. She begged that it might not be disturbed after her death, and she was buried with it intact near the high altar of the church of St. Gilles. Some years after it became necessary to repair the floor of the church in the proximity of the maiden's tomb. It was found that the coffin had fallen to pieces, and a gold coin was noticed, which led to a more careful examination of the spot. Thirty double louis-d'or were discovered, which had been hidden by the girl in her hair, thus proving that the supposed saint was at heart a miser. "Gold goes through all doors except heaven's doors"; and for this the girl had lost her heaven. In Stanza xxviii. Mr. Browning teaches a lesson of which he is never weary:—

> "Evil or good may be better or worse
> In the human heart, but the mixture of each
> Is a marvel and a curse."

Original sin, the innate corruption of man's heart, is illustrated says the poet, by this girl's avarice. The priest built a new altar with the discovered money.

Goldoni. (Published first in the *Pall Mall Gazette*, Dec. 8th, 1883; then in the *Browning Society's Papers.*) Carlo Goldoni (1707-93) was the most illustrious of the Italian comedy-writers, and the real founder of modern Italian comedy. He had a pension from the French King Louis XVI., which he lost at the Revolution, and he was reduced to the extremest misery. A monument was erected to him at Venice in 1883, and Browning wrote for the album of the Goldoni monument the following lines:—

> "Goldoni,—good, gay, sunniest of souls,—
> Glassing half Venice in that verse of thine,—
> What though it just reflect the shade and shine

Of common life, nor render, as it rolls,
Grandeur and gloom? Sufficient for thy shoals
Was Carnival: Parini's depths enshrine
Secrets unsuited to that opaline
Surface of things which laughs along thy scrolls.
There throng the People: how they come and go,
Lisp the soft language, flaunt the bright garb,—see,—
On Piazza, Calle, under Portico
And over Bridge! Dear king of Comedy,
Be honoured! Thou that didst love Venice so—
Venice, and we who love her, all love thee!

(VENICE, *Nov.* 27th, 1883.)

"Good to Forgive." (*La Saisiaz.*) The epilogue to *La Saisiaz* begins with these words. In Vol. II. of the *Selections* the poem forms No. 3 of *Pisgah Sights.*

Gottingen. The university town in Germany to a lecture hall in which Christ went in the vision on *Christmas Eve.* Here a consumptive lecturer was "demolishing the Christ-myth," but advising the audience to lose nothing of the Christ idea.

Grammarian's Funeral, A, shortly after the Revival of Learning in Europe. (*Men and Women*, 1855; *Romances*, 1863; *Dramatic Romances*, 1868.) Mr. Browning often describes a man as a typical product of his age and environment, and invests him with its characteristics, making him figure as an historical personage. He has done so in this case, and we seem to know the grammarian in all his pedantry and exclusive devotion to a minute branch of human knowledge. The revival of learning, after the apparent death-blow which it received when the hordes of Northern barbarism overran Southern Europe and destroyed the civilisation of the Roman empire, began in the tenth century—that century which, as Hallam says (*Lit. Europe*, i. 10), "used to be reckoned by mediæval historians the darkest part of this intellectual night." In the twelfth century much greater improvement was made. The attention of Europe was drawn to literature in this century, says Hallam, by, "1st, the institution of universities; 2nd, the cultivation of the modern languages, followed by the multiplication of books and the extension of the art of writing; 3rd, the investigation of the Roman law; and lastly, the return to the study of the Latin language in its ancient models of purity." All these factors were at work and progressing gradually down to the fifteenth century. A company of the grammarian's disciples are bearing his coffin for burial on a tall mountain, the appropriate lofty place of sepulture for an elevated man. As they carry the body, one of them tells his story, and dilates on the praises of the departed scholar. They cannot fitly bury their master in the plain with the common herd. Nor will a lower peak suffice: he shall rest on a peak whose soaring excels the rest. This high-seeking man is for the morning land, and as they bear him up the rocky heights they step together to a tune with heads erect, proud of their noble burden. He was endowed with graces of face and form; but youth had been given to learning till he had become cramped and withered. This man would eat up the feast of learning even to its crumbs. He would live a great life when he had learned all that books had to teach; meanwhile he despised what other men termed life. Before living he would learn how to live:—

"Leave Now for dogs and apes!
Man has Forever."

Deeper he bent over his books, racked by the stone (*calculus*): bronchitis (*tussis*) attacked him; but still he refused to rest. He had a sacred thirst. He magnified the mind, and let the body decay uncared for. That he long lived nameless, that he even failed, was nothing to him. He wanted no payment by instalment; he could afford to wait, and thus even in the death-struggle he "ground at grammar." And so where the

"Lightnings are loosened,
Stars come and go!"

this lofty man was left "loftily lying."

NOTES.—*Hotis' business*, *Properly based Oun*, *Enclitic De*. these are points in Greek grammar concerning which grammarians have written learned treatises.

Greek Poems. Mr. Browning had a peculiar power in rendering the ideas of the great Greek poets into strong resonant English verse. His lovely *Balaustion's Adventure*, the fascinating and picturesque *Aristophanes' Apology*, with the *Herakles* of Euripides, and the rough, robust, and perhaps over-literal *Agamemnon* of Æschylus, at once proclaim the Greek scholar and the English master-poet. Some extracts from Professor Mahaffy's criticism of Mr. Browning's Greek translations are given below from his *History of Classical Greek Literature*, vol. i. On the transcription of the *Agamemnon* (p. 258): "Mr. Robert Browning has given us an over-faithful version from his matchless hand,—matchless, I conceive, in conveying the deeper spirit of the Greek poets. But, in this instance, he has outdone his original in ruggedness, owing to his excess of conscience as a translator" (p. 277). Mr. Browning has turned his genius for reproducing Greek plays upon this masterpiece, and has given a version which will probably not permit the rest [Miss Anna Swanwick's, Mr. Morshead's, etc.] to maintain their well-earned fame, though it is in itself so difficult that the Greek original is often required for translating his English. I confess that, even with this aid, which shows the extraordinary faithfulness of the work, I had preferred a more Anglicised version from his master-hand." On the transcription of *Alcestis* (p. 329): "By far the best translation is Mr. Browning's, in his *Balaustion's Adventure;* but it is much to be regretted that he did not render the choral odes into lyric verse. No one has more thoroughly appreciated the mean features of *Admetus* and *Pheres*, and their dramatic propriety" (note, p. 335). On the transcription of *The Raging Hercules* (p. 348): "We can now recommend the admirable translation in Mr. Browning's *Aristophanes' Apology*, as giving English readers a thoroughly faithful idea of this splendid play. The choral odes are, moreover, done justice to, and translated into adequate metre—in this, an improvement on the *Alcestis*, to which I have already referred." Speaking afterwards, of the *Helena* of Euripides, Mr. Mahaffy remarks (p. 353): "The choral odes are quite in the poet's later style, full of those repetitions of words which Aristophanes derides,"—and he adds in a note: "Mr. Browning has not failed to reproduce this Euripidean feature with great art and admirable effect in his version of the *Herakles*." . . . p. 466: "Nothing is more cleverly ridiculed [in *Aristophanes*] than those repetitions of the same word which occur in the pathetic lyrical passages of Euripides. The modern poet, who best understands Euripides, has followed his example in this point:—

'Dances, dances, and banqueting,
To Thebes, the sacred city, through
Are a care! for change and change

Of tears and laughter, old to new,
Our lays, glad birth, they bring, they bring.'
Aristophanes' Apology, p. 266.

There are many more instances in this version of the *Hercules Furens*. This allusion to Mr. Browning suggests the remark that he has treated the controversy between Euripides and Aristophanes with more learning and ability than all other critics, in his '*Aristophanes' Apology*,' which is, by the way, an '*Euripides' Apology*' also, if such be required in the present day."

Guardian Angel, The: A Picture at Fano. (*Men and Women*, 1855; *Lyrics*, 1863.) Fano is a city of Italy in the province of Urbino-e-Pasaro. It is situated on the shores of the Adriatic, in a fertile plain at the mouth of the Metauro. Its population in 1871 was 6439. The splendid tombs of the Malatestas are contained in the church of St. Francesco. The cathedral and other churches possess valuable pictures by Domenichino, Guido, etc. The picture referred to in the poem is in the church of St. Augustine. It was painted by Guercino (so called from his squinting), properly called Giovanni Francesco Barbieri, who was born at Cento, near Bologna, in 1590. His first style was formed after that of the Carracci; he fell later under the influence of Caravaggio, whose strong colouring and shadows greatly impressed his mind. The nobles and princes of Italy, and his brother artists, very highly esteemed Guercino's work, and they classed him in the first rank of painters. He worked very rapidly, completing 106 large altar-pieces for churches, besides 144 other pictures. His greatest work is said to be his Sta. Petronilla, which is now in the Capitol at Rome. Guercino died in 1666, having amassed a large fortune by his labours. There is a good photograph of L'Angelo Custode, in the *Illustrations to Browning's Poems*, part i., published by the Browning Society. An angel with wings outspread is standing in a protecting attitude by a little child, and the angel's left arm embraces the infant, while the right hand encloses the hands of the child clasped in prayer. Cherubs look down from the clouds. In Guercino's first sketch of his Angel and Child, the angel points to heaven with his left hand, while he enfolds the child's hands with his right. Mr. Browning was staying at Ancona. He was greatly impressed by the picture, and forgetting that we all have a guardian angel, overlooked his own, and prayed, good Protestant as he was, to Guercino's angel to protect and direct him when he had done with the child. He, however, recognised Mrs. Browning as his own guardian angel, and with her went three times to see the painting. The Alfred referred to in Stanza vi. was Mr. Alfred Dommett, the Waring of the poem of that name. Mr. Dommett was then in New Zealand, by the Wairoa river of Stanza viii. Not only the consolatory doctrine of Holy Scripture and the Church as to the ministry of angels, but the soothing and elevating influence of religious art in conveying what words would fail to teach half so impressively, are well emphasised by Mr. Browning's poem. The beautiful figure "Bird of God" is from Dante (*Purgatorio*, Canto iv.).

Guelfs and Ghibellines. (*Sordello.*) The poem of *Sordello* is so full of references to the wars between the Guelfs and Ghibellines, that a knowledge of the origin of this celebrated feud will help to throw light on some paragraphs in the poem. Longfellow, in his notes to Dante's *Inferno*, gives the story:—"The following account of the Guelfs and Ghibellines is from the *Pecorone* of Giovanni Fiorentino, a writer of the fourteenth century. It forms the first Novella of the Eighth Day, and will be found in Roscoe's *Italian Novelists*, i. 322. 'There formerly resided in Germany two wealthy and well-born individuals, whose names were Guelfo and Ghibellino, very near neighbours, and greatly attached to each other. But returning together one day from the chase, there unfortunately arose some difference of opinion as to the merits of one of their hounds, which was maintained on both sides so very warmly that, from being almost inseparable friends and companions, they became each other's deadliest enemies. This unlucky division between them still increasing, they on either side collected parties of their followers, in order more effectually to annoy each other. Soon extending its malignant influence among the neighbouring lords and barons of Germany, who divided, according to their motives, either with the Guelf or the Ghibelline, it not only produced many serious affrays, but several persons fell victims to its rage. Ghibellino, finding himself hard pressed by his enemy, and unable longer to keep the field against him, resolved to apply for assistance to Frederick I., the reigning emperor. Upon this, Guelfo, perceiving that his adversary sought the alliance of this monarch, applied on his side to Pope Honorius II., who being at variance with the former, and hearing how the affair stood, immediately joined the cause of the Guelfs, the emperor having already embraced that of the Ghibellines. It is thus that the apostolic see became connected with the former, and the empire with the latter faction; and it was thus that a vile hound became the origin of a deadly hatred between the two noble families. Now, it happened that in the year of our dear Lord and Redeemer 1215, the same pestiferous spirit spread itself into parts of Italy, in the following manner. Messer Guido Orlando being at that time chief magistrate of Florence, there likewise resided in that city a noble and valiant cavalier of the family of Buondelmonti, one of the most distinguished houses in the state. Our young Buondelmonte having already plighted his troth to a lady of the Amidei family, the lovers were considered as betrothed, with all the solemnity usually observed on such occasions. But this unfortunate young man, chancing one day to pass by the house of the Donati, was stopped and accosted by a lady of the name of Lapaccia, who moved to him from her door as he went along, saying: "I am surprised that a gentleman of yuor appearance, Signor, should think of taking for his wife a woman scarcely worthy of handing him his boots. There is a child of my own, whom, to speak sincerely, I have long intended for you, and whom I wish you would just venture to see." And on this she called out for her daughter, whose name was Ciulla, one of the prettiest and most enchanting girls in all Florence. Introducing her to Messer Buondelmonte, she whispered, "This is she whom I have reserved for you"; and the young Florentine, suddenly becoming enamoured of her, thus replied to her mother, "I am quite ready, Madonna, to meet your wishes"; and before stirring from the spot he placed a ring upon her finger, and, wedding her, received her there as his wife. The Amidei, hearing that young Buondelmonte had thus espoused another, immediately met together, and took counsel with other friends and relations, how they might best avenge themselves for such an insult offered to their house. There were present among the rest Lambertuccio Amidei, Schiatta Ruberti, and Mosca Lamberti, one of whom proposed to give him a box on the ear, another to strike him in the face; yet they were none of them able to agree about it among themselves. On observing this, Mosca hastily arose, in a great passion, saying, "Cosa fatta capo ha," wishing it to be understood that a dead man will never strike again. It was therefore decided that he should be put to death, a sentence which they proceeded to execute in the following manner: M. Buondelmonte returning one Easter morning from a visit to the Casa Bardi, beyond the Arno, mounted upon a snow-white steed, and dressed in a mantle of the same colour, had just reached the foot of the Ponte Vecchio, or old bridge, where formerly stood a statue of Mars, whom the Florentines in their pagan state were accustomed to worship, when the whole party issued out upon him, and, dragging him in the scuffle from his horse, in spite of the gallant resistance he made, despatched him with a thousand wounds. The tidings of this affair seemed to throw all Florence into confusion; the chief personages and noblest families in the place everywhere meeting, and dividing themselves into parties in consequence; the one party embracing the cause of the Buondelmonti, who placed themselves at the head of the Guelfs; and the other taking part with the Amidei, who supported the Ghibellines. In the same fatal manner, nearly all the seigniories and cities of Italy were involved in the original quarrel between these two German families: the Guelfs still supporting the interests of the Holy Church, and the Ghibellines those of the Emperor. And thus I have made you acquainted with the history of the Germanic faction, between two noble houses, for the sake of a vile cur, and have shown how it afterwards disturbed the peace of Italy for the sake of a beautiful woman.'"

Gwendolen Tresham. (*A Blot in the 'Scutcheon.*) The cousin of Mildred Tresham.

Gypsy. (*The Flight of the Duchess.*) The old crone who is sent by the Duke to frighten the Duchess, and who rescues her from her unhappy life.

Hakeem or **Hakem.** (*Return of the Druses.*) He was the chief of the Druses. The first hakeem was the Fatimite Caliph B'amr-ellah. He professed to be the incarnate deity. He was slain near Cairo, in Egypt, on Mount Makattam.

Halbert and Hob. (*Dramatic Idyls,* First Series, 1879.) Two men, father and son, of brutal type, and the last of their line, are sitting quarrelling one Christmas night in their homestead. High words, followed by taunts and curses, led to an attack on the father by his furious son, who flew at his throat with the intention of casting him out in the snow. The father was strong and could have held his own in the scuffle, but suddenly all power left him: he was struck mute. This still more enraged the son, who pulled him from the room till they reached the house-door-sill. Slowly the father found utterance and told his son that on just such a Christmas night long ago he had attacked his father in a similar manner and had dragged him to the same spot, when he was arrested by a voice in his heart. ' I stopped here; and, Hob, do you the same!" The son relaxed his hold of his father's throat, and both returned upstairs, where they remained in silence. At dawn the father was dead, the son insane. "Is there a reason in nature for these hard hearts?" Certainly there is, says the mental pathologist. Persons born with such and such cranial and cerebral characteristics cannot help being brutal and criminal. They are handicapped heavily by nature from the hour of their birth, and they only follow out a law of their development, for which they are not responsible when they become criminal. The mental pathologist would have no difficulty in drawing the portraits of Halbert and Hob. There is a monotony and family likeness in the criminal physiognomy which does not require an expert to detect. When a specialist such as Dr. Down goes over a great prison like Broadmoor, he has no difficulty in indicating for us the precise aberrations from the normal type which distinguish between the honest man and the criminal. This would be a terrible reflection on the Divine providence, if we omitted to take into account the pregnant last line of Mr. Browning's poem:

"That a reason out of nature must turn them soft, seems clear."

As Nature is never without her compensations, so there is a reason above all our materialism, our facial angles, our oxycephalic and our microcephalic heads which justifies the ways of God to men. Doctors are slow to recognise this, but judges always act upon the principle. Experts in criminal pathology find responsibility with great difficulty in the men they are endeavouring to save from the gallows. The judge, however, keeps to the common-sense rule that if the criminal knew that he was doing what he ought not to do, he is responsible before the law for his crime. Halbert heard the voice in his heart—Hob relaxed his hold of the father's throat. Conscience rules supreme even over heredity and cerebral aberration. The basis of this story is found in Aristotle's *Ethics*, I., vii., c. 6.

"Heap Cassia, Sandal-buds, and Stripes." The first line of the song in *Paracelsus* iv.

Helen's Tower. Lines written at the request of the Earl of Dufferin and Clandeboye, on the tower which the Earl erected to the memory of his mother, Helen, Countess of Giffard. (Printed in the *Pall Mall Gazette*, Dec. 28th, 1883.)

Henry, Earl Mertoun. (*A Blot in the 'Scutcheon.*) He was Mildred Tresham's lover, and was killed by her brother, Earl Tresham.

Herakles = Hercules, who wrestles with death, conquers him, and restores Alkestis to her husband, in *Balaustion's Adventure*. The *Raging Hercules* of Euripides, which Balaustion read to Aristophanes, is translated by Mr. Browning in the volume *Aristophanes' Apology*.

Heretic's Tragedy, The; A Middle-Age Interlude. (*Men and Women*, 1855; *Romances*, 1863; *Dramatic Romances*, 1868.) "It would seem to be a glimpse from the burning of Jacques du Bourg Molay, at Paris, A.D. 1314; as distorted by the refraction from Flemish brain to brain during the course of a couple of centuries." [THE HISTORY.] Molay was Grand Master of the order of the Knights Templars, suppressed by a decree of Pope Clement V. and the general council of Vienne, in 1312. The Knights Templars were instituted by seven gentlemen at Jerusalem, in 1118, to defend the holy places and pilgrims from the insults of the Saracens, and to keep the passes free for such as undertook the voyage to the Holy Land. They took their name from the first house, which was given them by King Baldwin II., situated near the place where anciently the temple of Solomon stood. By the liberality of princes, immense riches suddenly flowed to this Order, by which the knights were puffed up to a degree of insolence which rendered them insupportable even to the kings who had been their protectors; and Philip the Fair, king of France, resolved to compass their ruin. They were accused of treasons and conspiracies with the infidels, and of other enormous crimes, which occasioned the suppression of the Order. The year following, the Grand Master, who was a Frenchman, was burnt at Paris, and several others suffered death, though they all with their last breath protested their innocence as to the crimes that were laid to their charge. These were certainly much exaggerated by their enemies, and doubtless many innocent men were involved with the guilty. A great part of their estates was given to the Knights of Rhodes or Malta. (*Butler's Lives of the Saints—sub* May 5.) For half a century before the suppression of the Order, horrible stories about various unholy rites practised at its midnight assemblies had been in circulation. It was said that every member on his initiation was compelled to deny the Lord Jesus Christ, to spit upon and trample under foot a crucifix, and submit to certain indecent ceremonies. It was charged against them that hideous four-footed idols were worshipped, and other things too terrible to narrate were said to be done at these assemblies. Whether these things were true or not, has been hotly disputed ever since the accusations were made. The spitting on the cross seems, at any rate in France, to have been admitted by the accused; many of the worst things confessed were admitted under the most cruel tortures, and are consequently more likely to have been false than true. In Carlyle's essay on the "Life and Writings of Werner" (*Critical and Miscellaneous Essays*, vol. i., p. 66: 1888), the whole story of these mysterious rites is discussed. After several pages of quotations from Werner's drama *The Templars in Cyprus*, Carlyle says, "One might take this trampling on the Cross, which is said to have been actually enjoined on every Templar at his initiation, to be a type of his secret behest to undermine that institution (the Catholic Church) and redeem the spirit of religion from the state of thraldom and distortion under which it was there held. It is known at least, and was well known to Werner, that the heads of the Templars entertained views, both on religion and politics, which they did not think meet for communicating to their age, and only imparted by degrees, and under mysterious adumbrations, to the wiser of their own order. They had even publicly resisted, and succeeded in thwarting, some iniquitous measure of Philippe Auguste, the French king, in regard to his coinage; and this, while it secured them the love of the people, was one great cause, perhaps second only to their wealth, of the hatred which that sovereign bore them, and of the savage doom which he at last executed on the whole body."

[THE POEM.] The Abbot Deodaet and his monks are singing in the choir of their church about the burning alive of the Master of the Temple two hundred years before. He has sinned the unknown sin, and sold the influence of the Order to the Mohammedan. In a graphic and lurid manner they picture the details of the execution. They have no pity for the victim, and seem to be gloating over his sufferings. They imagine that the victim calls in his agony on the Saviour whom he forsook and traitorously sold; he cries now "Saviour, save Thou me!" The Face upon which he had spat, the Face on the crucifix which he trampled upon, is revealed to the burning man feature by feature; he now sees his awful Judge, his voice dies, and John's soul flares into the dark. Said the Abbot, "God help all poor souls lost in the dark!"

NOTES.—i., *Organ: plagal cadence.* The cadence formed when a subdominant chord immediately precedes the final tonic chord. ii., *Emperor Aldabrod*, probably the family name of one of the Greek emperors, but I can find nothing about him. *Sultan Saladin*, of Egypt and Syria, whose portrait is so faithfully drawn by Sir Walter Scott, in *The Talisman. Pope Clement V.* (1305-14). Platina, in his life of this Pope, says only a few words on the Templars: "He took off the Templars, who were fallen into very great errors (as denying Christ, etc.), and gâve their goods to the Knights of Jerusalem"; *clavicithern:* an upright musical instrument like a harpsichord. iv., *Laudes:* a Catholic service associated with *Matins.* It consists, amongst other devotions, of five Psalms. vi., *Salvâ reverentiâ*: "saving reverence," like the "saving your presence" of the Irishman. vii., *Sharon's Rose*: *Solomon's Song*, ii. 1. The rose was the symbol of secrecy. viii., *leman:* a sweetheart of either sex.

Hervé Riel. (Published in the *Cornhill Magazine*, March 1871. Browning received £100 for it, which sum he gave to the Paris Relief Fund, to provide food for the starving people after the siege of Paris. Published in the *Pacchiarotto* volume in 1876.) The story told in the poem is strictly historical. Hervé Riel was a Breton sailor of Le Croisic, who, after the great naval battle of La Hogue in 1692, saved the remains of the French fleet by skilfully piloting the ships through the shallows of the Rance, and thereby preventing their capture by the English. For this splendid service he was permitted to ask whatever reward he chose to name. The brave Breton asked merely for a whole day's holiday, that he might visit his wife, the Belle Aurore. Dr. Furnivall says: "The facts of the story had been forgotten, and were denied at St. Malo, but the reports of the French Admiralty were looked up, and the facts established. The war between Louis XIV. and William III. was undertaken by the former with the object of restoring James II. to the English throne. Admiral Turnville engaged the English fleet off Cape La Hogue, and thereby wrecked the French fleet and the cause of James. Apropos of Hervé Riel, Mr. Kenneth Grahame says (*Browning Society's Papers*, March 30th, 1883, p. 68*): 'In Rabelais' *Pantagruel*, lib. IV., cap. xxi., Panurge says, '. . . quelque fille de roy . . . me fera exiger quelque magnificque cenotaphe, comme feit Dido à son mary Sychee; . . . Germain de Brie à Hervé, le nauctrier Breton,' etc. Then a note says, 'En 1515, dans un combat naval, le Breton Hervé Primoguet, qui commandoit *la Cordelière*, attacha son navire en feu au vaisseau amiral ennemi *la Regente d'Angleterre*, et se fit sauter avec lui. Germain de Brie ou Brice (*Brixius*) qui celebra ce trait heroique dans un poeme latin, etoit un des amis de Rabelais.' This was a forerunner of Browning's hero. The coincidence of names, etc., is curious."

Hippolytos. (See ARTEMIS PROLOGIZES.) The *Hippolytus* of Euripides is the chaste worshipper of Diana (Artemis), who will give no heed to Venus. His step-mother Phædra loves him, and kills herself when she discovers he will not succumb to her attentions.

Hohenstiel-Schwangau. See PRINCE HOHENSTIEL-SCHWANGAU.

Holy-Cross Day [On which the Jews were forced to attend an annual Christian Sermon in Rome]. (*Men and Women*, 1855; *Romances*, 1863; *Dramatic Romances*, 1868.)—[THE HISTORY.] Holy Cross Day, or the Festival of the Exaltation of the Holy Cross, falls on September 14th annually. It is kept in commemoration of the alleged miraculous appearance of the Cross to Constantine in the sky at midday. The discovery of the True Cross by St. Helen gave the first occasion of the festival, which was celebrated under the title of the Exaltation of the Cross on

September 14th, both by the Latins and Greeks, as early as in the fifth or sixth centuries at Jerusalem, from the year 335. (See for the history of the festival Butler's *Lives of the Saints*, under September 14th.) The particular details of this poem are not historical, but it is quite true that such a sermon was preached to Jews from time to time, and that they were driven to church to listen to it. A papal bull, issued in 1584, formerly compelled the Jews to hear sermons at the church of *St. Angelo in Pescheria*, close to the Jewish quarter. The Pescheria or fish market adjoins the Ghetto, the quarter allotted to the Jews by Paul IV. This pope compelled the Jews to wear yellow head-gear; and, among other oppressive exactions, they had to provide the prizes for the horse-races at the Carnival. In a note at the end of the poem Mr. Browning says, "The late Pope abolished this bad business of the Sermon." The conduct of the popes towards the Jews varied according to the policy or humanity in the character of the pontiff. "In 1442 Eugenius IV. deprived them of one of their most valuable privileges, and endeavoured to interrupt their amicable relations with the Christians: they were prohibited from eating and drinking together. Jews were excluded from almost every profession, were forced to wear a badge, to pay tithes; and Christians were forbidden to bequeath legacies to Jews. The succeeding popes were more wise or more humane. In Naples the celebrated Abarbanel became the confidential adviser of Ferdinand the Bastard and Alphonso II.; they experienced a reverse, and were expelled from that city by Charles V. The stern and haughty Pope Paul IV. renewed the hostile edicts; he endeavoured to embarrass their traffic by regulations which prohibited them from disposing of their pledges under eighteen months; deprived them of the trade in corn and in every other necessary of life, but left them the privilege of dealing in old clothes. Paul first shut them up in their Ghetto, a confined quarter of the city, out of which they were prohibited from appearing after sunset. Pius IV. relaxed the severity of his predecessor. He enlarged the Ghetto, and removed the restriction on their commerce. Pius V. expelled them from every city in the papal territory except Rome and Ancona; he endured them in those cities with the avowed design of preserving their commerce with the East. Gregory XIII. pursued the same course: a bull was published, and suspended at the gate of the Jews' quarter, prohibiting the reading of the Talmud, blasphemies against Christ, or ridicule against the ceremonies of the Church. All Jews above twelve years old were bound to appear at the regular sermons delivered for their conversion; where it does not seem, notwithstanding the authority of the pope and the eloquence of the cardinals, that their behaviour was very edifying. At length the bold and statesmanlike Sextus V. annulled at once all the persecuting or vexatious regulations of his predecessors, opened the gates of every city in the ecclesiastical dominions to these enterprising traders, secured and enlarged their privileges, proclaimed toleration of their religion, subjected them to the ordinary tribunals, and enforced a general and equal taxation." (Milman's *History of the Jews*, book xxvii.)

[THE POEM.] Part of the satire of the poem is in the fictitious extract from the *Diary by the Bishop's Secretary*, 1600, prefixed to it. The Bishop looks upon the matter as though he were compelling the Jews to come in and partake of the gospel feast; he flatters himself that many conversions have taken place in consequence of the enforcement of this law, and that the Church was conferring a great blessing on the Jews by permitting them to partake of the heavenly grace. What the Jews themselves thought of the business is told in the poem. The speaker describes the crowding of the church by the Israelites, packed like rats in a hamper or pigs in a stye; to the life the poet hits off the behaviour of the wretched audience, compelled to listen to that which they abhorred, and to pretend to be converted, and to affect compunction and interest in doctrines which they detested. Then the most serious part of the poem begins: the speaker complains that the hand which gutted his purse would throttle his creed, and for reward the men whom he has helped to their sins would help him to their God; then the pathos deepens, and while the pretended converts are going through the farce of acknowledging their conversion in the sacristy, the speaker meditates on Rabbi Ben Ezra's *Song of Death*. The night the Jewish saint died he called his family round him and said their nation in one point only had sinned, and he invokes Christ if indeed He really were the Messiah, and they had given Him the cross when they should have bestowed the crown, to have pity on them and protect them from the followers of His teaching, whose life laughs through and spits at their creed. Perhaps, indeed, they withstood Christ then: it is at least Barabbas they withstand now! Let Rome make amends for Calvary. Let Him remember their age-long torture, the infamy, the Ghetto, the garb, the badge, the branding tool and scourge, and this summons to conversion; by withstanding this they are but trying to wrest Christ's name from the devil's crew.

Home, D. D.: the Spiritualist medium. See MR. SLUDGE THE MEDIUM.

Home Thoughts from Abroad. (Published in *Dramatic Romances and Lyrics*, in *Bells and Pomegranates*, VII., 1845.) In praise of all the mighty ravishment of our English spring, and the lovely sister months April and May,—

> "May flowers bloom before May comes,
> To cheer, a little, April's sadness."

And nowhere, surely, are these months so delightful as in England! Melon-flowers do not make up "for the buttercups, the little children's dower." In many parts of Southern Europe the trees have all been ruthlessly cut down, lest they should harbour birds. The absence of our hedgerows does much to mar the beauty of a Continental landscape in spring.

Home Thoughts from the Sea. (*Dramatic Romances vnd Lyrics*, in *Bells and Pomegranates*, VII., 1845.) Patriotic reflections on passing the Bay of Trafalgar by one who, remembering how here England helped the Englishmen, asks himself "How can I help England?"

House. (*Pacchiarotto, with other Poems*: 1876.) If we accept Shakespeare's Sonnets in their natural sense, as the best authorities say we must, they open up to the public gaze passages in the life of the great poet which those who love an ideal Shakespeare would rather have not known. If, says Mr. Browning in the poem, Shakespeare unlocked his heart with a sonnet-key, the less Shakespeare he! For his own part, he will do nothing of the sort; and, though probably few men led purer and holier lives from youth to manhood than Mr. Browning, he declines to admit the vulgar gaze of the public into the secret chambers of his soul. In earthquakes, indeed, the fronts of houses often fall, and expose the private arrangements of the home to the impertinent observation of the passer-by. In earthquakes this cannot be helped; but a writer may keep his secrets to himself till an imprudent biographer gets hold of them to make "copy" of. As a fact, all that the world is really concerned with in Mr. Browning's life and opinions can be gathered "by the spirit-sense" from his works. The main idea of the poem is very similar to that of *At the Mermaid.*

Householder, The. (*Fifine at the Fair.*) The Epilogue to the poem, telling how Don Juan is at last united to his wife Elvire by death.

How it strikes a Contemporary. (*Men and Women:* 1855.) The faculty of observation is essential both to the poet and the spy. Lavater said that "he alone is an acute observer who can observe minutely without being observed." The poet of Valladolid was mistaken by the vulgar mob for an agent of the Government, because they were always catching him taking "such cognisance of men and things." His picture is sketched in a very few lines; but these are sufficient to show us the very man, in his scrutinising hat, crossing the Plaza Mayor of the dull and deserted city, in which there was—one would think—as little life to interest a poet as to employ a spy. We soon get to feel that the poet-evidences in the man's behaviour should have been sufficiently strong to save him from the reproaches of his neighbours. The dog at his heels, the note he took of any cruelty towards animals or cursing of a woman, the interest in men's simple trades, the poring over bookstalls, reveal to us the image of his soul. However, his fellow-citizens in all these things thought they had evidence of a chief inquisitor; and in the land of Spain, which for many centuries cowered under the shadow of the most terrible weapon ever forged against the liberties of man, inquisition and espionage were in the air. Men were better judges of spies than of poets; they were more familiar with them. So it was set down in their minds that all their doings were sent by this recording prowler to the king. All the mysteries of the town were traced to his influence: A's surprising fate, B's disappearing, C's mistress, all were traced to this "man about the streets." But it was not true, says the contemporary, that if you tracked the inquisitor home you would find him revelling in luxury. On the contrary, his habits were simple and abstemious; at ten he went to bed, after a modest repast and a quiet game of cribbage with his maid. And when the poor, mysterious man came to die in the clean garret, whose sides were lined by an invisible guard who came to relieve him, there was no more need for that old coat which had seen so much service. How suddenly the angels change the fashion of our dress—and how much better they understand us than do our neighbours!

How they brought the Good News from Ghent to Aix. (*Dramatic Romances and Lyrics*, in *Bells and Pomegranates*, 1845.) There is no actual basis in history for the incidents of this poem, though there is no doubt that in the war in the Netherlands such an adventure was likely enough. Three men go off on horse-back at their hardest, at moonset, from the city of Ghent, to save their town—through Boom, and Düffeld, Mecheln, Aerschot, Hasselt, Looz, Tongres, and Dalhem, to the ancient city of Aix. The hero of the work was the good horse Roland, who was voted the last measure of wine the city had left. Two of the horses dropped dead on the road, and the noble Roland, bearing "the whole weight of the news," with blind, distended eyes and nostrils, fell just as he reached the market-place of Aix, resting his head between the knees of his master.

Humility. (*Asolando*, 1889.) A flower-laden girl drops a careless bud without troubling to pick it up. She has "enough for home." "So give your lover," says the poet, "heaps of love," he thinking himself happy in picking up a stray bud, "and not the worst," which she has gladdened him by letting fall.

"I am a Painter who cannot Paint." (*Pippa Passes.*) Lutwyche's speech begins with these words.

"I go to prove my Soul." (*Paracelsus.*) The words of the hero of the poem when he starts on his career.

Ibn-Ezra = the historical person who forms the subject of the poem RABBI BEN EZRA (*q.v.*)

Imperante Augusto Natus Est. (*Asolando*, 1889.) In the reign of Augustus Octavianus Cæsar, second emperor of Rome, two Romans are entering the public bath together, and while the bath is being heated they converse in the vestibule about the great services which Octavianus has rendered to the city and the empire, and one of them refers to the panegyric on the Emperor read out in public on the previous day by Lucius Varius Rufus. He had praised the Emperor as a god, and the speaker goes on to say how he once met Octavianus as he was going about the city disguised as a beggar. At the end of the poem is the story told by Suidas, the author of a Greek lexicon, who lived before the twelfth century, and who was probably a Christian, as his work deals with Scriptural as well as pagan subjects. This myth narrates the visit of Augustus Cæsar to the oracle at Delphos. "When Augustus had sacrificed," said Suidas, "he demanded of the Pythia who should succeed him, and the oracle replied:—

"'A Hebrew slave, holding control over the blessed gods,
Orders me to leave this home and return to the underworld.
Depart in silence, therefore, from our altars.'"

Nicephorus relates that when Augustus returned to Rome after receiving this reply, he erected an altar in the Capitol with the inscription "Ara Primogeniti Dei." On this spot now stands the Church of S. Maria in Aracœli, a very ancient building, mentioned in the ninth century as S. Maria de Capitolio. The present altar also incloses an ancient altar bearing the inscription *Ara Primogeniti Dei*, which is said to have been the one erected here by Augustus. According to the legend of the twelfth century, this was the spot where the Sibyl of Tibur appeared to the Emperor, whom the Senate proposed to elevate to the rank of a god, and revealed to him a vision of the Virgin and her Son. This was the origin of the name "Church of the Altar of Heaven." It is historical that Augustus used to go about Rome disguised as a beggar. Jeremy Taylor's account of events in the Roman world, as recorded in his *Life of Christ*, sec. iv., will serve as a good introduction to the historical matters referred to in the poem:—"For when all the world did expect that in Judæa should be born their prince, and that the incredulous world had in their observation slipped by their true prince, because He came not in pompous and secular illustrations; upon that very stock Vespasian (Sueton. *In Vitâ Vesp.* 4; Vide etiam Cic., *De Divin.*) was nursed up in hope of the Roman empire, and that hope made him great in designs; and they being prosperous, made his fortunes correspond to his hopes, and he was endeared and engaged upon that future by the prophecy which was never intended him by the prophet. But the future of the Roman monarchy was not great enough for this prince designed by the old prophets. And therefore it was not without the influence of a

Divinity that his predecessor Augustus, about the time of Christ's nativity, refused to be called "lord" (*Oros.* vi. 22). Possibly it was to entertain the people with some hopes of restitution of their liberties, till he had griped the monarchy with a stricter and faster hold; but the Christians were apt to believe that it was upon the prophecy of a sibyl foretelling the birth of a greater prince, to whom all the world should pay adoration; and that prince was about that time born in Judæa. (Suidas *In histor. verb.* "*Augustus.*") The oracle, which was dumb to Augustus' question, told him unasked, the devil having no tongue permitted him but one to proclaim that 'an Hebrew child was his lord and enemy.'" Octavianus chose the title of Augustus on religious grounds, having assumed the exalted position of Chief Pontiff. The epithet Augustus was one which no man had borne before—a name only applied to sacred things. The rites of the gods were termed august, their temples were august, and the word itself was derived from the auguries. The cult of the Cæsar began to assume a ritual and a priesthood at the very time when the approaching birth of Christ was to destroy the empire and its religious belief. Mrs. Jameson, in her *Legends of the Madonna*, p. 197, says: "According to an ancient legend, the Emperor Augustus Cæsar repaired to the sibyl Tiburtina, to inquire whether he should consent to allow himself to be worshipped with divine honours, which the Senate had decreed to him. The Sibyl, after some days of meditation, took the Emperor apart and showed him an altar; and above the altar, in the opening heavens, and in a glory of light, he beheld a beautiful Virgin holding an infant in her arms, and at the same time a voice was heard saying, 'This is the altar of the Son of the living God!' whereupon Augustus caused an altar to be erected on the Capitoline Hill with this inscription, *Ara Primogeniti Dei*; and on the same spot, in later times, was built the church called the *Ara Cœli*—well known, with its flight of one hundred and twenty-four marble steps, to all who have visited Rome. This particular prophecy of the Tiburtine sybil to Augustus rests on some very antique traditions, pagan as well as Christian. It is supposed to have suggested the 'Pollio' of Virgil, which suggested the 'Messiah' of Pope. It is mentioned by writers of the third and fourth centuries. A very rude but curious bas-relief, preserved in the Church of the Ara Cœli, is perhaps the oldest representation extant. The Church legend assigns to it a fabulous antiquity; and it must be older than the twelfth century, as it is alluded to by writers of that period. Here the Emperor Augustus kneels before the Madonna and Child, and at his side is the sibyl Tiburtina pointing upwards." Of course, such a subject became a favourite one with artists. There is a famous fresco on the subject by Baldassare Peruzzi at Siena, Fonte Giusta. There is also a picture dealing with it at Hampton Court, by Pietro da Cortona. St. Augustine (*De Civitate Dei*, lib. xviii., cap. 23) describes the prophecy of Sibylla Erythrea concerning Christ:—"Flaccianus, a learned and eloquent man (one that had been Consul's deputy), being in a conference with us concerning Christ, showed us a Greek book, saying they were this sibyl's verses; wherein, in one place, he showed us a sort of verses so composed that, the first letter of every verse being taken, they all made these words: Ἰησοῦς Χριστος, Θεοῦ ὕιος σωτὴρ (Jesus Christ, Son of God, the Saviour)." Some think this was the Cumean Sibyl. Lactantius also has prophecies of Christ out of some sybilline books, but he does not give the reference. The Latin hymn sung in the Masses for the Dead, and well known as the *Dies Iræ*, has this verse:

> "Dies iræ, dies illa,
> Solvet sæclum in favilla,
> Teste David cum Sibylla."

NOTES.—*Publius:* not historical. *Lucius Varius Rufus* was a tragic poet, the friend of Virgil and Horace. He wrote a panegyric on the Emperor Augustus, to which Mr. Browning refers in the opening lines of the poem. *Little Flaccus* was Horace, who declared that Varius was the only poet capable of singing the praises of M. Agrippa. His tragedy *Thyestes* is warmly praised by Quintillian. *Epos:* heroic poem. *Etruscan kings.* The Rasena or Etrusci inhabited Etruria, in that part of Italy north of Rome. The kings were elected for life. Roman families were proud to trace back their ancestry to the Etruscan kings. *Mæcenas:* patron of letters and learned men, the adviser of Augustus. He was descended from the ancient kings of Etruria. *Quadrans:* a Roman coin, worth about half a farthing of our money. The price of a bath, paid to the keeper of the public bagnio. *Thermæ*, the baths. *Suburra:* a street in Rome, where the dissolute Romans resorted. *Quæstor*, the office of Quæstor, under the empire, was the first step to higher positions. *Ædiles*, magistrates. The baths were under their superintendence. *Censores*, officials whose duty it was to take the place of the consuls in superintending the five-yearly census. *Pol!* an oath. By Pollux! *Quarter-as:* in Cicero's time, the *as* was equal to rather less than a halfpenny. *Strigil*, a flesh brush. *Oil-drippers*, used after bathing.

In a Balcony. (Published in *Men and Women*: 1855.) A drama which is incomplete. Concentrated into an hour, we have the crises of three lives, which, passing through the fire, reveal a tragedy which has for its scene the balcony of a palace. A Queen has arrived at the age of fifty with her strong craving for love still unsatisfied. Constance, a cousin of the Queen and a lady of her court, is loved by Norbert, who is in the Queen's service. He has served the State well and successfully, and the Queen has set her heart upon him. Norbert is advised by Constance to act diplomatically, and pretend that he has served the Queen only for her sake. He must not permit her to see the love which he has for the woman to whom he has pledged himself. The Queen, who is already married in form, though not in heart, offers to dissolve the union, in an interview which she has with Constance, and shows how eagerly she grasps at the prospect of a new life which opens up before her. Constance is prepared to sacrifice herself for Norbert and the Queen. She seeks Norbert, and reveals to him the real state of affairs. The Queen discovers the lovers, and hears Norbert declare his love for Constance, which she tries to divert to the Queen. At once the Queen sees all her hopes dashed to the ground. She says nothing; but having left the balcony, the music of the ball, which is proceeding within, suddenly ceases, the footsteps of the guard approach, the lovers feel their impending doom; but one passionate moment unites them in heart for ever, and they are led away to death.

In a Gondola. (*Dramatic Lyrics*, in *Bells and Pomegranates*, No. III.: 1842.) In the fourth book of Forster's *Life of Dickens* is a letter which Dickens wrote to Maclise, from which we learn that Browning wrote the first verse of this poem, beginning, "I send my heart up to thee," to express Maclise's subject in the Academy catalogue. Dickens says, in a letter to the artist: "In a certain picture called the 'Serenade,' for which Browning wrote that verse in Lincoln's Inn Fields, you, O Mac, painted a sky. If you ever have occasion to paint the Mediterranean, let it be exactly of that colour." In the poem a lover and his mistress are singing in a gondola—conscious of their danger, for the interview is a stolen one, and the three who are referred to are perhaps husband, father, and brother, or assassins hired by one of them. The chills of approaching death avail not to cool the ardour of their passion in this precious hour in the gondola. They feel they have lived, let death come when it will; and as they glide past church and palace, reality is concentrated in their boat, the shams and illusions of life are on the banks. The lover is stabbed as he hands the lady ashore. He craves one more kiss, and dies. He scorns not his murderers, for they have never lived:

> "But I
> Have lived indeed, and so—can die!"

NOTES.—*Castelfranco* (born 1478) is Giorgione, one of the greatest Italian painters. His father belonged to the family of the Barbarella, of Castelfranco in the Trevisan. For his Life see VASARI. *Schidone* was an Italian painter of the sixteenth century. *Haste-thee-Luke* is the English of *Luca-fà-presto* ("Luke work-fast"), nickname of *Luca Giordano* (1632—1705), a Neapolitan painter. His nickname was given to him, not on account of his rapid method of working, but in consequence of his poor and greedy father urging him to increased exertions by constantly exclaiming "Luca, fà presto." The youth obeyed his father, and would actually not leave off work for his meals, but was fed by his father's hand while he laboured on with the brush. *Giudecca*: a great canal of Venice. "*Lido's wet, accursed graves.*" Byron desired to be buried at Lido. Ancient Jewish tombs are there, moss-grown and half covered with sand. The place is desolate and very gloomy. *Lory:* a species of parrot.

Inapprehensiveness. (*Asolando.*) The ruin referred to in the fourth line is that of the old palace of Queen Cornaro, who, having been driven out of her kingdom of Cyprus, kept up a shadow of royalty here, with Cardinal Bembo as her secretary. It was he who told the story, in his *Asolani*. Mr. Browning thought that there was no view in all Italy to compare with that from the tower of the old palace. Two friends stand side by side contemplating the scene. The lady's attention is attracted to a chance-rooted wind-sown tree on a turret, and to certain weed-growths on a wall. She is inapprehensive that by her side stands an incarnation of dormant passion, needing nothing but a look from her to burst into immense life. So little does one soul know of another. The Vernon Lee in the last line is a well-known authoress, Violet Paget, best known perhaps by her work entitled *Euphorion*.

In a Year. (*Men and Women*, 1855; *Dramatic Lyrics*, 1868.) Finely contrasts the constancy of a woman's love with the inconstancy of man's. Love is not love unless it be "an ever fixed mark." In exchange for the man's love, the woman gave health, ease, beauty, and youth, and was content to give "more life and more" till all were gone, and think the sacrifice too little. That was the woman's "ever fixed mark." The man asks calmly: "Can't we touch these bubbles, then, but they break?"

Incident of the French Camp. (*Dramatic Lyrics*, in *Bells and Pomegranates*, III.: 1842.) Ratisbon (German Regensburg) is an ancient and famous city of Bavaria, on the right bank of the Danube. It has endured no less than seventeen sieges since the tenth century, accompanied by bombardments, the last of which took place in 1809, when Napoleon stormed the town, which was obstinately defended by the Austrians. Some two hundred houses and much of the suburbs were destroyed. As the Emperor was watching the storming, a rider flew from the city full gallop, saluting the Emperor. He told him they had taken the city. The chief's eye flashed, but presently saddened as he looked on the brave youth who had brought the news. "You are wounded!" "Nay, I'm killed, sire!" and the lad fell dead.

Inn Album, The. (1875.) The chief features of this tragedy, "where every character is either mean, or weak, or vile," are taken from real life. It is "the story of the wrecked life of a girl who loved her base seducer as a god." This curious study in mental pathology opens with a description of the visitors' book of a country inn, filled with the usual idiotic entries which are found in such books. The shabby-genteel parlour of the inn is occupied by two men playing at cards—a young and a middle-aged man. The elder, a cultivated and accomplished *roué*, has just lost to the younger man ten thousand pounds at play. The loser has hitherto been pretty uniformly the winner; but his companion, who has succeeded in plucking the pigeon, has not deceived him. He has seen through his pretences, and is fully aware that he is accompanied on this trip to the village where the inn in which they are staying is situated, purely for the chance it offered of winning money from him for the last time before his approaching marriage. The polished snob who has won is inclined to be satirical at his companion's expense, and loftily desires him to consider the debt as cancelled: he is a millionaire, and can afford to do without it. This the elder man, with perfect politeness, declines, and assures him that it shall be paid. They leave the inn. The young man is to visit his intended bride; but he dare not introduce his companion, as his reputation has made it impossible to do so. As they walk towards the station the young man inquires how it is that his friend, with all his advantages in life, is in every way a failure. He then learns that his chances were missed four years ago, when he should have married a woman with whom he had certain relations, and who could have saved him from his aimless and wayward life. He had won the heart of a lofty-minded girl, had seduced her, and, though he had not intended marriage at first, had offered it. When she discovered that he had betrayed her without thinking of marrying her, she rejected his proposal, which had come too late to appease her wounded pride, and had settled down as the wife of an obscure country parson, old and poor. Weakly, she had neglected to secure her safety by telling her husband the story of her past, and in consequence was liable at any moment to be the victim of her seducer for the second time. The scoundrel had led the life of a woman-wrecker, and his love for his victim had turned to hate, as he told his companion, because she had disdained to save him from himself. When the elder man has unburdened himself, then the younger tells his story too. He has loved a peerless woman, who refused him, as she was vowed to another. There are points in his story which suggest to him that they have both loved the same woman, though he says that could not be, as he has heard that she married the man of whom she spoke. The young man now parts from his companion, and bids him return to the inn, there to await him for an hour, while he tries to induce his aunt to receive him as her guest. In the third part of the poem we are introduced to two women—an elder and a younger—who are talking in the parlour of the inn, just left vacant by the departure of the two card-players. The younger is the girl whom the young man of the story is to marry; and she has begged her old friend, the elder woman, to meet her, that she may see the man whom she is to marry. She has come by the train, has been met at the station by her young friend, and they adjourn to the little inn to talk matters over quietly. While the younger woman is absent from the parlour, and the elder is engaged in turning over the leaves of the visitors' book, she is terror-stricken at seeing her old lover enter the room. The lady is the clergyman's wife, and the man is the old *roué* who is waiting for his friend who has won his ten thousand pounds. She believes the whole affair is a scheme to entrap her, and bitterly reproaches the man who has ruined her life, and even now must drag her from her retirement for further persecution. He indulges in recriminations, pretending that it is his life which she has wrecked, and that she is inspired with hatred for him though he has not ceased to love her. She thanks God that she had grace to hurl contempt at the contemptible:

> "Rent away
> By treason from my rightful pride of place,
> I was not destined to the shame below.
> A cleft had caught me."

Revealing to him the bitterness of her position, hanging, as it were, over the brink of a yawning precipice, his old love for her is reawakened, and he kneels to the injured woman. He entreats her to fly with him to

> "A certain refuge, solitary home
> To hide in.
>
> . . . .
>
> Come with me, love, loved once, loved only, come,
> Blend loves there!"

But the woman sees through him, and says:

> "Your smiles, your tears, prayers, curses move alike
> My crowned contempt."

And while he is kneeling there, in bursts the young man, who has returned to say that his aunt declines to meet him. He is startled to see the lady to whom he had vainly offered his heart four years ago, and rushes to the conclusion that he too has been entrapped for some purpose. The fifth section of the poem opens with a scornful denunciation of the trick which he considers stands confessed in the scene which he beholds. "O you two base ones, male and female! Sir!" he exclaims; "half an hour ago I held your master for my best of friends, and four years since you seemed my heart's one love!" The woman explains to him that she has been sent for simply to counsel his cousin on the question of her proposed marriage. She finds him innocent save in folly, and will so report. The elder man she bids to leave the youth, and leave unsullied the heart she rescues and would lay beside another's. While she speaks the devil is tempting him to one more crime. He will turn affairs to his own advantage. He writes some lines in the album before him, closes the book, hands it to the indignant woman, and begs her to leave him alone with his friend while he discusses the situation. In the book which she receives he has written a note to her telling her that her young lover is still faithful to her, and threatening her that if she does not receive him on familiar terms the story of her past shame shall be exposed to her husband. Left alone with the young man, he opens out a scheme of infernal ingenuity, whereby at once he will pay his gambling debt and avenge himself for the contempt and scorn with which his unhappy victim has once more received the offer of his affection. He proposes to barter the woman who has unwittingly put herself into his power—to compel her to yield herself up to the man in exchange for the ten thousand pounds he cannot otherwise pay. He explains to him that she has deluded her parson husband—would have yielded to himself had he not determined to substitute his friend. "Make love to her; pick no phrase; prevent all misconception: there's the fruit to pluck or let alone at pleasure!" He leaves the room, and in superb composure the intended victim enters. Captive of wickedness, she warns him: "Back, in God's name!" "Sin no more!" she cries: "I am past sin now." She implores him to break the fetters which have bound him to the evil influence which has destroyed her life. Her noble bearing under the terrible circumstances assures him of her innocence of any complicity in a trick. He tells her the man has told heaps of lies about her, which he had not believed. Blushing and stumbling in his speech, he contrives to let her know the use that was to be made of her. Not knowing if there were truth in what was told him of her marriage, he offers her his hand if she is free to accept it,—any way, to take him as her friend. She gives him her hand. At that moment the adversary returns. "You accept him?" he asks. "Till death us do part!" she answers. "But before death parts, read here the marriage licence which makes us one." He then displays the awful words addressed to her in the fatal page she holds in her hand. She reads, and when she comes to the last line—

"Consent—you stop my mouth, the only way"—

turning to the young man, she pitifully asks, "How could mortal 'stop it'?" "So!" he cries. "A tiger-flash, and death's out and on him!" In the closing scene the wretched, hunted woman dies. She has secured her vindicator's acquittal on the charge of murder by writing in the album that he has saved her from the villain, righteously slain, who would have outraged her. As she dies the young girl who was to have married the defender of the dead woman appears on the scene, and the tragedy closes. In *Notes and Queries* for March 25th, 1876, Dr. F. J. Furnivall thus mentions the incidents on which the poem is based: "The story told by Mr. Browning in this poem is, in its main outlines, a real one—that of Lord De Ros, once a friend of the great Duke of Wellington, and about whom there is much in the *Greville Memoirs*. The original story was, of course, too repulsive to be adhered to in all its details—of, first, the gambling lord producing the portrait of the lady he had seduced and abandoned, and offering his expected dupe, but real beater, an introduction to the lady as a bribe to induce him to wait for payment of the money he had won; secondly, the eager acceptance of the bribe by the younger gambler, and the suicide of the lady from horror at the base proposal of her old seducer. The story made a great sensation in London over thirty years ago. Readers of *The Inn Album* know how grandly Mr. Browning has lifted the base young gambler, through the renewal of that old love, which the poet has invented, into one of the most pathetic creations of modern time, and has spared the base old *roué* the degradation of the attempt to sell the love which was once his delight, and which, in the poem, he seeks to regain, with feelings one must hope are real, as the most prized possession of his life As to the lady, the poet has covered her with no false glory or claim on our sympathy. From the first she was a law unto herself; she gratified her own impulses, and she reaped the fruit of this. Her seducer has made his confession of his punishment, and has attributed, instead of misery, comfort and ease to her. She has to tell him, and the young man who has given her his whole heart, that the supposed comfort and ease have been to her simply hell; and tell, too, why she cannot accept the true love that, under other conditions, would have been her way back to heaven and life. What, then, can be her end? No higher power has she ever sought. Self-contained, she has sinned and suffered. She can do no more. By her own hand she ends her life; and the curtain falls on the most profoundly touching and most powerful poem of modern times." The young girl of the poem is the invention of the poet; the other characters took part in the actual tragedy. In his *Memoirs*, first series, Greville mentions Lord De Ros from time to time, and they travelled together in Italy. Under date of "Newmarket, March 29th, 1839," Greville makes the following entry in the first volume of the second series of his *Memoirs*, concerning the death of his friend: "Poor De Ros expired last night soon after twelve, after a confinement of two or three months from the time he returned to England. His end was enviably tranquil, and he bore his protracted sufferings with astonishing fortitude and composure. Nothing ruffled his temper or disturbed his serenity. His faculties were unclouded, his memory retentive, his perceptions clear to the last; no murmur of impatience ever escaped him, no querulous word, no ebullition of anger or peevishness; he was uniformly patient, mild, indulgent, deeply sensible of kindness and attention, exacting nothing, considerate of others and apparently regardless of self, overflowing with affection and kindness of manner and language to all around him and exerting all his moral and intellectual energies with a spirit and resolution that never flagged till within a few hours of his dissolution, when nature gave way, and he sank into a tranquil unconsciousness, in which life gently ebbed away. Whatever may have been the error of his life, he closed the scene with a philosophical dignity not unworthy of a sage, and with a serenity and sweetness of disposition of which Christianity itself could afford no more shining or delightful example. In him I have lost, 'half lost before,' the last and greatest of the friends of my youth; and I am left a more solitary and a sadder man."

Instans Tyrannus = The Threatening Tyrant. (*Men and Women*, 1855; *Dramatic Romances*, 1868.) The title of this poem was suggested by Horace's Ode on the Just Man (*Od.* iii. 3. 1):—

> "Justum et tenacem propositi virum,
> Non civium ardor prava jubentium,
> Non vultus instantis tyranni," etc.

('The just man, firm to his purpose, is not to be shaken from his fixed resolve by the fury of a mob laying upon him their impious behests, nor by the frown of a threatening tyrant, etc.') These lines are said to have been repeated by the celebrated De Witte while he was subject to torture. When men or causes are suppressed by tyranny, the tyrant knows well in his heart that force alone, and not justice, enables him to crush opposition to his will; and he is the first to see, even if he do not acknowledge, the Divine Arm thrust forth from the heavens to protect his victims and avenge their wrongs. From some undefined cause a poor, contemptible man was the object of a tyrant's hate: he struck him, tried to bribe him, tempted his blood and his flesh. Having tried every way to extinguish the man, he contrived thunder above and mine below him to destroy, as a rat in a hole, this friendless wretch, when suddenly the man saw God's arm across the sky. The man

> —"caught at God's skirts, and prayed!
> So, *I* was afraid!"

[Archdeacon Farrar refers the incidents of this poem to the persecution of the early Christians.—*Browning Society Papers*, Pt. VII., p. 22*.]

In Three Days. (*Men and Women*, 1855; *Dramatic Lyrics*, 1868.) A lover anticipates that in three days he shall see his lady. He is aware that three days may change his future, as has often been changed the history of the world in the time. He knows, too, that though three days may cast no shadow in his way, still the years to follow may bring changes and chances of unimagined end. He reiterates that in three days he shall see her, and fear of all that the future may have in store is absorbed in the blissful anticipation.

Italian in England, The. (*Dramatic Romances and Lyrics*, in *Bells and Pomegranates*, No. VII., 1845.) The incident is not historical, though something of the kind might well have happened to any of the Italian patriots in their revolt against the Austrian domination. A prominent Italian patriot is hiding from the Austrian oppressors of his country after an unsuccessful rising. He has taken refuge in England, and the poem tells how the Austrians pursued him everywhere, and how he would have been taken if a peasant girl, to whom he confessed his identity, had not preferred humanity and the love of her country to the gold she might have earned by delivering him to his pursuers. [Mazzini must have gone through many such experiences, and the poem was one which he very highly appreciated.] Hunted by the Austrian bloodhounds, hiding in an old aqueduct, up to the neck in ferns for three days, the pangs of hunger induced him to attract the attention of a peasant girl going to her work with her companions: he threw his glove, to strike her as she passed. Without giving any sign that could acquaint her friends with her object, she glanced round and saw him beckon; breaking a branch from a tree, so as to recognise the spot, she picked up the glove and rejoined her party. In an hour she returned alone. He had not intended to confide in the woman, but her noble face led him to confess he was the man on whose head a great price was set. He felt sure he would not be betrayed. He bade her bring paper, pen and ink, and carry his letter to Padua, to the cathedral; then proceed to a certain confessional which he mentions, and whisper his password. If it was answered in the terms he named, then she was to give the letter to the priest. She promised to do as he desired. In three days more she appeared again at his hiding-place. She told him she had a lover who could do much to aid him. She brought him drink and food. In four days the scouts gave up the search, and went in another direction. At last help arrived from his friends at Padua. He kissed the maiden's hand, and laid his own in blessing on her head. When he took the boat from the seashore, on the night of his escape, she followed him to the vessel. He left, and never saw her more. And now that he is safe in England, he reflects that it is long since he had a thought for aught but Italy. Those whom he had trusted, those to whom he had looked for help, had made terms with the oppressors of his country; his presence in his own land would be awkward for his brethren. But there is one "in that dear, lost land" whose calm smile he would like to see; he would like to know of her future, her children's ages and their names, to kiss once more the hand that saved him, and once again to lay his own in blessing on her head, and go his way. "But to business!"

NOTES.—*Metternich:* the great Austrian diplomatist, and enemy of Italian independence. *Charles:* Carlo Alberto, King of Sardinia. He resorted to severe measures against the party known as "Young Italy," founded by Mazzini. He died in 1849. *Duomo,* the cathedral. *Tenebræ* = darkness: the office of matins and lauds, for the three last days in Holy Week. Fifteen lighted candles are placed on a triangular stand, and at the conclusion of each psalm one is put out, till a single candle is left at the top of the triangle. The extinction of the other candles is said to figure the growing darkness of the world at the time of the Crucifixion. The last candle (which is not extinguished, but hidden behind the altar for a few moments) represents Christ, over whom Death could not prevail.

Ivàn Ivànovitch. (*Dramatic Idyls,* First Series, 1879.) Ivàn Ivànovitch, or John Jackson, as his name would be in English, was skilled in the use of the axe, as the Russian workman is. Employed one day in his yard, in the village where he lived, suddenly over the snow-covered landscape came a burst of sledge bells, the sound of horse's hoofs galloping; then a sledge appeared drawn by a horse, which fell down as it reached the place. What seemed a frozen corpse lay in the vehicle: it was Dmitri's wife, without Dmitri and the children, who left the village a month ago. They restore the woman, who utters a loud and long scream, followed by sobs and gasps, as, with returning life, she takes in the fact that she is safe. "But yesterday!" she cries. "Oh, God the Father, Son and Holy Ghost, cannot You bring again my blessed yesterday? I had a child on either knee, and, dearer than the two, a babe close to my heart. Intercede, sweet Mother, with thy Son Almighty—undo all done last night!" Then she reminds them how, a month ago, she and her children had accompanied her husband, who had gone to work at a church many a league away: five of them in that sledge--Ivàn, herself, and three children. The work finished, they were about to return, when the village caught fire. Then Ivàn hurried his family into the sledge, and bade them hasten home while he remained to combat the flames. He bade them wrap round them every rug, and leave Droug, the old horse, to find his way home. They start; soon the night comes on; the moon rises. They pass a pine forest: a noise startles the horse—his ears go back, he snuffs, snorts, then plunges madly. Pad, pad, behind them are the wolves in pursuit—an army of them; every pine tree they pass adds a fiend to the pack; the eldest lead the way, their eyes green-glowing brass. The horse does his best; but the first of the band—that Satan-face—draws so near, his white teeth gleam, he is on the sledge—"perhaps her hands relaxed her grasp of her boy," she says; "for he was gone." The cursed crew fight for their share; they are too busy to pursue. She urges the horse to increased exertion. Alas! the pack is after them again; "Satan-face" is first, as before, and ravening for more. The mother fights with the monster, but the next boy is gone—plucked from the arms she clasped round him for protection. Another respite, while the fiends dispute for their share; but, as they fly over the snow, the leader of the pack tells his companions that their food is escaping; he leaves them to pick the bones, and—pad, pad!—is after the sledge again. All fight's in vain: the green brass points, the dread fiend's eyes, pierce to the woman's brain—she falls on her back in the sledge; but, wedging in and in, past her neck, her breasts, her heart, Satan-face is away with her last, her baby boy. She remembered no more. And now she is at home—childless, but with her life. And Ivàn the woodsman sternly looks; the woman kneels. Solemnly he raises his axe, and one blow falls—headless she kneels on still—

"It had to be.
I could no other: God it was bade 'Act for Me!'"

He wipes his axe on a strip of bark, and returns silently to his work. The Jews, the gipsies, the whole crew, seethe and simmer, but say no word. Then comes the village priest, and with him the commune's head, Stàrosta, wielder of life and death; they survey the corpse, they hear the story. The priest proclaimed

"Ivàn Ivànovitch God's servant!"

"Amen!" murmured the crowd, and "left acquittal plain adjudged." They told Ivàn he was free. "How otherwise?" he asked.

Notes.—*Ivàn Ivànovitch* is "an imaginary personage, who is the embodiment of the peculiarities of the Russian people, in the same way as *John Bull* represents the English and *Johnny Crapaud* the French character. He is described as a lazy, good-natured person." (*Webster's Dict.*) *A verst* is equal to about two-thirds of an English mile. *Droug:* the horse's name means friend, and is pronounced "drook." *Pope* should not be spelled with a capital; it is merely the Russian term for priest—*papa*, father. *Pomeschìk* means a landed proprietor. *Stàrosta*, the old man of the village, the overseer.

This is a variant of a Russian wolf-story which, in one form or another, we all heard in our childhood. The poet visited Russia in the course of his great tour in Europe in 1833, and he has told the familiar tale of the unhappy mother who saved her own life by throwing one after another of her children to the pursuing wolves, with all the local colouring and fidelity to the facts to which we are accustomed in the poet's work. Not merely as a tale dramatically told are we to consider the poem; but—as might be expected—we must look upon it as a problem in mental pathology. The superficial observer, looking upon the mere facts, and not troubling very much about the psychology of the case, will at once condemn the unhappy mother, and execute her as promptly in his own mind as did Ivàn Ivànovitch with his axe. But rough and ready judgments, however necessary in the conduct of our daily life, are frequently unsound; and the voice of the people is about the last voice that should be listened to in such a case as this. If a man who is usually considered a sane and decent member of society suddenly does some abnormal and outrageous thing, we at once ask ourselves, "Is he mad?" If a mother, any mother, suddenly violates the maternal instinct in a flagrant manner, we immediately suspect her of mental derangement. The maternal instinct is the strongest thing in nature; the ties which bind a woman to her offspring are stronger, in the ordinary healthy mother, than the ties which bind a man to decent and ordinary observance of the laws of society. Old Bailey judgments are not to be employed in such a case as this; it is one for a specialist. And we apprehend there is not a competent authority in brain troubles living who would not acquit Louscha on the ground of insanity.

Ixion. (*Jocoseria*, 1883.) Ixion, in Greek mythology, was the son of Phlegyas and king of the Lapithæ. He married Dia, daughter of Deioneus, and promised to make his father-in-law certain bridal presents. To avoid the fulfilment of his promise, he invited him to a banquet, and when Deioneus came to the feast he cruelly murdered him. No one would purify him for the murder, and he was consequently shunned by all mankind. Zeus, however, took pity on him, and took him up to heaven and there purified him. At the table of the gods he fell in love with Hera (Juno), and afterwards attempted to seduce her. Ixion was banished from heaven, and by the command of Zeus was tied by Mercury to a wheel which perpetually revolved in the air. Ixion, condemned to eternal punishment, is in the poem described as defying Zeus after the manner of Prometheus. It is impossible to doubt that Mr. Browning intends to represent the popular idea of God and his own attitude towards the doctrine of eternal punishment. It is, however, only the caricature of God created by popular misconception at which the poet aims, whatever may have to be said of his opinions concerning eschatology. As Caliban thought there was a *Quiet* above Setebos, so Ixion appeals to the Potency over Zeus. The truth is intended that both unsophisticated man in the savage state and the highest type of cultured man agree in their theological beliefs so far as to acknowledge a Supreme Being of a higher character than the anthropomorphic God of popular worship. Of course both Caliban and Ixion talk Browningese. Ixion is represented as comparing himself with his torturer :—

> "Behold us!
> Here the revenge of a God, there the amends of a Man"—

a man with bodily powers constantly renewed, to enable him to suffer. Above the torment is a rainbow of hope, built of the vapour, pain-wrung, which the light of heaven, in passing tinges with the colour of hope. Endowed with bodily powers intended to be God's ministers, Ixion has been betrayed by them. But he was but man foiled by sense; he has endured enough suffering to teach him his error and his folly. Why make the agony perpetual?" "To punish thee." Zeus may reply. Ixion says he once was king of Thessaly: he had to punish crime. Had he been able to read the hearts of the criminals whom he sent to their doom, and had plainly seen repentance there, would he not have given them

"Life to retraverse the past, light to retrieve the misdeed?"

Zeus made man, with flaw or faultless: it was his work. Ixion had been admitted, all human as he was, to the company of the gods as their equal. He had faith in the good faith and the love of Zeus, and for acting upon it was cast from Olympus to Erebus. Man conceived Zeus as possessing his own virtues: he trusted, loved him because Zeus aspired to be equal in goodness to man. Ixion defies him, tells him he apes the man who made him; it is Zeus who is hollowness. The iris, born of Ixion's tears, sweat and blood, bursting to vapour above, arching his torment, glorifies his pain; and man, even from hell's triumph, may look up and rejoice. He rises from the wreck, past Zeus to the Potency above him—

"Thither I rise, whilst thou—Zeus, keep the godship and sink!"

The Zeus of the poem bears no relation whatever to the Christian's God. The Potency over all is the All-Father, the God of Love, who yet, in Infinite Love, may punish rebellious man, who conceivably may reject His love, may never feel a touch of the repentance which Ixion declared he felt, who suffering and still sinning, hating and still rebelling, may conceivably be left to the consequences of the rebellion which knows no cessation, as the suffering no respite.

NOTES.—*Sisuphos*, "the crafty": son of Æolus, punished in the other world by being forced for ever to keep on rolling a block of stone to the top of a steep hill, only to see it roll again to the valley, and to start the toilsome task again. *Tantalos*, a wealthy king of Sipylus in Phrygia. He was a favourite of the gods, and allowed to share their meals; but he insulted them, and was thrown into Tartarus. He suffered from hunger and thirst, immersed in water up to the chin; when he opened his mouth the water dried up and the fruits suspended before him vanished into the air. *Heré*, in Greek mythology the same as Juno, queen of heaven and wife of Zeus or Jupiter. *Thessaly*, a country of Greece, bounded on the south by the southern parts of Greece, on the east by the Ægean, on the north by Macedonia and Mygdonia, and on the west by Illyricum and Epirus. *Olumpos*, a mountain in Thessaly. On the highest peak is the throne of Zeus, and it is there that he summons the assemblies of the gods. *Erebos*, in Greek mythology "the primeval darkness." The word is usually applied to the lower regions, filled with impenetrable darkness. *Tartaros-doomed* = hell-doomed.

Jacopo (*Luria*) was the faithful secretary of the Moorish mercenary who led the army of Florence.

Jacynth. (*Flight of the Duchess.*) The maid of the Duchess, who went to sleep while the gipsy woman held the interview with her mistress, and induced her to leave her husband's home.

James Lee's Wife. (*Dramatis Personæ*, 1864; originally entitled *James Lee.*) This is a story of an unfortunate marriage, told in a series of meditations by the wife. Mr. Symons describes the psychological processes detailed in the poem as "the development of disillusion, change, alienation, severance and parting." The key-notes of the nine divisions of the work are: I. Anxiety; II. Apprehension; III. Expostulation; IV. Despair; V. Reflection; VI. Change; VII. Self-denial; VIII. Resignation; IX. Self-Sacrifice.

I. At the Window.—The wife reflects that summer has departed. The chill, which settles upon the earth as the sun's warm rays are withheld, falls heavily on her heart. Her husband has been absent but a day, and as she thinks of the changing year, she asks, with apprehension, "Will he change too?"

II. By the Fireside.—He has returned, but not the sun to her heart. As they sit by the fire in their seaside home, she reflects that the fire is built of "shipwreck wood." Are her hopes to be shipwrecked too? Sailors on the stormy waters may envy their security as they behold the ruddy light from their fire over the sea, and "gnash their teeth for hate" as they reflect on their warm safe home; but ships rot and rust and get worm-eaten in port, as well as break up on rocks. She wonders who lived in that home before them. Did a woman watch the man with whom she began a happy voyage—see the planks start, and hell yawn beneath her?

III. In the Doorway.—The steps of coming winter hasten; the trees are bare; soon the swallows will forsake them. The wind, with its infinite wail, sings the dirge of the departed summer. Her heart shrivels, her spirit shrinks; yet, as she stands in the doorway, she reflects that they have every material comfort. They have neither cold nor want to fear in any shape, only the heart-chill, only the soul-hunger for the love that is gone. God meant that love should warm the human heart when material things without were cold and drear. She will

"live and love worthily, bear and be bold."

IV. Along the Beach.—The storm has burst; it is no longer misgiving, fear, apprehension: it is certainty. She meditates, as she watches him, that he wanted her love; she gave him all her heart. He has it still: she had taken him "for a world and more." For love turns dull earth to the glow of God. She had taken the weak earth with many weeds, but with "a little good grain too." She had watched for flowers and longed for harvest, but all was dead earth still, and the glow of God had never transfigured his soul to her. But she did love, did watch, did wait and weary and wear, was fault in his eyes. Her love had become irksome to him.

V. On the Cliff.—It is summer, and she is leaning on the dead burnt turf, looking at a rock left dry by the retiring waters. The deadness of the one and the barrenness of the other suit her melancholy; they are symbols of her position, and as she muses, a gay, blithe grasshopper springs on the turf, and a wonderful blue-and-red butterfly settles on the rock. So love settles on minds dead and bare; so love brightens all! So could her love brighten even his dead soul.

VI. Reading a Book, under the Cliff.—She is reading the poetry of "some young man" (Mr. Browning himself, who published these "Lines to the Wind" when twenty-three years old). The poet asks if the ailing wind is a dumb winged thing, entrusting its cause to him; and as she reads on she grows angry at the young man's inexperience of the mystery of life. He knows nothing of the meaning of the moaning wind: it is not suffering, not distress; it is change. That is what the wind is trying to say, and trying above all to teach: we are to

"Rejoice that man is hurled
From change to change unceasingly,
His soul's wings never furled!"

"Nothing endures," says the wind. "There's life's pact—perhaps, too, its probation; but man might at least, as he grasps 'one fair, good, wise thing,'—the love of a loving woman —grave it on his soul's hands' palms to be his for ever."

VII. Among the Rocks.—Earth sets his bones to bask in the sun, and smiles in the beauty with which the rippling water adorns him; and so she comforts herself by reflecting that we may make the low earth-nature better by suffusing it with our love-tides. Love is gain if we love only what is worth our love. How much more to make the low nature better by our throes!

VIII. Beside the Drawing-Board.—She has been drawing a hand. A clay cast of a perfect thing is before her. She has learned something of the infinite beauty of the human hand—has studied it, has praised God, its Maker, for it; and as she contemplates the world of wonders to be discovered therein, she is fain to efface her work and begin anew, for somehow grace slips from soulless finger-tips. The cast is that of a hand by Leonardo da Vinci. She has passionately longed to copy its perfection, but as the great master could not copy the perfection of the dead hand, so she has failed to draw the cast. And so she turns to the peasant girl model who is by her side that day, "a little girl with the poor coarse hand," and as she contemplates it she begins to understand the worth of flesh and blood, and that there is a great deal more than beauty in a hand. She has read Bell on the human hand, and she knows something of the infinite uses of the mechanism which is hidden beneath the flesh. She knows what use survives the beauty in the peasant hand that spins and bakes. The living woman is better than the dead cast. She has learned the lesson that all this craving for what can never be hers—for the love she cannot gain, any more than the perfection she cannot draw—is wasting her life. She will be up and doing, no longer dreaming and sighing.

IX. On Deck.—It was better to leave him! She will set him free. She had no beauty, no grace; nothing in her deserved any place in his mind. She was harsh and ill-favoured (and perhaps this was the secret of the trouble). Still, had he loved her, love could and would have made her beautiful. Some day it may be even so; and in the years to come a face, a form—her own—may rise before his mental vision, his eyes be opened, his liberated soul leap forth in a passionate "'Tis she!"

Jesus Christ. That Mr. Browning was something more than a Theist, a Unitarian, or a Broad Churchman, may be gathered from several passages in his works, as well as from direct statements to individuals. Three lines in the *Death in the Desert* (though often said to be used only dramatically), when taken in connection with the whole drift and purpose of the poem, seem to indicate a faith which is more than mere Theism:

"The acknowledgment of God in Christ, accepted by thy reason,
Solves for thee all questions in the earth and out of it,
And has so far advanced thee to be wise."

In the *Epistle of Karshish*, the Arab physician says concerning Jesus, who had raised Lazarus from the dead:—

"The very God! think, Abib, dost thou think?
So, the All-Great, were the All-Loving too—
So, through the thunder comes a loving voice
Saying, 'O heart I made, a heart beats here!
Face, my hands fashioned, see it in myself!
Thou hast no power nor may'st conceive of mine.
But love I gave thee, with myself to love,
And thou must love me who have died for thee!'
The madman saith He said so: it is strange."

Christmas Eve and *Easter Day* seem to be meaningless if they do not express the author's faith in the divinity of our Lord. Just as every believer in Him can detect the true ring of the Christian believer and lover of his Lord in the lines quoted from the *Epistle of Karshish*, so will his touchstone detect the Christian in many other passages of the poet's work.

In *Saul*, canto xviii., David says:—

"My flesh, that I seek
In the Godhead! I seek and I find it. O Saul, it shall be
A Face like my face that receives thee; a Man like to me,
Thou shalt love and be loved by, for ever: a Hand like this hand
Shall throw open the gates of new life to thee! See the Christ stand!"

David—to whom Christendom attributes the Psalms, even were he only the editor of that wonderful body of prayer and praise—as the utterer of sentiments like these, is permitted to express the orthodox opinion that he prophesied of the Christ who was to come. Mr. Browning would have hardly done this "dramatically." (What are termed "the Messianic Psalms" are ii., xxi., xxii., xlv., lxxii., cx.) Pompilia, in *The Ring and the Book*, a character which is built up of the purest and warmest faith of the poet's heart, says :—

> "I never realised God's truth before—
> How He grew likest God in being born."

The poem entitled "The Sun," in *Ferishtah's Fancies*, No. 5, may be studied in this connection.

Jews. Browning had great sympathy with the Jewish spirit. See RABBI BEN EZRA, JOCHANAN HAKKADOSH, BEN KARSHOOK, HOLY CROSS DAY, and FILIPPO BALDINUCCI.

Jochanan Hakkadosh. (*Jocoseria:* 1883.) The Hebrew which Mr. Browning quotes in the tale as the title of the work from which his incidents are derived, may be translated as "Collection of many Fables"; and the second Hebrew phrase means "from Moses to Moses [Moses Maimonides] there was never one like Moses." Although the story of this poem is not historical, it is founded on characters and events which are familiar to students of Jewish literature and history. Hakkadosh means "The Holy." Rabbi Yehudah Hannasi (the Prince) was the reputed author of the *Mishnah*, and was born before the year 140 of the Christian era. On account of his holy living he was surnamed Rabbenu Haḳḳadosh. Jochanan means John. In the *Jewish Messenger* for March 4th, 1887, the poem is reviewed from a Jewish point of view by "Mary M. Cohen," from which interesting study we extract the following particulars:—The scene of the poem is laid at Schiphaz, which is probably intended for Sheeraz, in Persia. "I think," says the authoress, "that, with artistic licence, Mr. Browning does not here portray any individual man, but takes the names and characteristics of several rabbis, fusing all into a whole. Jochanan finds old age a continued disappointment. He is represented as almost overtaken by death; his loving scholars, as was usual in the days of rabbinism, cluster about him for some worthy word of parting advice. One of the pupils asks: 'Say, does age acquiesce in vanished youth? The rabbi, groaning, answers grimly:

> "Last as first
> The truth speak I—in boyhood who began
> Striving to live an angel, and, amerced

For such presumption, die now hardly, man.
What have I proved of life? To live, indeed,
That much I learned."

It was suggested to the dying rabbi that if compassionating folk would render him up a portion of their lives, Hakkadosh might attain his fourscore years. Tsaddik, the scholar, well versed in the Targums, was foremost in urging the adoption of this expedient. By yielding up part of their lives, the pupils of Jochanan hope to combine the lessons of perfect wisdom and varied experience of life. But experience proves fatal to all the hopes, the aspirations, the high ideals of youth. Experience paralyses action. Experience chills the aspirations which animate the generous mind of the lover, the soldier, the poet, the statesman. When the men of experience contributed their quota, 'certain gamesome boys' must needs throw some of theirs also. This accounts for the rabbi being found alive unexpectedly after a long interval:

"Trailing clouds of glory do we come from God, who is our home."

The rabbi utters heaven-sent intuitions, the gift of these lads. Under the influence of the *Ruach*, or spirit, Jochanan declares that happiness, here and hereafter, is found in acting on the generous impulses, the noble ideals which are sent into the mind, in spite of the testimony of experience that we shall fail to realise our aspirations. 'There is no sin,' says the rabbi, 'except in doubting that the light which lured the unwary into darkness did no wrong, had I but marched on boldly.' What we see here as antitheses, or as complementary truths, are reconciled hereafter. This reconciliation cannot be grasped by our present faculties. The rabbi seems to 'babble' when he tries to express in words the truth he sees. The pure white light of truth, seen through the medium of the flesh, is composed of many coloured rays. Evil is like the dark lines in the spectrum. The whole duty of man is to learn to love. If he fails, it matters not; he has learned the art: 'so much for the attempt—anon performance.' Love is the sum of our spiritual intuitions, the law of our practical conduct."

NOTES.—*Mishna*, the second or oral Jewish law; the great collection of legal decisions by the ancient rabbis; and so the fundamental document of Jewish oral law. *Schiphaz*, an imaginary place; or perhaps *Sheeraz*, on the Bundemeer, referred to at end of poem. *Jochanan Ben Sabbathai*, not historical. *Khubbezleh*, a fanciful name of the poet's invention. *Targum*, a Chaldee version or paraphrase of the Old Testament. *Nine Points of Perfection*: Nine is a trinity of trinities, and is a mystical number of perfection; the slang expression "dressed to the nines" means dressed to perfection. *Tsaddik* = just, not historical. *Dob* = Bear (the constellation). *The Bear*, the constellation. *Aish*, the Great Bear. *The Bier*: the Jews called the constellation of the Great Bear "The Bier." *Three Daughters*, the tail stars of the Bear. *Banoth* = daughters. *The Ten*: Jewish martyrs under the Roman empire. *Akiba, Rabbi*, lived A.C. 117, and laid the groundwork of the Mishna. He was one of the greatest Jewish teachers, and was at the height of his popularity when the revolt of the Jews under Barcochab took place. (See for a history of the revolt, and of Akiba's influence, *Milman's History of the Jews*, Book xviii.) He was scraped to death with an iron comb. *Perida*: a Jewish teacher of such infinite patience that the Talmud records that he repeated his lesson to a dull pupil four hundred times, and as even then he could not understand, four hundred times more, on which the spirit declared that four hundred years should be added to his life. *Uzzean*: Job, the most patient man, was of the land of Uz. *Djinn*, a supernatural being. *Edom*: Rome and Christianity went by this name in the Talmud. "*Sic Jesus vult*," so Jesus wills. *The Statist* = the statesman. *Mizraim* = Egypt. *Shushan* = lily. *Tohu-bohu*, void and waste. *Halaphta*, Talmudic teachers. *Ruach*, spirit. *Bendimir*: no doubt the Bundemeer, one of the chief rivers of *Farzistan*, a province in Persia. *Og's thigh bone*: "Og was king of Bashan. The rabbis say that the height of his stature was 23,033 cubits (nearly six miles). He used to drink water from the clouds, and toast fish by holding them before the orb of the sun. He asked Noah to take him into the ark, but Noah would not. When the flood was at its deepest, it did not reach to the knees of this giant. Og lived 3000 years, and then he was slain by the hand of Moses. Moses was himself ten cubits in stature (15 feet), and he took a spear ten cubits long, and threw it ten cubits high, and yet it only reached the heel of Og. . . . When dead, his body reached as far as the river Nile. Og's mother was Enach, a daughter of Adam. Her fingers were two cubits long (one yard), and on each finger she had two sharp nails. She was devoured by wild beasts.—*Maracci.*"

Jocoseria. The volume of poems under this title was published in 1883. It contains the following works: "Wanting is—What?" "Donald," "Solomon and Balkis," "Cristina and Monaldeschi," "Mary Wollstonecraft and Fuseli," "Adam, Lilith and Eve," "Ixion," "Jochanan Hakkadosh," "Never the Time and the Place," "Pambo." In a letter to a friend, along with an early copy of this work, the poet stated that "the title is taken from the work of Melander (Schwartzmann)—reviewed, by a curious coincidence, in the *Blackwood* of this month. I referred to it in a note to 'Paracelsus.' The two Hebrew quotations (put in to give a grave look to what is mere fun and invention), being translated, amount to: (1) "A Collection of Many Lies"; and (2) an old saying, 'From Moses to Moses arose none like to Moses' (*i.e.* Moses Maimonides). . . ." One of the notes to *Paracelsus* refers to Melander's "Jocoseria" as "rubbish." Melander, whose proper name was Otho Schwartzmann, was born in 1571. He published a work called "Joco-Seria," because it was a collection of stories both grave and gay.

Johannes Agricola in Meditation. (First published in *The Monthly Repository*, and signed "Z.," in 1836. Reprinted in *Dramatic Lyrics*, in *Bells and Pomegranates*, 1842.) Johannes Agricola meditates on the thought of his election or choice by the Supreme Being, who in His eternal counsels has before all worlds predestined him as an object of mercy and salvation. God thought of him before He thought of suns or moons, ordained every incident of his life for him, and mapped out its every circumstance. Totally irrespective of his conduct, God having chosen of His own sovereign grace, uninfluenced in the slightest degree by anything which Johannes has done or left undone, to consider him as a guiltless being, is pledged to save him of free mercy. It would make no difference to his ultimate salvation were he to mix all hideous sins in one draught, and drink it to the dregs. Predestined to be saved, nothing that he can do can unsave him; foreordained to heaven, nothing he could do could lead him hell-wards. As a corollary, those souls who are not so predestined in the counsels of God to eternal salvation may be as holy, as perfect, in the sight of men as he (Agricola) might be vile in their sight; yet they shall be tormented for ever in hell, simply because God has mysteriously left them out of His choice. They are reprobate, non-elect, and nothing that they could possibly do could avail to save them. When Adam sinned, he sinned not only for himself, but for the whole human race, and the whole species was forthwith condemned in him, excepting only those whom God in His Sovereign mercy had from all eternity elected to save, and that without regard to their merit or demerit. These reprobate persons might try to win God's favour, might labour with all their might to please Him, and would only thereby add to their sin. Priest, doctor, hermit, monk, martyr, nun, or chorister,—all these, leading holy and before men beautiful lives, were eternally foreordained to be lost before God fashioned star or sun. For all this Johannes Agricola praises God, praises Him all the more that he cannot understand Him or His ways, praises Him especially that he has not to bargain for His love or pay a price for his salvation. Such is the terrible portrait which Mr. Browning has drawn of the teaching of a man who, as one of the Reformers, and as a friend of Luther, was the founder of what is known in religious history as Antinomianism. Hideous as is the perversion of gospel teaching which Agricola set forth, the doctrines of Antinomianism still linger on amongst certain sects of Calvinists in England and Scotland. The doctrine of reprobation is thus stated in the *Westminster Confession of Faith*, iii. 7: "The rest of mankind (*i.e.* all but the elect), God was pleased . . . to pass by, and to ordain them to dishonour and wrath, etc." Mosheim, in his *Ecclesiastical History* (century xvii., Sect. 11, Part II., chap. ii., 23), thus describes the Presbyterian Antinomians: "The Antinomians are over-rigid Calvinists, who are thought by the other Presbyterians to abuse Calvin's doctrine of the absolute decrees of God, to the injury of the cause of piety. Some of them . . . deny that it is necessary for ministers to exhort Christians to holiness and obedience of the law, because those whom God from all eternity elected to salvation will themselves, and without being admonished and exhorted by any one, by a Divine influence, or the impulse of Almighty grace, perform holy and good deeds; while those who are destined by the Divine decrees to eternal punishment, though admonished and entreated ever so much, will not obey the Divine law, since Divine grace is denied them; and it is therefore sufficient, in preaching to the people, to hold up only the gospel and faith in Jesus Christ. But others merely hold that the elect, because they cannot lose the Divine favour, do not truly commit sin and break the Divine law, although they should go contrary to its precepts and do wicked actions, and therefore it is not necessary that they should confess their sins or grieve for them: that adultery for instance, in one of the elect appears to us indeed to be a sin or a violation of the law, yet it is no sin in the sight of God, because one who is elected to salvation can do nothing displeasing to God and forbidden by the law." Very similar teaching may be discovered at the present day in the body of religionists known as Hyper-Calvinists or Strict Baptists. The professors are for the most part much better than their creed, and they are exceedingly reticent concerning their doctrines so far as they are represented by the term Antinomian; but the organs of their phase of religious belief, *The Gospel Standard* and *The Earthen Vessel*, frequently contain proofs of the vitality of Agricola's doctrines in their pages. For example, in the *Gospel Standard* for July 1891, p. 288, we find the following: "No hope, nor salvation, can possibly arise out of the law or covenant of works. Every man's works are sin,—his best works are polluted. Every page of the law unfolds his defects and shortcomings, nor will allow of a few shillings to the pound,—Pay the whole or die the death." The tendency of Antinomianism is to become an esoteric doctrine, and it is seldom preached in any grosser form than this, however sweet it may be to the hearts of the initiated.

John of Halberstadt. The ecclesiastic in *Transcendentalism* who was also a magician and performed the "prestigious feat' of conjuring roses up in winter.

Joris. One of the riders in the poem "How they brought the Good News from Ghent to Aix."

Jules. (*Pippa Passes*). The young French artist who married Phene under a misunderstanding, the result of a practical joke played upon him by his companions.

Karshish. (*An Epistle.*) The Arab physician who wrote of the interesting cases which he had seen in his travels to his brother leech, and who described Lazarus, who was raised from the dead, as having been in a trance.

King, A. The song in *Pippa Passes*, beginning "A king lived long ago," was originally published in *The Monthly Repository* (edited by W. J. Fox) in 1835.

King Charles I. of England. See STRAFFORD.

King Charles Emanuel, of Savoy (*King Victor and King Charles*), was the son of Victor Amadeus II., Duke of Savoy. He became king when his father suddenly abdicated, in 1730.

King Victor and King Charles: A Tragedy. (*Bells and Pomegranates*, II., 1842.) Victor Amadeus II., born in 1666, was Duke of Savoy. He obtained the kingdom of Sicily by treaty from Spain, which he afterwards exchanged with the Emperor for the island of Sardinia, with the title of King (1720). He was fierce, audacious, unscrupulous, and selfish, profound in dissimulation, prolific in resources, and a "breaker of vows both to God and man." He was, however, an able and warlike monarch, and had the interests of his kingdom at heart. He was, moreover, beloved by the people over whom he ruled, and under his reign the country made great progress in finances, education, and the development of its natural resouces. His whole reign was one of unexampled prosperity, and his life was a continued career of happiness until, in 1715, his beloved son Victor died. His daughter, the Queen of Spain, died shortly after. Charles Emanuel, his second son, had never been a favourite with the King. He was ill-favoured in appearance, and weak and vacillating in his conduct. When the Queen died, in 1728, Victor married Anna Teresa Canali, a widowed countess, whom he created Marchioness of Spigno. For some reasons or other which have never been satisfactorily explained, the King now decided to abdicate in favour of his son Charles Emanuel. He gave out that he was weary of the world and disgusted with affairs of State, and desired to live in retirement for the remainder of his days. It is more probable that his fiery and audacious temper, and his deceitfulness, dissimulation, and persistent endeavours to overreach the other powers with which he had intercourse, had involved him in difficulties of State policy from which he could only extricate himself by this grave step. Mr. Browning implies, in the preface to his tragedy, that his investigations of the memoirs and correspondence of the period had enabled him to offer a more reasonable solution of the difficulties connected with this strange episode in Italian history than any previous account has offered. When the King announced his intention to resign his crown, he was entreated by his people, his ministers and his son, to forego a project which every one thought would be prejudicial to the interests of the kingdom; but nothing would induce him to reconsider his decision, which he carried out with the completest ceremonial. After taking this step he retired with his wife to his castle at Chambéry; and, as might have been expected, he speedily grew weary of his seclusion. He had an attack of apoplexy, and when he recovered it was with faculties impaired and a temper readily irritated to outbursts of violent behaviour. The marchioness now began to suggest to him that he had done unwisely by resigning his crown; and, day by day, urged him to recover it. This was probably due to the desire she felt of being queen. He still remained on good terms with his son, who visited him at Chambéry; but he gave him to understand that he was not satisfied with his management of affairs, and constantly intervened in their direction. In the summer of 1731 Charles, accompanied by his queen (Polyxena) visited his father at the baths of Eviano, and before his return home he received private intimation that his father was about to proceed to Turin to resume the crown he had resigned. He lost no time in returning home, which he reached just before his father and the marchioness. He visited the ex-king on the following day, when he was informed that his reason for returning to Turin was the necessity for seeking a climate more suitable to his present state of health. Charles was satisfied with the explanation, and placed the castle of Moncalieri at his father's service: here the ex-king received his son's ministers, and hints were dropped and threatening expressions used by Victor, which left little doubt as to his intentions on the minds of his audience. It now became necessary for King Charles to seriously consider the best means to secure himself and his queen from the effects of his father's change of mind. Victor lost little time in declaring himself: on September 25th, 1731, he sent for the Marquis del Borgo, and ordered him to deliver up the deed by which he had resigned his crown. The minister evaded in his reply, and of course informed the King of the demand. Now it was that Charles was inclined to waver between his duty to his realm and his duty to his father. He was a good, obedient son, and of upright and generous disposition, and was inclined to yield to his father's wishes. He called the chief officers of state around him, and laid the matter before them. They were not forgetful of the threats which the old king had recently used towards them, and the Archbishop of Turin had little difficulty in convincing them and the king that it was impossible to comply with his father's demands. If anything were wanting to confirm them in their decision, it was forthcoming in the shape of news that the old king had demanded at midnight admittance into the fortress of Turin, but had been refused by the commander. The council of Charles Emanuel readily concurred in the opinion that Victor should be arrested. The Marquis d'Ormea, who had been the old king's prime minister, was charged with the execution of the warrant of arrest. He proceeded, with assistance and appropriate military precautions, to carry out the order, entering the king's apartments at Moncalieri. They captured the marchioness, who was hurried away screaming to a state prison at Ceva, with many of her relatives and supporters; and then secured the person of the old king. He was asleep, and when aroused and made acquainted with the mission of the intruders, he became violently excited, and had to be wrapped in the bedclothes and forced into one of the court carriages, which conveyed him to the castle of Rivoli, situated in a small town of five thousand inhabitants, near Turin. His attendants and guards were strictly ordered to say nothing to him: if he addressed them, they maintained an inflexible silence, merely by way of reply making a very low and submissive bow. He was afterwards permitted to have the company of his wife and to remove to another prison, but on October 31st, 1732, he died.

Laboratory, The: ANCIEN REGIME. First appeared in *Hood's Magazine,* June 1844, to which it was contributed to help Hood in his illness; afterwards published in *Dramatic Romances and Lyrics* (*Bells and Pomegranates,* VII.) This poem and *The Confessional* were printed together, and entitled *France and Spain.* Mr. Arthur Symons reminds us that Rossetti's first water-colour was an illustration of this poem, and has for subject and title the line "Which is the poison to poison her, prithee?" The keynote of the poem is jealousy, a distorted love-frenzy that impels to the rival's extinction. The story is told in the most powerful and concentrated manner. The jealous woman's whole soul is compressed into her words and actions; her emotion is visible; her voice, subdued yet full of energy, is audible in every line. The woman is a Brinvilliers, who has secured an interview with an alchemist in his laboratory, that she may purchase a deadly poison for her rival. We gather from the first verse that the poison consisted principally of arsenic. The "faint smokes curling whitely," to protect the chemist from which it was necessary to wear a glass mask, sufficiently supplement our knowledge of the old poisoner's art to enable us to indicate its nature. The patience of the woman, who in her eagerness for her rival's death has no desire to hurry the manufacture of the means of it, is powerfully described. She is content to watch the chemist at his deadly work, asking questions in a dainty manner about the secrets of his art. She has all the ideas of "a big dose" which the uninitiated think requisite for big patients. "She's not little—no minion like me!" "What, only a drop?" she asks. She is anxious to know if it hurts the victim. Is it likely to injure herself too? Reassured on that point, the glass mask is removed, and for reward the old man has all her jewels and gold to his fill. He may kiss her besides, and on the mouth if he will. There is a very remarkable instance in the second verse of the use made of antithesis by the poet. The proper emphasis can only be given when we rightly apprehend the ideas which oppose each other in the lines—

> "*He* is with *her*, and *they* know that *I* know
> Where they are, what they do: they believe *my tears* flow
> While *they laugh*, laugh at *me*, at me fled to the *drear*
> *Empty church*, to pray God in, for *them*!—I am *here*."

The antithesis of the several sets of ideas is the only safe guide to the emphasis—*he* as opposed to *her*, *tears* to *laughter*, *me* to *them*, the *church* to the *laboratory*.* Although the effects of some

* One of the most remarkable instances of the use made of antithesis I ever heard was at Friern Barnet Church, into the porch of which I strolled when walking one summer day some twenty-five years ago. I was just in time to hear the preacher use words which I have never forgotten. The antithesis of the sentence was perfect: If *thou* wouldst *hereafter be* where *Christ is*, see *thou* be not found

of the deadliest poisons were well known to the ancients, their detection and recovery from the body by chemical means is a branch of science of only modern discovery. The Greeks and Romans were well acquainted with mercury, arsenic, henbane, aconite and hemlock. The art of poisoning was brought to great perfection in India; but, though dissection of the living and the dead was practised by the Alexandrian School in the third century B.C., the Greek and Roman physicians were quite incapable of such a knowledge of pathology as would enable them to detect any but the coarsest signs of poisoning in a dead body. Much less were they able to detect or recover by analysis the particular poison used by the criminal. It is not surprising that, under such circumstances, professional poisoners usually escaped punishment. In the fourteenth century arsenic was generally employed. Of the great schools of poisoners which flourished in Italy in the sixteenth and seventeenth centuries, Venice was the earliest. Troublesome people were removed by the Council of Ten by means of convenient poisons. Toffana and others combined poisoning with the art of cookery; and T. Baptist Porta, in his book on "Natural Magic," under the section of cooking, shows that the trades of poisoner and cook were often combined. Toffana was the greatest of all the seventeenth-century poisoners. She made solutions of arsenic of various strengths, and sold them in phials under the name of "Naples Water" or "Acquetta di Napol." It is said that she poisoned six hundred persons, including Popes Pius III. and Clement XIV. There was practically no fear of detection, and the liquid was sold openly to any one willing to pay the price for a deadly compound; the purpose for which it could alone be employed being perfectly well understood. Mr. Browning's poem introduces us to a laboratory, where an arsenical preparation is being prepared. The glass

now where *He* is *not*, lest *when He come* he say to *you*, what *now* by your conduct you say to *Him* 'Depart from Me—where *I* am *you* can not come!'" If any one would investigate this principle of antithetic reading further, let him take Macaulay's "Essay on Von Ranke's Popes," vol. ii., p. 128, and beginning at the words, "There is not, and there never was," see how to place the correct emphasis by observation of the opposed ideas. This is the one great secret of good reading. Printers' punctuation is horribly misleading, and should usually be disregarded mask refered to in the first line was used to protect the purchaser from the white, deadly smoke which the mineral gave off. The poison for which the lady paid so lavishly could be prepared nowadays by any chemist's apprentice for a few pence; but, plentiful as it is, it is comparatively rarely used by criminals, as the same apprentice could infallibly detect it in the body after death, and reproduce in a test tube the very same poison used by the criminal.

Lady and the Painter, The. (*Asolando:* 1889.) A lady visiting an artist who has a picture on his easel of a nude female figure, protests against the irreverence to womanhood involved in his inducing a young woman to strip and stand stark-naked as his model. Before replying, he asks the lady what it is that clings half-savage-like around her hat. She, thinking he is admiring her headgear, tells him they are "wild-bird wings, and that the Paris fashion-books say that next year the skirts of women's dresses are to be feathered too. Owls, hawks, jays and swallows are most in vogue." Asking if he may speak plainly, and having been answered that he may, he tells Lady Blanche that it would be more to her credit to strip off all her bird-spoils and stand naked to help art, like his poor model, as a type of purest womanhood. "*You*, clothed with murder of His best of harmless beings, what have you to teach?" The poem is directed against the savage and wicked custom of wearing the plumage of birds, by which millions of God's beautiful creatures are doomed annually to slaughter; by wearing gloves made of skins stripped from the living bodies of animals (if report be true); and by the use of sealskin and other animal coverings, which necessitates the wholesale slaughter of countless thousands of happy creatures in Arctic seas. I recently asked Miss Frances Power Cobbe—the noble lady who was a friend of Mr. Browning, and who has devoted her life and splendid literary talents to befriending dumb animals and protesting against cruelty in high places—to furnish me with some account of the agitation against the foolish habit of wearing bird-plumage in women's bonnets. I have received from Miss Cobbe the following particulars: "The Plumage League began December 1885. It started with a letter in the *Times*, December 18th, 1885 (quoted *in extenso* in the *Zoophilist*, January 1886, p. 164), by the Rev. F. O. Morris, embodying one from Lady Mount Temple. Before May 1886 a long list of names (given in the *Zoophilist*) were given as patrons of the League, including Lady Mount Temple, Duchess of Sutherland, Lady Londesborough, Lady Sudeley, Hon. Mrs. R. C. Boyle, Louisa Marchioness of Waterford, Princess Christian, Lady Burdett Coutts, Lady Eastlake, Lady John Manners, Lady Tennyson, Lady Herbert of Lea, and about forty other ladies of rank. I should say that the League was originated by Lady Mount Temple and the Rev. F. O. Morris. There is another society in existence for the same purpose, working in London—the Birds' Protection Society—one of whose local secretaries lately applied to me for a subscription."

Lady Carlisle, Lucy Percy. (*Strafford.*) She was the daughter of the ninth Earl of Northumberland, and did her utmost to save Strafford's life.

Lapaccia. Mona Lapaccia was Fra Lippo Lippi's aunt, the sister of his father, who brought him up till he was eight years old, when, being no longer able to maintain him, she took him to the Carmelite Convent.

La Saisiaz (A. E. S., Sept. 14th, 1877).—Mr. Browning was staying during the autumn of 1877, with his sister, amongst the mountains near Geneva, at a villa called "La Saisiaz," which in the Savoyard dialect means "The Sun." They were accompanied on this occasion by Miss Ann Egerton Smith. The happiness of the visit to this beautiful spot was marred by the sudden death of Miss Smith, from heart disease, on the night of September 14th. The poem is the result of the poet's musings on death, God, the soul, and the future state. It is one of Mr. Browning's noblest and most beautiful utterances on the great questions of the Supreme Being and the ultimate destiny of the soul of man. It is Theism of the loftiest kind, and the grounds on which it is based are as philosophical as they are poetically expressed. The work has often been compared with the *In Memoriam* of Tennyson. The powerful optimism, the robust confidence and devout faith in the infinite love and wisdom of the Supreme Being, are in each poem emphasized again and again. After several pages of description of the scenery of the locality, Mr. Browning imagines that a spirit of the place bade him question, and promised answer, of the problems of existence—

> "Does the soul survive the body? Is there God's self—no
> or yes?"

He is weak, but "weakness never needs be falseness." He will go to the foundations of his faith; he will take stock—see how he stands in the matter of belief and doubt; will fight the question out without fence or self-deception. It shall not satisfy him to say that a second life is necessary to give value to the present, or that pleasure, if not permanent, turns to pain; in the presence of that recent death there must be rigid honesty, and it does not satisfy him to know there's ever some one lives though we be dead. Such a thought is repugnant to him,—not that repugnance matters if it be all the truth. He must, however, ask if there be any prospect of supplemental happiness? In the face of the strong bodies yoked to stunted souls, and the spirits that would soar were they not tethered by a fleshly chain; of the hindering helps, and the hindrances which are really helps in disguise,—the fact remains that hindered we are. However the fact be explained, life is a burthen; at best, more or less, in its whole amount is it curse or blessing? He thinks he has courage enough to fairly ask this question, and accept the answer of reason. He has questioned, and has been answered. Now, a question presupposes two things: that which questions and answers must exist. "I think, therefore I am" (*Cogito, ergo sum*), said Descartes. (And this is about the only thing in life of which we can be certain. Matter may be all illusion; as Bishop Berkeley said, we may be living in one long dream. But at least it takes a mind to do that. We therefore are; soul *is*, whatever else is not.) The second thing presupposed is, that the fact of being answered is proof that there must be a force outside itself:

"Actual ere its own beginning, operative through its course,
Unaffected by its end,—that this thing likewise needs must be."

Here, then, are two facts: the last we may call God; the first, Soul. If an objector demands that he shall *prove* these facts his answer is that, recognising they surpass his power of proving these facts, proves them such to him:

"Ask the rush if it suspects
Whence and how the stream which floats it had a rise,
and where and how
Falls or flows on still!"

If the rush could think and speak, it would say it only knows that it floats and is, and that an external stream bears it onward. What may happen to it the rush knows not: it may be wrecked, or it may land on shore and take root again; but this is mere surmise, not knowledge. Can we have better foundation for believing that, because we doubtless are, we shall as doubtless be? Men say we have, "because God seems good and wise." But there reigns wrong in life. "God seems powerful," they say; "why, then, are right and wrong at strife?" "Anyhow, we want a future life," say men; "without it life would be brutish." But wanting a thing, and hoping for it, are not proofs that our aspirations will be gratified; out of all our hopes, how many have had complete fulfilment? None. But "we believe," men sigh. So far as others are concerned the poet will not speak—he knows not. But he knows not what he is himself, which nevertheless is an ignorance which is no barrier to his knowing that he exists and can recognise what gives him pain or pleasure. What others are or are not is surmise; his own experience is knowledge. To his own experience, then, he appeals. He has lived, done, suffered, loved, hated, learned and taught this: there is no reconciling wisdom with a distracted world, no reconciling goodness with evil if it is to finally triumph, no reconciling power if the aim is to fail; if—and he only speaks for himself, his own convictions, and not for any other man's—if you hinder him from assuming that earth is a school-time and life a place of probation, all is chaos to him; he cannot say how these arguments and reasons may affect other men; he reiterates that he speaks for himself alone, because to colour-blind men the gras which is green to him may be red,—who is to decide which uses the proper term, supposing only two men existed, and one called grass green, the other red? So God must be the referee in His own case. The earth, as a school, is perhaps different for each individual; our pains and pleasures no more tally than our colour-sense. The poet, therefore, recognises that for him the world is his world, and no other man's; he is to judge what it means for himself. He will therefore proceed to estimate the world as it seems to him, exactly as he would judge of an artisan's work—is it a success or a failure? Was God's will or His power in fault when the vapours shrouded the blue heaven, and the flowers fell at the breath of the dragon? Death waits on every rose-bloom, pain upon every pleasure, shadow on every brightness. We cannot love, but death lurks hard by; cannot learn sympathy unless men suffer pain. If he is told that all this is necessity, he will bear it as best he can; if, on the other hand, you say it has been ordained by a Cause all-good, all-wise, all-potent, he protests as a man he will not acquiesce if, at the same time, you tell him that this life is all:

> "No, as I am man, I mourn the poverty I must impute:
> Goodness, wisdom, power, all bounded, each a human attribute!"

Speaking for himself, he counts this show of things a failure if after this life there be no other; if the school is not to educate for another sphere, all its lessons are fruitless pain and toil. But, grant a second life, he heartily acquiesces; he sees triumph in misfortune's worst assaults, and gain in all the loss. When was he so near to knowledge as when hampered by his recognised ignorance? Was not beauty made more precious by the deformities surrounding him? Did he not learn to love truth better when be contemplated the reign of falsehood? And for love, who knows what its value is till he has suffered by the death-pang? The poet here breaks off the argument to address the spirit of the lost friend, and express his hope that one day they may meet again:—

> "Can it be, and must, and will it?"

Then he recalls his thoughts from the region of surmise, to which they have wandered, home to stern and sober fact. He needs not the old plausibilities of the "misery done to man" and the "injustice of God," if another life compensate not for the ills of the present; he is prepared to take his stand as umpire to the champions Fancy and Reason, as they dispute the case between them. FANCY begins the amicable war by conceding that the surmise of life after death is as plain as a certainty, and acknowledges that there are now three facts—God, the soul, and the future life. REASON assents, sees there is definite advantage in the acknowledgment, admits the good of evil in the present life, detects the progress of everything towards good, and, as the next life must be an advance upon this one, suggests that, at the first cloud athwart man's sky, he should not hesitate, but die. FANCY then increases its concession, and sees the necessity of a hell for the punishment of those who would act the butterfly before they have played out the worm. Thus we have five facts now—God, soul, earth, heaven and hell. REASON declares that more is required: are we to shut our eyes, stop our ears, and live here in a state of nescience, simply waiting for the life to come, which is to do everything for the soul? FANCY protests that this present stage of our existence has worth incalculable—that every moment spent here means so much loss or gain for that next life which on this life depends. We have now six plain facts established. REASON points out that FANCY has proved too much by appending a definite reward to every good action and a fixed punishment to every bad one. We lay down laws as stringent in the moral as the material world. If we say, "Would you live again, be just," it is to put a necessity upon man as determined as the law of respiration—"Would you live now, regularly draw your breath.' If immortality were anything more than surmise, if heaven and hell were as plainly the consequences of our course of life here as a fall of a breach of the laws of gravity, then men would be compelled to do right and avoid evil. Probation would be gone, our freedom would be destroyed, neither merit nor discipline would remain—

"Thus have we come back full circle."

The poet says he hopes,—he has no more than hope, but hope—no less than hope. Standing on the mountain, looking down upon the Lake of Geneva, his eye falls on the places where dwelt four great men *Rousseau*, who lived at Geneva; *Byron*, lived at the villa called "Diodati," at Geneva; and wrote the *Prisoner of Chillon* at Ouchy, on the Lake; *Voltaire*, who built himself a château at Fernex; *Gibbon*, who wrote the concluding portion of his great work at Lausanne. The somewhat obscure reference to the "pine tree of Makistos," near the close of the poem, has caused considerable puzzling of brains amongst Browning students, none of whom have been able to assist me in solving the problem. So far as I am able to understand it, the solution seems to be this: The reference to Makistos is from the *Agamemnon* of Æschylus. The town of Makistos had a watch-tower on a neighbouring eminence, from which the beacon lights flashed the news of the fall of Troy to Greece. Clytemnestra says:

"sending a bright blaze from Ide,
Beacon did beacon send,
Pass on—the pine-tree—to Makistos' watch-place."

So the famous writers named as connected with that part of the Lake of Geneva contemplated by Mr. Browning, who were all Theists, passed on the pine-tree torch of Theism from age to age—Diodati, Rousseau, Gibbon, Byron, Voltaire, who—

"at least believed in Soul, was very sure of God."

(Voltaire built a church at Ferney, over the portal of which he affixed the ostentatious inscription, "*Deo erexit Voltaire.*") Many writers (Canon Cheyne for one, in the *Origin of the Psalter*, p. 410) have thought that by the lines beginning, "He there with the brand flamboyant," etc., the poet referred to himself. Of course, any such idea is preposterous; the reference was to Voltaire. Mr. Browning, apart from the question of the egotism involved, could not say of himself, "he at least believed in soul." There was no minimising of religious faith in the poet. Still less could he speak of himself as "crowned by prose and verse."

NOTES.—*Python*, the Rock-snake, the typical genus of Pythonidæ; "*Athanasius contra mundum*" = Athanasius against the world. St. Athanasius, Bishop of Alexandria, and one of the most illustrious defenders of the Christian faith, was born about the year 297. In defending the Nicene Creed he had so much opposition to contend with from the Arian heretics that, in the words of Hooker, it was "the whole world against Athanasius, and Athanasius against it."

Last Ride Together, The. (*Men and Women*, 1855; *Romances*, 1863; *Dramatic Romances*, 1868.) This poem is considered by many critics to be the noblest of all Browning's love poems; for dramatic intensity, for power, for its exhibition of what Mr. Raleigh has aptly termed Browning's "tremendous concentration of his power in excluding the object world and its relations," the poem is certainly unequalled. It is a poem of unrequited love, in which there is nothing but the noblest resignation; a compliance with the decrees of fate, but with neither a shadow of disloyalty to the ideal, nor despair of the result of the dismissal to the lover's own soul development. The woman may reject him,—there is no wounded pride; she does not love him,—he is not angry with her, nor annoyed that she fails to estimate him as highly as he estimates himself. He has the ideal in his heart; it shall be cherished as the occupant of his heart's throne for ever—of the ideal he, at least, can never be deprived. This ideal shall be used to elevate and sublimate his desires, to expand his soul to the fruition of his boundless aspiration for human love, used till it transfigures the human in the man till it almost becomes Divine. And so—as he knows his fate—since all his life seemed meant for, fails—his whole heart rises up to bless the woman, to whom he gives back the hope she gave; he asks only its memory and her leave for one more last ride with him. It is granted:

> "Who knows but the world may end to-night?"

(a line which no poet but Browning ever could have written. The force of the hour, the value of the quintessential moment as factors in the development of the soul, have never been set forth, even by Browning, with such startling power.) She lay for a moment on his breast, and then the ride began. He will not question how he might have succeeded better had he said this or that, done this or the other. She might not only not have loved him, she might have hated. He reflects that all men strive, but few succeed. He contrasts the petty done with the vast undone,

> "What hand and brain went ever paired?
> What heart alike conceived and dared?
> What act proved all its thought had been?
> What will but felt the fleshly screen?"

And the meaning of it all, the reason of the struggle, the outcome of the effort? The poet alone can tell: he *says* what we *feel.* "But, poet," he asks, "are you nearer your own sublime than we rhymeless ones? You sculptor, you man of music, have you attained your aims?" Then he consoles himself that if here we had perfect bliss, still there is the life beyond, and it is better to have a bliss to die with dim-descried—

> "Earth being so good, would heaven seem best?"

What if for ever he rode on with her as now, "The instant made eternity"?

Lazarus, who was raised from the dead, is the real hero of the poem *An Epistle.*

Léonce Miranda. (*Red Cotton Night-Cap Country.*) The principal actor in the drama was the son and heir of a wealthy

Paris jeweller. He formed an illicit connection with Clara de Millefleurs, and lived with her at St. Rambert, finally committing suicide from the tower on his estate. It is said that the real name of the firm of jewellers was "Meller Brothers," and that Clara de Millefleurs was Anna de Beaupré.

Levi Lincoln Thaxter. *Poet Lore*, vol. i., p. 598 (1889), states that Mr. Browning wrote an inscription for the grave of Levi Lincoln Thaxter, a well known American Browning reader, on the Maine sea-coast. The inscription runs thus:—"Levi Lincoln Thaxter. Born in Watertown, Massachusetts, Feb. 1st, 1824. Died May 31st, 1884.

"Thou, whom these eyes saw never! Say friends true
Who say my soul, helped onward by my song,
Though all unwittingly, has helped thee too?
I gave of but the little that I knew;
How were the gift requited, while along
Life's path I pace, couldst thou make weakness strong!
Help me with knowledge—for Life's Old——Death's New!"
R. B. to L. L. T., *April* 1885.

Life in a Love. (*Men and Women*, 1855, *Lyrics*, 1863; *Dramatic Lyrics*, 1868.) A man is content to spend his whole life on the chance that the woman whose heart he pursues will one day cease to elude him. When the old hope is dashed to the ground, a new one springs up and flies straight to the same mark. And what if he fail of his purpose here? How can life be better expended than in devotion to one worthy ideal?

Light Woman, A. (*Men and Women*, 1855; *Romances*, 1863 *Dramatic Romances*, 1868.) A wanton-eyed woman ensnares a man in her toils just to add him to the hundred others she has captured. The victim has a friend who feels equal to conquering the victor. It is a question which is the stronger soul; the woman of a hundred conquests lies in the strong man's hand as tame as a pear from the wall. But the game turns out to be a serious one: the light woman recognises her conqueror as the higher soul, and loves him accordingly. What is he to do? He does not wish to eat the pear; is he to cast it away? It is an awkward thing to play with souls. Light as she was, she had a heart, though the hundred others could not discover a way to it; this man did, and broke it. The question for the breaker is

What does he seem to himself? The last lines of the poem are interesting. The author says of himself:—

> "And Robert Browning, you writer of plays,
> Here's a subject made to your hand."

Likeness, A. (*Dramatis Personæ*, 1864.) As no two faces are exactly alike in every particular, so no two souls are ever cast in one mould. The very markings of our finger tips differ in every hand, and so each soul has its own language, which must be learned by whomsoever would discover its secret. And here science avails not; soul grammars and lexicons are not written for its tongue. A face, a glance, a word will do; but it must be the right glance, and the true open-sesame. The face which has spoken to us, the soul visitant who has penetrated to our solitude, the book, the deed which has formed the bond between us, speaks not to others as it spoke to us; and the face which is enshrined in our heart of hearts, to them is "the daub John bought at a sale." "Is not she Jane? Then who is she?" asks the stranger who intermeddleth not with our joys. But when that face is confessed to be one to lose youth for, to occupy age with the dream of, to meet death with; then, half in rapture, half in rage, we say, "Take it, I pray; it is only a duplicate!"

Lilith. (*Adam, Lilith, and Eve.*) "According to the Gnostic and Rosicrucian mediæval doctrine, the creation of woman was not originally intended. She is the offspring of man's own impure fancy, and, as the Hermetists say, 'an obtrusion.' . . . First 'Virgo,' the celestial virgin of the Zodiac, she became 'Virgo-Scorpio.' But in evolving his second companion, man had unwittingly endowed her with his own share of spirituality; and the new being whom his 'imagination' had called into life became his 'saviour' from the snares of Eve-Lilith, the first Eve, who had a greater share of matter in her composition than the primitive 'spiritual man.'"—Madame Blavatsky's *Isis Unveiled*, vol. ii., p. 445.

Lost Leader, The. (*Dramatic Romances and Lyrics, in Bells and Pomegranates*, No. VII., 1845; *Poems*, 1849; *Dramatic Lyrics*, 1868.) A great leader of a party has deserted the cause, fallen away from his early ideals and forsaken the teaching which has inspired disciples who loved and honoured him. They are sorrowful not so much for their own loss as for the moral deterioration he has himself suffered. The poem is a very popular one, and is generally considered to refer to Wordsworth, who in his youth had strong Liberal sympathies, but lost them, as Mr. John Morley says in his introduction to Wordsworth's poems:—"As years began to dull the old penetration of a mind which had once approached, like other youths, the shield of human nature from the golden side, and had been eager to 'clear a passage for just government,' Wordsworth lost his interest in progress. Waterloo may be taken for the date at which his social grasp began to fail, and with it his poetic glow He opposed Catholic emancipation as stubbornly as Eldon, and the Reform Bill as bitterly as Croker. For the practical reform of his day, even in education, for which he had always spoken up, Wordsworth was not a force." Browning used to see a good deal of Wordsworth when he was a young man, but there was no friendship between them. Wordsworth treated with contempt Browning's republican sympathies—a contempt heightened, as is usually the case with those who have lapsed from their former ideals, by the remembrance that he had once professed to follow them. But, though the poem has undoubted reference to Wordsworth, it has a certain application also to Southey, Charles Kingsley, and others, who in youth were Radicals and in old age became rigidly Conservative. Browning told Walter Thornbury that Wordsworth was "the lost leader," though he said "the portrait was purposely disguised a little; used, in short, as an artist uses a model, retaining certain characteristic traits and discarding the rest" (*Notes and Queries*, 5th series, vol. i., p. 213.) There is a letter published in Mr. Grosart's edition of Wordsworth's *Prose Works*, which is conclusive on this point:—

"19, WARWICK CRESCENT, W., *February 24th*, 1875.

"DEAR MR. GROSART,—I have been asked the question you now address me with, and as duly answered, I can't remember how many times. There is no sort of objection to one more assurance, or rather confession, on my part, that I *did* in my hasty youth presume to use the great and venerable personality of Wordsworth as a sort of painter's model; one from which this or the other particular feature may be selected and turned to account. Had I intended more—above all, such a boldness as portraying the entire man—I should not have talked about 'handfuls of silver and bits of ribbon.' These never influenced the change of politics in the great poet—whose defection, nevertheless, accompanied as it was by a regular face-about of his special party, was, to my private apprehension, and even mature consideration, an event to deplore. But, just as in the tapestry on my wall I can recognise figures which have *struck out* a fancy, on occasion, that though truly enough thus derived, yet would be preposterous as a copy; so, though I dare not deny the original of my little poem, I altogether refuse to have it considered as the 'very effigies' of such a moral and intellectual superiority.

"Faithfully yours,

"ROBERT BROWNING."

"Lost, lost! yet come." The first line of the "Song of April" in *Paracelsus*, Part II.

Lost Mistress, The. (*Dramatic Romances and Lyrics*, in *Bells and Pomegranates*, VII., 1845; *Lyrics*, 1863; *Dramatic Lyrics*, 1868.) A calm suppression of intensest feeling, the quiet resignation of a great love in a spirit of humility and sacrifice, by a man who has complete control over himself. The pretence of not feeling the blow is exquisitely represented, and the spirit which underlies it is that of the strong-souled contender with the trials of life who wrote the poem. The life's current frozen, the sun sunk in the heart to rise no more, the joy gone out of life, are summed up in "All's over, then!" He remarks the sparrow's twitter and the leaf buds on the vine; the snowdrops appear, but there is no spring in his heart; her voice will stay in his soul for ever, yet he may hold her hand "so very little longer" than may a mere friend.

Love among the Ruins. (*Men and Women*, 1855; *Lyrics*, 1863; *Dramatic Lyrics*, 1868.) While Mrs. Browning was staying with Mr. Browning in Rome, in the winter of 1853-54, she was writing *Aurora Leigh*, and he was busy with *Men and Women*, including this exquisite poem. It is a landscape by Poussin in words, and is melodious and soothing, as befits the subject. It is evening in the Roman Campagna, amid the ruins of cities once great and famous. The landscape cannot fail to touch the soul with deepest melancholy, as we reflect on the evanescence of all human things. A vast city, whose memorials have dwindled to a "so they say"; "the domed and daring palaces" represented by a few blocks of half-buried marble and the shaft of a column, overrun by a vegetation which is the symbol of eternal beauty, lovingly covering the decaying handiwork of a long vanished people. And amid the colonnades and temples, the turrets and the bridges, the spirit of the observer dwells with the mournful reflection that the hand of death and the devouring tooth of time reduce all earthly things to ruin, and the shadows of oblivion fall on the world of spirit and cover the deeds alike of glory and of shame. But from the wreck of the ages, and the scattered memorials of a forgotten metropolis, there came a golden-haired girl with eager eyes of love, and the sad-reflecting contemplator of the past learns, by the glance of her eye and the embrace which extinguishes sight and speech, that whole centuries of folly, noise, and sin, are not to be weighed against that moment when we recognise that Love is best.

Love in a Life. (*Men and Women*, 1855; *Lyrics*, 1863; *Dramatic Lyrics*, 1868.) A lover inhabiting the same house as his love, is constantly eluded by the charmed object of his pursuit. The perfume of her presence is in every room, and he is always promising his heart that she shall soon be found, yet the day wanes with the fruitless quest, for as he enters she goes out, and twilight comes with—

> "Such closets to search, such alcoves to importune!"

Thus do our ideals ever evade us.

Love Poems.—"One Word More," "Evelyn Hope," "A Serenade at the Villa," "In Three Days," "The Last Ride Together," "Numpholeptos," "Cristina," "Love among the Ruins," "By the Fire Side," "Any Wife to any Husband," "A Lovers' Quarrel," "Two in the Campagna," "Love in a Life," "Life in a Love," "The Lost Mistress," "A Woman's Last Word," "In a Gondola," "James Lee's Wife," "Rudel to the Lady of Tripoli," "O Lyric Love!" (in the first volume of the *Ring and the Book*), "Count Gismond," "Confessions," "The Flower's Name," "Women and Roses," "My Star," "Mesmerism." (These are by no means all, but are, perhaps, some of the best.)

Lover's Quarrel, A. (*Men and Women*, 1855; *Lyrics*, 1863; *Dramatic Lyrics*, 1868.) "A shaft from the devil's bow," in the shape of a bitter word, has divided two lovers who before were all the world to each other. It seems to him so amazing that the tongue can have power to sever such fond hearts as theirs. He comforts himself with the assurance that though in summer-tide's warmth heart can dispense with heart, the first chills of winter and the first approach of the storms of life will drive the loved one to his arms.

Lucrezia. (*Andrea del Sarto.*) She was the wife of the artist—cold, unsympathetic, but beautiful—and was the model for much of his work. In the poem Andrea is conversing with her, and indicating the causes which have arrested his power as an artist.

Luigi. (*Pippa Passes.*) The conspiring young patriot who meets his mother at evening in the turret on the hillside near Asolo. He believes he has a mission to kill the Emperor of Austria. His mother is trying to dissuade him, and he is about to yield, when Pippa's song as she passes re-inspires him, and he leaves the tower, and so escapes from the police who are on his track.

Luitolfo. (*A Soul's Tragedy.*) Chiappino's false friend, and Eulalia's lover.

Luria, A Tragedy. (*Bells and Pomegranates*, VIII., 1846.) Time 14—. The historical incidents which are to some extent the basis of this play had their rise in the constant struggles between the Guelf and Ghibelline factions in Italy, which involved the various republics which arose in consequence of those wars in the most bitter internecine struggles for supremacy. One of the most important of these was the war between the Florentine and the Pisan republics. Wars between different Italian cities were frequent in the middle ages; according to Muratori, the first conflict was waged in 1003, when Pisa and Lucca contended for the mastery. In the eleventh century the military and real importance of Pisa was greatly developed, and was doubtless due to the necessity of constantly contending against Saracenic invasions. The chroniclers assert that the first war with Florence, which broke out in 1222, arose from a quarrel between the ambassadors of the rival states at Rome over a lapdog. When so trifling an occasion led to such a result, it is evident there were deeper grounds for hatred and mistrust at work. It is not within the scope of this work to trace the causes which led to the war between the two great Italian republics in the beginning of the fifteenth century. In the early part of the fourteenth century Castruccio became lord of Lucca and Pisa, and was victorious over the Florentines. In 1341 the Pisans besieged Lucca, in order to prevent the entry of the Florentines, to whom the city had been sold by Martino della Scala. The Florentines obtained Porto Talamone from Siena, and established a navy of their own. They attacked the harbour of Pisa, and carried away its chains, which they triumphantly bore to Florence, and suspended in front of the Baptistery, where they remained till 1848. As the war continued the Pisans suffered more and more. In 1369 they lost Lucca; in 1399 Visconti captured Pisa, and in 1406 the Florentines made another attack upon the city, besieging it both by sea and land. As the defenders were starving, they succeeded in entering the city on October 9th. The orders of the Ten of War at Florence were to crush every germ of rebellion and drive out its citizens by measures of the utmost harshness and cruelty. Mr. Browning's play has for its object to show how Pisa fell under the dominion of its powerful rival. The characters are Luria, a Moorish commander of the Florentine forces; Husain, a Moor, his friend; Puccio, the old Florentine commander, now Luria's chief officer; Braccio, commissary of the republic of Florence; Jacopo, his secretary; Tiburzio, commander of the Pisans; and Domizia, a noble Florentine lady. The scene is Luria's camp, between Florence and Pisa. The time extends only over one day, and the five Acts are named "Morning," "Noon," "Afternoon," "Evening," and "Night." A battle is about to take place which will decide the issue of the war. Luria is Browning's Othello, and one of the noblest of his characters. He is a simple, honest, whole-souled creature, incapable of guile, and devoted to the welfare of Florence. Puccio was formerly at the head of the Florentine army; he has been deposed for some state reason, and the Moorish mercenary substituted, he remaining as the subordinate of that general. The reasons which have induced the Seigniory to abstain from entrusting the command of its army to a Florentine are the most despicable that could influence any public body. They were understood to be afraid that they would have to reward the victorious general, or that he might use his power and influence with the people to make himself master of their city. So they choose a man whom they merely pay to fight for them—a Moor, who can have no friends amongst the citizens, and a stranger who can have no other claim upon them than his wages. They go further: they proceed to try him secretly for treason before he has committed it; they set spies to watch his every movement and to record his every word; they employ for this purpose unscrupulous men, well versed in the art of manufacturing evidence; they weave their toils so skilfully that by the time Luria has won their battle for them, they will have accumulated all the evidence which is required, and the death sentence will be pronounced as the victory is won. The appointment of the displaced Puccio to a secondary position in command was one of the steps taken for this end: he would naturally be discontented, and become a ready tool in the hands of the cold, skilful Braccio, all intellect, and practised in the most devious ways of statecraft. Professor Pancoast, in his valuable papers on *Luria* in *Poet Lore*, vol. i., p. 555, and vol. ii., p. 19, says: "It is possible that Mr. Browning may have found the suggestion for this situation in a passage in Sapio Amminato's *Istoria Fiorentine*, relating to this expedition against Pisa. "And when all was ready, the expedition marched to the gates of Pisa, under the command of Conte Bartoldo Orsini, a Ventusian captain in the Florentine service, accompanied by Filippo di Megalotti, Rinaldo di Gian Figliazzi, and Maso degli Albizzi, in the character of commissaries of the commonwealth. For, although we have every confidence in the honour and fidelity of our general, you see it is always well to be on the safe side. And in the matter of receiving possession of a city, . . . these nobles with the old feudal names! We know the ways of them! An Orsini might be as bad in Pisa as a Visconti, so we might as well send some of our own people to be on the spot. The three commissaries therefore accompanied the Florentine general to Pisa." (Am. xvii., Lib. Goup. 675.) These words throw an instructive light on Mr. Browning's drama, and seem to justify its motive. From this background of treachery and deceit the grand figure of Luria, honest, transparently ingenuous, generous, and true to the core, boldly stands forth to claim our admiration and our esteem. He knows nothing of their devious ways, can only go straightforward to his aim, and on this eve of the great battle he receives from Tiburzio, the commander of the Pisan forces, a letter which has been intercepted from Braccio to the Florentine Seigniory; he is desired to read it, as it exposes the plots which the Florentines are hatching against him. Luria declines to read the letter, tears it to pieces, and gives battle to the enemy. The victory is a great one: Pisa is in his hands; then he sends for Braccio, charges him with the treachery, and learns what the letter would have told him if he had read it. Braccio does not deny what Luria divines; charges have been prepared against him,—he will be tried that night. He maintains the absolute right of Florence to do as she has done. Domizia, whose brothers suffered shame and death in such manner at the hands of Florence, protests that Florence needs must mistrust a stranger's faith. At this moment Tiburzio, the Pisan general, enters, testifies to the faith of the man who has defeated him, and offers to resign to him his charge, the highest office, sword and shield, with the help which has just arrived from Lucca. He begs him to adopt their cause, and let Florence perish in her perfidy. Here was temptation indeed to Luria: his own victorious troops would not have turned their arms against him, and Pisa would have eagerly accepted him. But Luria dismisses Tiburzio, thanks him, bids him go: he is free,—"join Lucca!" And then, he reflects, he has still time before his sentence comes; he has it in his power to ruin Florence. Would it console him that his Florentines walked with a sadder step? He has one way of escape left him: he has brought poison from his own land for use in an emergency such as this; he drinks,—

"Florence is saved: I drink this, and ere night,—die!"

Madhouse Cells. The two poems *Johannes Agricola in Meditation* and *Porphyria's Lover* were published in *Dramatic Lyrics, Bells and Pomegranates*, No. III., under the general title MADHOUSE CELLS. In the *Poetical Works* of 1863 the general title was given up.

Magical Nature. (*Pacchiarotto, with other Poems*: 1876.) The beauty of a flower is at the mercy of the destroying hand of time; the beauty of a jewel is independent of it. The petals drop off one by one, the flower perishes; every facet of the jewel may laugh at time. Mere fleshly graces are those of the flower; the soul's beauty is best symbolised by the gem.

Malcrais. (*Two Poets of Croisic.*) Paul Desforges Maillard assumed the name of Malcrais when he sent his poems to the Paris *Mercure*, pretending they were the work of a lady.

"**Man I am and man would be, Love.**" The fourth lyric in *Ferishtah's Fancies* begins with this line.

Marching Along. (No. I. of *Cavalier Tunes.*) Originally appeared in *Bells and Pomegranates*, 1842.

Martin Relph. (*Dramatic Idyls*, First Series: 1879.) This poem deals with a profound psychological problem. How far do we understand the mystery of our own heart? How far can we analyse our own motives? Out of two powerful motives, either of which may equally move us to do or leave undone a certain thing, can we infallibly tell which one has ultimately prompted our action? Are we less an enigma to ourselves than to others? The Scripture warns us that we may not trust our imaginations, by reason of the deceit which is within our breast. All his life the old man Martin Relph had been trying to solve a mystery of this kind. He wants to know whether he is a murderer or only a coward; and every year, till his beard is as white as snow, has he gone to a hill outside the town where he lived to ask this question, and to protest with all his power of speech—despite the misgiving at his heart—that he was a coward. And this was his story. When a youth he, with the rest of the villagers, had been crowded up in this spot by the soldiers who held the place, that they might see, for a terrible warning, the execution of a young woman for playing the spy, and so interfering in the King's military concerns. It was in the reign of King George, and there had been a rebellion, and the rebels had learned the strength of the troops sent against them by means of some spy. A letter had been intercepted written by a girl to her lover, and the poor creature had told him such news of the movements of the troops as she thought would interest him, not knowing she was doing any harm. In all this the authorities smelt treason. Her lover was Vincent Parkes, one of the clerks of the King, "a sort of lawyer," and therefore dangerous. To give the girl a chance of clearing herself from suspicion, the commander of the troops sent for this Parkes, who was in a distant part of the country, bidding him come and dispel the cloud hanging over the girl if he could, and giving him a week for the journey. The week is up. Parkes has taken no notice of the letter; and the girl, tried by court-martial, is to be shot that day. And now poor Rosamund Page, with pinioned arms and bandaged face, is left to die. Her faithless lover, who could have saved her, has not appeared, and there is no help for her but in God. The villagers are assembled to see the sight; and Martin Relph, who also loved the girl, is there also. The word is given: up go the guns in a line, and the paralysed spectators close their eyes and kneel in prayer,—all except Martin, who stands in the highest part of the hill and sees a man running madly, falling, rising, struggling on, waving something white above his head; and no one in all the crowd sees the messenger but Martin Relph. And he is speechless, makes no sign, for hell-fire boils in his brain; and the volley is fired and the woman dead, while stretched on the field, half a mile off, is Vincent Parkes, dead also, with the King's letter in his hand that proclaims his sweetheart's innocence. He had been hampered and hindered at every turn by formalities and frivolous delays on the part of the authorities, and so was too late. Martin Relph, had he called out, could have stayed the execution. Why did he remain silent? The thought had flashed through his mind, as he recognised the position, "She were better dead than his!" and so he had not spoken; but he has told his heart a thousand times that fear kept him silent, and he has passed his life in trying to convince himself it was so indeed. But, deceitful as the human heart may be, deep down in its recesses he knew he was a murderer.

Mary Wollstonecraft and Fuseli. (*Jocoseria*, 1883.) Mary Wollstonecraft was the foundress of the Women's Rights movement. She was born in 1759, and early gave evidence of the possession of superior mental powers and of bold ideas of her own. Her first attempt in literature was a pamphlet entitled *Thoughts on the Education of Daughters*. She was of a very energetic spirit, with considerable confidence in her own powers. "I am going to be the first of a new genus," she wrote to her sister Everina in 1788. "I tremble at the attempt; yet if I fail, I only suffer. Freedom, even uncertain freedom, is dear. This project has long floated in my mind. You know I am not born to tread in the beaten track; the peculiar bent of my nature pushes me on." At this time she had secured employment as literary adviser to Mr. Johnson, the publisher of her pamphlet. At this gentleman's house she met many interesting people; amongst others the author, William Godwin, and the artist, Henry Fuseli. She now began to attack the established order of society in the most violent manner. She heartily sympathised with the French Revolution, and denounced Lords and Commons, the clergy and the game laws, with great violence. She will be best remembered by her book *A Vindication of the Rights of Woman.* Her idea was that the women of her time were fools, and that men kept women in ignorance that they might retain their authority over them. "Strengthen the female mind by enlarging it," she pleads: her idea being that men kept women either as slaves or playthings. She now became greatly interested in Fuseli, who did not in the least reciprocate her affection, but was annoyed by it. He was a married man, and though, no doubt, he could see that at first her love for him was platonic, it was rapidly assuming a more ardent character. She wrote him many letters full of affection, and actually ventured to ask Mrs. Fuseli to accept her as an inmate in her family. Finding that Fuseli remained impervious to her attacks upon his heart, she went to Paris, sending him a letter asking his pardon "for having disturbed the quiet tenor of his life." In Paris she soon consoled herself with a gentleman named Gilbert Imlay, with whom she lived without taking what she termed the "vulgar precaution" of marriage. Shortly after forming this connection Imlay cruelly deserted her. She left Paris, hurried to London, found her worst fears confirmed, and attempted to commit suicide by throwing herself from Putney Bridge. She was picked up, living to regret the "inhumanity" which had rescued her from death. She heard no more of Imlay; but five years after meeting William Godwin for the first time at Mr. Johnson's she met him again by chance at the house of a mutual friend. As Mary's opinion about the "vulgar formality" of marriage remained unchanged, and as Godwin held with her on the subject, the formality was once more dispensed with; but ultimately it was considered advisable so far to conciliate the prejudices of society as to go through the ceremony, which was performed at Old St. Pancras Church, and Mary Wollstonecraft became Mrs. Godwin in due form. In September 1797 her troubled life came to a premature close. She died before completing her thirty-ninth year. Mary left two children; the younger of these, her daughter by Godwin, became the wife of the poet Shelley, The elder, Imlay's daughter, poisoned herself, leaving a slip of paper stating that she had done so "to put an end to the existence of a being whose birth was unfortunate." The authoress of the *Rights of Woman* had neglected to consider the rights of Mrs. Fuseli and of the fruit of her illicit connection with Imlay when she devoted herself to the emancipation of her sex. In the poem Mary prates vainly of what she would do if only she were loved; and as the Rev. John Sharpe, M.A., says in his paper on *Jocoseria* with reference to the question, "Wanting is——what?" (a question which seems to preside over all the poems in the volume to which it is a prologue): "Deeds, not words, are wanted. Perfect love awakens love in the indifferent by perfect deeds of loving self-sacrifice."

Master Hugues of Saxe-Gotha. (*Men and Women*, 1855; *Lyrics*, 1863; *Dramatic Lyrics*, 1868.) An organist in a church where they have just concluded the evening service determines to have a colloquy with the old dead composer Master Hugues as to the meaning of the compositions known as fugues for which he was celebrated. They were mountainous in their structure—the ideas were piled one upon another till their meaning was lost in cloudland. So, while the church is emptying and the altar ministrants are putting things to rights, he will look into the matter of the old quaint arithmetical music in fashion before Palestrina brought back music to the service of melody. There is but one inch of candle left in the socket, so the composer must tell him what he has to say quickly. First he delivers his phrase; he gives but a clause. He asserts nothing, puts forward no proposition; nevertheless there is an answer, though a needless one, and the two start off together. (It will be seen that the poet suggests five impersonations of characters taking part in the discussion or mangle of the composition.) A third interposes, and volunteers his help; a fourth must have his say, and a fifth must needs interfere. So the disputation is like that of a knot of angry politicians, who all want to speak at once, and will scarcely allow each other to utter a complete sentence. This is a perfect description of a fugue, which even to the uninstructed listener is a musical wrangle plainly enough. In the fugue the organist sees a moral of life, with its zigzags, dodges, and ins and outs. Truth and Nature are over our heads. God's gold here and there shines out in our soul-manifestations, if we would but let truth and Nature have their way with us, the gold would be all the plainer to see; but with our evasions, our pretences, shams and subterfuges we have all but obliterated it, just as the inventor of the fugue has buried his melody under a mountain of musical tricks and pedantic finger puzzles. The organist pauses; he will have no more of it as a moral of life. The Jesuit's casuistry, which went to prove that all sorts of evil things might under certain circumstances and under such and such restrictions become actual virtues, was swept away by Pascal's clear-sighted common sense. So Master Hugues and his fugues shall vanish before the full organ blaring out the *mode Palestrina*—the grave, pure, truthful music of the Church. As Pascal to Escobar, so is Palestrina to Master Hugues; quibbles, shams, fencings with truth, overlay God's gold with the cobwebs of tradition, and must be brushed away. "Rochell has quite correctly perceived that the approximate best symbol of the uncreated heaven is music. In the evolution of harmonies in the upper and lower notes, and their mutual conflict; in the solution of strife and tension into blessed calm; in the transmutation of the ever-recurring theme into new phrases; in the constant reappearance of the *motif*, of the question which seeks a reply through every evolution of the notes, and which leads the reply into a new process—in this we see the temporal symbol of the eternal rhythm, the eternal circular movement in God's heaven, where melodious colours and radiant notes are interwoven with each other; where nothing lies in stagnant repose, but all is in motion; where unity and harmony are eternally effected by means of the contrasted, movements and action." (Martensen's *Jacob Boehme*, page 167.)

NOTES.—*Hugues* is a purely imaginary composer. Verse i. "*mountainous fugues*": "A fugue is a short, complete melody, which *flies* (hence the name) from one part to another, while the original part is continued in counterpoint against it. The beginning of this art-form dates from very primitive times" (Sir G. Macfarren). Probably Bach's fugues are meant in the poem. vi., *Aloys and Jurien and Just*, sacristan's assistants; "*darn the sacrament lace*": the lace on the altar linen. The actual sacrament linen is washed by the clergy in the Roman Catholic Church. The church plate (*i.e.*, chalice, paten, etc.) is cleaned by the clergy also. viii., *claviers*, the keyboard of the organ ix., "*great breves as they wrote them of yore*": a breve is the longest note in music, and was formerly square in shape. In the old Spanish cathedrals I have seen the music-books used in the services of such a size that it required two men to carry them. The notes in such books are very large. xvi., "*O*

Danaides, O Sieve!" the Danaides were the daughters of Danaus, who were condemned for their crimes to pour water for ever in the regions below into a vessel with holes in the bottom. xvii., *Escobar*, y Mendoza, was a Spanish casuist, the general tendency of whose writings was to find excuses for human frailties. Pascal severely criticised him in his *Provincial Letters.* His doctrines were disapproved at Rome. Escobar himself was a most excellent man. He died in 1669. xviii., "*Est fuga, volvitur rota*" = it is a flight, the wheel rolls itself round. xix., *risposting* = riposting, a term in fencing; in this case equal to making a repartee. xx., *ticken* = ticking, a twill fabric very closely woven. xxviii., *meâ pœnâ* = at my risk of punishment; *Gorgon*, a monster with a terrible head, with hair and girdle of snakes; "*mode Palestrina*": Giovanni P. da Palestrina (1524-1594), now universally distinguished as the Prince of Music, emancipated his art from the trammels of pedantry, which, ignoring beauty as the most necessary element of music, was tending to reduce it to mere arithmetical problems.

May and Death. (Published first in *The Keepsake*, 1857; in 1864 published in *Dramatis Personæ*.) Mrs. Orr, in her *Life and Letters of Robert Browning*, says that the poet wrote this poem in remembrance of one of his boy companions, the eldest of "the three Silverthornes, his neighbours at Camberwell, and cousins on the maternal side." The name of Charles in the poem stands for the old familiar Jim. Mrs. Silverthorne was the aunt who paid for the printing of *Pauline*. The verses express the wish that all the delights of spring had died with his friend; yet he would except one plant of the woods in May which has in its leaves a streak of spring's blood. Where'er the leaf grows in a wood they know the red drop comes from the poet's heart. The question has often been asked "What is the plant referred to in the fourth stanza?" The following reply was given in the *Browning Society's Papers*:—"Surely the *Polygonum Persicaria* or Spotted Persicaria is the plant referred to. It is a common weed, with purple stains upon its rather large leaves; these spots varying in size and vividness of colour according to the nature of the soil where it grows." The Rev. H. Friend, in *Flowers and Flower Lore* (p. 5), says:—"Respecting the Virgin, I have recently found the country folk in one part of Oxfordshire retaining an interesting legend which connects the name of her ladyship with the *Spotted Persicaria.* It will be remembered that, in consequence of the dark spot which marks the centre of every leaf belonging to this plant, popular tradition asserts that it grew beneath the Cross, and received this distinction through the drops of blood which fell from the Saviour's wounds touching its leaves. The *Oxonian* however, says that the Virgin was wont of old to use its leaves for the manufacture of a valuable ointment, but that on one occasion she sought it in vain. Finding it afterwards, when the need had passed away, she condemned it, and gave it the rank of an ordinary weed. This is expressed in the local rhyme:—

> 'She could not find in time of need,
> And so she pinched it for a weed.'

The mark on the leaf is the impression of the Virgin's finger, and the persicaria is now the *only* weed that is not useful for something." Again (p. 191) he says, "We are told that in some parts of England the arum, commonly called lords and ladies, cows and calves, parson in the pulpit, or parson and clerk, is known as Gethsemane, because it is said to have been growing at the foot of the cross, and to have received on its leaves some of the blood:—

> 'Those deep unwrought marks,
> The villager will tell you,
> Are the flower's portion from the atoning blood
> On Calvary shed. Beneath the Cross it grew.'

The same tradition clings to the purple orchis and the spotted persicaria. We have already seen how many plants are supposed to have gained their purple hue or ruddy colour from blood of hero, god, or martyr. A similar legend seems to have been at one time attached to the purple-stained flowers of the wood-sorrel, which is by Italian painters, including Fra Angelico, occasionally placed in the foreground of their pictures representing the Crucifixion. This plant is called Alleluia in Italian, which may have had something to do, however, with its association with the Cross of Christ, 'as if the very flowers round the Cross were giving glory to God.' The wallflower, that 'scents the dewy air,' is in Palestine called 'the blood-drops of Christ'; and its deep hue has led to its being called by a similar name in the West of England. The rose-coloured lotus, or melilot, was said to have sprung in like manner from the blood of the lion slain by the Emperor Adrian. It is probable that the story was the modification of some earlier myth. Mr. Conway tells us he has somewhere met with a legend telling that the thorn-crown of Christ was made from rose-briar, and that the drops of blood that started under it and fell to the ground blossomed to roses. Mrs. Howe, the American poetess, beautifully alludes to this in the lines—

'Men saw the thorns on Jesus' brow,
But angels saw the Roses.'"

Meeting at Night and Parting at Morning. (Originally published as NIGHT AND MORNING in *Dramatic Romances and Lyrics*, *Bells and Pomegranates*, VII.: 1845.) The speaker is a man who joyfully seeks his happy seaside home at night, where he rejoins the wife from whom the demands of his daily work have separated him. In the sequel (*Parting at Morning*) the rising sun calls men to work: the man of the poem to work of a lucrative character; and excites in the woman (if we interpret the slightly obscure line correctly) a desire for more society than the seaside home affords. Commentators on these poems have evidently "jumped the difficulty."

Melander. The author whose work "Joco-Seria" suggested the title of Mr. Browning's volume of poems *Jocoseria* (*q.v.*).

Melon-Seller, The. (*Ferishtah's Fancies*, II.) The second of the lessons learned by Ferishtah on his way to dervishhood. He sees a well-remembered face in a melon-seller near a bridge. He was once the Shah's Prime Minister: he peculated, and was disgraced. Shocked at the contrast between what the man was and has now become, Ferishtah asks him if he did not curse God for the twelve years' bliss he enjoyed only to end in misery like that? The beggar contemptuously asked his questioner if he were unwise enough to think him such a fool as to repine at God's just punishment on sin, and to reproach Him with the happiness he had tasted in the past? Job said: "Shall we receive good at the hand of God, and evil not receive?" This was just what the melon-seller said. "But great wits jump"; and Ferishtah, having learned the great lesson, went his way to dervishhood. The Lyric asks for a little severity from Love: so much undeserved bliss has been imparted, that a little injustice seems requisite to balance things.

Memorabilia. (*Men and Women*, 1855—when the title was *Memorabilia (on Seeing Shelley)*; *Lyrics*, 1863; *Dramatic Lyrics*, 1868.) A man with a soul crosses a vast moor, a blankness of miles, but on one hand-breadth spot he spies an eagle's feather, which he cherishes. An eagle's feather meant something to the man with the soul, the miles of blank moor had nothing to say to him; and so once he saw Shelley plain, and even spoke to him. The man had lived long before and had lived long after, but the sight of Shelley and the words he spoke made just that hand-breadth of his life something different from all the colourless remainder. [Some there are who love to say the same of Robert Browning!] Mr. Browning early in his youth (1825) fell under the influence of Shelley. Mr. Sharp, in his *Life of Browning*, says that, as he was one day passing a bookstall, "he saw, in a box of second-hand volumes, a little book advertised as 'Mr. Shelley's Atheistical Poem,—very scarce.' He had never heard of Shelley, nor did he learn for a long time that the *Dæmon of the World* and the miscellaneous poems appended thereto constituted a literary piracy." He discovered that there was such a poet as Shelley; that he had written several volumes, and was dead. He begged his mother to procure him Shelley's works, which she had some difficulty in doing, as several booksellers to whom she applied knew nothing of them. The books were ultimately purchased at Ollier's shop, in Vere Street. Shelley, as Mr. Sharp says, "enthralled" Browning. His first work, *Pauline*, was written under the dominance of the Shelley passion. He refers to Shelley in *Sordello*. *Memorabilia* was composed in the Roman Campagna in the winter of 1853-54.

Men and Women. (Published in 1855, in two vols.; now dispersed in vols. iii., iv. and v. of *Poetical Works*, 1868.) The poems included under this general title were fifty-one in number.

Vol. I. contained the following:—"Love among the Ruins," "A Lovers' Quarrel," "Evelyn Hope," "Up at a Villa—Down in the City," "A Woman's Last Word," "Fra Lippo Lippi," "A Toccata of Galuppi's," "By the Fireside," "Any Wife to any Husband," "An Epistle of Karshish," "Mesmerism," "A Serenade at the Villa," "My Star," "Instans Tyrannus," "A Pretty Woman," "Childe Roland to the Dark Tower Came," "Respectability," "A Light Woman," "The Statue and the Bust," "Love in a

Life," "Life in a Love,' "How it Strikes a Contemporary," "The Last Ride Together," "The Patriot," "Master Hugues of Saxe-Gotha," "Bishop Blougram's Apology," "Memorabilia."

Vol. II.: "Andrea del Sarto," "Before," "After," "In Three Days," "In a Year," "Old Pictures in Florence," "In a Balcony," "Saul," "De Gustibus——," "Women and Roses," "Protus," "Holy-Cross Day," "The Guardian Angel," "Cleon," "The Twins," "Popularity," "The Heretic's Tragedy," "Two in the Campagna," "A Grammarian's Funeral," "One Way of Love," "Another Way of Love," "Transcendentalism," "Misconceptions," "One Word More."

In the six-volume edition of *Poetical Works* the poems comprised under the title of *Men and Women* are the following, and it is these which are generally understood now by the *Men and Women* poems:—"Transcendentalism," "How it Strikes a Contemporary," "Artemis Prologuises," "An Epistle containing the Strange Medical Experience of Karshish the Arab Physician," "Pictor Ignotus," "Fra Lippo Lippi," "Andrea del Sarto," "The Bishop orders his Tomb at St. Praxed's Church," "Bishop Blougram's Apology," "Cleon," "Rudel to the Lady of Tripoli," "One Word More."

Unquestionably in these works we have the very flower of Mr. Browning's genius. There is not one of them which the world will willingly let die. As Mr. Symons says, their distinguishing feature is "the monologue brought to perfection. Such monologues as *Andrea del Sarto*, or *The Epistle of Karshish*, never have been, and probably never will be, surpassed, on their own ground, after their own order."

Mesmerism. (*Dramatic Romances:* 1855.) A description of an influence of one mind upon another, which would in modern medical parlance be termed hypnotism. When an operator has this power, and has frequently exercised it upon his subject, it is undoubtedly true that what is here described in so lifelike a manner may actually take place. The subject may have been led to expect that she would be required to undertake the journey in question, and the mind in that case would contribute to the success of the operation. Hypnosis and somnambulism are not produced by any fluid which escapes from the mesmeriser's body, but by the fact that the subject has been induced to form a fixed idea that he is being hypnotised. Braid asserts that the imagination of the subject is an indispensable element in the success of the experiment; he declares that the most expert hypnotiser will exert himself in vain unless the subject is aware of what is passing and surrenders himself body and soul. Binet and Frere, in their valuable work on *Animal Magnetism*, p. 96, say that "a whole series of purely physical agents exist, which prove that sleep can be induced without the aid of the subject's imagination, against his will, and without his knowledge." The incidents of the poem may all be accounted for by the doctrine of expectant attention. The use of hypnotic suggestion for criminal purposes is referred to in stanzas xxvi. and xxvii.—a very real danger from a medico-legal point of view, as some think. At night, when all is quiet but the noises peculiar to the hours of darkness, the mesmeriser of the poem desires that the woman under the influence of his will-power shall forthwith make her way to him through the rain and mud straight to his house. In due time she enters without a word. Recognising the wonderful influence which one mind may exercise upon another, the operator prays that he may never abuse it, and he reflects that one day God will call him to account for its exercise.

Mihrab Shah. (*Ferishtah's Fancies*, 6.) THE MYSTERY OF EVIL AND PAIN. An inquirer, while culling herbs, has had his thumb nipped by a scorpion. He wishes to know "Why needs a scorpion be? Why, in fact, needs any evil or pain happen to man if God be wholly good and omnipotent?" Ferishtah replies that when he awoke in the morning he was thankful that his head did not tumble off his neck. "But," says the inquirer, "heads do not fall unchopped." Says the dervish, "They might do so by natural law; why might not a staff loosed from the hand spring skyward as naturally as it falls to the ground?" What would be the bond 'twixt man and man if pain were abolished? Take away from man thanks to God and love to man, what is he worth? The lyric explains the compensations of existence. The ardent soul is enshrined in feeble flesh, the sluggish soul in a robust frame. What one person lacks is found in another, and this creates a bond of sympathy between our spirits. No one has everything. What we lack we admire when present in another, and so our own defects are pardoned for what in us is excellent.

Mildred Tresham. (*A Blot in the 'Scutcheon.*) The lady who is loved by Lord Henry Mertoun, and visited by him in secret at night. She dies when she learns that her brother has killed her lover.

Misconceptions. (*Men and Women*, 1855.) A beautiful fancy of a branch on which a bird has rested a moment bursting into bloom for pride and joy that it has been so honoured. The poet treats it as symbolical of a heart which has thrilled for a moment under the smiles of a queen ere she went on to her true-love throne.

Mr. Sludge, "The Medium." (*Dramatis Personæ:* 1864.) Mr. Sludge is a "medium" who has been detected by his dupe in the act of cheating. He has worked upon his patron's love for his dead mother, has pretended that he has had communications with the spirit world, and has found it a profitable business. However, he is found out, the game is up, he is half throttled by the man whom he has swindled, and is about to be kicked out of his house. He admits the cheating, but tries to make out that it was prompted by a low species of spirit (*elementals* as they are called). He offers, if liberally paid, to explain how the fraud has been carried out. He pretends one moment that he is repentant, the next he proposes to increase his guilt by falsely accusing his too confiding benefactor. He is prepared to swear that he picked a quarrel with him to get back the presents he had given. The bargain is made; and the medium, seated again at the "dear old table" which has so often been the partner of his performances, proceeds to explain that it is much more the fault of the public that they are cheated, than that of the artful folk who are always ready to meet demand by supply. In many things, but especially in affairs relating to the unseen world, people are willing to be deceived; and, as Demosthenes said, "Nothing is more easy than to deceive ourselves, as our affections are subtle persuaders."

"It's all your fault, you curious gentlefolk!"

said Sludge. "Everybody is interested in ghosts, and everybody will listen to the ghost-seer. A poor lad, the son of a servant in your house, talks to you about money, and you immediately suspect him of having stolen some; if he talk to you about seeing spirits, you encourage him to tell his story, and you listen with open ears. You make allowances for the unexplained '*phenomena*,' and you are not disconcerted by his blunders. So the boy is encouraged to try again, to see more, hear more and stranger things. You have patience with the primary manifestations,' always weak at first; you discourage doubts as always fatal to them, and thus educate the boy in his cheating. He is compelled to invent; you prompt him, your readiness to be deceived confirms him in his readiness to deceive. It is not that the boy starts as a liar; he will soon enough develop into that; at first however,

> "'It's fancying, fable-making, nonsense-work—
> What never meant to be so very bad.'

He brightens up his dull facts till they shine, and you no longer recognise them as dull, but brilliant. He hears what other mediums have done, he estimates your demands of him; you push him to the brink, he is compelled to dive. Let him confess his deception, and he has to go back to the gutter from which you have taken him. Let him keep on, and he lives in clover. And so he manufactures for you all you demand. He has heard raps and seen a light. 'Shaped somewhat like a star?' you eagerly inquire. 'Well, like some sort of stars, ma'am.' 'So we thought!' you say. 'And any voice?' Not yet.' 'Try hard next time!' Next time you have the voice. The medium is launched in the rapids. The falls are hard by: nothing can hinder but he must go over. He becomes the medium which has been required of him. The spirits forthwith speak up and become familiar and confidential. If any complain that the spirits do not fulfil our expectation of what the ghosts of Bacon, Cromwell, or Beethoven should be and do, the answer is ready and assumes two forms. If Bacon is deficient in spelling, does not know where he was born or in what year he died, this is no argument against spiritualism. The spirits are of all orders; and many, perhaps most, are tricksy, undeveloped, and delight to deceive. Or, again, the explanation is put in this way:—What is a medium? He is the means, and the only means, by which the spirits can hold converse with mortals. They have no organs; they must use ours. The medium holding converse with the spirit of Beethoven, not being much of a musician, is, of course, only able very imperfectly to express the composer's musical soul. He pours in—to Sludge's soul—a sonata. If it comes out the Shakers' Hymn in G, that is the defect of the means or medium by which the master has been driven to express himself." Sludge tells his dupe that it was thus he helped him out of every scrape; and the fools who attended every séance did not criticise. Why should they? They did not criticise his wine or his furniture—why should they criticise his medium? Of course they sometimes doubted. "Ah!" says the host, "it was just this spirit of doubt pervading the circle which confused the medium and accounted for his errors!" Sludge often got out of his difficulties that way. Sometimes, however the awful aspect of truth would present itself so sternly before him as to spoil all the cockering and cosseting he received, and he would gnash his teeth at the thought of the ruin of his soul by the humbug forced upon him. The cheating was nursed out of the lying. He would have stopped, but his dupes were for progress; they always demanded fresh and more striking "phenomena"—from talking to writing, from writing to flowers from the spirit world. If he actually were detected in jogging the table, or making squeaks with his toes, he would be accused of joking; if he pretended he was not, then he was at once in the dupe's power. Then the cheating is so easy! A master of an ordinary trade can perform miracles to the untaught. The glass-blower, pipe maker, even the baker, by long practice, can puzzle the uninitiated; practise table-tilting, joint-cracking, playing tricks in the dark, and the phenomena of the medium's business become easy as an old shoe. But, apart from this actual trickery, can the hardest head detect where the cheating begins, even if he is on his guard? There is a real love of a lie, and liars have no difficulty in attracting those who are only waiting to be deceived, and the most sceptical are just the most likely to be caught. Then the Solomon of saloons, the philosophic diner-out,—these were his patrons. They "wanted a doctrine for a chopping-block." They had to be singular, and hack and hew common sense to show their skill in dialectics. These had Sludge injured. Then he reminds his patrons that the Bible teaches spiritualism. We all start with a stock of it; and stars even, we are taught, are not only worlds and suns, but stand for signs when we should set about our proper business. Sludge declares he has taught himself to live by signs: he is broken to the way of nods and winks. He has not waited for the tingle of the bell, but has obeyed the tap of knuckles on the wall. Suppose he blunders nine times out of ten as to the meaning of the knuckle summons, is he not a gainer if the tenth time he guesses right? Everybody blunders even as he. The thing is to imitate the ant-eater, and keep his tongue out to catch all nature's motes for food. It is wisdom to respect the infinitely little, for God comes close behind the animalcule, life simplified to a mere cell. All was not cheating either: he has told his lie and seen truth follow. He knows not why he did what he never tried to do, described what he never saw, spoke more than he ever intended; and though he believes everybody can and does cheat, he is not less sure that every cheat's every inspired lie contains a germ of truth. Pervade this world by an influx from the next, and all the dead, dry, dull facts of existence spring into life and freshness, as at the touch of harlequin's wand; and harlequin's wand is Sludge's lie, for which the inanimate world was waiting. You see the real world through the false, and so you have the golden age all by the help of a little lying. At most, Sludge is only a poet who acts the books which poets write. The more to his honour! But all his specious reasoning fails to reassure his awakened dupe, who gives him the notes he promised and dismisses him. No sooner is the medium out of the presence of the man whom he has deceived than he pours out a volley of abuse, and wishes he dare burn down the house; he will declare that he throttled his "sainted mother"—the old hag—in such a fit of passion as his throat had just felt the effects of; he reproaches himself for not having prophesied he would die within a year; but he consoles himself with counting his money, and reflecting that his awakened dupe is not the only fool in the world. "Sludge" is D. D. Home, the American medium. Mrs. Browning was an ardent spiritualist, and Mr. Browning, in consequence, had considerable experience of the ways of mediums and the talk and arguments of their followers. Although no medium ever reasoned with such skill and subtlety as Sludge, the main arguments used by this impostor are precisely those put forward by spiritualists. The mediums are a wretchedly weak, invertebrate order of beings, quite incapable of any such virile processes of thought as those expressed in the poem. There could be no greater mistake than to suppose that Mr. Browning intended to make any defence for any phase of spiritualism whatever: he has simply gathered into a poem the best which could be put forward for spiritualism, and directed it upon the personality of Sludge. Intimate friends of the Brownings assure me that Mr.

Browning with great difficulty restrained his disgust at the practices of spiritualists, and his annoyance at the fact that his wife devoted so much time and attention to this aspect of human folly. Perhaps the feature which angered him most was the habit of trading upon and outraging the most sacred feelings of the human heart, in the endeavour to gain clients for a money-making occupation.

NOTES.—*Catawba wine:* a white wine of American make, from grapes first discovered about 1801 near the banks of the Catawba river. Its praises have been sung by Longfellow. *Greeley:* Horace Greeley, the eminent American editor. His history was identified with the fortunes of his paper the *Tribune.* "*Nothing lasts, as Bacon came and said*": Bacon's Essay LVIII. is *Of the Vicissitude of Things. Phenomena:* the spiritualists' term for the antics of tables, pats, twitchings, ghostly lights, tinkling of bells, etc., at their *séances. The Horseshoe:* the great waterfall of that name at Niagara. *Pasiphae:* the daughter of the Sun and of Perseis, who married Minos, King of Crete. She was enamoured of a bull, or more probably of an officer named Taurus (a bull). *Odic Lights:* Od, the name given by Reichenbach to an *influence* he believed he had discovered; it was held to explain the phenomena of mesmerism, and to account for the luminous appearances at spirit-rapping circles. "*Canthus of my eye*" = the corner of the eye. *Stomach cyst,* an animalcule which is nothing more than a bag, without limbs or organs; one of the infusoria, the simplest of creatures endowed with animal life. "*The Bridgewater book*": The Earl of Bridgewater (1758-1829) devised by his will £8,000 at the disposal of the President of the Royal Society, to be paid to the authors of treatises "On the Power, Wisdom and Goodness of God as manifested in the Creation." Several of the treatises are now famous books, as Bell on *The Hand,* Kirby on *Habits and Instincts of Animals,* and Whewell's *Astronomy. Eutopia* = Utopia.

Molinos. *See* MOLINISTS.

Molinists, The (*Ring and the Book*), were followers of Michael Molinos, a Spanish priest and spiritual director of great repute in Rome, who was a cadet of a noble Spanish family of Sarragossa. He was born on December 21st, 1627. In 1675 he published, during his residence in Rome, his famous work entitled *The Spiritual Guide,* a book which taught the doctrine known as that of Quietism. This species of mysticism had previously been taught by John Tauler and Henry Suso, as also by St. Theresa and St. Catherine of Siena, but in a different and more orthodox form than that in which it was presented by Molinos. Butler, in his *Life of St. John of the Cross*, says that the system of perfect contemplation called Quietism chiefly turned upon the following general principles:—1. In perfect contemplation the man does not reason, but passively receives heavenly light, the mind being in a state of perfect inattention and inaction. 2. A soul in that state desires nothing, not even its own salvation; and fears nothing, not even hell itself. 3. That when the soul has arrived at this state, the use of the sacraments and of good works becomes indifferent. Pope Innocent XI., in 1687, condemned sixty-eight propositions extracted from this author as heretical, scandalous and blasphemous. Molinos was condemned by the Inquisition at Rome, recanted his errors, and ended his life in imprisonment in 1696.

Monaldeschi. (*Cristina and Monaldeschi.*) The Marquis Monaldeschi, the grand equerry of Queen Cristina of Sweden. He was put to death at Fontainebleau by order of Cristina, because he had betrayed her.

Monsignore the Bishop. (*Pippa Passes.*) He comes to Asolo to confer with his "Intendant" in the palace by the Duomo; he is contriving how to remove Pippa from his path, when her song as she passes stings his conscience, and he punishes his evil counsellor who suggested mischief concerning her.

Morgue, The, at Paris. (*Apparent Failure.*) The place by the Seine where the dead are exposed for identification.

Muckle-Mouth Meg ("Big-Mouth Meg"). (*Asolando*, 1889.) Sir Walter Scott was a descendant of the house of Harden, and of the famous chieftain *Auld Watt* of that line. Auld Watt was once reduced in the matter of live stock to a single cow, and recovered his dignity by stealing the cows of his English neighbours. Professor Veitch says "the Scots' Border ancestry were sheep farmers, who varied their occupation by 'lifting' sheep and cattle, and whatever else was 'neither too heavy nor too hot.'" The lairds of the Border were, in fact, a race of robbers. Sir Walter Scott was proud of this descent, and his fame as a writer was due to his Border history and poetry. The poem describes the capture red-handed of the handsome young William Scott, Lord of Harden, who was defeated in one of these forays, and taken prisoner by Sir Gideon Murray of Elibank, who ordered him to the gallows. But the Laird's dame interposed, asking grace for the callant if he married "our Muckle-mouth Meg." The young fellow said he preferred the gallows to the wide-mouthed monster. He was sent to the dungeon for a week; after seven days of cold and darkness he was asked to reconsider his decision. He found life sweet, and embraced the ill-favoured maiden.

Muléykeh, (*Dramatic Idyls*, Second Series, 1880.) A tale of an Arab's love for his horse. The story is a common one, and seems adapted from a Bedouin's anecdote told in Rollo Springfield's *The Horse and his Rider.* Hóseyn was despised by strangers for his apparent poverty. He had neither flocks nor herds, but he possessed Muléykeh, his peerless mare, his Pearl: he could afford to laugh at men's land and gold. In the race Muléykeh was always first, and Hóseyn was a proud man. Now, Duhl, the son of Sheybán, withered for envy of Hóseyn's luck, and nothing but the possession of the Pearl would satisfy him: so he rode to Hóseyn's tent, told him he knew that he was poor, and offered him a thousand camels for the mare. Hóseyn would not consider the proposal for a moment. "*I love Muléykeh's face*," he said, and dismissed her would-be purchaser. In a year's time Duhl is back again at Hóseyn's tent. This time he would not offer to buy the Pearl. He tells him his soul pines to death for her beauty, and his wife has urged him to go and beg for the mare. Hóseyn said, "It is life against life. What good avails to the life bereft?" Another year passes, and the crafty Duhl is back again—this time to steal what he can neither buy nor beg. It is night. Hóseyn lies asleep beside the Pearl, with her headstall thrice wound about his wrist. By Muléykeh's side stands her sister Buhéyseh, a famous mare for fleetness too: she stands ready saddled and bridled, in case some thief should enter and fly with the Pearl. Now Duhl enters as stealthily as a serpent, cuts the headstall, mounts her, and is "launched on the desert like bolt from bow." Hóseyn starts up, and in a minute more is in pursuit on Buhéyseh. They gain on the fugitive, for Muléykeh misses the tap of the heel, the touch of the bit—the secret signs by which her master was wont to urge her to her utmost speed. Now they are neck by croup, what does Hóseyn but shout—

"Dog Duhl. Damned son of the Dust,
Touch the right ear, and press with your foot my Pearl's left flank!"

Duhl did so: Muléykeh redoubled her pace and vanished for ever. When the neighbours saw Hóseyn at sunrise weeping upon the ground, he told them the whole story, and when they laughed at him for a fool, and told him if he had held his tongue, as a boy or a girl could have done, Muléykeh would be with him then:—

"'And the beaten in speed!' wept Hóseyn: 'You never have loved my Pearl.'"

Music Poems. The great poems dealing with music are "Abt Vogler," "Master Hugues of Saxe-Gotha," "A Toccata of Galuppi's," and "Charles Avison." Other poems which are musical in a lesser degree are "Saul," "A Grammarian's Funeral," "The Serenade," "Up at a Villa," "The Heretic's Tragedy." "Balaustion's Adventure" and "Fifine" also have incidental music references.

My Last Duchess—Ferrara. (Published first in *Bells and Pomegranates*, III., under *Dramatic Lyrics*, with the title "Italy," in 1842; *Dramatic Romances*, 1868.) A stern, severe, Italian nobleman, with a nine-hundred-years' name, is showing his picture gallery, to the envy of a Count whose daughter he is about to marry. He is standing before the portrait of his last duchess, for he is a widower, and is telling his companion that "the depth and passion of her earnest glance" was not reserved for her husband alone, but the slightest courtesy or attention was sufficient to call up "that spot of joy" into her face. "Her heart," said the duke, "was too soon made glad, too easily impressed." She smiled on her husband (she was his property, and that was right); she smiled on others (on every one, in fact), and that was an infringement of the rights of property which this dealer in human souls could not brook, so he "gave commands,"—"then all smiles stopped together." The concentrated tragedy of this line is a good example of the poet's power of compressing a whole life story in two or three words. The heartless duke instantly dismisses the memory of his duchess and her fount of human love sealed up "by command." "We'll go together down, sir,"—and as they descend he draws his guest's attention to a fine bronze group, and discusses the question of the dowry he is to receive with the woman who is *to succeed* his last duchess.

NOTE.—*Fra Pandolf* and *Claus of Innsbruck* are imaginary artists. Without very careful attention several delicate points in this poem will be lost. When the duke said "Fra Pandolf" by design, he desired to impress on the envoy, and his master the Count, the sort of behaviour he expected from the woman he was about to marry. He intimated that he would tolerate no rivals for his next wife's smiles. When he begs his guest to "Notice Neptune——taming a sea horse," he further intimated how he had tamed and killed his last duchess. All this was to convey to the envoy, and through him to the lady, that he demanded in his new wife the concentration of her whole being on himself, and the utmost devotion to his will.

My Star. (*Men and Women*, 1855; *Lyrics*, 1863; *Dramatic Lyrics*, 1868.) To one observer a beautiful star may appear in iridiscent colours unobserved by others; just as, by looking at a prism from a certain angle, we catch a play of rainbow tints which they might miss by adopting a different point of view. Where strangers see a world, the singer obtains access to a soul which opens to him all its glory, as the prism reveals the constituent colours which combine to make the cold white ray of light. The poem has been considered to be a tribute to Mrs. Browning.

My Wife Gertrude. See BOOT AND SADDLE.

Naddo (*Sordello*) was a troubadour, and the Philistine friend and counsellor of Sordello. He told Sordello not to try to introduce his own ideas to the world: poetry should be founded in common-sense and deal with the common ideas of mankind. The poet should, above all things, try to please his audience. People like calm and repose. He must not attempt to rise to an intellectual level his readers have not reached. Sordello, he said, should be satisfied with being a poet, and not aim at being a leader of men as well. Mr. Browning is in all this defending himself and satirising the popular view of the poet's province.

Names, The. A poem written for the "Show-Book" of the Shakespearean Show at the Albert Hall, May 1884, held on behalf of the Hospital for Women in the Fulham Road, London:—

"Shakespeare!—to such name's sounding, what succeeds
Fitly as silence? Falter forth the spell,—
Act follows word, the speaker knows full well,
Nor tampers with its magic more than needs.
Two names there are: That which the Hebrew reads
With his soul only: if from lips it fell,
Echo, back thundered by earth, heaven, and hell,
Would own, 'Thou didst create us!' Nought impedes
We voice the other name, man's most of might,
Awesomely, lovingly: let awe and love
Mutely await their working, leave to sight
All of the issue as—below—above—
Shakespeare's creation rises: one remove,
Though dread—this finite from that infinite."

ROBERT BROWNING, *March 12th*, 1884.

Reprinted in the *Pall Mall Gazette* of May 29th.

The Hebrews will not pronounce the sacred tetragrammaton יהוה They substitute Adonai in reading the ineffable name. Jahwé (with the J pronounced as Y) is the correct pronunciation of the unspeakable name. Yet the learned hold that the true mirific name is lost, the word "Jehovah" dating only from the Masoretic innovation. See a discussion of the whole matter in *Isis Unveiled* (Blavatsky), vol. ii. p. 398,—a work which contains a good deal of real learning mixed with infinite rubbish.

Napoleon III. See PRINCE HOHENSTIEL-SCHWANGAU.

Nationality in Drinks. Under this title we have three poems, originally published separately—namely, *Claret, Tokay*, and *Beer*. The first and second were published in *Hood's Magazine*, in June 1844. In 1863 the poems were brought under their present title in the *Poetical Works*. In *Claret* the fancy of the poet sees in his claret-flask, as it drops into a black-faced pond, a resemblance to a gay French lady, with her arms held beside her and her feet stretched out, dropping from life into death's silent ocean. In *Tokay* the bottle suggests a pygmy castle-warder, dwarfish, but able and determined, strutting about with his huge brass spurs and daring anybody to interfere with him. *Beer* is in memory of the beverage drunk to Nelson's memory off Cape Trafalgar: it includes an authentic anecdote given to the poet by the captain of the vessel. He said they show a coat of Nelson's at Greenwich with tar still on the shoulder, due to the habit he had of leaning one shoulder up against the mizzen-rigging.

Natural Magic. (*Pacchiarotto and other Poems*, 1876.) Hindū conjurors are exceedingly clever, and will produce a tree from apparently nothing at all, in all stages of growth. In the case described the narrator locks a nautch girl in an empty room and takes his stand at the door; in a short time the conjuror is embowered in a mass of verdure, fruit and flowers. In the same way, by the magic of a charming personality, the singer's life has been transformed from coldness and gloom to warmth and beauty. The poem illustrates the supreme power which spirit exerts over matter. The power of the ideal world, the all-absorbing influence of faith in the unseen to the Christian, is always being exerted to produce such effects in the souls of men and women whose lives are spent in the most squalid and unlovely surroundings.

"Nay, but you who do not love her." (*Dramatic Romances and Lyrics*, in *Bells and Pomegranates*, 1845; *Lyrics*, 1863; *Dramatic Lyrics*, 1868.) The first line of a song in praise of some tresses of a lady's hair. Even those who do not love her must admit she is pure gold. As for him, he cannot praise her, he loves her so much: he will leave the praise for those who do not.

Ned Bratts. (Published in *Dramatic Idyls*, first series, 1879; written at Splügen.) The story is taken from *The Life and Death of Mr. Badman*, by John Bunyan, the author of the *Pilgrim's Progress*, and published in London 1680. "At a Summer Assizes holden at Hartfort, while the Judge was sitting upon the Bench, comes this old Tod into the Court, cloathed in a green suit, with a Leathern Girdle in his hand, his bosom open and all in a dung sweat, as if he had run for his Life; and being come in, he spake aloud as follows: 'My Lord,' said he, 'Here is the veriest rogue that breathes upon the face of the earth. I have been a thief from a child; when I was but a little one I gave myself to rob orchards, and to do other such-like wicked things, and I have continued a thief ever since. My Lord, there has not been a robbery committed these many years, so many miles of this place, but I have either been at it, or privy to it.' The Judge thought the fellow was mad, but after some conference with some of the Justices, they agreed to indict him; and so they did, of several felonious actions, to all which he heartily confessed Guilty, and so was hanged with his wife at the same time." In the poem, *Ned Bratts*, the scene is laid at Bedford. The assizes are held on a broiling day in June; the court-house is crammed; horse stealers, rogues, puritans and preachers are being tried and sentenced, when through the barriers there burst Publican Ned Bratts and Tabitha his wife, loudly confessing they were the "worst couple, rogue and quean, unhanged," and detailing the various high crimes and misdemeanours of which they had long been guilty. He tells of the laces they had bought of the Tinker in the Bedford cage, and of

> "His girl,—the blind young chit who hawks about his wares";

tells of the Book which the girl gave him, the Book her father wrote in prison, which told of "Christmas" [he meant "Christian"]. "Christmas was meant for me," he says,—he must get rid of his burden and hurry from "Destruction," which to him is Bedford town. So fearful are the converted couple that they will fall again into their old sins, and so miss Heaven's gate, they beg the judges to

> "Sentence our guilty selves; so, hang us out of hand!"

Ned sank upon his knees in the old court-house, while his wife Tab wheezed a hoarse "Do hang us, please!" The Lord Chief Justice wondered what judge ever had such a case before him since the world began, and having thought the matter over, said—

> "Hanging you both deserve, hanged both shall be this day!"

And so they were.

Never the Time and the Place. (*Jocoseria*, 1883.) It is impossible to doubt that in this exquisite poem is enshrined the memory of Mrs. Browning. Joy and beauty are all around, time and place are all that heart could wish, but the loved one is absent, and nothing can fill her place. Yet beyond the reach of storms and stranger they will meet! The eternal value of human love is again asserted in this poem.

Norbert. (*In a Balcony.*) The young man with whom the Queen has fallen in love, but whose heart is given to Constance.

"Not with my Soul Love." The tenth lyric in *Ferishtah's Fancies* begins with these words.

Now. (*Asolando*, 1889.) The value of "the quintessential moment," a theme on which Mr. Browning frequently dilates, is emphasized in this poem—

"The moment eternal—just that and nothing more,"

when the assurance comes that love has been definitely won despite of time future and time past.

Nude in Art, The, is defended by the poet in *Francis Furini* and *The Lady and the Painter.*

Numpholeptos. (*Pacchiarotto, with other Poems,* 1876.) The word means "caught or entranced by a nymph." Primitive man always has invested natural objects with some form of life more or less resembling our own. The Greeks and Romans believed the hills, the woods and the streams to be the peculiar dwelling-places of nymphs, the spirits of external Nature. They were the maidens of heaven, daughters of Zeus. The nymphs of the rivers and fountains were called Naiads; those of the forests and mountains were Dryads, Hamadryads, and Oreades. Plutarch, in his *Life of Aristides,* says that "when the hero sent to Delphi to inquire of the oracle, he was told that the Athenians would be victorious if they addressed prayers to Jupiter, Juno, Pan, and the nymphs Sphragitides. The cave of these nymphs was "in one of the summits of Mount Cithæron, opposite the quarter where the sun sets in the summer; and it is said in that cave there was formerly an oracle, by which many who dwelt in those parts were inspired, and therefore called Nympholepti." There was an unnatural idea about a human being enchained by a nymph, just as in the Rhine legends the connection of sailors with the water maidens always brought mischief to the human being so fascinated. It was thought by the Greeks that the Nympholepti lost their reason, though they gained superior wisdom of the inferior gods. See De Quincey on the Nympholeptoi. (Works, Masson's Ed., vol. viii., pp. 438, 442.) In Mr. Browning's poem the nymph is a pure, superhuman woman creature, who has entranced a young man enamoured of her heavenly perfections. She has set him an impossible task; from the centre of pure white light she bids him trace ray after ray of light, which is broken into rainbow tints; and she bids him return to her untinctured by the coloured beams he has been compelled to traverse. The poem is one of the most difficult, if not the most difficult, of Mr. Browning's works. It is his largest use of his favourite light metaphor—the breaking up of pure white light into the coloured rays of the solar spectrum. A ray of white light (it is unnecessary, perhaps, to explain) is composed of the seven primary colours—violet, indigo, blue, green, yellow, orange and red. A solar ray of light can be separated by a prism into these seven colours. These again, when painted side by side upon a disc which is rapidly revolved, are, as the poet says, "whirled into a white." The nymph dwells in a realm of this white light. Before the light reaches the young man the imperfection of the medium which conveys it, or of his soul which receives it, breaks up the white light into its constituent coloured rays. He is bidden by her to travel down each red and yellow ray line, and work in its tint, but return to her without a stain, as pure as the original beams which rayed forth from her dwelling-place. This he is unable to do. He returns again and again, exciting her disgust at his appearance; and he starts off on another path, only to return coloured by the medium in which he has lived, as before. I have discussed this poem at length in my chapter on "Browning's Science, as shown in *Numpholeptos*," in my *Browning's Message to his Time*, second edition, 1891. The poem was debated at the Browning Society on May 31st, 1891; and so many different explanations were suggested, none of them in the least satisfactory, that the meeting requested Dr. Furnivall to ask Mr. Browning's assistance in the matter. He did so, and received the following reply:—"Is not the key to the meaning of the poem in its title, νυμφοληπτος [caught or entranst by a nymph], not γυναικεραστής [a woman lover]? An allegory, that is, of an impossible ideal object of love, accepted conventionally as such by a man who, all the while, cannot quite blind himself to the demonstrable fact that the possessor of knowledge and purity obtained without the natural consequences of obtaining them by achievement—not inheritance,—such a being is imaginary, not real, a nymph and no woman; and only such an one would be ignorant of and surprised at the results of a lover's endeavour to emulate the qualities which the beloved is entitled to consider as pre-existent to earthly experience, and independent of its inevitable results. I had no particular woman in my mind; certainly never intended to personify wisdom, philosophy, or any other abstraction; and the orb, raying colour out of whiteness, was altogether a fancy of my own. The 'seven spirits' are in the Apocalypse, also in Coleridge and Byron,—a common image."

"Oh Love! Love!" The lyric of Euripides in his *Hippolytus* (B.C. 428). Translated in J. P. Mahaffy's "Euripides," in Macmillan's *Classical Writers.* After quoting Euripides' two stanzas, Mr. Mahaffy says (p. 115):—"Mr. Browning has honoured me (Dec. 18th, 1878), with the following translation of these stanzas, so that the general reader may not miss the meaning or the spirit of the ode. The English metre, though not a strict reproduction, gives an excellent idea of the original one"—

I.

"Oh Love! Love, thou that from the eyes diffusest
Yearning, and on the soul sweet grace inducest—
Souls against whom thy hostile march is made—
Never to me be manifest in ire,
Nor, out of time and tune, my peace invade!
Since neither from the fire—
No, nor the stars—is launched a bolt more mighty
Than that of Aphrodité
Hurled from the hands of Love, the boy with Zeus for sire.

II.

"Idly, how idly, by the Alpherian river,
And in the Pythian shrines of Phœbus, quiver
Blood-offering from the bull, which Hellas heaps:
While Love we worship not—the Lord of men!
Worship not him, the very key who keeps
Of Aphrodité when
She closes up her dearest chamber-portals:
Love, when he comes to mortals,
Wide-wasting, through those deeps of woes beyond the deep!"

Og. See note to *Jochanan Hakkadosh* in the Sonnets on the Talmudic legend of the giant Og's bones and bedstead. Jewish scholars say the Hebrew work quoted has no existence, and that Mr. Browning's stock of Hebrew was very small.*

Ogniben. (*A Soul's Tragedy.*) He was the astute Pope's legate who went to Faenza to suppress the insurrection. He smoothed matters by getting Chiappino to leave the city, and he then complacently went away, saying he had known "*four*-and-twenty leaders of revolt."

Old Gandolf. (*The Bishop orders his Tomb at St. Praxed's*

* See *Browning Society's Papers*, Pt. XII., p. 81.

Church.) The Bishop's predecessor in his see, and the man whose tomb he desires to outdo.

Old Pictures in Florence. (*Men and Women*, 1855; *Lyrics*, 1863; *Dramatic Lyrics*, 1868.) On a warm March morning the poet from a height looks down upon Florence, gleaming in the translucent air, with all the glory of the beautiful city lying on the mountain side; and of all he saw the startling bell-tower of Giotto was the best to see. But he reproaches Giotto because he has played him false. This was unkind, as he loved him so. And this reflection, in its turn, leads him to think upon Giotto's brother artists. He recalls the ancient masters, and sees them haunting the churches and cloisters where their work was done, and lamenting the decay and neglect of their frescoes. In particular, he reflects on the wronged great soul of a painter whose work is peeling from the walls,—"a lion who dies of an ass's kick." The world wrongs its forgotten great souls, and hums round its famous Michael Angelos and its Raphaels; but perhaps they do not regard it, safe in heaven seeing God face to face, and all, as Browning hopes, attained to be poets. He thinks they can hardly be "quit of a world where their work is all to do," where the little wits have no ability to understand the relationship of artist to artist, and how one whom the world is pleased to honour derives in direct line from another who is forgotten. Not a word is heard now of men who in their day were as famous as the rest—Stefano, for example,—

> "Called Nature's Ape and the world's despair
> For his peerless painting."

He then reflects on the development of the artist. Greek art reuttered the truth of man, and Soul and Limbs, each betokened by the other, were made new in marble. Our weakness is tested by the strength, our meagre charms by the beauty of the matchless forms of Greek sculpture. This taught us the perfection of the body, but the artists one day awoke to the beauty and perfection of Soul, and then they worked for eternity, as the Greeks for time. This Greek art was perfect; these bodies could be no more beautiful. Consequently, so far there was arrest of development; they could never change, being whole and complete. Having learned all they have to teach, we shall see their work abolished. But in painting Souls, the artificer's hand can never be arrested, for soul develops eternally, and things learned on earth are practised in heaven. This is illustrated by the case of Giotto. At a stroke he drew a perfect O. This could be done no better: it was perfect, complete, not to be surpassed. But Giotto planned a bell-tower, wonderful for beauty, but not even yet completed. The conception outran the power to bring to perfection. Round O's can be completed; campaniles are still to finish. And so the Greeks finished their bodies. The early masters who began by depicting souls have their work still to finish. Their work is not completed—can, in fact, never be finished—because the soul is infinite. No doubt, he says, the early painters had to meet the objection, "What more can you want than Greek art?" They answered, "To paint man—to make his new hopes shine through his flesh." New fears glorify his rags. To bring the invisible full into daylight, what matters if the visible go to the dogs? How much they dared, these early masters! The first of this new development, however imperfect, beats the best of the old. Then he reflects that there is a fancy which some lean to (it is an Eastern fancy, now popularised by the Theosophists), that when this life is over we shall begin a fresh succession of lives—lives wherein we shall repeat in large what here we practise in little; and so through an infinite series of lives on a scale that is to be changed. But this is not at all to the poet's mind. He thinks he has learned his lesson here. He has seen

"By the means of evil that good is best,"

and considers that the uses of labour may consequently be garnered. He hopes there is rest; he has had troubles enough. And now he turns away from abstract conceptions on this deep problem to concrete matters—to the actual men who have carved and painted the forms he loves; and he brings up the memories of Nicolo the Pisan sculptor, and of the painter Cimabue, and goes on to speak of Ghiberti and Ghirlandajo. Alas! their ghosts are watching their peeling frescoes, their blistered or whitewashed works. He recalls the names of many a draughtsman and craftsman whose works are left to stealers and dealers. Suddenly the poet remembers the grudge he has against Giotto. There was a precious little picture, which Michael Angelo eyed like a lover, which was lost, but which has just turned up; and

Browning wanted it, he thinks that he ought to have been prompted by the spirit of Giotto to go to the right quarter for it, and now it is sold—to whom?—he cannot discover. But he shall have it yet, his jewel! Then he expresses his hope that Italy may soon see the last of the hated Austrian; and then wha will not the new Italian republic accomplish for man and art The Bell-tower of Giotto shall soar up to its proper stature,

"Completing Florence, as Florence Italy."

He wonders if he will be alive the morning the scaffold is taken down, and the golden hope of the world springs from its sleep.

NOTES.—Verse 8, *Da Vinci:* Leonardo Da Vinci, born 1452, died 1519, artist, sculptor, architect, musician, and man of letters; in addition to these he was a scientist and explorer. 9, *Dello*, the Florentine painter, born towards the end of the fourteenth century, registered under the name of Dello di Niccolo Delli. He was a sculptor as well as a painter, and was employed by the king of Spain: *Stefano:* a celebrated Italian painter of Florence (1301 ?—1350 ?); his naturalism earned him the title of "Scimia della Natura" (Ape of Nature). Vasari says, "He not only surpassed all those who preceded him in the art, but left even his master, Giotto himself, far behind. Thus he was considered, and with justice, to be the best of all the painters who had appeared down to that time." He excelled in perspective and foreshortening; *Nature's Ape:* Christofano Landino, in the Apology preceding his commentary on Dante, says, "Stefano is called 'The Ape of Nature' by every one, so accurately does he express whatever he designs to represent"; *Vasari, Georgio*, the author of the *Lives of the Painters*; *Theseus*, one of the statues of the Parthenon of Athens, now in the British Museum. 13, *Son of Priam* = Paris; *Apollo*, the snake-slayer, the Belvedere as described in the *Iliad*; *Niobe*, chief figure of the celebrated group of statues "Niobe all tears for her children," in the Uffizi gallery at Florence; *the Racer's frieze* of the Parthenon; *dying Alexander*, a fine piece of ancient Greek sculpture at Florence. 17, *Giotto and the "O"*: Pope Benedict XI. sent a messenger to Giotto to bring him a proof of the painter's power. Giotto refused to give him any further example of his talents than a O, drawn with a free sweep of the brush from the elbow.

The Pope was satisfied, and engaged Giotto at a great salary to adorn the palace at Avignon (Professor Colvin); *Campanile*, the bell-tower by the side of the Duomo at Florence. This is greatly praised by Ruskin, who says: "The characteristics of power and beauty occur more or less in different buildings, some in one and some in another. But altogether, and all in their highest possible relative degrees, they exist, as far as I know, only in one building of the world—the Campanile of Giotto." 23, *Nicolo the Pisan:* born between 1205 and 1207, died 1278; a sculptor and architect; *Cimabue*, Giotto's teacher (1240-1302), the great art reformer; *Ghiberti, Lorenzo* (1381-1455): he executed the wonderful bronze gates of the Baptistery at Florence, which were said by Michael Angelo to be worthy to have been the gates of Paradise; *Ghirlandajo, Domenico*, Florentine painter (1449-98), was the son of Tommaso del Ghirlandajo. 26, *Bigordi:* this is stated by some to have been the family name of Ghirlandajo, but it is disputed; *Sandro Botticelli*, born at Florence in 1457, died 1515; a celebrated Florentine painter; "*the wronged Lippino*," or Filippo Lippi, known as Filippino or Lippino (1460-1505), a Florentine painter, son of Fra Lippo Lippi, Some of his pictures were attributed to other artists, hence the expression "wronged"; *Frà Angelico* (1387-1455)—Il Beato Fra Giovanni Angelico da Fiesole—was the great Dominican Friar-Painter of Florence, the greatest of all painters of sacred subjects. He was a most holy man, shunning all advancement, and devoted to the poor. He never painted without fervent prayer; *Taddeo Gaddi:* an Italian painter and architect of the Florentine school (1300-1366), son of Gaddo Gaddi; he was one of Giotto's assistants for twenty-four years; when Giotto died he carried on the work of the Campanile; *intonaco*, rough cast, plaster, paint; *Jerome*, St. Jerome, the translator of the Scriptures into Latin; *Lorenzo Monaco*, Don Lorenzo, painter and monk, of the Angeli of Florence. First noticed as a painter, 1410. He executed many works in the Camaldoline monastery of his order. He was highly esteemed for his goodness. Verse 27, *Pollajolo, Antonio* (1433-98), a great painter and sculptor of Florence. He began life, as many of the great Italian artists did, as a goldsmith; *tempera*, a mixture of water and the yoke ot eggs—used to give body to colours: the same as *distemper; Alesso Baldovinetti*, a Florentine painter (1422-99): he worked in fresco and mosaic. 28, *Margheritone of Arezzo*, painter, sculptor, and architect (1236-1313); held in high estimation by painters who worked in the Greek manner. He was the first in painting on wood to cover the surface with canvas; *barret*, a cloak. 29, *Zeno*, the founder of the sect of the Stoics; *Carlino*, a painter. 30, "*a certain precious little tablet*," a lost picture which turned up while Mr. Browning was in Florence; *Buonarroti* = Michael Angelo. 31, *San Spirito* = "Holy Spirit," a church in Florence, so named; *Ognissanti* = "All Saints'," name of a church of Florence; "*Detur amanti*," let it be given to the lover; "*Jewel of Giamschid*": Byron calls it "the jewel of Giamschid," Beckford "the carbuncle of Giamschid" (see Brewer's *Reader's Handbook*); *Persian Sofi*, the name of a dynasty (1499-1736). 32, "*worst side of Mont St. Gothard*," the Swiss side; *Radetzky*, Count, field-marshal Austria (1766-1858), and famous in the wars against the insurrections against Austria by the Lombardians; *Morello*, a mountain near Florence; 33, *Witanagemot*, the great national council, the assent of which was necessary for all the laws of the Anglo-Saxon kings; so in Mrs. Browning's poem she refers to "a parliament of lovers of Italy"; *Ex: "Casa Guidi"*: Mrs. Browning's noble poem on Italian liberty; "*quod videas ante*," the which see above; *Loraine's*, *i.e.*, the Guises of unrivalled eminence in the sixteenth century; *Orgagna* (1315-76), a painter of Florence. 34, *prologuize*, to introduce with a formal preface; *Chimæra*, a fabulous animal. 35, "*curt Tuscan*": Tuscan is the literary language of Italy, therefore more dignified and freer from colloquialisms and vulgarisms than more modern forms; *-issimo*, termination of the superlative degree; *Cambuscan*, king of Sarra, in Tartary, the model of all royal virtues (see Brewer's *Handbook*); "*alt to altissimo*," high to the highest; *beccaccia*, a woodcock; "*Duomo's fit ally*": Giotto's lovely Bell-tower is a fit companion to the cathedral; *braccia*, a cubit.

"O Lyric Love, half-angel and half-bird." The first line of the invocation to the spirit of Mrs. Browning in Book I. of *The Ring and the Book*. Some stupid readers have thought this poem an invocation to our Lord, catching at the words "to drop down, to toil for man, to suffer, or to die." They thought they detected some familiar words heard in church; and one incompetent critic went so far as to write, "Though Lyric Love is here a quality personified, it seems to be so interchangeably with Christ . . . This is the interpretation we attach to the lines, though we have heard that some interpreters have actually considered them to be addressed to his wife!" (*The Religion of our Literature*, by George McCrie, p. 87.) There is really no difficulty about the lines until we come to parse them. Dr. Furnivall has done this in his grammatical analysis of the poem (*Browning Society's Papers*, No. IX., p. 165). An old lady who had read and profited by Bunyan's *Pilgrim's Progress* was advised to read Dr. Cheever's *Lectures* in explanation of the allegory; asked how she liked the latter work, she said she understood the *Pilgrim's Progress*, and hoped, before she died, to understand Dr. Cheever's interpretation. I think I understand 'O Lyric Love': I can never hope to understand Dr. Furnivall's analysis. It was called, at the time he wrote it, "Furnivall's Jubilee Puzzle."

"Once I saw a Chemist take a Pinch of Powder" (*Ferishtah's Fancies*). The first line of the eighth lyric.

One Way of Love. (*Men and Women*, 1855; *Lyrics*, 1863; *Dramatic Lyrics*, 1868.) A song of unrequited love. The lover has strewn the month's wealth of June roses on his lady's path: she passes them without notice. For months he has striven to learn the lute: she will not listen to his music. His whole life long he has learned to love, and he has lost. Let roses lie, let music's wing be folded: he will but say how blest are they who win her. A noble, dignified way of accepting defeat in love! *Another Way of Love* is a sequel to this poem. In this case the roses of June are actually tiresome to the man to whom they are offered. The woman in the first poem did not notice her roses, the man in the sequel confesses himself weary of their charms. His lady is satirical at his expense, and severely says he may go, and she will be recompensed if June mend the bower which his hand has rifled. June may also bestow her favours on a more appreciative recipient. She may also revenge herself by the lightning she uses to clear away insects and other rose-bower spoilers.

NOTE.—Verse 2, *Eadem semper*, always the same.

One Word More. (To E. B. B. [Elizabeth Barrett Browning] 1855.) This poem was originally appended to the collection of poems called *Men and Women* (*q.v.*) Browning's *Men and*

Women, containing amongst other noble poems his *Epistle to Karshish*, *Cleon*, *Fra Lippo Lippi*, and *Andrea del Sarto*, were fifty in number, and the concluding poem, *One Word More*, formed the dedication to his wife. The volume was in one sense a return for her *Sonnets from the Portuguese*, in which she poured out her love to Mr. Browning. In this poem he not less warmly declares his love for his wife, his "moon of poets." The dedication is happy, because his interest in men and women had been quickened and deepened by his marriage. They had studied human nature together, and each poetic soul had re-acted upon the other. He explains why he has desired to give something of his best, some gift which is not a gift to the world but to the woman he loves; and as the meanest of God's creatures—

> "Boasts two soul-sides: one to face the world with
> One to show a woman when he loves her!"

The poor workman, the most unskilful artisan, will strive to do something which shall express his utmost effort, to present to his love, and the greatest geniuses of the world have been actuated by a similar motive. Raphael, not content with painting, must pour out his soul in poetry for the woman of his heart (did she love the volume of a hundred sonnets all her life?), and Mr. Browning says he and his poet-wife would rather read that volume than wonder at the Madonnas by which his name will be ever known. But that volume will never be read. Guido Reni treasured it, but, as treasures do disappear, it vanished. Dante once proposed to paint for Beatrice an angel—traced it perchance with the corroded pen with which he pricked the stigma in the brow of the wicked—"Dante, who loved well because he hated": hating only wickedness, and that because it hinders loving. Mr. Browning would rather study that angel than read a fresh *Inferno*, but that picture we shall never see. No artist lives and loves who desires not for once and for one to express himself in a language natural to him and the occasion, but which to others is but an art; and so the painter will forgo his painting and write a poem, the writer will try to paint a picture "once and for one only"—

> "So to be the man and leave the artist."

Why is this? When a man comes before the world as leader,

teacher, prophet, artist or poet, in any capacity which is his proper business, he is open to the unsympathetic criticism of a world which is ever exacting and always ungrateful in exact proportion to the magnitude of the work done for it. Under these circumstances the real self in the man seldom appears; when, however, he presents himself before the sympathetic soul of the woman who loves him, he no longer works for the critic, no longer acts a part, no longer appears in a character distasteful to himself. When Moses smote the rock and saved the Israelites, he had mocking and sneering for his reward: the ungrateful and unbelieving multitude behaved after their manner. Could Moses forget the ancient wrong he bore about him? Dare the man ever put off the prophet? But were there in all that crowd a woman's face—a woman he could love—he would for her sake lay down the wonder-working rod, for he would be as the camel giving up its store of water with its life. But the poet says he shall never paint pictures, carve statues, nor express himself in music: for his wife he stands on his power of verse alone, and so he bids her take the lines of this love poem, which he has written for her, as the artist in fresco will steal a hair-pencil and cramp his spirit into missal painting for his lady, and the musician who sounds the martial strain will breathe his love through silver to serenade his princess; so he—the Browning men knew for other work—may this once whisper a love song to the ear of his wife. He will speak to her not dramatically, as he spoke in the poems in his book, but in his own true person. She knows him under both aspects, as the moon of Florence is the same which shines in London, though she has put off her Italian glory, and hurries dispiritedly through the gloomy skies of England. Could the moon really love a mortal, she has a side she could turn towards him, unseen as yet by herdsman or astronomer on his turret. Dumb to Homer, to Keats even, she would speak to *him*. And so the poet has for his love

> "A side the world has never seen,"

the novel

> "Silent silver lights and darks undreamed of."

NOTES.—Verse 2, *Century of Sonnets*. I can find no evidence that Raphael wrote a hundred sonnets. Some three, or at most four, are all about which I can find anything. Michael Angelo wrote many impassioned sonnets, and was undoubtedly a fine poet; but if Raphael wrote many sonnets, they are, as Mr. Browning says, lost. Probably the whole story is an example of poetical licence. There is a very mediocre sonnet (as Mr. Samuel Waddington describes it in the notes to his *Sonnets of Europe*) by Raphael, which he has inscribed on one of his drawings now exhibited at the British Museum :—

SONNET.

BY RAPHAEL.

" Un pensier dolce erimembrare e godo
Di quello assalto, ma più gravo el danno
Del partir, ch'io restai como quei c' anno
In mar perso la stella, s' el ver odo.
Or lingua di parlar disogli el nodo
A dir di questo inusitato inganno
Ch' amor mi fece per mio grave afanno,
Ma lui più ne ringratio, e lei ne lodo.
L'ora sesta era, che l' ocaso un sole
Aveva fatto, e l' altro sur se in locho
Ati più da far fati, che parole.
Ma io restai pur vinto al mio gran focho
Che mi tormenta, che dove lon sole
Desiar di parlar, più riman fiocho."

"There are also two other sonnets," says Mr. Waddington, "attributed to Raphael, but they can hardly be considered worthy of his illustrious name." Raphael's "*lady of the sonnets*" was Margherita (La Fornarina), the baker's daughter, of whom Raphael was devotedly fond, and whose likeness appears in several of his most celebrated pictures. "*Else he only used to draw Madonnas*:" Mrs. Jameson, in her *Legends of the Madonna*, gives the following list of Raphael's famous Madonnas: del Baldacchino, delle Candelabre, del Cardellino, della Famiglia Alva, di Foligno, de Giglio, del Passeggio, dell' Pesce, della Seggiola, di San Sisto. Verse 3, "*Her San Sisto names*": the Madonna di S. Sisto is the glory of the Dresden gallery. Little is known of its history; no studies or sketches of it exist. It much resembles the Madonna di Foligno, but is less injured by restoration. "*Her, Foligno*": the Madonna di Foligno was dedicated by Sigismund Corti, of Foligno, private secretary to Pope Julius II., and a distinguished patron of learning. Sigismund, having been in danger, vowed an offering to Our Lady, to whom he attributed his escape. The picture is in the Vatican. It was painted in 1511. "*Her that visits Florence in a Vision*": Mr. Browning, in a letter to Mr. W. J. Rolfe, said: "The Madonna at Florence is that called *del Granduca*, which represents her 'as appearing to a votary in a vision'—so say the describers; it is in the earlier manner, and very beautiful." It is in the Pitti Palace, Florence. Painted about 1506. "*Her that's left with lilies in the Louvre*" (Paris): on this Mr. Browning explained that, "I think I meant *La Belle Jardinière*—but am not sure—from the picture in the Louvre." This is a group of three figures: the Mother and Child and St. John. Painted in 1508. Verse 4, "*That volume Guido Reni . . . guarded*": this does not appear to have been a book of Sonnets, as Browning says, but a volume with a hundred designs drawn by Raphael. Reni left this book to his heir Signorini. Verse 5, "*Dante once prepared to paint an angel*": Dante was master of all the science of his time. He was a skilful draughtsman, and tells us that on the anniversary of the death of Beatrice he drew an angel on a tablet. He was an intimate friend of Giotto, who has recorded that it was from him he drew the inspiration of the allegories of Virtue and Vice for the frescoes of the Scrovegni Palace at Padua. He was also a musician. Verse 7, *Bice* is Beatrice, Dante's "gentle love." Verse 9, "*Egypt's flesh-pots*" (Exod. xvi. 3). Verse 10, "*Sinai-forehead's cloven brilliance*" (Exod. xxxiv. 29, 30). Verse 11, *Jethro*, the father-in-law of Moses (Exod. iii. 1); "*Æthiopian bond-slave*" (Numb. xii. 1). Verse 14, "*Karshish, Cleon, Norbert, and the Fifty*": there is a distinct caution here to those who seek for Browning's real opinions on religion and the various subjects with which he deals, that he is speaking dramatically in these poems, and not "in his true person." Verse 15, *Samminiato* = San Miniato, a well-known church in Florence. Verse 16, "*Zoroaster on his terrace*": the celebrated founder of the doctrine of the Persian Magi. Very little is known about him personally, but his religion is well understood. Ancient historians say he lived five thousand years before the Trojan War. His scriptures are the *Zend Avesta*. He studied at night the aspect of the heavens. "*Galileo on his turret*": Galileo, as an astronomer, required an observatory. *Keats*: Browning was much influenced by "the human rhythm" of Keats. There is abundant trace of this in *Pauline*, and in the second of the *Paracelsus* songs, "Heap cassia, sandal-buds, etc." "*Moonstruck mortal*": see Keats' poem *Endymion*, the fable of Endymion's amours with Diana, or the Moon. The fable probably originated from Endymion's study of astronomy requiring him to pass the night on a high mountain, to observe the heavenly bodies. "*Paved work of a sapphire*" (Exod. xxiv. 10). Mr. W. M. Rossetti explains some of the allusions in this poem in the *Academy* for January 10th, 1891:—"I understand the allusions, but Browning is far from accurate in them. 1. Towards the end of the *Vita Nuova*, Dante says that, on the first anniversary of the death of Beatrice, he began drawing an angel, but was interrupted by certain people of distinction, who entered on a visit. Browning is therefore wrong in intimating that the angel was painted 'to please Beatrice.' 2. Then Browning says that the pen with which Dante drew the angel was perhaps corroded by the hot ink in which it had previously been dipped for the purpose of denouncing a certain wretch—*i.e.*, one of the persons named in his *Inferno*. This about the ink, as such, is Browning's own figure of speech not got out of Dante. 3. Then Browning speaks of Dante's having 'his left hand i' the hair o' the wicked,' etc. This refers to *Inferno*, Canto 32, where Dante meets (among the traitors to their country) a certain Bocca degli Abati, a notorious Florentine traitor, dead some years back, and Dante clutches and tears at Bocca's hair to compel him to name himself, which Bocca would much rather not do. 4. Next Browning speaks of this Bocca as being a 'live man.' Here Browning confounds two separate incidents. Bocca is not only damned, but also dead; but further on (Canto 33) Dante meets another man, a traitor against his familiar friend. This traitor is Frate Alberigo, one of the Manfredi family of Faenza. This Frate Alberigo was, though damned, not, in fact, dead; he was still alive, and Dante makes it out that traitors of this sort are liable to have their souls sent to hell before the death of their bodies. A certain Bianca d'Oria, Genoese, is in like case—damned but not dead. 5. Browning proceeds to speak of 'the wretch going festering through Florence.' This is a relapse into his mistake—the confounding of the dead Florentine Bocca degli Abati with the living (though damned) Faentine and Genoese traitors, Frate

Alberigo and Bianca d'Oria, who had nothing to do with Florence."

On the Poet, Objective and Subjective; on the latter's Aim; on Shelley as Man and Poet. By Robert Browning. (The introductory essay to *Letters of Percy Bysshe Shelley*. Moxon: 1852.) Dr. Furnivall says: "The cause of Browning's writing this essay was (I believe) as follows:—In or before 1851, a forger clever enough to take in the publishers wrote some 'letters of Shelley and Byron.' Moxon bought the forged Shelley letters, and John Murray the Byron ones. Before they were proved spurious, Moxon printed the Shelley letters, and got Browning to write an introductory essay to them. Murray was slower, and, by the discovery of the forgery, was saved the exposure and annoyance that Moxon incurred in publishing, and then having to suppress, his book. The spurious Shelley letters were, as might have been expected, nugatory, barren of any new revelations of Shelley's character. Browning could actually make nothing of them, and therefore wrote his Essay, not on the Letters, but on the two classes of poets, objective and subjective, and on Shelley. He wanted a chance of writing on the poet he admired; the Letters gave him the chance; and, being told that they were genuine, he accepted them as such without inquiry. Moreover, being in Paris at the time, he had no opportunity of consulting English experts, had even any suspicion of forgery crossed his mind. The worth of his Essay is no way weakened by its having been set before spurious letters." A brief extract from Mr. Browning's Essay will indicate his estimate of the poetic method which he selected as his own. Speaking of the subjective poet, he says: "He, gifted like the objective poet with the fuller perception of nature and man, is impelled to embody the thing he perceives, not so much with reference to the many below, as to the One above him, the supreme Intelligence which apprehends all things in their absolute truth—an ultimate view ever aspired to, if but partially attained by the poet's own soul. Not what man sees, but what God sees—the *Ideas* of Plato, seeds of creation lying burningly in the Divine Hand—it is toward these that he struggles. Not with the combination of humanity in action, but with the primal elements of humanity he has to do; and he digs where he stands—preferring to seek them in his own soul as the nearest reflex of that absolute Mind, according to the intuitions of which he desires to perceive and speak. Such a poet does not deal habitually with the picturesque groupings and tempestuous tossings of the forest-trees, but with their roots and fibres naked to the chalk and stone. He does not paint pictures and hang them on the walls, but rather carries them on the retina of his own eyes: we must look deep into his human eyes to see those pictures on them. He is rather a seer, accordingly, than a fashioner; and what he produces will be less a work than an effluence. That effluence cannot be easily considered in abstraction from his personality,—being indeed the very radiance and aroma of his personality, projected from it but not separated." In these words we have not only Mr. Browning's defence of his work (if any could be needed), but an explanation of the reason why he seems as much interested in dissecting the soul of a villain or a scamp as of a saint and hero. Count Guido in his complex wickedness, brooding in his prison cell, is more interesting to such an analyst than Pompilia fluttering her wings on the borders of heaven. The old *roué* in the Inn Album, has root fibres worth tracing till they grip the stones. Simple old Rabbi Ben Ezra has nothing to dissect; his innocent soul lies basking in the smile of God. He has nothing to do with him but sit at his feet and listen. This "Essay on Shelley" has been reprinted and published in Part I. of the *Browning Society's Papers.*

Optimism. Browning's optimism is that which perhaps more than anything else distinguishes his whole work from first to last. Most eloquently has this been acknowledged by James Thomson, a pessimist of the pessimists. Unhappily he could not himself feel this confidence in "everything being for the best in the best of all possible worlds," but he could admire it in another. "Browning," he said, "has conquered life, instead of being conquered by it: a victory so rare as to be almost unique, especially among poets in these latter days." It would be easy to give examples of Browning's optimism, which would fill many pages of this work. The following will suffice:—

"God's in His heaven—all's right with the world!"
Song in "Pippa Passes."

"There shall never be one lost good! What was, shall live as before;
The evil is null, is nought, is silence implying sound;

What was good, shall be good, with, for evil, so much good more;
On the earth the broken arcs; in the heaven, a perfect round."

Abt Vogler.

"Let us cry 'All good things
Are ours, nor soul helps flesh more, now, than flesh helps soul!'"

Rabbi Ben Ezra.

"My own hope is, a sun will pierce
The thickest cloud earth ever stretched;
That, after Last, returns the First,
Though a wide compass round be fetched
That what began best, can't end worst,
Nor what God blessed once, prove accurst.'

Apparent Failure.

Orchestrion. The musical instrument invented by Abt Vogler (*q.v.*).

Ottima. (*Pippa Passes.*) The woman who, with her paramour Sebald, murdered her husband Luca.

"Overhead the Tree-Tops meet." (*Pippa Passes.*) Pippa sings these words as she passes the Bishop's house.

"Over the Sea our Galleys went." (*Paracelsus.*) The hero sings the song of which these are the opening words in Part IV., *Paracelsus Aspires.*

Pacchiarotto, and how he worked in Distemper. (Published July 1876, in a volume with *Other Poems.*) They were: "At the Mermaid," "Home," "Ship," "Pisgah-Sights," "Fears and Scruples," "Natural Magic," "Magical Nature," "Bifurcation," "Numpholeptos," "Appearances," "St. Martin's Summer," "Hervé Riel," "A Forgiveness," "Cenciaja," "Filippo Baldinucci on the Privilege of Burial," "Epilogue."

Pacchiarotto (or **Pacchiarotti**) **Jacopo,** has been confused in history with **Girolamo del Pacchia,** and this fact is referred to in the beginning of the poem. The following account of these painters, who lived about the same time, from the *Encyclopædia Britannica,* will help to clear the way for the comprehension of this rather difficult poem,—difficult not on account of the story, which is told clearly enough, but for the extraneous matter with which it is intermingled.

[THE MAN.] "Pacchia, Girolamo Del, and Pacchiarotto (or Pacchiarotti) Jacopo. These are two painters of the Sienese school, whose career and art-work have been much mis-stated till late years. One or other of them produced some good pictures, which used to pass as the performance of Perugino; reclaimed from Perugino, they were assigned to Pacchiarotto; now it is sufficiently settled that the good works are by G. del Pacchia, while nothing of Pacchiarotto's own doing transcends mediocrity. The mythical Pacchiarotto, who worked actively at Fontainebleau, has no authenticity. Girolamo del Pacchia, son of a Hungarian cannon-founder, was born probably in Siena, in 1477. Having joined a turbulent club named the Bardotti, he disappeared from Siena in 1535, when the club was dispersed, and nothing of a later date is known of him. His most celebrated work is a fresco of the Nativity of the Virgin, in the chapel of St. Bernardino, Siena: graceful and tender, with a certain artificiality. Another renowned fresco, in the church of St. Catherine, represents that saint on her visit to St. Agnes of Montepulciano, who, having just expired, raises her foot by miracle. In the National Gallery of London there is a Virgin and Child. The forms of G. del Pacchia are fuller than those of Perugino (his principal model of style appears to have been in reality Francialigio); the drawing is not always unexceptionable. The female heads have sweetness and beauty of feature, and some of the colouring has noticeable force. Pacchiarotto was born in Siena in 1474. In 1530 he took part in the conspiracy of the Libertini and Popolani, and in 1533 he joined the Bardotti. He had to hide for his life in 1535, and was concealed by the Observantine fathers in a tomb in the church of St. John. He was stuffed in close to a new-buried corpse, and got covered with vermin and dreadfully exhausted by the close of the second day. After a while he resumed work. He was exiled in 1539, but recalled in the following year; and in that year, or soon afterwards, he died. Among the few extant works with which he is still credited is an Assumption of the Virgin, in the Carmine of Siena."

[THE POEM.] Pacchiarotto must needs take up "Reform." He thought it was his vocation to set things in general to rights. The world he considered needed reforming, and he was quite ready to undertake the task. He found mankind stubborn, however, and not much inclined to listen to him. So he constructed himself a workshop, and painted its walls in fresco with all sorts and conditions of men, from beggar to noble. He drew kings, clowns, popes, emperors, priests, and ladies; then washed his brushes, cleaned his pallet, took off his working dress, and began to lecture his figures which he had painted. He put arguments into their mouths, and of course readily refuted them. He found his figures very meek and complaisant, and he had no trouble at all in disposing of their replies to his own satisfaction. He stripped them one by one of their "cant-clothed abuses," exposed the sophistry of their excuses, and left their vices without a leg to stand upon. Paint-bred men being so easily upset, he was now prepared to deal with those of flesh and blood, so he wished mortar and paint good-bye and descended to the streets. It happened just at this time that there fell upon Siena a famine. This public distress afforded our artist his opportunity: he blamed the authorities for the famine, and set himself to the task of teaching them to manage things better. Now, there was at that time a club of disaffected citizens, who called themselves *Bardotti*, or "spare-horses"—those which walk by the side of the waggon drawn by the working team—horses doing nothing to draw the load, but ready in case of emergency. Such were these gentry; they did not work, but they were ready for such an emergency as the present. And their advice to the authorities was simply to turn things upside down, make servant master, poverty wealth, and wealth poverty; then things would be righted. Pacchiarotto placed himself in the midst of these folk, and suggested that what they wanted was the right man in the right place, and he was the right man. The words were not out of his mouth ere the Spare-Horses flew at him, and he had to run for his life. Looking everywhere for some place of shelter, he found himself at the cemetery of a Franciscan monastery; and the only place where he could hide himself with safety from the pursuers was in a vault with a recently-buried corpse, so he was obliged to creep through a hole in the brickwork and habituate himself to the strange bedfellow. In this stinking atmosphere, and covered with vermin from the corpse, he lay in misery for two days, praying the saints to set him free, and promising for ever to abandon the attempt to preach change to his fellow-citizens. When he was starved into sanity, he scrambled out of this loathsome hiding-place, looking like a spectre, only much more "alive." He then found his way to the superior of the brotherhood, who had him well cleansed and rubbed with odoriferous unguents. They fed him, clothed him, and then he told his story all unvarnished. Be sure the good monk gave him sound advice. He told him how he had had hopes of converting men by his own preaching, and how hard he had found the task. He had come to the conclusion that work for work's sake was the real need of men: let men work, but not dream, and they would succeed; if present success merely were intended, heaven would begin too soon. He advised him not to be a spare-horse, but a working-horse—to stick to his paint brush and work for his living. Pacchiarotto was mute; he had no need of conversion. He was reformed already, not by a live man's arguments, but by the dead thing—the clay-cold grinning corpse, that had asked him why he was in such a hurry to leave the warm light and join him in the grave. The corpse had told him how earth was a place of rehearsal, at which things seldom go smoothly. The Author, no doubt, had His reasons, which would come out when he play was produced. Meanwhile he advised him not to interfere with its production; he was suffering from a swelling called Vanity, which he would prick and relieve him of. And so Pacchiarotto, having partaken of the monks' good cheer, was restored to sanity and said good-bye. Mr. Browning now addresses his critics. He has told them a plain story, and tried therewith to content them. He considers them as an assembly of May-day sweeps, with tongs and bellows, calling at his house and announcing themselves as

"We critics as sweeps out your chimbly!'

They relieve his flue of the soot, suggest that he burns a deal of coal in his kitchen, and the neighbours do say he ought to consume his own smoke! Browning tells them that his housemaid says they bring more dirt into the house than they remove. But he will not be hard upon them: "'twas God made you dingy," he says. He will give them soap, however, and let them dance away and make a rattle with their brushes, which is a large share of their whole business, he thinks. He bids them not trample his grass, and flings out a liberal largess and bids them be off, or his housemaid will serve them as Xantippe served Socrates once; she will take the first thing that comes to her hand.

NOTES.—Verse 2, "*my Kirkup*": this was Baron Kirkup, an admirer of art and letters, who was on friendly terms with Browning at Florence. He received a title of nobility from the

King of Italy for his services to literature. It was he who discovered Dante's portrait in the Bargello at Florence. *San Bernardino:* St. Bernardino of Siena became, at the age of twenty-three, one of the most celebrated and eloquent preachers among the Franciscans, but he refused all ecclesiastical honours. He founded the Order of the "*Observants*" (see note to v. 17). He was born 1380. *Bazzi:* the Italian painter Giannantonio Bazzi (who, until recent years, was erroneously named *Razzi*) bore the name "*Sodona*," or "*Il Sodoma*," as a family name, and signed it upon some of his pictures. Bazzi was corrupted into Razzi, and "Sodona" into "Sodoma." He lived *c.* 1479—1549. *Beccafumi:* a distinguished painter of the Siena school, who lived at the beginning of the sixteenth century. v. 3, *Sopra sotto*, topsy-turvy. v. 5, *Quiesco*, I rest; "*priest armed with bell, book, and candle*": in the major excommunication the bell is rung, the sentence read from the book, and the lighted candle extinguished. v. 6, *frescanti*, painters in fresco. v. 8, *Boanerges:* sons of Thunder—an appellation given by Jesus Christ to His disciples James and John. v. 9, *Juvenal:* the celebrated Roman satirist; flourished at Rome in the latter half of the first century. He severely chastised the follies and vices of his times. He was particularly outspoken concerning the licentiousness of the Roman ladies. "*Quæ nemo dixisset in toto, nisi (ædepol) ore illoto*": which things no one would have spoken about fully, unless (by Gad) he had a dirty mouth. (Juvenal's satires about the Roman ladies are inconceivably filthy, and if the things were true it was ill to speak of them in this manner. St. Paul was equally severe, but adopted another method.) *Apage:* away! begone! v. 11, "*non verbis sed factis*": not by words but by deeds. v. 12, "*fetch grain out of Sicily*": Sicily has always been famous for its wheat. Even at the present day the best wheat for making Naples macaroni comes from this beautiful island, and the people take in return the inferior wheat of Italy. Sicily was in ancient times sacred to Ceres, the goddess of the corn-lands. v. 13, "*Freed Ones*," "*Bardotti*": a revolutionary club so called, which was broken up by the authorities in 1535. Pacchia and Pacchiarotto both seem to have had some connection with it; *bailiwick:* the precincts in which a bailiff has jurisdiction. v. 15, "*kai tà loipa*," Και τα λειπόμενα = and so forth; *kappas, taus, lambdas* (κ.τ.λ.): the initial letters of the above Greek words, commonly used in learned books. **v.** 16, "*per ignes incedis*" : thou art treading upon fires. Not quite correctly quoted, as to the order of the words, from Horace (*Od.* II. i. 6), "Et incedis per ignes, suppositos cineri doloso." v. 17, *St. John's Observance:* "The Italians call the Franciscans *Osservanti*, in France *Pères ou Frères de l'Observance*, because they observed the original rule as laid down by St. Francis, went barefoot, and professed absolute poverty. This order became very popular" (Mrs. Jameson's *Monastic Orders*). v. 18, "*haud in posse sed esse mens*" : mind as it is, not as it might be. **v.** 21, *thill-horse* a thiller horse, a horse which goes between the shafts, or thills. v. 22, *imposthume*, an abscess or boil. v. 23, "*sæculorum in sæcula!*" for ever and ever; *Benedicite:* Bless ye! May you be blessed. v. 27, *aubade* [Fr.], open-air music performed at daybreak before the window of the person whom it is intended to honour. v. 27, *skoramis*, a vessel of dishonour. v. 28, *karterotaton belos*, the strongest dart (see Pindar's 1st Olympic Ode). "*which Pindar declares the true melos*" = mode. *ad hoc*, hitherto. *os frontis*, the forehead. "*hebdome, hieron emar*," the seventh, the holy day. "*tei gar Apollona chrusaora, egeinato Leto*" : on which the golden-sworded Apollo was born of Latona.

Painting Poems. The *great poems* of this class are *Andrea del Sarto*, *Pictor Ignotus*, and *Fra Lippo Lippi*. (Vasari's *Lives of the Painters* should be read in connection with the poems which deal with the Italian artists.)

Palma. The heroine of *Sordello*. She was the daughter of Eccelino, the Ghibelline, by Agnes Este. The historical personage represented by Browning's Palma was Cunizza.

Pambo. (*Jocoseria*, 1883.) The poem is based upon a passage in the *Ecclesiastical History of Socrates Scholasticus*, Lib. iv., cap. xviii., "concerning Ammon the Monk, and divers religious men inhabiting the Desert." In the time of St. Antony, in the Nitrian desert, A.D. 373, there was a monk named "Pambo, a simple and an unlearned man, who came unto his friend to learn a Psalm; and hearing the first verse of the thirty-ninth Psalm, which is there read: 'I said, I will take heed unto my ways, that I offend not with my tongue'—would not hear the second, but went away saying, 'This one verse is enough for me, if I learn it as I ought to do.' And when his teacher blamed him for absenting himself a whole six months, he answered for himself that he had not well learned the first verse. Many years after that, when one of his acquaintances demanded of him whether he had learned the verse, he said again, that in nineteen years he had scarce learned in life to fulfil that one line." His life is taken from Palladius, in Lausiac and Rufin. *Hist. Patr. Sozomen.* Alban Butler, in his *Lives of the Saints*, under the date September 6th, gives the following interesting account of the character, whose history was apparently only partially known by Mr. Browning, as in the second verse of the poem he says he does not know who he was:—"St. Pambo betook himself in his youth to the great St. Antony in the desert, and, desiring to be admitted among his disciples, begged he would give him some lessons for his conduct. The great patriarch of the ancient monks told him he must take care always to live in a state of penance and compunction for his sins, must perfectly divest himself of all self-conceit, and never place the least confidence in himself or in his own righteousness; must watch continually over himself, and study to act in everything in such a manner as to have no occasion afterward to repent of what he had done; and that he must labour to put a restraint upon his tongue and his appetite. The disciple set himself earnestly to learn the practice of all these lessons. The mortification of gluttony was usually laid down by the fathers as one of the first steps towards bringing the senses and the passions into subjection: this, consisting in something exterior and sensible, its practice is more obvious, yet of great importance towards the reduction of all the sensual appetites of the mind, whose revolt was begun by the intemperance and disobedience of our first parents. Fasting is also, by the Divine appointment, a duty of the exterior part of our penance. What a reproach are the austere lives which so many saints have led to those slothful and sensual Christians whose god is the belly, and who walk enemies to the Cross of Christ, or who have not courage, at least by frequent self-denials, to curb this appetite! No man can govern himself who is a slave to this base gratification of sense. St. Pambo excelled most other ancient monks in the austerity of his continual fasts. The government of his tongue was no less an object of his watchfulness than that of his appetite. A certain religious brother to whom he had applied for advice began to recite to him the thirty-ninth psalm: 'I said, I will take heed to my ways, that I sin not with my tongue.' Which words Pambo had no sooner heard, but, without waiting for the second verse, he returned to his cell, saying that was enough for one lesson, and that he would go and study to put it in practice. This he did by keeping almost perpetual silence, and by weighing well, when it was necessary to speak, every word before he gave any answer. He often took several days to recommend consultations to God, and to consider what answer he should give to those who addressed themselves to him. By his perpetual attention not to offend in his words, he arrived at so great a perfection in this particular that he was thought to have equalled, if not to have excelled, St. Antony himself; and his answers were seasoned with so much wisdom and spiritual prudence that they were received by all as if they had been oracles dictated by heaven. Abbot Poemen said of our saint: 'Three exterior practices are remarkable in Abbot Pambo: his fasting every day till evening, his silence, and his great diligence in manual labour.' St. Antony inculcated to all his disciples the obligation of assiduity in constant manual labour in a solitary life, both as a part of penance and a necessary means to expel sloth and entertain the vigour of the mind in spiritual exercises. This lesson was confirmed to him by his own experience, and by a heavenly vision related in the Lives of the Fathers as follows: 'Abbot Antony, as he was sitting in the wilderness, fell into a grievous temptation of spiritual darkness; and he said to God: "Lord, I desire to be saved; but my thoughts are a hindrance to me. What shall I do in my present affliction? How shall I be saved?" Soon after he rose up, and, going out of his cell, saw a man sitting and working, then rising from his work to pray; afterward sitting down again and twisting his cord, after this rising to pray. He understood this to be an angel sent by God to teach him what he was to do, and he heard the angel say to him: "Do so, and thou shalt be saved." Hereat the Abbot was filled with joy and confidence, and by this means he cheerfully persevered to the end.' St. Pambo most rigorously observed this rule, and feared to lose one moment of his precious time. Out of love of humiliations, and a fear of the danger of vain-glory and pride, he made it his earnest prayer for three years that God would not give him glory before men, but rather contempt. Nevertheless

God glorified him in this life, but made him by His grace to learn more perfectly to humble himself amidst applause. The eminent grace which replenished his soul showed itself in his exterior by a certain air of majesty, and a kind of light which shone on his countenance, like what we read of Moses, so that a person could not look steadfastly on his face. St. Antony, who admired the purity of his soul and his mastery over his passions, used to say that his fear of God had moved the Divine Spirit to take up His resting-place in him. St. Pambo, after he left St. Antony, settled in the desert of Nitria, on a mountain, where he had a monastery. But he lived some time in the wilderness of the Cells, where Rufinus says he went to receive his blessing in the year 374. St. Melania the Elder, in the visit she made to the holy solitaries who inhabited the deserts of Egypt, coming to St. Pambo's monastery on Mount Nitria, found the holy abbot sitting at his work, making mats. She gave him three hundred pounds weight of silver, desiring him to accept that part of her store for the necessities of the poor among the brethren. St. Pambo, without interrupting his work, or looking at her or her present, said to her that God would reward her charity. Then, turning to his disciple, he bade him take the silver and distribute it among all the brethren in Lybia and the isles who were most needy, but charged him to give nothing to those of Egypt, that country being rich and plentiful. Melania continued some time standing, and at length said: 'Father, do you know that here is three hundred pounds weight of silver?' The Abbot, without casting his eye upon the chest of silver, replied: 'Daughter, He to whom you made this offering very well knows how much it weighs without being told. If you give it to God, who did not despise the widow's two mites, and even preferred them to the great presents of the rich, say no more about it.' This Melania herself related to Palladius. St. Athanasius once desired St. Pambo to come out of the desert to Alexandria, to confound the Arians by giving testimony to the divinity of Jesus Christ. Our saint, seeing in that city an actress dressed up for the stage, wept bitterly; and being asked the reason of his tears, said he wept for the sinful condition of that unhappy woman, also for his own sloth in the Divine service, because he did not take so much pains to please God as she did to ensnare men. When Abbot Theodore begged of St. Pambo some words of instruction: 'Go,' said he, 'and exercise mercy and charity toward all men. Mercy finds confidence before God.' To the priest of Nitria who asked him how the brethren ought to live, he said: 'They must live in constant labour and the exercise of all virtues, watching to preserve their conscience free from stain, especially from giving scandal or offence to any neighbour.' St. Pambo said, a little before his death: 'From the time that I came into this desert, and built myself a cell in it, I do not remember that I have ever ate any bread but what I had earned by my own labour, nor that I ever spoke any word of which I afterward repented. Nevertheless, I go to God as one who has not yet begun to serve Him.' He died seventy years old, without any sickness, pain, or agony, as he was making a basket, which he bequeathed to Palladius, who was at that time his disciple, the holy man having nothing else to give him. Melania took care of his burial, and having obtained this basket, kept it to her dying day. St. Pambo is commemorated by the Greeks on several days. It was a usual saying of this great director of souls in the rules of Christian perfection, 'If you have a heart, you may be saved.' The extraordinary austerities and solitude of a St. Antony or a St. Pambo are not suitable to persons engaged in the world,—they are even inconsistent with their obligations; but all are capable of disengaging their affections from inordinate passions and attachment to creatures, and of attaining to a pure and holy love of God, which may be made the principle of their thoughts and ordinary actions, and sanctify the whole circle of their lives. Of this all who have a heart are, through the Divine grace, capable. In whatever circumstances we are placed, we have opportunities of subduing our passions and subjecting our senses by frequent denials, of watching over our hearts by self-examination, of purifying our affections by assiduous recollection and prayer, and of uniting our souls to God by continual exterior and interior acts of holy love. Thus may the gentleman, the husbandman, or the shopkeeper, become an eminent saint, and make the employments of his state an exercise of all heroic virtues, and so many steps to perfection and to eternal glory."—Mr. Browning, in the last verse, addresses his critics in a jocular manner. He owns he is very much like Pambo,—he has spent much time in *looking to his ways*; yet, as he is so often reminded by his reviewers and critics, he still feels, he says, that he *offends with his tongue!*

NOTE.—"*Arcades sumus ambo*": "we are both alike eccentric." From Vergil's *Eclogues* (vii.), where Corydon and Thyrsis are described as *both Arcadians.*

Pan and Luna. (*Dramatic Idyls*, Second Series, 1880.) Pan was the god of shepherds, of huntsmen, and of all the inhabitants of the country. He was a monster in appearance, had two small horns on his head, his complexion was ruddy, his nose flat, and his legs, thighs, and feet and tail, were those of a goat. The god of shepherds lived chiefly in Arcadia, and he is described by the poets as frequently occupied in deceiving and entrapping the nymphs of the neighbourhood. Luna was the same as Diana or Cynthia—names given to the moon. Mr. Browning quotes from Vergil, *Georgics*, iii., 390, at the head of the poem the words, "Si credere dignum est" (if we may trust report), the context giving the account according to Vergil—

> "'Twas thou, with fleeces milky-white, (if we
> May trust report) Pan, god of Arcady,
> Did bribe thee, Cynthia; nor didst thou disdain,
> When called in woody shades, to cure a lover's pain."

The legend was the poetical way of accounting for an eclipse of the moon. The naked maid-moon flying through the night sought shelter in a fleecy cloud mass caught on some pine-tree top. "Shamed she plunged into its shroud," when she was grasped by rough red Pan, the god of all that tract, who had made a billowy wrappage of wool tufts to simulate a cloud. Vergil says that Luna was a not unwilling conquest; Mr. Browning does more justice to the supposed austerity of the goddess of night. It is evident, however, that the moral of the poem is that she yielded herself to the love of Pan out of compassion. Pan exalted himself in aspiring to her austere purity; Luna voluntarily subjected herself to the lower nature out of sympathy, thus preserving her modesty by sanctifying it with sacrifice.

Paracelsus. [THE MAN.] Paracelsus was the son of a physician, William Bombast von Hohenheim, who taught him the rudiments of alchemy, surgery, and medicine; he studied philosophy under several learned masters, chief of whom was Trithemius, of Spanheim, Abbot of Wurzburg, a great adept in magic, alchemy, and astrology. Under this teacher he acquired a taste for occult studies, and formed a determination to use them for the welfare of mankind. He could hardly have studied under a better man in those dark days. Tritheim himself was well in advance of most of the teachers of his time; he was of the Theosophists or Mystics, for they are of the same class, and probably, in their German form, derived their origin from the labours of Tauler of Strasburg, who afterwards, with "the Friends of God," made their headquarters at Basle. The mysticism which is so dear to Mr. Browning, and which perhaps finds its highest expression in the poem which we are considering, is not therefore out of place. When he left his home he went to study in the mines of the Tyrol. There, we are told, he learned mining and geology, and the use of metals in the practice of medicine. "I see," he says, "the true use of chemistry is not to make gold, but to prepare medicines." Paracelsus is rightly termed "the father of modern chemistry." He discovered the metals zinc and bismuth, hydrogen gas, and the medical uses of many minerals, the most important of which were mercury and antimony. He gave to medicine the greatest weapon in her armoury—the tincture of opium. His celebrated *azoth* some say was magnetised electricity, and others that his *magnum opus* was the science of fire. He acted as army surgeon to several princes in Italy, Belgium, and Denmark. He travelled in Portugal and Sweden, and came to England; going thence to Transylvania, he was carried prisoner to Tartary, visiting the famous colleges of Samarcand, and went thence with the son of the Khan on an embassy to Constantinople. All this time he had no books. His only book was Nature; he interrogated her at first-hand. He mixed with the common people, and drank with boors, shepherds, Jews, gipsies, and tramps, so gaining scraps of knowledge wherever he could, and giving colourable cause to his enemies to say he was nothing but a drunken vagabond fond of low company. He would rather learn medicine and surgery from an old country nurse than from a university lecturer, and was denounced accordingly and—naturally. If there was one thing he detested more than another, it was the principle of authority. He bent his head to no man. Paracelsus, as we find him in his works, was full of love for humanity, and it is much more probable that he learned his lessons while travelling, and mixing amongst the poor and wretched, and while a prisoner in Tartary, where he doubtless imbibed much Buddhist and occult lore from the philosophers of Samarcand, than that anything like the Constantinople drama was enacted. Be this as it may, we have abundant evidence in the many extant works of Paracelsus that he was thoroughly imbued with the spirit and doctrines of the Eastern occultism, and was full of love for humanity. A quotation from his *De Fundamento Sapientiæ* must suffice: "He who foolishly believes is foolish; without knowledge there can be no faith. God does not desire that we should remain in darkness and ignorance. We should be all recipients of the Divine wisdom. We can learn to know God only by becoming wise. To become like God we must become attracted to God, and the power that attracts us is love. Love to God will be kindled in our hearts by an ardent love for humanity, and a love for humanity will be caused by a love to God." In the year 1525 Paracelsus went to Basle, where he was fortunate in curing Froben, the great printer, by his laudanum, when he had the gout. Froben was the friend of Erasmus, who was associated with Œcolampadius; and soon after, upon the recommendation of Œcolampadius, he was appointed by the city magnates a professor of physics, medicine and surgery, with a considerable salary; at the same time they made him city physician, to the duties of which office he requested might be added inspector of drug shops. This examination made the druggists his bitterest enemies, as he detected their fraudulent practices: they combined to set the other doctors of the city against him, and as these were exceedingly jealous of his skill and success, poor Paracelsus found himself in a hornet's nest. We find him then at Basle University in 1526, the earliest teacher of science on record. He has become famous as a physician, the medicines which he has discovered he has successfully used in his practice; he was now in the eyes of his patients at least,

> "The wondrous Paracelsus, life's dispenser,
> Fate's commissary, idol of the schools and courts."

In 1528 we find him at Colmar, in Alsatia. He has been driven by the priests and doctors from Basle. He had been called to the bedside of some rich cleric who was ill; he cured him, but so speedily that his fee was refused. Though not at all a mercenary man (for he always gave the poor his services gratuitously) he sued the priest, but the judge refused to interfere, and Paracelsus used strong language to him, and had to fly to escape punishment. The closing scene of the drama is laid in a cell in the hospital of Salzburg. It is the year 1541, his age but forty-eight, and the divine martyr of science lies dying. Recent investigations in contemporary records have proved that he had been attacked by the servants of certain physicians who were his jealous enemies, and that in consequence of a fall he sustained a fracture of the skull, which proved fatal in a few days. He was buried in the churchyard of St. Sebastian at Salzburg, but in 1752 his bones were removed to the porch of the church, and a monument was erected to his memory by the archbishop. When his body was exhumed it was discovered that his skull had been fractured during life. Writers on magic, of whom Dr. Hartmann is one, describe *azoth* as being "the creative principle in Nature; the universal panacea or spiritual life-giving air—in its lowest aspects, ozone, oxygen, etc." Much ridicule has been cast upon Paracelsus for his belief in the possibility of generating homunculi; but after all he may only mean that chemistry will succeed in bridging the gulf between the living and the not-living by the production of organic bodies from inorganic substances. Paracelsus held that the constitution of man consists of seven principles: (1) The elementary body; (2) The archæus (vital force); (3) The sidereal body; (4) The animal soul; (5) The rational soul; (6) The spiritual soul; (7) The man of the new Olympus (the personal God). Those who are familiar with Indian philosophy will recognise this anthropology as identical with its own. Paracelsus, in his *De Natura Rerum*, says, "The external man is not the real man, but the real man is the soul in connection with the Divine Spirit." We understand now what Mr. Browning means when he says that "knowing is opening the way to let the imprisoned splendour escape." His idea that all Nature was living, and that there is nothing which has not a soul hidden within it—a hidden principle of life—led him to the conclusion that, in place of the filthy concoctions and hideous messes that were in vogue with the doctors of his time, it was possible to give tinctures and quintessences of drugs, such as we now call active principles,—in a word, that it is more reasonable and pleasant to take a grain or two of quinine than a tablespoonful of timber. He set himself to study the causes and the symptoms of disease, and sought a remedy in common-sense methods. Mr. Browning is right when he makes him say he had a "wolfish hunger after knowledge"; and surely there never lived a man whose aim was to devote its fruits to the service of humanity more than his. There are many hints in his works that he knew a great deal more than he cared to make known. Take this example. He said: "Every peasant has seen a magnet will attract iron. I have discovered that the magnet, besides this visible power, has another and a concealed power." Again: "A magnet may be prepared out of some vital substance that will attract vitality." Mesmer, who lived nearly three hundred years after him, reaped the glory of a discovery made, as Lessing says, by the martyred fire-philosopher who died in Salzburg hospital. "Matter is the visible body of the invisible God," says Paracelsus. Matter to him was not dead. "Matter is, so to say, coagulated vapour, and is connected with spirit by an intermediate principle which it receives from the spirit." We cannot understand Paracelsus and the science of his time without a little inquiry as to what was meant by the search for the philosopher's stone, the elixir of life, and the universal medicine. It is very difficult to discern what was really intended by these phrases. Dr. Anna Kingsford, who paid considerable attention to the hermetic philosophy, says: "These are but terms to denote pure spirit and its essential correlative, a will absolutely firm, and inaccessible alike to weakness from within and assault from without." Another writer ingeniously tries to explain the universal solvent as really nothing but pure water, which has the property of more or less dissolving all the elements. His *alcahest*—as he termed it—as far as I can make out was nothing more than a preparation of lime; but writers of this school only desired to be understood by the initiated, and probably the words actually used meant something quite different. There was a reason for using an incomprehensible style for fear of the persecutions of the Church, and these books, like the rolls in Ezekiel, were "written within and without." Many great truths, we know, were enshrouded in symbolic names and fanciful metaphors. It is certain that Paracelsus, like his predecessors, sought to possess the elixir of life. It does not appear from his writings that he thought it possible to render the physical body immortal; but he held it to be the duty—as the medical profession holds it still—of the physician to preserve life as long as possible. A great deal of matter attributed to Paracelsus on this subject is spurious, but there are some of his authentic writings which are very curious and entertaining. He describes the process of making the *Primum Ens Melissæ*, which after all turns out to be nothing but an alkaline tincture of the leaves of the common British plant known as the Balm or *Melissa officinalis*. Some very amusing stories are told of the virtues of this concoction by Lesebure, a physician to Louis XIV., and which speak volumes for the credulity of the doctors of those times. Another of his great secrets was his *Primum Ens Sanguinis*. This is extremely simple, being nothing more than the venous injection of blood from the arm of "a healthy young person." In this we see that he anticipated our modern operation of transfusion. His doctrine of signatures was very curious and most absurd. He thought that "each plant was in a sympathetic relation with the Macrocosm and consequently with the Microcosm." "This signature," he says, "is often expressed even in the exterior forms of things." So he prescribed the plant we call euphrasy or "eye bright" for complaints of the eyes, because of the likeness to an eye in the flower; small-pox was treated with mulberries because their colour showed that they were proper for diseases of the blood. This sort of thing still lingers in country domestic medicine. *Pulmonaria officinalis* or Lungwort, so called from its spotted leaves looking like diseased lungs, has long been used for chest complaints. (See my "Paracelsus the Reformer of Medicine" in *Browning's Message to his Time.*)

Paracelsus. [THE POEM, 1835.] PARACELSUS ASPIRES: BOOK I. (*Würzburg*, 1512.) Paracelsus the student is talking with his friends Festus and Michal on the eve of his departure to seek knowledge of the deeper sort, that cannot be learned from books,—in the great world of men. It is a time to arouse young men. The dark night of ignorance yields to the rising sun of learning, for the art of printing and the glories of the Revival of Learning have liberated the minds of men. Authority no longer suffices: the men of Germany will see for themselves. So Paracelsus, pupil of the learned Abbot Trithemius, resolves to forsake the monastery cell and the ancient books, and go out to seek for himself knowledge in the byways of the world. His friends are timid. They mistrust his method; they call him proud and too self-confident, advise him to stick to the beaten ways of learning, nor venture into the tangled forests and pathless deserts which God has evidently closed against man's rash intrusion. Paracelsus, on the contrary, feels that he has a great commission from God: he dare not subdue the vast longings which fill his soul. God's command is laid upon him, and he must answer to His will. Festus objects that a man must not presume to serve God save in the appointed channels. God looks to means as well as ends, and Paracelsus ought not to scorn the ordinary means of learning. The impatient student suggests that his fierce energy, his striving instinct, the irresistible force which works within him, are proofs that he possesses a God-given strength never imparted in vain. He will abjure the idle arts of magic. New hopes animate him, new light dawns upon him: he is set apart for a great work. "Then," replies his friend, "pursue it in an approved retreat; turn not aside from the famed spots where Learning dwells. Rome and Athens shall teach you; leave seas and deserts to their desolation." Paracelsus declares his aspiration to be no less than a passionate yearning to comprehend the works of God, God Himself, all God's intercourse with the human mind. He goes to prove his soul. God, who guides the bird in his trackless way, will guide him: he will arrive in God's good time. His friends think that all this may be but self-delusion; at least, he is selfish to attempt this work alone. Festus declares that were he elect for such a task he would encircle himself with the love of his fellows, and not cut himself off from human weal; for there is nothing so monstrous in the world as a being not knowing what love is. Michal, the tender woman friend, urges him to cast his hopes away—warns him that he is too proud. He will find what he seeks, but will perish so! Paracelsus protests that he does not lightly give up either the pleasures of life or the love they praise. Truth, he says, is within ourselves; knowing consists in opening a way where the splendour imprisoned within the soul may escape. It comes not from outward things. He offers, therefore, no defiance to God in desiring to know. Humanity may beat the angels; yet, if once man rises to his true stature, Festus believes, and so does Michal, that

Paracelsus will succeed. He plunges for the pearl; they wait his rise.

Paracelsus Attains: Book II. The scene is laid in a Greek conjuror's house at Constantinople, 1521. Paracelsus is mentally taking stock of his attainments—what gained, what lost. He has made discoveries, but the produce of his toil is fragmentary—a confused mass of fact and fancy. He can keep on the stretch no longer: he will learn by magic what he has failed to learn by labour. His overwrought brain demands rest; even in failure he will have rest. True, he had hoped for attainment once, but that is past. His heart was human once. He had loving friends in Würzburg; but love has gone, and his life's one idea has absorbed him, to obtain at all costs his reward in the lump. God may take pleasure in confounding such pride. He may have been fighting sleep off for death's sake. Is his mind stricken? He believes that God would warn him before He struck. And now from within he hears a voice. It is that of Aprile, the spirit of a departed poet, who has aspired to love beauty only. As Paracelsus has sought knowledge alone, Aprile would love infinitely all forms of art and all the delights of Nature. Paracelsus demands he should do obeisance to him, the Knower. Aprile refuses to acknowledge the kingship of one who knows nothing of the loveliness of life. Paracelsus now sees the error into which both have fallen. He has excluded love, as Aprile has excluded knowledge. They are two halves of one dissevered world. Paracelsus, learning now wherein lies his defect, feels that he has attained.

Paracelsus: Book III. At Basle, 1526. Paracelsus meets his friend Festus, who has come to the famous university town to see the wondrous physician, whom they call "life's dispenser, idol of the courts and schools." He has heard him lecture from his Professor's chair; has seen the benches thronged with eager students; has gathered from their approving murmurs full corroboration of his hopes: his pupils worship him. Paracelsus admits his outward success, but confides to his friend that he is indeed most miserable at heart. The hopes which fed his youth have not been realised. He aspired to know God: he has attained—a professorship at Basle! He has wrought certain cures by means of drugs whose uses he has discovered; he has a pile of diplomas and licences; he has received (what he values most) a generous acknowledgment of his merit from Erasmus; and he has a crowded class-room, and, in place of his high aims, there have sprung up in his soul like fungi at the roots of a noble tree, a host of petty, vile delights. As for his eager following, mere novelty and ignorant amazement, coupled with innate dulness and the opposition to the regular system of the schools, will account for it. Seeing all this, and feeling that the work to which he has addressed himself is too hard for him, he has sunk in his own esteem, fallen from his ambition, and has become brutal, half-stupid and half-mad. He feels that he precedes his age in his contempt and scorn for all who worked before him on the same path. He has in public burned the books of Aetius, Oribasius, Galen, Rhasis, Serapion, Avicenna, and Averroes.

PARACELSUS ASPIRES. BOOK IV. The scene is at Colmar, in Alsatia, at an inn, 1528. Yet once more Paracelsus aspires. He has sent for his friend Festus to tell him that he is exposed to the world as a quack, that he is cast off by those who erstwhile worshipped him, and denounced by those whom he has served. He has saved the life of a church dignitary, who not only refused afterwards to pay his fee, but made Basle impossible for him. His pupils grew tired of him when he attempted to teach them and gave up amusing them. The faculty drew off from him when their old methods were interfered with; and so he turned his back on the university. And once more the philosopher has started on his travels, seeking to know with all the enthusiasm of his youth—with the old aims, but not by the same means. No longer the lean ascetic, debarring his soul of her rightful pleasures; but embracing all the joys of life, and combining pleasure with knowledge. This is to be his new method. His appetites, he must own, are degraded—his joys impure. Festus warns him that the base pleasures which have superseded his nobler aims will never content him. Paracelsus declares he lives to enjoy all he can and to know all he can. He has cast off his remorseless care, is hardened in his fault; and as he sings the song of—

> "The men who proudly clung
> To their first fault, and perished in their pride,"

his friend Festus, alarmed at this impiety, urges him to renounce the past, to wait death's summons amid holy sights, and return with him to Einsiedeln. Paracelsus declares this to be impossible: his baser life forbids; a sneering devil is within him; he is weary; the wine-cup, in which he has long tried to drown his disappointment, fails him now; he can hardly sink deeper. Festus attempts to comfort and advise: he too has felt sorrow: sweet Michal is dead. This rouses Paracelsus to endeavour on his part to comfort Festus by declaring his faith in the soul's immortality.

PARACELSUS ATTAINS. BOOK V. In a cell in the hospital of Salzburg, in 1541, Paracelsus lies dying. His faithful friend is by his side, watching through the weary night; and as he watches the patient, he prays for the tortured champion of man. He has sinned, but surely he has sought God's praise. Had God granted him success, it must have been to His honour. Say he erred, God fashioned him and knew how he was made. Festus could have sat quietly at the feet of God. He could never have erred in this great way. God is not made like us. It will be like Him to save him! Now Paracelsus awakes; his failing strength struggles like the flame of an expiring taper. At first, in half-delirious phrases, he tells of the hissing and contempt which struck at his heart at Basle—the measureless scorn heaped on him, as they called him quack and cheat and liar. And now he cries that human love is gone; he dreams of Aprile; he calls on God for one hour of strength to set his heart on Him and love. And then, with a clearer consciousness, he recognises Festus, who tells him that God will take him to His breast, and on earth splendour shall rest upon his name for ever,—the name of the master-mind, the thinker, the explorer. He sings of the gliding Mayne they knew so well; and the simple words loose the dying man's heart, for he knows he is dying, and his varied life drifts by him. There is time yet to speak; but he will rise and speak standing, as becomes a teacher of men. He has sinned, he feels his need for mercy, and he can trust God. It was meant to be with him as had fallen out. His fevered thirst for knowledge was born in him. He has learned so much of God: His joy in creation; His intentions with regard to man His final work the product of the world's remotest ages; its æons of preparation; the love mingling with everything that tended towards the highest work of creation; the progress which is the law of life. The tendency to God he can descry even in man's present imperfection. He sees now where his error lay: how he overlooked the good in man; how he had failed to note the good in evil, and to detect the love beneath the mask of hate; how he had denied the half-reasons, the faint aspirings, the struggles for truth; the littleness in man, despite his errors; the upward tendency in all his weakness. All this he knew not, and he failed. Yet if he

> "Stoop
> Into a dark, tremendous sea of cloud,
> It is but for a time."

He "shall emerge one day." And so he sinks to rest. And this is Browning's *Paracelsus.*

It is in *Paracelsus* (the work that posterity will probably estimate as Browning's greatest) that we must look for the strongest proof of his sympathy with man's desire to know and bend the forces of Nature to his service. To some students this magnificent work will appear only the string of pearls and precious stones that some of us consider *Sordello* to be. To others it is a drama illustrating the contending forces of love and knowledge; others, again, find in it only an elaborate discussion on the Aristotelian and Platonic systems of philosophy. It is none of these alone: rather, if a single sentence could describe it, it is the Epic of the Healer, not of the hero who stole from heaven a jealously-guarded fire, but of him who won from heaven what was waiting for a worthy recipient to take and help us to. In so far as *Paracelsus* came short, it was deficiency of love that hindered him; of his striving after knowledge, and what he won for man, the epic tells in words and music that, to me at least, have no equal in the whole range of literature. It is most remarkable that long before the scientific men of our time had given Paracelsus credit for the noble work he did for mankind, and the lasting boon many of his discoveries conferred upon the race, Mr. Browning, in this wonderful poem, recognised both his labours and their results at their true value, and raising his reputation at this late hour from the infamy with which his enemies and biographers had covered it, set him in his proper place amongst the heroes and martyrs of science. We owe the poet a debt of gratitude for this rehabilitation. No man could have written this transcendent poem who had less than Browning's power of thrusting aside the accidents and accretions of a character, and getting at the naked germ from which springs the life of the real man. That no follower of medicine, no chemist, no disciple of science, did this for Paracelsus is, in the splendid light of Mr. Browning's research and penetration, a remarkable instance of the fact that the unjust verdicts of a time and a class need to be reversed in a clearer atmosphere, and in freedom from class prejudices not often accorded to contemporary biographers. A poet alone could never have done us this service; and a single attentive perusal of this work is enough to show that the intimate blending of the scientific with the poetic faculty could alone have effected the restoration. How lovingly the poet has taken this world-benefactor's remains from the ditch into which his profession had cast them, and laid them in his own beautiful sepulchre, gemmed, chiselled, and arabesqued by all the lovely imagery of his fancy, no reader of Browning's *Paracelsus* needs to be told.

[For a complete study of the life and work of Paracelsus, and Mr. Browning's poem thereon, see the chapter " Paracelsus, the Reformer of Medicine," in my *Browning's Message to his Time* (Sonnenschein).]

NOTES TO BOOK I.—*Würzburg* is one of the most ancient and historically important towns of Germany. Its bishops were made dukes of Franconia in 1120. Its university was founded in 1582. *Trithemius* of Spanheim was abbot of Würzburg, and was a great astrologer and alchemist. *Einsiedeln*, in Canton Schwyz, Switzerland, is a noted place of pilgrimage on the Alpbach, thirty miles from Zurich, under the Herrenberg, with an abbey founded in 861, containing a black statue of the Virgin. Immense quantities of missals, rosaries, etc., are produced there. Zwingle was a priest here 1515-19; and not far from the town is the house where Paracelsus was born. Population now about 7650. *Gier-eagle:* supposed to be a small vulture (Lev. xi. 18). *Black arts:* Black magic = sorcery, as opposed to white magic = science. *The Stagirite:* Aristotle, who was born at Stagira, in Macedon.

NOTES TO BOOK II.—*Constantinople*, the city of the East where many astrologers practised their art. "*A Turk verse along a scimitar*": the Arabs use verses of the Koran in the decoration of their walls, pottery, arms, etc. The Alhambra at Granada is profusely decorated in this way. The Arabic, Persian, and Turkish letters lend themselves admirably to ornamental purposes. *Arch-genethliac:* a *genethliac* is a calculator of nativities —an astrologer.

NOTES TO BOOK III.—*Pansies:* if these flowers were, as is said, favourites with Paracelsus, the choice was appropriate. *Pensées* for "the thinker, the explorer," and "heartsease" for the anxious and overworked man. *Rhasis*, or *Rhazes*, was a distinguished physician of Bagdad (925-6). *Basil* = Basel, Basle. *Œcolampadius*, a Reformer of Basle, friend of Erasmus. *Castellanus* was Pierre Duchatel, a French prelate. When at Basle, Erasmus procured him employment as a corrector of the press with Frobenius. He was bishop of Tulle in 1539, of Maçon in 1544, and in 1551 of Orleans. He was a tolerant man in an intolerant age. *Munsterus*, a Christian Socialist, connected with the Peasants' War; executed 1525. *Frobenius*, the friend of Erasmus, cured by Paracelsus. He was a famous printer at Basle. *Rear mice:* probably a device in the arms on the gate. *Lachen*, a village of 1200 inhabitants, on the margin of the lake of Zurich. The holy hermit Meinrad, the founder of Einsiedeln, originally lived on the top of the Etzel, near here. "*Cross-grained devil in my sword*": the long sword of Paracelsus is famous:—

> "Bumbastus kept a devil's bird
> Shut in the pummel of his sword,
> That taught him all the cunning pranks
> Of past and future mountebanks."
>
> (HUDIBRAS, Part II., Cant. 3.)

Naudæus (in his "History of Magic") observes of this familiar spirit, "that though the alchymists maintain that it was the secret of the philosopher's stone, yet it were more rational to believe that, if there was anything in it, it was certainly two or three doses of his laudanum, which he never went without, because he did strange things with it, and used it as a medicine to cure almost all diseases." "*Sudary of the Virgin*": a handkerchief, a relic of the Blessed Virgin Mary. *Suffumigation*, a medical fumigation, such as was used by Hippocrates. *Erasmus* was born at Rotterdam in 1466. The home of his old age was Basel, to which place he was attracted by the fame of the printing press of Frobenius. Here he made the acquaintance of Zwingle and Holbein, and other men full of the desire for learning. "*Ape at the bed's foot*" patients who suffer from delirium frequently see apes, rats, cats, and other animals and figures, mocking them at the foot of the bed. "*Spain's cork-groves*": cork is the bark of the cork-oak (*Quercus suber*). It grows in Spain, and is most abundant in Catalonia and Valencia. "*Præclare! Optime!*" = Bravo! well done! "*I precede my age*": it has only recently been discovered how much our modern science owes to the labours and researches of Paracelsus. *Aëtius* was an Arian doctor, who was very skilful in medical disputation. He died at Constantinople in 367. *Oribasius* was the court physician of Julian the Apostate (326—403). *Galen* was a great anatomist and a physiological physician. *Rhasis* (see note, p. 324). *Serapion*, an Alexandrian physician, "a great name in antiquity." *Avicenna*, an Arabian philosopher and physician, born about A.D. 980, who presented to his countrymen the doctrines of Galen blended with those of Aristotle. *Averröes*, an Arabian philosopher and physician, born at Cordova in 1126, the interpreter of the Aristotelian philosophy to the Mohammedans. *Zuinglius* = Zwingle the Reformer, of Zurich. *Carolstadius*, or *Carlstadt*, one of the first Reformers. He was professor of divinity at Wittemberg, and early joined Luther in the new religion. He became the leader of the fanatical sect of iconoclasts at Wittemberg, and excited them to excesses. He was banished, and died at Basle in 1541. *Suabia*, the name of an ancient duchy in the south-west part of Germany. *Oporinus*: lived two years in close intimacy with Paracelsus as his secretary, and has been suspected of defaming his memory. "*Sic itur ad astra*": such is the way to immortality. *Liechtenfels*, a canon who was cured by Paracelsus when he was in danger of death, and refused afterwards to pay the stipulated fee.

NOTES TO BOOK IV.—"*Quid multa?*" why say more? *Cassia*, an inferior kind of cinnamon. "*Sandal-buds*": the sandal is a low tree, like a privet, and has a great fragrance. "*Stripes of labdanum*" or *ladanum*: a fragrant, resinous exudation from the plants *Cystus creticus* and *Cystus ladaniferus*. *Aloes*: the fragrant resin of the *agalloch* or *lign-aloe* of Scripture. *Nard* = spikenard; very fragrant. "*Sweetness from Egyptian shroud*": the faint odour from the spices used to embalm the mummy. "*Fiat experientia corpore vili*," or *fiat experimentum in corpore vili*: Let the experiment be made on a body of no value (a hospital patient, *e.g.*!)

NOTES TO BOOK V.—*Salzburg:* the beautifully situated old city of Austria, eighty-seven miles S.E. of Munich. "*Jove and the Titans*": the Titans were the sons of Saturn, who made war against Jupiter; and though they were of gigantic size, they were subdued. *Phæton*, the son of Phœbus and Clymene, who requested his father to give him leave to drive his chariot. The rash youth was unable to bear the light and heat, and dropped the reins. To prevent a general conflagration Jupiter struck him with thunder, and he dropped into the river Eridanus. *Galen of Pergamos:* an eminent physician of the time of Trajan. *Persic Zoroaster* "was one of the greatest teachers of the East, the founder of what was the national religion of the Perso-Iranian people from the time of the Achæmenidæ to the close of the Sassanian period." He founded the wisdom of the Magi. The *Zend-Avesta* is the great Zoroastrian bible. "*Thus he dwells in all,*" etc., down to "*Man begins anew a tendency to God,*" is a faithful representation of the teaching of the Kabbalah (see *Encyc. Brit.*, vol. xiii., p. 812, last ed.): "The whole universe, however, was incomplete, and did not receive its finishing stroke till man was formed, who is the acme of the creation and the microcosm. 'Man is both the import and the highest degree of creation, for which reason he was formed on the sixth day. As soon as man was created everything was complete, including the upper and nether worlds, for everything is comprised in man. He unites in himself all forms'" (*Zohar*, iii., 48).

Parleyings with Certain People of Importance in their Day. To wit: Bernard de Mandeville, Daniel Bartoli, Christopher Smart, George Bubb Dodington, Francis Furini, Gerard de Lairesse, and Charles Avison. Introduced by A Dialogue between Apollo and the Fates; concluded by Another between John Fust and his Friends. The title-page stands thus, and the following dedication is on the next page: "In Memoriam J. Milsand. Obiit iv. Sept. MDCCCLXXXVI. *Absens absentem auditque videtque.*" Published 1887. M. Milsand was a well-known French critic, and was an early admirer of Mr. Browning's works. *Sordello* was dedicated to M. Milsand in its revised edition. The *Parleyings* volume is dealt with in a lucid and sympathetic manner in Mr. Nettleship's *Essays and Thoughts.*

Parting at Morning. See MEETING AT NIGHT, to which this poem is the sequel.

Patriot, The. AN OLD STORY. (*Men and Women*, 1855; *Romances*, 1863; *Dramatic Romances*, 1868.) A patriot who has been the people's idol, and now, having fallen from his pedestal, is on his way to execution. A year ago that very day they would have given him the sun from their skies had he asked it in that city whose air was a mist of joy bells. He strove his hardest to pluck down that sun to give them, and to-day the year is run out, and he goes bound, with bleeding forehead from the pelting stones, to the shambles. But God will repay, and he feels safe with that. It has been thought that this poem refers to Arnold of Brescia. Mr. Browning contradicted this.

Paul Desforges Maillard. (*Two Poets of Croisic.*) He is the second of the Poets, René Gentilhomme being the first. He competed for a prize at the French Academy, and was unsuccessful. The poem tells how he made his name known through his sister's influence.

Pauline: A Fragment of a Confession (1832). The first work of the poet, and his embryonic work, because it contains in their rudiments all the peculiarities and powers of his genius. He wrote nothing which was not the legitimate development of the forces which we see in this inchoate work. It is nebulous, but it is a nebula which has within itself the potentiality of worlds of thought. Misty and vague as it everywhere seems, it is influenced by laws which will concentrate its thought into stars and planets, such as *Paracelsus*, and the *Ring and the Book.* It is autobiographical, and admits us into the laboratory of the writer's thought; it is marvellously consistent with the latest utterances of the poet on the subjects nearest to his heart. High thoughts, which through the years of a long life will live in royal splendour in his brain, are born here in travail, as regal things are wont to be. It was a boy's work,—the poet was only twenty years old when he wrote it,—but a competent critic could have detected evidence that in the anonymous author of *Pauline* a psychological poet had arisen, one who determined to probe to their depths the mysteries of the human soul. From Mr. Gosse's article in *The Century Magazine* we learn that the young poet had produced a quantity of verses while a mere child, and had planned a number of soul-studies of a similar character to *Pauline.* He published the poem anonymously in 1833, when he was twenty years old. It was reprinted in 1867, with the following note: "The first piece in the series (*Pauline*) I acknowledge and retain with extreme repugnance, indeed purely oi necessity; for not long ago I inspected one, and am certified of the existence of other transcripts, intended sooner or later to be published abroad: by forestalling these I can at least correct some misprints (no syllable is changed), and introduce a boyish work by an exculpatory word. The thing was my earliest attempt at 'poetry, always dramatic in principle, and so many utterances of so many imaginary persons, not mine,' which I have written since according to a scheme less extravagant and scale less impracticable than were ventured upon in this crude preliminary sketch—a sketch that, on reviewal, appears not altogether wide of some hint of the characteristic features of that particular *dramatis persona* it would fain have reproduced; good draughtsmanship, however, and right handling were far beyond the artist at that time." With the "good draughtsmanship" and "right handling" of the work we need not concern ourselves; what is of paramount importance is the fact that in *Pauline* we have "the god, though in the germ." If the mature artist was ashamed of his puerile performance, his disciples have always loved and admired it, and his deeper students have delighted to trace in its pages the nuclei of principles which have in his maturer works dowered the world with a priceless treasure. The poem is a fragment of a confession from a young man to a young woman whom he loves. It concerns Pauline very little, but is the revelation of the man as a study of the poet's own naked soul. It is not a confession of deeds, but of moods and mental attitudes. He who could unpack his own heart so completely would be likely to reveal the innermost recesses of the characters with which he should deal in the future. It is the revelation of a soul all self-centred. A soul's awakening, a soul in terror at its own capabilities, desires and forces too hard to be controlled—"made up of an intensest life"—imbued with "a principle of restlessness which would be all, have, see, know, taste, feel all"—a soul terrified at its own vast shadow, fearing to face its own spectres, and instinctively "building up a screen" of woman's love to be shut in with from a brood of fancies with which he dare not wrestle. Had he never left her side he had been spared this shame. He is sure of her love, though ghosts of the past haunt them. He has not the love to offer which befits her; but he has faith, and he trusts her as we trust the east for morning light. He has communed with her, but she knew not the shame which lurked behind his words and smiles, and she drove away despair from him. He has fallen, is ruined; he has felt in dreams he was a fiend chained in darkness, till, after ages had passed came a white swan to remain with him, and it contented him. And again, he had seemed to be a young witch who drew down a god to sing of heaven, and as he sang he perished grinning, but murmuring "I am still a god to thee." He has thought that his early life, his songs and wild imaginings, were the only worthy things standing out distinct amid the fever of the after years. And this was his (Shelley's) award. He, the Sun-treader, had drawn out from his worshipper the one spark of love remaining in his soul, and in his tears he praises him. He loved Shelley in his shame, and now he is renowned he watches him as a star, as one altered and worn and full of tears looks to heaven. He strips his mind bare, has a most clear consciousness of self, and recognises that of all his powers an imagination which has been an angel to him is the one which saves his soul from utter death. He feels a need, a trust, a yearning after God, which somehow is reconciled with a neglect of all he deemed His laws. He sees God everywhere, yet can love nothing; has had high dreams and low aims, and so lost himself. Then he turned to song, he gazed without fear on the works of mighty bards, for in them he recognised thoughts his own heart had also borne; then came the outburst of the soul's power, a key to a new world, a sound as of angelic mutterings. He vowed himself to liberty. Men should be gods, earth,—heaven. His soul rose to meet the new life. As one watches for a fair girl that comes forth a withered hag, so all these high-born fancies dwindled into nothing; faith in man, freedom, virtue, motives, power, human loves, all vanished. They were not missed, for wit and mockery and pleasure came in their stead. His powers grew, his soul became as a temple; only God was gone, and a dark spirit sat in His seat, and mocking shadows cried "Hail!" to him. He resolved to wear himself out with joy, then to win men's praise by undying song, and the mockery laughed out again. Then he met Pauline and knew she loved him; he looked in his heart for a love to return, and love and faith were gone, and selfishness wears him as a flame, and hunger for pleasure has become pain. Then came a craving after knowledge, as a sleepless harpy. He begins now to know what hate is. Yet with it all he has learned the great truth that his restless longings, his all encompassing selfishness, only prove that earth is not his sphere, because he cannot so narrow himself but he exceeds it. Hateful as his selfishness has grown to be, he can pass from such thoughts. Andromeda, rock-chained, awaiting the snake, causes you no fear for her safety: God will come in thunder from the stars to save her, so he will triumph over his decay; when the calm comes again after the fever has subsided, he will do something equal to his conjecture. He can project himself into all forms of Nature, live the life of plants, mount bird-like, breathe in a fish the morning air in the sun-warm water. He will build a thought-world; he is inspired. Pauline shall come with him to the world of fancy through the ghostly night and sun-warmed morning; he is concentrated, he drinks in the life of all, yet cannot be immortal for all these struggling aims. What is this passionate hunger for the All—this insatiable thirst for utmost pleasure? It is man's cry for the satisfying presence of God in his soul. The alone to the Alone; nothing intervening can give peace and rest to the spirit of man; flame-like it tends upwards to its source. The only ONE, the Crucified, the Risen Christ—"Christus Consolator" is recognised as the remedy for his sense of infinite loss; and as he recognises the Divine love he is united with the purest earthly soul he knows:—"Pauline, I am thine for ever." "Love me, Pauline—leave me not." And so the hideous past shall be the past, and he will go forward with her—

> "Feeling God loves us, and that all that errs
> Is a strange dream which death will dissipate."

Again he will go o'er the tracts of thought, again will beauteous shapes come to him and unknown secrets be divulged,—priest and lover as of old—"Shelley, Sun-treader," he cries, "I believe in God, and truth, love—I would lean on thee." Professor Johnson, in his paper on "Conscience and Art in Browning," gives the following as the theme of the poem:—"The Divine call and anointing of the poet, so to speak; his sin, which consists in a self-divorce; his decline and degradation as he sinks into the 'dim orb of self'; finally, his redemption and restoration by Divine love, mediated to him by human love."

NOTES.—"*His award*," "*Him whom all honour*," "*Thou didst smile, poet*," "*Sun-treader*" (lines 142, 144, 151, 1020): all these refer to Shelley. "*A god wandering after beauty*" (line 321): Apollo seeking Daphne. Apollo pursued Daphne, who fled from him, seeking the aid of the gods, who changed her into a laurel. "*A giant standing vast in the sunset*" (line 322): Atlas, one of the Titans, is referred to here.

> "*A high-crested chief*
> *Sailing with troops of friends to Tenedos*" (line 324):

"After the fall of Troy, many of the Greek chiefs, among them Nestor, set sail for home, while others, at the desire of Agamemnon, remained behind to sacrifice to Pallas. Those who set sail went to the island of Tenedos, where they made offerings to the gods" (*Poet Lore*, vol. i., p. 244; Homer, *Odyssey*, iii.). "*The dim clustered isles in the blue sea*" (line 321): the islands of the Ægean Sea, east of Greece.

> "*Who stood beside the naked swift-footed,*
> *Who bound my forehead with Proserpine's hair*" (line 334)

the *swift-footed* was Hermes, the name of Mercury among the Greeks. He was the messenger of the gods. He was presented by the King of Heaven with a winged cap, called *petasus*, and with wings for his feet, called *talaria*. *Proserpine* was the daughter of Ceres by Jupiter. "*As Arab birds float sleeping in the wind*" (line 479): this is considered by some to refer to the pelican, by others to the Birds of Paradise.

> "*The king*
> *Treading the purple calmly to his death*" (line 568):

Agamemnon, to whom his loved Cassandra foretells his doom in vain:—

> "Well, sire, I yield me vanquished by thy voice;
> I go, treading on purple, to my house."
> (Potter's "Agamemnon" of *Æschylus*, 1017.)

The boy with his white breast," etc. (line 574): see Potter's "Choephoræ" ot *Æschylus*, 1073: Orestes avenged his father's death by assassinating his mother Clytemnestra and the adulterer

Ægisthus. *Andromeda* (line 656): Andromeda was ordered to be exposed to a sea-monster, and was tied naked to a rock; but Perseus delivered her, changed the monster into a rock, and married her. "*The fair pale sister went to her chill grave*" (line 963): Antigone interred by night the remains of her brother Polynices against the orders of Creon, who commanded her to be buried alive. She, however, killed herself before the sentence could be executed (see "Antigone" of *Sophocles*). The long Latin preface to *Pauline* from the *Occult Philosophy* of Cornelius Agrippa is thus englished in Mr. Cooke's *Browning Guide-Book*:—"I doubt not but the title of our book, by its rarity, may entice very many to the perusal of it. Among whom many of hostile opinions, with weak minds, many even malignant and ungrateful, will assail our genius, who in their rash ignorance, hardly before the title is before their eyes, will make a clamour. We are forbidden to teach, to scatter abroad the seeds of philosophy, pious ears being offended, clear-seeing minds having arisen. I, as a counsellor, assail their consciences; but neither Apollo nor all the Muses, nor an angel from heaven, would be able to save me from their execrations, whom now I counsel that they may not read our books, that they may not understand them, that they may not remember them, for they are noxious—they are poisonous. The mouth of Acheron is in this book: it speaks often of stones: beware, lest by these it shape the understanding. You, also, who with fair wind shall come to the reading, if you will apply so much of the discernment of prudence as bees in gathering honey, then read with security. For, indeed, I believe you about to receive many things not a little both for instruction and enjoyment. But if you find anything that pleases you not, let it go that you may not use it, for I do not declare these things good for you, but merely relate them. Therefore, if any freer word may be, forgive our youth; I, who am less than a youth, have composed this work." The preface is dated London, January 1833. V.A. XX. is the Latin abbreviation of *Vixi annos viginti*, I was twenty years old.

Pearl, A, a Girl. (*Asolando*, 1889.) According to Eastern fable there is a great power in a pearl: if you could speak the right word, you could call a spirit from the simple-looking stone which would make you lord of heaven and earth. Be this as it may, the poet says if you utter the right word, that evokes for you the love of a girl—held, perhaps, in little esteem by the world—her soul escapes to you, and you are creation's lord!

"Periods" of Browning. It is usual with students to divide the poet's work into some four or five periods. Mr. Fothering-ham's classification is as good as any: he makes the periods five.—Period I., "*a time of youth and prelude*" (1832—1840), the time of *Pauline*, *Paracelsus*, and *Sordello*. During this time the poet was trying the nature and compass of his theme and forming his style.—Period II., "*the time of early manhood*" (1841—1846), the time of the dramas and early dramatic lyrics. All the dramas except *Strafford* belong to this time. In this period he was studying how best to use his poetical powers.—Period III. is "*the time of maturity*," his manhood and married life (1846—1869). Now he has found his standpoint; he is firm, vigorous, and confident. During this time he gave us *Christmas Eve*, *Men and Women*, *Dramatis Personæ*, and *The Ring and the Book*.—Period IV. is "*the time of his later maturity*" (1870—1878). Now the casuistic and argumentative element becomes more prominent; the dramatic aspect retires into the background, the philosophical teacher advances. "His hardest and least poetic work," it has been said, was put forth in this period: *Hohenstiel-Schwangau*, *Red Cotton Night-Cap Country*, etc.—Period V. (1879—1889), "*the time of the latest works*." A period of criticism of life, as in *Ferishtah* and the *Parleyings*.

Peter Ronsard. (*The Glove.*) He tells the story of Sir De Lorge, and how he leaped amongst the lions to recover his lady's glove.

Pheidippides. (*Dramatic Idyls, First Series*, 1879.) Pheidippides, an athlete, has been commissioned by the Athenian government to run a race,—to reach Sparta for military assistance in a great crisis in Greek history. Persia has invaded Greece: in her extremity she implores help from the neighbouring Spartans; for two days and two nights Pheidippides the fleet-footed youth ran over hills and along the dales, as fire runs through stubble, and so he bounded on his way with his message. He broke into the midst of the Spartan assembly, told his story, and prayed the prayer of Athens; but Sparta, ever jealous and mistrustful of her great neighbour, heard it coldly, and cast about for excuses. Then the passionate runner cried to the gods of his country—to Pallas Athene, protector of the city, to Apollo, to Diana—to influence the deliberations of the council gathered to hear his message, and to say to them "Ye must!" And no bolt fell from heaven, as they still delayed. At last they gave their answer,—their religion forbade them to go to war while the moon was half-orbed in the sky; her circle must be full ere they could assist; Athens must wait in patience! The youth wasted neither word nor look on the false and vile Spartans, but turned his face homewards, crying to the gods of his land; rushing past the woods and streams where they had often manifested themselves to mortals he reproached them with faithlessness and ingratitude,—his countrymen had honoured them with sacrifice and libation, and in their extremity they disregarded their cry for help. All at once, as he ran by the ridge of Parnassus, there in the cool of a cleft was seated the majestical god Pan! Grave, kindly were his eyes, his face amused at the mortal's awe of him. "Halt, Pheidippides!" he cried; and with his brain in a whirl the youth stood still. "Hither to me! Why pale in my presence?" he graciously began. "How is it Athens only in Hellas holds me aloof?" Then the god told the young man how they might trust him; that he was to bid Athens take heart, —that when the Persians were not only lying dead on their soil, but cast into the sea, then they were to praise great Pan, who had fought in their ranks and made one cause with the free and the bold Athenians. And for a pledge he gave him the fennel he grasped in his hand. He went on to speak of reward for himself, but of that Pheidippides would not speak; if he ran before, now he flew indeed; he touched not the earth with his foot, the air was his road. "Praise Pan!" he cried, as he reached Athens, "we stand no more in danger!" Then Miltiades asked him what his own reward should be? What had the god promised for him? "Release from the racer's toil," he said. "But he would fight and be foremost in the field of fennel, pounding Persia to the dust; then marry a certain maid when Athens was free, and in the coming days tell his children how the god was awful, yet so kind." The brave youth fought at Marathon; and when Persia was dust. "Once more run," they cried, "Pheidippides, to Akropolis, say Athens is saved, thank Pan,—go shout!" Then the youth flung down his shield and ran as before. "Rejoice! we conquer!" he cried; and with joy bursting his heart he died.

He had gained the reward promised by Pan,—release from the racer's toil, no vulgar reward in praise or in pelf,—he could desire no greater bliss. Herodotus tells the whole story (Book VI., 94—106). Darius was desirous of subduing those people of Greece who had refused to give him earth and water. He sent against Eretria and Athens Datis, who was a Mede by birth, and Artaphernes, son of Artaphernes, his own nephew; and he despatched them with strict orders, having enslaved Athens and Eretria, to bring the bondsmen into his presence. 102. "Having subdued Eretria, and rested a few days, they sailed to Attica, pressing them very close, and expecting to treat the Athenians in the same way as they had the Eretrians. Now, as Marathon was the spot in Attica best adapted for cavalry, and nearest to Eretria, Hippias, son of Pisistratus, conducted them there. 103. But the Athenians, when they heard of this, also sent their forces to Marathon; and ten generals led them, of whom the tenth was Miltiades. . . . 105. And first, while the generals were yet in the city, they despatched a herald to Sparta, one Pheidippides, an Athenian, who was a courier by profession, one who attended to this very business. This man, then, as Pheidippides himself said, and reported to the Athenians, Pan met near Mount Parthenion, above Tegea; and Pan, calling out the name of Pheidippides, bade him ask the Athenians why they paid no attention to him, who was well inclined to the Athenians, and had often been useful to them, and would be so hereafter. The Athenians, therefore, as their affairs were then in a prosperous condition, believed that this was true, and erected (after Marathon presumably), a temple to Pan beneath the Akropolis, and in consequence of that message they propitiate Pan with yearly sacrifices and the torch race. 106. This Pheidippides, being sent by the generals at that time when he said Pan appeared to him, arrived in Sparta on the following day fter his departure from the city of the Athenians, and on coming in presence of the magistrates, he said, 'Lacedæmonians, the Athenians entreat you to assist them, and not to suffer the most ancient city among the Greeks to fall into bondage to barbarians; for Eretria is already reduced to slavery, and Greece has become weaker by the loss of a renowned city.' He accordingly delivered the message according to his instructions, and they resolved indeed to assist the Athenians; but it was out of their power to do so immediately, as they were unwilling to violate the law; for it was the ninth day of the current month, and they said they could not march out on the ninth day, the moon's circle not being full. They therefore waited for the full moon." How the Athenians won the famous battle of Marathon, "following the Persians in their flight, cutting them to pieces, till, reaching the shore, they called for fire and attacked the ships," should be read also. Herodotus says the Persians lost about six thousand four hundred men; the Athenians only one hundred and ninety-two. Mr. Browning seems unduly severe on the Spartans, for Herodotus tells us (120) that "two thousand of the Lacedæmonians came to Athens after the full moon, making haste to be in time; that they arrived in Attica on the third day after leaving Sparta. But having come too late for the battle, they nevertheless desired to see the Medes; and having proceeded to Marathon, they saw the slain; and afterwards, having commended the Athenians and their achievement, they returned home."

NOTES.—*Χαίρετε, νικῶμεν:* Rejoice! we conquer! *Zeus, the Defender:* Jupiter was worshipped under many aspects, such as "the Lightning Flasher," "the Thunderer," "the Flight Stayer," "the Best and Greatest," etc. "*Her of the aegis and spear*" = Minerva, who was represented with a shield and spear. "*Ye of the bow and the buskin*" = Diana, who was represented with a bow and buskined legs of a huntress. *Pan*, the goat-god. "*Archons of Athens, topped by the tettix*" (*tettix*, a grasshopper): the Athenians sometimes wore golden grasshoppers in their hair as badges of honour, because these insects are supposed to spring from the ground, and thus they showed they were sprung from the original inhabitants of the country. *Sparta*, the capital of Laconia, also called Lacedæmon. The distance from Athens to Sparta is from 135 to 140 miles. The trained couriers had great physical strength and powers of endurance, being regularly employed for such occasions as this. "*Persia bids Athens proffer slaves'-tribute*": "Darius (B.C. 493) sent heralds into all parts of Greece to require earth and water in his name. This was the form used by the Persians when they exacted submission from those they were desirous of bringing under subjection." (Rollins' *Ancient History*, vol. ii., p. 267.) *Eretria*, one of the principal cities of Eubœa, which is the largest Island in the Ægean Sea, now called Negroponte. *Hellas* = Greece. *Athené*, Minerva.

Phoibos, an epithet of Apollo; *Artemis*, the Greek name of Diana. *Olumpos* = Olympus, the mountain in Greece believed to be the seat of the gods. *Filleted victim:* sacrificial victims were generally decked out with ribbons and wreaths, and sometimes the cattle had their horns gilded. *Fulsome libation*—fulsome in the sense of rich, liberal. Libations were offerings of oil or wine poured on the ground in honour of the deity. *Parnes:* the mountain is called Parthenion above Tegea, by Herodotus. *Ivy:* the Greeks highly esteemed the ivy. It was consecrated to Apollo, and Bacchus had his brows and spear decked with it; *Miltiades*, the Greek general who commanded the Athenians at the battle of Marathon; *Marathon day:* "The victory of Marathon preserved the liberties of Greece, and perhaps of Europe, from the dominion of Persia; was fought in the month of September, B.C. 490" (Wordsworth's *Greece*, p. 109). *Akropolis*, the citadel or stronghold of Athens. *Fennel-field:* Marathon in Greek meant this; when Pan gave the handful of fennel to the courier he gave him Μαραθρον—that is to say, the fennel field where the battle was to be. "*Rejoice!*" χαίρετε: the first of the two Greek words which are at the head of the poem. *Pan* (*lit.* "the pasturer"—from the same root as the Lat. *pastor*, shepherd, and *panis*, bread). He was the protecting deity of flocks and herds and hunters. He was represented by the ancients with a pug nose, very hairy, and with horns and feet of a goat. He was described as wandering about in the woods and dales and hills, playing with the nymphs and looking after the flocks. He was sleepy in the noonday sun, and did not like to be disturbed; at such times, therefore, shepherds did not play their pipes. His voice and appearance used to frighten those who saw him—so much so, that our word "panic" is derived from his name. It is said that he won the fight at Marathon for the Athenians by causing a "panic" amongst the Persians. He was the god of prophecy, and there were oracles of Pan. Pan as the Universe, the All, is a misinterpretation of his name. The Romans identified Pan with their Faunus. [Mrs. Browning's fine poem *The Dead Pan* should be read in this connection.]

Pictor Ignotus. FLORENCE, 15—. (*Dramatic Romances and Lyrics* in *Bells and Pomegranates*, VII., 1845.) The subject is not historical, but is conceived in the true spirit which animated the work of the great religious (chiefly monastic) painters of the middle ages. The speaker says he could have painted pictures like those of a certain youth whose praise is in every one's mouth. He could have executed all his soul conceived: hand and brain were pair, and all he saw he could have committed to his canvas. Each passion written on the countenance, whether Hope a-tiptoe for embrace, or Rapture with drooping eyes, or Confidence lighting up the forehead, all that human faces gave him, has he saved. He has dreamed of going forth in his pictures to pope or kaiser, to the whole world, with flowers cast upon the car which bore the freight, through streets re-named from the triumphal passing of his picture, to the house where learning and genius should greet his coming; and the thought has frightened him, and he has shrunk from the popularity as a nun shrinks from the gaze of rough soldiery; it terrified him to think of his works dragged forth to be bought and sold as household stuff, to have to live with people sunk in their daily pettiness, to see their faces, listen to their prate, and hear his work discussed. If at times he feels his work monotonous, as he goes on filling the cloisters and eternal aisles with the same Virgins, Babes, and Saints, with the same cold, calm, beautiful regard, at least no merchant traffics in his neart. The sacredness of the place where his pictures moulder and grow black will protect him from vain tongues which would criticise and discuss his work. This poem has been much misunderstood. Some have seen in it the bitter complaint and the wail of half-suppressed longing of one whom fame has passed unnoticed; he has failed to please the world, and will now retire to pursue his art in the cloister. Nothing could be further from the poet's purpose in this work. Others, and those the majority of critics, have found in the poem a revelation of the true art-spirit, as though Mr. Browning had made a great discovery in this connection. The plain fact is that this spirit of retirement, this abhorrence of working for the praise of men, this hatred of applause-seeking and of self-advertisement, was that which animated the men of old Catholic times who built our cathedrals and our abbeys, and who painted our great pictures and glorified all Europe with works of art. The poem might fairly be considered as uttered by a Fra Angelico with reference to Raffaele. The great monastic painters, like Angelico, painted under the eye of God, looking upon their work as immediately inspired by His Spirit: for God and through God, not through men and for men, was their work done. It has been the life-work of Mr. Ruskin to point this out. These men were not actuated by the vain advertising spirit which animates so much of our modern work of all kinds. Humility is a virtue now little appreciated: it was the life of these old artists' souls. Pictor Ignotus was not jealous of the popular youth whose pictures were decked with flowers by the people as they were borne through the streets which were re-named in their honour. He did not want the mob's applause; he shrank from the appreciations of the thoughtless street folk as a nun would shrink from the compliments of a band of rough soldiery. All this beautiful spirit is fast dying out. When a writer like Browning reminds us that there were once, in "15—," in a place like Florence, men animated by it, critics cry out, "What a discovery! How wonderful!" It is a discovery like ours of gold in South Africa, where the men of old time went to Ophir to find the precious metal.

NOTE.—Vasari says that the Borgo Allegri at Florence took its name from the joy of the inhabitants when a Madonna by Cimabue was carried through it in procession.

Pied Piper of Hamelin, The. (*Dramatic Lyrics*, 1842.) Written to amuse little Willie Macready. The story told in the poem is one of a class of legends dealing with the subject of cheating magicians of a promised reward for services rendered. Verstegan, in his *Restitution of Decayed Intelligence* (1634), has the story on which apparently Mr. Browning's poem is written. "A piper named Bunting undertook for a certain sum of money to free the town of Hamelin, in Brunswick, of the rats which infested it; but when he had drowned all the rats in the river Weser, the townsmen refused to pay the sum agreed upon. The piper, in revenge, collected together all the children of Hamelin, and enticed them by his piping into a cavern in the side of the mountain Koppenberg, which instantly closed upon them, and a hundred and thirty went down alive into the pit (June 26th, 1284). The street through which Bunting conducted his victims was Bungen, and from that day to this no music is ever allowed to be played in this particular street." The same tale is told of the fiddler of Brandenberg: the children were led to the Marienberg, which opened upon them and swallowed them up. When Lorch was infested with ants, a hermit led the multitudinous insects by his pipe into a lake, where they perished. As the inhabitants refused to pay the stipulated price, he led their pigs the same dance, and they, too, perished in the lake. Next year a charcoal burner cleared the same place of crickets; and when the price agreed upon was refused, he led the sheep of the inhabitants into the lake. The third year came a plague of rats, which an old man of the mountain piped away and destroyed. Being refused his reward, he piped the children of Lorch into the Tannenberg. There are similar Persian and Chinese tales. (See Dr. Brewer's *Reader's Handbook.* Hamlin or Hamelin is a town in the province of Hanover, Prussia. "Some trace the origin of the legend to the 'Child Crusade,' or to an abduction of children. For a considerable time the town dated its public documents from the event" (*Encyc. Brit.*). Julius Wolff wrote a poem on the subject (Berlin, 1876). See S. Baring Gould's *Curious Myths of the Middle Ages*, 2nd ser., 1868; Grimm's *Deutsche Sagen*, Berlin, 1866; and Reitzenstein's edition of Springer's *Geschichte der Stadt Hameln*, Hameln, 1861. Some authorities consider the story a myth of the wind.

Pietro Comparini (*The Ring and the Book*) was the reputed father of Pompilia, and was murdered with his wife by Count Guido.

Pietro of Abano. (*Dramatic Idyls*, second series, 1880.) [THE MAN.] Dr. Furnivall, in a note to Mr. Sharpe's excellent paper on Pietro of Abano in the *Browning Society's Reports*, No. V., gives the following particulars of the character from the *Nouvelle Biographie Universelle*, Paris, 1855, i. 29—31. "Pietro of A'bano, Petrus de A'pano or Aponensis, or Petrus de Padua, was an Italian physician and alchemist; born at Abano, near Padua, in 1246, died about 1320. He is said to have studied Greek at Constantinople, mathematics at Padua, and to have been made Doctor of Medicine and Philosophy at Paris. He then returned to Padua, where he was Professor of Medicine, and followed the Arabian physicians, especially Averroes. He got a great reputation, and charged enormous fees. He hated milk and cheese, and swooned at the sight of them. His enemies, jealous of his renown and wealth, denounced him to the Inquisition as a magician. They accused him of possessing the philosopher's stone, and of making, with the devil's help, all money spent by him come back to his purse, etc. His trial was begun; and had he not died naturally in time, he would have been burnt. The Inquisitors ordered his corpse to be burnt; and as a friend had taken that away, they had his portrait publicly burnt by the executioner. In 1560 a Latin epitaph in his memory was put up in the church of St. Augustine. The Duke of Urbino set his statue among those of illustrious men; and the Senate of Padua put one on the gate of its palace, beside those of Livy, etc. His best-known work is his *Conciliator Differentiarum quæ inter Philosophos et Medicos versantur* (Mantua, 1472, and Venice, 1476, fol.); often reprinted. Other works are: 1. *De Venenis, eorumque Remediis*, translated into French by L. Boet (Lyons, 1593, 12mo); 2. *Geomantia* (Venice, 1505, 1556, 8vo); 3. *Expositio Problematum Aristotelis* (Mantua, 1475, 4to); 4. *Hippocrates de Medicorum Astrologia Libellus*, in Greek and Latin (Venice, 1485, 4to); 5. *Astrolabium planum in tabulis ascendens, continens qualibet hora atque minutæ æquationes Domorum Cœli*, etc. (Venice, 1502, 4to); 6. *Dioscorides digestus alphabetico ordine* (Lyons, 1512, 4to); 7. *Heptameron* (Paris, 1474, 4to); 8. *Textus Mesues noviter emendatus*, etc. (Venice, 1505, 8vo); 9. *Decisiones physionomiæ* (1548, 8vo); 10. *Questiones de Febribus* (Padua, 1482); 11. *Galeni tractatus varii a Petro Paduano, latinitate donati*, MS. in St. Mark's Library, Venice; 12. *Les Eléments pour opérer dans les Sciences magiques*, MS. in the Arsenal Library, Paris." Murray's *Guide to Northern Italy* says that "Abano may be visited either from Padua or from Monselice. Its baths have retained their celebrity from the time of the Romans. The place is also remarkable as being the birthplace of Livy, and also of the physician and reputed necromancer, Pietro d'Abano, in whom the Paduans take almost equal pride. This village is about three miles from the Euganean hills." The medicinal springs procured this place its ancient name of *Aponon*, derived from *α*, privative, and πονος, pain. At Padua is the *Palazzo della Ragione*, built by *Pietro Cozzo* between 1172 and 1219, a vast building standing entirely upon open arches, surrounded by a loggia. Murray says: "The history of this hall is as remarkable as its aspect. It was built in 1306 by an Austin friar, *Frate Giovanni*, a great traveller; and he asked no other pay for his work than the wood and tiles of the old roof which he was to take down. The interior of the hall is covered by strange, mystical paintings designed by Giotto according to the instructions of *Pietro d'Abano.*" Pietro d'Abano was the first reviver of the art of medicine in Europe; and he travelled to Greece for the purpose of learning the language of Hippocrates and Galen, and of profiting by the stores which the Byzantine libraries yet contained. He practised with the greatest success; and his medical works were considered as amongst the most valuable volumes of the therapeutic library of the middle ages. His bust is over one of the doors of the hall; the inscription placed beneath it indignantly repudiates the magic and sorcery ascribed to him; but the votaries of the occult sciences smiled inwardly at this disclaimer. His treatises upon necromancy, geomancy, amulets and conjuration, were circulated from hand to hand. When at Padua, some years since, the Rev. John Sharpe found a stone set in the wall of the vestibule of the Sacristy of the Church of the Eremitani, to Pietro of Abano. It bore the following inscription:—

PETRI APON
CINERES
OB. AN. 1315
AET. 66.

[THE POEM.] Peter was a magician. He had been of all trades, architect, astronomer, astrologer, beside physician. Even worse than astrologer, for men scrupled not to accuse him of having dealings with the devil. This was the Middle Age way with men of science, and it must be confessed that the mystical manner of their writings and the uncanny nature of some of their doings give colour to the accusation. It was convenient, also, to accuse Peter of diabolic arts. When he had built a tower or cured a prince, it was an economical way of discharging the debt to accuse the old man of wizardry. So they cursed him roundly and then rid themselves of their liability. But Peter grinned and bore it all. He seems to have invented a steamboat which would have whirled through the water had not the priests broken up his evil-looking machine, and bastinadoed him beside. One night, as he reached his lodgings, some one plucked his sleeve and asked an interview with him. It was a young Greek, who professed great admiration for the mage. He tells him that he has heard that the price he pays for his potent arts is that he may not drink a drop of milk; but he has discovered this is not to be taken literally,—it is to be considered figuratively, as he will explain. He asks the master leave to become the friend of mankind, and that by being himself their model. He begs, therefore, to be taught the true magic, to learn the art of making fools subserve the man of mind. A prince is inspired with the idea of building a palace by an architect. The architect uses the prince as the means of furthering his own interests—his ambition to be honoured as a great architect. The workmen who build the mansion are animated by their desire for wages, and so the architect uses both prince and artisan as his tools. The young Greek wants to use men of high and low degree for similar ends. The magician says if he were to comply with his desire he would only make one ingrate more; he has been so often deceived this way. The Greek replies that what he wants is the milk of human kindness. He has not been animated by love of his species in what he has done for mankind. He has wrought wonders, but not for love. This is the meaning of his enforced abstinence from milk; but let him confer upon his supplicant this favour he asks, and he will earn his love and gratitude, which will remove from him his curse. Every step he lifts him up, by so much greater will the reward of the benefactor be. The magician determines to comply: he will test this man's heart. "Shuffle the cards once more," he says. Suddenly the young man becomes aware that he has undergone a great change. He was talking Plato to the master but a while ago; now he is surrounded by wealth, and has many friends. A year has passed when one day, lounging at his ease in his villa, his servant announces an old friend who desires to speak with him. It is old Peter, who is sore beset by his enemies, who want to burn him. He has come to the young man who owes him everything, to beg a hiding-place and a crust. The ingrate will not for a moment listen to his plea; he cannot think of harbouring him, as if it were to be discovered it would compromise him. He takes the opportunity, however, to ask for a greater favour,—he wishes to learn how to rule men and subject them to his pleasure. Then, if he will wait awhile, he may be able to show his gratitude. The old man turns his back and leaves the house. He is no sooner away than the spell begins to work. Politics were the prize now. He became a statesman and a friend of the Emperor. One day, after a council, he was pacing his closet, when there was a knock at the door, and Peter entered. He reminds him that ten years have passed since he refused him the favour he demanded. He had given him a mansion, out of which he only begged the use of a single chamber, that will no longer suffice. He now comes to beg a stronghold where he may be safe from his enemies: grant him this, and he will trouble the young man no more. But the latter is concerned only with thoughts of more power for himself: he wants now to rule the souls of men; from the temporal power he would rise to the spiritual; he would be no less than Pope. Having then reached the highest rung of the ladder, he promises to pay the debt he owes to the full. Once more old Peter turns to go, and already the influence is felt. He is at Rome, has been elected Pope, and has reached the summit of his desires. Seated in the palace of the Lateran, one day an intruder pushes aside the arras. It is old Peter again; he is ninety now, and does not care if they burn him; he has lived his day. He has, however, a favour to ask: he has written a great book, and he wants it preserved for the use of posterity. Will the Pope see to this? The Pontiff eyes the frowsy parchment with disgust, and when the old man kneels to kiss his foot, he spurns him. "We're Pope,—once Pope, you can't unpope us!" In a moment the vision was over. The three trial scenes of the Greek's life were played out: he was himself again. The magic was dissolved; he had been tested, had been shown the corruption of his own heart in a moment, though it seemed a lifetime in the passing of the vision. Peter lived out his life, but he had never yet learned love. Perhaps in another life that lesson was to come. As for the Greek, nothing is recorded of him. The poet says he may go his way—he is too selfish not to thrive! The moral of the story is that to win men's love we must not merely help them, not merely fling favours at them, but must consecrate ourselves to their service. In the loving service of, and the self-sacrificing endeavour to benefit our fellow-men, lies the secret of winning happiness for ourselves. It is more blessed to give than to receive only when the giving is to man for God's sake—for the love of God manifested by efforts on behalf of our fellow-men.

NOTES.—Verse 2, *Petrus ipse*, Peter the very same. v. 9, *True moly:* "A fabulous herb of secret power, having a black root and white blossoms, said by Homer to have been given by

Mercury to Ulysses, as a counter-charm against the spells of Circe" (*Webster's Dict.*). v. 10, "*Mark within my eye its iris mystic-lettered*": Letters of the alphabet have been seen marked on the human eye as figures on a dial. Mr. Browning said, "that there was an old superstition that, if you look into the iris of a man's eye, you see the letters of his name or the word telling his fate." (See *Echo*, 23rd March, 1896.) v. 14, "*Petri en pulmones*," Behold, the lungs of Peter! v. 15, "*Ipse dixi*," I have said. v. 16, *Hans of Halberstadt*: a canon of Halberstadt, in Germany, who was a magician who rode upon a devil in the shape of a black horse, and who performed the most incredible feats. (See Browning's poem *Transcendentalism*.) v. 19, "*De corde natus haud de mente*," born of heart, not of mind. *Bene*: the first syllables of Benedicite; here the charm begins to work. v. 23, *Plato on "the Fair and Good"*: Emerson, in his essay on Plato, says: Plato taught this as "the cause which led the Supreme Ordainer to produce and compose the universe. He was good; and he who is good has no kind of envy. Exempt from envy, He wished that all things should be as much as possible like Himself. Whosoever, taught by wise men, shall admit this as the prime cause of the origin and foundation of the world, will be in the truth. All things are for the sake of the good, and it is the cause of everything beautiful." v. 26, *Sylla*: the debauched Roman dictator, who gave up his command and retired to a solitary retreat at Puteoli. v. 27, "*Hag Jezebel and her paint and powder*": Jezebel, the wife of Ahab, who "painted her face and tired her head, and looked out at a window (2 Kings ix. 30). *Jam satis*, already, enough! v. 33, "*Tantalus's treasure*": Tantalus was tortured in hell by having food and drink apparently always within his reach, but always eluding his grasp. v. 37, "*Per Bacco*": by Bacchus,—an Italian oath. v. 38, "*Salomo si nôsset*," if Solomon had but known this! "*Teneor vix*," I can hardly contain myself! v. 39, *hactenus*, up to this time. "*Nec ultra plus!*" nothing further. *Spelter*, zinc. *Peason*, peas. v. 43, "*Pou sto*," where I may stand. Archimedes said he could move the world if he had a place to stand on. v. 46, *Lateran*: the church of St. John Lateran, in Rome; "the mother and head of all the city and the world," as it is called, was the principal church of Rome after the time of Constantine. Five important councils have been held here.

Adjoining it is the Lateran Palace. "*Gained the purple*": *i.e.*, the cardinalate, from the scarlet hat, stockings, and cassock worn by cardinals. "*Bribed the Conclave*": the meeting of the members of the Sacred College of Cardinals for the election of a pope is called a *conclave.* "*Saw my coop ope*": the cardinals go into conclave on the tenth day after the death of the Pope, attended usually by only one person. No access to the conclave is permitted. An opening is left for food to be passed in. The voting must all be done in this assembly. Each cardinal has a boarded cell in the Vatican assigned him by lot. Voting is carried on till some cardinal is found who has the requisite majority of two-thirds of those who are present. v. 47, *Tithon:* a son of Laomedon, king of Troy. He was so beautiful that Aurora fell in love with him and carried him away. He begged her to make him immortal, and the goddess granted the favour. As he forgot to ask her also to preserve his youth, he became old and decrepid, and begged to be removed from the world. As he could not die, she changed him into a grasshopper. v. 48, "*Conciliator Differentiarum*," conciliator of differences. "*De Speciebus Ceremonialis Magiæ*": concerning the kinds of the ceremonial of magic. "*The Fisher's ring, or foot that boasts the Cross*": one of the titles of the Pope is "the Fisherman," after St. Peter. His signet is the ring of the Fisherman; the cross is worked on his slipper. v. 49, "*Apage, Sathanas!*" begone Satan! "*Dicam verbum Salomonis*," I command it in the name of Solomon. Peculiar significance is attached by mystical writers to this word Sol-Om-On (the name of the sun in three languages). *Dicite:* the closing syllables of "benedicite," so that the visions had all taken place between *bene*—and—*dicite.* v. 50, *Benedicite!* a word of good omen, a blessing. "*Idmen, idmen!*" we know, we know! v. 51, *Scientiæ Compendium*, compendium of science. "*Admirationem incutit*": it inspires admiration. *Antipope:* an opposition pope, of which there have been several examples in history; they were usurpers of the popedom. v. 53, *Tiberius Cæsar* (born 42 B.C., died 37 A.D.): Emperor of Rome. When at Padua he consulted the oracle of Geryon, he drew a lot by which he was required to throw golden tali into the fountain of Aponus for an answer to his questions; he did so, and the highest numbers came up. The fountain is situated in the Euganean hills, near Padua.

Oracle of Geryon: Geryon was a mythical king in Spain who had three bodies, or three heads. *Suetonius Tranquilius:* author of the biographies of the first twelve Roman emperors. v. 54, *Venus:* the highest throw with the four *tali*, or three *tesseræ*. The best cast of the *tali* (or foursided dice) was four different numbers; but the best cast of the *tesseræ* (or ordinary dice) was three sixes. The worst throw was called *canis*—three aces in *tesseræ*, and four aces in *tali*. (Brewer's *Handbook*.)

Pillar at Sebzevah, A. (*Ferishtah's Fancies*, 11. Key-note: "Love is better than knowledge.") Sage and pupil argue as to which is the better, knowledge or love. The sage says that love far outweighs knowledge; it is objected that an ass loves food, and perhaps the hand that feeds it—why depose knowledge in favour of love? Ferishtah says that all his knowledge only suffices to enable him to say that he loves boundlessly, endlessly. He had knowledge when a youth, but better knowledge came as he grew older, and pushed it aside; it has been so ever since—the gain of to-day is the loss of to-morrow. It is, in fact, no gain at all: knowledge is not golden, it is but lacquered ignorance. It has a prize: the process of acquiring knowledge is the only reward. But love is victory. In love we are sure to succeed,—there is no delusion there. A child grasps an orange, though he fails to grasp the sun he strives to reach; he may find his orange not worth holding, but the joy was in the shape and colour, and these were better for him than the sun, which would have only burned his fingers. If we can say we are loved in return for the love we bestow, this is to hold a good juicy orange, which is better than seeking to know the mystery of all created things: if we succeeded, it would only be to our own hurt, as the sun would have scorched the child who cried for it. There was a pillar in Sebzevah with a sun-dial fixed upon it. Suppose the townsmen had refused to make use of the dial till they knew the history of the man and his object in erecting the pillar? Better far to go to dinner when the dial says "Noon," and ask no questions. If we love, we know enough. Suppose in crossing the desert we are thirsty, we stoop down and scoop up the sand, and water rises: what need have we to dig down fifty fathoms to find the spring? The best thing we can do is to quench our thirst with the water which is before us: we do not, under the circumstances, require a cisternful. There is one unlovable thing, and that is hate. If out of the sand we get nothing but sand, let us not pretend to be finding water; let us not nickname pain as pleasure. If knowledge were all our faculty, God must be ignored; but love gains God at first leap. The lyric bids us not ask recognition for our love: the deepest affection is the most silent. Words are a poor substitute for the silence of a long gaze and the touch which reveals the soul.

NOTES.—*Mushtari*, the planet Jupiter (Persian). *Hudhud:* fabulous bird of Solomon, according to Eastern legend: the lapwing, a well-known bird in Asia. *Sitara:* Persian for a star.

Pippa Passes: A Drama. (*Bells and Pomegranates*, No. I., 1841.) Pippa is the name of a girl employed at the silk mills at Asolo, in the Trevisan, in Northern Italy. In the whole year she has but one holiday: it is New Year's day, and she determines to make the most of it. She springs out of bed as day is breaking, mapping out as she dresses herself what she will do with Morning, Noon, Evening, and Night. She thinks of the four persons whose lot is most to be envied in the little town, and will imagine herself each of these in turn. But she claims that the day will be fine and not ill-use her. There is the great, haughty Ottima, whose husband, old Luca, sleeps in his mansion while his wife makes love; her lover Sebald will be just as devoted, however the rain may beat on the home. Jules, the sculptor, will wed his Phene to-day: nothing can disturb their happiness, their sunbeams are in their own breasts. Evening may be misty, but Luigi and his lady mother will not heed it. Monsignor will be here from Rome to visit his brother's house: no storm will disturb his holy peace. But for Pippa, the silk-winder, a wet day would darken her whole next year. So her morning fancy starts her as Ottima: all the gardens and the great storehouse are hers. But this is not the kind of love she envies; there's better love, she knows. Her next choice shall give no cause for the scoffer—wedded love, like that of Jules and Phene, for example. But still improvement can be made even upon that: it is, after all, but new love; hers should have lapped her round from the beginning: "only parents' love can last our lives." She will be Luigi, communing with his mother in the turret. But if we come to that, God's love is better even than that of Monsignor the holy and beloved priest, for to-night Pippa will in fancy have her dwelling in the palace by the Dome.—

I. MORNING. Ottima is with her paramour, the German Sebald, in the shrub-house. They have murdered Luca, and are talking calmly of their sin, and contrasting their present freedom with the restraint of last New Year's day. Ottima's husband can no longer fondle her before her lover's face. But there is the corpse to remove, and as Sebald reflects, he begins to regret his treachery to the man who fed and sheltered him. Ottima tells him she loves him better for the crime. They caress each other, and as Sebald fondles Ottima the voice of Pippa singing as she passes is heard from without: "God's in His heaven." Sebald starts, conscience-stricken; Ottima says it is only "that ragged little girl!" At once Sebald is disenchanted; he sees the woman in all the naked horror of her crimes; all her grace and beauty are gone; he hates and curses her. The woman takes the guilt all upon her own head, and prays for him, not for herself: forgetting self, she thinks only of Sebald. "Not me—to him, O God, be merciful!" To her guilty soul also comes the reflection, "God's in His heaven." In self-sacrifice begins her redemption. Pippa has converted both. While Pippa is passing to Orcana, some students from Venice are discussing a jest they have played off on Jules. They have, by means of sham letters which they have concocted between them and sent him as coming from the girl he loves, induced him to believe she was a cultivated woman, and he has been deceived into marrying her.—II. NOON. When the ceremony is over the truth is told him. He gives his bride gold, and is preparing to separate from her, when Pippa passes, singing "Give her but a least excuse to love me!" Jules reasons, Here is a woman with utter need of him. She has an awakening moral sense, a soul like his own sculptured Psyche, waiting his word to make it bright with life—he will evoke this woman's soul in some isle in far-off seas! He forgives her. Pippa's song has worked the reconciliation.—III. EVENING. Luigi and his mother are conversing in the turret on the hill above Asolo. Luigi is what has been termed a "patriot"; he is suspected of belonging to the secret society of the Carbonari, and is at the moment actually discussing with his mother a plot to kill the Emperor of Austria. His mother tells him that half the ills of Italy are feigned, that patriotism seems the easiest virtue for a selfish man to acquire. She urges him to delay his journey to Vienna till the morning. Endeavouring to dissuade him thus, he is on the point of yielding, when Pippa passes, singing "No need the king should ever die!" "Not that sort of king," says Luigi. "Such grace had kings when the world began!" continues the passing Pippa. Luigi says, "It is God's voice calls," and he goes away. He thereby escapes the police, who had just arranged that if he remained at the turret over the night, he was to be arrested at once. Pippa goes on from the turret to the Bishop's brother's home, near the Cathedral.—IV. NIGHT. And here we are shown how little we poor puppets know of the strings which prompt our movements. Pippa would be Ottima, the murderess; and as she, the poor but good and happy silkwinder, trudges on her way to make the holiday of the year, the voluptuous murderess is purifying her wicked soul in agony. She sings in the lightness of her heart, and a line of her morning hymn is the arrow of God to two sinful souls. She would be the bride of Jules—the bride who has just been detected in fraud, on the point of rejection, and who has been redeemed by the snatch of Pippa's innocent monition. She would be the happy Luigi, who would have failed in a purpose he deemed to be a noble one, and would have been a prisoner in the hands of the Austrian police if he had not been nerved by her careless eulogy of good kings. And now, as she approaches her ideally perfect persons, the holy Monsignor is actually engaged in taking steps for her ruin. His superintendent is explaining a plan he has elaborated for getting rid of Pippa, who is the child of his brother, and to whom the property he is holding rightfully belongs. The superintendent has found an English scoundrel named Bluphocks, residing in the locality, who will entrap the girl and take her to Rome to lead a vicious life, which will kill her in a few years. The bishop is listening to the tempter, when Pippa passes, singing one of her innocent little songs, ending with the line—

"Suddenly God took me."

This awakens the conscience of the ecclesiastic, who calls his servants to arrest the villain. All unconscious, as night falls Pippa re-enters her chamber. She has been in fancy the holy Monsignor, Luigi's gentle mother, Luigi himself, Jules the sculptor's bride, and Ottima as well. Tired of fooling, she notices that the sun has dropped into a black cloud, and as night comes on she wonders how nearly she has approached these people of her fancy, to do them good or evil in some slight way; and as she falls asleep she murmurs—

> "All service ranks the same with God—
> With God, whose puppets, best and worst,
> Are we: there is no last nor first."

The drama shows us how near God is to us in conscience. "God stands apart," as the poet says, "to give man room to work"; but in every great crisis of our life, if we listen we may hear Him warning, threatening, guiding, revealing. Not near to answer problems of existence, or to solve the mystery of life: this would interfere with our development of soul; but near to save us from the dangers that await us at every step. The drama shows us, too, our mutual interdependence. Pippa, the silk-girl, had a mission to convert Ottima, Sebald, Jules, and the Bishop. We look for great things to work for us: it is ever the unseen, unfelt influences which are the most potent. We are taught, also, that there is nothing we do or say but may be big with good or evil consequences to many of our fellows of whom we know nothing. People whom we have never seen, of whose very existence we are ignorant, are affected for good or evil eternally by our lightest words and our most thoughtless actions.

NOTES.—For an account of *Asolo* see p. 49 of this work. Silk in large quantities is manufactured in this part of Italy. There is no historical foundation for any of the incidents of the poem. The song in Part II., which Jules and Phene hear, relates, however, to Caterina Carnaro, the exiled Queen of Cyprus. *Possagno:* an obscure village situated amongst the hills of Asolo, famous as the birthplace of Canova, the sculptor. *Cicala:* a grasshopper.—I. MORNING. "*The Capuchin with his brown hood*": the Capuchin monks are familiar to all travellers in Italy. They are a branch of the great Franciscan Order. The habit is brown. The Order was established by St. Francis in the thirteenth century. "Cappuccino" means playfully "little hooded fellow." "*Campanula chalice*": the bell of a flower, as of a Canterbury-bell. "*Bluphocks*": the name means "Blue Fox," and is a skit on the *Edinburgh Review*, which is bound in a cover of blue and fox. "*Et canibus nostris*," even to our dogs. *Canova, Antonio* (1757—1822), one of the greatest sculptors of modern times. He was born at Passagno, near

Asolo, the scene of Pippa's drama. "*Psiche-fanciulla*": Psyche as a young girl with a butterfly, the personification of man's immaterial part. This sculpture is considered as the most faultless and classical of Canova's works. *Pietà:* sculpture representing the Virgin Mary holding the dead body of Christ on her knees. *Malamocco:* "The Lagoon, immediately opposite to Venice, is closed by a long shoaly island, Malamocco" (*Murray*). *Alciphron:* lived in the age of Alexander the Great. He was a philosopher of Magnesia. *Lire:* the lira is an Italian coin of the value of a franc (say, tenpence). *Tydeus*, a son of Œneus, king of Colydon. He was one of the great heroes of the Theban war.—II. NOON. *Coluthus*, a native of Lycopolis, in Egypt, who wrote a poem on the rape of Helen of Troy. He lived probably about the beginning of the sixth century. *Bessarion:* Cardinal Bessarion discovered the poem of Coluthus in Lycopolis in the fifteenth century. *Odyssey:* Homer's poem which narrates the adventures of Ulysses. *Antinous:* One of the suitors of Penelope during the absence of Odysseus. He attempted to seize the kingdom and was killed by Odysseus on his return. *Almaign Kaiser:* the German Emperor. *Hippolyta:* a queen of the Amazons, who was conquered by Hercules, and by him given in marriage to Theseus. *Numidia:* a country of North Africa, now called Algiers. *Hipparchus:* a son of Pisistratus, and tyrant of Athens. He was a great patron of literature. His crimes led to his assassination by a band of conspirators, the leaders of which were Harmodius and Aristogiton. *Archetype:* the pattern or model of a work. *Dryad:* a wood-nymph. *Primordial*, original. *Cornaro:* Queen of Cyprus. Venice took her kingdom from her, and compelled her to resign, assigning her a palace at Asolo. *Ancona:* a city of central Italy, on the shores of the Adriatic. *Intendant*, a superintendent. "*Celarent, Darii, Ferio*": coined words used in logic. "*Bishop Beveridge*": there was a bishop of that name; but this is a pun, and means beverage (drink). *Zwanziger:* a twenty-kreuzer piece of money. "*Charon's wherry*": Charon was a god of hell, who conducted souls across the river Styx. *Lupine-seed*, in plant-lore "lupine" means wolfish, and is suggestive of the Evil One. (*Flower-lore*, by Friend, p. 59.) *Hecate*, a goddess of Hell, to whom offerings were made of eggs, fish, and onions. *Obolus*, a silver coin of the Greeks, worth 8*d.*

They used to put it into the mouth of the corpse as Charon's fee. "*To pay the Stygian ferry*": the river Styx, in the infernal regions, across which Charon conducted the souls, and received an obolus for his fee. *Prince Metternich* (1773-1859): a celebrated Austrian statesman. *Panurge:* a character of Rabelais'. He was a companion of Pantagruel's. He was an impecunious rake and dodger, a boon companion and licentious coward. *Hertrippa:* one of Rabelais' characters in his *Gargantua and Pantagruel. Carbonari:* the name of an Italian secret society which arose in 1820. *Spielberg:* the name of a hill near Brünn, in Moravia, on which stands the castle wherein Silvio Pellico the patriot was confined. III. EVENING. *Lucius Junius Brutus,* whose example animated the Romans to rise against the tyranny of the infamous Tarquin. *Pellicos:* Silvio Pellico was an Italian dramatist and patriot (1788-1854). He was arrested as a member of a secret society by the Austrian Government, and imprisoned for fifteen years in Spielberg Castle, near Brünn. "*The Titian at Treviso*": Treviso is a town in Italy, seventeen miles from Venice. In the cathedral of San Pietro there is a fine Annunciation by Titian (1519). *Python:* the monster serpent slain by Apollo near Delphi. *Breganze wine:* of Breganza, a village north of Vicenza.—IV. NIGHT. *Benedicto benedicatur:* a form of blessing. *Assumption Day:* the festival of the Assumption of the Virgin into Heaven. It is kept on August 15th. *Correggio:* one of the great Italian painters (1494-1534). *Podere,* a manor. *Cesena:* an episcopal city lying between Bologna and Ancona. *Soldo,* a penny. "*Miserere mei, Domine,*" "Have mercy on me, O God!" *Brenta,* a river of North Italy. *Polenta,* a pudding of chestnut flour, etc.

Pisgah-Sights. (*Pacchiarotto* volume, 1876.) 1. From a high mountain the roughness and smoothness of the distant landscape seem to blend into a harmonious picture, the uncouthness is hidden by the grace, the angles are blunted into roundness, its harshness is reconciled into a beautiful whole. If we could be taken by angelic hands and be borne a few miles beyond the surface of the earth, all her mountains would dwindle down till the rough, scarred and furrowed earth would become a perfect orb. A little nearer heaven, and a little farther away from the scene of our pilgrimage here, and evil and sorrow and pain and want will all soften down and be lost in good and joy and blessedness. We are too close to things here to get the right view of their proportions; a handbreadth off, and things which are mysteries to us now will be clear as the daylight. All will be seen as lend and borrow, good will be recognised as the brother of evil, and joy will be seen to demand sorrow for its completion. Why man's existence must so be mixed we cannot say; the majority only begin to see the round orb of things as they near the end o their journey. 2. If we could live our life over again, would we strive any longer? Would we exercise greed and ambition, burrow for earth's treasures, soar for the sun's rights, or not rather be content with turf and foliage—just plain learners of life's lessons, with no attempt to teach, with no desire to rearrange anything at all? Should we not be stationary while the march of hurrying men defiling past us, made us complacent at our post, reflecting that the only possibility of fearing, wondering at, or loving anything at all, lay in our keeping, at a respectful distance from everything which men were hurrying to seek? 3. If it be better to forget than to forgive, so is it better than living to die, to let body slumber while soul, as Indian sages tell, wanders at large, fretless and free, encumbered nevermore by body's grossness, soul in sunshine and love, body under mosses and ferns.

NOTE.—V. 2, *Deniers*, small copper French coins of insignificant value.

Plot-Culture. (*Ferishtah's Fancies*, 10: "God's All-Seeing Eye.") "If all we do or think or say be marked minute by minute by the Supreme, may not our very making prove offence to the Maker's eye and ear?" Thus argued a disciple. The Dervish answers, "There is a limit-line rounding us, severing us from the immensity, cutting us from the illimitable. All of us is for the Maker; all the produce we can within the circle produce for the Master's use is His in autumn. He wants to know nothing of the manure which fertilises the soil—of this we are masters absolute; but we must remember doomsday. In the lyric the singer indicates the uses of Sense as distinguished from Soul. "Soul, travel-worn, toil-weary," is not for love-making; for that let Sense quench Soul!

Poetics. (*Asolando*, 1889.) The singer says the foolish call their Love "My rose," "My swan," or they compare her to the maid-moon blessing the earth below. He will have none of this: he tells the rose there is no balm like breath; bids the swan bend its neck its best,—his love's is the whiter curve. Let the moon be the moon,—he is not afraid to place his Love beside it. She is her human self, and no lower words will describe her.

Polyxena. (*King Victor and King Charles.*) The wife of King Charles: full of resolution, and instinctively sees the right thing, and does it at the appropriate moment. Her "noble and right woman's manliness," as Mr. Browning calls it, enables her to counteract her husband's weakness and to clear his mental vision. Magnanimous and loyal to all, especially to herself and truth, she is one of the poet's finest female characters.

Pompilia. (*The Ring and the Book.*) She was the wife of Count Guido Franceschini, and he killed her, with her foster-parents, when she escaped from his cruel treatment and fled to Rome with the good priest Caponsacchi. She is Browning's noblest and most beautiful female character. There is an excellent study of Pompilia in *Poet Lore*, vol. i., p. 263. The keynote of her character is found in the line of the poem—

> "I knew the right place by foot's feel;
> I took it, and tread firm there."

Ponte dell' Angelo (Venice) = The Angel's Bridge. (*Asolando*, 1889.) Boverio, in his *Annals*, 1552, n. 69, relates this legend of Our Lady. It is recorded at length in *The Glories of Mary*, by St. Alphonsus Liguori (p. 192), a curious work which contains a great number of such stories, which have for their moral the efficacy of prayers to Our Lady as a protection from the devil. On one of the large canals at Venice is a house with the figure of an angel guarding it from harm. Once upon a time (says Father Boverio in his *Annals*) this house belonged to a lawyer, who was a cruel oppressor of all who sought his advice; never was such an extortionate rascal, though a devout one. On one occasion, after a particularly lucrative week, he determined to ask some holy man to dinner, as he could not get the memory of a widow whom he had wronged out of his mind; so he invited the chief of the Capucins to disinfect his house by his holy presence. The monk duly presented himself, and was informed that a most admirable helpmate in the house was an ape, who worked for him indefatigably. The host leaves his guest for awhile, that he may go below to see how the dinner progresses. No sooner had the lawyer left the room than the monk, by the instinct which saints possess for detecting the devil under every disguise, adjures the ape to come out of his hiding-place and show himself *in propriâ personâ.* Satan stands forth, and explains that he is there to convey to hell the lawyer who plagued the widows and orphans by his exactions. The monk asks how it came to pass that he had so long delayed God's commission by acting as servant where he should have been a minister of justice. The devil explains that the lawyer had placed himself under the Virgin's protection by the prayers which he never intermitted; thus the man is armed in mail, and cannot be lugged off to hell while saying, "Save me, Madonna!" If he should discontinue that prayer, Satan would pounce on him at once. He waits, therefore, hoping to catch him napping. The holy man adjures him to vanish. The fiend says he cannot leave the house without doing some damage to prove that his errand had been fulfilled. The saint bade him make his exit through the wall, and leave a gap in the stone for every one to see, which, having duly been done, the monk goes downstairs to dinner with a good appetite. The host asks what has become of the ape, whose assistance he requires, and is terrified to see his guest wringing blood from the table napkin. It is explained that the miracle is performed to show him how he has wrung blood from his clients, and the host is bidden to go down on his knees and swear to make restitution. The man consents, and absolution following, he is forthwith taken upstairs to see the hole in the wall left by the devil exorcised by his saintship. The lawyer fears that Satan may use the aperture of exit for an entry to his dwelling at a future time, when the Capucin bids him erect the figure of an angel and place it by the aperture, which holy sign will frighten the fiend away. And this is why the house by the bridge has the angel on the escutcheon, and why the bridge itself is called the Angel's Bridge, though Mr. Browning thinks the Devil's Bridge would have been as good a name for it.

Pope, The. (*The Ring and the Book.*) The final appeal in the Franceschini murder case being to the Pope, he has to decide the fate of the Count. He reviews the whole case in the tenth book, and gives his decision for the execution of the murderers. Browning's old men are some of his greatest creations, and *The Pope* is perhaps the finest of such conceptions. There is an excellent essay on *The Pope* in *Poet Lore*, vol. i., p. 309, by Professor Shackford.

Pope, The, and the Net. (*Asolando*, 1889.) It is generally supposed that this poem refers to Pope Sixtus V. Mr. Browning possibly obtained the idea from Leti's well-known biography of the Pope, which is full of fables. Dr. Furnivall, however, thinks that Mr. Browning invented the story. It is said that the character of Sixtus V. suits the poem better than any other. The pope in question—Felice Peretti—was born in 1521, of poor parents, but the story of his having been a swineherd in his youth seems to be mere legend. The *Encyclopædia Britannica* (9th edition) says he was created cardinal in 1570, when he lived in strict retirement; affecting, it is said, to be in a precarious state of health. According to the usual story, which is probably at least exaggerated, this dissimulation greatly contributed to his unexpected elevation to the papacy on the next vacancy (April 24th, 1585). "Sixtus V. left the reputation of a zealous and austere pope—with the pernicious qualities inseparable from such a character in his age—of a stern and terrible, but just and magnanimous temporal magistrate, of a great sovereign in an age of great sovereigns, of a man always aiming at the highest things, and whose great faults were but the exaggerations of great virtues." The best view of his character is that given by Ranke. Mr. Browning makes his Pope to be the son of a fisherman, who, on his elevation to the cardinalate, kept his fisher-father's net in his palace-hall on a coat-of-arms, as token of his humility. When, however, he became Pope, the net was removed because it had caught the fish.

Popularity. (*Men and Women*, vol. ii., 1855.) This poem is a tribute to Keats. Shelley and Keats soon displaced Pope and Byron from the mind of the youthful poet who gave us *Pauline*: it is not difficult to trace in that first work of Browning's the influence of both. When, as a boy, he made acquaintance with the then little-known works of Keats, we can guess, even if biographers had not told us, how the author of *Endymion* and *The Eve of St. Agnes* would charm the young poet's soul. "Remember," he says here, "one man saw you, knew you, and named a star!" Then he fancies him as a fisherman on Tyrian seas, plundering the ocean of her purple dye: kings' houses shall be made glorious and their persons beautiful with the product of the coloured conchs. Then he sees merchants bottling the extract and selling it to the world. They eat turtle and drink claret, but who fished up the murex? How does he live? What mean food had John Keats all his struggling life? He taught men to paint their ideas in glowing word-tints and images luxuriant. These men gorge, while the man who ransacked the ocean of thought and the world of fancy is left to starve.

NOTES.—Verse 6, *Tyrian shells:* the genera Murex and Purpura have a gland called the "adrectal gland, which secretes a colourless liquid, which turns purple upon exposure to the atmosphere, and was used by the ancients as a dye" (*Encyc. Brit.*). It was a discovery of the Phœnicians, and was known to the Greeks in the Homeric age. The juice collected from the shells was placed in salt, and heated in metal vessels; then the wool or silk was dyed in it. Tyrian purple wool in Cæsar's time cost £43 10*s.* a pound. Purple robes were used from very early times as a mark of dignity. Tyre was a very ancient city of Phœnicia, with great harbours and very splendid buildings. *Astarte:* the Venus of the Greeks and Romans, a powerful Syrian divinity. She had a great temple at Hieropolis, in Syria, with three hundred priests. v. 12, *Hobbs, Nobbs, Stokes, and Nokes:* fancy names, of course—meaning the men who profit by other men's labours. They bottle and sell the precious things for which the brave fisherman risks his life and spends his days and nights, after all receiving but a miserable fraction of the gain. v. 13, *Murex:* the genus of molluscs from which the Tyrian purple dye was obtained. It was of the class GASTROPODA, order AZYGOBRANCHIA, sub-order *Siphonochlamyda*, **Rachiglossa*, family *Muricidæ*. *Purpura* also was used (hence *purple*), of the same sub-order—family *Buccinidæ*. "*What porridge had John Keats?*" John Keats, the poet, was born Oct. 29th, 1795, and died of consumption in Rome, Feb. 23rd, 1821, when only twenty-six years old. His *Ode to a Nightingale* will serve to immortalise him, even if he had written nothing else. After this his best poems are his *Endymion*, *Hyperion*, and the *Eve of St. Agnes*. His straitened circumstances and his ill-health made him hysterical and fretful; but though he was certainly cruelly used by his reviewers, it is only a ridiculous legend that he was killed by an article against him in the *Quarterly Review*. Bitter reviews of our books do not introduce to our lungs the microbes of tuberculosis.

Porphyria's Lover. (Published first in Mr. Fox's *Monthly Repository* in 1836, over the signature "Z." Reprinted as II.

"Madhouse Cells," in *Dramatic Lyrics*, *Bells and Pomegranates*, 1842.) In the midst of a storm at night, to a man sitting alone by a burnt-out fire in his room, enters the woman whom he loves, but of whose love he has never been sure in return. She glides in, shuts out the storm, kneels by the dull grate and makes a cheerful blaze, takes off her dripping cloak, lets down her damp hair, sits by his side, speaks to him, puts her arm around him, rests his cheek on her bosom, and murmuring that she loves him, gives herself to him for ever. At last, then, he knows it; his heart swells with joyful surprise, he realises the tremendous wealth of which he is thus suddenly possessed; and lest change should ever come, lest the wealth should ever be squandered, the possession ever be lost, he will kill her that moment: and so, as she reposes there, he winds her beautiful long hair in a cord thrice round her little throat, and she is strangled—painlessly, he knows, but his unalterably, because dead. And God, he says, has watched them as they sat the night through, and He has not said a word! This poem was Browning's first monologue.

Potter's Wheel, The. The figure of the potter's wheel in *Rabbi Ben Ezra* is taken from Isaiah lxiv. 8, Jeremiah xviii. 2—6, and Romans ix. 20, 21. See a similar use of the figure in Quarles' *Emblems* (Book III., Emblem 5).

Pretty Woman, A. (*Men and Women*, 1855; *Dramatic Lyrics*, 1868.) Here is a beautiful woman—simply a beauty, nothing more. What, then, is not that enough? Why cannot we let her just adorn the world like a beautiful flower? Why do we demand more of her than to gladden us with her charms? So the craftsman makes a rose of gold petals with rubies in its cup, all his fine things merely effacing the rose which grew in the garden. The best way to grace a rose is to leave it; not gather it, smell it, kiss it, wear it, and then throw it away. Leave the pretty woman just to beautify the world,—it needs it!

Prince Berthold. (*Colombe's Birthday*.) He claims, by right, the duchy which is held by Colombe.

Prince Hohenstiel-Schwangau, Saviour of Society (1871). Prince Hohenstiel-Schwangau represents the Emperor Napoleon III. Hohenstiel-Schwangau represents France. The name is formed from that of one of the Bavarian royal castles called Hohen-Schwangau. Visitors to the Ober-Ammergau Passion Play will remember the beautiful and luxurious castles which the mad king built and furnished in so costly a manner in the midst of the picturesque scenery of the Bavarian Alps. The poem deals with the subjective processes which Browning supposed animated Napoleon III. in his character as Saviour of Society. *Prince Hohenstiel-Schwangau* is not precisely a soul-portrait of the Emperor Napoleon III. Mr. Browning does not draw portraits—he analyses characters. He has therefore used the Emperor as a model is used by an artist. The artist does not simply paint the model's portrait, he uses him for a higher purpose of art. Mrs. Browning was greatly interested in Louis Napoleon, enthusiastically entered into the spirit of his ambitions, and considered him as "the Saviour of Society." She loved Italy so passionately that the destroyer of the power of Austria over the land which she loved could not fail to win her admiration; and this, probably, was the chief reason of her esteem for him. Her poem *Napoleon III. in Italy* should be read in this connection; each verse ends "Emperor Evermore." She says:—

> "We meet thee, O Napoleon, at this height
> At last, and find thee great enough to praise.
> Receive the poet's chrism, which smells beyond
> The priest's, and pass thy ways!
> An English poet warns thee to maintain
> God's word, not England's;—let His truth be true,
> And all men liars! with His truth respond
> To all men's lie."

She goes on to call him "Sublime Deliverer," and praises him for that "he came to deliver Italy."

[THE MAN.] For some of my younger readers, who may not be familiar with the career of the late Emperor of France, it may be necessary to remind them of the following facts in his history. He was born at Paris on April 20th, 1808. The revolution of 1830, which dethroned the Bourbons, first launched Louis Napoleon on his eventful career. With his elder brother he joined the Italian bands who were in revolt against the pope. This revolt was suppressed by Austrian soldiers. The law banishing the Bonapartes exiled him on his return to Paris, and he came to England at the age of twenty-three. In a few weeks he went to Switzerland, and wrote an essay on that country. Returning to France, he was arrested and sent to America by Louis Philippe in 1836. He returned to Switzerland next year, but shortly after left for England again, living this time in Carlton Terrace. In 1840 he made his descent upon France; his party were shot or imprisoned, Louis being condemned to perpetual imprisonment in the castle of Ham, on the Somme. He escaped after six years, and once more went to London, living at 10, King Street, St. James's. When Louis Philippe died, in 1848, Louis went to France and offered himself to the provisional government. He was ordered to withdraw from France, which he did. In April 1848 he acted as a special constable in London at the time of the Chartist disturbances. Soon after, he was elected in France to the Assembly, in three departments. In December 1848 he was elected president of the Republic by above five million votes. On the 2nd December, 1851, he executed the *coup d'état*, and soon after was made Emperor by the votes of nearly eight million persons. For eighteen years Louis Napoleon was sovereign of France. He married Eugénie de Montigo, Countess of Teba, Jan. 30th, 1853. On the 4th June was fought the battle of Magenta, for the liberation of Italy; and he entered Milan the next morning in company with Victor Emmanuel. He met the Emperor of Austria at Villafranca on July 11th, and the preliminaries of peace were arranged. He was hurried into the war with Germany by the clerical party at court in 1870, his advisers seeing no hope for the permanence of his dynasty but in a successful war. At the defeat of Sedan he was made prisoner, with ninety thousand men. He was incarcerated at Wilhelmshöhe, near Cassel, from which he subsequently retired to England. He lived with the Empress at Chislehurst, dying there on Jan. 9th, 1873.

[THE POEM.] The Prince is talking with Lais, an adventuress, in a room near Leicester Square. He is explaining that he has not been actuated in his past life by any desire to make anything new, but merely to conserve things, and carry on what he found ready for him: thus he has been a conserver, a saviour of society. He has lived to please himself, though he recognises God and considers himself as His instrument. God is not to every one the same; to the woman of the town with whom he is conversing, He is the Providence that helps her to pay her way. God is to all men just what they conceive him to be: a shopkeeper's God and a king's God differ,—it is just as they conceive Him. For his own part he has tried on a large scale to please himself; but he has an eye to another world also, so he must carry out God's wishes so far as he understands them,—he must preserve what he found established. He thinks himself a great man because a great conservator of order. There have been changes by God's acts, but he has held it his object in life to find out the good already existing, and preserve it. It is only the inspired man who can change society from round to square; he is himself only the man of the moment; if he succeeds, the inspired man will be the first to recognise the value of his work. He will touch nothing unless reverently; he has no higher hope than to reconcile good with hardly-quite-as-good; he will not risk a whiff of his cigar for Fourier and Comte, and all that ends in smoke. He thinks it best to be contented with what is bad but might be worse. For twenty years he has held the balance straight, and so has done good service to humanity; he has not trodden the world into a paste, that he might roll it out flat and smooth; it has been no part of his task to mend God's mistakes. All else but what a man feels is nothing, and the thing on which he congratulates himself as a ruler of men is that everything he knows, feels, or can conceive, he can make his own. He thinks that God made all things for him, and himself for Him. To learn how to set foot decidedly on some one path to heaven makes it worth while to handle things tenderly; we might mend them, but also we might mar them; meanwhile they help on so far, and therefore his end is to save society. He has no novelties to offer, he creates nothing, has no desire to renew the age,—his task is to co-operate, not to chop and change. All the good we know comes from order; he will not interfere with evil, because good is brought about by its means. When a chemist wants a white substance, and knows that the dye can be obtained from black ingredients, what a fool he would be if he were to insist that these also should be white! The Prince does not disapprove this bad world, and has no faith in a perfectly good one here. Is there any question as to the wisdom of saving society? Did he work aright with the powers appointed him for this end? On reviewing his work he finds more hope than discouragement: what he found he left, what was tottering he kept stable. It is God's part to work great changes. He discovered that a solitary great man was worth the world. It was his work to tend the cornfield, to feed the myriads of hungry men who sought for daily bread and nothing more. Was he to turn aside from that to play at horticulture, look after the cornflowers and rear the poppies? "I am Liberty, Philanthropy, Enlightenment, Patriotism," cried each: "flaunt my flag alone!" He objected, "What about the myriads who have no flag at all?" If he had to choose between faith and freedom, aristocracy and democracy, or effecting the freedom of an oppressed nation, he would ask, "How many years on an average do men live in the world?" "Some score," he is told. To this he replies, if he had a hundred years to live he might concentrate his energies on some great cause. But he has a cause, a flag and a faith: it is Italy. There was a time when he was voice and nothing more, but only like his censors; then he was full of great aims. Has he failed in promise or performance? He thinks in neither; he found that men wanted merely to be allowed to live, and so he consulted for his kind that have the eyes to see, the mouths to eat, the hands to work. Nature told him to care for himself alone in the conduct of his mind; he was to think as if man had never thought before, and act as if all creation watched him. Nature has evolved her man from the jelly-fish through various stages, till he has reached the headship of creation. He, too, the Prince, has been evolved, and can sympathise with all classes of men. Men in the main have little wants, not large; it was his duty to help the least wants first: if only he could live a hundred years instead of the average twenty, he could experiment at ease. Men want meat; they can't chew Kant's *Critique of Pure Reason* in exchange. Obstacles, he has discovered, are good for mankind; medicines are impeded in their action, and so are state remedies; it is not possible always to effect precisely what is intended, neither would it be always best in the long run. He illustrates this by a story of an artist's trick he saw in Rome once. An artist had covered up the sons and serpents of a Laocoön group, leaving only the central figure, with nothing to show the purpose of his gesture; then a crowd was called to give their opinion of the gesture of the figure. Every one thought it showed a man yawning, except one man, who said "I think the gesture strives against some obstacle we cannot see." Prince Hohenstiel-Schwangau would like this far-sighted individual to write his history: he would be able to tell the world how he who was so misunderstood has tried to be a man. And here, he says, ends his autobiography. He will now give some idea to his companion (Lais, a not unsuitable auditor for his apologia) of what he might have been if his visions had become realities. Had his story been told by an historian of the Thiers-Hugo sort, he might have appeared thus. The nation chose the Assembly first to serve her, chose the President afterward chiefly to see that her servants did good service; when the time came that the head servant must vacate his place, and it was patent that his fellow-servants were all knaves or fools, seeing that everybody was working to serve his own purposes, that they were only waiting for the president's term of office to expire, to see their own longings crowned, he appealed to the Assembly, showed how his fellow-servants had been plotting and scheming while he alone had been faithful to the nation which had trusted him, and suggested that he should be made "master for the moment." Let him be entrusted with the utmost power they could confer upon him, he would use it faithfully. And the nation answered, with a shout,—

"The trusty one! no tricksters any more!"

Up to the time when his term of office as president must expire he had let things go their own way, knowing all, seeing everything, but letting things develop. Not that this was unsuspected by his enemies: they guessed that he was meditating some stroke of state; they saw through him, as he through them, and were on their guard. He was re-elected, and there was uprising. "The knaves and fools, each trickster with his dupe," dropped their masks, unfurled their flags, and brandished their weapons. Then fell his fist on the head of craft and greed and impudence; the fancy patriot, and the night hawk prowling for his prey, all alike were reduced to order and obedience. Of course it was demurred that he was too prodigal of life and liberty, too swift, too thorough; and Sagacity complained that he had let things go on unnoticed till severe measures had been required: he should have frustrated villainy in the egg; so for want of the by-blow had to come the butcher's work. To all this he replies that his oath had restrained him; he had rather appealed to the people for the commission to act as he had done. And then began his sway; and his motto had been, Govern for the many first, think of the poor mean multitude, all mouths and eyes primarily, and then proceed to help the few, the better favoured. His aim had been to try to equalise things a little, and this by way of reverence. He did his work with might and main, and not a touch of fear, but with confidence in God who comes before and after; irresolute as he was at first, now that the cankers of society were laid bare before him, he wrenched them out without a touch of indecision. And so, when the Republic, violating its own highest principle, bade Hohenstiel-Schwangau (really France) fasten in the throat of a neighbour (Italy), and deprive her of liberty, in this he saw an infamy triumphant; and when he came into power, he saw, too, that it demanded his interference. Sagacity said, "Let the wrong stand over,—he was not to blame for the wrong, it was there before his time." But he was prompt to act. Out came the canker, root and branch, with much abuse for him from friend and foe. Sagacity said he had been precipitate, rash, and rude, though in the right: he should have blown a trumpet-blast to let the wrong-doers know they must set their house in order. He replies that he would have broken another generation's heart by the respite to the iniquity. And so the war came. "But France," said Sagacity, "had ever been a fighter, and would continue to be so till the weary world interfered." Prince Hohenstiel-Schwangau recognises this, and says war for war's sake is damnable. He will prevent the growth of this madness. This, however, does not imply that there shall be no war at all, when the wickedness he denounces comes from the neighbour. He will deliver Italy from the rule of Austria, smite her oppressor hip and thigh till he leaves her free from the Adriatic to the Alps. Sagacity suggests that this should not be all for nought: "there ought to be some honorarium paid—Savoy and Nice, for example." But the Prince says "No; lèt there be war for the hate of war." So Italy was free. But there were other points noteworthy and commendable in the man's career: he was resolute, fearless, and true, and by his rule the world had proof a point was gained. He had shown he was the fittest man to rule; chance of birth and dice-throw had been outdone here. Sagacity often advised him to confirm the advance, and bade him wed the pick of the world; if he married a queen, he might tell the world that the old enthroned decrepitudes acknowledged that their knell had sounded, and that they were making peace with the new order. Or let him have a free wife for his free state. Sagacity desires to prop up the lie that the son derives his genius from the sire, but God does not work like this. He drops His seed of heavenly flame where He wills on earth; the rock all naked and unprepared is as likely to receive it as the accumulated store of faculties:

> "The great Gardener grafts the excellence
> On wildings where He will."

He tells the story of the manner in which the succession of priests was maintained at an old Roman temple. Each priest obtained his predecessor's office by springing from ambush and slaying him,—his initiative rite was simply murder under a religious sanction; so he says it is, and ever shall be with genius and its priesthood in the world, the new power slays the old. Thus did the Prince refute Sagacity, always whispering in his ear that Fortune alternates with Providence, and he must not reckon on a happy hit occurring twice. But he will trust nothing to right divine and luck of the pillow; rulers should be selected by supremacy of brains; a blunder may ensue; it cannot be worse than the rule of the legitimate blockhead. By this time poor Lais has gone to sleep (little wonder!). The Prince leaves off imagining what the historian of the Thiers-Hugo school might have written, of the life he might have led, and the things he might have done. All this was in cloud-land. In the inner chamber of the soul the silent truth fights the battle out with the lie, truth which unarmed pits herself against the armoury of the tongue. We must use words though; and somehow—as even do the best rifled cannon—words will deflect the shot.

NOTES.—*Œdipus*, son of Laius, king of Thebes, and Jocasta. He was exposed to the persecutions of Juno from his birth. He murdered his father and committed incest with his mother. *Riddle of the Sphinx:* Œdipus solved the riddle of the Sphinx, a terrible monster which devoured all those who attempted its solution and failed. The enigma was this: "What animal in the morning walks upon four feet, at noon upon two, and in the evening upon three?" Œdipus said: "Man, in the morning of his life, goes on all fours; when grown to manhood, he walks erect; and in old age, the evening of life, supports himself with a stick." "*Home's stilts*": the spirit-rapper, D. D. Home, is here referred to. (See, for Mr. Browning's opinion of Spiritualism, his poem *Mr. Sludge the Medium.* Sludge is really Home.) *Corinth*, an ancient city of Greece, celebrated for its wealth and the luxury of its inhabitants. *Thebes:* the Sphinx resorted to the neighbourhood of this city. It was the capital of Bœotia, and one of the most ancient cities of Greece. *Laïs*, a celebrated courtesan who lived at Corinth, and ridiculed the philosophers. *Thrace*, an extensive country between the Ægean, Euxine and Danube. *Residenz* (Ger.): the residence of a prince and count. *Pradier Magdalen:* the statue of St. Mary Magdalen by James Pradier, in the Louvre. Pradier was born at Geneva in 1790, and died in Paris 1852. He was a brilliant and popular sculptor. His chief works are the Son of Niobe, Atalanta, Psyche, Sappho (all in the Louvre), a bas-relief on the triumphal arch of the Carousel, the figures of Fame on the Arc de l'Etoile, and Rousseau's statue at Geneva. *Fourier:* Charles Fourier was a Frenchman who recommended the reorganisation of society into small communities, living in common. *Comte, Auguste:* the author of the Positive Philosophy, the key to which is "the Law of the Three States' —that is to say, there are three different ways in which the human mind explains phenomena, each way succeeding the other. These three stages are the Theological, the Metaphysical, and the Positive. The Positive stage is that in which the relation is established between the given fact and some more general fact. "*But, God, what a Geometer art Thou!*" This is Plato's. Browning uses the same idea in *Easter Day* (see the notes to that poem). *Hercules*, substituting his shoulder for that of Atlas: Atlas was one of the Titans, and was fabled to support the world on his shoulders. Hercules was said to have eased for some time the labours of Atlas by taking upon his shoulders the weight of the heavens. *Œta*, a mountain range in the south of Thessaly. *Proudhon* was a revolutionary writer (1809-65). His answer to the question, "Qu'est ce-que la Propriété?" is famous: "La Propriété, c'est le vol," he replied. His greatest work was the "*Système des Contradictions économiques, ou Philosophie de la Misère.*" His violent utterances led to his imprisonment for three years. *Great Nation:* to the French their country is "La Grande Nation." *Leicester Square:* all the foreign refugees in England gravitate towards Leicester Square. *Cayenne:* the capital of French Guiana, and a penal settlement for political offenders. It is anything but "cool," the temperature throughout the year being from 76° to 88° Fahr. It is fever-stricken, and very unhealthy generally. *Xerxes and the Plane-tree:* Xerxes going from Phrygia into Lydia, observed a plane-tree, which on account of its beauty, he presented with golden ornaments. (*Herodotus* vii. 31.) *Kant:* Emmanuel Kant, author of the *Critique of Pure Reason* (1724-1804). He was the greatest philosopher of the eighteenth century. This celebrated work of Kant's penetrated to all the leading universities, and its author was hailed by some as a second Messiah. The falls of *Terni*, on the route from Perugia to Orte, in Central Italy, have few rivals in Europe in point of beauty and volume of water. They are the celebrated falls of the Velino (which here empties itself into the Nera) called the Cascate delle Marmore, and are about 650 feet in height. *Laocoön*, a Trojan, priest of Apollo, who was killed at the altar by two serpents. The famous group of sculpture called by this name is in the Vatican Museum, in the *Cortile del Belvedere.* According to Pliny, it was executed by three Rhodians, and was placed in the palace of Titus. It was discovered in 1506, and was termed by Michael Angelo a marvel of art. *Thiers, Louis Adolphe* (1797-1877), "liberator of the territory," as France calls him. He wrote the *History of the French Revolution. Victor Hugo*, born 1802, a famous politician and novelist of France, was exiled by Louis Napoleon after the *coup d'état.* He fulminated against the Emperor from Jersey his book *Napoleon the Little.* He was detested almost fanatically by Napoleon III. "*Brennus in the Capitol*": Brennus was a leader of the Gauls, and conqueror at the Allia, a small river eleven miles north of Rome, on the banks of which the Gauls inflicted a terrible defeat on the Romans on July 16th, B.C. 390. After this defeat the Romans, terrified by this sudden invasion, fled into the Capitol and left the whole city in the possession of the enemy. The Gauls climbed the Tarpeian rock in the night, and the Capitol would have been taken if the Romans had not been alarmed by the cackling of some geese near the doors, when they attacked and defeated the Gauls. *Salvatore*, = Salvator Rosa, a renowned painter of the Neapolitan school. *Clitumnus*, a river of Italy, the waters of which, when drunk, were said to render oxen white. *Nemi:* the lake of Nemi, in the Alban mountains, near Rome, was anciently called the *Lacus Nemorensis*, and sometimes the Mirror of Diana, from its extreme beauty. Remains have been discovered of a temple to that goddess in the neighbourhood, and from her sacred grove, or *nemus*, the present name is derived.

"**Prize Poems.**" Dining one day last year at Trinity College, Cambridge, with that enthusiastic young Browning scholar, Mr. E. H. Blakeney (himself a poet of great promise), we discussed the question of the comparative popularity of Browning's shorter poems, and it was decided that he should ask the editor of the *Pall Mall Gazette* to put it to the vote in his columns. A prize was offered for the list of fifty poems which came nearest to the standard list obtained by collating the lists of all the competitors. The fifty "prize poems" selected by the *plébiscite* as Browning's best, arranged in the order of the votes they severally received, were the following:—

1. How they brought the Good News from Ghent to Aix.
2. Evelyn Hope.
3. { Abt Vogler. / Saul.
5. Rabbi Ben Ezra.
6. The Lost Leader.
7. The Pied Piper of Hamelin.
8. Prospice.
9. Hervé Riel.
10. Andrea del Sarto.
11. The Last Ride Together.
12. A Grammarian's Funeral.
13. Home Thoughts from Abroad.
14. The Boy and the Angel.
15. Epilogue to Asolando.
16. { By the Fireside. / Fra Lippo Lippi.
18. Caliban upon Setebos.
19. One Word More.
20. Any Wife to Any Husband.
21. An Epistle of Karshish.
22. Incident of the French Camp.
23. The Guardian Angel.
24. Love among the Ruins.
25. { Apparent Failure. / A Forgiveness.
27. { A Death in the Desert. / A Woman's Last Word.
29. Count Gismond.
30. In a Gondola.
31. The Patriot.
32. A Toccata of Galuppi's.
33. My Last Duchess.
34. { The Worst of It. / Truth and Art.
36. The Statue and the Bust.
37. The Bishop orders his Tomb at St. Praxed's Church.
38. Cristina.
39. Clive.
40. Confessions.
41. Two in the Campagna.
42. Summum Bonum.
43. After.
44. { Holy Cross Day. / The Italian in England.
46. Up at a Villa.
47. Before.
48. { James Lee's Wife. / Soliloquy of the Spanish Cloister.
50. Old Pictures in Florence.

Prologue to Dramatic Idyls. (*Second Series.*) When we are suffering from bodily illness, doctors often disagree as to the diagnosis of our complaint. We go from specialist to specialist, and each physician declares that we are suffering from that disorder which he makes his special study: the brain doctor says it is all brain trouble; the heart man, the liver and lung specialists, are all pretty certain to diagnose their own favourite malady. And so even the wisest are ignorant of man's body. But when we come to soul, there is no difficulty at all: they pounce on our malady in a trice. They can see the body, and cannot tell what is the matter with it; the soul, which they cannot see, presents no difficulties whatever to their wise heads! Mr. Sharp, in his paper on *Dramatic Idyls* II., says this Epilogue is the key to the leading idea of each poem in the volume. *Echetlos* deals with patriotic action. We think Miltiades and Themistocles true patriots, but history shows that they only served their own turn. *Clive* dreaded death less than a lie, yet committed suicide: was this due to courage or fear? *Mulyekeh* loved his mare, but sacrificed her to his pride. *Pietro of Abano* did benevolent actions, yet had no love in his heart. *Doctor* —— did good actions from a motive of hate. *Pan and Luna:* this poem deals with an act of love from opposite extremes—Pan gross and brutal, Luna pure and modest; yet she does not spurn Pan. This was not due to want of modesty, but to the power of love, and Pan was not actuated by brute passion. *The Epilogue* is to oppose the idea that poets sing spontaneously about anything. Browning says his rocks are hard and forbidding, yet they hold, like Alpine crags, pine seeds of truth.

Prologue to Ferishtah's Fancies. This is intended to describe the peculiar construction of the volume of poems. The poet tells his readers how ortolans are eaten in Italy: the birds are stuck on a skewer, some dozen or more, each having interposed between himself and his neighbour on the spit a bit of toast and a strong sage leaf; and the eater is intended to bite through crust, seasoning, and bird altogether, so the lusciousness is curbed and the full flavour of the delicacy is obtained. The poem, we are told, is dished up on the same principle. We have sense, sight and song here, and all is arranged to suit our digestion. We have the fancy or fable, then a dialogue, and a melodious lyric to conclude; so, in the twelve poems, we may see twelve ortolans, with their accompanying toast and sage leaf.

NOTES.—*Ortolans* (*Emberiza hortulana*): the garden bunting, a native of Continental Europe and Western Asia. It is very much like the yellowhammer. They are netted, and fed in a darkened room with oats and other grain. They soon become very fat, and are then killed for the table; the birds are much prized by gourmands. *Gressoney*, a village in the valley of the Aosta. *Val d'Aosta*, valley of the Aosta, in northern Piedmont.

Prologue to Pacchiarotto. The poet is imprisoned on a long summer day with his feet on a grass plot and his eyes on a red brick wall. True, the wall is clothed with a luxuriant creeper through which the bricks laugh, and the robe of green pulsates with life, beautifying the barrier. He reflects that wall upon wall divide us from the subtle thing that is spirit: though cloistered here in the body-barrier, he will hope hard, and send his soul forth to the congenial spirit beyond the ring of neighbours which, like a fence of brick and stone, divides him from his love.

Prospice = "Look forward" (*Dramatis Personæ*, 1864) was written in the autumn following Mrs. Browning's death. St. Paul speaks of those "who through fear of death were all their lifetime subject to bondage": the author of *Prospice* and the Epilogue to *Asolando* was not of this class. Few men have written as nobly as he on the awful "minute of night," and its fight with the "Arch Fear." Estimating it at its fullest import, as only a great imaginative mind can do, he is in face of "the black minute" and "the power of the night"—the Mr. Greatheart of the pilgrims to the dark river. Nothing grander has been written on the subject than the poems we have named. In the short poem *Prospice* is concentrated the strength of a great soul and the courage of one who is prepared for the worst, with eyes unbandaged. As an example of the poet's power nothing can be finer. The dramatic intensity of the opening lines—the fog, the mist, the snow, and the blasts which indicate the journey's end, "the post of the foe"—is unsurpassed even by Shakespeare himself. It is a defiance of death, a challenge to battle.

Protus. (*Men and Women*, 1855; *Romances*, 1863; *Dramatic Romances*, 1868.) There is no historical foundation for the poem. In the declining years of the Roman Empire such rapid transitions of power were not uncommon. A baby Emperor Protus is described in some ancient work as absorbing the interest of the whole empire: queens ministered at his cradle. The world rose in war till he was presented at a balcony to pacify it. Greek sculptors and great artists strove to impress his graces on their work, his subjects learned to love the letters of his name; and on the same page of the history it was recorded how the same year a blacksmith's bastard, by name John the Pannonian, arose and took the crown and wore it for six years, till his sons poisoned him. What became of the young Emperor Protus was then but mere hearsay: perhaps he was permitted to escape; he may have become a tutor at some foreign court, or, as others say, he may have died in Thrace a monk. "Take what I say," wrote the annotator, "at its worth."

Puccio. (*Luria.*) The officer in the Florentine army who was superseded by the Moorish leader Luria.

Queen, The. (*In a Balcony.*) The middle-aged woman who, though married, falls in love with Norbert, the lover of Constance. She prepares to divorce her husband and marry her officer. When, however, she discovers the truth about the young lovers, she is the prey of jealousy and offended dignity, and the drama closes with ominous prospects for the unfortunate couple.

Queen Worship. Under this title were originally published two poems: i., *Rudel and the Lady of Tripoli;* and ii., *Cristina.*

Quietism. See MOLINISTS.

Rabbi Ben Ezra. (*Dramatis Personæ*, 1864.) The character is historical. The *Encyclopædia Britannica* gives the name as Abenezra, or Ibn Ezra, the full name being Abraham Ben Meir Ben Ezra; he was also called Abenare or Evenare. "He was one of the most eminent of the Jewish literati of the Middle Ages. He was born at Toledo about 1090, left Spain for Rome about 1140, resided afterwards at Mantua in 1145, at Rhodes in 1155 and 1166, in England in 1159, and died probably in 1168. He was distinguished as a philosopher, astronomer, physician, and poet; but especially as a grammarian and commentator. The works by which he is best known form a series of *Commentaries* on the books of the Old Testament, which have nearly all been printed in the great Rabbinic Bibles of Bomberg (1525-26), Buxtorf (1618-19), and Frankfurter (1724-27). Abenezra's commentaries are acknowledged to be of very great value. He was the first who raised biblical exegesis to the rank of a science, interpreting the text according to its literal sense, and illustrating it from cognate languages. His style is elegant, but is so concise as to be sometimes obscure; and he occasionally indulges in epigram. In addition to the commentaries, he wrote several treatises on astronomy or astrology, and a number of grammatical works." He appears to have possessed extraordinary natural talents; to these he added "indefatigable ardour and industry in the pursuit of knowledge, and he enjoyed besides, in his youth, the advantage of the best teachers, among whom was the Karaite, Japhet Hallevi or Levita, to whom he is believed to have owed his taste for etymological and grammatical investigation, and his preference for the literal to the allegorical and cabalistic interpretation of Scripture. He was afterwards married to Levita's daughter." He did not consider his life a fortunate one as men look upon life. "I strive to grow rich," he said; "but the stars are against me. If I sold shrouds, none would die. If candles were my wares the sun would not set till the day of my death." The cause of his leaving Spain was an outbreak against the Jews. Hitherto, he said of himself, he had been "as a withered leaf; I roved far away from my native land, from Spain, and went to Rome with a troubled soul." He seems to have written no books until after his exile, and then he actively engaged in literary work. The most complete catalogue of his works is contained in Furst's *Bibliotheca Judaica* (Leipzig, 1849). "Maimonides, his great contemporary, esteemed his writings so highly for learning, judgment, and elegance, that he recommended his son to make them for some time the exclusive object of his study. By Jewish scholars he is preferred, as a commentator, even to Raschi in point of judiciousness and good sense; and in the judgment of Richard Simon, confirmed by De Rossi, he is the most successful of all the rabbinical commentators in the grammatical and literal interpretation of the Scriptures" (*Imp. Dict. Biog.*). According to Rabbi Ben Ezra, man's life is to be viewed as a whole. God's plan in our creation has arranged for youth and age, and no view of life is consistent with it which ignores the work of either. Man is not a bird or a beast, to find joy solely in feasting; care and doubt are the life stimuli of his soul: the Divine spark within us is nearer to God than are the recipients of His inferior gifts. So our rebuffs, our stings to urge us on, our strivings, are the measure of our ultimate success: aspiration, not achievement, divides us from the brute. The body is intended to subserve the highest aims of the soul: it will do so if we live and learn. The flesh is pleasant, and can help soul as that helps the body. Youth must seek its heritage in age; in the repose of age he is to take measures for his last adventure. This he can do with prospect of success proportionate to his use of the past. Wait death without fear, as you awaited age. Sentence will not be passed on mere "work" done: our purposes, thoughts, fancies, all that the coarse methods of human estimates failed to appreciate, these will be put in the diamond scales of God and credited to us. God is the Potter; we are clay, receiving our shape and form and ornament by every turn of the wheel and faintest touch of the Master's hand. The uses of a cup are not estimated by its foot or by its stem; but by the bowl which presses the Master's lips to slake the Divine thirst. We cannot see the meaning of the wheel and the touches of the potter's hand and instrument; we know this, and this only,—our times are in His hand who has planned a perfect cup.—I am indebted to Mr. A. J. Campbell for the following notes, the result of his researches in endeavouring to trace the real Rabbi Ibn Ezra in the poem *Rabbi Ben Ezra*. His fellow-religionists say of the Rabbi that he was "a man of strongly marked individuality and independence of thought, keen in controversy, yet genial withal; and it is in words such as these that the final estimate of his own people is given. 'He was the wonder of his contemporaries and of those who came after him . . . profoundly versed in every branch of knowledge, with unfailing judgment, a man of sharp tongue and keen wit' (Dr. J. M. Jost, *Geschichte des Judenthums*, 2nd Abth., p. 419). And again: 'This man possessed an immense erudition; but his masterly spirit is far more to be wondered at than the mass of knowledge he acquired' (Id., *Geschichte des Israeliten*, 6te Theil, p. 162)." Mr. Campbell thinks that the distinctive features of the Rabbi of the poem were drawn by Mr. Browning from the writings of the real Rabbi, and that the philosophy which he puts into the mouth of Rabbi Ben Ezra was actually that of Rabbi Ibn Ezra. "It was no worldly success that gave peace to his age; but he had won a spiritual calm, no longer troubled by the doubts that at one time or another must come to all who think. 'While this remarkable man was roving about from east to west and from north to south, his mind remained firm in the principles he had once for all accepted as true. . . . His advocacy of freedom of thought and research, his views concerning angels, concerning the immortality of the soul, are the same in the earlier commentaries . . . as with [those] which were written later; the same in his grammatical works as in his theological discourses'" (Dr. M. Friedlander, *Essays on Ibn Ezra*, Preface and p. 139). "Our times are in His hand," says Browning's Rabbi; so, too, Ibn Ezra, in a poem quoted by Dr. Michael Sachs (*Die Religiose Poesie der Juden in Spanien*, p. 117)—"In deiner Hand liegt mein Geschichte." Says Dr. Friedlander, "He had very little money, and very much wit, and was a born foe to all superficiality. So he had spent his youth in preparing himself for his future career by collecting and storing up materials, in cultivating the garden of his mind so that it might at a later period produce the choicest and most precious fruits" (Ibn Ezra's *Comment.*, *Isaiah*, Introduction by Dr. Friedlander). Mr. Campbell says that the keynote of Ibn Ezra's teaching is that the essential life of man is the life of the soul. "Man has the sole privilege of becoming superior to the beast and the fowl, according to the words 'He teacheth him to raise himself above the cattle of the earth'" (Ibn Ezra, *Comment.*, *Job* xxxv. 11). "He ascribes to man's soul a triple nature, or three faculties roughly corresponding to the division of St. Paul of man into body, soul and spirit. The soul of man, he holds, can exist with or without the body, and did, in fact, preexist" (Friedlander, *Essays on Ibn Ezra*, pp. 27-8). This is Browning's theory in verse 27. In Browning's poem the Rabbi describes man's life as the *lone* way of the soul (verse 8). Ibn Ezra, in his *Commentary*, *Psalm* xxii. 22, says, "The soul of man is called lonely because it is separated during its union with the body from the universal soul, into which it is again received when it departs from its earthly companion." When Rabbi Ben Ezra, in Mr. Browning's poem, speaks of the body at its best projecting the soul on its way (verse 8), he is uttering the thought of Ibn Ezra, who says, "It is well known that, as long as the bodily desires are strong, the soul is weak and powerless against them, because they are supported by the body and all its powers: hence those who only think of eating and drinking will never be wise. By the alliance of the intellect with the animal soul [sensibility, the higher quality of the body] the desires [the lower quality or appetite of the body] are subordinated, and the eyes of the soul are opened a little, so as to comprehend the knowledge of material bodies; but the soul is not yet prepared for pure knowledge, on account of the animal soul which seeks dominion and produces all kinds of passion; therefore, after the victory gained with the support of the animal soul over the desires, it is necessary that the soul should devote itself to wisdom, and seek its support for the subjection of the passions, in order to remain under the sole control of knowledge" (Ibn Ezra, *Comment.*, *Eccl.* vii. 3). Mr. Campbell has shown how much Mr. Browning has assimilated Ibn Ezra's philosophy in many other points in the poem. (For an extended explanation of the poem see my *Browning's Message to his Time*, pp. 157-72.)

Rawdon Brown. "Mr. Rawdon Brown, an Englishman of culture, well known to visitors in Venice, died in that city in the summer of 1883. He went to Venice for a short visit, with a definite object in view, and ended by staying forty years. During one of his rare runs to England, I met him at Ruskin's at Denmark Hill, somewhere about 1860. He englished, abstracted, and calendared for our Record Office, a large number of the reports of the Venetian Ambassadors in England in the days of Elizabeth, etc. His love for Venice was so great, that some one invented about him the story which Browning told in the following sonnet, which was printed by Browning's permission, and that of Mrs. Bronson—at whose request it was written—in the *Century Magazine* 'Bric-à-Brac' for February 1884" (Dr. Furnivall in *Browning Society's Papers*, vol. i., p. 132*).

"Tutti ga i so gusti, e mi go i mii."—*Venetian Saying.*

(*Tr.* Everybody follows his taste, and I follow mine.)

Sighed Rawdon Brown: "Yes, I'm departing, Toni!
I needs must, just this once before I die,
Revisit England: *Anglus* Brown am I,
Although my heart's Venetian. Yes, old crony—
Venice and London—London's 'Death the bony'
Compared with Life—that's Venice! What a sky,
A sea, this morning! One last look! Good-bye.
Cà Pesaro! No, lion—I'm a coney
To weep—I'm dazzled; 'tis that sun I view
Rippling the—the—*Cospetto*, Toni! Down
With carpet-bag, and off with valise-straps!
Bella Venezia, non ti lascio più!"
Nor did Brown ever leave her: well, perhaps
Browning, next week, may find himself quite Brown!

Nov. 28th, 1883. ROBERT BROWNING.

Reason and Fancy. The discussion between Reason and Fancy is in *La Saisiaz*.

Red Cotton Night-cap Country, or Turf and Towers (1873). This may be termed a pathological poem, a study of suicidal mania and religious insanity in a young man of dissipated habits whose "mind" was scarcely worthy of the poet's analysis. The title given to the work was so bestowed in consequence of Mr. Browning having met Miss Thackeray in a part of Normandy which she jokingly christened "White Cotton Night-cap Country," on account of its sleepiness. Mr. Browning having heard the tragedy which his story tells, said "Red Cotton Night-cap Country" would be the more appropriate term. The alternative title, "Turf and Towers," is much more likely to have been suggested by the scenery of the place than by the more fanciful reasons which have sometimes been imagined for it. The scene of the story is in the department of Calvados, close to the city of Caen. The whole country is very interesting, from its historical associations and architectural remains, and the scenery is exceedingly beautiful. M. de Caumont, the distinguished archæologist of Caen, enumerates nearly seventy specimens of the Norman architecture of the eleventh and twelfth centuries existing in it. Battlemented walls furnished with towers, picturesque chateaux, old churches and tall spires in a landscape of luxuriant pastures and grey and purple hills, justified the title "Turf and Towers," even apart from the particular circumstances connected with the story. Mr. Browning visited St. Aubin's in 1872, and was interested in the singular history of the family which owned Clairvaux, a restored priory in the locality. Léonce Miranda, the son and heir of a wealthy Paris jeweller, led a dissipated life in his times of leisure, but industriously pursued his calling in strictly business hours. After devoting his attentions to a number of light-o'-loves, he one day fell in love with an adventuress, one Clara Mulhausen, who succeeded in securing him in her toils. As she was already married, the connection was of a nature to be carried on in seclusion, and the jeweller accordingly left a manager in charge of his business, retiring with the woman to Clairvaux, where his father had already purchased property. For five years the couple lived together in what was considered to be happiness. Then Miranda was suddenly called to Paris to account to his mother for his extravagance: he had spent large sums in building operations, having amongst other things erected a Belvedere (a sort of tower above the roof built for viewing the scenery). He so felt the reproaches of his mother that he attempted to commit suicide by throwing himself into the Seine. He was saved, however, and having been restored by Clara's nursing, was convalescent when he was again urgently summoned to his mother, only to find her dead. He was told that his conduct was responsible for his mother's death; and his relatives, careless of the consequences to a mind so unhinged as Miranda's, spared him none of their upbraidings. All this had the anticipated effect: he gave up the bulk of his property to his relatives, reserving only enough for his decent support and that of Clara. When the day arrived for the legal arrangements to be completed, he was found in a room reading and burning in the fire a number of letters. He had afterwards, so it was discovered, placed a number of the papers in a bag and held it in the fire till his hands were destroyed, at the same time crying, "Burn, burn and purify my past." If anything more than what had already happened were necessary to prove the man's insanity, the fact that he inflicted this terrible injury upon himself was sufficient evidence on the point. He declared that he was working out his salvation, and had to be dragged from the room protesting that the sacrifice was incomplete: "I must have more hands to burn!" He lay in a fevered condition for three months, raving against the temptress. When he was sufficiently restored to health he took her back to his heart, saying, however, "Her sex is changed: this is my brother—he will tend me now." He disposed of the jeweller's shop to his relatives, and went back to Clairvaux with the woman. At this point Mr. Browning brings the would-be suicide under the influence of religion; the man devoted his substance liberally to the poor, and made many gifts to the Church: it was "ask and have" with this kind Miranda, who was striving to save his soul by acts of charity. It happened that there was a pilgrimage chapel of *La Déliverande* near Clairvaux, called in the poem, rather oddly, "The Ravissante." The Norman sailors and peasants have resorted to this place of devotion for the last eight hundred years. Murray says: "It is a small Norman edifice. The statue of the Virgin, which now commands the veneration of the faithful, was resuscitated in the reign of Henry I. from the ruins of a previous chapel destroyed by the Northmen, through the agency of a lamb constantly grubbing up the earth over the spot where it lay. Such is the tenor of the legend. The reputation of the image for performing miracles, especially in behalf of sailors, has been maintained from that time to the present." Of course Miranda paid many visits to Our Lady's shrine; many prayers had been heard and answered there,—why should not La Déliverande help him? One splendid day in spring he mounts the stairs of his view-tower, and, as the poet imagines, addresses the Virgin in exalted phrase. He declares that he burned his hands off because she had prompted, "Purchase now by pain pleasure hereafter in the world to come." He had lightened his purse even if his soul still retained forbidden treasure, and "Where is the reward?" He reproaches Our Lady that she has done nothing to help him. She is Queen of Angels: will she suspend for him the law of gravity if he casts himself from the tower? He tells her it will restore religion to France, to the world, if this miracle is worked. He sees Our Lady smile assent: he will trust himself. He springs from the balustrade, and lies stone dead on the turf the next moment. "Mad!" exclaimed a gardener who saw him fall. "No! Sane," says Mr. Browning. "He put faith to the proof. He believed in Christianity for its miracles, not for its moral influence on the heart of man; better test such faith at once—'kill or cure.'" By a later will Miranda had bequeathed all his property to the Church, reserving sufficient for the support of Clara. Of course the relatives interfered, with the idea of securing the property for themselves. This led to a trial, which was decided in the lady's favour, and she was châtelaine of Clairvaux where Browning saw her in 1872. The real names of the persons and places are not given in the poem, and there is no good purpose to be served by giving a key to them.

NOTES.—[The pages are those of the first edition of the Poem.] Page 2, "*Un-Murrayed*": unfrequented by tourists who carry Murray's or Bædeker's guide-books. p. 4, *Saint-Rambert* = St. Aubin, a pretty bathing-place in Calvados, Normandy; *Joyous-Gard:* the estate given by King Arthur to Sir Launcelot of the Lake for defending Guinevere. p. 6, *Rome's Corso:* the principal modern thoroughfare of Rome is the Corso. p. 18, *Guarnerius*, Andreas, and his son Giuseppe, early Italian violin makers; *Straduarius*, Antonio: a famous violin maker of Cremona (1649-1737). p. 19, *Corelli* (1653-1713): a celebrated violin player and composer; *cushat-dove* = the ring-dove or wood-pigeon; *giga* = *gigg:* a jig, a dance; *Saraband:* a grave Spanish dance in triple time. p. 23, "*Quod semel, semper, et ubique*": what was once, and is always and everywhere. This would seem to be intended for the celebrated rule of St. Vincent of Lerins as to the Catholic Faith—"Quod ubique, quod semper, quod ad omnibus creditum est. Hoc est etenim vere proprieque catholicum" (*Comm.*, c. 3)—that is to say, the Catholic doctrine is that which has been believed in all places, at all times, and by all the faithful. p. 24, *Rahab-thread:* see Joshua ii. 18. p. 25, *Octroi:* a tax levied at the gate of Continental cities on food, etc., brought within the walls. p. 29, *The Conqueror's country:* Normandy, the native country of William the Conqueror. p. 30, *Lourdes* and *La Salette:* celebrated places of pilgrimage in France. p. 37, *Abaris:* a priest of Apollo; he rode through the air, invisible, on a golden arrow, curing diseases and giving oracles. p. 42, *Madrilene*, of Madrid. p. 73, *Father Secchi:* the great Jesuit astronomer of Rome. p. 83, *Acromia:* in anatomy, the outer extremities of the shoulder-blades. p. 84, *Sganarelle:* the hero of Molière's comedy *Le Mariage Forcé.* A man aged about fifty-four proposes to marry a fashionable young woman, but he has certain scruples which, however, are allayed by the cudgel of the lady's brother. p. 87, *Caen:* an ancient and celebrated city of Normandy. p. 88, "*Inveni ovem* [*meam*] *qua perierat*": "I have found my sheep which was lost" (St. Luke xv. 6). p. 108, *Favonian breeze:* the west wind, favourable to vegetation; *Auster:* an unhealthy wind, the same as the Sirocco. p. 140, *L'Ingegno*, Andrea Luigi. p. 141, *Boileau:* the great French poet, born at Paris 1636; *Louis Quatorze:* Louis XIV., king of France; *Pierre Corneille:* the great dramatic poet (1606-84), born at Rouen. p. 177, "*Religio Medici*": a doctor's religion; the title of the celebrated book of Sir Thomas Browne, a devout Christian writer; the new religion of the hyper-scientific school of doctors is mere materialism. p. 193, *Rouher*, Eugene: French politician (1814-84); *Œcumenical Assemblage at Rome:* a general or universal council of the bishops of the Roman Catholic Church. p. 202, *fons et origo:* the fount and origin. p. 203, "*On Christmas morn—three Masses*": the first is the midnight mass, the second at break of day, the third is the Christmas morning mass. p. 204, *Cistercian monk:* of an Order established at Citeaux, in France, by Robert, abbot of Moleme. The Order is very severe; but its rule is similar to that of the Benedictines; *Capucin:* a monk of the Order of St. Francis; *Benedict:* St. Benedict, "the most illustrious name in the history of Western monasticism": he was born at Nursia, in Umbria, about the year 480; *Scholastica:* St. Scholastica was the sister of St. Benedict: she established a convent near Monte Cassino. p. 210, *Star of Sea:* Stella Maris, one of the titles of Our Lady, because *mare* means "the sea" in Latin. p. 229, *Commines* (more correctly Comines): Philippe de Comines (1445-1509), called "the father of modern history." Hallam says that his *Memoirs* "almost make an epoch in modern history." p. 234, "*Queen of Angels*": one of the titles of the Blessed Virgin Mary. p. 235, "*Legations to the Pope*": ambassadors or envoys to the Pope of Rome. p. 238, *Alacoque:* the Ven. Margaret Mary Alacoque, who founded the devotion to the Sacred Heart of Jesus in France; "*Renan burns his book*": Ernest Renan, born 1823, the famous French philologist and historian, author of the Rationalistic *Life of Jesus*, which of course he did not burn! "*Veuillot burns Renan*": Louis Veuillot (1813-83), a celebrated French writer of the Ultramontane school, who would gladly have suppressed Renan if he had had the opportunity; "*The Universe*": the famous Catholic journal edited by Veuillot. p. 245, *Lignum vitæ:* Guaiacum wood, used in rheumatism, etc.; *grains of Paradise:* an aromatic drug with carminative properties, like ginger. p. 268, "*Painted Peacock*": the butterfly whose scientific name is the *Vanessa io*; *Brimstone-wing*: the species of butterfly so called from its bright yellow colour. Its scientific name is the *Rhodocera Rhamna.*

Religious Belief of Browning. There was little or no dogmatism in Browning's religious faith. He was at least a Theist. "He believed in Soul, and was very sure of God." Whether the orthodox would consider him a Christian in the sense of the old churches is a matter we cannot discuss here; in the widest sense, however, he has given abundant evidence that he was a Christian. Those who maintain him to be a believer in the Divinity of Christ ground their opinion on such poems as *A Death in the Desert* and *The Epistle of Karshish*—which, nevertheless, it is objected, are merely dramatic utterances, and cannot fairly be held to set forth the poet's own convictions; to such an opponent I should be content to point to the following letter, published just after the poet's death in *The Nonconformist*, and reprinted in the Transactions of the Browning Society. It was written by Browning in 1876 to a lady, who, believing herself to be dying, wrote to thank him for the help she had derived from his poems, mentioning particularly *Rabbi Ben Ezra* and *Abt Vogler*, and giving expression to the deep satisfaction of her mind that one so highly gifted with genius should hold, as Browning held, to the great truths of our religion, and to a belief in the glorious unfolding and crowning of life in the world beyond the grave:—" 19, *Warwick Crescent, W., May 11th*, 1876. Dear Friend,—It would ill become me to waste a word on my own feelings, except inasmuch as they can be common to us both in such a situation as you described yours to be—and which, by sympathy, I can make mine by the anticipation of a few years at most. It is a great thing—the greatest—that a human being should have passed the probation of life, and sum up its experience in a witness to the power and love of God. I dare congratulate you. All the help I can offer, in my poor degree, is the assurance that I see ever more reason to hold by the same hope—and that, by no means in ignorance of what has been advanced to the contrary; and for your sake I would wish it to be true that I had so much of 'genius' as to permit the testimony of an especially privileged insight to come in aid of the ordinary argument. For I know I myself have been aware of the communication of something more subtle than a ratiocinative process, when the convictions of 'genius' have thrilled my soul to its depth, as when Napoleon, shutting up the New Testament, said of Christ—'Do you know that I am an understander of men? Well, He was no man! ('Savez-vous que je me connais en hommes? Eh bien, celui-là ne fut pas un homme.') Or as when Charles Lamb, in a gay fancy with some friends as to how he and they would feel if the greatest of the dead were to appear suddenly in flesh and blood once more—on the final suggestion, 'And if Christ entered this room?' changed his manner at once, and stuttered out—as his manner was when moved, 'You see—if Shakespeare entered, we should all rise; if *He* appeared, we must kneel.' Or, not to multiply instances, as when Dante wrote what I will transcribe from my wife's Testament—wherein I recorded it fourteen years ago—'Thus I believe, thus I affirm, thus I am certain it is, that from this life I shall pass to another better, there, where that lady lives, of whom my soul was enamoured.' Dear Friend, I may have wearied you in spite of your good will. God bless you, sustain, and receive you! Reciprocate this blessing with yours affectionately, ROBERT BROWNING." The Agnostic school is indefatigable in endeavouring to secure Browning as a great representative of their "know-nothingism," whatever that may be. They might as reasonably claim Robert Browning on the side of Agnosticism as John Henry Newman on the side of Atheism, which also certain wiseacres in their crass hebetude or vain affectation have pretended to do.

Religious Poems. (1) More or less expressions of the poet's own faith are "La Saisiaz," "Christmas Eve and Easter Day," "The Epistle of Karshish," "Rabbi Ben Ezra," "The Pope" (in *The Ring and the Book*), and "Prospice." (2) Dramatic utterances concerning religion may be found in "Caliban upon Setebos," "A Death in the Desert," "Saul," and "Johannes Agricola," amongst many others.

Renan (Epilogue to *Dramatis Personæ*). The "second speaker" in the Epilogue is described as Renan. Joseph Ernest Renan, philologist, member of the Institute of France, was born Feb. 27th, 1823. He is best known by his *Life of Jesus*.

Rephan (*Asolando*, 1889). "Suggested," as the poet says in a note prefixed to the poem, "by a very early recollection of a pure story by the noble woman and imaginative writer, Jane Taylor, of Norwich."* It will assist the reader to understand the poem if I give an outline of the story which lived so long in Browning's memory and suggested these verses. "Rephan" is the star mentioned in Jane Taylor's beautiful story "How it Strikes a Stranger," contained in the first volume of her work entitled *The Contributions of Q. Q.* Mrs. Oliphant, in her *Literary History of the Nineteenth Century*, vol. ii., p. 351, thus describes "How it Strikes a Stranger." "A little epilogue in which the supposed impression made upon the mind of an angel whose curiosity has tempted him, even at the cost of sharing their mortality, to descend among men, is the theme, recurs to our mind from the recollections of youth with considerable force." In one of the most ancient and magnificent cities of the East there ap-

* This is a mistake: it should be Ongar, not Norwich.

peared, in a remote period of antiquity, a stranger of extraordinary aspect. He had no knowledge of the language of the country, and was ignorant of its customs. One day, when residing with one of the nobles of the city, after having been taught the language of the people and having learned something of their modes of thought, he was seen to be gazing with fixed attention upon a certain star in the heavens. He explained that this was his home: he was lately an inhabitant of that tranquil planet, from whence a vain curiosity had tempted him to wander. When the first idea of death was explained to him, he was but slightly moved; but when he was informed that the happiness or misery of the immortal life depended upon a man's conduct in the present stage of existence, he was deeply moved, and demanded that he should be at once minutely instructed in all that was necessary to prepare himself for death. He lost all interest in wealth and pleasures, and astonished his friends by his absorption in the thoughts which concerned another life. Soon, people treated him with contempt, and even enmity; but this did not annoy him,—he was always kind and compassionate to those about him. To every invitation to do anything inconsistent with his real interests, his one answer was, "I am to die! I am to die!" As we might expect, Mr. Browning takes this simple and beautiful story, and imbues it with his own philosophy till he has made it his own. In the poem the wanderer from the star (Rephan), in compliance with the request of his friends, gives some account of the manner of his life before his human existence began upon our planet. In the land he has left—his native realm—all is at most, nowhere deficiency or excess; on this planet we but guess at a mean. In "Rephan" there is no want; whatever should be, *is*. There is no growth, for that is change; nothing begins and nothing ends; it fell short in nothing at first, no change was required to mend anything. The stranger explains that, to convey his thoughts, he has to use our language: his own no one who heard him could understand. In "Rephan" better and worse could not be contrasted; all was perfection. Blessing and cursing were alike impossible. There are neither springs nor winters. Time brings no hope and no fear: as is to-day so shall to-morrow be. All were happy, all serene. None were better than he: that would have proved that he lacked somewhat; none worse, for he was faultless. How came it that his perfection grew irksome? How was it his desire arose to become a mortal on our earth? How did soul's quietude burst into discontent? How long had he stagnated there, where weak and strong, wise and foolish, right and wrong are merged in a neutral Best? He could not say, neither could he tell how the passion arose in his breast. He knew not how he came to learn love by hate, to aspire yet never reach, to suffer that one whom he loved might be happy, to wing knowledge for ignorance. He tells his hearers that they fear, they agonise and die, and he asks them have they no assurance that after this earth-life wrong will prove right? Do they not expect that making shall be mending in the sphere to which their yearnings tend? And so when in his pregnant breast the yearnings grew, a voice said to him: "Wouldst thou strive, not rest? burn and not smoulder? win by contest; no longer be content with wealth, which is but death? Then you have outlived "Rephan," you are beyond this sphere. There is a higher plane for you. Thy place now is Earth!" It is the old Browning story, the true mark of his highest teaching: the necessity of evil to evoke the highest good, the need of struggle for development, of contest for strength and victory. Simple, good Jane Taylor would not recognise her pretty fable as it comes from Browning's alembic in the form of *Rephan*.

Respectability. (*Men and Women*, 1855; *Lyrics*, 1863; *Dramatic Lyrics*, 1868.) The world will let us do just what we like, provided only we take out its licence; import what we like, only we must pay the customs duty; bring into the place what we please, only we must not omit the *octroi*. Defy or evade these, and the stamp of respectability being withheld, we lose caste. Everything depends on the Government stamp which the officers chalk-mark on our baggage. By conforming we gain the guinea stamp, but run a risk of losing the gold itself. The world proscribes not love, allows the caress, provided only we buy of it our gloves. What the world fears is our contempt for its licence. It is, however, exceedingly placable, and is quite ready to license anything if we pay it the fee and do it the homage. At the Institute, for example, Guizot, hating Montalembert (as Liberalism hates Ultramontanism in theory), will receive him with courtesy, not to say affection. "We are passing the lamps: put your best foot foremost!"

Return of the Druses, The. A TRAGEDY. (*Bells and Pomegranates*, IV., 1843.) [THE HISTORICAL FACTS.] The Syrian Druses occupy the mountainous region of the Lebanon and Anti-Lebanon. They are found also in the Auranitis and in Palestine proper, to the north-west of the Sea of Tiberias. Crypto-Druses —Druses not by race, but by religion—are believed to dwell in Egypt, near Cairo. It is said that the Syrian Druses number over eighty thousand warriors. They covet no proselytes, and are an exceedingly mysterious, uncommunicative people, though they keep on good terms, as far as possible, with their Christian and Mahometan neighbours. They respect the religion of others, but never disclose the secrets of their own. Of their origin very little has with certainty been ascertained. They do not accept the name of Druses, and regard the term as insulting. They call themselves "disciples of Hamsa," who was their Messiah, who came to them in the tenth century from the Land of the word of God. Next in rank to Hamsa are the four throne-angels. One of these was the missionary Bohaeddin. Mr. Browning probably refers to him under the name of Bahumid the Renovator. Moktana Bohaeddin committed the Word to writing, and intrusted it to a few initiates. They speak Arabic; but the Druses are not considered by ethnologists to belong to the Semitic family. They have a tradition that they belonged originally to China. Whatever may have been the origin of this people, it is evident that they are now a very mixed race, as their religion also is compounded of Judaism, Christianity, and Mahometanism. Mackenzie says: "They have a regular order of priesthood, and a kind of hierarchy. There is a regular system of passwords and signs." It is certain that there are to be found in their religion traces of Gnosticism and Magianism. One theory of their origin, to which the poet refers in the drama, is to the effect that the Druses are the descendants of a crusader, Count Dreux, who left Godfrey de Bouillon's army to settle in the Lebanon. "The rise and progress of the religion which gives unity to the race," according to the *Encyclopædia Britannica*, 9th edition, vol. vii., p. 484, "can be stated with considerable precision. As a system of thought it may be traced back in some of its leading principles to the Shiite sect of the Batenians, or Batiniya, whose main doctrine was that every outer has its inner, and every passage in the Koran an allegorical sense; and to the Karamatians, or Karamita, who pushed this method to its furthest limits; as a creed it is somewhat more recent. In the year 386 A.H. (996 A.D.) Hakim Biamrillahi (*i.e.*, he who judges by the command of God), the sixth of the Fatimite caliphs, began to reign; and during the next twenty-five years he indulged in a tyranny at once so terrible and so fantastic, that little doubt can be entertained of his insanity. As madmen sometimes do, he believed that he held direct intercourse with the Deity, or even that he was an incarnation of the Divine intelligence; and in 407 A.H., or 1016 A.D., his claims were made known in the mosque at Cairo, and supported by the testimony of Ismael Darazi.* The people showed such bitter hostility to the new gospel that Darazi was compelled to seek safety in flight; but even in absence he was faithful to his god, and succeeded in winning over the ignorant inhabitants of Lebanon. According to Druse authority this great conversion took place in the year 410 A.H. Meanwhile, the endeavours of the caliph to get his divinity acknowledged by the people of Cairo continued. The advocacy of Hasan ben Haidara Fergani was without avail; but in 408 A.H. the new religion found a more successful apostle in the person of Hamze ben Ali ben Ahmed, a Persian mystic, feltmaker by trade, who became Hakim's vizier, gave form and substance to his creed, and by his ingenious adaptation of its various dogmas to the prejudices of existing sects, finally enlisted an extensive body of adherents. In 411 the caliph was assassinated by contrivance of his sister Sitt Almulk; but it was given out by Hamze that he had only withdrawn for a season, and his followers were encouraged to look forward with confidence to his triumphant return. Darazi, who had acted independently in his apostolate, was branded by Hamze as a heretic; and thus, by a curious anomaly, he is actually held in detestation by the very sect which probably bears his name. The propagation of the faith, in accordance with Hamze's initiation, was undertaken by Ismael ben Muhammed *Temimi*, Muhammed ben *Wahab*, Abulkhair *Selama*, ben Abdalwahab ben Samurri, and Moktana Bohaeddin, the last of whom was known by his writings from Constantinople to the borders of India. In two letters addressed to the Emperor Constantine VIII. and Michael the Paphlagonian,

* The name Druses is generally, but not universally, believed to be derived from this Darazi.—E. B

he endeavours to prove that the Christian Messiah reappeared in the person of Hamze (or Hasam)." The Druses call themselves Unitarians or Muahhidin, and believe in the absolute unity of God. He is the essence of life, and although incomprehensible and invisible, is to be known through occasional manifestations in human form. Like the Hindūs, they hold that he was incarnated more than once on earth. Hamsa was the *precursor* of the last manifestation to be (the tenth *avatar*), not the inheritor of Hakem, who is yet to come. Hamsa was the personification of the "universal wisdom." Bohaeddin, in his writings, calls him the Messiah. They hold ideas on transmigration which are Pythagorean and cabalistic. They have seven great commandments, which are imparted equally to all the initiated. These would seem to be incorrectly given by most of the encyclopædias. Professor A. L. Rawson, of New York, who is an initiate into the mysteries of the religion of the Druses, gives the following as the actual tenets of the faith. (They are termed the seven "tablets").—1. The unity of God, or the infinite oneness of Deity; 2. The essential excellence of truth; 3. The law of toleration as to all men and women in opinion; 4. Respect for all men and women as to character and conduct; 5. Entire submission to God's decrees as to fate; 6. Chastity of body and mind and soul; 7. Mutual help under all conditions. The Druses believe that all other religions were merely intended to prepare the way for their own, and that allegorically it may be discovered in the Jewish and Christian Scriptures. They treat with the utmost reverence what are called the Four Books on Mount Lebanon. These are the Pentateuch, the Psalms, the Gospels, and the Koran. All are bound to keep the seven commandments of Hamsa above mentioned. [THE DRAMA.] Mr. Browning's drama does not appear to be founded upon any historical facts. The time occupied by the tragedy is one day. Djabal is an initiated Druse, a son of the last Emir, who, when his family was massacred in the island which is the scene of the drama, had made his escape to Europe. He has resolved to return to this islet of the southern Sporades, colonised by the Lebanon Druses and garrisoned by the Knights Hospitallers of Rhodes. He has felt within him a Divine call to liberate his countrymen and restore them to the land from which they are exiled. He dwells upon the wrongs which the people have suffered at the hands of their oppressors, and in his passionate love for his country, and a desire to gratify his revenge for the slaughter of his kindred, has determined to become their liberator. The tragedy opens with the deliberations of the Druse initiates, who are expecting the manifestation of the Hakeem, the incarnation of the vanished Khalif who is to free their people, and who is believed by them to have appeared in the person of Djabal, now returned to the oppressed tribe. The island is governed by a prefect appointed by the Knights of Rhodes in Europe. This prefect has used his authority in a cruel and oppressive manner. Djabal has taken upon himself the redemption of his people, and during his stay in Europe has made a firm friend of a young nobleman, Lois de Dreux, who is about to join the Order of the Knights of Rhodes. His period of probation is to be passed in the island, and for this purpose he has accompanied Djabal on his return. Djabal has secretly resolved that upon his return to his people the cruel prefect, who has almost extirpated the sheikhs, shall be slain. He has secured also the alliance of the Venetians, who have promised that a fleet of their ships shall be prepared to transport the Druses to their home in the Lebanon, and shall be in readiness to receive them when the murder of the prefect shall have liberated his countrymen. The complicated part of the story now begins. Anael is a Druse maiden whose devotion to her nation is the strongest passion of her soul, and who has vowed to wed no one but the man who has delivered her people from the tyranny which oppresses them. That he may win her heart Djabal has declared himself to be the Hakeem, who has become incarnate for the salvation of the Druse nation. He has declared himself to be the long hoped and prayed for divinity, and offered himself to the people in that character. His plan has perfectly succeeded. Anael and her tribe believe that Djabal is the real Hakeem, and that he will liberate the people, show himself as Divine, and exalt her with himself when the work is perfected. He has decreed the death of the tyrant, and Anael knows this. To Anael, Djabal is her God as well as her lover; yet she cannot worship him as Divine. "'Oh, why is it,' she asks,

> 'I cannot kneel to you?
> Never seem you—shall I speak the truth?—
> Never a God to me!
> 'Tis the man's hand,
> Eye, voice!'"

Djabal has deceived himself into a half belief in the sanctity of his mission; but as the day approaches when he is to fulfil his promises his heart fails him, and he loses faith in himself. He struggles with his own heart, and endeavours to be true to himself and people; but he has gone too far, the circumstances in which he is placed are too strong for him, and he is driven forward on the course on which he has entered. He now resolves to solve the difficulty by flight. He will make his escape, but before he does so will kill the prefect with his own hands. He is on his way to the tyrant's chamber when he meets Anael, and learns from her that she has slain the prefect. He now tells her everything. At first she declines to believe in his falseness; but when a conviction of the truth is forced upon her she refuses to drive him from her heart. The Divine nature of Djabal has been in a sense an obstacle to her love in his character as Hakeem. He has seemed too remote for her merely human affection, and she has never deemed herself worthy to be associated with him in his exaltation. In her determination to kill the tyrant, and in the accomplishment of that act of patriotism, she has been actuated principally by her desire to elevate herself to his level, so that she might have a principal share in the liberation of her nation. They now discover that the murder need not have been committed. Lois de Dreux, the young nobleman who has accompanied Djabal from Europe, has fallen in love with Anael also; and though prohibited by the rules of the Order of knighthood of which he is a postulant, to entangle himself with women, he has aspired to win her love. Lois has represented to the chapter of the Order the cruelties inflicted by their prefect on the people, and has succeeded in obtaining an order for his removal. The young Frankish knight has been elevated by the Order to the position occupied by the deposed governor, so that the liberation of the Druses is now close at hand. Anael urges Djabal to confess his deception and own his imposition to his people. This he refuses to do. She cannot forgive him. When she finds him false and cowardly she takes upon herself to denounce him to the European rulers of the island. Djabal is brought to trial. His accuser is Anael, who is closely veiled till the appropriate moment, when the veil drops, and he is confronted by his lover. His life hangs upon her words. He urges her to speak them; but this she cannot do. Djabal is now man, and man only: he is not separated from her by his Divine nature. She could hardly hope to be one with him in his glory: she can at least be united with him in his degradation and disgrace. All her love for him rises within her, and she hails him "Hakeem!" and falls dead at his feet. The human heart has proved victorious, and the man has conquered the god. Djabal, committing the care of the Druses to his friend Lois, and bidding him guard his people home again and win their blessing for the deed, stabs himself as he bends over the body of the faithful Anael. As he dies the Venetians enter the place and plant the Lion of St. Mark. Djabal's last cry mingles with their shouts, "On to the mountain! At the mountain, Druses!"

NOTES.—Act i., *Rhodian cross:* that of the Knights of St. John (see below). *Osman,* who founded the Ottoman empire in Asia. *White-cross knights:* the Knights Hospitallers. They wore a white cross of eight points on a black ground. From 1278 till 1289, when engaged on military duties, they wore a plain straight white cross on a red ground. *Patriarch:* in Eastern churches a dignitary superior to an archbishop, as the Patriarch of Constantinople, Alexandria, etc. *Nuncio:* an ambassador from the Pope to an emperor or king. *Hospitallers:* an order of knights who built a hospital at Jerusalem, in A.D. 1042, for pilgrims. They were called *Knights of St. John,* and after the removal of the order to Malta *Knights of Malta.* *Candia:* the ancient Crete. It was sold to the Venetians in 1194. *Rhodes:* an island of the Mediterranean. "*pro fide*": for the faith. "*Bouillon's war*": the crusade of Godfrey de Bouillon.—Act ii., "*sweet cane*": Acorus calamus. It grows in the Levant and in this country; is very aromatic, having a smell when trodden on like incense. Miss Pratt says it has been used from time immemorial for strewing the floors of Norwich Cathedral. *Lilith:* Adam's first wife (see note to ADAM, LILITH and EVE, and art. LILITH). "*incense from a mage-king's tomb*": students of occult science say that sweet odours have been known to issue from the tombs of magicians, and lamps have been found burning therein when broken open. *khandjar:* an Eastern weapon.—Act. iii., *The venerable chapter:* the meeting of an order or community. *Bezants:* gold coins of Byzantium. "*Red-cross rivals of the Temple*": the order of the "Knights Templars" (see notes to *The Heretics' Tragedy*). They wore a red cross of eight points.—Act iv., *Tiar:* a tiara.—Act v., *Biamrallah*. Hakem Biamr Allah, sixth Fatimite Caliph of Egypt. *Fatemite*, or *Fatimite:* named from Fatima, the daughter of Mohammed and wife of Ali, from whom the founder of the dynasty of Fatimites professed to have sprung. "*Romaioi, Ioudaioite kai proselutoi*" (*Gr.*, Acts ii. 10, 11): "Strangers of Rome, Jews and proselytes."

Reverie. (*Asolando*, 1889.) In Mr. Browning's last volume, published in London as he lay dying in Venice, the two closing poems seem strangely and nobly intended to gather into a focus his whole philosophy of life, and give to the world, in two of his most exquisite poems, his fullest and clearest expressions of the faith of his heart and the quintessence of his teaching. Had the poet known they were the last lines he should write, had he foreseen that these were the last accents of his message, it is impossible to imagine that he could have risen higher than he has done in *Reverie* and the "Epilogue." The purport of *Reverie* is to reconcile the ideas of Power and Love—to reconcile by proving them indeed to be one. "Power is Love." When power is no longer limited, then is the reign of love. As Mr. Browning says in *Paracelsus*, "with much power always much more love." That "The All-Great" is "The All-Loving too," is the teaching of Christianity. That power, in its perfection, must *necessarily* be love, is a point in Mr. Browning's philosophical system arrived at independently of dogma. It is the monistic conception of the forces that mould life, as opposed to the dualistic conception. The Power everywhere visible in the universe, pervading everything, in all things from the atom to the sun, making man feel his utter helplessness and insignificance, requires no further demonstration. We are assured that Power is dominant. Our only difficulty is about Love. In face of the evil in the world, the inequalities in life, the dominance of evil, can we say with truth that the All-Powerful is the All-Loving too? Browning in *Reverie* says that truth comes before us here "fitful and half guessed, half seen, grasped at, not gained, held fast." Notwithstanding this defect, a single page of the world's wide book, properly deciphered, explains the whole. We must try the clod ere we test the star; know all our earth elements ere we apply the spectroscope to Mars. It is true that good struggles but evil reigns; yet earth's good is proved good and incontrovertibly worth loving, and evil can be nothing but a cloud stretched across good's orb—no orb itself. There is no doubt whatever about the infinity of the power. There is equally no doubt about the value of the good so far as it goes. Let power "but enlarge good's strait confine," and perfection stands revealed. "Let on Power devolve Good's right to co-equal reign!" What is wanted is some law which abolishes everywhere that which thwarts good. And the poet avows his confidence that somewhen Good will praise God unisonous with Power.

Richard, Count of St. Bonifacio (father and son). (*Sordello.*) Guelfs. In a secret chamber in his palace Palma and Sordello hold earnest conference with each other in the first book of the poem.

Ring and the Book, The. In twelve books. Published in four volumes, each consisting of three books, from 1868 to 1869.

Book I.—When a Roman jeweller makes a ring, he mingles his pure gold with a certain amount of alloy, so as to enable it to bear file and hammer; but, the ring having been fashioned, the alloy is dissolved out with acid, and the ring in all its purity and beauty of pure gold remains perfect. So much for the Ring. For the Book it happened thus:—Mr. Browning was one day wandering about the Square of St. Lorenzo, in Florence, which on that occasion was crammed with booths where odd things of all sorts were for sale; and in one of them he purchased for eightpence an old square yellow book, part print, part manuscript, with this summary of its contents:—

"A Roman murder case;
Position of the entire criminal cause
Of Guido Franceschini, nobleman,
With certain Four the cut-throats in his pay,
Tried, all five, and found guilty and put to death
By heading or hanging as befitted ranks,
At Rome, on February Twenty-Two,
Since our Salvation Sixteen Ninety-Eight:
Wherein it is disputed if, and when,
Husbands may kill adulterous wives, yet 'scape
The customary forfeit."

As before the ring was fashioned the pure gold lay in the ingot, so the pure virgin truth of the murder case lay in this book; but it was not in a presentable form and such as a poet could use.

As the jeweller adds a little alloy to permit the artistic working of the Ring, so the poet must mix his poetic fancy with the simple legal evidence contained in the Book, and in this manner work up the history for popular edification. And thus we have *The Ring and the Book.* The simple, hard, legal documents opened the story thus. The accuser and the accused said, in the persons of their advocates, as follows:—The Public Prosecutor demands the punishment of Count Guido Franceschini and his accomplices, for the murder of his wife. Then the Patron of the Poor—the counsel acting on behalf of the accused—protests that Count Guido ought rather to be rewarded, with his four conscientious friends, as sustainers of law and society. It is true, he says, that he killed his wife, but he did it laudably. Then the case was postponed. It was argued that the woman slaughtered was a saint and martyr. More postponement. Then it was argued that she was a miracle of lust and impudence. More witnesses, precedents, and authorities called and quoted on both sides:

> "Thus wrangled, brangled, jangled they a month,"—

only on paper—all the pleadings were in print. The Court pronounced Count Guido guilty, his murdered wife Pompilia pure in thought, word and deed; and signed sentence of death against the whole five accused. But Guido's counsel had a reserve shot. The Count, as was the frequent custom in those days, was in one of the minor orders of the priesthood, and claimed clerical privilege. Appeal was therefore made to the Pope. Roman society began to talk, the quality took the husband's part, the Pope was benevolent and unwilling to take life: Guido stood a chance of getting off. But the Pope was shrewd and conscientious; and having mastered the whole matter, said, "Cut off Guido's head to-morrow, and hang up his mates." And it was so done. Thus much was untempered gold, as discovered in the little old book. But we want to know more of the matter, and in four volumes (of the original edition) Mr. Browning satisfies us. Who was the handsome young priest, Canon Caponsacchi, who carried off the wife? Who were the old couple, the Comparini, Pietro and his spouse, who, on a Christmas night in a lonely villa, were murdered with Pompilia? Mr. Browning has ferreted it out for us and mixed his fancy with the facts to bring them home to us the better. He has been to Arezzo, the Count's city—the wife's "trap and cage and torture place." He stopped at Castelnuovo, where husband and wife and priest for first and last time met face to face. He passed on to Rome the goal, to the home of Pompilia's foster-parents. He conjures up the vision of the dreadful night when Guido and his wolves cried to the escaped wife, "Open to Caponsacchi!" and the door was opened, showing the mother of the two-weeks'-old babe and her parents the Comparini. He ponders all the story in his soul in Italy, and in London when he returns home, till the ideas take clear shape in his mind, and the whole story lives again in his brain, and he can reproduce for us the facts as they must have occurred. Count Guido Franceschini was descended of an ancient though poor family. He was

> "A beak-nosed, bushy-bearded, black-haired lord,
> Lean, pallid, low of stature, yet robust,
> Fifty years old."

He married Pompilia Comparini—young, good, beautiful—at Rome, where she was born; and brought her to his home at Arezzo, where they lived miserable lives. That she might find peace, the wife had run away, in company of the priest Giuseppe Caponsacchi, to her parents at Rome; and the husband had followed with four accomplices, and catching her in a villa on a Christmas night with her parents (putative parents really), had killed the three; the wife being seventeen years old, and the Comparini, husband and wife, seventy. There was Pompilia's infant, Guido's firstborn son, but he had previously put it in a place of safety.

NOTES.—Line 7, *Castellani:* a celebrated Roman jeweller (Piazza di Trevi 86), who executes admirable imitations from Greek, Etruscan, and Byzantine models. *Chiusi:* a very ancient Etruscan city, full of antiquities and famous for its tombs. l. 27, *rondure*, a round. l. 45, *Baccio Bandinelli*, a sculptor of Florence (1497-1559). l. 47, "*John of the Black Bands*"*:* Father of Cosimo I., Giovanni delle Bande Neri. l. 48, *Riccardi:* the palace of one of the great families of Florence. l. 49, *San Lorenzo*, the great church so named in Florence. l. 77, *Spicilegium*, a collection made from the best writers. l. 114, "*Casa Guidi, by Felice Church*"*:* this was the residence of the Brownings at Florence when he bought the little book. l. 223, *Justinian*,

Emperor of the East A.D. 527. His name is immortalised by his code of laws; *Baldo*, an eminent professor of the civil law, and also of canon law, born in 1327; *Bartolo* of Perugia, a professor of civil law, under whom Baldo studied; *Dolabella*, the name of a Roman family; *Theodoric*, king of the Ostrogoths (*c.* A.D. 454-526); *Ælian*, a writer on natural history in the time of Adrian. l. 263, *Presbyter*, *Primæ tonsuræ*, *Subdiaconus*, *Sacerdos*: these are some of the different steps to the priesthood in the Roman Church —that is to say, First tonsure, subdeacon, deacon, priest. l. 284, *Ghetto*, the Jewish quarter in Rome. l. 300, *Pope Innocent XII.* was *Antonio Pignatelli.* He reigned from 1691 to 1700. He introduced many reforms into the Church, and, after a holy and self-abnegating life, died on September 27th, 1700; *Jansenists*, followers of Jansen, who taught Calvinism in the Catholic Church; *Molinists*, followers of Molinos, who taught Arminianism in the Catholic Church; *Nepotism*, favouritism to relations. l. 435, *temporality*: the material interests of the Catholic Church. l. 490, "*gold snow Jove rained on Rhodes*": as the Rhodians were the first who offered sacrifices to Minerva, Jupiter rewarded them by covering the island with a golden cloud, from which he sent showers of treasures on the people. l. 495, *Datura*: the thorn apple—stramonium. l. 496, *lamp-fly* = a fire-fly. l. 868, *Æacus*, son of Jupiter; on account of his just government made judge in the lower regions with Minos and Rhadamanthus. l. 898, "*Bernini's Triton fountain*:" in the great square of the Barberini Palace, the Tritons blowing the water from a conch-shell. l. 1028, "*chrism and consecrative work*": Chrism is the oil used in ordination, etc., in the Roman and Greek Catholic Churches. l. 1030, *lutanist*, one who plays on the lute. l. 1128, "*Procurator of the Poor*": a proctor, an attorney who acts on behalf of the poor. l. 1161, *Fisc*, a king's solicitor, an attorney-general. l. 1209, *clavicinist*, one who plays on the clavichord. l. 1212, *rondo* = rondeau, a species of lively melody with a recurring refrain; *suite*, a connected series of musical compositions. l. 1214, *Corelli*, *Arcangelo*, Italian musical composer; *Haendel*, Handel the musician. l. 1311, "*Brotherhood of Death*": the Confraternity of the Misericordia, or Brothers of Mercy, who prepare criminals for death and attend funerals as an act of charity. l. 1328, *Mannai*, a sort of guillotine.—This seems a fitting place in which to insert the following note, which serves to explain the origin of the great poem:—

In *The Christian Register* of Boston for Jan. 19th, 1888, there is an article entitled "An Eagle Feather," by the Rev. John W. Chadwick, of Brooklyn. This clergyman visited Mr. Browning and asked him, "And how about the book of *The Ring and the Book*? Had he made up that, too, or was there really such a book? There was indeed; and would we like to see it? There was little doubt of that; and it was produced, and the story of his buying it for 'eightpence English just' was told, but need not be retold here, for in *The Ring and the Book* it is set down with literal truth. The appearance and character of the book, moreover, are exactly what the poem represents. It is part print, part manuscript, ending with two epistolary accounts, if I remember rightly, of Guido's execution, written by the lawyers in the case. It was an astonishing 'find,' and it is passing strange that a book compiled so carefully should have been brought to such a low estate. Mr. Browning did not seem at all inclined to toss it in the air and catch it, as he does in verse. He handled it very carefully, and with evident affection. I asked him if it did not make him very happy to have created such a woman as Pompilia; and he said, 'I assure you that I found her just as she speaks and acts in my poem, in that old book.' There was that in his tone that made it evident Caponsacchi had a rival lover without blame. Of the old pope of the poem, too, he spoke with real affection. He told us how he had found a medal of him in a London antiquary's shop, had left it meaning to come back for it; came back, and found that it had gone. But the shopman told him Lady Houghton (Mrs. Richard Monckton Milnes) had taken it. 'You will lend it to me,' said Mr. Browning to her, 'in case I want it some time to be copied for an illustration?' She preferred giving it to him; had most likely intended doing so when she bought it. It was in a pretty little box, and had a benignant expression, exactly suited to the character of the good pope in the poem. As a further proof that all is grist that comes to some folks' mills, there was a picture of the miserable Count Guido Franceschini on his execution day, which some one had come upon in a London printshop and sent to Mr. Browning."

Mr. Browning having told the incidents of the story in all their principal details, might, in the ordinary way, have considered this sufficient. He has reserved nothing till the last, and in the usual way would have destroyed the interest of his remaining volumes had he been a mere story-teller. His purpose, however, was different. He will now take the principal actors in the tragedy, and separately and at length let them give their account of it in their own language and according to their own view of the case. He will, moreover, give his readers the opposing views of the two halves into which the Roman populace have been divided on the murders. He will introduce us to the Pope considering the course of action he is called upon to pursue as supreme judge of the matter; and the very lawyers, who are preparing their briefs and getting up their speeches, will also have their say. We shall thus have this many-sided subject put before us in every possible way; and we shall be enabled to follow the windings of the human mind on such a subject as though we were centred in the breast, in turn, of each of the actors in the dreadful drama We have, therefore, in

Book I., The dry facts of the case in brief;

Book II., HALF ROME (the view of those antagonistic to the wife);

Book III., THE OTHER HALF ROME (representing the opinion of those who take her part);

Book IV., TERTIUM QUID (a third party, neither wholly on one side nor the other);

Book V., COUNT GUIDO FRANCESCHINI (his own defence);

Book VI., GIUSEPPE CAPONSACCHI (the Canon's explanation);

Book VII., POMPILIA (her story, as she told it on her death-bed to the nuns);

Book VIII., DOMINUS HYACINTHUS DE ARCHANGELIS (Count Guido's counsel and his speech for the defence);

Book IX., JURIS DOCTOR JOHANNES-BAPTISTA BOTTINIUS (the Public Prosecutor's speech);

Book X., THE POPE (who in this book reviews the whole case, and gives his decision in Guido's appeal to him);

Book XI., GUIDO (his last interview in prison with his spiritual advisers);

Book XII., THE BOOK AND THE RING (the conclusion of the whole matter).

BOOK II., HALF ROME.—A great crowd had assembled at the church of St. Lorenzo-in-Lucina, hard by the Corso, to view the bodies of the murdered Comparini exposed to view before the altar. It was at this very church where Pompilia was baptised, brought by her pretended mother, who had purchased her to palm off on her husband in his dotage, and so cheat the heirs. To this very altar-step whereon the bodies lie did Violante, twelve years after, bring Pompilia to marry the Count clandestinely. It is four years since the marriage, and from dawn till dusk the multitude has crowded into the church, coming and going, pushing their way, and taking their turn to see the victims and talk over the tragedy. We have the story told by a partisan of the husband, who does not think he was so prodigiously to blame, he says. The Comparini (the wife's reputed parents) were of the modest middle class, born in that quarter of Rome, and citizens of good repute, childless and wealthy; possessed of house and land in Rome, and a suburban villa. But Pietro craved an heir, and seventeen years ago Violante announced that, spite of her age, an heir would soon be forthcoming. By a trick, Pompilia, the infant, was produced at the appropriate time—whereat Pietro rejoiced, poor fool! As Violante had caught one fish, she must try again, and find a husband for the girl. Count Guido was head of an old noble house, but not over-rich. He had come up to Rome to better his fortune, was friend and follower of a certain cardinal, and had a brother a priest, Paolo. Looking out for some petty post or other, he waited thirty years, till, as he was growing grey, he thought it time to go and be wise at home. At this moment Violante threw her bait, Pompilia. She thought it a great catch to find a noble husband for the child and the shelter of a palace for herself in her old age; and so old Pietro's daughter became Guido Franceschini's lady-wife. Pietro was not consulted till all was over, when he pretended to be very indignant. All went to Arezzo to enjoy the luxury of lord-and-lady-ship. They were soon undeceived. They discovered that they had exchanged their comfortable bourgeois home for a sepulchral old mansion, the street's disgrace, to pick garbage from a pewter plate and drink vinegar from a common mug. They sighed for their old home, their daily feast of good food and their festivals of better. Robbed, starved and frozen, they declared they would have justice. Guido's old lady-mother, Beatrice, was a dragon; Guido's brother, Girolamo, a bad licentious man. Four months of this purgatory was sufficient. Pietro made his complaints all over the town; Violante exposed the penurious housekeeping to every willing ear. Bidding Arezzo rot, they departed for home. Once more at Rome, Violante thought of availing herself of the Jubilee and making a full confession and restitution. She told the truth about Pompilia: how she had been purchased by her several months before birth from a disreputable laundry-woman, partly to please her husband, partly to defraud the rightful heirs. Was this due to contrition or revenge? Prove Pompilia not their child, there was no dowry to pay according to agreement. Guido would then be the biter bit. Guido took the view that all this was done to cheat him. He protested, and being left alone with his wife, revenged his wrongs on her. The case came before the Roman courts. Guido being absent, the Abate, his clerical brother, had to take his part. The courts refused to intervene. Appeals and counter-appeals followed. Pompilia's shame and her parents' disgrace were published to the world; and so it went on. Pompilia, left alone with her old husband, looked outside for life; and lo! Caponsacchi appeared—a priest, Apollos turned Apollo. He threw comfits to her at the theatre, at carnival time—no great harm—but he was, moreover, always hanging about the street where Guido's palace was. Pompilia observed him from her window. People began to talk, the husband to open his eyes. Things went on, till one April morning Guido awoke to find his wife flown. He had been drugged, he said. Caponsacchi, the handsome young priest, had brought a carriage for her: they had gone by the Roman road eight hours since. Guido started in pursuit, coming up with the fugitives just as they were in sight of Rome. Caponsacchi met the husband unabashed: "I interposed to save your wife from death, yourself from shame." Fingering his sword, he offered fight, or to stand on his defence at Rome. The police came up and secured the priest, and they went upstairs to arouse the wife. She overwhelmed her husband with invective, turning to her side even the very *sbirri*. "Take us to Rome," both prisoners demanded. Love letters and verses were produced, and husband and wife fought out their case before the lawyers. The accused declared that the letters were not written by them. The court found much to blame, but little to punish. The priest was sentenced to three years' exile at Civita Vecchia; the wife must go into a convent for a while. Guido was not satisfied: he claimed a divorce. Pompilia did the same. On account of her health a little liberty was allowed her, and she left the convent to reside with her pretended parents at their villa. Here she gave birth to a child. Guido was furious when he heard all this, and went to Rome to the villa with four confederates, pretending to be Caponsacchi. The door was opened, when he rushed in with his braves and killed them all; and so the two Comparini are lying in the church, and Pompilia is in the hospital dying of her wounds.

NOTES.—Line 84, *Guido Reni*, a painter of the Bolognese school, 1574-1642. The Crucifixion referred to is above the high altar. l. 126, "*Molino's doctrine*": a form of Quietism. l. 300, "*tacked to the Church's tail*": it was the custom in this age for gentlemen who desired the protection of the Church for their own purposes to take one of the minor orders, without any intention of going into the diaconate or priesthood. Count Guido was thus, in a sense, under the Church's protection. l. 490, "*novercal type*": pertaining to a step-mother; *cater-cousin*, or *quater-cousin*: a cousin within the first four degrees of kindred; *sib*: a blood relation (A.-S., *sibb*, alliance). l. 537, *Papal Jubilee*: this is observed every twenty-fifth year. ll. 892-3, "*ears plugged*," etc.: a good description of the effects of a strong dose of opium. l. 907, *osteria*: Italian name of an inn. l. 1044, *Sbirri*: Papal police. l. 1159, "*Apage*": away! begone! l. 1198, "*Convertites'*: nuns who devote themselves to the rescue of fallen women. l. 1221, "*as Ovid a like sufferer*": Ovid was banished by Augustus to Tomus, on the Euxine Sea, either for some amour or imprudence; *Pontus*: a kingdom of Asia Minor, bounded on the north by the Euxine Sea. l. 1244, "*Pontifex Maximus whipped vestals once*": the high priest severely scourged the vestal virgins if they let the sacred fire go out. l. 1250, "*Caponsacchi*": in English "Head i' the Sack": this family is mentioned in Dante's *Paradise*, xvi.; in his time they lived at Florence, in the Mercato Vecchio, having removed from Fiesole; *Fiesole*, an ancient town near Florence. l. 1270, "*Canidian hate*": Canidia was a Neapolitan, beloved by Horace. When she deserted him he held her up to contempt as an old sorceress (Horace, *Epodes*, v. and xvii.). See Notes to "White Witchcraft." l. 1342, "*domus pro carcere*": a house for a prison. l. 1375, "*hoard i' the heart o' the toad*": Fenton says, "There is to be found in the heads of old and great toads a stone they call borax or stelon, which, being used as rings, give forewarning against venom." See also Brewer's *Phrase and Fable*, art. "Toads." l. 1487, "*male-Grissel*": Griselda was the patient lady in Chaucer's *Clerk of Oxenford's Tale*. She came forth victoriously from the repeated trials of her maternal and conjugal affections. l. 1495, "*Rolando-stroke*": Roland, the hero of Roncesvalles. His trusty sword was called Durandal:—

> "Nor plated shield, nor tempered casque defends,
> When Durindana's trenchant edge descends."
>
> (ORLANDO FURIOSO, bk. x.)

l. 1496, *clavicle*: the collar-bone.

BOOK III., THE OTHER HALF ROME.—Little Pompilia lies dying in the hospital, stabbed through and through again. She had prayed that she might live long enough for confession and absolution. "Never before successful in a prayer," this had been answered. She has overplus of life to speak and right herself from first to last, to pardon her husband and make arrangements for the welfare of her child. The lawyers came and took her depositions; the priests, also, to shrive her soul. The other half Rome make excuses for Pietro and Violante. Their lives wanted completion in a child: Violante's fault was not an unnatural one. Her husband was acquiescent—natural too. Violante's confession was but right and proper; and if she wronged an heir, who was he? As for the wooing, it was all done by the Count: a wife was necessary alike for himself, his mother, and his palace; and so he dazzled the child Pompilia with a vision of greatness. The crowd said she might become a lady, but the bargain was but a poor one at best. Pompilia, aged thirteen years and five months, was secretly married to the Count one dim December day. Pietro was told when it was too late, and had to surrender all his property in favour of Guido, who was to support his wife's belongings. Four months' insolence and penury they had to endure at Arezzo, and then Pietro went back to beg help from his Roman friends, who laughed and said things had turned out just as they expected. Violante went to God, told her sin, and reaped the Jubilee's benefit. Restitution, however, said the Church, must be made: the sin must be published and amends forthcoming. Pompilia's husband must be told that his contract was null and void. Pietro's heart leaped for joy at the prospect of recovering all his surrendered estate. Guido naturally pronounced the whole tale "one long lie"—lying for robbery and revenge—and threw himself on the courts. The courts held the child to be a changeling. Pietro's renunciation they made null: he was no party to the cheat; but Guido is to retain the dowry! More proceedings naturally followed this strange decision. Then the Count forms the diabolical plan to drive his girl-wife, by his cruelty, into the sin which will enable him to be rid of her without parting with her money. Guido concocts a pencilled letter to his brother the Abate, which he makes his wife trace over with ink, he guiding her hand because she could not write, wherein she states—not knowing a word she pens—that the Comparini advised her, before they left Arezzo, to find a paramour, carry off what spoil she could, and then burn the house down. The Abate took care to scatter this information all over Rome. At Arezzo Guido set himself to make his wife's life there intolerable, at the same time setting a trap into which she could not avoid falling. The Other Half Rome thinks it probable that the priest Caponsacchi pitied and loved Pompilia, who wept and looked out of window all day long; for there were passionate letters (prayers, rather), addressed to him by the suffering wife; though it is true she avers she never wrote a letter in her life, still she abjured him, in the name of God, to help her to escape to Rome. If not love, this was love's simulation, and calculated to deceive the Canon. Pompilia, however, protested that she had never even learned to write or read; nor had she ever spoken to the priest till the evening when she implored him to assist her to escape. On the other hand, the priest admitted having received the letters purporting to come from Pompilia. He did write to her: as she could not read she burned the letters—never bade him come to her, yet accepted him when Heaven seemed to send him. When Guido's cruelty first sprang on Pompilia, she had appealed to the secular Governor and the Archbishop; but both were friends of Guido, and both refused to interfere between husband and wife, so she went to confess to a simple friar, told him how suicide had tempted her, begged him to write to her pretended parents to come and save her. He promised; but by nightfall was more discreet, and withdrew from the dangerous business. So the woman, thus hard-beset, looked out to see if God would help, and saw Caponsacchi; called him to her—she at her window, he in the street below—and at nightfall fled with him for Rome. The world sees nothing but the simple fact of the flight. The implicated persons protest that the course they took, though strange, was justified for life and honour's sake. Absorbed in the sense of the blessedness of the flight, she had said little to her preserver through the long night. As daybreak came they reached an inn: he whispered, "Next stage, Rome!" Prostrate with fatigue, she could go no farther; stayed to rest at the osteria, fell asleep, and awoke with Count Guido once more standing betwixt heaven and her soul—awoke to find her room full of roaring men, her preserver a prisoner. Then she sprang up, seized the sword which hung at the Count's side, and would have slain him, but men interposed. The priest avers that the flight had no pretext but to get Pompilia free: how should it be otherwise? If they were guilty, as Guido would have the world believe, what need to fly? or, if they must, why halt with Rome in sight? He vindicates Pompilia's fame. Guido's tale was to the effect that he and his whole household had been drugged by the wife, which gave the fugitives time to get thus far on their way. He expected easy execution probably; thought he would find his wife cowering under her shame. When she turned upon him, and would have slain him he had to invent another story; produce love letters from a woman who could not write, replies from the priest, who could happily defend his character and prove the forgery. Then the story of the investigation before the courts was told: how Pompilia owned she caught at the sole hand stretched out to snatch her from hell; how Caponsacchi proudly declared that as man, and much more as priest, he was bound to help weak innocence; how he exposed the trap set by Guido for them both; how he had never touched her lip, nor she his hand, from first to last, nor spoken a word the Virgin might not hear. Then they discussed the decision of the court—the sentence, the relegation of the priest, the seclusion of the wife in the convent at Guido's expense. They discussed the five months' peace which Pompilia passed with the nuns, the application made by the sisters on behalf of Pompilia's waning health, and her residence with Pietro and his wife at their villa. They tell of the determination of Guido, after the birth of his child, to avail himself of the propitious minute and rid himself of his wife and her putative parents, that the child remaining might inherit all and repair his losses. The sympathisers with Pompilia dwelt on the fact that, while the bells were chiming good-will on earth and peace to man, the dreadful five stole by back slums and blind cuts to the villa, asking admission in Caponsacchi's name. Then follow the murders. Violante was stabbed first, Pietro next; and then came Pompilia's turn, It was told how the murderers escaped, till at Baccano they were overtaken and cast red-handed into prison.

NOTES.—Line 59, *Maratta:* Carlo Maratti was the most celebrated of the later Roman painters of the seventeenth century. He was born 1625. The great number of his pictures of the Virgin procured him the name of "Carlo delle Madonne." l. 95, "*That doctrine of the Philosophic Sin*": "Philosophical Sin," is a breach of the dignity of man's rational nature. Theological Sin offends against the Supreme Reason. (See Rickaby's *Moral Philosophy*, p. 119.) l. 385, "*Hesperian ball, ordained for Hercules to taste and pluck*": the golden apples of the Hesperides plucked by Hercules, were probably oranges. l. 439, *Danae*, the daughter of Acrisius, and mother of Perseus by Jupiter. l. 555, "*The Holy Year*": the Jubilee at Rome, first instituted by Boniface VIII., elected Pope 1294. The Jubilee occurs every twenty-five years, and is a time of special indulgences. l. 556, "*Bound to rid sinners of sin*": no indulgence forgives sin, nor gives permission to commit sin; but it is "the remission, through the merits of Jesus Christ, of the whole or part of the debt of temporal punishment due to a sin, the guilt and everlasting punishment of which sin has, through the merits of Jesus Christ, been already forgiven in the Sacrament of penance" (*Catholic Belief*, by J. Bruno, D.D., p. 183). l. 567. "*The great door, new-broken for the nonce*": according to the special ritual, the Pope, at the commencement of the Jubilee year goes in solemn procession to a particular walled-up door (the Porta Aurea, or golden door of St. Peter's), and knocks three times, using the words of Psalm cxviii. 19, "Open to me the gates of righteousness." The doors are then opened and sprinkled with holy water, and the Pope passes through. When the Jubilee closes, the special doorway is again built up, with appropriate solemnities" (*Encyc. Brit.*). l. 572, "*Poor repugnant Penitentiary*": a penitentiary is an "officer in some cathedrals, vested with power from the bishop to absolve in cases reserved to him. The Pope has a *grand penitentiary*, who is a Cardinal, and is chief of the other *penitentiaries*" (*Webster's Dict.*). That this particular ecclesiastic was "repugnant" is a gratuitous assumption of the poet: he probably took as much interest in his business as any other clergyman takes in his. 1413, *Civita*, Civita Vecchia, a seaport near Rome. 1445, "*Hundred Merry Tales*": the tales or novels of Franco Sacchetti. 1450, *Vulcan*, the god of fire and furnaces, son of Jupiter and Juno.

BOOK IV., TERTIUM QUID.—"A third something," siding neither wholly with Guido nor with his victim, attempts to arrive at a judicial conclusion apportioning in a superior manner blame now on one side now on the other, and, by granting on each side something, endeavours to reconcile opposing views, and from the contending forces produce something like order. The speaker is addressing personages of importance, and his phrase is courtly and polite. He refers with a sort of contempt to this "episode in burgess-life." His account of the business is as follows:—This Pietro and Violante, living in Rome in a style good enough for their betters, indulge themselves with luxury till they get into debt and creditors begin to press. Driven to seek the papal charity reserved for respectable paupers, they become pensioners of the Vatican, and Violante casts about for means to restore the fortunes of her household. Certain funds only want an heir to take, which heir Violante takes measures to supply by the aid of a needy washerwoman who ekes out her honest trade by a vile one, and who for a price will sell, in six months' time, the child of her shame, meantime pocketing the earnest money and promising secrecy. Violante returns flushed with success, and reaches vespers in time to sing *Magnificat*. Then home to Pietro, to whom is delicately confided the enrapturing but puzzling news that at last an heir will be born to him. In due time the infant is put in evidence, and Francesca Vittoria Pompilia is baptised; and so "lies to God, lies to man," lies every way. The heirs are robbed, foiled of the due succession. When twelve years have passed, the scheming Violante has next to arrange a good match for her daughter, with her savings and her heritage. This, with all Rome to choose from, may be proudly done, and then *Nunc Dimittis* may be sung. Miserably poor as Count Guido was, the family was old enough to afford the drawback. The Church helped the second son, Paolo, and made a canon of him—even took Guido under its protection so far as one of the minor orders went. A cardinal gave him some inferior post, but afterwards dispensed with his services. What was to be done? Youth had gone, age was coming on. His brother advised him to look out for a rich wife, told him of Pompilia, and offered his assistance in the suit. The burgess family's one want being an aristocratic husband for their girl Violante, eagerly accepted the Count, and they got the marriage done. Pietro had to make the best of things. Who was fool, who knave, it was difficult to decide: perchance neither or both. Guido gives the wealth he had not got, and the Comparini the child not honestly theirs—each cheated the other. It turned out that one party saw the cheat of the other first, and kept its own concealed. Which sinned more was a nice point. The finer vengeance which became old blood was Guido's, the victim was the hard-beset Pompilia, the hero of the piece Caponsacchi. "Out by me!" he cried. "Here my hand holds you life out!" Whereupon Pompilia clasped the saving hand. Then as to the love letters, Guido protests his wife can write. How could he, granting him skill to drive the wife into the gallant's arms, bring the gallant to play his part so well—a man to whom he had never spoken in his life?

NOTES.—Line 31, "*Trecentos inseris: ohe, jam satis est! Huc apelle!*" (Horace, *Sat.* i. 5): "Here, bring to, *ye dogs*, you are stowing in hundreds; hold, now *sure* there is enough." (Smart's trans.). l. 54, "*basset-table:* basset was a game at cards invented by a Venetian noble; it was introduced into France in 1674. l. 147, "*posts off to vespers, missal beneath arm*": a rather absurd line; a missal is a mass-book, and does not contain the vesper services; mass is always said in the morning. l. 437, "*notum tonsoribus*," the common gossip—(Pr.); *tonsor*, a barber; *zecchines:* sequins, Venetian coins worth from 9*s.* 2*d.* to 9*s.* 6*d.* l. 731, *devil's-dung:* assafœtida, an evil-smelling drug. l. 761, "*cross buttock*": a blow across the back; *quarter staff:* a long stout staff used as a weapon of offence or defence. l. 834, "*Hophni and the ark*": "And the ark of God was taken; and the two sons of Eli, Hophni and Phinehas, were slain" (1 Sam. iv., 11 etc.). "*Correggio and Ledas*": Correggio's picture of "Leda and the Swan," in the Berlin Museum. l. 1054, "*cui profuerint!*" Whom they might profit! l. 1069, "*acquetta* = Aqua Tofana, a poisonous liquid much used in Italy in the seventeenth century by women who wished to get rid of their husbands or their rivals. l. 1131, *Rota:* a superior Papal court. l. 1144, *Paphos:* a city of Cyprus where Venus was worshipped. l. 1322, *Vicegerent:* an officer deputed by a superior to take his place. l. 1408, *Patrizj:* the captain of the police who arrested the criminals. l. 1577, "*fons et origo malorum*": fount and origin of the evils.

BOOK V., COUNT GUIDO FRANCESCHINI.—We are now introduced to the persons of the drama themselves; and first to the Count, who is on his defence before the court for the murder. He has just been put to the torture, and with bones all loosened by the rack is cringing and trembling before the arbiters of life and death. He confesses that he killed his wife and the Comparini, who called themselves her father and mother to ruin him. What he has now to do is to put the right interpretation on his deed. He reminds the court that he comes of an ancient family, descended from a Guido who was Homager to the Empire. His family had become poor as St. Francis or our Lord. He had cast about for some means to restore the fallen fortunes of his house, and sought advice of his fellows how this might be done. He had thoughts of a soldier's life; but they said that, as eldest son and heir, his post was hard by the hearth and altar. He should "try the Church, and contend against the heretic Molinists, and so gain promotion," said one; but others said this would not do—"he must marry, that his line might continue; let him make his brothers priests, and seek his own fortune in the great world of Rome." And so to Rome he came. Humbly, he pleads, he has helped the Church: he has disposed of his property that he might have means to bribe his way to favour at Rome; for the better protection of his person and the advancement of his fortunes, he has taken three or four of the minor orders of the Church, which commit to nothing, yet help to flavour the layman's meat. Thus for the Church. On the world's side he danced, and gamed, and quitted himself like a courtier. At this time he was only sixteen, and was willing to wait for fortune. He waited thirty years, hung about the haunts of cardinals and the Pope, and made friends wherever he could. One day he grew tired of waiting any longer; he was hard upon middle life; he must, he saw, be content to live and die only a nobleman; and so, as his mother was growing old, his sisters well wedded away, and both his brothers in the Church, he resolved to leave Rome, return to Arezzo, and be content. He was like a gamester who has played and lost all. The owners of the tables do not like a man to leave the place penniless. "Let him leave the door handsomely," they say; and so his brother Paul whispered in his ear, told him to take courage and a wife—at least, go back home with a dowry. Paul's advice was weighty, and he listened to him; and before the week was out the clever priest found Pietro and Violante, who had just the daughter, and just the dowry with her, for his brother. "She is young, pretty, and rich," he said; "you are noble, classic, choice." "Done!" said Guido. All the priest proposed he accepted, and the girl was bought and sold—a chattel. "Where was the wrong step?" he asks the court: "if all his honour of birth, his style and state, went for nothing, then society and the law had no reward nor punishment to give. The social fabric falls like a card-house. He thought he had dealt fairly; the others found fault, and wanted their money back, just as the judge, disappointed with a picture for which he had given a great price, wanted his cash returned. Perhaps, also, the judge grew tired of the cupids. When he had purchased his wife he expected wifeliness; just as when, having bought twig and timber, he had bought the song of the nightingale too. Pompilia broke her pact; refused from the first to unite with him in body or in soul. More than this, she published the fact to all the world: said she had discovered he was devil and no man, and set all the town laughing at his meanness and his misery; said he had plundered and cast out her parents; and that she was fain to call on the stones of the street to save her, not only from himself, but the satyr-love of his own brother, the young priest. Was it any marvel that his resentment grew apace? Yet he was not a man of ice: women might have reached the odd corners of his heart, and found some remnants of love there. Pompilia was no dove of Venus either, but a hawk he had purchased at a hawk's price. He does not presume to teach the court what marriage means: it was composed of priests who had eschewed the marriage state with Paul; but the court knew how monks were dealt with who became refractory. If he were over-harsh in bringing his wife to due obedience it was her own fault; she should have cured him by patience and the lore of love. When the Comparini had returned to Rome, they boasted how they had cheated him who cheated them; boasted that Pompilia, his wife, was a bye-blow bastard of a nameless strumpet, palmed off upon him as the daughter with the dowry. Dowry? It was the dust of the street. Under these circumstances Pompilia's duty was no doubtful one: she ought to have recoiled from them with horror. She had been their spoil and prey from first to last, and had aided him in maintaining her cause and making it his own. He admits the trick of the false letter: it was his, and not hers; yet he protests that Pompilia, from window, at church and theatre, launched looks forth and let looks reply to Caponsacchi. And so, in his struggles to extricate his name and fame, this gad-fly must be stinging him in the face. Pricked with shame, plagued with his wife and her parents, what was he to do? Ever was Caponsacchi gazing at his windows. Was he to play at desperate doings with a wooden sword, or shorten his wife's finger by a third, for listening to a serenade? He did nothing of that sort: he only called her a terrible name; and the effect was, when he awoke next morning he found a crowd in his room, fire in his throat, wife gone, and his coffers ransacked. The servants had been drugged too. His wife had eloped with Caponsacchi. He discovered that all the town was laughing at the comedy. They told him how the priest had come at daybreak, while all the household slept; how the wife had led the way out of doors on to the gate where, at the inn, a carriage waited, and took the two to the gate San Spirito, on the Roman road. He told the court how he had set out alone on horseback, floundered through two days and nights, and so at last came up with the fugitives at an inn, saw his wife and her gallant together waiting to start again for Rome. "Does the court suggest," he asks, "that that was, if ever, the time for vengeance?" But he was content with calling in the law to help. He pleads guilty to cowardice: he might have killed them then; but cowardice was no crime. He urges that he had been brought up at the feet of law, and so had slain them not. He had searched the chamber where they passed the night, and found love-laden letters with such words on: "Come here, go there, wait, we are saved, we are lost"; even to details of the sleeping potion which was to drug his wine. The fugitives declared they had not written these; they were forged, they said. Then he tells how he had appealed in vain to the courts. The most he gained was that the priest was relegated to Civita for three years, and Pompilia was sent to a sisterhood. He reminds the court of its severity in cases of heresy and the like, and of its mildness in a case like his. Advice was given to him how to proceed with fresh trials from time to time, and he tried to play the man and bear his trouble as best he might; and then one day he learned that Pompilia's durance was at an end,—she was transferred to her parents' house. He reflected then how the Comparini had beaten him at every point: they gained all; he lost all, even to the wife, the lure; had caught the fish and found the bait entire. And now another letter from Rome, with the news that he is a father; his wife has borne a son and heir,—the reason plain why she left the convent. Then he rose up like fire; his troubles were but just beginning: the child he had longed for was stolen too, and scorn and contempt would be heaped on him full measure. He told the story to his servants, who all declared they would avenge their master's wrongs. He picked out four resolute youngsters, and off they went to Rome. They reached the city on Christmas-eve, as the festive bells rang for the "Feast of the Babe." This arrested him; he dropped the dagger. "Where is His promised peace?" he asked. Nine days he waited thus, praying against temptation, while the vision of the Holy Infant was before him. Soon this faded in a mist, and the Cross stood plain, and he cried, "Some end must be!" He reached the house where Pompilia lived; he knocked, asked admittance for "Caponsacchi," and the door was opened. Had Pompilia even then fronted him in the doorway in her weakness, had even Pietro opened, he had paused; but it was the hag, the mother who had wrought the mischief, who appeared. Then he told the court how the impulse to kill her had seized him, and how, having begun, he had made an end. He was mad, blind, and stamped on all. He told the court how the officers of justice had come upon him twenty miles off, when he was sleeping soundly as a child; and wherefore not? He was his own self again. His soul safe from serpents, he could sleep. He protests he has but done God's bidding, and health has returned and sanity of soul. He declares that he stands acquitted in the sight of God. If his wife and her lover were innocent, why did the court punish them? Their punishment was inadequate, and as soon as their backs were turned the evil began to grow again. He demands the court should right him now; thank and praise him for having done what they should have done themselves. He has doubled the blow they had essayed to strike. He urges them to protect their own defender. He was law's mere executant, and he demands his life, his liberty, good name, and civic rights again. He is for God; the game must not be lost to the devil. He has work to do: his wife may live and need his care; his brother to bring back to the old routine; his infant son to rear—and when to him he tells his story, he will say how for God's law he had dared and done.

NOTES.—"*Vigil torment*": this torment is referred to in the speech of Dominus Hyacinthus, line 329 *et seq.*, as "the Vigiliarum." Line 149, *Francis:* St. Francis of Assisi, founder of the Order of Franciscans; *Dominic:* St. Dominic, founder of the Order of Dominicans: "*Guido, once homager to the Empire*": *i.e.*, he held lands of the Emperor by "homage." l. 207, "*suum cuique*": let each have his own; *omoplat:* shoulder-blade. l. 285, "*utrique sic paratus*": so prepared either way. l. 401, "*sors, a right Vergilian dip*": scholars used to open their Vergil at random for guidance, as people nowadays open their Bible to see what text will turn up. l. 542, *baioc* = bajocco: a Roman copper coin worth three farthings. l. 559, *Plautus:* a famous comic poet of Rome, who died 184 B.C.; *Terence:* a celebrated writer of comedies, a native of Carthage; he died 159 B.C. l. 560, "*Ser Franco's Merry Tales*": Sacchetti's novels and tales, somewhat in the manner of Boccaccio (1335-1400). l. 627, *Caligula:* Emperor of Rome, who delighted in the miseries of mankind, and amused himself by putting innocent persons to death. He was murdered A.D. 41. l. 672, *Thyrsis:* a young Arcadian shepherd (Vergil, *Ecl.* vii. 2); *Neæra:* a country maid, in Vergil. l. 811, *Locusta:* a vile woman, skilled in preparing poisons; who helped Nero to poison Britannicus. l. 850, *Bilboa:* a flexible-bladed rapier from Bilboa. l. 922, "*stans pede in uno*," standing on one foot. l. 1137, *spirit and succubus:* evil spirit, demon, or phantom. l. 1209, *Catullus:* a learned but wanton poet. l. 1264, *Helen and Paris:* Paris, the son of Priam, king of Troy, who eloped with Helen, the wife of Menelaus, carried her to Troy, and so occasioned the war between the Greeks and Trojans. l. 1356, *Ovid's art:* (of love). l. 1358, "*more than his Summa*": the "*Summa Theologiæ*," the famous work of St. Thomas Aquinas, from which every priest of the Roman Church has to study his theology. l. 1359, *Corinna:* a celebrated woman of Tanagra, who seven times obtained a poetical prize when Pindar was her rival. l. 1365, *merum sal*, pure salt. l. 1549, "*Quis est pro Domino?*" "Who is on the Lord's side?" l. 1737, *acquetta:* euphemism for the acqua-tofana, a deadly liquid, colourless poison. l. 1760, "*ad judices meos*," to my judges. l. 1780, *Justinian's Pandects:* the digest of Roman jurists, made by order of Justinian in the sixth century. l. 2009, *soldier bee:* a bee which fights for the protection of the hive, and sacrifices his life in the act of using his sting. l. 2010, *exenterate:* to disembowel. l. 2333, *Tozzi:* physician to the Pope. He succeeded Malpighi. l. 2339, *Albano:* Guido was right; Albano succeeded Innocent XII. as Pope in 1700.

BOOK VI., GIUSEPPE CAPONSACCHI.—The court now hears the story of Caponsacchi: he has been sent for to repeat the evidence which he gave on a former occasion, and to counsel the court in this extremity. It was six months ago, he says, that in the very place where he now stands, he told the facts, at which they decorously laughed, the stifled titter that so plainly meant "We have been young too,—come, there's greater guilt!" Now they are grave enough,—they stare aghast; as for himself, in this sudden smoke from hell he hardly knows if he understands anything aright. He asks why are they surprised at the ending of a deed whose beginning they had seen? He had his grasp on Guido's throat; they had interfered, they saw no peril, wanted no priest's intrusion; he had given place to law, left Pompilia to them,—and there and thus she lies! What do they want with him? he asks: is it that they understand at last it was consistent with his priesthood to endeavour to save Pompilia? It was well they had even thus late seen their error. He owns he talks to the court impertinently, yet they listen because they are Christians; and even a rag from the body of the Lord makes a man look greater, and be the better. He will be calm and tell the simple facts. He is a priest, one of their own body, and of a famous Florentine descent; he had been brought up for the priesthood from his youth, but had trembled when he came to take the vows, and would have shrunk from doing so had not the bishop quieted his qualms of conscience, and satisfied him there was an easier sense in which the vows could be taken than had appeared in his first rough reading. Nobody expected him in these days to break his back in propping up the Church: the martyrs built it; all that priests had to do now was to adorn its walls. He must therefore cultivate his gift of making madrigals, that he may please the great ladies, and make the bishop boast that he was theirs. And so he became a priest, a fribble, and a coxcomb, but a man of truth. He said his breviary and wrote the rhymes, was regular at service, and as regular at his post where beauty and fashion ruled. One night, after three or four years of this life, he found himself at the theatre with a brother Canon; he saw enter and seat herself,—

"A lady, young, tall, beautiful, strange, and sad,"

like a Rafael over an altar. As he stared, his companion the Canon said he would make her give him back his gaze; and straightway tossed a packet of comfits to her lap, and dodged behind him, nodding from over Caponsacchi's shoulder. The lady turned, looked their way, and smiled—a strange, sad smile. "Is she not fair, my new cousin?" said Canon Conti. The fellow at the back of the box is Guido; she's his wife, married three years since. He cautioned him to do nothing to make her husband treat her more cruelly than he already did; but this was not required,—the sight of Pompilia's 'wonderful white soul' shining through the sadness of her face had filled him with disgust for the frivolity and the vanity of his former life. Lent was near; he would live as became a priest. His patron, when he found him absent from the assemblies of fashion and reproved him, reproached him with playing truant, Caponsacchi said he had resolved to go to Rome, and look into his heart a little. One evening, as he sat musing over a volume of St. Thomas, contrasting his past life with that required of him by his office, his thoughts recurred to the sad, strange lady. There was a tap at the door, and a masked, muffled mystery entered with a letter; it purported to come from her to whom the comfits had been thrown, and assured him the recipient had a heart to offer him in return. Inquiring who the messenger might be, she said she was Guido's "kind of maid"; all the servants hated him, she added, and she had offered her aid to bring comfort to the sweet Pompilia. Caponsacchi said he then took pen and wrote, "No more of this!" explaining that once on a time he should not have proved so insensible to her beauty, but now he had other thoughts. Caponsacchi said that he saw Guido's mean soul grinning through this transparent trick. Next morning a second letter was brought by the same messenger; it urged him to visit the lovesick lady, and no longer cruelly delay; it declared she was wretched, that she had heard he was going to Rome, and implored him to take her with him. He asked the maid "what risk they ran of the husband?" "None at all," she answered; "he is more stupid than jealous." He took a pen and wrote that she solicited him in vain; he was a priest and had scruples. After that in many ways he was still pursued, and ever his reply was "Go your ways, temptress!" Urged to pass her window, and glance up thereat, if only once, he resolved to expose the trick and punish the Count. He went. There at the window, with a lamp in hand, stood Pompilia, grave and grief-full; like Our Lady of all the Sorrows, she was there but a moment, and then vanished. He knew she had been induced by some pretence to watch a moment on the balcony. He was about to cry, "Out with thee, Guido!" when all at once she reappeared, just on the terrace overhead; so close was she that if she bent down she could almost touch his head; and she did bend, and spoke, while he stood still, all eye, all ear. She told him that he had sent her many letters; that she had read none, for she could neither read nor write; that she was in the power of the woman who had brought them; that she had explained their purport, that she had made her listen while she told her that he, a priest, had dared to love her, a wife, because he had seen her face a single time. This wickedness she thinks cannot be true,—it were deadly to them both; but if indeed he had true love to offer, did he indeed mean good and true, she might accept his help. It was so strange, she said, that her husband, whom she had not wronged, should hate her so, should wish to harm her: for his own soul's sake would the priest hinder the harm? Then she told him how happily she had dwelt at Rome, with those dear Comparini whom she had been wont to call father and mother; she could not understand what it was that had prompted his soul to offer her his help, but, as he had done so, would he render her just aid enough to save her life with? To leave the man who hated her so were no sin. "Take me to Rome!" she cried. "You go to Rome: take me as you would take a dog!" She told him how she had turned hither and thither for aid,—to great good men, Archbishop and Governor, she had opened her heart. They only smiled: "Get you gone, fair one!" they said. In her despair she went to an old priest, a friar who confessed her; to him she told how, worse than husband's hate, she had to bear the solicitations of his young idle brother. "Write to your parents," said the friar. She said she could neither read nor write. "I will write," he promised; but no answer came. She ended with repeating her entreaty that he should take her to the Comparinis' home at Rome. Caponsacchi promised at once to do this thing for her; it was settled he should find a carriage, and the money for the purpose, and return when he had made arrangements for the flight. [The messenger who had brought him the Count's letters was shown to be his mistress; the Count had forged the notes from Pompilia, and the replies thereto.] Then the priest went home to meditate on this strange matter, and the more he thought of what he had agreed to do, the more incongruous with his sacred office did it seem. Was he not wedded to the mystic bride—the Church? Did it not say to him, "Leave that live passion; come, be dead with me"? Then came the voice of God, His first authoritative word: "I had been lifted to the level of her!" he exclaimed. Now did he perceive the function of the priest: to leave her he had thought self-sacrifice; to save her, was the price demanded, and he paid it. "Duty to God is duty to her." Yet, when the morning broke, his heart whispered, "Duty is still wisdom," and the day wore on. When evening came he determined to see her again, to advise her, to bid her not despair. He went. There she stood as before, and now reproached him for not returning earlier; and when he saw her sadness, and heard her piteous pleading, he said

"Leave this home in the dark to-morrow night."

He told her the place of meeting and the way thereto, promising to be ready at the appointed time. Then he secured a carriage, made all arrangements, and, at the time agreed, Pompilia draped in black, but with the soul's whiteness shining through her veil, was there. She sprang into the carriage, he beside her —she and he alone, and so began the flight through dark to light, through day and night, again to night, once more on to the last dreadful dawn. He told the court the incidents of the weary journey,—all her weakness and her craving for rest at Rome,—how she urged him to continue, till they were at last within twelve hours of the city, and there seemed no fear of pursuit. Then he entreated her to descend and take some rest. For a while she waited at a roadside inn, nursed a woman's child, sat by the garden wall and talked, then off again refreshed. On they went till they reached Castelnuovo. "As good as Rome!" he cried. She was sleeping as he spoke, and woke with a start and scream—

> "Take me no further; I should die: stay here!
> I have more life to save than mine!"

then swooned. The people at the inn urged him to let her rest the night with them. He could not but choose. All the night through he paced the passage, keeping guard. "Not a sound, nor movement," they said. At first pretence of gray in the sky he bade them have out the carriage, while he called to break her sleep; and as he turned to go there faced him Count Guido, as master of the field encamped, his rights challenging the world, leering in triumph, scowling with malice. He was not alone. With him were the commissary and his men. At once he was arrested. Then "Catch her!" the husband bade. That sobered Caponsacchi. "Let me lead the way!" he cried, explaining he was privileged, being a priest, and claiming his rights. Then they went to Pompilia's chamber. There she lay sleeping, "wax-white, seraphic." "Seize and bind!" hissed Guido. Pompilia started up, stood erect, face to face with her tormentor. "Away from between me and hell!" she cried. "I am God's, whose knees I clasp,—hence!" Caponsacchi tried to reach her side, but his arms were pinioned fast; the rabble poured in and took the husband's part, heaping themselves upon the priest. Springing at the sword which hung at Guido's side, she drew and brandished it. "Die, devil, in God's name!" she cried; but they closed round her, twelve to one. Then Guido began his search for the gold, the jewels, and the plate of which he declared he had been robbed, and for the amorous letters he had reason to expect to find. They could not refuse the priest's appeal to be judged by the Church, and so he was sent to Rome with Pompilia; and to separate cells in the same prison they were borne. He told his judges then that he had never touched Pompilia with his finger-tip, except to carry her that evening to her couch, and that as sacredly as priests carry the vessels of the altar. He tells the court he might have locked his lips and laughed at its jurisdiction, for when this murder happened he was a prisoner at Civita. She had only the court to trust to when Guido hacked her to pieces. He had come from his retreat as friend of the court, had told his tale for pure friendship's sake. He reminds them how in the first trial he had disproved the accusation of the letters, and the verses they contained: if any were found, it was because those who found had hidden first. Then he tells how, as in relegation he was studying verse, suddenly a thunderclap came into his solitude. The whirlwind caught him up and brought him to the room where so recently the judges had dealt out law adroitly, and he learned how Guido had upset it all. In a frank and dignified appeal to the court, he explains how it was that God had struck the spark of truth from contact between his and Pompilia's soul, daring him to try to be good and show himself above the power of show. Had they not acted as babes in their flight? Had they been criminals, was there not opportunity for sin without a flight at all? or, if it were necessary to fly, where had they stayed for sin? Had he saved Pompilia against the law?—against the law Guido slays her. Deal with him! If they say he was in love, unpriest him then; degrade, disgrace him: for himself no matter; for Pompilia let them "build churches, go pray!" They will find him there. He knows they too will come. He sees a judge weeping: he is glad—they see the truth. Pompilia helped him just so. As for the Count, he had him on the fatal morning in arms' reach; he could have killed him It was through him (Caponsacchi) he had survived to do this deed. He asks them not to condemn the Count to death. Leave him to glide as a snake from off the face of things, and be lost in the loneliness. He stops the rapid flow of words, owns he has been rash in what he has said, fears he has been but a poor advocate of the woman, protests they had no thought of love, and begs them to be just. Even while he pleads for Pompilia they tell him she is dead. Why did they let him ramble on?—his friends should have stopped him. Then he grows almost incoherent in his mental distress; asks them if they will one day make Pope of the friar who heard Pompilia's dying confession, and declares he had never shriven a soul

"so sweet and true, and pure and beautiful."

Then he grows calm again, speaks of being as good as out of the world now he is a relegated priest, and concludes with a despairing cry to the God whom he is no longer permitted to serve.

NOTES.—*Arezzo*, the ancient Arretium, is the seat of a bishop and a prefect. The present population of the town is about eleven thousand, or, if the neighbouring villages are included, about thirty-nine thousand inhabitants. In the middle ages the town suffered severely in the wars of the Guelfs and Ghibellines; in this struggle it usually took the side of the Ghibellines. Caponsacchi's church is that of S. Maria della Pieve, said to be as old as the beginning of the ninth century, with a tower and façade dating from 1216. The façade has four series of columns, arranged rather incongruously. Many ancient sculptures are over the doors. The interior of the church consists of a nave, with aisles and a dome. Petrarch was born at No. 22 in the Via dell' Orto; the house bears an inscription to the effect that "Francesco Petrarca was born here, July 20th, 1304." The cathedral is a fine Italian Gothic building, dating from 1177; the façade is still unfinished. The interior has no transept, but is of fine and spacious proportions, with some good stained-glass windows of the early part of the sixteenth century. Pope Gregory X. died at Arezzo, and his tomb is in the right aisle. There is a marble statue of Ferdinand de' Medici in front of the cathedral, which was erected in 1595 by John of Douay. Arezzo is about a hundred miles north of Rome. In the story of the flight from Arezzo towards Rome, Caponsacchi indicates the chief places which they passed on the road. The first halt was at *Perugia*, the capital of the province of Umbria, with a population of some fifty thousand. It is the residence of a prefect, a military commandant, the seat of a bishop and a university. The city is built partly on the top of a hill and partly on the slope. *Assisi* may well be called "holy ground" (*Caponsacchi*, line 1205). Here was born St. Francis in 1182. "He was the son of the merchant Pietro Bernardine, and spent his youth in frivolity. At length, whilst engaged in a campaign against Perugia, he was taken prisoner, and attacked by a dangerous illness. Sobered by adversity, he soon afterwards (1208) founded the Franciscan order." St. Francis was one of the most beautiful characters in religious history. His whole life was devoted to the poor and sick, and his order, to the present day, is the most charitable monastic order in the world. The monastery of St. Francis at Assisi has existed for six centuries. *Foligno* is an industrial town of twenty-one thousand inhabitants, and is the seat of a bishop. The cathedral was erected in the twelfth century. The church of S. Anna, or Delle Contesse, once contained Rafael's famous Madonna di Foligno, now in the Vatican. *Castelnuovo:* at this place Guido overtook the travellers. It is situated about fifteen miles from Rome, and is only a village, with an inn. Line 230, "*Capo-in-Sacco, our progenitor*": see note to Book II., "HALF ROME," l. 1250. l. 234, *Old Mercato:* the old market-place in Florence, where the Caponsacchi formerly resided. l. 249, *Grand-duke Ferdinand:* the marble statue of Ferdinand in front of the cathedral was erected by Giovanni da Bologna in 1595. l. 251, *Aretines:* the men of Arezzo. l. 280, "*The Jews and the name of God*": the Jews do not pronounce the name of Jehovah, or Jahveh, out of reverence; they substitute the word Adonai, Lord. l. 333, *Marinesque Adoniad:* a celebrated poem called *Adonis* was written by Giovanni Marini, who lived at the beginning of the seventeenth century. l. 346, *Pieve:* the parish church of S. Maria della Pieve, said to have been built in the ninth century on the site of a temple of Bacchus. l. 389, *Priscian* was a great grammarian of the fifth century, whose name was almost synonymous with grammar. "To break Priscian's head" was to violate the rules of grammar. l. 402, *facchini:* porters, or scoundrels. l. 449, *in sæcula sæculorum*, "world without end": the concluding words of the "Glory be to the Father," etc., chanted at the end of each psalm. l. 467, *canzonet:* a short song in one, two, or three parts. l. 559, *Thyrsis*, a shepherd of Arcadia; *Myrtilla*, a country maid in love with Thyrsis. l. 574, "*At the Ave*": at the hour of evening prayer, when the "Hail Mary" and hymns to the Virgin are sung. l. 707, "*Our Lady of all the Sorrows*": the Blessed Virgin is called "Our Lady of Sorrows," and is painted with a sword piercing her heart, from the words of the Gospel, "A sword shall pierce through thine own soul also" (St. Luke xi. 35). l. 828, *The Augustinian:* the friar of the order of St. Augustine. l. 960, *St. Thomas with his sober grey goose-quill:* St. Thomas Aquinas is referred to here. He was a famous Dominican theologian. His *Sum of Theology* is the standard text-book of the divine science in all Catholic countries. Aquinas was called "the angelic doctor." l 961, "*Plato by Cephisian reed*": the

Cephisus was a river on the west side of Athens, falling into the Saronic Gulf; the largest river in Attica. l. 988, "*Intent on his corona*": the rosary or chaplet of beads is in Italy and Spain called the "corona." The monk was intent on his rosary. l. 1102, *Our Lady's girdle*: legend says that the Blessed Virgin, as she was being assumed into heaven, loosened her girdle, which was received by St. Thomas. (See Mrs. Jameson's *Legends of the Madonna.*) l. 1170, *Parian*: a pure and beautiful marble of Parcs; *coprolite*: the petrified dung of carnivorous reptiles. l. 1203, *Perugia*: a city about thirty-five miles from Arezzo, on the road to Rome. l. 1205, "*Assisi—this is holy ground*": because there was the monastery founded by St. Francis of Assisi. l. 1266, *The Angelus*: a prayer consisting of the angelical salutation to Mary, with versicle and response and collect, said three times a day, at morning, noon and night; in Catholic countries and religious houses a bell is rung in a peculiar manner to announce the hour of this prayer. l. 1275, *Foligno*: a small town near Perugia. l. 1666, "*Bembo's verse*": Cardinal Bembo. (See notes to *Asolo*, p. 51.) l. 1667, "*De Tribus*": the title of a scandalous pamphlet, called "The Three Impostors," which was well known in the seventeenth century: Moses, Christ, and Mahomet were thus designated. (This explanation was sent me by the late Mr. J. A. Symonds.) l. 1747, "*De Raptu Helenæ*": concerning the rape of Helen of Troy.

BOOK VII., POMPILIA.—From her deathbed Pompilia tells the story of her life: says how she is just seventeen years and five months old: 'tis writ so in the church's register, where she has five names—so laughable, she thinks. There will be more to write in that register now; and when they enter the fact of her death she trusts they will say nothing of the manner of it, recording only that she "had been the mother of a son exactly two weeks." She has learned that she has twenty-two dagger wounds, five deadly; but she suffers not too much pain, and is to die to-night; thanks God her babe was born, and better, baptised and hid away before this happened, and so was safe; he was too young to smile and save himself. Now she will never see her boy, and when he grows up and asks "What was my mother like?" they will tell him "Like girls of seventeen"; but she thinks she looked nearer twenty. She wishes she could write that she might leave something he should read in time. Her name was not a common one: that may serve to keep her a little in memory. He had no father that he ever knew at all, and now—to-night—will have no mother and no name, not even poor old Pietro's. This is why she called the boy Gaetano. A new saint should name her child. Those old saints must be tired out with helping folk by this time. She had five, and they were! How happy she had been in Violante's love, till one day she declared she had never been their child, was but a castaway and unknown! People said husbands love their wives: hers had killed her! They said Caponsacchi, though a priest, did love her, and "no wonder you love him," shaking their heads, pitying and blaming not very much. Then she tells the tale of six days ago, when the New Year broke: how she was talking by the fire about her boy, and what he should do when he was grown and great. Pietro and Violante had assisted her to creep to the fireside from her couch, and they sat wishing each other more New Years. Pietro was telling, too, of the cause he expected to gain against the wicked Count, and Violante scolded him for tiring Pompilia with his chatter: she was so happy that friendly eve. Then, next morning, old Pietro went out to see the churches. It was snowing when he returned, and Violante brought out a flask of wine and made up a great fire; and he told them of the seven great churches he had visited, and how none had pleased him like San Giovanni. He was just saying how there was the fold and all the sheep as big as cats, and shepherds half as large as life listening to the angel,—when there was a tap at the door. The rest, she said, they knew. . . . Pietro at least had done no harm, and Violante, after all, how little! She did wrong, she knows; she did not think lies were real lies when they had good at heart: it was good for all she meant. She sees this now she is dying: she meant the pain for herself, the happiness all for Pompilia. And now the misery and the danger are over; as she sinks away from life, she finds that sorrows change into something which is not altogether sorrow-like. Her child is safe, her pain not very great. She is so happy that she is just absolved, washed fair. "We cannot both have and not have." Being right now, she is happy, and that colours things. She will tell the nuns, who watch by her and nurse her, how all this trouble came about. Up to her marriage at thirteen years, the days were as happy as they were long. Then, one day, Violante told her she meant next day to bring a cavalier whom she must allow to kiss her hand. He would be the same evening at San Lorenzo to marry her: but all would be as before, and she would still live at home. Till her mother spoke she must hold her tongue: that was the way with girl-brides. So, like a lamb, she had only to lie down and let herself be clipped. Next day came Guido Franceschini—old, not so tall as herself, hook-nosed, and with a yellow bush of beard, much like an owl in face; and his smile and the touch of his hand made her uncomfortable, though she did not suppose it mattered anything. Once, when she was ill, an ugly doctor attended her: he cured her, so his appearance did not affect his skill. Then, on the deadest of December days, she was hurried away at night to San Lorenzo. The church door was locked behind the little party, and the priest hurried her to the altar, where was hid Guido and his ugliness. They were married; and she, silent and scared, joined her mother, who was weeping; and they went home, saying no word to Pietro. "Girl-brides," said Violante, "never breathe a word!" For three weeks she saw nothing of Guido. Nothing was changed. She was married, and expected all was over. The scarecrow doctor did not return: she supposed that Guido would keep away likewise. Then, one morning, as she sat at her broidery frame alone, she heard voices, and running to see, found Guido and the priest who had married her. Pietro was remonstrating, and Guido was claiming his wife, and had come to take her. Then she began to see that something mean and underhand had happened. Her mother was to blame, herself to pity. She was the chattel, and was mute. She retired to pray to God. Violante came to her, told her that she would have a palace, a noble name, and riches; that young men were volatile; that Guido was the sort ot man for housekeeping; and it had been arranged they were not to separate, but should all live together in the great palace at Arezzo, where Pompilia would be queen. And so she went with Guido to his home. Since then it was all a blank, a terrific dream to her. The Count had married for money, and the money was not forthcoming; and he became unkind to his wife to punish the Comparini who had cheated him. So he accused her of being a coquette, of licentious looks at theatre and church. She knew this was a false charge, but could not divine his purpose in making it, so made matters worse by never going out at all. When the maid began to speak of the priest and of the letters they said he had written, she begged her to ask him to cease writing, even from passing through the street wherein she lived. The Count's object she did not know was that they might be compromised. In her trouble she went to the Archbishop, begging him to place her in a convent. It was all so repugnant to her, barely twelve years old at marriage. But the Church could give no help: to live with her husband, she was told, was in her covenant. Then she told the frightful thing—of the advances of her husband's brother, who solicited, and said he loved her; told him that her husband knew it all, and let it go on. The Archbishop bade her be more affectionate to her husband, and to let his brother see it. So home she went again, and her husband's hate increased. Henceforth her prayers were not to man, but to God alone. She had been, she told them, three dreary years in that gloomy palace at Arezzo, when one day she learned that there could be a man who could be a saviour to the weak, and to the vile a foe. It was at the play where she first saw Caponsacchi. She saw him silent, grave, and almost solemn; and she thought had there been a man like that to lift her with his strength into the calm, how she could have rested. At supper that night her husband let her know what he had seen: the throwing of the comfits in her lap, her smile and interest in the priest; told her she was a wanton, drew his sword and threatened her. This was not new to her. He told her that this amour was the town's talk, and he menaced the person of Caponsacchi. A week later, Margherita, her maid, who it was said was more than servant to her lord, began to tell her of the priest who loved her and urged her to send him some token in return. Pompilia bade her say no more; but ever and again the woman reverted to the subject, and she at last produced letters said to have been sent by him. And when the importunity continued, she declared she knew all this of Caponsacchi to be false. The face which she had seen that night at the play was his own face, and the portrait drawn of him she was sure was false. And then, when April was half through, and it was said every one was leaving for Rome, and Caponsacchi too, a light sprang up within her: was it possible she also could reach Rome? How she had tried to leave the hateful home! She had appealed to the Governor of the city, to the Archbishop, to the poor friar, to Conti her husband's relative, and he alone suggested a way of escape. "Ask Caponsacchi," he said: "he's your true St. George, to slay the monster." Then to Margherita she said, "Tell Caponsacchi he may come!" And so again she saw the silent and solemn face, and told him all her trouble: how she was in course of being done to death. She trusted in God and him to save her—to take her to Rome and put her back with her own people. He said "he was hers." The second night, when he came as arranged, he said the plan was impracticable,—he dare not risk the venture for her sake. But she urged him, and he yielded. "To-morrow, at the day's dawn," he would take her away. That night her husband, telling her how he loathed her, bade her not disturb him as he slept. And then she spoke of the flight, her prayers, her yearning to be at rest in Rome. Then all the horrors of the fatal night. She pardoned her husband: she knew that her presence had been hateful to him; she could not help that. She could not love him, but his mother did. Her body, but never her soul, had lain beside him. She hopes he will be saved. So, as by fire, she had been saved by him. As for her child, it should not be the Count's at all—"only his mother's, born of love, not hate!" Then, with her fast-failing mind-sight, she turns to the image of "the lover of her life, the soldier-saint." Death shall not part her from him: her weak hand in his strong grasp shall rest in the new path she is about to tread. She bids them tell him she is arrayed for death in all the flowers of all he had said and done. He is a priest, and could not marry; nor would he if he could, she thinks: the true marriage is for heaven.

"So, let him wait God's instant men call years;
Meantime hold hard by truth and his great soul,
Do out the duty! Through such souls alone
God stooping shows sufficient of His light
For us i' the dark to rise by. And I rise!"

NOTES.—Line 423, *Master Malpichi:* probably Marcello Malpighi (1628-1694), a great physician of Bologna. He was the founder of microscopic anatomy. In 1691 he removed to Rome to become physician to Pope Innocent XII. l. 427, "*The lion's mouth:* Via di Bocca di Leone—the name of a street near the Corso. l. 607, *The square o' the Spaniards :* Piazza di Spagna is the centre of the strangers' quarter in Rome. It derives its name from the palace of the Spanish Ambassador. l. 1153, *Mirtillo*, probably a minor poet of the period. l. 1303, *The Augustinian :* an order of monks following the rule of St. Augustine. l. 1377, *The Ave Maria :* the "Hail Mary"—an evening devotion, wherein the prayer occurs of which these are the first words.

BOOK VIII., DOMINUS HYACINTHUS DE ARCHANGELIS, PAUPERUM PROCURATOR.—In this book we have the counsel on behalf of Count Guido at work in his study, preparing the defence which he is to make on behalf of his client. He is a family man, and his life is bound up in that of his son, whose birthday it is, the lad being eight years old. He will devote himself to his case, and when his work is done will enjoy the yearly lovesome frolic feast with little Cinuolo. "Commend me," says the man of law, "to home joy, the family board, altar and hearth!" He is very anxious to make a good figure in the courts over this case, his opponent, old bachelor Bottinius, shall be made to bite his thumb; and he expresses his gratitude to God that he has Guido to defend just when his boy is eight years old, and needs a stimulus to study from his sire. He chuckles at his good fortune: a noble to defend, a man who has almost with parade killed three persons; it is really too much luck to befall him, and on his son's birthday too! he prays God to keep him humble, and mutters "*Non nobis Domine !*" as he turns over his papers. He determines to beat the other side, if only for love, as a tribute to little Cinotto's natal day (the boy was called by half a dozen pet names). He will astonish the Pope himself with his eloquence and skill; and the day shall be remembered when his son becomes of age. Then he bethinks himself of the night's feast: the wine, the minced herbs with the liver, goose-foot, and cock's-comb, cemented with cheese; he rubs his hands again, as he thinks of all the good things getting ready. But now to work: he must puzzle out this case. He is particular about the Latin he will use; he would like to bring in Vergil, but that will not do well in prose. His son shall attack him with Terence on the morrow. Then he curbs his ardour, and sets himself to deal in earnest with the case. Bottinius will deny that Pompilia wrote any letter at all. Anticipating what his opponent will say, he says he had rather lose his case than miss the chance of ridiculing his Latin and making the judge laugh, who will so enjoy the joke. If it comes to law, why, he is afraid he cannot "level the fellow": he sees him even now in his study, working up thrusts that will be hard to parry, he is sure to deliver a bowl from some unguessed standpoint. And now he stops to rub some life into his frozen fingers, hopes his boy will take care of his throat this cold day, and reflects how chilly Guido must be in his dungeon, despite his straw. Carnival time too: what a providence, with the city full of strangers! He will do his best to edify and amuse them: they may remember Cintino some day! But to the case. "Where are we weak?" he asks. The killing is confessed: they tortured Guido, and so got it out of him,—he shall object to that; nobles are exempt from torture. A certain kind of torture like that called *Vigiliarum*, is excellent for extracting confession; he has never known any prisoner stand it for ten hours; they "touched their ten," 'tis true, "but, bah! they died!" If the Count had not confessed, he should have set up the defence that Caponsacchi really murdered the three, and fled just as Guido, touched by grace,—consequent upon having been a good deal at church at the holy season—hastened to the house to pardon his wife, and so arrived just in time—to be charged with the murders. Yes, he could have done very well on this line, he thinks; but the confession has spoiled all that. Wonderful that a nobleman could not stand torture better! Why, he has known several brave young fellows keep a rack in their back garden, and take a turn at it for an hour or two at a time, just to see how much pain they could stand without flinching: he thinks men are degenerating. And so he meanders on, pulling himself up in the midst of a nice point to wonder whether his cook has remembered how excellently well some chopped fennel-root goes with fried liver. "But no; she cannot have been so obtuse as to forget!" He shall begin his speech with a pretty compliment to His Holiness, then he shall quote St. Jerome, St. Gregory, Solomon, and St. Bernard, who all say that a man must not be touched in his honour. Our Lord Himself said, "My honour I to nobody will give!" (He stops to reflect that a melon would have improved the soup, but that the boy wanted the rind to make a boat with.) He shall continue, that a husband who has a faithless wife *must* raise hue and cry,—the law is not for such cases,—these are for gentlemen to deal with themselves. Of course the other side will object that Guido allowed too long an interval to elapse between the capture of the fugitives and the killing; but he *shall* show that there really was no interval between the inn and the Comparinis' villa at Rome: Pompilia was inaccessible between these places. If they object that Guido, when he arrived at Rome on Christmas Eve, should have sought his vengeance at once, he shall ask, "Is no religion left?" A man with all those Feasts of the Nativity to occupy his mind could not be expected to go about his private business. (He pauses to reflect that a little lamb's fry will be very toothsome in an hour's time.) The charge is that "we killed three innocents"; as to the manner of the killing, that matters nothing, granted we had the right to kill. Eight months since they would have been held to blame if they had let this bad pair escape: true, that was the time to have killed them, but the Count had not the proper weapons handy. He shall say, too, that he did not instruct his confederates to kill any one of the three, but merely to disfigure them; they had been too zealous. He next proceeds to dispose of a number of points in which it is charged the offence was aggravated,—such as slaying the family in their own house, and lastly that the majesty of the sovereign has received a wound. (Here he fervently hopes the devil will not instigate his cook to stew the rabbit instead of roasting him: he will have to go and see after things himself—he really must.) But, if the end be lawful, the means are allowed. (The Cardinal has promised to go and read the speech to the Pope, and point its beauties out, so he must be adroit in his words.) As he stands forth as the advocate of the poor, he must put in a word or two for the four assassins who did the deed. On their behalf he pleads that, as the husband was in the right in what he did, those who helped him could not be in the wrong. (On which more Latin and neat phrases.) He will be reminded that Guido went off without paying the men the stipulated fee for the murders. "What fact," he shall ask, "could better illustrate the perfect rectitude of the Count?" The men were not actuated by malice, but by a simple desire to earn their bread by the sweat of their brow. As for the Count, so absorbed was he in vindicating his honour, that paltry, vulgar questions of money wholly escaped him; "he spared them the pollution of the pay." In conclusion, he shall urge that Guido killed his wife in defence of the marriage vow, that he might creditably live. "There's my speech," he cries, as he dashes down the pen; "where's my fry, and family, and friends? What an evening have I earned to-day!" And off he goes to supper, singing "Tra-la-la, lambkins, we must live!"

NOTES.—Line 8, "*And chews Corderius with his morning crust*": the *Colloquies of Corderius* were used in every school of any consequence in the time of Shakespeare's boyhood. It was the most popular Latin book for boys of the time. l. 14, *Papinianian pulp*: Papinian was the most celebrated of Roman jurists, and an intimate friend of the Emperor Septimius Severus. l. 58, *Flaccus:* Horace, whose full name was Quintus Horatius Flaccus. l. 94, "*Non nobis, Domine, sed Tibi laus*": "Not unto us, Lord, but to Thee be the praise!" l. 101, *Pro Milone:* the celebrated oration of Cicero on behalf of Milo, a friend of his. l. 115, *Hortensius Redivivus:* Hortensius, the Roman orator. l. 117, "*The Est-est*": a wine so called because a nobleman once sent his servant in advance to write "Est," *it is!* on any inn where the wine was particulary good; at one place the man wrote "Est-est," *It is! it is!* in token of its superlative excellence, and the vintage has ever since gone by this designation. l. 329, "*Questions,*" tortures; *Vigiliarum:* torture by incessant jerking of the body and limbs. l. 482, *Theodoric:* king of the Ostrogoths (*c.* A.D. 454-526); he caused the celebrated Boethius to be put to death. l. 483, *Cassiodorus:* a Roman historian, statesman, and monk, who lived about 468 A.D.; he was raised by Theodoric to the highest offices. He was one of the first of literary monks, and his books were much used in the middle ages. l. 498, *Scaliger:* Julius Cæsar Scaliger (1484-1558), a man of the greatest eminence in the world of letters, and as a man of science, and a philosopher. He had a son, *Joseph Justus Scaliger*, not less eminent, who wrote the work referred to. l. 503, *The Idyllist* is Theocritus, the Sicilian poet. l. 513, *Ælian:* a Roman, in the reign of Adrian, surnamed the honey-tongued, from the sweetness of his style; he wrote seventeen treatises on animals. l. 948, *Valerius Maximus,* a Latin writer, who made a collection of historical anecdotes, and published his work in the reign of Tiberius. It was called *Books of Memorable Deeds and Utterances.* Most of the tales are from Roman history. *Cyriacus:* patriarch of the Jacobites, monk of the convent of Bizona, in Syria; died at Mosul in 817 A.D.

He wrote homilies, canons, and epistles. l. 1542, *Castrensis:* a distinguished professor of civil and canon law; he died in 1441. He was a professor at Vienna, Avignon, Padua, Florence, Bologna, and Perugia. His most complete work is his readings on the *Digest. Butringarius:* a jurisconsult (1274-1348). [I have not considered it necessary to translate the many Latin lines in this and the following section of the work, because in nearly every case their sense is given in the context, and therefore those who do not read Latin will lose nothing, as practically they have it all englished in the text.]

BOOK IX., JURIS DOCTOR JOHANNES-BAPTISTA BOTTINIUS (FISCI ET REV. CAM. APOSTOL. ADVOCATUS).—Bottinius is the Public Prosecutor, and has to present the case against the Count and his confederates. He is not a family man, and seems to have but a low ideal of feminine virtue. He admires the sex, but from a superior masculine standpoint; their weaknesses are amiable. Of girls he says—

> "Know one, you know all
> Manners of maidenhood: mere maiden she.
> And since all lambs are like in more than fleece,
> Prepare to find that, lamb-like, she too frisks——"

He mixes up references to the Holy Family, Joseph, Mary, her Babe, Saint Anne and Herod; with whom he compares Pompilia, the Comparini family, and the Count; and all this with illustrations from the classics not greatly to the honour of women. The view of Bottinius, in short, is that of the bachelor man of the world, with no very lofty ideals about anything. His philosophy is summed up in his last words, "Still, it pays." He says he feels his strength inadequate to paint Pompilia; but we know this is a professional way of speaking, for he soon relapses into "melting wiles, deliciousest deceits"—very incongruous with our ideas of what Pompilia really was. No doubt, he thinks, there were some friskings, for which Guido naturally threatened the whip, and considers Guido to have been impatient. He supposes that Pompilia smiled upon everybody, till, when three years of married life had run their course, she smiled on Caponsacchi; and as he was a priest, and the court was more or less ecclesiastical, Bottinius makes light of the affair. He will grant that the lady somewhat plied "arts that allure," "the witchery of gesture," and the like. This was within the right of beauty, for the purpose of securing a champion. He will grant, for argument's sake, that she did write to Caponsacchi. What of it?—it was but to say her life was not worth an hour's purchase. It was not likely that Caponsacchi fell in love—he who might be Pope some day—yet the lady, being in such a case, was bound to offer him nothing short of love, as his great service was to save her. What was she to offer him—money? To escape death she might well have feigned love, and offered such a reward as the Idyl of Moschus makes Venus promise to any who should bring back lost Cupid. As it was wiser to choose a priest for the rescue of her life, if the cleric were young, handsome, and strong, so much the better, surely. Suppose it were true that Pompilia administered an opiate to her husband the night before she left him? Well, that was to protect him from rough usage if he aroused and interfered. This, says Bottinius, is how he would argue if the things which are but fables had been true: of course Guido never slept a wink, and Pompilia, equally of course, knew nothing about opiates. Then, when she started with her rescuer on the road to Rome, even granting what the suborned coachman said about the kissing which he saw—the one long embrace which constituted the journey—a sage and sisterly kiss were surely allowable, and this is probably what was exaggerated by the drowsy, tired driver. Then, when the pale creature, exhausted with the long journey, fainted at the inn, and Caponsacchi carried her to the chamber, what if he "stole a balmy breath, perhaps"? "why curb ardour here?" He could but pity her, and "pity is so near to love!" As Pompilia was asleep, she could neither know nor care. Were he to concede that Pompilia did write the incriminating letters, she, for self-protection, might deny she did so. "Would that I had never learned to write!" said one; Pompilia, splendidly mendacious, merely out-distanced him with, "To read or write I never learned at all!" Bottinius cannot resist a thrust or two at his "fat opponent's" love of good living; calls him "thou archangelic swine," and reminds him that he had not invited him to last night's birthday feast, when all sorts of good things were going. Turning to the action of Caponsacchi, he reminds the court that Archbishop and Governor, gentle and simple, did nothing to extricate Pompilia from her troubles; they all went their ways and left her to her fate; Caponsacchi alone, bursting through the impotent sympathy of Arezzo, caught Virtue up, and carried her off. He had not soiled her with the pitch alleged: the marks she bore were the evanescent black and blue of the necessary grasp. Then he must tell a tale how Peter, John, and Judas, being on a journey, were footsore and hungry; how they reached at night an inn for rest where there was but one room; for food but a solitary fowl, a wretched sparrow of a thing. Peter suggested they should all go to sleep till the fowl was ready, then he who had had the happiest dream should eat the entire fowl, as there was not enough for three; so each rested in his straw. When they awoke, John said he had dreamed he was the Lord's favourite disciple, and claimed the meal. Peter had dreamed he had the keys of heaven and hell, and thought the fowl must clearly be his. But Judas dreamed that he had descended from the chamber where they slept and had eaten the fowl. And so the traitor really had: he had left nothing but the drumstick and the merry-thought; and that is how the bone called merry-thought earned its name, to put us in mind that the best dream is to keep awake sometimes. So, said Bottinius, the great people of Arezzo never meant Innocence to starve while Authority sat at meat. They meant Pompilia to have something—in their dreams; they were willing to help her—in their sleep. Caponsacchi did wiser than dream or sleep: he brought a carriage, while the Archbishop and the Governor wondered what they could do. Then the Advocate bursts into a fit of admiration for the majesty and sanctity of the law, and what it would have done for Guido if only he had been content to wait. He comments on the penance which Pompilia had undergone; and though he cannot believe that Caponsacchi ever went near her when she left the convent, is inclined to ask, Suppose he did? Is it a matter for surprise that he would feel lonely at Civita, and pine a little for the feminine society to which he had been accustomed? And so he goes on denying all the accusations, but always adding, "And suppose it were otherwise?" He says, if he must speak his mind, it had been better that Pompilia had died upon the spot than lived to shame the law. Does he credit her story?—no! Did she lie?—still no! He explains it this way: She had made her confession at the point of death, and was absolved; it was only charity in her to spend her last breath by pretending utter innocence, and thus rehabilitate the character of Caponsacchi. Had she told the naked truth about him, it would have doubtless injured him, and she was not bound to do that; and as the Sacrament had obliterated the sin, she was justified in the course he believes she took.

NOTES.—Line 115, *The Urbinate:* Rafael. l. 116, *The Cortonese:* Luca da Cortona, Italian painter. l. 117, *Ciro Ferri,* Italian painter (1634-1689). l. 170, *Phryne,* a celebrated beauty of Athens. She was the mistress of Praxiteles, who made a statue of her, which was one of his greatest works, and was placed in the temple of Apollo at Delphi. l. 226, *The Teian:* the Greek poet Anacreon was born at Teos, in Ionia. l. 284, *The Mantuan* = Vergil. l. 394, *Commachian eels* were anciently, and are still, very celebrated. l. 400, *Lernæan snake,* the famous hydra which Hercules slew. l. 530, *Idyllium Moschi,* the first Idyl of the Greek poet Moschus, entitled "Love a Runaway." l. 541, *Myrtilus,* the son of Mercury and Phæthusa: for his perfidy he was thrown into the sea, where he perished; *Amaryllis,* the name of a countryman mentioned by Theocritus and Vergil. l. 873, *Demodocus,* a musician at the court of Alcinous: the gods gave him the power of song, but denied him the blessing of sight. l. 875, "*foisted into that Eighth Odyssey*": see Pope's Homer's *Odyssey,* Book VIII., with the first note thereto. l. 887, *Cornelius Tacitus,* a celebrated Roman historian, born in the reign of Nero. l. 893, "*Thalassian-pure*": Thalassius was a beautiful young Roman in the reign of Romulus. At the rape of the Sabines, a virgin captured by one of the ravishers was declared to be reserved for Thalassius, and all were eager to reserve her pure for him. l. 968, *Hesione,* a daughter of Laomedon, king of Troy. It fell to her lot to be exposed to a sea monster. Hercules killed the monster and delivered her, but Laomedon refused to give him the promised reward. l. 989, *Hercules and Omphale:* Omphale was queen of Lydia, and Hercules loved her so much that he used to spin by her side amongst her women, while she wore the lion's skin and bore the club of the hero. l. 998, *Anti-Fabius, i.e.,* opposed to the policy of Quintus Fabius Maximus, the Roman general who opposed the progress of Hannibal, not by fighting, but by harassing counter-marches and ambuscades; for which he received the name of the *delayer.* A Fabian policy, therefore, is a waiting policy. Caponsacchi acted promptly. l. 1030, "*Sepher Toldoth Yeschu*": the Italians have an endless store of tales and legends of this character. See, for many such, *Mr. Crane's Italian Popular Stories* (Macmillan). l. 1109, "*Thucydides and his sole joke*": Thucydides was a celebrated Greek historian, born at Athens. He wrote the history of the Peloponnesian war, in which he tells the story of Cylon (I. 126). l. 1345, *Maro* = Vergil; *Aristæus*, a son of Apollo, said to have learnt from nymphs the art of the cultivation of olives and management of bees, which he communicated to mankind. l. 1494, *Triarii*, old soldiers that were kept in reserve to assist in case of hazard. l. 1573, "*famed panegyric of Isocrates*". Isocrates was one of the ten Attic orators, and one of the most remarkable men in the literary history of Greece. He was born B.C. 436. His splendid panegyric was delivered B.C. 380, for the purpose of stimulating the people of Greece to unite against the power of Asia.

BOOK X. [THE POPE.] As to a court of final appeal, the case has now come before the Pope, Guido having claimed "benefit of clergy." The Supreme Pontiff has made a prolonged study of the evidence adduced on the trials, and of the whole circumstances surrounding the case; now he has to decide the fate of the Count and his accomplices in the murder. And that he may give judgment without bias, in the sight of God and of the world, he nerves himself for the task by recalling the history of his predecessors in the Chair of Peter who have, from the Apostle up to Alexander, the last Pope, dared and suffered. How judged this one, how decided that? did he well or ill? He remembers that no infallibility attaches to such a decision as he must give in the case in which he is called upon to act: judgment must be given in his own behoof; so worked his predecessors. And now appeal is made from man's assize to him acting, speaking in the place of God. He must be just, and dare not let the felon go scot free. It is not possible to reprieve both criminal and Pope. Guido was furnished for his life with all the help a Christian civilisation could bestow: he had intellect, wit, a healthy frame, and all the advantages of family and position. He accepted the law that man is not here to please himself, but God; placed himself under obedience to the Church, which is the embodiment of that principle, and then deliberately clothed himself with the protection of the Church that he might violate the law with impunity. Three-parts consecrate, he sought to do his murder in the Church's pale. Such a man—religious parasite

—proves "irreligiousest of all mankind." His low instincts make him believe only in "the vile of life." He is clothed in falsehood, scale on scale. The typical actuating principle of his life was plainly exhibited in his marriage. He was prompted to that by no single motive which should have suggested matrimony. In this he had sunk far below the level of the brute, "whose appetite, if brutish, is a truth." This lust of money led him to lie, rob and murder; to pursue with insatiate malice the parents of his wife by punishing their child, putting day by day and hour by hour,

"The untried torture to the untouched place,"

goading her to death and bringing damnation by rebound to those who loved her. Ruining the three, he enjoyed luck and liberty, person, rights, fame, worth, all intact; while these poor souls must waste away, be blown about as dust. Such cruelty needed only as its complement, as a masterpiece of hell, the craft of this simulated love intrigue,—these false letters, false to body and soul they figure forth—as though the man had cut out some filthy shapes to fasten below the cherubs on a missal-page. But Pompilia's ermine-like soul takes no pollution from all this craft. It arose that in the providence of God were born new attributes to two souls. Priest and wife—both champions of truth—developed new safeguards of their noble natures. Then does the law step in, secludes the wife and gives the oppressor a new probation. It only induces Guido to furbish up his tools for a fresh assault. He has a son. To other men the gift brings thankfulness; Guido saw in the babe but a money-bag. Even in the deepest degradation of his sinful career he has another grace vouchsafed from God. When he fled from the scene of the murders, he took with him the money which he had agreed to pay his confederates. They came near to his hiding-place, intending to kill him for the gold, but were too late: the agents of the law were too quick for them. He had another chance of repentance. So stands Guido; and this master of wickedness has for pupils his "fox-faced, horrible brother-brute the Abate," and his younger brother, neither wolf nor fox, but the hybrid Girolamo, and

"The hag that gave these three abortions birth,
Unmotherly mother and unwomanly
Woman,"

and lastly the four companions in the murder, who acceded at once to the crime, as though they were set to dig a vineyard. Then the Pope recalls the only answer of the Governor to whom Pompilia appealed—a threat and a shrug of the shoulder. He has a severe word for the Archbishop, as a hireling who turned and fled when the wolf pressed on the panting lamb within his reach. It comforts him to turn to Pompilia, "perfect in whiteness," as he pronounces. It makes him proud in the evening of his life as "gardener of the untoward ground," that he is privileged to gather this "rose for the breast of God."

> "Go past me
> And get thy praise,—and be not far to seek
> Presently when I follow if I may!"

Nor very much apart from her can be placed Caponsacchi, his "warrior-priest." He finds much amiss in this freak of his. He disapproves the masquerade, the change of garb; but it was grandly done—that athlete's leap amongst the uncaged beasts set upon the martyr-maid in the mid-cirque. Impulsively had he cast every rag to the winds; but he championed God at first blush, and answered ringingly, with his glove on ground, the challenge of the false knight. Where, then, were the Church's men-at-arms, while this man in mask and motley has to do their work? When temptation came he had taken it by the head and hair, had done his battle, and has praise. Yet he must ruminate. "Work, be unhappy, but bear life, my son!" He turns to God, "reaches into the dark," "feels what he cannot see"; renews his confidence in the Divine order of the universe, but not without a pause, a shudder, a breathing space while he collects his thoughts and reviews his grounds of faith. The mind of man is a convex glass, gathering to itself

> "The scattered points
> Picked out of the immensity of sky."

He understands how this earth may have been chosen as the theatre of the plan of redemption; as he in turn represents God here, he can believe that man's life on earth has been devised that he may wring from all his pain the pleasures of eternity. "This life is training and a passage," and even Guido, in the world to come, may run the race and win the prize. It does not stagger him, receiving and trusting the plan of God as he does, that he sees other men rejecting and disbelieving it, any more than it surprises him to find fishers who might dive for pearls dredging for whelks and mud-worms. But, alas for the Christians!—how ill they figure in all this! The Archbishop of Arezzo—how he failed when the test came! The friar, who had forsaken the world, how he shrank from doing his duty, for fear of rebuke! Women of the convent to whom Pompilia was consigned,—their kiss turned bite, and they claimed the wealth of which she died possessed because the trial seemed to prove her of dishonest life: so issue writ, and the convent takes possession by the Fisc's advice. Their fine speeches were all unsaid—their "saint was whore" when money was the prize. All this terrifies the aged Pope—not the wrangling of the Roman soldiers for the garments of the Lord, but the greed in His apostles. But are not mankind real? Is the petty circle in which he moves, after all, the world? The instincts of humanity have helped mankind in every age; they will do so still. If, because Christianity is old, and familiarity with its teachings has bred a confidence which is ill grounded, the Christian heroism of past times can no longer be looked for, yet the heroism of mankind springs up eternally, and will suffice for all its needs. And now he hears the whispers of the times to come. The approaching age (the eighteenth century) will shake this torpor of assurance; discarded doubts will be re-introduced; the earthquakes will try the towers of faith; the old reports will be discredited. Then what multitudes will sink from the plane of Christianity down to the next discoverable base, resting on the lust and pride of life! Some will stand firm. Pompilias will "know the right place by the foot's feel"; Caponsacchis by their mere impulses will be guided aright; the vast majority will fall. But the Vicar of Christ has a duty to perform, whatever may be in store in the womb of the coming age. With Peter's key he holds Peter's sword:

"I smite
With my whole strength once more ere end my part,"

he says. Men pluck his sleeve, urge him to spare this barren tree awhile; others point out the privileges of the clergy, the right of the husband over the wife, the offence to the nobility involved in condemning one of their order, the danger to his own reputation for mercy. He brushes away with a sweep of his hand all these busy oppositions to his sense of duty, and signs the order for the execution of Guido and his companions. On the morrow the men shall die—not in the customary place, where die the common sort; but Guido, as a noble, shall be beheaded where the quality may see, and fear, and learn. He has no hope for Guido—

> "Except in such a suddenness of fate.
> I stood at Naples once, a night so dark
> I could have scarce conjectured there was earth
> Anywhere, sky or sea, or world at all:
> But the night's black was burst through by a blaze—
> Thunder struck blow on blow, earth groaned and bore,
> Through her whole length of mountain visible:
> There lay the city, thick and plain, with spires,
> And, like a ghost disshrouded, white the sea.
> So may the truth be flashed out by one blow,
> And Guido see, one instant, and be saved.
> * * * *
> "Carry this forthwith to the Governor!"

NOTES.—Line 1, *Ahasuerus:* Esther vi. 1. l. 11, "*Peter first to Alexander last*": St. Peter to Pope Alexander VIII., who died 1691. l. 25, *Formosus Pope* (891-6): he was bishop of Porto, and succeeded Stephen. He had formerly, from fear of Pope John, left his bishopric and fled to France. As he did not return when he was recalled, he was anathematised, and deprived of his preferments. He returned to the world, and put on the secular habit. Pope Martin (882-4) absolved him, and restored him to his former dignity; he then came to the popedom by bribery. (See *Platina.*) l. 32, *Stephen VII.* (The Pope, 896-7): "he persecuted the memory of Formosus with so much spite, that he abrogated his decrees and rescinded all he had done; though it was said that it was Formosus that conferred the bishopric of Anagni upon him. Stephen, because Formosus had hindered him before of this desired dignity, exercised his rage even upon his dead body; for Martin the historian says he hated him to that degree that, in a council which he held, he ordered the body of Formosus to be dragged out of the grave, to be stripped of his pontifical habit and put into that of a layman, and then to be buried among secular persons, having first cut off those two fingers of his right hand which are principally used by priests in consecration, and thrown into the Tiber, because, contrary to his oath, as he said, he had returned to Rome and exercised his sacerdotal function, from which Pope John had legally degraded him. This proved a great controversy, and of very ill example; for the succeeding popes made it almost a constant custom either to break or abrogate the acts of their predecessors, which was certainly far different from the practice of any of the good popes whose lives we have written." (Platina's *Lives of the Popes*, Dr. Benham's edition, vol. i., p. 237.) l. 89, "ΙΧΘΥΣ, *which means Fish*": the letters of this word, the Greek for fish, make the initials of the words Jesus, Christ, of God, Son, Saviour. The fish emblem for our Lord is common in the Roman catacombs, and is still used in ecclesiastical art. l. 91, "*The Pope is Fisherman*": because he is the successor of St. Peter the fisherman, and Christ said He would make Peter a fisher of men (Mark i. 17). l. 108, *Theodore II.* (Pope 898) restored the decrees of Formosus, and preferred his friends. l. 122, *Luitprand:* a chronicler of Papal history. l. 128, *Romanus* (Pope 897-8): as soon as he received the pontificate he disavowed and rescinded all the acts and decrees of Stephen. Platina calls such men "popelings," *Ponti-ficuli* (ed. 1551). l. 132, *Ravenna:* Pope John IX. removed to Ravenna in consequence of the disturbances in Rome. He called a synod of seventy-four bishops, and condemned all that Stephen had done; he restored the decrees of Formosus, declaring it irregularly done of Stephen to re-ordain those on whom Formosus had conferred holy orders. (See *Platina*.) l. 138, *De Ordinationibus* = concerning Ordinations. l. 142, *John IX.* (Pope 898-900) reasserted the cause of Formosus, in consequence of which great disturbances arose in Rome. *Sergius III.* (Pope 904-11) "totally abolished all that Formosus had done before; so that priests, who had been by him admitted to holy orders, were forced to take new ordination. Nor was he content with thus dishonouring the dead pope; but he dragged his carcase again out of the grave, beheaded it as if it had been alive, and then threw it into the Tiber, as unworthy the honour of human burial. It is said that some fishermen, finding his body as they were fishing, brought it to St. Peter's church; and while the funeral rites were performing, the images of the saints which stood in the church bowed in veneration of his body, which gave them occasion to believe that Formosus was not justly persecuted with so great ignominy. But whether the fishermen did thus, or no, is a great question; especially it is not likely to have been done in Sergius' lifetime, who was a fierce persecutor of the favourers of Formosus, because he had hindered him before of obtaining the pontificate." (Platina, *Lives of the Popes.*) l. 293, "*The sagacious Swede*": this was Swedenborg, born at Stockholm 1688, died 1772: the mathematical theory of Probability is referred to here. (See *Encyc. Brit.*, vol. xix., p. 768.) l. 297, "*dip in Vergil here and there, and prick for such a verse*": just as people open the Bible at random to find a verse to foretell certain events, so scholars used Vergil for this purpose; *sortes Vergilianæ*: Vergilian lots. l. 466, *paravent:* Fr. a screen; *ombrifuge:* a place where one flies for shade. l. 510, *soldier-crab:* the same as *hermit-crab.* Named from their combativeness, or from their possessing themselves of the shells of other animals. l. 836, *Rota:* a tribunal within the Curia, formerly the supreme court of justice and the universal court of appeal. It consists of twelve members called auditors, presided over by a dean. The decisions of the Rota, which form precedents, have been frequently published (*Encyc. Dict.*). l. 917, *she-pard:* a female leopard. l. 1097, "*The other rose, the gold*": this is "an ornament made of wrought gold and set with gems, which is blessed by the Pope on the fourth Sunday of Lent, and usually afterwards sent as a mark of special favour to some distinguished individual, church, or civil community" (*Encyc. Brit.*, x. 758). l. 1188, "*Lead us into no such temptations, Lord*": "It is lawful to pray God that we be not led into temptation, but not lawful to skulk from those that come to us. *The noblest passage in one of the noblest books of this century* is where the old Pope glories in the trial—nay, in the partial fall and but imperfect triumph—of the younger hero." (R. L. Stevenson's *Virginibus Puerisque*, p. 43.) l. 1596: Missionaries to China have always had great difficulty in expressing the word God with our idea of the Supreme Being in the Chinese language. l. 1619, *Rosy cross:* Dr. Brewer says this is "not *rosa-crux* = rose-cross; but *ros crux*, dew cross. Dew was considered by the ancient chemists as the most powerful solvent of gold; and cross in alchemy is the synonym of light, because any figure of a cross contains the three letters L V X (light). 'Lux' is the menstruum of the red dragon (*i.e.* corporeal light), and this sunlight properly digested produces gold, and dew is the digester. Hence the

Rosicrucians are those who use dew for digesting lux or light for the purpose of coming at the philosopher's stone." (*Brewer's Dict. of Phrase and Fable*, p. 765.) l. 1620, *The great work* = the *magnum opus:* "to find the absolute in the infinite, the indefinite, and the finite. Such is the *magnum opus* of the sages; such is the whole secret of Hermes; such is the stone of the philosophers. It is the great Arcanum." (*Mysteries of Magic*, A. E. Waite, p. 196.) This is the "Azoth" of Paracelsus and the sages. Magnetised electricity is the first matter of the *magnum opus*. l. 1698, "*Know-thyself*": *e cœlo descendit* Γνῶθι σεαυτὸν — "Know thyself came down from heaven" (Juvenal, *Sat.* xi. 24); "*Take the golden mean,*" "*Est modus in rebus*": "There is a mean in all things." (Horace, *Sat.* i. 106.) l. 1707, "*When the Third Poet's tread surprised the two*": "the talents of Sophocles were looked upon by Euripides with jealousy, and the great enmity which unhappily prevailed between the two poets gave an opportunity to the comic muse of Aristophanes to ridicule them both on the stage with humour and success" (*Lemprière, Eur.*). l. 1760, *schene* or sheen = brightness or glitter. l. 1762, *tenebrific:* causing or producing darkness. l. 1792, "*Paul,—'tis a legend,'—answered Seneca*": Butler, *Lives of the Saints*, under date June 30th, says: "That Seneca, the philosopher, was converted to the faith and held a correspondence with St. Paul, is a groundless fiction." l. 1904, *antimasque* or *anti-mask:* a ridiculous interlude; *kibe:* a crack or chap in the flesh occasioned by cold. l. 1942, *Loyola:* St. Ignatius Loyola, founder of the Order of the Jesuits. l. 1986-7, "*Nemini honorem trado*": Isaiah xlii. 8, xlviii. 11 — "I will not give mine honour to another," or "my glory" (as A.V.). l. 2004, *Farinacci:* Farinaccius was procurator-general to Pope Paul V., and his work on torture in evidence, "*Praxis et Theorica Criminalis* (Frankfort, 1622)," is a standard authority. l. 2060, "*the three little taps o' the silver mallet*": when the Pope dies it is the duty of the *camerlingo* or chamberlain to give three taps with a silver mallet on the Pope's forehead while he calls him; it is a similar ceremony to that used at the death of the kings of Spain; where the royal chamberlain calls the dead sovereign three times, "Señor! Señor! Señor!" l. 2088, *Priam:* the last king of Troy; *Hecuba:* the wife of Priam, by whom he had nineteen children according to Homer; "*Non tali auxilio*": this is from Vergil's *Æneid*, ii., 519

—"Non tali auxilio, nec defensoribus istis tempus eget," "The crisis requires not such aid nor such defenders as thou art." l. 2111, *The People's Square:* Piazza del Popolo, at the north entrance to Rome. It is reached from the Corso.

BOOK XI., GUIDO—is now in the prison cell awaiting execution. He is visited by Cardinal Acciaiuoli and Abate Panciatichi, who are to remain with him till the fatal moment. He is pleading with them for their aid; he reminds them of his noble blood, too pure to leak away into the drains of Rome from the headsman's engine. He protests his innocence; he has only twelve hours to live, and is as innocent as Mary herself. He denounces the Pope, who could have cast around him the protection of the Church, whose son he is. His tonsure should have saved him. It was the Pope's duty to have shown him mercy, but he supposes he is sick of his life, and must vent his spleen on him. He asks the Abate if he can do nothing? They used to enjoy life together, but he concludes that his companions have hearts of stone. He wishes he had never entangled himself with a wife; he was a fool to slay her. Why must he die? It need not be if men were good. If the Pope is Peter's successor, he should act like Peter. Would Peter have ordered him to death when there was his soul to save? What though half Rome condemned him? the other half took his part. The shepherd of the flock should use the crumpled end of his staff to rescue his sheep, not the pointed end wherewith to thrust them. The law proclaims him guiltless, but the Pope says he is guilty; and he supposes he ought to acquiesce and say that he deserves his fate. Repent? not he! What would be the good of that? If he fall at their feet and gnash and foam, will that put back the death engine to its hiding-place? He reflects that old Pietro cried to him for respite when he chased him about his room. He asked for time to save his soul: Guido gave him none. Why grant respite to him if he deserves his doom? Then he reproaches his companions: had they not sinned with him if he had done wrong? had they ever warned him, not by words, but by their own good deeds? He declares that he does not and cannot repent one particle of his past life. How should he have treated his wife? Ought he to have loved or hated her? When he offered her his love, had she not recoiled with loathing from him? Had she not acted as a victim at the sacrifice? Was it not her desire to be anywhere apart from him? What was called his wife was but "a nullity in female shape"—a plague mixed up with the "abominable non-descripts" she called her father and her mother. It was intended that he should be fooled; it happened that he had anticipated those who wished to fool him: yet this boast was premature. All Rome knows that the dowry was a derision, the wife a nameless bastard; his ancient name had been bespattered with filth, and those who planned the wrong had revealed it to the world. Yes, he had punished those who fooled him so. He had punished his wife, too, who had no part in their crime; and why? Her cold, pale, mute obedience was so hateful to him. "Speak!" he had demanded, and she obeyed; "Be silent!" and she obeyed also, with just the selfsame white despair. Things were better when her parents were present; when they left she ran to the Commissary and the Archbishop to beg their interference, and then committed the "worst offence of not offending any more." Her look of martyr-like endurance was worse than all: it reminded him of the "terrible patience of God." All that meant she did not love him; —she might have shammed the love. As it was, his wife was a true stumbling-block in his way. Everything, too, went against him. It was so unlucky for him that he did not catch the pair at the inn under circumstances when he could lawfully have slain them both together. There is always some—

> "Devil, whose task it is
> To trip the all-but-at perfection."

Unhappily, he had just missed his chance of appearing grandly right before the world. When he took his assassins to the villa he was fortunate, it is true, in finding all at home—the three to kill; but he had been unlucky in not escaping, as he had arranged. Then, when he thought he had killed his wife (with his knowledge of anatomy too!), she must linger for four whole days, the surgeon keeping her alive that every soul in Rome might learn her story. All the world could listen then. Had it not been for that he would have had a tale to tell that would have saved his head: he would have sworn he had caught Pompilia in the embraces of the priest, who had escaped in the darkness. And now she has lived to forgive him, commend him to the mercies of God, while fixing his head upon the block. And then at his trial all was against him: the dice were loaded, and the lawyers of no service to him. Yet he is sure that the Roman people approve his deed, though the mob is in love with his murdered wife. He says "there was no touch in her of hate." The angels would not be able to make a heaven for her if she knew he were in hell, she would pray him into heaven against his will; for it is hell which he demands, so heartily does he hate the good! Yes, he is impenitent,—no spark of contrition. Would the Church slay the impenitent? He passionately tells the Cardinal that he knows he is wronged, yet will not help him. As he sees no chance of their relenting, he tries to influence them by suggesting how he could have helped their chances at the next election of a Pope, which cannot be long delayed. Then he falls to entreaty again: "Save my life, Cardinal; I adjure you in God's name!" begs him go, fall at the Pope's feet, tell him he is innocent; and if that serve him not, say he is an atheist, and implore him not to send his soul to perdition. "Take your crucifix away!" he cries. Then, when all seems hopeless, he begins to abuse the Pope, the Cardinals, and all. He hates his victims too, he protests, as much as when he slew them; and while he curses, impenitent, scornful and full of malice, he hears the chant of the Brotherhood of Mercy, who sing the Office of the Dying at his cell-door. Then he shrieks that all he had been saying was false; he was mad:

"Don't open! Hold me from them! I am yours,
I am the Grand Duke's—no, I am the Pope's!
Abate,—Cardinal,—Christ,—Maria,—God, . . .
Pompilia, will you let them murder me?"

NOTES.—Line 13, *Certosa:* a Carthusian monastery, La Certosa, in Val' Emo, is situated about four miles from Florence. It was founded about 1341. It is Gothic, and is built in a grand style, like that of a castle. l. 186, *mannaia:* an instrument for beheading criminals, much like the guillotine. l. 188, "*Mouth-of-Truth*"—*Bocca della Verità:* S. Maria in Cosmedin, in ancient Rome. From the mouth of a fountain to the left is the portico, into which, according to a mediæval belief, the ancient Romans thrust their right hands when taking an oath. l. 261, "*Merry Tales*": the novels and tales of Franco Sacchetti (1335-1400). He wrote some three hundred *novelle* in pure Tuscan. l. 272, *Albano,* or *Albani, Francesco* (1578-1660): a celebrated

Italian painter, who was born at Bologna. He lived and taught in Rome for many years. Among the best of his sacred pictures are a "St. Sebastian" and an "Assumption of the Virgin," both in the church of St. Sebastian at Rome. l. 274, "*Europa and the bull*": Europa was the daughter of Agenor, king of Phœnicia. Jupiter became enamoured of her, and assumed the form of a beautiful bull. When Europa mounted on his back he carried her off. l. 291, *Atlas* and *axis* are bones of the neck on which the head turns: the *atlas* is the first cervical vertebra, the *axis* is the second cervical vertebra; *symphyses*, the union of bones with each other. l. 327, "*Petrus, quo vadis?*" "Peter, whither goest thou?" On the Appian Way at Rome there is a small church called Domine Quo Vadis, so named from the legend that St. Peter, fleeing from the death of a martyr, here met his Master, and inquired of Him, "Domine, quo vadis?" ("Lord, whither goest Thou?") to which he received the reply, "Venio iterum crucifigi" ("I come to be crucified again")—whereupon the apostle, ashamed of his weakness, returned. l. 569, *King Cophetua:* an imaginary king of Africa, who fell in love with a beggar girl. He married her, and lived happily with her for many years. l. 683, "*and tinkle near*": at the mass, when the priest consecrates the elements, a small bell is rung by the server to acquaint the worshippers with the fact that the consecration has taken place. This, of course, is the most solemn part of the mass, when the worshippers are most attentive. l. 685, *Trebbian:* from Trevi, in the valley of the Clitumnus. l. 786, "*Hocus-pocus*"; Nares says these words represent Ochus Bochus, an Italian magician invoked by jugglers; but there are other explan tions. *Vallombrosa Convent:* a famous convent near Florence. Milton says, "Thick as autumnal leaves that strew the br oks in Vallombrosa" (*Paradise Lost*, i. 302). But the trees are pines, and *not deciduous*. l. 1119, "*the Etruscan monster*": Mr. Browning was a student of Etruscan art and archæology. The Etruscans were the nation conquered by the Romans, and their antiquities are abundant in the district between Rome and Florence. The monster is the Chimæra, represented with three heads—those of a lion, a goat, and a dragon. Bellerophon, mounted on the horse Pegasus, attacked and overcame it. l. 1413, *Armida:* a beautiful sorceress, a prominent character in Tasso's *Jerusalem Delivered*. l. 1416, *Rinaldo*, in the same poem, was the Achilles of the Crusaders' army. He ran away from home at the age of fifteen, and was enrolled in the adventurers' squadron. Rinaldo fell in love with Armida, and wasted his time in voluptuous pleasures. l. 1420, *zecchines*, or *sequins:* Venetian gold coins, worth about 9*s.* 6*d.* l. 1669, *stinche:* a prison. l. 1808, "*Helping Vienna*": this refers to the second siege of Vienna by the Turks in 1683, when 150,000 Turks sat down before the city, Cara Mustapha being their leader. Pope Innocent XI. and John Sobieski, king of Poland, entered into a league to oppose the common enemy of Christian Europe. The whole Turkish army was defeated, and fled in the utmost disorder after the great battle fought under the walls of Vienna on Sept. 12th, 1683. l. 1850, *Gaudeamus,* "let us be glad." l. 1925, *Jove Ægiochus:* Jupiter was surnamed Ægiochus because, according to some authors, he was brought up by a goat. Properly the name is from the *ægis* which the god bore. l. 1928, "*Seventh Æneid*": Virgil's great poem was the "Æneis," which has for its subject the settlement of Æneas in Italy. The passage referred to is in the *Eighth Book* (426), and begins "His informatum, manibus jam parte politâ." l. 2034, "*Romano vivitur more*": Life goes on in the Roman way. l. 2051, "*Byblis in fluvius*": Byblis fell in love with her brother, and was changed into a fountain. l. 2052, "*sed Lycaon in lupum*": a cruel king of Arcadia, named Lycaon, was changed into a wolf by Jupiter, because he offered human sacrifices on the altar of the god Pan. l. 2144, *Paynimrie,* heathendom. l. 2184, *Olimpia,* in *Orlando Furioso:* Countess of Holland and wife of Bireno: when her husband deserted her she was bound naked to a rock by pirates, but Orlando delivered her and took her to Ireland. *Bianca:* wife of Fazio. She tried to save her husband from death; failed, went mad, and died of a broken heart. l. 2185, *Ormuz wealth:* the island Ormuz, in the Persian Gulf, is a mart for diamonds. l. 2211, *Circe:* a sorceress, who turned the companions of Ulysses into swine. Ulysses resisted the metamorphosis by virtue of the herb *moly*, given him by Mercury. l. 2214, *Lucrezia di Borgia:* she was thrice married, her last husband being Alfonso, Duke of Ferrara. Through her influence many persons were put to death. Her natural son Gennaro having been poisoned, she died herself as he expired. l. 2414, "*Who are these you have let descend my stair?*" They were the Brothers of Mercy, whose duty it was to attend criminals on the scaffold. Their chant was the Office of the Dying.

BOOK XII., THE BOOK AND THE RING.—On Feb. 22nd, 1698, Guido and his confederates were executed. We have, in the concluding book of this long poem, the reports of the execution, and the comments made concerning it in Rome, from four persons. The first which the poet gives is a letter from a stranger, a man of rank, on a visit to Rome from Venice. He begins his letter on the evening of the day in question, by stating that the Carnival is nearly over, the city very full of strangers, the old Pope tottering on the verge of the grave, and the people already beginning to discuss his probable successor. The Pope took daily exercise a week ago by the river-side, for the weather was like May. Then, after more gossip about politics, he says he has lost his bet of fifty sequins by the execution of the Count: he had felt, up to two days ago, that he would win the wager, as everybody seemed to think the Count would save his head; but the Pope's was the one deaf ear to every appeal for a reprieve, and so "persisted in the butchery." One of the writer's friends was so annoyed at the Pope's refusal to spare the life of a man with whom he had dined, that he would have actually stayed away from the execution, had it not been for a lady, whose presence on that occasion made it a desirable amusement for him. Of course, everybody of any importance was there, and the people made a general holiday of the occasion. Then he narrates how the ecclesiastics who had attended Guido on the eve of his execution considered that their efforts to prepare him for the next world had been crowned at last with complete success. The procession from the prison to the place of execution is described; and severe exception is taken to the choice of the Piazza del Popolo, as a deliberate affront to the aristocracy residing there. Still, it had its compensations, as it afforded a fine spectacle, and made, on the whole, a very pleasant day. There were the usual incidents of a street crowd: the man run over and killed; the pushing and struggling for good places; outcries there were, also, against the Pope for forbidding the Lottery; and a miracle was worked upon a lame beggar by the prayer of the holy Guido as he glanced that way. The Count was the last to mount the scaffold steps, and the nobility were so occupied with observing him and his behaviour in the presence of death, that they paid no attention to the peasants who dangled on their respective ropes at the gallows. The Count made a speech to the multitude, and comported himself as became a good Christian gentleman. He begged forgiveness of God, and hoped his fellow-men would put a fair construction on his acts; asked their prayers for his soul, suggesting that they should forthwith say an "Our Father" and a "Hail, Mary!" for his sake. Then he turned to his confessor, made the sign of the cross, and cast a fervent glance at the church over the way; rose up, knelt down again, bent his head, and with the name of Jesus on his lips received the headsman's blow. That functionary showed the head to the populace in due form, and the spectacle was over. The strangers present were a little disappointed at the Count's height and general appearance. They understood he was fully six feet high, and youngish for his years, and if not handsome, at least dignified; but his face was not one to please a wife. No doubt something was due to the rough costume in which he committed the murder,—a coarse and shabby dress enough. His end was peace. If his friend wishes to bet on the next Pope, he will give him a hint; and now will conclude with the last new pasquinade which has amused the city.

There were three letters which were bound up with Mr. Browning's famous "find" at Florence. One of these was written by the Count's advocate, De Archangelis, concerning certain fresh points intended to be used in mitigation of the sentence; but the lawyer explains that the Pope had set every plea aside, and had hastened the execution. The letter is addressed to the friends of the Count, and the client is referred to as a gallant man, who died in faith in an exemplary manner. He considers that no blot has fallen on the escutcheon of his noble house, as he had respect and commiseration from all Rome, and from the cultivated everywhere. He concludes by hoping that God may compensate for this direful blow by sending future blessings on the family. Enclosed with this communication is another, not intended for the noble persons to whom the above polite effusion is addressed. This is for their lawyer, and is to be kept to himself. He tells him that their "Pisan aid" was of no avail: the Pope was determined to see Guido's head drop off, and would not listen to reason. Especially annoying was it that his superb defence was wasted: he got nothing for his work, and he does not care how soon the obstinate and inept Pope dies. He tells his correspondent, who is his boy's godfather, how much the lad enjoyed the fine sight at the execution. He had promised him, if his defence failed to save the Count's head, that he should go and see it chopped off. This was exactly to the boy's taste; and he sat at a window with a great lady, who twitted the boy on the triumph of his father's opponent Bottini, saying that his "papa, with all his eloquence, cannot be reckoned on to help as before." The boy cleverly replied that his "papa knew better than offend the Pope and baulk him of his grudge against the Count; he would else have argued off Bottini's nose." He would have his opponent see that he was a man able to drive right and left horses at once.—The next letter is from the Fisc Bottini, who says the case ended as he foresaw: Pompilia's innocence was easily proved. Guido had made very good sport, and "died like a saint, poor devil!" Bottini regrets he had not been on the other side. Pompilia gave him no opportunity to show his skill; he could have done better with the Count. He can imagine how De Archangelis crows and boasts that he kept the Fisc a month at bay; he knows how he would grin and bray; but the thing which most annoys him is the behaviour of the monk, whose report of the dying Pompilia's words took all the freshness from his best points; and then, when preaching at San Lorenzo yesterday about the case, from the text "Let God be true, and every man a liar," said this, which he encloses from a printed copy of the sermon all Rome is reading to-day. "Do not argue from the result of this trial," said the preacher, "that truth may look for vindication from the world. God seems to acquiesce with those who say 'He sleeps,' and will not always put forth His hand and be recognised:

> "Because Pompilia's purity prevails,
> Conclude you, all truth triumphs in the end?"

Of all the birds that flew from the ark, one only returned: how many perished? So—

> "How many chaste and noble sister-fames
> Wanted the extricating hand, and lie
> Strangled, for one Pompilia proud above
> The welter, plucked from the world's calumny?"

Truth has to wait God's time; for how long did the pagans of old

Rome point to the Catacombs and say, "Down there, below the ground, foul and obscene rites are practised, far from the sight of men"? The most hideous and fearful practices were charged upon the early Christians, who worshipped in those places of refuge; but not for ages did God's lightning expose to the world those holy receptacles for the mangled remains of His martyred saints, and permit the gaze of the multitude to penetrate the sacred chambers, where the faith of Christ was kept alive in those dreadful centuries of persecution. Then, when God did call the world to see the whole secret so long preserved from the world above, what was there to behold?—a poor earthen lump by the rock where the corpse lay, the grave which held the treasured blood of the martyr:

> "The rough-scratched palm branch, and the legend left
> *Pro Christo.*"

And so these abhorred ones turned out to be saints. The best defence the law can make for Pompilia is to say that wickedness was bred in her, and after this specimen of man's protection, one wave of God's hand bids the mists dispel, and the true instinct of a good old man, who hates the dark and loves the light, adduces another proof that "God is true, and every man a liar": he who trusts to human testimony for a fact thereby proves himself a fool: man is false, man is weak, and "truth seems reserved for heaven, not earth." As for himself, added the friar, "he has long since renounced the world, yet he is not forbidden to estimate the value of that which he has forsaken. If any one were to press him as to his content in having put the pleasures of the world aside, he would answer that, apart from Christ's assurances, he dare not say whether he had not failed to taste much joy; how much of human love in varied forms he had lost; how much joy, from 'books that teach and arts that help,' he had missed. He might have learned how to grow great as well as good. Many precious things, no doubt, he had forsaken; but there was one—the chief object of men's ambition—earthly praise and the world's good repute; in renouncing these, his loss, he is sure, was light, and in choosing obscurity he was convinced he had chosen well." Bottini thinks this is vanity and spite: how dare he say "every man is a liar"! What next? He finds that the sermon has already had its effect for Gomez, who had decided to appeal to another court, and declines to have any more to do with lawyers; he has resolved to let the liars possess the world, and so he must whistle for his job and his fee. He is happy to say, however, that he shall soon be able to show the rabid monk whether law be powerless or not; for by a great piece of luck the convent to which Pompilia was first sent has claimed all her property which she had willed to those who were to act as trustees for her son and heir; as Pompilia had not been relieved at the trial from her imputed fault, the convent had a right to claim its due, and take the whole of the property. It has therefore become the lawyer's duty to institute procedure against this very Pompilia, whom last week he held up as a saint, and charging her with having been a very common sort of sinner, perform a volte-face before the selfsame court which he had so recently addressed, and show this "foul-mouthed friar" that his white dove is a sooty raven. The Pope, however, soon rectified this bad business, and issued an "instrument," which the poet says is contained in his precious little account of the trial, by which the Supreme Pontiff restores the perfect fame of the dead Pompilia, and quashes all proceedings brought or threatened to be brought against the heir, by the Most Venerable Convent of the Convertites in the Corso. So was justice done a second time. Two years later died good Innocent XII., after a rule of nine years in Rome; and so there is an end of the story. Mr. Browning is unable to say what became of the boy Gaetano, the child of Guido and Pompilia.

NOTES.—Line 12, *Wormwood Star:* a star which (it was fabled) appeared at the approach of death. l. 43: If the writer did bet on Spada for Pope he lost, as Cardinal Albani became the next Pope, in 1700. l. 62, *Holy Doors:* certain doors in St. Peter's, at Rome, which are opened only at the commencement of a Papal jubilee, and at its close are at once bricked up again. l. 65, "*Fenelon will be condemned*": Fenelon was one of the Jansenist leaders in France, and Jansenism was on its trial in Rome. l. 89, *Dogana-by-the-Bank:* a new customhouse. l. 104, *Palchetto:* a balcony made of scaffolding, used for public spectacles. l. 105, *The Pincian:* the Pincian hill, beyond the Piazza del Popolo, is a hill of gardens. Here were once the gardens of Lucullus, in which Messalina celebrated her orgies. This is a fashionable drive in the evening for the modern Romans. l. 114. *The Three Streets* diverge from the Piazza del

Popolo on the south; to the right is the *Via di Ripetta;* to the left the *Via del Babuino,* leading to the Piazza di Spagna; in the centre is the *Corso.* l. 139, *The New Prisons—Carceri Nuovi:* these were built by Pope Innocent X. They are situated in the Via Giulia, leading to the Bridge of St. Angelo. l. 140, *Pasquin's Street:* the street in Rome where there stands a mutilated statue in a corner of the palace of Ursini; so called from a cobbler who was remarkable for his sneers and gibes, and near whose shop the statue was dug up. On this statue it has been customary to paste satiric papers. Hence a lampoon *à Pasquinade* is a piece of satirical writing (*Webster's Dict.*). *Place Navona:* the Piazza Navona is the largest in Rome after that of St. Peter. It is officially called Circo Agonale. The name is said to be derived from the *agones* (corrupted to Navone, Navona), or contests which took place in the circus. l. 158, *Tern Quatern:* a tern is a prize in a lottery, resulting from the favourable combination of three numbers in the drawing; a quatern is a combination of four numbers; and a combination of these is, I presume, some very exceptional prize for the holders of the tickets. l. 178: "*Pater,*" the Lord's Prayer; "*Ave,*" the angelical salutation to the Virgin. l. 179, "*Salve Regina Cœli*": a hymn to the Virgin, sung at Vespers, which begins with the words "Hail, Queen of Heaven!" l. 184, This is a satire against relic-worship, and not in very good taste. l. 199, *just-a-corps:* a short coat fitting tightly to the body. l. 208, *quatrain:* a stanza of four lines rhyming alternately. l. 217, *socius:* an ally, a confederate. l. 224, *Tarocs:* a game at cards played with seventy-eight cards. l. 277, "*Quantum est hominum venustiorum*": and all men who have any grace. l. 290, "*hactenus senioribus*": hitherto for our superiors. l. 320, *Themis:* a daughter of Cœlus and Terra, who married Jupiter against her own inclination. She is represented as holding a sword in one hand and a pair of scales in the other. l. 326, "*case of Gomez*": this was a legal matter before the courts, and which was referred to in one of the manuscripts consulted by Mr. Browning when engaged upon the poem. l. 327, "*reliqua differamus in crastinum!*" the rest let us put off till to-morrow; *estafette:* courier. l. 361, "*Bartolus-cum-Baldo*": the names of two eminent Italian jurists. l. 367, "*adverti supplico humiliter quod*": I have observed, I humbly beg that. l. 435, *Spreti:* the subordinate of "De Archangelis"; he is "advocate of the poor." l. 504, "*their idol god an ass*": the early Christians were accused by their pagan persecutors of all sorts of horrible and degrading superstitions, amongst other things of worshipping the head of an ass. There has recently been discovered amongst the wall scratchings on some relics of ancient Roman buildings the figure of a crucified man with the head of an ass; and an inscription roughly scratched implying that this was the god of some Christian thus held up to ridicule. l. 520, "*the rude brown lamp*": used in the Catacombs, both for light and for burning at the martyrs' tombs to honour them. l. 521, *the cruse*: thousands of these have been discovered, and are exhibited in the museum at the Church of St. John Lateran in Rome. l. 522, "*the palm branch*": graven in countless parts of the Roman catacombs, as a sign that the martyr buried beneath it had won the victory, and had conquered by his faith. l. 523, "*pro Christo*," for Christ: that is to say, the martyrs had shed the blood presented in the cruse for Christ's sake. l. 647, *ampollosity*: windbag behaviour. l. 679, "*claim every paul*": paolo, an Italian coin worth sixpence. l. 715, "*Astræa redux*": justice brought back. l. 745, "*Martial's phrase*": *Mart.* iv. 91. l. 787, *Gonfalonier*: Lord Mayor, who bore the standard, or *gonfalon*. l. 811, *Buonarotti* = Michael Angelo. l. 812, *Vexillifer*, standard-bearer. l. 813, *The Patavinian*: *i.e.*, Livy of Padua. l. 815, "*Janus of the double face*": Janus, a Roman deity represented with two faces, because he was acquainted with the past and future, or because he was taken for the sun who opens the day at his rising and shuts it at his setting (*Lemprière*). l. 865, "*Deeper than ever the Andante dived*": a movement or piece in *andante* (rather slow) time, as the *andante* in Beethoven's fifth symphony. l. 872, "*Lyric Love*": the poet's dead wife invoked in the first part of this work. Her poems on Italy are referred to in the last line.—The *Encyclopædia Britannica*, vol. xiii., p. 85, says that Innocent XI. was the Pope of *The Ring and the Book*. Mr. Browning, however, says that Antonio Pignatelli (Innocent XII.) was the Pope in question. The character of the earlier sovereign pontiff certainly agrees better with the story told by the poet than does that of the latter. It may be, as has been suggested by Mr. George W. Cooke, in his *Guide-Book to Browning*, that the poet confounded the two men with each other, or, what is more probable, that he deliberately gave to Innocent XII. qualities which belonged only to Innocent XI. (p. 339). The following sketch of the life of Innocent XI. (Benedetto Odelscalchi) is taken from the *Encyclopædia Britannica:* "He was Pope from 1676 to 1689; was born at Como in 1611, studied law at Rome and Naples, [and] held successively the offices of protonotary, President of the Apostolic Chamber, Commissary of the Marca di Roma, and Governor of Macerta; in 1647 Innocent X. made him cardinal, and he afterwards successively became legate to Ferrara and bishop of Novara. In all these capacities the simplicity and purity of character which he displayed had, combined with his unselfish and open-handed benevolence, secured for him a high place in the popular affection and esteem; and two months after the death of Clement X. he was (Sept. 21st, 1676), in spite of French opposition, chosen his successor. He lost no time in declaring and practically manifesting his zeal as a reformer of manners and a corrector of administrative abuses. He sought to abolish sinecures, and to put the papal finances otherwise on a sound footing; beginning with the clergy, he endeavoured to raise the laity also to a higher moral standard of living. Some of his regulations with the latter object, however, may raise a smile as showing more zeal than judgment. In 1679 he publicly condemned sixty-five propositions, taken chiefly from the writings of Escobar, Suarez, and the like, as '*propositiones laxorum moralistarum,*' and forbade any one to teach them under pain of excommunication. Personally not unfriendly to Molinos, he nevertheless so far yielded to the enormous pressure brought to bear upon him as to confirm in 1687 the judgment of the inquisitors by which sixty-eight Molinist propositions were condemned as blasphemous and heretical. His pontificate was marked by the prolonged struggle with Louis XIV. of France on the subject of the so-called 'Gallican Liberties,' and also about certain immunities claimed by ambassadors to the papal court. He died after a long period of feeble health on August 12th, 1689. Hitherto repeated attempts at his canonisation have invariably failed, the reason popularly assigned being the influence of France. The fine moral character of Innocent has been sketched with much artistic power, as well as with historical fidelity, by Mr. Robert Browning in *The Ring and the Book.*"—Innocent XII. (Antonio Pignatelli), whose name Mr. Browning expressly gives, as fixing the identity of the Pope whose character he portrayed, was born at Naples in 1615. He took Innocent XI. for his model. This pontiff made him, in 1681, cardinal, bishop of Faenza, legate of Bologna, and archbishop of Naples. "His election as pope took place February 12th, 1691. At the beginning of his reign he endeavoured to abolish nepotism by means of a bull, in 1692. His nepotes were the poor—the Lateran his hospital. The Bullarium *magnum* contains many rules relating to cloister discipline and the life of the secular clergy. His efforts for the restoration of discipline were so great, that scoffers boasted he had reformed the Church both in its head and members. He died on September 27th, 1700. Shortly before his decease he settled a large sum on the hospital he had erected, and ordered that his goods should be sold and the proceeds given to the poor. He was a benevolent and pious prelate" (*Imp. Dict. Univ. Biog.*). There is such frequent reference to Molinos and the doctrines of Molinism or Quietism in *The Ring and the Book*, and the subject is so unfamiliar to the general reader, that I have thought it wise to extract the following admirable note on the question from Butler's *Lives of the Saints*, under the date November xxiv., "St. John of the Cross':— "Quietism was broached by Michael Molinos, a Spanish priest and spiritual director in great repute at Rome, who, in his book entitled *The Spiritual Guide*, established a system of perfect contemplation. It chiefly turns upon the following general principles. 1. That perfect contemplation is a state in which a man does not reason, or reflect, either on God or himself, but passively receives the impression of heavenly light without exercising any acts, the mind being in a state of perfect inaction and inattention, which this author calls quiet. Which principle is a notorious illusion and falsity: for even in supernatural impressions or communications, how much soever a soul may be abstracted from her senses, and insensible to external objects, which act upon their organs, she still exercises her understanding and will, in adoring, loving, praising, or the like, as is demonstrable both from principle and from the testimony of St. Teresa, and all true contemplatives. 2. This fanatic teaches, that a soul in that state desires nothing, not even his own salvation; and fears nothing, not even hell itself. This principle, big with pernicious consequences, is heretical; as the precept and constant obligation of hope of salvation through Christ is an article of faith. The pretence that a total indifference is a state of perfection is folly and impiety, as if solicitude about things of duty was not a precept. And so if a man could ever be exempt from the obligation of that charity which he owes both to God and himself, by which he is bound, above all things, to desire and to labour for his salvation and the eternal reign of God in his soul. A third principle of this author is no less notoriously heretical: that in such a state the use of the sacraments and good works becomes indifferent; and that the most criminal representations and motions in the sensitive part of the soul are foreign to the superior, and not sinful in this elevated state; as if the sensitive part of the soul was not subject to the government of the rational or superior part, or as if this could be indifferent about what passes in it. Some will have it that Molinos carried his last principles so far as to open a door to the abominations of the Gnostics; but most excuse him from admitting that horrible consequence (see F. Avrigny, Honoré of St. Mary, etc.). Innocent XI., in 1687, condemned sixty-eight propositions extracted from this author as respectively heretical, scandalous and blasphemous. Molinos was condemned by the Inquisition at Rome, recalled his errors, and ended his life in imprisonment in 1696 (see Argentere, *Collect. Judiciorum de Novis Erroribus*, t. iii., part 2, p. 402; Stevaert, *Damnat. Prop.*, p. 1). Semi-Quietism was rendered famous by having been for some time patronised by the great Fenelon. Madame Guyon, a widow lady, wrote *An Easy and Short Method of Prayer*, and *Solomon's Canticle of Canticles interpreted in a Mystical Sense*, for which, by order of Lewis XIV., she was confined in a nunnery, but soon after enlarged. Then it was that she became acquainted with Fenelon; and she published the Old Testament with explanations, her own life by herself, and other works, all written with spirit and a lively imagination. She submitted her doctrine to the judgment of Bossuet, esteemed the most accurate theologian in the French dominions. After a mature examination, Bossuet, bishop of Meaux, Cardinal Noailles, Fenelon, then lately nominated archbishop of Cambray, and M. Trowson, superior of S. Sulpice, drew up thirty articles concerning *the sound maxims of a spiritual life*, to which Fenelon added four others. These thirty-four articles were signed by them at Issy in 1695, and are the famous 'Articles of Issy' (see Argentere, *Collectio Judiciorum de Novis Erroribus*, t. iii.; Du Plessis, *Hist. de Meaux*, t. l., p. 492; *Mémoires Chronol.*, t. iii., p. 28). During this examination Bossuet and Fenelon had frequent disputes for and against disinterested love, or divine love of pure benevolence. This latter undertook in some measure the patronage of Madame Guyon, and in 1697 published a book entitled *The Maxims of the Saints*, in which a kind of Semi-Quietism was advanced. The clamour which was raised drew the author into disgrace at the court of Lewis XIV., and the book was condemned by Innocent XII. in 1699, on the 12th of March, and on the 9th of April following, by the author himself, who closed his eyes to all the glimmerings of human understanding to seek truth in the obedient simplicity of faith. By this submission he vanquished and triumphed over his defeat itself, and, by a more admirable greatness of soul, over his vanquisher. With the book, twenty-three propositions extracted out of it were censured by the Pope as rash, pernicious in practice, and erroneous respectively; but none were qualified as heretical. The principal error of Semi-Quietism consists in this doctrine,—that, in the state of perfect contemplation, it belongs to the entire annihilation in which a soul places herself before God, and to the perfect resignation of herself to His will, that she be indifferent whether she be damned or saved; which monstrous extravagance destroys the obligation of Christian hope. The Divine precepts can never clash, but strengthen one another. It would be blasphemy to pretend that because God, as a universal ruler, suffers sin, we can take a complacence in its being committed by others. God damns no one but for sin and final impenitence; yet, whilst we adore the Divine justice and sanctity, we are bound to reject sin with the utmost abhorrence, and deprecate damnation with the greatest ardour, both which by the Divine grace we can shun. Where, then, can there be any room for such a pretended resignation, at the very thought of which piety shudders? No such blasphemies occur in the writings of St. Teresa, St. John of the Cross, or other approved spiritual authors. If they are, or seem to be, expressed in certain parts of some spiritual works, as those of Bernieres, or in the Italian translation of Boudon's *God Alone*, these expressions are to be corrected by the rule of solid theology. Fenelon was chiefly deceived by the authority of an adulterated edition of *The Spiritual Entertainments of St. Francis of Sales*, published at Lyons, in 1628, by Drobet. Upon the immediate complaint and supplication of St. Francis Chantal and John Francis Sales, brother of the saint, then bishop of Geneva, Lewis XIII. suppressed the privilege granted for the said edition by letters patent given in the camp before Rochelle in the same year, prefixed to the correct and true edition of that book made at Lyons by Cœurceillys in 1629, by order of St. Francis Chantal. Yet this faulty edition, with its additions and omissions, has been sometimes reprinted; and a copy of this edition imposed upon Fenelon, whom Bossuet, who used the right edition, accused of falsifying the book (see *Mem. de Trev.* for July, anno 1558, p. 446). Bossuet had several years before maintained in the schools of Sorbonne, with great warmth, that a love of pure benevolence is chimerical. Nothing is more insisted on in theological schools than the distinction of the love of chaste desire and of benevolence. By the first, a creature loves God as the creature's own good—that is, upon the motive of enjoying Him, or because he shall possess God and find in Him his own complete happiness,—in other words, because God is good to the creature himself, both here and hereafter. The love of benevolence is that by which a creature loves God purely for His own sake, or because He is in Himself infinitely good. This latter is called pure or disinterested love, or love of charity; the former is a love of an inferior order, and is said by most theologians to belong to hope, not to charity; and many maintain that it can never attain to such a degree of perfection as to be a love of God above all things; because, say they, he who loves God merely because He is his own good, or for the sake of his enjoyment, loves Him not for God's own increated goodness, which is the motive of charity; nor can he love Him more than he does his own enjoyment of Him, though he makes no such comparison, nor even directly or interpretatively forms such an act, that he loves Him not more than he does his own possession of Him—which would be criminal and extremely inordinate. So this love is good, and of obligation, as a part of hope; and it disposes the soul to the love of charity. Bossuet allowed the distinct motives of the loves of chaste desire and of benevolence; but said no act of the latter could be formed by the heart which does not expressly include an act of the former; because, said he, no man can love any good without desiring to himself at the same time the possession of that good or its union with himself, and no man can love another's good merely as another's. This all allow, if this other's good were to destroy or exclude the love of his own good. Hence the habit of love of benevolence must include the habit of the love of desire. But the act may be and often is exercised without it, for good is amiable in itself and for its own sake; and this is the general opinion of theologians. However, the opinion of Bossuet, that an act of the love of benevolence or of charity is inseparable from an actual love of desire is not censured, but is maintained also by F. Honoratus of St. Mary (*Tradition sur la Contempl.*, t. iii., ch. iv., p. 273). Mr. Morris carries this notion so far as to pretend that creatures, in loving God, consider nothing in His perfections but their own good (Letter 2, 'On Divine Love,' p. 8). Some advised Fenelon to make a diversion by attacking Bossuet's sentiments and books at Rome, and convicting him of establishing theological hope by destroying charity. But the pious archbishop made answer that he never would inflame a dispute by recriminating against a brother, whatever might have seemed prudent to be done at another season. When he was put in mind to beware of the artifices of mankind, which he had so well known and so often experienced, he made answer: "Let us die in our simplicity" (*moriamur in simplicitate nostrâ*). On this celebrated dispute the ingenious Claville (*Traité du Vrai Mérite*) makes this remark, —that some of those who carried the point were condemned by the public as if they lost charity by the manner in which they carried on the contest; but if Fenelon erred in theory he was led astray by an excess in his desire of charity. By this adversity and submission he improved his own charity and humility to perfection, and arrived at the most easy disposition of heart, disengaged from everything in the world, bowed down to a state of pliableness and docility not to be expressed, and grounded in a love of simplicity which extinguished in him everything besides. Those who admired these virtues in him before were surprised at the great heights to which he afterwards carried them: so much he appeared a new man, though before a model of piety and humility. As to the distinction of the motives in our love of God, in practice, too nice or anxious an inquiry is generally fruitless and pernicious; for our business is more and more to die to ourselves, purify our hearts, and employ our understanding in the contemplation of the Divine perfections and heavenly mysteries, and our affections in the various acts of holy love—a boundless field in which our souls may freely take their range. And while we blame the extravagances of false mystics, we must never fear being transported to excesses in practice by the love of God. It can never be carried too far, since the only measure of our love to God is to 'love without measure,' as St. Bernard says. No transports of pure love can carry souls aside from the right way, so long as they are guided by humility and obedience. In disputes about such things, the utmost care is necessary that charity be not lost in them, that envy and pride be guarded against, and that sobriety and moderation be observed in all inquiries; for nothing is more frequent than for the greatest geniuses, in pursuing subtleties, to lose sight both of virtue, of good sense and reason itself. (See Bossuet's works on this subject, t. vi., especially his *Mystici in Tuto*, in which he is more correct than in some of his other pieces; also Du Plessis, *Hist. de l'Eglise de Meaux*, t. l., p. 485; the several lines of Fenelon, etc.)" Mr. Browning in this poem is like a demonstrator of anatomy in a famous school of dissection—some Sir Charles Bell lecturing to a crowded room full of students; taking up nerve after nerve, following it through all its ramifications, tracing it from its origin in brain or spinal cord, and never leaving it till it is lost in microscopic fibres at the periphery. He is as impartial as the anatomist, who asks no questions as to the presence of the subject on his table: all he has to do with is the science to which he is devoted. Mr. Browning is as happy with Guido in his dungeon as with the Pope in the Vatican, or Pompilia in the presence of the angels waiting to conduct her to God. The matter in hand is the human soul; and as the greatest poet of the soul that the world has ever seen, he is lost in his work. Count Guido never could have thought or said so much for himself as Browning has said for him. Pompilia's innocent, unsophisticated heart never attempted to formulate such a meditation on her brief history. Caponsacchi, we may be sure, never rose from his sonnets and gallantry to such a conscious elevation of soul as burst suddenly forth in the splendour of Pompilia's soldier-saint on his defence. If the Pope himself, the Vicar of Christ, came to his decision by any such conscious process of reasoning and high-toned Christian philosophy—Catholic because it is the highest expression of the highest thought and noblest impulse of the human heart—as that with which Mr. Browning has invested him, then Innocent XII. was a man of genius second only to the poet who has "created" him nearly two hundred years after he died. But no! These people lived indeed; they wrought all which their histories tell of them; but how and why, they never knew. God alone perfectly reads the human heart; and a few men like Browning are privileged to catch a word of the record here and there.

Roland. (See CHILDE ROLAND TO THE DARK TOWER CAME.)

Rosny. (*Asolando*, 1889.) Love, pure and passionate, unrestrained by thought of self, and gluttonous of sacrifice, was the undoing of the hero. No prudence could keep Rosny from his fate. Strength in love, and its victory in death is judged by the maiden to be the best. Although there does not seem to be any historical incident referred to in the poem, it may be advisable to say that Maximilian de Béthune, duke of Sully (1560-1641), the French statesman, was born at the château of Rosny, near Mantes. The title of his baronetcy was derived from the name of his birthplace, and he was commonly known by the name of Rosny all his life. Murray says that "Rosny is a dirty little village about half-way between Mantes and Bonnières. The château was the birthplace of Sully, where he was frequently visited by his friend and master, Henri IV., who slept here the night after his victory at Ivry. The king, having overtaken Sully on the road desperately wounded, carried on a litter, accompanied by his squires in a like plight, fell on his neck and affectionately embraced him. The château is a plain, solid building of red brick, with stone quoins and a high tent roof, surrounded by a deep ditch. It was rebuilt by Sully at the beginning of the seventeenth century. From 1818 down to the Revolution of 1830 Rosny was the favourite residence of the Duchesse de Berri, who erected here a chapel to contain the heart of her husband."

Rosamund Page. (*Martin Relph.*) She was the young girl who was shot by the military for supposed treason, and whose innocence would have been proved by her lover Parkes, if Mr. Martin had made known his presence when he saw him arrive at the village from the eminence on which he was standing.

"Round us the Wild Creatures." (*Ferishtah's Fancies.*)

The lyric to the first poem, "The Eagle," commences with this line.

Rudel to the Lady of Tripoli. (*Dramatic Lyrics*, in *Bells and Pomegranates*, No. III., 1842. Since transferred to *Men and Women* in *Poetical Works*, 1863.) Geoffrey de Rudel was a gentleman of Blieux, in Provence, and one of those who were presented to Frederick Barbarossa in 1154. He was a troubadour. Sismondi, in his *Literature of the South of Europe*, vol. i., p. 87 (Bohn's Edit.), gives the following account of Rudel:—"The knights who had returned from the Holy Land spoke with enthusiasm of a Countess of Tripoli, who had extended to them the most generous hospitality, and whose grace and beauty equalled her virtues. Geoffrey Rudel, hearing this account, fell deeply in love with her without having ever seen her, and prevailed upon one of his friends, Bertrand d'Allamanon, a troubadour like himself, to accompany him to the Levant. In 1162 he quitted the court of England, whither he had been conducted by Geoffrey, the brother of Richard I., and embarked for the Holy Land. On his voyage he was attacked by a severe illness, and had lost the power of speech when he arrived at the port of Tripoli. The Countess, being informed that a celebrated poet was dying of love for her on board a vessel which was entering the roads, visited him on shipboard, took him kindly by the hand, and attempted to cheer his spirits. Rudel, we are assured, recovered his speech sufficiently to thank the Countess for her humanity, and to declare his passion, when his expressions of gratitude were silenced by the convulsions of death. He was buried at Tripoli, beneath a tomb of porphyry which the Countess raised to his memory, with an Arabic inscription. I have transcribed his verses on "Distant Love," which he composed previous to his last voyage:—

"Angry and sad shall be my way,
 If I behold not her afar:
And yet I know not when that day
 Shall rise—for still she dwells afar.
God! who hast formed this fair array
 Of worlds, and placed my love afar,
Strengthen my heart with hope, I pray,
 Of seeing her I love afar

"Oh Lord! believe my faithful lay,
For well I love her, though afar;
Though but one blessing may repa
The thousand griefs I feel afar,
No other love shall shed its ray
On me, if not this love afar;
A brighter one, where'er I stray
I shall not see, or near, or far."

In Mr. Browning's poem, Rudel chooses for his device a sun flower, which, by ever turning towards the sun, has parted with the graces of a flower to become a mimic sun. He says that men feed on his songs; but the sunflower's concern is not for the bees which gather the sweetness of the flower's breast,—its concern is solely for the sun. So turns Rudel longingly to the East, where his lady dwells afar.

St. John. (*A Death in the Desert.*) The poem is a monologue of the dying saint in the desert near Ephesus. He records what he has seen of our Lord, and sadly anticipates the time when men will ask, "Did he say he saw?"

St. Martin's Summer. (*Pacchiarotto, with Other Poems*, 1876.) A husband and wife, both young, are reflecting on the fact that they have each buried love under some tomb now moss-grown and forgotten. The man admits that somehow, somewhere, he has pledged his "soul to endless duty, many a time and oft." Grief is fickle, for time is a traitor. Love, being mortal, must pass away, and he does not think either of them so very guilty; they grieved over their lost love at the time, though now it is forgotten. Yet, though Love's corpse lies quiet, its ghost sometimes escapes, and it is not well to build too durable a monument over it; trellis-work is better. It is better to own the power of first love, recognise its permanence in the soul, and let the succeeding love be estimated at its value, which to the poet does not seem to be very high. Dead loves are the potent, though living loves are ghost dispellers. From the oft-repeated expressions of Mr. Browning's opinion, and from the drift of this poem, we might be warranted in concluding that he believed only in first love.

NOTES.—*St. Martin's Summer;* or, *St. Martin's Little Summer.* From October 9th to November 11th. At the close of autumn we generally have a month of magnificent summer weather. "Expect St. Martin's summer, halcyon days" (*Shakespeare*, 1 *Hen. VI.*, Act i., sc. 2), and, "Farewell thou latter spring! farewell All-hallown summer!" It is also called "St. Luke's Summer," and Martinmas, and Martilmasse, because the feast of St. Martin is kept on November 11th. St. Luke's Day is October 18th. Verse 12, *Penelope* was the wife of Ulysses. During the long absence of her husband she was several times importuned by suitors to marry them. She told them that she could not marry again, even if she were assured that Ulysses were dead, until she had finished weaving a shroud for her aged father-in-law. Every night she pulled out what she had woven during the day, and so her work made no progress. *Ulysses:* is a corrupt form of Odusseus, the king of Ithaca. He is one of the principal heroes in the Iliad of Homer, and the chief hero of the Odyssey.

St. Peter's at Rome. (*Christmas Eve.*) The great colonnade on either side of St. Peter's Square is of semicircular form, and is beautifully described by the poet as

> "Arms wide open to embrace
> The entry of the human race.

Saul. This is perhaps the grandest and most beautiful of all Mr. Browning's religious poems. It is a Messianic oratorio in words. The influence of music in the cure of diseases has long been a subject of study by physicians. Disraeli, in his *Curiosities of Literature*, has an article on "Medical Music." In Dr. Burney's *History of Music* there is a chapter on "The Medicinal Powers attributed to Music by the Ancients." Dr. Burney thought this influence was partly due to its occasioning certain vibrations of the nerves, as well as its well-known effect in diverting the attention. Depression of mind, delirium and insanity, were anciently attributed to evil spirits, which were put to flight by suitable harmonies. It was for this reason that David was sent for to cure the mental derangement of Saul. The influence of music on the lower animals is often exceedingly marked, and can scarcely in their case, as in our own, be due to the association of ideas. The peculiar and sweet melancholy inspired by distant church bells on a calm summer evening in the country, though difficult to account for, is not less real than is the inspiring and invigorating effect produced by march music on weary soldiers. Life is a harmonious process; where there is most health there is most harmony in the way in which the bodily functions are performed. A great physician has described health as "going easy." It would be strange, therefore, if animal life were not attuned to sympathy with mechanical harmony. The most modern theory is that "Music is one of the stimuli which regulates the vaso-motor activity employed in tissue nutrition." (See *Lancet*, May 9th, 1891, p. 1055.) In another article in the same journal, for May 23rd, the subject is still further treated. The writer says: "The value of music as a therapeutic method cannot yet be so precisely stated that we may measure it by dosage or by an invariably similar order of effects. Of its wholesome influence in various forms of disease, however, there can be little or no doubt. In making this assertion we do not, of course, assign to it any specific or peculiar action. It is no quack's nostrum, no reputed conqueror of ache or ailment. It is only, as we have already shown in a recent article, one of those intangible but effective aids of medicine which exert their healthful properties through the nervous system. It is as a mental tonic that music acts. Accordingly, we may naturally expect it to exert its powers chiefly in those diseases, or aspects of disease, which are due to morbid nervous action. The evidence of its utility on occasions where fatigue or worry has disturbed the proper balance and relation between the mind and body of the so-called healthy will explain its action in disease. We can readily understand how a pleasing and lively melody can awake in a jaded brain the strong emotion of hope and energising by its means the languid nerve-control of the whole circulation, strengthen the heart-beat and refresh the vascularity of every organ. We can picture the same brain in forced irritation fretfully stimulating the service of the vaso-motor nerves, and starving the tissues of their blood-supply. Here, again, it is easy to comprehend the regulating effect of quieter harmony, which brings at once a rest and a diversion to the fretting mind. Even aches are soothed for a time by a transference of attention; and why, then, should not pain be lulled by music?" That it sometimes is thus relieved, we cannot doubt. It is especially in the graver nervous maladies, however, that we should look for benefit from this remedy. Definite statistics on the subject may not be forthcoming, but all that we have said goes to show that states of insanity, which are largely influenced by the condition of the sympathetic system, should find some part of their treatment in the hands of the musician. It is, therefore, for such cases especially that we would enlist his services. In nervous diseases music produces a stimulating effect on the trophic nerves, these are so called because they are supposed to govern or control the normal metabolism of their tissues (or the phenomena whereby living organisms assimilate their food into their tissues). Depressing news will impede or even arrest digestion, as is well known; cheerful conversation and music assist the assimilation of our sustenance. The almost total ignorance of the ancients concerning physiological processes caused them to attribute to demons the maladies which they could not comprehend. Music was prescribed for Saul empirically: it mattered little to the patient, so long as he was cured, whether music expelled a demon who was tormenting him, or lubricated the wheels of his nervous mechanism. David took his harp to Saul's tent, untwisted the lilies which were twined round the strings to keep them cool, and began by playing the tune all the sheep knew, appealing to his mere animal nature, and bringing him into harmony with the lower forms of healthy life; for there are points in our lives touched alike by men and sheep. Then he played the tune which the quails love, and that which delights the crickets, and the music which appeals to the quick jerboa; for there is a bond of sympathy between these creatures of our Father's hand and ourselves which we do ill to overlook; it is well for us sometimes to allow ourselves to be influenced by those things which God has made to delight the beautiful dumb creatures whom St. Francis of Assisi delighted to call his brothers and sisters. It was another step towards Saul's recovery when his soul achieved the harmony of a quail and a jerboa. Then he advanced his theme: he led the patient by his melody to the help tune of the reapers; brought before his saddened soul the good friendship of the toilers at their merry-making; expanded his heart in the warmth of brotherliness, the sympathy of man with man. But higher yet! The march of the honoured dead is played,—the praise of the men who have forgotten the faults in the work the man completed. And after that the joyful marriage chant, the abounding life and cheerfulness of the maidens; the march, too, of the comradeship of man in his greater task, the compulsion of the mechanical forces to aid the progress of the race. More exalted strains follow when, in the spirit of the worship of the one God of Israel, the Levites ascend the altar steps to appease Jehovah in sacrifice. By slow degrees the music had done the first part of its work: the sluggish forces of his life began to tremble, the quiverings of returning vital force began to thrill his torpid nerves. The song went forward: the wild joys of living were celebrated, the value of man's life, the good providence of God, the friendship, the kingship, the gifts combined to dower one head with the wealth of the world,—the stimulus of high ambition, the surpassing deeds, the crowning fame all concentrated in Saul, king of Israel. And the leap of David's heart voicing itself in the cry "Saul!" went to his wintry soul as "spring's arrowy summons to the vale, making it laugh in freedom and flowers." Saul was "released and aware," the despair was gone; pale and worn, he stood by the tent pole, once more himself; he was recalled to life, but not yet fitted to enjoy it. David pushes his advantage: the future, with its glorious prospect, the reward which God shall give to the successors of the king; and as David sings of the ages to come, which will ring with his praises and the fame of his mighty deeds, the life stream courses through his veins, he begins to live once more, he puts out his hand, touches tenderly the brow of the harpist, and as he looks on David the beautiful soul of the youthful singer goes out to the king in love, the magnetism of his sympathy touches him, and he longs to impart to him more than the past and present; he would give him new life altogether ages hence as at the moment. If he would do this, how much more would God do!

"Have I knowledge? confounded it shrivels at Wisdom laid bare.
Have I forethought? how purblind, how blank, to the Infinite Care!"

If he would fain do so much for this suffering man, would save, redeem and restore him, interpose to snatch Saul the mistake, the failure, from ruin, and bid him win by the pain-throb, the intensified bliss of the next world's reward and repose, if he would starve his own soul to fill up Saul's life, surely God would exceed all that David could desire to do, as the Creator in everything surpasses the creature, and as the Infinite transcends the finite. Then, in a magnificent prophetic burst, the singer tells Saul:

> "O Saul, it shall be
> A Face like my face that receives thee; a Man like to me,
> Thou shalt love and be loved by, for ever; a Hand like this hand
> Shall throw open the gates of new life to thee! See the Christ stand!"

The singer leaves the tent, goes to his home through the night, but not alone: clouds of witnesses hover around him, angels have come to listen to his prophecy, and the air is full of yearning spirits; the earth has awakened; hell has heard the echoes of his song,—her crews are loosed with alarm at the danger which impends; the stars in their courses beat with emotion; all creation palpitates with excitement; but the Hand which impelled him "quenched it with quiet," and earth in rapture sank to rest. But the world was the better for the blessed news, "felt the new law"; the flowers rejoiced, the heart of the cedars and the sap of the vines responded to the thrill of joy the brooks murmured, "E'en so, it is so!" (What are known as the Messianic Psalms, or those in which David sings of the Christ, who was to come, are the following: Psalm ii., xxi., xxii., xlv., lxxii., and cx.)—In Longus's romance of *Daphnis and Chloe* there occur two passages which may have furnished Browning with the suggestion of this series of tunes. The first is found on pp. 303-4 (I quote from Smith's translation, in the Bohn edition): "He ran through all variations of pastoral melody; he played the tune which the oxen obey, and which attracts the goats,—that in which the sheep delight. The notes for the sheep were sweet, those for the oxen deep, those for the goats were shrill. In short, his single pipe could express the tones of every pipe which is played upon. Those present lay listening in silent delight; when Dryas rose up, and desired Philetas to strike up the Bacchanalian tune, Philetas obeyed; and Dryas began the vintage-dance in which he represented the plucking of the grapes, the carrying of the baskets, the treading of the clusters, and the drinking of the new-made wine. . . . Upon losing sight of her, Daphnis, seizing the large pipe of Philetas, breathed into it a mournful strain as of one who loves; then a lovesick strain as of one who pleads; lastly, a recalling strain, as of one who seeks her whom he has lost." The other is from pp. 332-4: "Daphnis disposed the company in a semicircle; then standing under the shade of a beech-tree, he took his pipe from his scrip, and breathed into it very gently. The goats stood still, merely lifting up their heads. Next he played the pasture tune, upon which they all put down their heads and began to graze. Now he produced some notes soft and sweet in tone: at once his herd lay down. After this he piped in a sharp key, and they ran off to the wood, as if a wolf were in sight." Again, may not the impulse to write this poetry have been derived from Heber's *Spirit of Hebrew Poetry*? On p. 197, vol. ii., of the translation, there is a kind of challenge to poets in general: "Take David in the presence of Saul. More than one poet has availed himself of the beauty of this situation; but no one to my knowledge has yet stolen the harp of David, and produced a poem, such even as Dryden's ode in the composition of Handel, where Timotheus plays before Alexander. If Browning did accept the challenge, it was only to refute the observation by his success." —*Pall Mall Gazette.*

NOTES.—The Bible story of David playing before Saul is found in 1 Samuel xvi. 14-23. Stanza i., *Abner:* the son of Ner, captain of Saul's host (1 Samuel xxvi. 5). Stanza vi., *jerboa:* a small jumping rodent animal, called also the jumping hare. Stanza viii., *Male-Sapphires:* the asterias or star-stone, a semi-transparent sapphire. Stanza xiv., *Hebron:* the most southern of the three cities of refuge west of Jordan; *Kidron:* a brook in Jerusalem.

Science in Browning. The following are some references to scientific matters in the poet's works appended to my essay on "Browning as a Scientific Poet" in *Browning's Message to his Time.* The list of references makes no pretension to be an exhaustive one—it could be considerably amplified by a careful reperusal of the works—but it will suffice for the purpose:—

Anatomy.—Poems, v., p. 152; vi., p. 158. Fifine, p. 68.

Astronomy.—Prince H. S., p. 96. Sordello, pp. 187, 188.

Botany.—Poems, i., p. 194; v., pp. 193, 208, 228, 312. Fifine, p. 14. Sordello, p. 20.

Chemistry.—Poems, iii., pp. 219, 220; iv., p. 238; v., pp. 155, 156. Prince H. S., pp. 44, 91. Red Cotton, p. 196. Croisic, pp. 90, 92. Fifine, pp. 65, 97, 130. Ferishtah, pp. 39, 40, 45, 76. Pippa P., p. 250. Sordello, p. 194. Ring and Book, i., p. 2

Electricity.—Poems, vi., pp. 183, 203. Red Cotton, p. 196. Fifine, p. 115.

Evolution.—Poems, i., p. 188. Prince H. S., p. 68. Fifine. p. 162. La Saisiaz, p. 57.

Light.—Poems, iii., p. 170. Jocoseria, p. 124. Fifine, pp. 65, 29. Numpholeptos, p. 101. Ring and Book, i., p. 71; iii., p. 170; iv., pp. 57, 79.

Materia Medica and Therapeutics.—Pietro of Abano, p. 84. Prince H. S., p. 77. Paracelsus, p. 111.

Medicine.—Poems, iv., p. 273; v., p. 220. Dramatic Idyls, ii., preface. Red Cotton, p. 199. Ferishtah, pp. 27, 55, 56. Ring and Book, iv., p. 12.

Pharmacy.—Poems, iii., p. 96; v., p. 220.

Physiology.—Poems, v., p. 191. Sordello, p. 195. Tray.

Scientific Matters in General.—Poems, v., pp. 128, 302; vi., p. 203. Dramatic Idyls, ii., p. 68. Fifine, pp. 51, 86. La Saisiaz, pp. 69, 82. Ferishtah, p. 131. Sordello, pp. 25, 203. Ring and Book, iv., pp. 61, 77, 180.

The references are to the six-volume edition of the poems, and to the original separate editions of the larger works.

Sebald. The man in *Pippa Passes* who murdered Ottima's husband.

Serenade at the Villa, A. (*Men and Women*, 1855; *Lyrics*, 1863; *Dramatic Lyrics*, 1868.) A lover serenades his lady on a sultry summer night; and the burden of his song is that, as he watches through the dark night at her villa, so he vows to watch through life over her path, and shield her from danger and serve her in secret devotion, as he sings to her now while she sleeps. The lady dreamed of music, but slept on, though "the earth turned in her sleep in pain." Earth has heard many serenades and many vows made only to be broken. The iron gate which ground its teeth to let the serenader pass seemed to be disputing the lover's protestations; and one fears that if his mistress was like the earth, and "turned in her sleep" too, she would derive little satisfaction from his music.

Setebos. (*Caliban and Setebos.*) The god of the Patagonians, whom Caliban worships because his mother did so. Caliban thinks he lives in the moon, and has made mankind for his amusement.

Shah 'Abbas. (*Ferishtah's Fancies, III.*) Shah 'Abbas, surnamed the Great, was one of the most celebrated of the sovereigns of Persia. He came to the throne at the age of eighteen, in the year 1585. He defeated the predatory Uzbeks, who occupied Khorassan, after a long and severe struggle, in a great battle near Herat (1597), and drove them out of his dominions. He was successful in the wars he waged against the Turks, and thereby greatly extended his dominions. He defeated the united armies of the Turks and Tartars in 1618. Baghdad was taken in 1623. When he died, in 1628, his dominions reached from the Tigris to the Indus. The circumstances narrated in Mr. Browning's poem are not historical. The subject of the poem is Belief. "It is beautiful, but is it true?" Ferishtah has now achieved dervishhood, and a pupil asks, "Was this life lived, was this death died, not dreamed?" It was answered, "Many attested it for fact." A cup-bearer left on record a story of the death of the brave Shah 'Abbas of simple fear at discovering a spider in his wine. The cup-bearer was eye-witness of the fact. The Dervish says we must distinguish between the noble act of belief, and mere easy acquiescence. Twenty soldiers testify to the death of a comrade; yet he comes home safe and sound after the wars. He had two sons. One who heard that his father was living rejoiced; the other preferred the evidence of the twenty men who saw him die. Ten years later home comes Ishak. The townsmen bid the man of ready faith go and welcome his father, and the unbelieving one to hide his head. The father would praise the loving heart in preference to the sceptical head. "Is God less wise?" asks Ferishtah. The lyric teaches that the true light of life is love. The dark ways of life and the mysteries of the human heart will prove stones of stumbling and rocks of offence where love is not the guide. With love and truth our obstacles disappear.

Shakespeare. The poem which Mr. Browning wrote for the *Shakespearean Show-Book*, 1884, commenced with the word "*Shakespeare!*" See NAMES, THE.

Shop. (*Pacchiarotto, with other Poems*, 1876.) "As even in science all roads," it has been said, "lead to the mouth," so is it with Art and Letters. The poet deplores the life of a tradesman who knows no other use of life but to enable him to drive a roaring business, his "meat and drink but money chink,"—and so, because flesh must be fed, spirit is chained to the counter.

The poet would have the tradesman brighten his daily life with art and song, as men do who let their good angels sometimes converse with them, in lands where poets and painters think more of art than money. The danger and wickedness of compelling the soul to be the eternal slave of sordid desires and petty anxieties is pointed out in this poem, and by "shop" we are not only to think of tradesmen, but of all the large class of those who are, like the man in the *Pilgrim's Progress*, too busy with the muck-rake to look at the heavens above them, and losing their higher selves in their absorption in earthly employments.

Sibrandus Schafnaburgensis. (See GARDEN FANCIES.) The name of some old scholar, who has written a book, which is read by a profane fellow in a garden, who throws it into a decaying tree, there to be in company with congenial fungi.

"Sighed Rawdon Brown." (See RAWDON BROWN.)

Soliloquy of the Spanish Cloister. [*Dramatic Lyrics*, in *Bells and Pomegranates*, *III.*, 1842, under the title of "Camp and Cloister—I. Camp (French), II. Cloister (Spanish)."] There is, of course, no historical basis for the subject-matter of this poem; but there is no reason why such things should not occur in a convent or monastery. Human nature, we find, is pretty much the same, under whatever conditions we examine it; and petty malice, ill-nature, and evil passions, find their congenial soil alike in the cloister and the world. Some of the most unpleasant failings of our nature are no doubt directly fostered by cloister life, just as religious people of every class are often censorious, uncharitable in their judgments, pharisaical and severe. Unless monks and nuns are regularly and entirely employed in useful labour, these evil weeds are certain to spring up in the untilled soil of the human heart. Work is the only remedy for pettiness of spirit, and active employment the only atmosphere for the nobler products of the soul. It must never be forgotten, however, that thousands of the most beautiful characters which have blessed the world have been formed in the cloister; such are being formed now, and will continue to be so formed, in direct proportion to the useful work in which its inmates are employed.—To inferior and evil natures the lofty and noble soul is generally an object of hatred and jealousy. In this poem we have a coarse-minded Spanish monk, boiling over with abhorrence of a good, gentle brother, who loves his flowers, trims his bushes and waters his rose trees with tender solicitude for the welfare of his plants, the only things in the monastery he can love. The simple talk of the hated friar at meal-time and recreation disgusts him; he knows in his heart that the good brother is a saint, though he tries in his malice to rake up some remembrance of a wandering look at odd times, and is not so ritualistically exact as he is himself. He spites him by damaging his plants all he can in a sly and ingenious way. He would like him to lose his chances of sa - vation if he could, so he will endeavour to pervert his orthodoxy and trip him up on his way to heaven; he will slip in amongst his greengages a wicked French novel; or he will even go so far as to ask Satan's aid,—when, as he meditates all this evil doing, the vesper bell rings and the wicked old fellow goes to his prayers.

NOTES.—Verse ii., "*Salve tibi*": a salutation, "Hail to thee!" Verse v., *Cross-wise*: the use of the sign of the cross is traceable to the earliest Christian times; "*The Trinity illustrate*": when the sign of the cross is made it is usual to add internally "In the name of the Father, and of the Son, and of the Holy Ghost. Amen." A Catholic remembers the Trinity in numberless ways; *Arian*: "One who adheres to the doctrines of Arius, a presbyter of the Church in the fourth century, who held Christ to be a created being, inferior to God the Father in nature and dignity, though the first and noblest of created beings." (*Mosheim.*) Verse vii., "*The great text in the Galatians*" I take to be the tenth verse of the third chapter: "For as many as are of the works of the law are under the curse: for it is written, 'Cursed is every one that continueth not in all things which are written in the book of the law to do them.'" "It is written,"—that is to say, in the book of Deuteronomy, xxviii., 15 to 68, wherein are set forth at length the curses for disobedience. Those arithmetically-minded commentators on this poem who have been disappointed in finding only some "seventeen works of the flesh" in Galatians v. 19-21 will find an abundant opportunity for their discrimination in the chapter of Deuteronomy to which I refer. The question to settle is "the twenty-nine distinct damnations." St. James says in his epistle (ii. 10), that "he who offends against the law in one point is guilty of all." If, therefore, the envious monk could induce his brother to trust to his works instead of to his faith, he would fall under the condemnation of the law, as explained by St. Paul in his epistle. *Manichee:* "A follower of Manes, a Persian, who tried to combine the Oriental philosophy with Christianity; and maintained that there are two supreme principles: the first of which, *light*, was held to be the author of all good; the second, *darkness*, the author of all evil" (*Webster's Dict.*). Verse viii., *Belial:* an evil spirit; "*Plena gratiâ Ave, Virgo!*": probably intended to represent "the angelical salutation," which is "Ave Maria, gratiâ plena"—"Hail, Mary, full of grace!"

Solomon and Balkis. (*Jocoseria*, 1883.) The Queen of Sheba sits on Solomon's ivory throne, and talks of deep mysteries and things sublime; she proves the king with hard problems, which he solves ere she has finished her questions. He humiliates the Queen by making her difficulties appear so childish that there is no spirit in her; but she musters up strength enough for just one more hard question: "Who are those," she asks, "who of all mankind should be admitted to the palace of the wisest monarch on application?" Solomon says the wise are the equals of the king; those who are kingly in craft should be his friends. He in turn asks the Queen, "Who are those whom she would admit on similar terms?" "The good," replies the Queen; and as she speaks she contrives to jostle the king's right hand, so that the ring which he wore was turned from inside now to outside. The ring bore the "truth-compelling Name" of Jehovah; then the King was obliged to confess that those only would be considered wise who came to offer him the incense of their flattery.—"You cat, you!" he adds; and then, turning the Name towards her, makes her also tell the truth. Promptly she is compelled to answer that by the good she means young men, strong, tall, and proper: these she enlists always as her servants. Then sighed the King: the soul that aspires to soar, yet ever crawls, can discern the great, yet always chooses the small; there is earth's rest, as well as heaven's rest; above, the soul may fly; here, she must plod heavily on earth. Solomon proposes to resume their discourse; but the Queen tells him that she came to see Solomon the wise man; not to commune with mind, but body—and, if she does not make too bold, would rather have a kiss!

NOTES.—*Conster:* Old English for construe. "*spheteron do*":

(Greek), his home: the idea of Balkis talking Greek to Solomon is to show what a prig she was. *Solomon's Seal*, as Solomon's ring is commonly called, was celebrated for its potency over demons and genii. It is probably of Hindu origin, and bore the double triangle sign of the Kabalists. (See *Isis Unveiled* (Blavatsky), vol. i., pp. 135-6.) "*You cat, you!*" Solomon descending to this is exquisitely funny. *Habitat:* a suitable dwelling-place. *Hyssop* (1 Kings iv. 33): a plant which grows in crevices of walls. Dr. J. Forbes Royle considers it to be the caper (*Capparis spinosa*), the *asuf* of the Arabs. According to the *Encyclopædia Britannica*, vol. xxiv., p. 738, the land of Sheba is Yemen, in Arabia. The ancient name of the people of Yemen was Saba (Sheba). "The Queen of Sheba who visited Solomon may have come with a caravan trading to Gaza, to see the great king whose ships plied on the Red Sea. The Biblical picture of the Sabæan kingdom is confirmed and supplemented by the Assyrian inscriptions. Tiglath Pileser II. (733 B.C.) tells us that Teima, Sabá, and Haipá (= Ephah, Gen. xxv. 4 and Isa. lx. 6) paid him tribute of gold, silver, and much incense. Similarly Sargon (715 B.C.), in his *Annals*, mentions the tribute of Shamsi, queen of Arabia, and of Itamara of the land of Sabá, gold and fragrant spices, horses and camels." The following is the Talmudic legend concerning the visit of the Queen of Sheba to Solomon. "It is said that Solomon ruled the whole world, and this verse is quoted as proof of the assertion: 'And Solomon was ruling over all the kingdoms, which brought presents, and served Solomon all the days of his life' (1 Kings iv. 21). All the kingdoms congratulated Solomon as the worthy successor of his father, David, whose fame was great among the nations; all save one, the kingdom of Sheba, the capital of which was called Kitore. To this kingdom Solomon sent a letter: 'From me, King Solomon, peace to thee and to thy government. Let it be known to thee that the Almighty God has made me to reign over the whole world, the kingdoms of the north, the south, the east, the west. Lo, they have come to me with their congratulations, all save thee alone. Come thou also, I pray thee, and submit to my authority, and much honour shall be done thee; but if thou refusest, behold, I shall by force compel thy acknowledgment. —To thee, Queen Sheba, is addressed this letter in peace from me, King Solomon, the son of David.' Now, whe

Queen Sheba received this letter, she sent in haste for her elders and councillors, to ask their advice as to the nature of her reply. They spoke but lightly of the message and the one who sent it; but the Queen did not regard their words. She sent a vessel, carrying many presents of different metals, minerals, and precious stones, to Solomon. It was after a voyage of two years' time that these presents arrived at Jerusalem; and in a letter intrusted to the captain, the Queen said 'After thou hast received the message, then I myself will come to thee.' And in two years after this time Queen Sheba arrived at Jerusalem. When Solomon heard that the Queen was coming, he sent Benayahu, the son of Jehoyadah, the general of his army, to meet her. When the Queen saw him she thought he was the King, and she alighted from her carriage. Then Benayahu asked, 'Why alightest thou from thy carriage?' And she answered, 'Art thou not his majesty, the King?' No, replied Benayahu, 'I am but one of his officers.' Then the Queen turned back and said to her ladies in attendance, 'If this is but one of the officers, and he is so noble and imposing in appearance, how great must be his superior, the King!' And Benayahu, the son of Jehoyadah, conducted Queen Sheba to the palace of the King. Solomon prepared to receive his visitor in an apartment laid and lined with glass; and the Queen at first was so deceived by the appearance that she imagined the King to be sitting in water. And when the Queen had tested Solomon's wisdom * and witnessed his magnificence, she said: 'I believed not what I heard; but now I have come, and my eyes have seen it all, behold, the half has not been told to me. Happy are thy servants who stand before thee continually to listen to thy words of wisdom. Blessed be the Lord thy God, who hath placed thee on a throne to rule righteously and in justice.' When other kingdoms heard the words of the Queen of Sheba, they feared Solomon exceedingly, and he became greater than all the other kings of the earth in wisdom and in wealth. Solomon was born in the year 2912 A.M., and reigned over Israel forty years. Four hundred and thirty-three years elapsed between the date of Solomon's reign and that of the Temple's destruction." (From Polano's translation of selections from the Talmud.)

* By means of riddles, as related in the Bible.

Sonnet:*—

"Eyes, calm beside thee, (Lady could'st thou know!)
May turn away thick with fast-gathering tears:
I glance not where all gaze: thrilling and low
Their passionate praises reach thee—my cheek wears
Alone no wonder when thou passest by;
Thy tremulous lids bent and suffused reply
To the irrepressible homage which doth glow
On every lip but mine: if in thine ears
Their accents linger—and thou dost recall
Me as I stood, still, guarded, very pale,
Beside each votarist whose lighted brow
Wore worship like an aureole, 'O'er them all
My beauty,' thou wilt murmur, 'did prevail
Save that one only:'—Lady could'st thou know!

August 17*th*, 1834. Z."

Sordello. [THE MAN.] Sordello was a troubadour, and we have to thank Dante for having made, in his *Purgatorio*, such frequent reference to him as will preserve his name from oblivion as long as the *Divina Commedia* is known to the world. Sordello is referred to in the *Purgatorio* eight times: viz., in Canto vi. 75; vii. 2, 52; viii. 38, 43, 62, 93; ix. 53 (Cary's translation). In the sixth Canto we are introduced to Sordello thus:—

"But lo! a spirit there
Stands solitary, and toward us looks;
It will instruct us in the speediest way."
We soon approach'd it. O thou Lombard spirit!
How didst thou stand, in high abstracted mood,
Scarce moving with slow dignity thine eyes.
It spoke not aught, but let us onward pass,
Eying us as a lion on his watch.
But Vergil, with entreaty mild, advanced,
Requesting it to show the best ascent.
It answer to his question none return'd;
But of our country and our kind of life
Demanded—When my courteous guide began,

---

* The above sonnet, by Robert Browning, is copied from *The Monthly Repository* (edited by W. J. Fox) for 1834, New series, vol. viii., p. 712.

> 'Mantua,' the shadow, in itself absorb'd,
> Rose towards us from the place in which it stood,
> And cried, 'Mantuan! I am thy countryman,
> Sordello.' Each the other then embraced."

Cary's note is valuable: "The history of Sordello's life is wrapt in the obscurity of romance. That he distinguished himself by his skill in Provençal poetry is certain; and many feats of military prowess have been attributed to him. It is probable that he was born towards the end of the twelfth, and died about the middle of the succeeding century. Tiraboschi, who terms him the most illustrious of all the Provençal poets of his age, has taken much pains to sift all the notices he could collect relating to him; and has particularly exposed the fabulous narrative which Platina has introduced on this subject in his history of Mantua. Honourable mention of his name is made by our poet in the treatise *De Vulg. Eloq.*, lib. i. cap. 15, where it is said that, remarkable as he was for eloquence, he deserted the vernacular language of his own country, not only in his poems, but in every other kind of writing. Tiraboschi had at first concluded him to be the same writer whom Dante elsewhere (*De Vulg. Eloq.*, lib. ii. c. 13) calls Gottus Mantuanus, but afterwards gave up that opinion to the authority of the Conte d'Arco and the Abate Bettinelli. By Bastero, in his *Crusca Provenzale*, (ediz. Roma., 1724, p. 94), amongst Sordello's MS. poems in the Vatican, are mentioned "Canzoni, Tenzoni, Cobbole," and various "Serventesi," particularly one in the form of a funeral song on the death of Blancas, in which the poet reprehends all the reigning princes in Christendom.—Many of Sordello's poems have been brought to light by the industry of M. Raynouard, in his *Choix des Poésies des Troubadours* and his *Lexique Roman*." Sismondi, in his *Literature of Europe*, vol. i., p. 103, says that the real merit of Sordello as a troubadour "consists in the harmony and sensibility of his verses. He was amongst the first to adopt the ballad form of writing; and in one of these which has been translated by Millot, he beautifully contrasts, in the burthen of his ballad, the gaieties of nature, and the ever-reviving grief of a heart devoted to love. Sordel, or Sordello, was born at Goïto, near Mantua, and was for some time attached to the household of the Count of S. Bonifazio, the chief of the Guelf party, in the march of Treviso. He afterwards passed into the service of Raymond Berenger, the last count of Provence of the house of Barcelona. Although a Lombard, he had adopted in his compositions the Provençal language, and many of his countrymen imitated him. It was not at that time believed that the Italian was capable of becoming a polished language. The age of Sordello was that of the most brilliant chivalric virtues and the most atrocious crimes. He lived in the midst of heroes and monsters. The imagination of the people was still haunted by the recollection of the ferocious Ezzelino, tyrant of Verona, with whom Sordello is said to have had a contest, and who was probably often mentioned in his verses. The historical monuments of this reign of blood were, however, little known; and the people mingled the name of their favourite poet with every revolution which excited their terror. It was said that he had carried off the wife of the Count of S. Bonifazio, the sovereign of Mantua; that he had married the daughter or sister of Ezzelino; and that he had fought this monster, with glory to himself. He united, according to popular report, the most brilliant military exploits to the most distinguished poetical genius. By the voice of St. Louis himself he had been recognised, at a tourney, as the most valiant and gallant of knights; and at last the sovereignty of Mantua had been bestowed upon this noblest of the poets and warriors of his age. Historians of credit have collected, three centuries after Sordello's death, these brilliant fictions, which are, however, disproved by the testimony of contemporary writers. The reputation of Sordello is owing, very materially, to the admiration which has been expressed for him by Dante; who, when he meets him at the entrance of Purgatory, is so struck with the noble haughtiness of his aspect, that he compares him to a lion in a state of majestic repose, and represents Virgil as embracing him on hearing his name."—I am indebted to Professor Sonnenschein for the following account of the man Sordello, as well as for the valuable notes on the period, and the persons with whom the poem deals. The notes distinguished by the initial [S.] are also due to Professor Sonnenschein's generous assistance: "All that is known of the real Sordello is that he was a troubadour of the thirteenth century mentioned by his contemporary Rolandin, who states that he eloped with Cuniza, wife of Count Richard de Saint Bonifazio, and sister of

Ezzelino da Romano. Some of his poems still survive, and from them a few more facts relating to the poet may be gleaned; and that is the whole of our real knowledge of him. For some reason, however, the poets and romantic historians have made much more of him. First, Dante met him at the portals of Purgatory among those who had perished by violence without a chance of repenting them of their sins. When he saw Vergil he cried: '*O Montovano io son Sordello, della tua terra*' (Oh Mantuan, I am Sordello of thy country!') Dante, in his poem says he had the appearance and aspect of a lion; and the same author, in a prose treatise on the vulgar tongue, says Sordello excelled in all kinds of poetry and aided in founding the Italian language by numerous words skilfully borrowed from the dialects of Cremona, Brescia and Verona. A century later Benvenuto d'Imola, in a commentary on the works of Dante, says Sordello was a citizen of Mantua, an illustrious and able warrior and a courtier, who lived in the reign of Ezzelin da Romano, whose sister Cuniza fell in love with him and invited him to a rendezvous. Ezzelino, disguised as a servant, discovered them together, but permitted Sordello to escape upon promising not to return. Yielding, however, again to the entreaties of Cuniza, he was again discovered by her watchful brother, and fled. He was pursued and slain by the emissaries of Ezzelino. Benvenuto, who gives no authority for his statements, also says that Sordello was the author of a book which he admits never to have seen, called *Thesaurus thesaurorum.* About the same time some biographical notices of the troubadours, written in the language of Provence, mention Sordello as having been the son of a poor knight of Mantua. At an early age he composed numerous songs and poems, which gained him admittance to the court of the Count of St. Boniface. He fell in love with the wife of that lord, and eloped with her. The fugitives were received by the lady's brothers, who were at war with St. Boniface. After a time he left the lady there, and passed into Provence, where his talents obtained such brilliant recognition that he was soon the owner of a château, and made an honourable marriage. Early in the next century Aliprando wrote a fabulous rhyming chronicle of Milan, in which Sordello plays a conspicuous part. In this he is a member of the family of Visconti, born at Goïto. He began his literary career in early youth by producing a book called *The Treasure.* Arms proving more attractive, by the time he was twenty-five he was distinguished for his bravery, his address, his nobility, and the grace of his demeanour, although he was small of stature. Accepting many challenges, he was always victorious, and sent the vanquished knights to tell his deeds of valour to the King of France. At the invitation of that prince he was about to cross the Alps, when he yielded to the entreaties of Ezzelino and went to reside with him at Verona. There he long resisted the advances, the prayers, the entreaties of Ezzelino's sister Beatrice. At last he fled to Mantua, but was followed by Beatrice disguised as a man. He finally yielded, and married her. A few days later he left her, and went to France, where he spent several months with the court at Troyes, where his valour, his gallantry and his poetic talents were greatly admired. After being knighted by the King, who gave him three thousand francs and a golden falcon, he returned to Italy. All the towns received him with pomp, as the first warrior of his time. The Mantuans came out to meet him, but he passed on to Verona to reclaim his bride. When he returned with her, he was welcomed with eight days of public rejoicing. After that, Ezzelino laid siege to Mantua, but was driven away by Sordello, who afterwards aided the Milanese against him and gave him the wound of which he died. What became of him afterwards does not appear; but this chronicle, which was a mass of anachronisms, romances, and fictions, was largely drawn upon by the historic writers of the next century, many of whom have adopted the story of Sordello as therein told, and of the Lady Beatrice who never existed. In the sixteenth century, Nostradamus, in his *Lives of Provençal Poets*, says: Sordello was a Mantuan, who at the age of fifteen years entered the service of Berenger, Count of Provence. His verses were preferred to those of Folquet de Marseille, Perceval Doria, and all the other Genoese and Tuscan poets. He made very beautiful songs, not about love, but on subjects relating to philosophy. He translated into Provençalese a digest of the laws, and wrote a historical treatise on the Kings of Aragon and Provence. Darenou, to whom I am indebted for most of my information, after examining all of these and some later authorities, considers that the only certain facts are those written by Rolandin shortly after Sordello's death. Dante was so nearly contemporaneous that he also may be taken as an authority. Of his Italian poems, and his prose works, nothing is known to have survived; but at least thirty-four of his Provençalese poems still exist. Of these one-half are love songs of the most pronounced type, despite the statement of Nostradamus to the contrary. Several have been translated into French, and some are said to be of a high character. In one, the poet boasts of his conquests and his fickleness. Some are in the form of dialogues, in which he discusses such questions as, Whether it be better for a lover to die or continue to exist after the loss of his beloved; or Whether it be right to sacrifice love to honour, or to prefer the glory of knightly combat to love. In a poetic letter to the Count of Provence, he begs that prince not to send him to the Crusades, as he cannot make up his mind to cross the seas, and wishes to delay as long as possible entering into life eternal. In several of his poems he violently attacks Pierre Vidal, the troubadour, whom he seems to have hated bitterly. The whole story is a curious instance of development. Originally a troubadour, apparently with most of the vices, faults, and virtues of the typical troubadour of the thirteenth century, he gradually became, as the centuries advanced, first a hero of romance, a *preux-chevalier* and model Italian knight-errant, and finally that which we see Mr. Browning has made of him. In *Sismondi* I find the following concerning Sordello: "Two men, superior in character to these court parasites, about this time attained great reputations in the Lombard republics, through their Provençalese songs. One of these, Ugo Cattola, devoted his talents to combating the corruption and tyranny of princes; the other, Sordello de Mantua, is enveloped in mysterious obscurity. The writers of the following century speak of him with profound respect, without giving us any details of his life. Those who came later have made him a magnanimous warrior, a valiant defender of his country, and some even a prince of Mantua. The nobility of his birth and his marriage with a sister of Eccelino da Romana, are attested by his contemporaries. His violent death is obscurely indicated by the great Florentine poet; and the only claims to immortality that remain to Sordello to-day are his words and actions mentioned by Dante in the *Purgatorio*." The following is also given in *Sismondi* as one of the few surviving specimens of Sordello's poetry. It is called:

TENSA DE SORDEL ET DE PEYRE GUILHEM.

GUILHEM.

En Sordel que vous en semblan
De la pros contessa preysan?
Car tout dison, et van parlan
Que per s'amor etz in vengutz,
E quen cujatz esser son drutz,
En blanchatz etz por ley canutz.

GUILLAUME.

Eh bien, Sordel, que vous en semble de cette aimable comtesse si prisée? Car tous disent, tous vous rèpétant que pour son amour vous êtes veni ici, que vous avez cru pouvoir être son amant, et que pour elle vos cheveux blanchissent, et vos forces vous abandonnent.

SORDEL.

Peyre Guilhem tot son affan
Mist Dieu in ley for per mon dan.
Les beautatz que les autratz an
En menz, et el pres son menutz.
Ans fos ab emblanchatz perdutz
Che esso non fos advengutz.

SORDELLO.

Pierre Guillaume, Dieu mit en elle tout son travail, pour en faire mon tourment. Les beautés qu'ont toutes les autres ne sont rien; leur prix est peu de chose. Plutôt fussé-je perdu par la vieillesse, que d'avoir éprouvé ce que j'éprouve.

The poem of *Sordello* is a picture of the troublous times of the early part of the thirteenth century in North Italy, and is the history of the development of Sordello's soul. Frederick II. is Emperor and Honorius III. is Pope. Frederick II., the noblest of mediæval princes, the man who suffered much because he was centuries in advance of his time, is too well known to need any description. To understand the causes of the conflicts in which Lombardy was engaged, we must go back to the time of Charlemagne, who took the Lombard king Desiderius prisoner, in 774, and destroyed the Lombard kingdom. Luitprand, the sovereign of the Lombards from 713 to 726, had extended the dominion of Lombardy into Middle Italy. The Popes found this dominion too formidable, so they solicited the assistance of the Frankish kings. The whole of Upper Italy had been conquered by the Lombards in the sixth century. "Charles, with the title of King of the Franks and Lombards, then became the master of Italy. In 800, the Pope, who had crowned Pepin King of the Franks, claimed to bestow the Roman Empire, and crowned his greater son Emperor of the Romans" (*Encyc. Brit.*). Now began a vast system in North Italy of episcopal "immunities," which made the bishops temporal sovereigns. In the eleventh century the Lombard cities had become communes and republics, managing their own affairs and making war on their troublesome neighbours. Leagues and counter-leagues were formed, and confederacies of cities even dared to challenge the strength of Germany. Otto the Great's empire, in the early years of the tenth century, consisted of Germany and Lombardy, with the Romagna and Burgundy; and it was Otto who fixed the principle, that to the German king belonged the Roman crown. The crown of Germany was at this period elective, although it often passed in one family for several generations. Struggles for supremacy between the two powers took place in the reign of the Emperor Henry IV. of Franconia and the papacy of Gregory VII., the famous Hildebrand. It was the struggle between Church and State destined to be fraught with so much misery. The contest ended at this period in a compromise; but most of the gains were on the side of the Pope. It was renewed with great fierceness in the reign of Frederick I. of Hohenstaufen, called Barbarossa or "Red Beard," who came to the throne in 1152. He bestowed on the Empire the title of Holy. The cities of Lombardy were commonwealths, somewhat after the fashion of those of ancient Greece; they had grown very rich and powerful, and whilst they admitted the Emperor's authority in theory, were averse to the practice of submission. The city of Milan, by her attacks on a weaker neighbour, who appealed to Frederick for aid, began a war which resulted in the Peace of Constance in 1183, by which the Emperor abandoned all but a nominal authority over the Lombard League. The son and successor of Frederick—Henry VI.—began to reign in 1190; he married Constance, heiress of the Norman kingdom of Sicily, which was a fief of the papal crown. After the death of Henry VI., Philip, his brother, began to reign, in 1198. In 1208, Otho IV., surnamed the Superb, ascended the throne, and was crowned Emperor. The next year he was excommunicated and deposed. In 1212, Frederick II., King of Sicily, who was the son of Henry VI., began his reign, he received the German crown at Aix-la-Chapelle, 1215, and the Imperial crown of Rome, 1230. When he died he possessed no fewer than six crowns,—the Imperial crown, and the crowns of Germany, Burgundy, Lombardy, Sicily, and Jerusalem. He had assumed the cross, and in 1220 he left his Empire for a space of fifteen years, to accomplish the crusade and to carry on the war with the Lombard cities and the Pope (Gregory IX.). John of Brienne, the dethroned King of Jerusalem, who was afterwards Emperor of the East, had a daughter named Yolande, whom Frederick married. He sent a bunch of dates to Frederick to remind him of his promised crusade. When that sovereign formed the army of the East, he left his young son Henry to represent him in Germany. Frederick was deposed by his subjects, and died in 1250, naming his son Conrad as his successor. In the beginning of the reign of Conrad III., 1138, the Imperial crown was contested by Henry the Proud Duke of Saxony. It was at this time that the contests between the factions, afterwards so famous in history as those of the Guelfs and the Ghibellines, began. Duke Henry had a brother named Welf, the leader of the Saxon forces. They used his name as their battle cry, and the Swabians responded by crying out the name of the village where their leader, the brother of Conrad, had been born—namely, Waibling. The Welfs and the Waiblings were therefore the originals of the terms Guelfs and Ghibellines.—" *The Romano Family.* During the reign of Conrad II. (1024-39) a German gentleman, named Eccelino, accompanied that Emperor to Italy, with a single horse, and so distinguished himself that, as a reward for his services, he received the lands of Onaro and Romano in the Trevisan marches. This founder of a powerful house, famous for its crimes, was succeeded by Alberic, and he by another Eccelino, called the First and also le Bègue—'the Stammerer.' These gentlemen largely augmented their patrimony, acquiring Bassano, Marostica, and many other estates situated to the north of Vicenza, Verona, and Padua; so that their fief formed a small principality, equal in power to either of its neighbouring republics; and as the factions of the towns sought to strengthen themselves by alliances with them, the Seigneurs de Romano were soon regarded as the chiefs of the Ghibelline party in all Venetia. Eccelin le Bègue and Tisolin de Campo St. Pierre, a Paduan noble, were warm friends, and the latter was married to a daughter of the former, and had a son grown to manhood. Cecile, orphan daughter and heiress of Manfred Ricco d'Abano, was offered in marriage, by her guardians, to the young St. Pierre; but the father before concluding the advantageous alliance, thought it proper to consult his friend and father-in-law, Eccelino. That gentleman, however, wished to obtain this great fortune for his own son, and secretly bribed the lady's guardians to deliver her up to him, when he carried her off to his castle of Bassano and then hurriedly married her to his son. This treachery made the whole family of Campo St. Pierre indignant, and they vowed vengeance. They had not long to wait for their opportunity. Several months after the marriage, the wife of the young Eccelino went on a visit to her estates in the Paduan territory, with a suite more brilliant than valiant. Tisolin's son, Gerard, who was to have been Cecile's husband, and was now her nephew, seized her and carried her off from the midst of her retinue to his castle of St. André. Cecile, escaping after a time, returned to Bassano and related her terrible misfortune to her husband, who at once repudiated her, and she afterwards married a Venetian nobleman. The two families had, however, thus founded a mutual hate, which descended from father to son, and cost many lives and much blood. In the meantime, Eccelino II.'s power was augmented by this marriage and the one he afterwards contracted. He made alliances with the republics of Verona and Padua; and he soon required their aid, for in 1194, when one of his enemies was chosen podesta of Vicenza, he, his family, and the whole faction of Vivario, were exiled from the city. Before submitting, he undertook to defend himself by setting fire to his neighbours' houses; and a great portion of the town was destroyed during the insurrection. These were the first scenes of disorder and bloodshed which greeted the eyes of Eccelino III. or the Cruel, who was born a few weeks before. Exile from Vicenza was not a severe sentence for the lords of Romano; for they retired to Bassano, in the midst of their own subjects, and called around them their partisans, who were persecuted as they themselves were, without the same resources. By the aid thus given with apparent generosity, they degraded their associates, transforming their fellow-citizens into mercenary satellites, and increasing their influence in the town, from which their exile could not be of long duration. The Veronese interfered to establish peace in Vicenza. They had the Romanos recalled, with all their party; and an arrangement was made by which two podestas were chosen at the same time, one by each party. In 1197, however, the Vicenzese again chose a single podesta, hostile to Eccelino, and this time not only banished the Romanos, but declared war against them, and sent troops to besiege Marostica. Eccelino, placed between three republics, could choose his own allies; and decided now upon Padua. The Paduan army attacked that of Vicenza, near Carmignano, and took two thousand prisoners. The Vicenzese called upon the Veronese to assist them, and together they invaded the Paduan territory, desolating it up to the very walls of the city, and so frightening the Paduans that they delivered up all of their prisoners without waiting to consult Eccelino. That prince took this opportunity to break with Padua, and called upon Verona to arbitrate between him and Vicenza, giving them as hostages his young daughter and his strongest two castles, Bassano and Anganani. By this thorough confidence he so won the affection of the podesta of Verona that he concluded peace for him with Vicenza and the whole Guelf party, and then returned his castles to him. The Paduans revenged themselves by confiscating Onaro, the first estate possessed by the Romano family in Italy.—*Salinguerra.* William Marchesella des Adelard, chief of the Guelf party in Ferrara, had the misfortune to see all the male heirs of his house, his brother and all his sons, perish before him. An only daughter of his brother, named Marchesella, remained, and he declared her the sole heiress to his immense estates, naming the son of his sister as heir should Marchesella die without children. Tired of warfare, and hoping to ensure peace to his distracted country, he determined to do so by uniting the leading families of the two factions. Salinguerra, son of Torrello, was at the head of the Ghibellines in Ferrara; and William not only offered his niece to him in marriage, but actually before his death placed her, then a child of seven years, in his hands to be reared and educated. The Guelfs were, however, unwilling to permit the heiress of their leading family to remain in the hands of their enemies; and they could not consent to transfer their affection and allegiance to those with whom they had fought for so long a time. They therefore found an opportunity to surprise Salinguerra's palace, and abduct Marchesella, whom they placed in the palace of the Marquis d'Este, choosing Obizzo d'Este to be her husband, and placing her property in the hands of the Marquis. In the end Marchesella died before she was married; her cousins, designated by William, in this event, to be his heirs, were afraid to claim the estates, and the whole property continued in the hands of the Este family. In the meantime the insult offered to Salinguerra was keenly resented. The abduction took place in 1180, and for nearly forty years afterwards civil war continued within the walls of Ferrara without ceasing. During those years, ten times one faction drove the other out of the city, ten times all the property of the vanquished was given up to pillage, and all their houses razed to the ground.—*Eccelino and Salinguerra.* In 1209 Otho IV. entered Italy, and held his court near Verona. All the chief lords of Venetia—but especially Eccelino II., de Romano, and Azzo VI., Marquis d'Este—were summoned to attend. Those two gentlemen had profited by the long interregnum which preceded Otho's reign to increase their influence in the marches, and the factions were more bitter against each other than ever. These factions had different reasons for existing in the different towns; but they quickly adopted the newly introduced names of Guelf and Ghibelline, and a common tie was thus suddenly formed between the factions in the various places. Thus, by the mere adoption of a name, Salinguerra in Ferrara and the Montecci in Verona, found themselves allies of Eccelino; and, on the other hand, the Adelards of Ferrara, Count St. Bonifazio at Verona and Mantua, and the Campo St. Pierre at Padua, were all allies of the Marquis d'Este. The year before, Este, after a short banishment, had re-entered Ferrara, and had succeeded in being declared lord of that city,—the first time that an Italian republic abandoned its rights for the purpose of voluntarily submitting to a tyrant. About the same time the Marquis had gained an important victory over Eccelino and his party; but, at the moment when the Emperor entered Italy, Eccelino had gained some advantages over the Vicenzese, and thought himself on the point of capturing the city. Azzo marched against him, whereupon Salinguerra entered Ferrara and drove out all of Azzo's adherents. The summons sent to the chiefs to meet the Emperor no doubt prevented a bloody battle and a useless massacre. (See note, p. 500; see also the article, TAURELLO SALINGUERRA, in this work.) In 1235, after a long and turbulent reign, full of vicissitudes, Eccelino II. retired into a monastery, and divided his principality between his two sons, Eccelino III. and Alberic. The latter remained at Treviso; but Eccelino III. became very powerful, kept all

Italy in turmoil, and was notorious for his infamous tyrannies and cruelties. In 1255 he was excommunicated by the Pope, Alexander IV., and a crusade was preached against him. He fought against his enemies from that time, with varying success and stubborn courage, until 1259, when he was wounded in battle and taken prisoner. The leaders of the enemy with difficulty protected him from the fury of the soldiers and the people; but he himself tore the bandages from his wounds, and died on the eleventh day of his captivity. All the cities which he had conquered and oppressed at once revolted; and Treviso, where Alberic had reigned ever since his father's abdication, revolted and drove him out. Alberic, with his family, took refuge in his fortress of San Zeno, in the Euganean mountains; but the league of Guelf cities declared against him, and the troops of Venice, Treviso, Vicenza, and Padua surrounded the castle, where they were soon joined by the Marquis d'Este. Traitors delivered up the outworks; but Alberic and his wife, two daughters and six sons, took refuge on the top of a tower. After three days, compelled by hunger, he delivered himself up to the Marquis, at the same time reminding him that one of his daughters was the wife of Renaud d'Este. In spite of this, however, he and his family were all murdered and torn to pieces, and their dismembered bodies divided among all the cities over which the hated Romano family had tyrannised. In 1240 Gregory IX. preached a crusade against the Emperor Frederick II., and a crusading army surrounded Ferrara, where Salinguerra, then more than eighty years old, had reigned for some time as prince and as head of the Ghibellines. He successfully defended the city for some time; but when attending a conference, to which he was invited by his enemies, he was treacherously captured and sent to Venice, where, after five years' imprisonment, he died." [S.]

[THE POEM.] *Sordello* is Browning's *Hamlet*, and is the most obscure of all Mr. Browning's poems. It has been aptly compared to a vast palace, in which the architect has forgotten to build a staircase. Its difficulties are not merely those which are inseparable from an attempt to trace the development of a soul,—such a work without obscurity could only deal with a very simple soul,—but are consequent on the remoteness of time in which the political events and historical circumstances which formed the environment of Sordello's existence took place, and the partial interest which the majority of readers feel concerning those events. The work deals with the struggles of the Guelfs and Ghibellines; and it is necessary to possess a fair knowledge of the history of the times, places, and persons concerned before we can grasp the mere outlines of the story. It must be admitted, whether we allow the charge of obscurity or not, that Mr. Browning never helps his reader. He may or may not actually hinder him : it is certain that he does not go out of his way to assist him. The first step towards understanding Sordello, then, is to gain some acquaintance with the period and personages of the story. The work is full of beauty. Probably no poet ever poured out such wealth of richest thought with such princely liberality as Mr. Browning has done in this much discussed poem. It is like a Brazilian forest, in which, though we shall almost certainly lose our way, it will be amidst such profusion of floral loveliness that it will be a delight to be buried in its depths.

Book I.—The poem in its first scene places us in imagination in Verona six hundred years ago. A restless group has gathered in its market-place to discuss the news which has arrived,—that their prince, Count Richard of St. Boniface, the great supporter of the cause of the Guelfs, who had joined Azzo, the lord of Este, to depose the Ghibelline leader, Tauzello Salinguerra, from his position in Ferrara, has become prisoner in Ferrara; and in consequence immediate aid is demanded from the "Lombard League of fifteen cities that affect the Pope." The Pope supported the Guelf cause, the Kaiser that of the Ghibellines. The leaders of the two causes are described, and the principles of which each was the representative. We are next introduced to Sordello; not in his youth, but in a supreme moment before the end of his career—a moment which has to determine his future. How this pregnant moment has come about, and how the past has fashioned the present, the poet now proceeds to explain. We are taken back to the castle of Goïto, when Sordello was a boy already of the regal class of poets, musing by the marble figures of the fountain, and finding companions in the embroidered figures on the arras. Adelaide, wife of Eccelino da Romano, the Ghibelline prince, was mistress of the castle. Sordello was only a page, known only as the orphan of Elcorte, an archer, who, in the slaughter of Vicenza, had saved his mistress and her new-born son at the cost of his own life. The son was afterwards known as Eccelin the Cruel. Sordello led the ideal life of a poet child at Goïto. All nature was a scene of enchantment to him, was endowed with form and colour from his own rich fancy. But Sordello was not content with living his own life, he must combine in his person the lives of his imaginary heroes. He will be perfect: he chooses Apollo as his ideal: he must love a woman to match his high ambition. He aims at Palma, Eccelin's only child by his former wife, Agnes Este, but who has been already set apart, for reasons of state, as the wife of Count Richard of St. Boniface, the Guelf. Palma, however, it is reported in the castle, will refuse him. Sordello anxiously awaits his opportunity. The return of Adelaide to the castle demands the services of the troubadours: Sordello's chance lies this way.

Book II. shows us Sordello setting forth on a bright spring day, full of hope that he will meet Palma. Arriving at Mantua, he finds a Court of Love, in which his lady sits enthroned as queen, and the troubadour Eglamor contending for her prize against all comers. Eglamor seems to make but a poor affair of the story he is singing. He ceases. Sordello knows the story too, and feels that he can do better with it. He springs forward, and with true inspiration sings a new song to the old idea transfigured. He has won the prize from Palma's hands. Swooning with joy, he is carried back to Goïto, the poet's crown on his brow and Palma's scarf round his neck. Eglamor is dead with spite, and the troubadours have a new chief. Thus was Sordello poet, Master of the Realms of Song. He will slumber: he can arise in his strength any day. He is summoned to Mantua to sing to order. He finds the idea of work distasteful; but he conquers, and is crowned with honours. But he feels he has only been loving song's results, not song for its own sake; his failure to reach his ideal destroys the pleasure derived from his success. Soon the true Sordello vanished, sundered in twain, the poet thwarting the man. The man and bard was gone; internal struggles frittered his soul; he became too contemptuous, and so he neither pleased his patrons nor himself. He falls lower and lower, abjures the soul in his songs, and contents himself with body. His degradation is complete. Meanwhile Adelaide dies, and Eccelin resolves to forsake the world and the

Emperor, and come to terms with the Pope. Taurello rages furiously at this news, and returns to Mantua. Sordello is chosen to sound his praises. "'Tis a test, remember," says Naddo. But Sordello loathes the task: he will not sing at all, and runs away to Goïto.

BOOK III.—Once more at his old home, Mantua becomes but a dream. Sordello, well or ill, is exhausted: rather than imperfectly reveal himself, he will remain unrevealed. He will remain himself, instead of attempting to project his soul into other men. He spent a year with Nature at Goïto, but as one defeated,—youth gone, love and pleasure foregone, and nothing really done. With an all-embracing sympathy he has not himself really lived. When Nature makes a mistake she can rectify it. He must perish once, and perish utterly. He should have brought actual experience of things obtained by sterling work to correct his mere reflections and observations. He may do something yet: though youth is gone, life is not all spent. He has the will to do—what of the means? Resolution having thus been taken, the means are suddenly discovered. Naddo arrives as messenger from Palma, telling how Eccelin has distributed his wealth to his two sons, has married them to Guelf brides, and has retired to a monastery; that Palma is betrothed to Richard of St. Boniface, and Sordello must compose a marriage hymn. Sordello seizes the opportunity, and hastens to meet Palma at Verona. We have now arrived at the point at which the poem of Sordello opens in Book I. He has to hear a strange confession from the lips of Palma. If Sordello had been paralysed by indecision, she too had done nothing, because she was awaiting an "outsoul." Weary with waiting for her complement, which should enable her to live her proper life, she had conceived a great love for Sordello when he burst upon the scene at the Love Court. To win Sordello for herself and her cause henceforth was her life-object. When Adelaide died this became practicable. She had heard the astonishing dying confession of Adelaide, and had witnessed Eccelin's visit to the death-chamber when he came to undo everything which Adelaide had done. He had resolved to reconcile the Guelf and Ghibelline factions. Taurello determined to use Palma to support the Ghibellines. Palma, as head of the house, agreed to this; but it was arranged that the project should not at present be made public. She must profess her intention to carry out the arrangement which Taurello had made, before he entered on the religious life, of marrying the Guelf, Count Richard. Taurello has thus entrapped the Count, and has him in prison at Ferrara. Palma's father, Eccelin, blots out all his old engagements. All now rests with Palma, and she arranges to fly with Sordello on the morrow as arbitrators to Taurello at Ferrara. Now is one round of Sordello's life accomplished. Mr. Browning here makes a long digression, beginning, "I muse this on a ruined palace-step at Venice." The City in the Sea seems to him a type of life:—

> "Life, the evil with the good,
> Which make up living, rightly understood;
> Only do finish something!"

No evil man is past hope; if he has not truth, he has at least his own conceit of truth; he sees it surely enough: his lies are for the crowd. Good labours to exist; though Evil and Ignorance thwart it. In this life we are but fitting together an engine to work in another existence. He sees profound disclosures in the most ordinary type of face: the world will call him dull for this, as being obscure and metaphysical. There are poets who are content to tell a simple story of impressions; another class presents things as they really are in a general, and not, as in the previous class, in an individual sense; but the highest class of all brings out the deeper significance of things which would never have been seen without the poet's aid. These are the Makers-see—obviously a higher type of genius than the Seers. "But," asks the objector, "what is the use of this? It is quite true that men of action, like Salinguerra, are not unwisely preferred to dreamers like Sordello: they, at least, *do* the world's work somehow; this is better than talking about it. But, at any rate, there is no harm done in compelling the Makers-see to do their duty. It is their province to gaze through the "door opened in heaven," and tell the world what they see, and make us see it too, as did John in Patmos Isle. And so Mr. Browning has analysed for us the soul of Sordello; but he expects no reward for it. The world is too indolent to look into heaven with John, or into hell with Dante.

Book IV.—The description of the unhappy position of Ferrara, "the lady city," for which both Guelf and Ghibelline contended, opens the fourth book. Sordello is here with Palma. He has seen the dreadful condition of the people, and has espoused their cause. Here, in the midst of carnage and ruin, Sordello learns his altruism. He appeals to Taurello Salinguerra, but nothing comes of it. The more he sees of the misery of the people, the more he vows himself to an effort to raise them. The soldiers ask him to sing at their camp-fire. He sings, and Palma hears and takes him back to Taurello Salinguerra. The poet here describes the chief and tells his story. He is the doer, as contrasted with Sordello the visionary; but he has led a life of misfortune and adventure. At the burning of Vicenza he lost wife and child; he embraced the cause of Eccelin and the Ghibellines. As Eccelin had gone into a monastery, all Taurello's plans were disarranged. He ponders as to whom shall be given the Emperor's badge of the prefectship; and what shall he do with his prisoner Richard; Sordello asks Palma what are the laws at work which explain Ghibellinism. He feels he has been a recreant to his race: Taurello has the people's interest at heart; all that Sordello *should* have done he *does*. Are Guelfs as bad as Ghibellines, or better? Both these do worse than nothing, is a reflection which comforts the do-nothing poet. What if there were a Cause higher and nobler than either, and he (Sordello) were to be its true discoverer? A soldier, at this point, suggests to Sordello a subject for a ballad: a tale of a dead worthy long ago consul of Rome, Crescentius Nomentanus, who—

"From his brain,
Gave Rome out on its ancient place again."

Sordello resolves to build up Rome again—a Rome which should mean the rights of mankind, the realisation of the People's cause.

BOOK V.—The splendid dream of a New Rome has vanished from Sordello's mind ere night; his enthusiasm is chilled, and arch by arch the vision has dissolved. Mankind cannot be exalted of a sudden; the work of ages cannot be done in a day. The New Rome is one more thing which Sordello could imagine, but could not make. His heart tells him that the minute's work is the first step to the whole work of a man: he has purposed to take the last step first: he may be a man at least, if he cannot be a god. The world is not prepared for such a violent change; society has never been advanced by leaps and bounds. Charlemagne had to subject Europe by main force, then Hildebrand was enabled to rule by brain power. Strength wrought order, and made the rule of moral influence possible; in its turn, moral power allied itself with material power. The Crusaders learned the trick of breeding strength by other aid than strength; and so the Lombard League turned righteous strength against pernicious strength. Then comes, in its turn, God's truce to supersede the use of strength by the Divine influence of Religion. All that precedes is as scaffolding, indispensable while the building is in progress, but a thing to spurn when the structure is completed: that, however, is not yet. As talking is Sordello's trade, he endeavours to persuade Salinguerra to join the Guelfs, as this, to Sordello, seems the more popular cause. Taurello hears him with patience, mixed with a contemptuous indifference. His scornful demeanour rouses Sordello to make the highest claims for the poet's authority: "A poet must be earth's essential king." To bend Taurello to the Guelf cause, Sordello would give up life itself. He knows that "this strife is right for once." Taurello is impressed at last: the argument hits him, not the man; himself must be won to the Ghibellines. Palma, being a woman, is impossible as leader of the party; her love for Sordello may, however, be cast in the balance, and in an inspired moment Taurello invests Sordello with the Emperor's badge, which he casts upon his neck. Palma now tells Taurello that Adelaide, on her death-bed, confessed that Sordello was Taurello's own son, who did not perish, as he believed, at Vicenza. Adelaide, for her own purposes, had concealed his rescue. "Embrace him, madman!" Palma cried; thoughts rushed, fancies rushed. "Nay, the best's behind," Taurello laughed. Palma hurries Taurello away, that Sordello may collect his thoughts awhile. Sordello is crowned. They hear a foot-stamp as they discuss the future, in the room where they left Sordello, and "out they two reeled dizzily."

Book VI.—Now has arisen the great temptation of Sordello Is it to be the Great Renunciation or the Fall? With the magnificent prospect before him of Chief of the Ghibellines, the Emperor cause; with the Emperor's badge on his neck; with Palma, his Ghibelline bride, he, Taurello Salinguerra's son, might at last do something! After all, what was the difference between Guelf and Ghibelline? Why should he give up all the joy of life that the multitude might have some joy? "Speed their Then." "But how this badge would suffer!—you improve your Now!" So Sordello lovingly eyes the tempter's apple. After all, evil is just as natural as good; and without evil no good can accrue to men. Sordello may then as well be happy while he may. Soul and body have each alike need of the other: soul must content itself without the Infinite till the earth-stage is over. He has tried to satisfy the soul's longing, and has failed: why not seek now the common joys of men? Salinguerra and Palma reach the chamber door and dash aside the veil, only to find Sordello dead, "under his foot the badge." Has he lost or won? He learned how to live as he came to die: he made the Great Renunciation, and in seeming defeat he achieved his soul's success.

NOTES TO BOOK I.—Line 6, *Pentapolin*, "o' the naked arm," king of the Garamanteans, who always went to battle with his right arm bare. (See *Don Quixote*, I. iii. 4; "*The friendless-people's friend*," etc.: Don Quixote is here spoken of, and "*Pentapolin named o' the Naked Arm*" is mentioned by Don Quixote when he sees the two flocks of sheep: "Know, friend Sancho, that yonder army before us is commanded by the Emperor Alifanfaron, sovereign of the Island of Trapoban; and the other is commanded by his enemy the king of the Garamanteans, known by the name of Pentapolin with the naked arm, because he always engages in battle with the right arm bare." l. 12, *Verona:* a city of North Italy, on the Adige, under the Lombard Alps. l. 66, "*The thunder phrase of the Athenian*," etc.: Æschylus, who fought at Marathon. l. 70, "*The starry paladin*": Sir Philip Sidney's love poems to Stella were written under the *nom de plume* of Astrophel (the lover of the star). [S.] l. 80, *The Second Friedrich* = Holy Roman Emperor (1194-1250), surnamed *the Hohenstauffen*, the most remarkable historic figure of the middle ages. He was the grandson of Barbarossa, and was crowned in 1220. l. 81, *Third Honorius* = Pope Honorius III (1216-1227): he was a Guelf. l. 104, *Richard of St. Boniface*, Count of Verona, was of the Guelfs; *Lombard League:* the famous alliance of the great Lombard cities began in 1164. l. 117, "*Prone is the purple pavis*": a pavise is a large shield covering the whole body: when the shield was *prone*—*i.e.* fallen flat on its face—its owner was defenceless. l. 124, "*Duke o' the Rood*": of the

Order of the Holy Cross. l. 126, *Hell-cat* = Eccelin. l. 131, *Ferrara:* an ancient city of North Italy, twenty-nine miles from Bologna and seventy from Venice. l. 131, *Osprey:* a long-winged eagle. "An osprey appears to have been the coat of arms of Salinguerra, as the 'ostrich with a horseshoe in his beak' was that of Eccelin." [S.] l. 142, *Oliero:* the monastery which Eccelin the monk entered. It is situated near Bassano, in the Eastern Alps. ll. 148 and 149, *Cino Bocchimpane* and *Buccio Virtù:* citizens. l. 149, *God's Wafer:* an oath (Ostia di Dio). l. 150, "*Tutti Santi*" = "All Saints!" an exclamation. l. 153, *Padua:* a famous city of Lombardy, said to be the oldest in North Italy; *Podesta* = governor of a city. l. 197, *Hohenstauffen:* this dynasty of Germany began with Conrad III. (1137-52). Frederick II. was the most illustrious man of this illustrious family. l. 198, *John of Brienne:* crusader and titular king of Jerusalem (1204). He was afterwards Emperor of the East. His daughter Yolande or Iolanthe married Frederick II. l. 201, *Otho IV.*, Holy Roman Emperor (*c.* 1174-1218). l. 202, *Barbaross* = Frederick Barbarossa: one of the greatest sovereigns of Germany (1152-90). There is a German tradition that he is not dead, but only sleeping, and that when he starts from his slumbers a golden age will begin for Germany. l. 205, *Triple-bearded Teuton* Barbarossa: the legend runs that his beard has already grown through the table slab, but must wind itself thrice round the table before his second advent. l. 253, *Trevisan:* of the province of Treviso; its chief town, Treviso, is distant seventeen miles from Venice. l. 257, *Godego:* a town in Venetia, amongst the Asolan hills. *Marostica:* a town of North Italy, fifteen miles north-east of Vicenza, at the foot of Mount Rovero. l. 258, *Castiglione:* a town at the Italian end of the Lago di Garda (Cartiglion in the text, but evidently a misprint); *Bassano:* a city of Italy, in the province of Vicenza, on the Brenta. In the centre of the town is the Tower of Ezzelino. *Loria*, or Lauria: a city of Italy in the province of Potenza. The castle was the birthplace of Ruggiero di Loria. l. 259, *Suabian:* the struggle for the Imperial throne between Philip of Swabia and Otto of Brunswick (1198-1208) enlisted the sympathies of Italy, and some of the Guelfic towns took the part of the Guelf Otto. l. 262, *Vale of Trent:* Trent or Tridentum was once the wealthiest town in Tyrol; it lies between Botzen and Verona.

l. 263, *Roncaglia*, near Piacenza, where Frederick I. held the Diet in 1154, and received the submission of the Lombards. l. 265, *Asolan and Euganean hills:* in the Trevisan, a district of North Italy, between Trent and Venice. l. 266, *Rhetian*, of the country of the Tyrol and the Grisons; *Julian* mountains: between Venetia and Noricum. l. 288, *Romano:* Eccelino da Romano. l. 304, *Rovigo:* a city of Italy, about twenty-seven miles S.S.W of Padua. From the eleventh to the fourteenth century the Este family was usually in authority. l. 305, *Ancona's March:* the frontier or boundary of Ancona, a city of Central Italy on the Adriatic. l. 315, *Hildebrand:* Pope Gregory VII. (1073-85). l. 317, *Twenty-four:* the magistrates of Verona who managed the affairs of the city. l. 324, *Carroch*, or *caroccio:* a Lombard war carriage, which was drawn by oxen, and bore a great bell, the standard of the army, and the Sacred Host, forming a rallying point. l. 373, "*John's transcendent vision*" — Book of Revelation. ll. 382 and 385, *Mantua* and *Mincio:* about seven hundred years ago the river Mincio formed a great marsh round the city of Mantua; this separated the city from the mountains, on the slope of which stood the castle of Goïto. l. 420, *Caryatides:* figures of women serving to support entablatures. l. 587, "*That Pisan Pair*"*:* Niccolo Pisano, and Giovanni Pisano, his son were great sculptors and architects of Pisa (*circ.* 1207-78). "Nicolo was born about 1200, and was one of the first to seek after the truer forms of art in the general quickening of the century. He was a great sculptor, as his works and those of his son Giovanni (architect of the Campo Santo at Pisa) and his school bear witness at Pisa, Orvieto, Pistoia, and many other towns. After he had met with an example of the genuine antique—a sarcophagus now at Pisa—he brought his future work into accordance with its rules." [S.] l. 589, "*while at Sienna is Guidone set*"*:* "The name Guido da Sienna and the date 1221, mark a picture now at Sienna; and this, with other works attributed to the same painter, show him to have been one of the earliest artists who express a feeling independent of Byzantine influence." [S.] l. 591, "*Saint Euphemia*"*:* a fine brick church at Verona, dating from the thirteenth century. The interior has now been entirely remodelled. [S.]. *Saint Eufemia:* of Chalcedon: her body was said to have been miraculously conveyed to Rovigno, in the sixth century. l. 606, "*so they found at Babylon*": "It is said that after the city (of Seleucia) was burnt, the soldiers searching the temple (of Apollo) found a narrow hole, and when this was opened in the hope of finding something of value in it, there issued from some deep gulf, which the secret magic of the Chaldeans had closed up, a pestilence laden with the strength of incurable disease, which polluted the whole world with contagion, in the time of Verus and Marcus Antoninus, and from the borders of Persia to Gaul and the Rhine."—Ammianus Marcellinus. [S.] l. 607, "*Colleagues, mad Lucius and sage Antonine*": during the joint reign of Marcus Aurelius Antoninus (the philosopher) and the scapegrace Lucius Verus; the latter was in command of the Roman forces in the east, and engaged in a war with Parthia. His generals sacked Seleucia, and he was himself present in the neighbourhood of Babylon during the winters of A.D. 163-5 (*v.* Clinton, *Fasti Romani*). [S.] l. 608, "*Apollo's shrine*": "Seleuceus, one of Alexander's generals, and himself a Macedonian, founded the Syrian empire, and built the town of Seleucia. A good deal is told of the Hellenization of the East under Seleucus. He, no doubt, founded the temple of Apollo, who was claimed as an ancestor of the family." [S.] l. 617, *Loxian*: surname of Apollo. l. 671, *Orpine*: a yellow plant, commonly called *Livelong* (Sedum Telephium). l. 679, "*adventurous spider*": the geometric spiders (Orbitelariæ), are almost the only ones whose method of forming a snare have been at all minutely recorded. The garden spider (Epeira) spins a large quantity of thread, which, floating in the air in various directions, happens, from its glutinous quality, at last to adhere to some object near it—a lofty plant, or the branch of a tree. When the spider has one end of the line fixed, he walks along part of it, and fastens another, then drops and affixes the thread to some object below; climbs again, and begins a third, fastening that in a similar way. Mr. Browning is in error when he makes the spider shoot her threads from depth to height, from barbican to battlement. l. 707, "*eat fern seed*": this was anciently supposed to make the eater invisible, *Naddo*: appears as Sordello's friend and adviser: Mr. Browning makes him a representative of the "Philistine" party, and puts into his mouth the words of mere conventional, superficial wisdom. l. 720, "*Poppy—a coarse brown rattling crane*".

the cranium or skull-like poppy head, when it contains the seed and is dry. l. 784, *Valvassor*, or *vavasour:* in feudal law a principal vassal, not holding immediately of the sovereign, but of a great lord; *suzerain:* a feudal lord, a lord paramount. l. 835, "*The Guelfs paid stabbers, etc.*": "In 1209 Otho IV. entered Italy, and held his court near Verona. All the chief lords of Venetia, but especially Eccelino II., da Romana, and Azzo VI., Marquis d'Este, were summoned to attend. Those two gentlemen had profited by the long interregnum which preceded Otho's reign. They had used the various discords between the towns to increase each his own faction; and the hatred between the two was more bitter than ever. A dramatic scene took place at the meeting before the Emperor. When Eccelino saw Azzo, he said, in the presence of the whole court, 'We were intimate in our youth, and I believed him to be my friend. One day we were in Venice together, walking on the Place o St. Mark, when his assassins flung themselves upon me to stab me; and at the same moment the Marquis seized my arms, to prevent me from defending myself; and if I had not by a violent effort escaped, I should have been killed, as was one of my soldiers by my side. I denounce him, therefore, before this assembly as a traitor; and of you, Sire, I demand permission to prove by a single combat his treachery to me as well as to Salinguerra, and to the podesta of Vicenza.' Shortly afterwards, Salinguerra arrived, followed by a hundred men at arms, and throwing himself at the feet of the Emperor, he made a similar accusation against the Marquis, and also demanded the ordeal of battle. Azzo replied to him, that he had on his hands plenty of gentlemen more noble than Salinguerra ready to fight for him if he was so anxious for battle. Then Otho commanded all three to be silent, and declared that he should not accord to any of them the privilege of fighting for any of their past quarrels. From these two chiefs the Emperor expected greater service than from all other Italians; and he secured their allegiance by confirming the lordship of the Marches of Ancona upon the Marquis, and by declaring Eccelino to be imperial deputy and permanent podesta of Vicenza." [S.] Line 857, *Malek*, a Moor. l. 885, *Miramoline:* a Saracen prince, whose territory was situated in North Africa: in the year 1214, St. Francis of Assisi set out for Morocco to preach the gospel to this famous Mahometan, but was taken seriously ill on the way. l. 888, "*dates plucked from the bough John Brienne sent*": he sent a bunch of dates to remind Frederick of his promise to join the crusade. l. 924, *crenelled:* embattled, crenellated. l. 935, *Damsel-fly:* the dragon-fly, so called from its elegant appearance. l. 946, *Python:* a monstrous serpent which haunted the caves of Parnassus, and was slain by Apollo. l. 950, "*Girls—his Delians*": at the island of Delos the festival of Apollo was celebrated. The girls were priestesses of Apollo. l. 956, "*Daphne and Apollo*": Daphne was a nymph who, being pursued by Apollo, was at her own entreaty changed into a bay tree—the tree consecrated to Apollo. l. 1008, *Trouvères* = troubadours.

BOOK II.—Line 68, *Jongleurs:* minstrels who accompanied the troubadours, and who sometimes did a little jugglery. l. 71, *Elys:* "Elys, then, is merely the ideal subject, with such a name, of Eglamour's poem, and referred to in other places as his (Sordello's) type of perfection, realised according to his faculty (*El-lys*—the lily)"—Robert Browning. [S.] l. 156: "The rhymes 'Her head that's sharp . . . sunblanched the livelong summer' are referred to Book V., l. 246, 'the vehicle that marred Elys so much,' etc., and 'his worst performance, the Goïto as his first.' l. 980 of the same book." [S.] l. 94, "*spied a scarab*": one of the marks of Apis, the sacred bull of ancient Egypt. The marks were "a black coloured hide with a white triangular spot on the forehead, the hair arranged in the shape of an eagle on the back, and a knot under the tongue in the shape of a scarabæus, the sacred insect and emblem of Ptah, and a white spot resembling a lunar crescent at his right side" (Dr. S. Birch). l. 183, "*A Roman bride*": "on the wedding day, which in early times was never fixed upon without consulting the auspices, the bride was dressed in a long white robe with purple fringe and a girdle at the waist; her veil was of a bright yellow, and shoes likewise; her hair was divided with the point of a spear, which the antiquarians explained as emblematic of the husband's authority, or as typical of the guardianship of Juno Curitico (Juno with the lance)." "But while these rites are being performed, remain unwedded, ye damsels; let the torch of pinewood await auspicious days, and let not the curved spear part thy virgin ringlets" (Ovid, *Fasti*, ii. 160. [S.] l. 218, "*Perseus*"—rescuing Andromeda when chained to the rock in the sea. l. 222, "*gnome*": the Rosicrucians imagined gnomes to be sprites presiding over mines, etc. l. 224, "*Agate cup, his topaz rod, his seed pearl*": amongst the various superstitions connected with precious stones the agate was held to be an emblem of health and long life, and to possess certain medicinal uses. The topaz, said the old doctor, "is favourable to hæmorrhages, to impart strength, and promote digestion"; it was an emblem of fidelity. l. 307, "*Massic jars dug up at Baiæ*": Massic wine was famous in old Roman days. Baiæ, an ancient town near Naples; in old Roman days a health and pleasure resort of the wealthy; innumerable relics of these times have been unearthed. "Mons Massicus was a vine-clad hill in the Campagna, where the Falernian wine was grown." [S.] l. 297, "*A plant they have*": The day-lily—St. Bruno's lily—the *Hemerocallis liliastrum*, in French, belle de jour. l. 329, *Vicenza*: a city of Northern Italy of great antiquity; the first encounter between the Guelfs and Ghibellines took place here, about 1194. l. 330, *Vivaresi*: a Lombard family. l. 331, *Maltraversi*: a noble family of Padua. l. 435, *Machine*: see l. 1014. l. 460, "*some huge throbbing stone*": In one of Ossian's poems a description is given of bards walking around a rocking stone, and by their singing making it move as an oracle of battle." [S.] l. 483, *truchman* = an interpreter. l. 527, *rondel, tenzon, virlai, or sirvent*: forms of Provençal poetry. "*Rondel*, a thirteen-verse poem, in which the beginning is repeated in the third and fourth verses—from *rotundus*; *tenzon*, a contest in verse before a tribunal of love—from *tendo*, in the sense of to strive; *virlai*, or *virelay*, a short poem, always in short lines, and wholly in two rhymes, with a refrain—from *virer*; *sirvent*, a poem of praise or service, sometimes satirical; from *servire*." (*Imp. Dict.*) [S.] l. 529, *angelot*: an instrument of music somewhat resembling a lute. l. 625, "*sparkles off*": intransitive verb,—"his mail sparkles off and it rings, whirled from each delicatest limb it warps." [S.] l. 627, "*Apollo from the sudden corpse of Hyacinth*": Apollo was one day teaching Hyacinthus to play at quoits, and accidentally killed him. l. 630, *Montfort*: the father of Simon de Montfort, who fought against the Albigenses. l. 729, *Vidal*: Pierre Vidal, of Toulouse, a poet of varied inspiration, was loaded with gifts by the greatest nobles of his time (see Sismondi, *Lit. Eur.*, vol. i., p. 135). Professor Sonnenschein says he was a Provençal troubadour, who died about 1210. He was a sort of caricature of the usual troubadour excellence and foolishness. Some of his poems are the best remaining of the Provençal poetry. He went twice to Palestine, once with a crusade. He was hated by Sordello, and referred to in some of his poems which are extant. l. 730, *filamot:* yellow-brown colour; from *feuille-morte*; *murrey-coloured:* of a dark-red or mulberry colour (*morus*, mulberry). l. 755, *plectre*, or plectrum: a staff of ivory, horn, etc., for playing with on a lyre. l. 784, "*Bocafoli's stark-naked psalms*": not merely *plain* song, but *naked* song. l. 785, *Plara's sonnets.* Both personages are imaginary. l. 786, *almug:* "probably the red sandalwood of China and India" (Dr. W. Smith). l. 788, *river-horse:* the hippopotamus. l. 792, *pompion-twine:* pumpkin. l. 843, *Pappacoda:* a nickname. *Tagliafer*, or *Taillefer:* the favourite minstrel-knight of William of Normandy, who rode in front of the invading army at the battle of Senlac, and sang the song of Roland. l. 846, *o'ertoise:* overstretch? l. 877, *Count Lori*, or Loria of Naples. l. 883, "*The Grey Paulician*": "Eccelino II. found the Paterini or Paulicians, a Manichæan sect, who were driven from the East by the Empress Theodora (who had a hundred thousand of them killed) and her successors. They were slowly forced westward, and at last settled in Italy, and in Languedoc, in the neighbourhood of Albi. They are credited with planting the first seeds of the Reformation in the Latin Church. Innocent III., alarmed at their doctrines and increasing numbers, opposed them, and instructed St. Dominic and St. Francis to preach against them. The result was the cruel crusade of 1206, which continued in the form of more or less spasmodic persecution for many years,—at least thirty." [S.] l. 899, *Romano:* the birthplace of Ezzelino, near Bassano. Eccelino Romano was chief of the Ghibellines. l. 901, *Azzo's sister Beatrix:* married Otho IV. l. 902, *Richard's Giglia:* a Guelf lady. l. 929, *Retrude:* wife of Salinguerra. l. 948, *Strojavacca:* a troubadour? l. 986, "*Cat's head and Ibis' tail*": "Egyptian symbols in mosaic on the porphyry floor." [S.] l. 989, *Soldan:* Sultan. l. 1009, "*Iris root the Tuscan grated over them*" orris-root. l. 1013, *Carian group:* the Caryatides—women dressed as at the feasts of Diana Caryatis. Carya was a town in Arcadia.

Book III.—Line 2, *moonfern and trifoly:* plants which have supposed magical and healing properties [S.]; *moonfern*, the same as moonwort—*Rumex lunaria*; *mystic trifoly* = trefoil;

"Herb Trinity" was used by St. Patrick to teach the mystery of the Holy Trinity. l. 12, *painted byssus:* silky fibres of a mollusc which has sometimes been spun with silk. l. 14, *Tyrrhene whelk:* the celebrated Tyrian purple, formerly prepared from a shell fish at Tyre. l. 14, *trireme:* a galley or vessel with three benches of oars on a side. l. 15, *satrap* = the governor of a province (Persian). l. 87, "*Marsh gone of a sudden*": when the lake appeared in its place. l. 88, "*Mincio in its place laughed*": when the river occupied the place of the marsh. l. 121, *Island house:* "a villa outside Palermo called La Favara" [S.]; *Nuocera:* between Pompeii and Amalfi. It was called "de Pagani," from a Saracenic colony of Frederick II., who was sometimes contemptuously called the Sultan of Nocera. Villani preserves the quaint words of the famous taunt which Charles of Anjou addressed to Manfred, before the bath of Benvinutum: "Alles e dit moi a li Sultan de Nocere hoggi metorai lui en enfers o il mettar moi en paradis." [S.] l. 123, *Palermitans:* citizens of Palermo. l. 124, *Messinese:* citizens of Messina. l. 125, "*dusk Saracenic clans Nuocera holds*": Frederick, who was afterwards the renowned Frederick II., Emperor of Germany, was crowned at Palermo, in Sicily, in 1198; during his minority the land was torn by turbulent nobles, and revolted Saracens; in 1220 the Emperor-King planted a colony of Saracens at Nocera on the mainland. l. 132, *mollitious alcoves* = soft alcoves. l. 133, *Byzant domes:* Byzantine architecture, in which the dome was a feature, developed about A.D. 300. l. 135, "*August pleasant Dandolo*": "Enrico Dandolo, one of the patrician family of that name in Venice, was chosen doge in 1192, although already blind and seventy-two years old. After naval successes against the Pisans, he was applied to at the time of the fourth crusade to furnish vessels for transport to Constantinople. After making terms most advantageous to the Republic, he himself led the enterprise to success, and shared with the French in the pillage of the city, and very largely in booty and privileges accruing. The four horses of St. Mark's Church were brought over to Venice by him." [S.] l. 140, "*Transport to Venice square*": St. Mark's Church in Venice is adorned with precious columns brought from temples and buildings in all parts of the ancient world. l. 225, "*The bulb dormant, etc.*": "It was the custom to bury the hyacinth bulb with mummies." [S.] l. 85, *The Carroch:* "during the war of the Milanese with Conrad, the Salic archbishop,

Eribert, invented the Carroccio, which was at once adopted by all the cities of Italy. He placed it at the head of the army, and it was an imitation of the ark of the covenant of the tribes of Israel. The carroccio was a four-wheeled car drawn by four yokes of oxen. It was painted red; the oxen were dressed in red clothes to their heels; a very high mast, also painted red, was in the midst; it terminated in a golden ball. Below, between two white veils, floated the standard of the commune, and below that again was a crucifix, with the Saviour extending His arms to bless the army. A sort of platform in the front of the car was devoted to some of the bravest soldiers appointed for its defence. Another platform in the rear was occupied by musicians and trumpeters. Mass was said upon the carroccio before it left the town, and there was frequently a special chaplain attached to it." [S.] l. 312, "*the candle's at the gateway*": "compare with King Alfred's measurement of time. It is still the custom at Bremen for property to be sold at an auction by the candle—that is, the bidding goes on till the candle goes out." [S.] l. 314, *Tiso Sampier:* "Eccelin I. and Tissolin di Campo St. Pierre had been warm friends until, a difference occurring about a marriage portion, Eccelin proved treacherous and grasping, and a lasting feud arose between the two families." [S.] l. 315, "*Ferrara's succoured Palma!*" "The preceding passages in quotation marks are all in the Guelf spirit; this explanation is Ghibelline, say from Browning himself." [S.] l. 386, *Cesano:* a city of Emilia, between Bologna and Ancona, Dante, in *Inferno*, canto xxvii., characterises Cesano as living midway between tryanny and freedom. l. 456, *Fomalhaut:* a star of the first magnitude, in the constellation Priscus Australis, one of the brightest visible in the midnight meridian of September. [S.] l. 476, *Conrad:* the Swabian (1138-52). l. 486, *Saponian:* Mr. Browning explained this puzzling term as referring to the Saponi, who were a branch of the Eccelini family, which settled in Lombardy before the time of Sordello. l. 496, *Vincentines:* the people of Vicenza. l. 514,

"... *just*
As Adelaide of Susa could entrust
Her donative ...
... *to the superb*
Matilda's perfecting."

"The *Biographie Universelle* says: 'Adelaide, Marchioness of Susa, was contemporary with Matilda the great Countess of Tuscany, and governed Piedmont with wisdom and firmness. She endeavoured more than once to make peace between the Emperor and Popes. She was married three times—to a Duke of Swabia, a Marquis of Montferrat, and a Count of Maurienna; and partly through her inheritance from the husbands, all of whom she survived, partly on account of her wise management, her fief Susa became the most important in Italy. Matilda, the great Countess of Tuscany, was one of the most famous characters of her age. Absolute ruler of the most powerful country in Italy, she defended Hildebrand, and adhered to the Pope against all enemies, proffers or threats. During her lifetime she transferred the greater part of her possessions by deed of gift to the papacy; and that deed was the foundation of Papal claims to many lands in Italy throughout the following centuries. She owned the Castle of Canozza, where the Pope took refuge from Henry IV., who had married Adelaide's daughter; and it was to Canozza that that Emperor was obliged to resort, when later he sought the Pope's forgiveness, and when he was left standing barefoot in the snow awaiting the Pope's pleasure. Matilda conveyed her estates to the Pope in 1102, was made sovereign of all Italy in 1110, and died 1115.' There appears to be no mention of any donative entrusted to the superb Matilda, either in the *Biographie Universelle*, or in Sismondi." [S.] Line 501, "*lion's crine*" = lion's hair. l. 583, "*like the alighted Planet Pollux wore.*" Castor and Pollux were generally represented mounted on two white horses, armed with spears, and riding side by side with their heads covered with a bonnet, on the top of which glittered a star. The twins took part in the Argonautic expedition, and when a violent storm arose two flames of fire appeared, and were seen to play around their heads. Pollux was the son of Jupiter, whilst Castor was only his half-brother; but he obtained from Jupiter, for Castor, the gift of immortality, and a place with him amongst the constellations. St. Elmo's fire, which frequently appears and plays about masts and yards of ships during storms, was called Castor and Pollux by Roman sailors" (Lemprière, *Class. Dict.*). l. 590,

"*For thus*
I bring Sordello."

See Book I., l. 353. l. 616, "*Verona's Lady*" is a statue on the top of a fountain at one end of the Piazza d'Erbe. The fountain was put up in 916, at the completion of the aqueduct by Berenger. It was restored in 1368. The statue was first erected by Theodosius in 1380. It is called by the people *Donna Verona*, and wears a steel crown as a symbol that the town was an imperial residence. l. 617, *Gaulish Brennus*, who besieged Rome B.C. 385. l. 621, *Manlïus:* Manlius Marcus, a celebrated Roman who defended the Capitol against the Gauls. l. 625, *platan:* the plane tree. l. 626, *Archimage:* the high priest of the Magi or fire-worshippers. l. 687, *colibri:* humming birds. l. 712, *Bassanese*, of Bassano, a noble town on the Brenta. l. 797, *Basilic:* the Basilica, St. Mark's great Cathedral. l. 798, "*God's great day of the Corpus Domini*" (or *Body of the Lord*): the Feast of Corpus Christi, the Holy Sacrament of the Eucharist. It is held on the Thursday following Trinity Sunday. l. 811, *losel* = a wasteful, worthless fellow. l. 813,

"*God spoke,*
Of right hand, foot, and eye."
(See St. Matthew v. 29, 30) [S.]

l. 837, *mugwort* = a herb of the genus *Artemisia*. l. 839, "*Zin the Horrid*"*:* the Syrian wilderness where the Israelites found no water (Num. xx. 1). l. 847, "*potsherd and Gibeonites*"*:* see Joshua ix. l. 852, *Meribah:* see Exod. xvii. 7 and Num. xxvii. 14. l. 898, "*Prisoned in the Piombi*"*:* horrible torture cells on the leads of the Ducal Palace at Venice, where the prisoners were roasted in the sun. l. 924, "*Tempe's dewy vale*"*:* a beautiful valley in Thessaly. l. 964, *Hercules—in Egypt:* in his quest for the golden apples of the Hesperides, Hercules journeyed through Egypt—Busiris, the king, was about to sacrifice Hercules to Zeus, but he broke his bonds and slew Busiris, his sons and servants. l. 975, *patron-friend:* Walter Savage Landor, who warmly praised Browning's poetry when others abused it; the reference is to Empedocles, a Greek poet. l. 977, *Marathon, Platæa, and Salamis:* celebrated Greek battle-places. l. 987, "*The king who lost the ruby*"*:* Polycrates of Samos. He was advised to throw into the sea the most precious of his jewels, a beautiful seal; he grieved much at the loss, but in a few days he had a present of a large fish, in the belly of which his ring was found.

l. 992, *English Eyebright*: the botanical name of the plant is *Euphrasia officinalis*. Euphrasia, was the name of a lady who was an old friend of Mr. Browning's (Dr. Furnivall). l. 1021, *Xanthus:* a disciple of St. John the Evangelist. l. 1024, *Polycarp*, an early Christian martyr, A.D. 166; and a disciple of St. John. l. 1025, *Charicle:* also a disciple. l. 1045, "*twy prong*" was one of the instruments used by necromancers in "raising the devil." "To procure the magic fork.—This is a branch of a single beam of hazel or almond, which must be cut at a single stroke with the new knife used in the sacrifice. The rod must terminate in a fork." (Waite's *Mysteries of Magic*, p. 260.) *Pastoral Cross:* the cross on a priest's vestment is sometimes Y-shaped. Hargrave Jennings, in his *Rosicrucians*, says it is now used as an anagram exemplifying the Athanasian Creed; exactly, in fact, like the magic twy prong in shape. An Archbishop's crozier or pastoral staff terminates in a cross at the top.

BOOK IV.—Line 24, *quitch-grass* = couch-grass or dog-grass; it roots deeply, and is not easily killed. l. 24, "*loathy mallows*": loathsome mallows, probably because they grow in ditches and in churchyards. l. 34, *Legate Montelungo:* Gregorio di Montelongo, Pontifical legate for Gregory IX. l. 50, *arbalist*, a cross-bow; *manganel*, an engine of war for battering down walls and hurling stones; and *catapult*, a war engine. l. 72, *Jubilate:* rejoice ye! *Jubilate Deo*, 66th Psalm. l. 83:

> " . . . . *What cautelous*
> *Old Redbeard sought from Azzo's sire to wrench vainly.*"

The Lombard League had built Alexandria to defy Barbarossa, who was twice unsuccessful in taking it. l. 89, *Brenta:* a river of North Italy, passing near Padua. *Bacchiglione:* the river on which stand Vicenza and Padua. l. 98, *San Vitale:* a small town near Vicenza. l. 147, "*Messina marbles Constance took delight in*": the marbles of Sicily. For variety and beauty they rival those of any country of Europe. l. 229, *Mainard*, or *Meinhard:* Count of Görz, in the Tyrol. l. 280, *Concorezzi:* a knightly family of Padua. l. 395, "*Crowned grim twy-necked eagle*": the two-headed eagle, symbol of the empire. l. 479, *The Adelardi:* were a noble Guelf family of Ferrara and Mantua. Marchesella was heiress of the Adelardi family; Obizzo I. carried her off, and married her to his son Azzo V. l. 483, *Blacks and*

Whites: the Neri, the black party, and the Bianchi the white. The Bianchi are called the *Parte selvaggia*, because its leaders, the Cerchi, came from the forest lands of Val di Sieve. The other party, the Neri, were led by the Donati. (See Longfellow's Dante—Notes to *Inferno*, vi. 65.) l. 511, "*goshawk*": a short-winged slender hawk (*Falco palumbarius*). l. 533, *Pistore:* Pistoia. l. 577, *Matilda:* Countess of Tuscany (1046-1114), known as the Great Countess; she was the champion of the Church and the ally of Hildebrand. l. 585, *Heinrich:* "Henry VI., married Constance, daughter of the King of Naples and Sicily. He reigned from 1190 to 1197." [S.] "*Philip and Otho*": "the latter conspired against Frederick II., who was brought up by Innocent III., and after Philip's death made Emperor, in 1212. He lived till 1250. His son Henry, King of the Romans, rebelled against him." [S.] l. 614, *Bassano:* a city of Italy, in the province of Vicenza, on the Brenta. "There is a church of St. Francis at Bassano. Lanze says, 'It is the peculiar boast of Bologna that she can claim three of the few artists of the earliest times: one Guido, one Ventura, and one Ursone, of whom there exist memorials as far back as 1248." [S.] l. 615, *Guido the Bolognian:* Guido Reni, the great painter of Bologna (1575-1642). l. 645, *Guglielm*=William; *Aldobrand* or *Aldovrandino:* Governor of Ferrara, in conjunction with Salinguerra (1231). l. 735, *San Biagio:* St. Biase, a place near the Lake of Garda. l. 797, *Constance:* wife of Henry VI. of Germany; by this marriage Frederick hoped that his empire would soon include Naples and Sicily. l. 837, *Moorish lentisk:* the mastich tree. l. 884, *poison-wattles:* the baggy flesh on the animal's neck, an excrescence or lobe. l. 977, *Crescentius Nomentanus:* a Roman tribune, who, in the absence of Pope John and King Otho, tried to restore consular Rome. But the Pope and King returned, and crucified him, A.D. 998. (See Gibbon's *Decline and Fall*, chap. xlix.) Professor Sonnenschein sends me the following further note: "Crescentius was a Roman who, towards the end of the tenth century, endeavoured to restore his country's liberty and ancient glory. The power of the Eastern emperors had long ceased in Rome, that of the Western emperors had been suspended by long interregnas. Rome was a republic in which the citizens, the neighbouring nobles, and the Pope, disputed the authority. Crescentius, who was of the family of the Counts of the Tusculum, placed himself at the head of the anarchic government about 980, with the title of Consul. He had, to dispute his rank, Boniface VII., who, murderer of two popes, had become Pope himself. This pontiff was stained by the most shameful crimes, and as his authority was not well founded, the nobles and the people aided Crescentius in breaking the yoke. Boniface died 985. John XV., who succeeded him, was detained by Crescentius far from Rome, in exile, until he recognised the sovereignty of the people. Upon his return he did not seek to trouble the government; and, as well as one can judge through the obscurity of ages, the Roman republic enjoyed until 996, under the Consul Crescentius, such peace, order, and security, as it had not known for a long time. John XV. died the year Otho III. went from Germany to Italy, to receive the imperial crown. The young monarch chose his relative, Gregory V., to succeed John. None of the rights or privileges of Rome were known to the new pontiff, who, long accustomed to regard the popes as gods on earth, having now himself become pope, could not conceive of any resistance to his will. Crescentius refused to recognise a pope whose election and conduct were alike irregular. He opposed to him another pope, a Greek by birth, who took the name of John XVI., and he asked the Emperor of the East to send troops to his assistance. Otho III. entered Rome with an army in 998. He condemned John XVI. to horrible torture, and besieged Crescentius in the castle of St. Angelo; and as he could not conquer the latter, he offered him an honourable capitulation. However, he no sooner had him in his hands than he put him to death and ill-treated his wife. Three years later, on his return from a penitential pilgrimage, she succeeded in causing his death by poison." l. 1006, *wranal:* a lantern. l. 1032, "*Rome of the Pandects*" *:* "The digest or abridgment in fifty books of the decisions and opinions of the old Roman jurists, made in the sixth century, by order of the Emperor Justinian, and forming the first part of the body of the civil law." (Webster.)

BOOK V.—Line 6, *Palatine*, one invested with royal privileges and rights. l. 16, *atria*, halls or principal rooms in Roman houses. l. 17, *stibadium*, a half-round reclining couch used by Romans near their baths. l. 18, *lustral vase:* used in purification at meals, etc. l. 34, *pelt*, a skin of a beast with the hair on. l. 43, *obsidion*, a kind of black glass produced by volcanoes.

l. 58, *Mauritania*, an ancient country of North Africa = land of the Moors, celebrated for the wood called Citrus, for tables of which the Romans gave fabulous prices. l. 61, *Demiurge:* a worker for the people; so God, as Creator of the world. *Mareotic:* of the locality of Lake Mareotis, in Egypt. Mareotic wine was very famous; *Cæcuban:* Cæcubum, a town of Latium. Cæcubus Ager was noted for the excellence and plenty of its wines. l. 82, *Pythoness:* the priestess who gave oracular answers at Delphi, in Greece. l. 83, *Lydian king:* Lydia was a kingdom of Asia Minor. The king referred to was Crœsus, who interpreted in his own favour the ambiguous answer of the oracle, and was destroyed by following the advice he thought was given to him. l. 115, *Nina and Alcamo:* Sicilian poets of the period. In the life of Joanna, Queen of Naples, we read of "the Poetess Nina, whose love of her art caused her to become enamoured of a poet whom she had never seen. This fortunate bard (who returned her poetical passion) was called Dante; but we cannot plead in her excuse that he had anything else in common with the great poet of that name. Nina was the most beautiful woman of the day, and the first female who wrote verse in Italian. She was so engrossed by her passion for her lover that she caused herself always to be called 'The Nina of Dante.'" [S.] "Sismondi only mentions C. d'Alcamo as a Sicilian poet, apparently nearly contemporary with Frederick II. See Ginguené for a full account of Sicilian poetry." [S.] l. 145, *Castellans*, governors of castles. l. 146, *Suzerains*, feudal lords. l. 163, "*Hildebrand of the huge brain mask*": Pope Gregory VII. He was one of the most famous of the popes, and he lived in the latter part of the eleventh century. l. 174, *Mandrake:* Mandragora—a plant with a bifurcated root, concerning which many singular superstitions have accumulated. l. 186, "*Three Imperial Crowns*": the Imperial Crown proper, the German crown, and the Italian or Lombard crown. There seems a little confusion here in the order of the different metals. The Imperial Crown was of gold. The German is always spoken of as the silver crown. The Italian or Lombard crown was known as the iron crown, because one of the nails of Christ's cross was inserted into its gold frame." (*Encyc. Brit.*) l. 188, *Alexander IV.*, Pope of Rome (1254-61); *Innocent IV.*, Pope (1243-54). l. 189, *Papal key:* the keys of Peter in the papal arms. l. 194, "*The* *hermit Peter": Peter, the Hermit of Amiens, who preached up the first Crusade. l. 195, *Claremont* = Clermont, a city of France, in which, at a council held in 1095, Pope Urban II. first formally organised the great Crusade. l. 200, *Vimmercato*, a town on the Molgova, fourteen miles north-east of Milan. l. 203, "*Mantuan Albert*": Blessed Albert founder of the Order of Canons Regular. But it was Albert, patriarch of Jerusalem, who was umpire between Pope and Emperor. l. 204, *Saint Francis*, of Assisi, born 1182; one of the most beautiful characters who ever lived. All living creatures to him were his "brothers and sisters." l. 205, "*God's truce*": "The Pax Ecclesiæ," or "Treuga Dei"—a suspension of arms, putting a stop to private hostilities within certain periods. The treaty called the "Truce of God" was set on foot in A.D. 999. It was agreed, among other articles, that "churches should be sanctuaries to all sorts of persons, except those who violated this truce; and that from Wednesday till Monday morning no one should offer violence to any one, not even by way of satisfaction for any injustice he had received" (Butler's *Lives of the Saints*, *sub* "St. Odilo," Jan. 1st.) l. 281, *hacqueton:* a quilted jacket, worn under a coat of mail. l. 298, *trabea:* a regal robe. l. 384, *thyrsus:* a spear wrapped about with ivy, carried at feasts of Bacchus. l. 405, *baldric:* a richly ornamented belt, passing only over one shoulder. l. 453, "*Caliph's wheel work man*": an automaton. l. 509, *Typhon*, a giant. l. 660, *Lombard Agilulph:* a king of Lombardy, A.D. 601. l. 712, "*changed the spoils of every clime at Venice*": the great Cathedral of St. Mark's, Venice, contains columns and ornaments of various kinds, brought from heathen temples in all parts of the Roman world. Pillars from the Temple of Jerusalem, and precious marbles from ancient Roman palaces, combine to make the interior of St. Mark's one of the strangest and richest Christian churches in the world. So these spoils from many lands, taken from temples devoted to alien worship, have been "changed" to Christian uses in this church. l. 718, "*earth's reputed consummations*": that is to say, the noblest works which the world at the time could produce. "The temple at Thebes was the consummate achievement of one age; of another, that of the Temple of Jupiter Tonans; of another, the Parthenon at Athens. All these were 'earth's reputed consummations.'" l. 719, "*razed a seal*": Thebes being despoiled like Rome,

Athens rifled like Byzant, until St. Mark's at Venice having razed a seal (*i.e.* broken the seal, or, as it were, extracted the nails that fixed the most famous works in the world to their original site) lo! the glittering symbols of the all-purifying Trinity blazed above them: so the "horned and snouted god," the "cinerary pitcher," became part of the Christian edifice. l. 719, "*The All-transmuting Triad blazed above*": that is, they were consecrated by reason of the new faith in the Trinity. The three persons of the Holy Trinity are represented in the mosaics of St. Mark's Church."* l. 750, *Treville* or Treviglio: a town in Lombardy, fourteen miles south of Bergamo. l. 751. *Cartiglione:* is this a misprint for Castiglione? l. 788, *writhled* = wrinkled. l. 794, *pauldron:* a defence of armour-plate over the shoulders. l. 909, *Gesi* or Jesi: a city in the Italian province of Ancona. It was the birthplace of Frederick II. in 1194. l. 943, *Valsugan:* a town on the Brenta, on the road from Trent to Venice. l. 970 *Torriani:* a faction of Valsassina of Lombardy, contending with the *Visconti* (l. 971): Otho Visconti, Archbishop of Milan (1262), founded the house of Visconti. The Torriani were democrats, the Visconti aristocrats. l. 1065, "*Trent upon Apulia*": *i.e.*, Northern upon Southern Italy. l. 1071, *Cunizza:* called Palma throughout the poem (see p. 123). l. 1090, *Squarcialupo:* not historical.

BOOK VI.—Line 100, *jacinth* = hyacinth in mineralogy; a name given to several kinds of stone—topaz, etc.; *lodestone:* magnetic oxide of iron. l. 101, *flinders:* fragments (of shining metal). l. 142, *Cydippe:* an Athenian girl who met Acontius at a festival of Artemis. He wrote a promise of marriage from the girl to himself on an apple, and threw it at her feet. The girl read the words aloud, and the oracle told her father she would have to comply with the words she had read. l. 143, *Agathon*—evidently meant for Acontius in the above story. l. 184, *Dularete:* not historical. l. 323, "*brakes at balm-shed*": brake ferns at seed time—*i.e.*, autumn. l. 387, *reate* = a waterweed, as water crow-foot. l. 388, *gold-sparkling grail:* gravel gold-coloured. l. 417, *citrine* = crystals: a yellow pellucid variety of quartz; "*fierce pyropus-stone*" = a carbuncle of fiery redness. l. 590, *King-bird:* "The Phœnix travels (in an egg of myrrh) to Heliopolis to die." [S.] l. 614, "*an old fable,*" etc. See Pindar's,

* For the above suggestions I am indebted to the *Notes of the Browning Society*, Part VII., p. 42*.

"Fourth Pythian Ode." l. 630, *Hermit-bee*—a species of Apidæ; some of the best known of this species are solitary in their habits. The Carpenter-bee (*Xylocopa*) excavates nests and cells in wood; the Mason-bee (*Osmia* and *Megachill*) forms nests with particles of sand. l. 677-8, "*Henry of Egna*," "*Sofia*," "*Lady of the Rock*," *etc.*: Sofia was the "youngest daughter of Eccelin the monk, widow of Henry of Egna, the 'Lady of the Rock,' or of the Trentine Pass" (W. M. Rossetti). l. 698, *Campese*: a town on the Brenta, near Bassano. l. 699, *Solagna*: a village in the province of Vicenza, in the Eastern Alps. l. 787, *Valley Rù*: in the valley of Enneberg or Gaderthal, on the Eastern Alps. l. 788, *San Zeno*: the basilica of St. Zeno, an early bishop of Verona. l. 792, *raunce*, or rance, a bar or rail. l. 799, *cushat's chirre*—the ringdove's coo. l. 802, *barrow*: a tomb. l. 803, *Alberic*: brother of Eccelin. He was tortured to death. l. 858, *Hesperian fruit*: of the Western land (Italy or Spain). The golden apples of the Hesperides probably were oranges. l. 894, "*rifle a musk pod and 't will ache like yours*": a freshly-opened musk pod has a most powerful and pungent ammoniacal odour. Musk requires to be smelt in minute quantity. Sordello's story deals with political troubles and horrors of war, too powerful a dose for reading at one sitting.

"So, the head aches and the limbs are faint!" (*Fenshtah's Fancies.*) The sixth lyric begins with these words.

Soul, The. It "existed ages past" (*Cristina*); "is resting here an age" (*Cristina*); "on its lone way" (*Cristina* and *Rabbi ben Ezra*); "its nature is to seek durability" (*Red Cotton Night-cap Country*); "is independent of bodily pain" (*Red Cotton*); "is here to mate another soul" (*Cristina*); "shall rise in its degree" (*Toccata of Galuppi's*); "it craves all" (*Cleon*); and "can never taste death" (*Paracelsus*). *La Saisiaz* is *the* poem for proof of its existence and immortality.

Soul's Tragedy, A: Act I. being what was called the poetry of Chiappino's life, and Act II. its prose (London, 1846). The incidents are not all historical; they are imagined to have occurred at Faenza, a city of Italy about twenty miles south-west of Ravenna, in the sixteenth century. Chiappino is a patriot—so far as words and fine sentiments go. He is a good type of the men who in all popular movements seek their own interest while pretending to be concerned only for the welfare of the people.

Having fomented popular feeling against the Provost of Faenza he has been sentenced to exile. He has, however, an influential friend, Luitolfo, who has volunteered to exert his good offices with the Provost, with whom he is on good terms, with the view of obtaining a pardon. The first Act opens with a dialogue between Eulalia and Chiappino in Luitolfo's house, concerning the cause of the latter's prolonged absence on his errand of friendly intercession. Luitolfo and Eulalia are betrothed lovers. Chiappino, while his friend is absent endeavouring to save him, is bragging of his humanitarian courage and daring, and depreciating his friend while making love to his betrothed. Eulalia listens, but begs for "justice to him that's now entreating, at his risk, perhaps, justice for you!" Chiappino hates Luitolfo for the favours he has done him, the fines he has paid for him, the intercession he has made; and so he endeavours to make himself important in the woman's eyes, to pose as the martyr of humanity, while he belittles her betrothed lover, and tries to prove that his acts of kindness were unimportant. While they discuss, a knocking is heard without; the door is opened, and Luitolfo rushes in with blood upon him. He declares he has killed the Provost, and the crowd are in pursuit of him. Chiappino offers his protection, and talks bravely as usual; forces Luitolfo to fly in his disguise while he remains with Eulalia and meets the angry pursuers. The populace enter, and Chiappino, without hesitation, declares it was he who killed the Provost: he knows the people will bless him as their saviour, so he takes the credit of Luitolfo's act of vengeance. Eulalia is anxious he should give the credit to Luitolfo, as the murder turns out to be popular; but Chiappino defers the explanation till the morrow. Act II. is in prose; the scene is laid a month after, in the market-place of Faenza: Luitolfo is mingling in disguise with the populace assembled outside the Provost's palace. A bystander tells him that Chiappino will be the new Provost: it is he who was the brave friend of the people; Luitolfo the coward, who ran away from them and their cause. Ravenna, he says, governs Faenza, as Rome governs Ravenna; and the Papal legate, Ogniben, has entered the town, saying satirically: "I have known three-and-twenty leaders of revolts!" He wishes to know what the revolters want. The soldiers came into Ravenna, bearing their wounded Provost (he had not been killed, as

Luitolfo supposed). The Legate had come to arrange matters amicably. He will have no punishments for the insurrection. What he desires to know is, Do they wish to live without any government at all? or if not, do they wish their ruler to be murdered by the first citizen who conceives he has a grievance? Chiappino puts himself forward as spokesman, and declares he is in favour of a republic. "And you the administrator thereof?" asks the Legate. After a little fencing, Chiappino agrees to this; and so the crowd is waiting to see him invested with the provostship. He is to marry Luitolfo's love and succeed to his property. Luitolfo will not believe all this till he sees Eulalia and his quondam friend. Chiappino enters with Eulalia, making excuses for his *volte-face* both in politics and love, and shows that he falls completely into the trap the clever and satirical ecclesiastic has set for the pretended patriot. After much cutting sarcasm at Chiappino's expense on the part of the brilliant legate, who evidently knows his man to the marrow, the waiting populace are informed that the provostship will be conferred on Chiappino as soon as the name of the person who attempted to kill the late Provost is given up. Luitolfo comes from his place in the crowd to own and justify his act, much to the confusion of the man who has claimed all the credit of the deed. The Legate orders Luitolfo to his house, and recommends the patriot to rusticate himself awhile. Then, demanding the keys of the Provost's palace, and advising profitable meditation to the people, he leaves them chuckling that he has known *four-and-twenty* leaders of revolts. The character of the ecclesiastic Ogniben is one of the finest inventions of Mr. Browning.

NOTES.—Act I. *Scudi:* dollars. Act II.: *Brutus the Elder:* who conspired with Cassius against Julius Cæsar. "*Dico vobis!*" I tell you! "*St. Nepomucene of Prague*" = St. John Nepomucen of Prague (1383), martyr. He was an anchorite and an apostle. The Emperor Wenceslaus had him put to death because he refused to betray what the Empress had told him under the seal of confession. *Ravenna:* a very celebrated and very ancient city of North-east Italy. Its great historical importance began early in the fifth century, when Honorius transferred his court thither. From 402 to 476 A.D. Ravenna was the chief residence of the Roman emperors. It was subject to papal rulers in the period of this story. "*Cur fremuere gentes?*" (Psalm ii. 1): "Why do the heathen so furiously rage together?" *Pontificial Legate:* an ambassador sent by the Pope to the court of a foreign prince or state. "*Western Lands*": The allusion is to the discovery of America and the treasures and curiosities brought by Columbus to Spain.

Speculative. (*Asolando*, 1889.) Could the inspirations and pure delights of the past return, and remain with some great souls who have learned the divine alchemy of turning to gold the pains and pleasures of earth's old life, it would be for them all that lower minds seek in a new life in what they call heaven; the real heaven being a state, and not a place. Love has inspired the poem.

Spiritualism. Browning's opinions on this subject are to be found in his poem *Mr. Sludge the Medium.*

Spring Song. The poem commencing

"Dance, yellows and whites and reds!"

was published under the title of "Spring Song" in the *New Amphion*, 1886. In 1887 it was published at the end of *Gerard de Lairesse* in the "*Parleyings*" volume.

Statue and the Bust, The. The Riccardi Palace in Florence is the scene of the story told in this poem. A lady who has just been married to the head of the noble Riccardi house notices one who rides past her window with a "royal air." The bridesmaids whisper that it is the great Duke Ferdinand; who in his turn directs his glance at the bride the head of the house of Riccardi had that day brought home. As he looked at the woman and she at the man, her past was a sleep—her life that day only began. That night there was a feast in the house of the bride, and the Grand Duke was present. The lovers stood face to face a minute. In accordance with the courtly custom of the time, he was privileged to kiss the bride. Whether a word was spoken or not cannot be said. The husband, who stood by, however, saw or heard something which mortally offended him; and when, at night, he led his bride to her chamber, he told her calmly that the door which was then shut on her was closed till her body should be taken thence for burial. She could watch the world from the window, which faced the east, but could never more pass the door. The bride as calmly assented:

"Your window and its world suffice,"

she said. It would be easy, she thought, to fly to the Duke, who loved her: it would only be necessary to disguise herself as a page, and she would save her soul. She reflected, however, that next day her father was to bless her new condition; and she must tarry for a day, consoling herself with the reflection that she should certainly see the Duke ride past. And so she turned on her side, and went to sleep. That night the Duke resolved to ruin body and soul, if need might be, for the sake of this beautiful woman; and on the morrow he addressed the bridegroom, whose duties at court brought him into his presence, suggesting that he, with his wife, should visit him at his country seat at Petraja. The bridegroom quietly declined the invitation, giving as his reason that the state of his lady's health did not permit her to quit the palace, the wind from the Apennines being particularly dangerous for her. The Duke was foiled in his project; but promised himself it should not be long before he met the bride again, yet he must wait a night, for the envoy from France was to visit him. He too reflects that he shall see the lady as he rides past her palace. They saw each other, and each resolved that next day they would do more than glance at a distance; but next day and the next passed, and as constantly was the project of union deferred; the weeks grew months, the years passed by, till age crept on, and each perceived they had been dreaming. One day the lady had to confess that her beauty was fading: her hair was tinged with grey, her mouth was puckered, and she was haggard-cheeked; and as she beheld herself in her glass she bade her servants call a famous sculptor to fix the remains of her beauty, so that it should no more fade. Della Robbia must make her a face on her window waiting, as ever, to watch her lover pass in the square below. But long before the artist's work was finished, and the cornice in its place, the Duke had sighed over the escape of his own youth; and he too set John of Douay to make an equestrian statue of him, and to place it in the square he had crossed so often, so that men should admire him when he had gone to his tomb. The figure looks straight at one of the windows of the Riccardi Palace: the attitude suggests love for the lady and contempt of her husband. In connection with all this the poet reflects on the condition of the spirits of these two awaiting the Last Judgment. Do they reflect on the greatness of the gift of life—how they had seen the proper object of their lives, and yet had missed it? "But," the poet hears us object, "their end was a crime, and delay was best." The test, however, of our use of life can be as well attained by a crime as a virtue. A game can be played without money: where a button answers, it would be vain to use a sovereign. Whether we play with counters or coins, we must do our best to win:—

> "If you choose to play!—is my principle,
> Let a man contend to the uttermost
> For his life's set prize, be it what it will."

These people as surely lost their counter as if it were lawful coin. This moral has been much disputed by Browning students. So far as society was concerned the lady and the Duke did well: so far as their own souls were concerned they undoubtedly did ill. The Duke would have been more manly and the woman truer to her human instincts if he and she had let love have its way. Both dwarfed and withered their souls by looking and longing and pining for what they had not courage to grasp. The sin in each case was as great in the sight of God. It was simply prudence and conventionality which restrained the lovers; and these things count for nothing with the poet-psychologist. But conventionality counts for a great deal in our conduct of life. It may have been "the crowning disaster to miss life" for the man and woman: if so, it was a sacrifice justly due to human society. If every woman flew to the arms of the man whom she liked better than her own husband, and if every governor of a city felt himself at liberty to steal another man's wife merely to complete and perfect the circle of his own delights, society would soon be thrown back into barbarism. The sacrifice to conventionality and the self-restraint these persons practised may have atoned for much that was defective in their lives. "*Pecca fortiter*" (sin bravely), said Luther; but it would be difficult to defend the doctrine on any principle of ethics. Many readers have found difficulties in understanding this poem. One such wrote to an American paper to inquire: "(1) When, how, and where did it happen? Browning's divine vagueness lets one gather only that the lady's husband was a Riccardi. (2) Who was the lady? who the Duke? (3) The magnificent house where Florence lodges her Préfet is known to all Florentine ball-goers as the

Palazzo Riccardi. It was bought by the Riccardi from the Medici in 1659. From none of its windows did the lady gaze at her more than royal lover. From what window, then, if from any? Are the statue and the bust still in their original positions?" These queries fell into the hands of Mr. Wise, who forwarded them to Mr. Browning, who sent the following answer:— "Jan. 8th, '87. DEAR MR. WISE,—I have seldom met with such a strange inability to understand what seems the plainest matter possible. 'Ball-goers' are probably not history readers; but any guide-book would confirm what is sufficiently stated in the poem. I will append a note or two, however. (1) 'This story the townsmen tell': 'when, how, and where' constitutes the subject of the poem. (2) The lady was the wife of Riccardi, and the Duke—Ferdinand, just as the poem says. (3) As it was built by and inhabited by the Medici till sold, long after, to the Riccardi, it was not from the Duke's palace, but a window in that of the Riccardi, that the lady gazed at her lover riding by. The statue is still in its place, looking at the window under which is 'now the empty shrine.' Can anything be clearer? My 'vagueness' leaves *what* to be 'gathered' when all these things are put down in black and white? Oh, 'ball-goers'!—Yours very sincerely, ROBERT BROWNING." The Medicean palace in the Via Larga, now called the Via Cavour, is meant as the *duke's* palace. See articles on this question in *Poet Lore*, vol. iii., pp. 284 and 648. It is an error to suppose that but one palace is referred to in the poem. The Piazza della Annunziata in Florence is the square referred to in the first verse. The Church of the Annunciation of the Blessed Virgin was built in 1250, and adorned at the expense of Pietro de' Medici from the designs of Michelozzi. The loggia of the church forms the north side. On the east is the Foundling Hospital, *Spedale degli Innocenti*, dating from the year 1421. In the centre of the square is an equestrian statue of Ferdinand I., cast from cannon taken by the Knights of St. Stephen from the Turks.

NOTES.—"*Great Duke Ferdinand*": Ferdinand I. was Grand Duke of Florence, an honour first conferred on Cosimo (dei Medici) I. by Pope Pius V., who conferred the patent and crown upon him in Rome. Ferdinand was a cardinal from the age of fourteen, but he had never taken holy orders. He was an amiable and capable ruler, and Tuscany flourished under his government.

He was thirty-eight years old when, in 1587, he succeeded his brother on the throne. *Riccardi:* a noble family of Florence. "The Palazzo Riccardi, a proud and stately residence, was begun in 1430 by Cosimo dei Medici. It remained in the possession of the family till 1659. when they sold it to Gabriele Riccardi; but towards the end of the last century it was bought by the Grand Duke, and is now employed as a species of Somerset House, partly for literary purposes and partly for government offices. It is a noble building, and is most imposing in appearance. The window-sills are by Michael Angelo" (see Murray's *Handbook to North Italy*). *Via Larga:* this was overshadowed by the Medici Palace, symbolical of the shadow cast by the crime of its owners in destroying the liberties of the city. *Encolure* (Fr.): the neck and shoulders of a horse. *Emprise:* undertaking, enterprise. "*Cosimo and his cursed son*": Cosimo dei Medici was called "the father of his country," his grandson was "Lorenzo the Magnificent." *Arno:* the river which flows through Florence. *Petraja:* a suburban residence near Florence. *Apennine:* the mountain range in the valley of which Florence is seated. "*Robbia's craft,*" "*Robbia's cornice*": Della Robbia is the name of a family of great distinction in the art history of Florence. "Robbia's craft" would seem to be a term applied to the kind of work done, and does not refer to the artist himself, as the last famous Della Robbia (Girolamo) died in 1566. The work called Robbia ware was terra-cotta relief covered with enamel. *John of Douay* (1524-1608), usually called Giovanni da Bologna: a celebrated sculptor of Italy. "*stamp of the very Guelph*": English money of our time, our royal family being Guelfs. "*de te fabula*": the fable is told concerning yourself.

Strafford. [The Statesman and the Historical Period of the Poem.] It is so important that the reader of the tragedy of *Strafford* should start with a clear idea of the historical facts with which it deals, that I have included in my article the following extract from Professor Gardiner's Life of Strafford in the *Encyclopædia Britannica.* For the benefit of such of my readers as may have forgotten the fact, I may state that, before the earldom was conferred on Strafford, he was Sir Thomas Wentworth:—"High-handed as Wentworth was by nature, his rule in Ireland made him more high-handed than ever. As yet he had never been consulted on English affairs, and it was only in

February 1637 that Charles asked his opinion on a proposed interference in the affairs of the Continent. In reply, he assured Charles that it would be unwise to undertake even naval operations till he had secured absolute power at home. The opinion of the judges had given the King the right to levy ship-money; but, unless his Majesty had 'the like power declared to raise a land army, the crown' seemed 'to stand upon one leg at home, to be considerable but by halves to foreign princes abroad.' The power so gained, indeed, must be shown to be beneficent by the maintenance of good government; but it ought to exist. A beneficent despotism supported by popular gratitude was now Wentworth's ideal. In his own case Wentworth had cause to discover that Charles' absolutism was marred by human imperfections. Charles gave ear to courtiers far too often, and frequently wanted to do them a good turn by promoting incompetent persons to Irish offices. To a request from Wentworth to strengthen the position of the deputy by raising him to an earldom he turned a deaf ear. Yet, to make Charles more absolute continued to be the dominant note of his policy; and, when the Scottish Puritans rebelled, he advocated the most decided measures of repression, and in February 1639 he offered the king £2000 as his contribution to the expenses of the coming war. He was, however, too clear-sighted to do otherwise than deprecate an invasion of Scotland before the English army was trained. In September 1639, after Charles' failure in the first Bishops' War, Wentworth arrived in England, to conduct in the Star Chamber a case in which the Irish chancellor was being prosecuted for resisting the deputy. From that moment he stepped into the place of Charles' principal adviser. Ignorant of the extent to which opposition had developed in England during his absence, he recommended the calling of a parliament to support a renewal of the war, hoping that by the offer of a loan from the privy councillors, to which he himself contributed £20,000, he would place Charles above the necessity of submitting to the new parliament if it should prove restive. In January 1640 he was created Earl of Strafford, and in March he went to Ireland to hold a parliament, where the Catholic vote secured a grant of subsidies to be used against the Presbyterian Scots. An Irish army was to be levied to assist in the coming war. When, in April, Strafford returned to England, he found the Commons holding back from a grant of supply, and tried to enlist the peers on the side of resistance. On the other hand, he attempted to induce Charles to be content with a smaller grant than he had originally asked for. The Commons, however, insisted on peace with the Scots; and on May 9th, at the Privy Council, Strafford, though reluctantly, voted for a dissolution. After this Strafford supported the harshest measures. He urged the King to invade Scotland; and, in meeting the objection that England might resist, he uttered the words which cost him dear: 'You have an army in Ireland'—the army which, in the regular course of affairs, was to have been employed to operate in the west of Scotland—'you may employ here to reduce this kingdom.' He tried to force the citizens of London to lend money. He supported a project for debasing the coinage, and for seizing bullion in the Tower, the property of foreign merchants. He also advocated the purchasing a loan from Spain by the offer of a future alliance. He was ultimately appointed to command the English army, but he was seized with illness, and the rout of Newburn made the position hopeless. In the great council at York he showed his hope that, if Charles maintained the defensive, the country would still rally round him; whilst he proposed, in order to secure Ireland, that the Scots of Ulster should be ruthlessly driven from their homes. When the Long Parliament met, it was preparing to impeach Strafford, when tidings reached its leaders that Strafford, now Lord Lieutenant of Ireland, had come to London, and had advised the King to take the initiative by accusing his chief opponents of treason. On this the impeachment was hurried on, and the Lords committed Strafford to the Tower. At his trial in Westminster Hall he stood on the ground that each charge against him, even if true, did not amount to treason; whilst Pym urged that, taken as a whole, they showed an intention to change the government, which in itself was treason. Undoubtedly the project of bringing over the Irish army—probably never seriously entertained—did the prisoner most damage; and, when the Lords showed reluctance to condemn him, the Commons dropped the impeachment, and brought in a bill of attainder. The Lords would probably have refused to pass it if they could have relied on Charles's assurance to relegate Strafford to private life if the bill were rejected. Charles unwisely took part in projects for effecting Strafford's escape, and even for raising a military force to accomplish that end. The Lords took alarm and passed the bill. On May 9th, 1641, the King, frightened by popular tumults, reluctantly signed a commission for the purpose of giving to it the royal assent, and on the 12th Strafford was executed on Tower Hill."

[THE TRAGEDY.] (Published 1837, and dedicated to William C. Macready.) *Strafford*, a tragedy in five acts (written for the stage at Macready's request), has for its plot the impeachment of the Earl of Strafford and his condemnation and execution. It tells the story of the faithful statesman who loved his sovereign, and sacrificed his life from an almost insane devotion to an utterly unworthy man. The tragedy deals with a period of English history which was richer than any other in the assertion of the rights of the people against the tyranny of their rulers. We are introduced to the band of patriots who secured for us the rights which are to-day the most precious heritage of every Englishman—the brave men who, like Hampden and Pym, resisted the system of forced loans, and the obnoxious tax called "ship-money." Strafford has been carrying fire and sword through Ireland, and Charles is proposing to persecute the Scotch with similar severity. Wentworth has answered the summons of the king, and has yielded to his request to undertake the Scotch war. He now begins to see how treacherous his sovereign is. Charles, by bribes and promises, has detached him from the people's cause only to use him as a catspaw, to bear the hatred and fury of the people in his stead. Pym tries to win back "the apostate" to the cause of liberty. They loved each other as David and Jonathan; and the efforts of Pym to touch the heart of his friend, and win him from his chivalrous devotion to Charles to his duty to his country, are finely described in the play. But neither duty, danger, nor the imminent approach of death itself, can divert for a single moment the nobleman who is devoted body and soul to the wretchedest semblance of a "king by right divine" who ever secured such devoted service. Strafford, deaf alike to the calls of friendship and patriotism, serves one man only—Charles,—and leaves the patriots to fight for England as best they may. Lady Carlisle interposes her influence, warns Strafford of his danger, and begs him to secure his retreat while he may; but he is as little moved by the appeals of a woman's love as by those more powerful and legitimate motives which he has refused to entertain. Such blind devotion to an ideal founded on so insecure a base could have only ruin for its end. Strafford leads the army to the north, is ignominiously defeated, finds that Charles has treacherously listened to proposals of reconciliation with the Scotch, and that the patriots are in league with them; returns to London, and determines to impeach the patriots, but finds his move anticipated. He is himself impeached, a bill of attainder against him is passed, and he is arrested and imprisoned in the Tower. Charles, who had promised that Strafford should not suffer in life, liberty, or estate for his devotion to his cause, makes no effort to save him, though nothing could have been easier than to have done so; and actually, after a little show of hesitation, signs his death warrant at the request of Pym. Passionately and entirely devoted to Strafford, Lady Carlisle has conceived a plan by which, with the King's connivance, he may escape from the Tower. A boat has been brought to the river entrance of the fortress, and arrangements made for his escape to France; but Strafford refuses to run away from the country which demands his life, and will not let it be said to his children in after years that their father broke prison to save his head; and so, while he delays the acceptance of Lady Carlisle's assistance, he is led to execution. He sees that not he alone, but the master who has betrayed him, must incur the vengeance of the outraged people of England; and his last words addressed to Pym are to implore him (on his knees) to spare the King's life. He feels that nothing will move the stern patriot from his sense of duty, and thanks God that it is himself who dies first. He expresses no word of ill-feeling against Pym, and goes bravely to death, the victim of a misplaced affection almost without parallel in our history. *Strafford* is a presentation of "naked souls," as Dr. J. Todhunter called it. "They are almost like Hugo's personages, monomaniacs of ideas—Strafford of loyalty to Charles; Lady Carlisle of loyalty to Strafford's infatuation; Pym of loyalty to an ideal England . . . Browning has not left the King even a rag of conventional royalty to cover his nakedness. He has stript him with a vengeance." How far Browning's representation of the circumstances attendant on the impeachment and condemnation of Strafford is true to the actual facts must be left to the decision of the greatest authority on the history of the period—Professor

Gardiner. In his introduction to Miss E. H. Hickey's *Strafford*, he says: "We may be sure that it was not by accident that Mr. Browning, in writing this play, decisively abandoned all attempt to be historically accurate. Only here and there does anything in the course of the drama take place as it could have taken place at the actual court of Charles I. Not merely are there frequent minor inaccuracies, but the very roots of the situation are untrue to fact. The real Strafford was far from opposing the war with the Scots at the time when the Short Parliament was summoned. Pym never had such a friendship for Strafford as he is represented as having; and, to any one who knows anything of the habits of Charles, the idea of Pym or his friends entering into colloquies with Strafford, and even bursting unannounced into Charles's presence, is, from the historical point of view, simply ridiculous. So completely does the drama proceed irrespectively of historical truth, that the critic may dispense with the thankless task of pointing out discrepancies. He will be better employed in asking what ends those discrepancies were intended to serve, and whether the neglect of truth of fact has resulted in the highest truth of character.—For myself I can only say that, every time I read the play, I feel more certain that Mr. Browning has seized the real Strafford, the man of critical brain, of rapid decision, and tender heart, who strove for the good of his nation without sympathy for the generation in which he lived. Charles I., too, with his faults perhaps exaggerated, is the real Charles. Of Lady Carlisle we know too little to speak with anything like certainty; but, in spite of Mr. Browning's statement that his character of her is purely imaginary, there is a wonderful parallelism between the Lady Carlisle which history conjectures rather than describes. There is the same tendency to fix the heart upon the truly great man, and to labour for him without the requital of human affection; though in the play no part is played by that vanity which seems to have been the main motive with the real personage." It has frequently been said that Browning, in this play, has closely followed the story as given in the *Life of Strafford* by the late John Forster. The reason for this undoubted fact has recently been given to the world. In the *Pall Mall Gazette*, in the month of April 1890, Dr. F. J. Furnivall published the following letter, which asserts the late poet's right to almost the whole of the *Life of Strafford* that has hitherto gone under the name of the late John Forster, in the second volume of the *Lives of Eminent British Statesmen* in Lardner's "Cabinet Cyclopædia," pp. 178-411, with the Strafford Appendix, pp. 412-21: "This volume was published in 1836. John Forster wrote the life of Eliot, the first in the volume, and began that of Strafford. He then fell ill; and as he was anxious to produce the book in the time agreed on, Browning offered to finish *Strafford* for him, on his handing over all the material he had accumulated for it. Forster was greatly relieved by Browning's kindness. The poet set to work, completed Strafford's life on his own lines, in accordance with his own conception of Strafford's character, but generously said nothing about it till after Forster's death. Then he told a few of his friends—me among them—of how he had helped Forster. On my telling Prof. Gardiner of this, I found that he knew it; and had been long convinced that the conception of Strafford in this Lardner *Life* was not John Forster's, but was Robert Browning's. The other day Prof. Gardiner urged me to make the fact of Browning's authorship public; and I do so now, though I have frequently mentioned it to friends in private; and at the Browning Society, when a member has said, 'It is curious how closely Browning has followed his authority, Forster's *Life of Strafford*,' I have answered, 'Yes, because he wrote it himself.' We thus understand why, when Macready asked Browning, on May 26th, 1836, to write him a play, the poet suggested Strafford as its subject; and why, the *Life* being finished in 1836, the play was printed and played in 1837. The internal evidence will satisfy any intelligent reader that almost all the prose *Life* is the poet's. It is not only little touches like these on pp. 182-3, describing James I., which reveal Browning, —'He was not an absolute fool, and little more can be said of him . . . whenever an obvious or judicious truth seemed likely to fall in his way, *his pen infallibly waddled off from it*'; on p. 227, 'divers ill-spelt and solemn sillinesses from the King,' the reference to the 'Sordello' Ezzelin * on p. 229, etc.,— but it is the conception and working-out of the character of Strafford, '*that he was consistent to himself throughout*,' p. 228, etc., and that his one object was to make Charles

* Browning stopped his work on *Sordello* to write *Strafford*.

'the most absolute lord in Christendom,' and that this explains all apparent inconsistencies and vanities in his conduct. Let any one read the following last paragraph of the *Life*, and ask himself if it is not the poet's hand. Page 411: 'A great lesson is written in the life of this truly extraordinary person. In the career of Strafford is to be sought the justification of the world's "appeal from tyranny to God." In him Despotism had at length obtained an instrument with mind to comprehend, and resolution to act upon, her principles in their length and breadth; and enough of her purposes were effected by him to enable mankind to see "as from a tower the end of all." I cannot discern one false step in Strafford's public conduct, one glimpse of a recognition of an alien principle, one instance of a dereliction of the law of his being, which can come in to dispute the decisive result of the experiment, or explain away its failure. *The least vivid fancy will have no difficulty in taking up the interrupted design, and by wholly enfeebling, or materially emboldening, the insignificant nature of Charles, and by according some half-dozen years of immunity to the "fretted tenement" of Strafford's "fiery soul,"—contemplate then, for itself, the perfect realisation of the scheme of "making the prince the most absolute lord in Christendom." That done,—let it pursue the same course with respect to Eliot's noble imaginings, or to young Vane's dreamy aspirings, and apply in like manner a fit machinery to the working out the project which made the dungeon of the one a holy place, and sustained the other in his self-imposed exile.* The result is great and decisive! It establishes, in renewed force, those principles of political conduct which have endured, and must continue to endure, "like truth from age to age."' Take again a couple of passages of two and a half lines each on Strafford's illnesses, on page 369, and recollect that Browning owed much to Donne:—'The soul of the Earl of Strafford was indeed lodged, to use the expression of his favourite Donne, within a "low and fatal room" . . . But even by the side of the body's weakness we find a witness of the spirit's triumph,—a vindication of the mightiness of will!' And on page 370—'Then, when every energy was to be taxed to the uttermost, the question of his fiery spirit's supremacy was indeed put to the issue, by a complication of ghastly diseases.' Are these and like passages by John Forster? No! They are Robert Browning's

Plenty of others have his mark, especially those passages analysing and philosophising on character. I have appealed to Messrs. Smith & Elder to reprint this *Life of Strafford*, with an Introduction by Prof. Gardiner; but I suppose that there is no copyright in it, as it has always gone under John Forster's name. Assuredly all students of Browning should have this *Life* on their shelves. I should say that Forster did not write more than the first four pages of it, and that Browning began with 'James I. . . . came to this country in an ecstasy of infinite relief,' on page 182." In this *Life of Strafford* there is a striking passage on the question of that statesman's "apostacy." "In one word, what it is desired to impress upon the reader, before the delineation of Wentworth in his after years, is this—*that he was consistent to himself throughout.* I have always considered that much good wrath is thrown away upon what is usually called 'apostacy.' In the majority of cases, if the circumstances are thoroughly examined, it will be found that there has been 'no such thing.' The position on which the acute Roman thought fit to base his whole theory of æsthetics—

> "Humano capiti cervicem pictor equinam
> Jungere si velit, et varias inducere plumas,
> Undique collatis membris, ut turpiter atram
> Desinat in piscem mulier formosa supernè,
> Spectatum admissi risum teneatis, amici ?" etc.

is of far wider application than to the exigencies of an art of poetry; and those who carry their researches into the moral nature of mankind cannot do better than impress upon their minds, at the outset, that in the regions they explore they are to expect no monsters—no essentially discordant termination to any 'Mulier formosa supernè.' Infinitely and distinctly various as appear the shifting hues of our common nature when subjected to the prism of CIRCUMSTANCE, each ray into which it is broken is no less in itself a primitive colour, susceptible, indeed, of vast modification, but incapable of further division.* Indolence, however, in its delight for broad classifications, finds its account in overlooking this; and among the results none is more conspicu-

* Compare this use of the Light metaphor with Browning's frequent use of it in his poems, as I explain in the article on "Browning as a Scientific Poet" in my *Browning's Message to his Time.*

ous than the long list of apostates with which history furnishes us. It is very true, it may be admitted, that when we are informed by an old chronicler that 'at this time Ezzelin changed totally his disposition,'—or by a modern biographer that 'at such a period Tiberius first became a wicked prince,'—we examine too curiously if we consider such information as in reality regarding other than the act done and the popular inference recorded; beyond which it was no part of the writer to inquire.—Against all such conclusions I earnestly protest in the case of the remarkable personage whose ill-fated career we are now retracing. Let him be judged sternly, but in no unphilosophic spirit. In turning from the bright band of patriot brothers to the solitary Strafford —'a star which dwelt apart'—we have to contemplate no extinguished splendour, razed and blotted from the book of life. Lustrous, indeed, as was the gathering of the lights in the political heaven of this great time, even that radiant cluster might have exulted in the accession of the 'comet beautiful and fierce,' which tarried a while within its limits ere it 'darted athwart with train of flame.' But it was governed by other laws than were owned by its golden associates, and impelled by a contrary, yet no less irresistible force, than that which restrained them within their eternal orbits,—it left them, never to 'float into that azure heaven again.'"—John Forster's *Life of Strafford*, in the "Cabinet Cyclopædia" (conducted by Dr. Lardner), pp. 228-9.

NOTES.—Act i., Scene 1. *Pym*, the great and learned champion of English liberty, was an intimate friend of Wentworth, and deeply felt his desertion of the popular cause. *Sir Benjamin Rudyard* was a prominent member of the Long Parliament. When the quarrel broke out between Charles and the Parliament, Rudyard quitted his parliamentary pursuits and joined Hampden and Pym's party. He opposed the attainder of Strafford. He ultimately became anxious for a compromise between the King and the Commons; he acted, however, to the last with the patriots. *Henry Vane*, Sir, the younger, was a disciple of Pym, and was of considerable talents and equal fanaticism. He purloined from his father's cabinet a very important document, which was used against Strafford on his trial. After the Restoration he was brought to trial and executed. *Hampden, John*, a gentleman of Buckinghamshire, quiet, courteous, and submissive; but with a correct judgment, an invincible spirit, and the most consummate address.

In 1626 he was imprisoned for refusing to contribute towards the forced loan; he resisted the payment of ship-money. He threw himself heartily into the work of the Long Parliament, and commanded a troop in the parliamentary army. He was a great patriot and defender of the rights of the people. *Denzil Hollis, Lord:* "In 1629, when the Speaker refused to put to the vote Sir John Eliot's remonstrance against the illegal levying of tonnage and poundage, and against Catholic and Arminian innovations, Hollis read the resolutions, and was one of two members who forcibly held the Speaker in the chair till they were passed. He was in consequence committed to the Tower. He was one of the 'five members,' as they were called, whom Charles accused of high treason in January 1642. He took no part in the proceedings against Strafford, who was his brother-in-law" (*Imp. Dict. Biog.*). *The Bill of Rights:* the third great charter of English liberties must not be confounded with "the Petition of Right." "The Bill of Rights" was passed in the reign of William and Mary, in 1689. "*much worn Cottington*": he was ambassador to Madrid. "*maniac Laud*": Archbishop Laud was detested by the Puritans because he endeavoured to assimilate the doctrines and ritual of the Church of England to those of Rome. He was charged by Holles with high treason, and executed. *Runnymead:* the place where Magna Charta was signed. *renegade:* one faithless to principle or party; a deserter of a cause. *Haman:* see the Book of Esther. Haman resolved to extirpate the Jews out of the Persian empire, but Haman fell and Mordecai was advanced to his place. *Ahitophel* was a conspirator with Absalom against David, who prayed the Lord to turn the counsel of Ahitophel into foolishness (2 Sam. xv. 31); whence the term "Ahitophel's counsel." *League and Covenant:* the "Solemn League and Covenant" was designed by the Scotch to carry out in their integrity the principles of the Reformation and to establish the Presbyterian in lieu of the Episcopal Church. *Eliot:* Sir John Eliot compared Buckingham to Sejanus in lust, rapacity and ambition, in the House of Commons, and seconded the motion for his impeachment. Eliot was sent to the Tower. "*The Philistine*": the giant slain by David. "*Exalting Dagon where the ark should be*" (1 Sam. v.). Dagon was an idol, half man and half fish. He was worshipped by the Philistines. When they captured the "ark" from the Jews, it was placed in his temple, the idol fell, and the palms of his hands were broken off. *scourge and gag:* instruments of torture well understood in those days. "*The Midianite drove Israel into dens*" (Judges vi. 2): the Israelites for their sins were oppressed by Midian, and were compelled to hide from them in dens and caves of the mountains. *Gideon:* the Israelites prayed to God for deliverance from their enemies, and an angel sent Gideon, who destroyed Baal's altar and delivered Israel (Judges vi.). *Loudon:* Scottish lord and covenanter; committed to the Tower for soliciting the aid of the king of France: he was sent to Scotland by Charles. *Hamilton*, Marquess of: sent by Charles to Scotland as commissioner to suppress the Covenant, he dared not land; was suspected of treason, and fled; was restored to the King's favour, and became a leader of the royalists; was defeated by the parliamentary troops; fined £100,000, and executed. *Joab:* David, when dying, gave charge to Solomon to put his enemy Joab to death, which was done (1 Kings ii. 28-34). "*No Feltons*": J. Felton assassinated Villiers, Duke of Buckingham, and was executed. *Gracchus:* Tiberius and Caius Gracchus, the celebrated Roman tribunes, were after their death worshipped as gods, and their mother esteemed herself the happiest of Roman matrons in having given birth to such illustrious sons. *The Petition of Right*, the second great charter of English liberties, was directed against those grievances which Wentworth thus described in his speech in the third parliament: "the raising of money by loans, strengthened by commission, with unheard-of instruction; the billeting of soldiers by the lieutenants. . . . Our persons have been injured both by imprisonment without law (the King exercised an absolute right to imprison any one without legal proceedings), and by being designed to some office, charge, and employment, foreign or domestic, as a brand of infamy and mark of disgrace" (Prof. Gardiner). *Aceldama:* "a field said to have lain south of Jerusalem, purchased with the bribe which Judas took for betraying his Master, and therefore called the *field of blood*;—sometimes used in figurative sense" (*Webster's Dict.*). *Nathaniel Fiennes* was the second son of William Fiennes; he was a lawyer, and in 1640 sat in the House of Commons for Banbury. He was a rigid Presbyterian, and a member of nearly all Cromwell's parliaments. *Ship money:* "An imposition formerly charged on the ports, towns, cities, boroughs and counties of England, for providing and furnishing certain ships for the king's service. The attempt made by Charles I. to revive and enforce this imposition was resisted by John Hampden, and was one of the causes which led to the death of Charles. It was finally abolished" (*Webster's Dict.*). "*Wentworth's influence in the North*": Wentworth represented Yorkshire in parliament, and had great influence in the north of England.—Scene ii. "*Old Vane*" was secretary of state and comptroller of the household under Charles I. *Savill:* George Savill, Marquis of Halifax (?). *Holland, Earl of:* raised forces against the parliament after espousing its cause against Charles; he was tried after the King's death and executed. "*Lady Carlisle* was the daughter of the ninth Earl of Northumberland. In 1639 she had been for three years a widow. Her husband was James, Lord Hay, created successively Viscount Doncaster and Earl of Carlisle" (from Miss Hickey's *Strafford*). *Weston, Sir Richard,* Chancellor of the Exchequer, made Earl of Portland; denounced by Sir J. Eliot as an enemy of the Commonwealth. "*This frightful Scots affair*": Professor Gardiner shows that Strafford opposed peace with the Scots, supported the harshest measures, and urged the King to invade Scotland (*Encyc. Brit.*, vol. xxii., p. 586). "*In this Ezekiel chamber*": in the eighth chapter of Ezekiel the prophet has a vision of the chambers of imagery where he saw "wicked abominations." "*The Faction,*" a party acting in opposition to the constituted authority.—Act II., Scene i. "*Subsidies,*" says Blackstone, were taxes, not immediately on property, but on persons in respect of their reputed estates, after the nominal rate of 4*s.* in the pound for lands and 2*s.* 8*d.* for goods. *cockatrice:* "The basilisk; a fabulous serpent, said to be produced from a cock's egg brooded by a serpent. Its breath, and even its look, is fabled to be fatal" (*Webster's Dict.*). *Star Chamber:* "The origin of this court is derived from the most remote antiquity. Its title was derived from the *Camera Stellata* or Star Chamber, an apartment in the king's palace at Westminster, in which it held its sittings; it exercised an illegal control over the ordinary courts of justice, and in the reign of Charles I. became very tyrannical and offensive as a means of asserting the royal prerogative. It was abolished by the Long Parliament" (*Student's Hume*, p. 358).—Scene ii. *The George:* a figure of St. George on horseback, worn by knights of the Garter. *A masque,* a species of dramatic entertainment. Fletcher and Ben Jonson wrote many masques which were acted at Court. The most beautiful work of this kind is the Comus of Milton. Act III., Scene i.—*The new Parliament:* "The Long Parliament," which met Nov. 3rd, 1640; it voted the House of Lords as useless. *The Great Duke:* Buckingham.—Scene ii. *Windebank,* one of the secretaries of state, was impeached by the Commons for treason, and escaped to France. "*sly, pitiful intriguing with the Scots*": "Charles, in his eagerness to conclude the negotiation, was induced to concede many points which he would otherwise have refused" (Lingard, *Hist. Eng.*, vol. vii., p. 232). "*The Crew and the Cabal*": the "crew" was a number of people associated together; the "cabal" a number of persons united to promote their private views in church or state by intrigue. What is usually understood by the "cabal" was a name given to a ministry under Charles II., the initial letters of the names of its members forming the word cabal. *Mainwaring, Dr.*, a clergyman who preached in favour of the general loan. He was impeached by the Commons. *Goring, Colonel:* he was Governor of Portsmouth, was an officer of distinguished merit, and devoted to the King.—Scene iii., *rufflers,* bullies, swaggerers. "*Are we in Geneva?*": Calvin's city, where all sorts of puritanical restrictions were enforced against harmless amusements as well as breaches of morality. *St. John, Oliver:* St. John was Solicitor-General; he was one of the leaders of the Independents. *stockishness,* hardness, stupidity, blockishness (rare). *Maxwell, Usher of the Black Rod.* He received Strafford as his prisoner, after his impeachment, and required him to deliver his sword.—Act IV., Scene i. *Hollis:* Strafford was his brother-in-law, and so he took no part in the proceedings against him. "*A blind moth-eaten law*": Strafford said on his trial that "it was two hundred and forty years since any man was touched for this crime."—Scene ii. "*Prophet's rod*": "Moses took the rod of God in his hand" (Exod. iv. 20). *Haselrig, Sir Arthur:* was one of the five members of the House of Commons whom Charles tried to impeach. *Laud, Archbishop:* had been impeached by Sir Harry Vane, and was a prisoner in the Tower. *Bill of attainder: The Student's Hume* says (p. 399): "The student should bear in mind the difference between an *Impeachment* and a *Bill of Attainder.* In an impeachment the Commons are the accusers, and the Lords alone the judges. In a bill of attainder the Commons are the judges as well as the Lords; it may be introduced in either House; it passes through the same stages as any other bill; and when agreed to by both Houses it receives the assent of the Crown."—Act V., Scene ii. "*O bell' andare*": "The Italian boat-song is from Redi's *Bacco*, long since naturalised in the joyous and delicate version of Leigh Hunt." (R. B.) *Term*, or *Terminus:* the Roman god of bounds, under whose protection were the stones which marked boundaries. *Genius:* the Italian peoples regarded the Genius as a higher power which creates and maintains life, assists at the begetting and birth of every individual man, determines his character, tries to influence his destiny for good, accompanies him through life as his tutelary spirit, and lives on in the *Lares* after his death. (Seyffert's *Dict. Class. Ant.*) "*Garrard—my newsman*": was a clergyman who, when Wentworth went to Ireland as Lord Deputy, in 1633, was instructed to furnish him with news and gossip. (Miss Hickey.) *Tribune:* in ancient Rome, a magistrate chosen by the people to protect them from the oppression of the patricians or nobles. *Sejanus, Ælius:* distinguished himself at the court of Tiberius, who made a confidant of this fawning favourite, who made himself the darling of the senate, and the army. He was commander of the prætorian guards, and used every artifice to make himself important. He became practically head of the empire. He ridiculed the Emperor by introducing him on the stage; Tiberius then ordered him to be accused before the senate; he was subsequently imprisoned and strangled, A.D. 31. *Richelieu, Cardinal:* fomented the first commotions in Scotland, and secretly supplied the Covenanters with money and arms. He was prime minister to Louis XIII. of France. "*A mask at Theobald's*": Theobald's, in Hertfordshire, was a beautiful house, inherited by Robert Cecil, Earl of Salisbury, from his father, William Cecil, Lord Burleigh. King James liked this house so much that, in 1607, he offered Robert Cecil the Queen's dower-house at Hatfield in exchange for it. Several of Ben Jonson's masques were written for performance at Theobald's. (Prof. Morley.) *Prynne:* William Prynne was a barrister of Lincoln's Inn, of a morose and gloomy disposition, and a thorough-going Puritan; he particularly hated theatres, dancing, hunting, card playing, and Christmas festivities. He wrote a great book against all these things, which he called *Histrio-Mastix*. He was indicted as a libeller of the Queen, condemned to stand in the pillory, to lose both his ears, to pay £5000 fine to the King, and to be imprisoned for life. "*Strafford shall take no hurt*": Charles had said to Strafford, "Upon the word of a king you shall not suffer in life, honour, or fortune." "*Put not your trust in princes*": Psalm cxlvi. 3. *Wandesford:* Sir Christopher Wandesford was Master of the Rolls, and Privy Councillor in Ireland, and had been deputy there during Strafford's absence. He was an intimate friend of Strafford's, and is said to have died of grief at hearing of Strafford's arrest. (Miss Hickey's *Strafford.*) *Radcliffe, Sir George:* was appointed by Strafford guardian of his children; he was charged by Pym with treason. *Balfour:* Lieutenant of the Tower. "*Too late for sermon at St. Antholin's*": the Government had appropriated the Church of St. Antholin to the use of the Scotch commission. (Miss Hickey.) *Billingsley:* Balfour was desired by the King to admit Captain Billingsley and one hundred men to the Tower to effect Strafford's escape. (Miss Hickey's notes.) "*I fought her to the utterance*": the last or utmost extremity—the same as Fr. *à outrance*. "*David not more Jonathan*": were inseparable friends. The allusion is to David the psalmist and Jonathan the son of Saul. David's lamentation at the death of Jonathan was never surpassed in pathos and beauty. (2 Sam. i. 19-27.) "*His dream—of a perfect church.*" Laud wished to make the Church of England "Catholic"; he endeavoured to assimilate its doctrines and ceremonies to those of the Catholic Church, ignoring the fact that "the Tudor settlement" was Protestant. Laud desired to appropriate all that to him appeared valuable in the Roman Catholic system, and to reject all that to him seemed objectionable. His "perfect church" was, as Browning puts it, "a dream."

Summum Bonum. (*Asolando*, 1889.) A Latin phrase meaning the chief or ultimate good. "In ethics it was a phrase employed by ancient philosophers to denote that end in the following and attainment of which the progress, perfection and happiness of human beings consist. Cicero treated of the subject very fully in his *De Finibus*." (*Encyc. Dict.*) Concentration is the key-note of the poem: in the honey-bag of one bee there is the breath and bloom of a year; in a single gem is represented all the chemistry of nature, from the condensation of the gases which went to form the earth; in the beauty of a single pearl is all the wonder of the sea, just as in a lump of coal are the imprisoned sun-rays of prehistoric forests. But truth and trust are brighter and purer than gems and pearls; in the love of a young girl Mr. Browning sees the concentration of the brightest truth and purest trust in the universe, so holy a thing to him is love. The *Summum Bonum* of St. Augustine is, of course, the true, ultimate good of man—the Love of God—of which the love of the purest of mankind is but a dim reflection.

Sun, The. (*Ferishtah's Fancies*, 5.) Some one told one of Ferishtah's pupils that it had been reported that "God once assumed on earth a human shape," and he desired to know how the strange idea arose. Ferishtah replied that in days of ignorance men took the sun for God. "Let it be considered as the symbol of the Supreme," said the Dervish. "There must be such an Author of life and light somewhere: let us suppose the sun to be that Author. This ball of fire gives us all we enjoy on earth, and so inspires us with love and praise. If we eat a fig we praise the planter; and so on up to the sun, which gathers to himself all love and praise. The sun is fire, and more beside. Does the force know that it gives us what it does? Must our love go forth to fire? If we must thank it, there must be purpose with the power —a humanity like our own. Power has no need of will or purpose; and no occasion for beneficence when all that is, so is and so must be. As these qualities imply imperfection, let us 'eject the man, retain the orb, and then 'what remains to love and praise?' We cannot be expected to thank insentient things. No! man's soul can only be moved by what is kindred soul: man's way it receives good; man's way it must make acknowledgment. If man were an angel, his love and praise, right and fit enough now, would go forth idly. Man's part is to send love forth, even if it go astray." "But," says the objector, "man is bound by man's conditions, can only judge as good and right what his faculty adjudges such: how can we then accept in this one case falsehood for truth? We lack an union of fire with flesh; but lacking is not gaining: is there any trace of such an union recorded?" Ferishtah replies, "Perhaps there may be; perhaps the greatly yearned-for once befell; perhaps the sun was flesh once.' The pupil demands "An union inconceivable once was fact?" The Dervish replies, "There is something pervading the sun which it does not consume: is it not fitter to stand appalled before a conception unattainable by man's intelligence?" Firdausí, in the Sháh Námeh, records that Húsheng was the first who brought out fire from stone; and from that circumstance he founded the religion of the fire-worshippers, calling the flame which was produced the light of the Divinity. Húsheng was the second king of the Peshadian dynasty; from his time the fire faith seems to have slept till the appearance of Zerdusht, in the reign of Gushtasp, many centuries afterwards, when Isfendiyár propagated it by the sword. After Húsheng had discovered fire by hurling a stone against a rock, thereby producing a spark, which set light to the herbage, he made an immense fire, and gave a royal entertainment, calling it the Feast of Siddeh. The lyric explains that the divine element of fire is enshrined in the earthly flint when the spark escapes; the relationship is difficult to remember. So God was once incarnate in the form of man; and this some find it as hard to believe.

Tab. (*Ned Bratts.*) Tabitha Bratts, who was converted by John Bunyan, and who went with her husband to the Chief Justice at the assizes, asking to be hanged, and whose request was favourably entertained.

Tale, A. The Epilogue to the *Two Poets of Croisic* is included in the second series of *Selections* under this title.

Taurello Salinguerra. (*Sordello.*) His name, says Mr. W. M. Rossetti, may be translated as "Bullock Sally-in-war," or "Dash-into-fight." He belonged to the family of the Torelli, one of the two leading families of Ferrara. He married Sofia, a daughter of Eccelin the Monk, and he became the ruler of his native city. He was the right-hand man of Eccelin, and also of his son. The great authority on this character is Muratori (*Annali d' Italia, compilati da Lodovico Antonio Muratori*). Mr. W. M. Rossetti read a paper to the Browning Society in November 1889 on "Taurello Salinguerra," and I am indebted to this valuable essay for the following dates and particulars concerning this interesting character. He was born about the year 1160. In 1200, when he was head of the Ghibelline faction in Ferrara, he suddenly assailed the town of Argenta with the Ferrarese army, and having taken it, sacked it. In 1205 the head of the Guelf faction, both in Ferrara and the March of Verona, was Azzo VI.,

Marquis of Este. Naturally they quarrelled, and Azzo took the castle of La Fratta from Salinguerra and dismantled it. This was the beginning of the many dissensions between them. In 1207 Azzo VI. was compelled by Eccelino da Onara and others to retire from Verona. Then it was that Salinguerra, head of the Ghibellines in Ferrara, declaring himself the intimate friend of Eccelino, expelled from that city all the adherents of Marquis Azzo; and, leaving no room for him, began to act as Lord of Ferrara. In 1208 Marquis Azzo VI. re-established himself in Verona. Reaching Ferrara with an army, he expelled Salinguerra. In 1209 Salinguerra re-entered Ferrara, stripped Azzo VI. of Este of its dominion, and sent his partisans into exile. In 1210, the Emperor Otho IV. professing that the March of Ancona belonged to the empire, Azzo obtained the investiture of it from the Emperor. Probably at this time peace was re-established between Azzo VI. and Salinguerra, the competitors for the lordship of Ferrara. In 1213 Aldrovandino, Marquis of Este and Ancona, succeeded his father Azzo VI. and continued to hold, along with Count Richard of San Bonifazio, the dominion of Verona, where he was created Podestà in this year. He had contests with Salinguerra in Ferrara. In 1215 Aldrovandino, Marquis of Este, died, and was succeeded by Azzo VII., a minor. In 1221 Azzo VII. and his adherents assailed Salinguerra at Ferrara, and forced him to abandon the city, and consigned the palace of Salinguerra to the flames. After mediation, the expelled men returned to their homes. In 1222 the Ghibelline cause prevailed at Ferrara: Azzo and the Guelfs had to leave the city. He collected an army at Rovigo, and returned to Ferrara. Salinguerra, a crafty fox, made peace, for fear the people should turn against him. The peace was only a trap, however, by which to catch Azzo. In 1224 Azzo VII. returned to lay siege to Ferrara. The astute Salinguerra sent embassies to Count Richard of San Bonifazio, to induce him, with a number of horsemen, to enter Ferrara under pretext of concluding a friendly pact. But on entering he was at once made prisoner, with all his company; and therefore the Marquis of Este, disappointed, retired from the siege. Enraged at this result, Marquis Azzo proceeded to the siege of the castle of La Fratta, a favourite stronghold of Salinguerra, and starved it into submission. Salinguerra complained of this to Eccelino da Romana, his brother-in-law, and they both studied more assiduously than ever how best to crush the Guelfs, of which the Marquis of Este was chief. In 1225 the Lombard League procured the release of Count Richard, who returned to Verona; but he was expelled, when he took refuge in Mantua. He ultimately returned to Verona. In 1227 Eccelino the younger was established in Verona, and Count Richard again expelled. In 1228 Eccelino da Onara, father of Eccelino da Romana and of Alberic, had become a monk, and led the life of a hypocrite, finally showing himself to be a Paterine heretic. In 1230 Verona was in trouble: the Ghibellines raised a riot and imprisoned Count Richard; Salinguerra was made Podestà. In 1240 Pope Gregory IX. incited the Lombards and the Marquis of Este to besiege Ferrara. The Doge of Venice attended in person; the Mantuans concurred, as also did Alberico da Romana. After some months peace was proposed; and Salinguerra came to the camp of the confederates to ratify them. Salinguerra was entrapped, and was transferred as a prisoner to Venice; where, treated courteously, he ended his days in holy peace; and the House of Este, after so many years, re-entered Ferrara.

Templars. The poem *The Heretic's Tragedy* deals with the suppression of the order of the Knights Templars.

Theocrite. (*The Boy and the Angel.*) The boy who wishes to praise God "the Pope's great way," and who leaves his common task, and is replaced by the angel Gabriel. As neither boy nor angel please God in their changed positions, each returns to his appropriate sphere.

"The Poets pour us wine." (Epilogue to *Pacchiarotto.*) These words are the beginning of the Epilogue named, and are quoted from a poem of Mr. Browning's entitled *Wine of Cyprus*, the last verse but one, the last line of which is "And the poets poured us wine."

"There's a Woman like a Dewdrop." (*A Blot in the 'Scutcheon.*) The song in Act I., Scene iii., begins with this line. It is sung by Earl Mertoun as he climbs to Mildred Tresham's chamber.

"The Year's at the Spring." (*Pippa Passes.*) The song which Pippa sings as she passes the house of Ottima, and thereby brings conviction to her lover Sebald.

Thorold, Earl Tresham. (*A Blot in the 'Scutcheon.*) The brother of Mildred Tresham, who challenges Mertoun, her lover, on his way to a stolen interview with his sister, and kills him, thinking he has disgraced the family.

Through the Metidja to Abd-el-Kader. (1842.) The Metidja is an extensive plain near the coast of Algeria, "commencing on the eastern side of the Bay of Algiers, and stretching thence inland to the south and west. It is about sixty miles in length by ten or twelve in breadth" (*Encyc. Brit.*). Algiers was conquered by the French in 1830; but, after the conquest, constant outbreaks of hostilities on the part of the natives occurred, and in 1831 General Bertherene was despatched to chastise the rebels. Later in the same year General Savary was sent with an additional force of 16,000 men for the same purpose. He attempted to suppress the outbreaks of hostilities with the greatest cruelty and treachery. These acts so exasperated the people against their new ruler that such tribes as had acquiesced in the new order of things now armed themselves against the French. It was at this time that the world first heard of Abd-el-Kader. He was born in 1807, and was a learned and pious man, greatly distinguished amongst his people for his skill in horsemanship and athletic sports. He now rapidly collected an army of ten thousand men, marched to Oran and attacked the French, who had taken possession of the town; but was repulsed with great loss. He was so popular with his people that he had little difficulty in recruiting his forces, and he made himself so dangerous to the French that they found it expedient to offer him terms of peace, and he was recognised as emir of the province of Mascara. The peace did not last long, and hostilities broke out, leading to a defeat of the French in 1835. Constant troubles were caused the French by the opposition of Abd-el-Kader, and reinforcements on a large scale were sent against him from France. After varying fortunes, Abd-el-Kader was at last reduced to extremities, and was compelled to hide in the mountains with a few followers; at length he gave himself up to the French, and was imprisoned at Pau, and afterwards at Amboise. He afterwards obtained permission to remove to Constantinople, and from thence to remove to Damascus. The poem describes an incident of the war which took place in 1842, when the Duke d'Aumale fell upon the emir's camp and took several thousand prisoners, Abd-el-Kader escaping with difficulty.

"Thus the Mayne glideth." (*Paracelsus.*) The song which Festus sings to Paracelsus in the closing scene in his cell in the Hospital of St. Sebastian.

Tiburzio. (*Luria.*) The general of the army of the Pisans, who exposes to Luria the treachery of the Florentines, and whose letter the Moor destroys without reading it.

Time's Revenges. A SOLILOQUY. (*Dramatic Romances and Lyrics*, in *Bells and Pomegranates*, VII., 1845; *Romances*, 1863; *Dramatic Romances*, 1868.) "Love begets love," they say: probably this is not much truer than proverbs usually are. The speaker in the poem has a friend who would do anything in the world for him; in return, he barely likes him. As a compensation, inasmuch as "human love is not the growth of human will," the lady to whom the soliloquiser is passionately devoted, the woman for whom he is prepared to sacrifice body, soul, everything he holds dear, cares nothing at all for him; she would roast him before a slow fire for a coveted ball-ticket. And why not? if love be what the poet says it is—the merging by affinity of one soul in another—where no affinity exists no union can result. Lovers should study the elements of chemistry, and the laws which govern the affinities of the elementary bodies; or, if they are not inclined to so serious a task, let them take to heart the Spanish proverb, "Love one that does not love you, answer one that does not call you, and you will run a fruitless race."

Toccata of Galuppi's, A. (*Men and Women*, 1855.) Baldassare Galuppi (1706-85) was a celebrated Italian composer, who was born in 1706 near Venice. His father was a barber with a taste for music, and he taught his son sufficient of the elements of music to enable him to enter the Conservatorio degli Incurabile, where Lotti was a teacher. He produced an opera at the age of sixteen, but it was a failure; seven years after, however, he produced a comic opera *Dorinda*, which was a great success. The young composer's great abilities were now everywhere recognised, and his fame assured. He was a most industrious writer, and left no less than seventy operas; which, however, have not survived to our time. Galuppi resided and worked in London from 1741 to 1744. He went to Russia, where he lived at the court of the Empress Catherine II. (at whose invitation he went) in great honour, and did much for the improvement of musical taste in that country. In 1768 he left Russia, and became organist of St. Mark's, Venice. He died in 1785, and left fifty thousand lire to the poor of that city. His best comic opera is his *Il Mondo della Luna.* *A Toccata* is a "*Touch*-piece," a prelude or overture. "It does but *touch* its theme rapidly, even superficially, for the most part; so that the interpolation of solemn chords and emotional phrases, inconsistent with its traditional character, may naturally, by force of contrast, lead to some suggestion or recognition of the many irregularities of life" (Mrs. Alexander Ireland). In the admirable paper on this poem written by Mrs. Alexander Ireland for the Browning Society, she continues: "*A Toccata of Galuppi's* touches on deep subjects with a mere feather-touch of light and capricious suggestiveness, interwoven with the graver mood, with the heart-searching questionings of man's deep nature and mysterious spirit. The *Toccata* as a form of composition is not the measured, deliberate working-out of some central musical thought, as is the *Sonata* or *sound*-piece, where the trained ear can follow out the whole process to its delightful and orderly consummation, where the student marks the introduction and development of the subject, its extension, through various forms, and its whole sequence of movement and meaning, to its glorious rounding-off and culmination, spiritually noting each stage of the climbing structure and acknowledging its perfection with the inward silent verdict, 'It is well.' The *Toccata*, in its early and pure form, possessed no decided subject, made such by repetition, but bore rather the form of a capricious Improvisation or "Impromptu." It was a very flowing movement, in notes of equal length, and a homophonous character, the earliest examples of any importance being those by Gabrieli (1557-1613), and those by Merulo (1533-1604); while Galuppi, who was born in 1706 and died in 1785, produced a further advanced development of this particular form of musical composition, with chords freely introduced and other important innovations." Vernon Lee, in her *Studies of the Eighteenth Century in Italy* (III. "The Musical Life") says of the Venetian, Baldassare Galuppi, surnamed Buranello, that he was "an immensely prolific composer, and abounded in melody, tender, pathetic and brilliant, which in its extreme simplicity and slightness occasionally rose to the highest beauty. . . . He defined the requisites of his art to Burney in very moderate terms: 'Chiarezza, vaghezza, e buona modulazione'—clearness, beauty, and good modulation, without troubling himself much about any others. . . . Galuppi was a model of the respectable, modest artist, living quietly on a moderate fortune, busy with his art and the education of his numerous children, beloved and revered by his fellow-artists; and when some fifteen years later [than 1770] he died, honoured by them with a splendid funeral, at which all the Venetian musicians performed; the great Pacchiarotti writing to Burney that he had sung with much devotion to obtain a rest for Buranello's (Galuppi's) soul" (p. 101). In a note Vernon Lee adds: "Mr. Browning's fine poem, 'A Toccata of Galuppi's,' has made at least his name familiar to many English readers. Ritter, in his *History of Music* (p. 245), has a concise but expressive notice of Galuppi." *Balthasar Galuppi*, called Buranello (1706-85), a pupil of Lotti, also composed many comic operas. The main features of his operas are melodic elegance and lively and spirited comic forms; but they are rather thin and weak in their execution. He was a great favourite during his lifetime." The poem deals with two classes of human beings—the mere pleasure-takers with their balls and masks (Stanza iv.), and the scientists (Stanza xiii.) with their research and their 'ologies. The Venetians—who seemed to the poet merely born to blow and droop, who lived frivolous lives of gaiety and love-making—lived lives which came to nothing, and did deeds better left undone—heard the music which dreamily told them they must die, but went on with their kissing and their dancing till death took them where they never see the sun. The other class, immersed in the passion for knowledge, the class which despises the vanities and frivolities of the butterfly's life, and consecrates itself to science, not the less surely dissipates its energies and misses the true end of life if it has nothing higher to live for than "physics and geology."

NOTES.—ii., *St. Mark's.* The great cathedral of Venice, named after St. Mark, because it is said that the body of that Evangelist was brought to Venice and enshrined there. "*where the Doges used to wed the sea with rings*": the Doge was the chief magistrate of Venice when it was a republic. "The ceremony of wedding the Adriatic was instituted in 1174 by Pope Alexander III., who gave the Doge a gold ring from off his own finger in token of the victory achieved by the Venetian fleet at

Istria over Frederick Barbarossa, in defence of the Pope's quarrel. When his Holiness gave the ring, he desired the Doge to throw a similar ring into the sea annually, in commemoration of the event" (Dr. Brewer). iii., "*the sea's the street there*": there are neither horses nor carriages in Venice; you go everywhere by gondola—to church, to theatre, to market; your gondola meets you at the railway station; in a word, the sea is the street. *Shylock's Bridge:* they show you Shylock's house in the old market place by the Rialto Bridge. vi., *clavichord*, a keyed and stringed instrument, not now in use, being superseded by the pianoforte. viii., *dominant's persistence.* The dominant in music is the name given to the fifth note of the scale of any key, counting upwards. The dominant plays a most important part in cadences, in which it is indispensable that the key should be strongly marked (Grove). "*dear dead women*": the ladies of Venice are celebrated for their beauty. An article in *Poet Lore*, October 1890, p. 546, thus explains the technical musical allusions in *A Toccata of Galuppi's*. These are all to be found in the seventh, eighth, and ninth verses. "The lesser thirds are, of course, minor thirds, and are of common occurrence; but the diminished sixth is an interval rarely used. So rare is it, that I have seen it stated by good authorities that it is never used harmonically. Ordinarily a diminished sixth (seven semitones), exactly the same interval as a perfect fifth, instead of giving a plaintive, mournful, or minor impression, would suggest a feeling of rest and satisfaction. As I have said, however, there is one way in which it can be used—as a suspension, in which the root of the chord on the *lowered* super-tonic of the scale is suspended from above into the chord with added seventh on the super-tonic, making a diminished sixth between the root of the first and the third of the second chord. The effect of this progression is most dismal, and possibly Browning had it in mind, though it is doubtful almost to certainty if Galuppi knew anything of it. Whether it be an anachronism or not, or whether it is used in a scientifically accurate way or not, the figure is true enough poetically, for a diminished interval —namely, something less than normal—would naturally suggest an effect of sadness. *Suspensions*, as may already have been guessed by the preceding example, are notes which are held over from one chord into another, and must be made according to certain musical rules as strict as the laws of the Medes and Persians. This holding over of a note always produces a dissonance, and must be followed by a concord,—in other words, a *solution*. Sevenths are very important dissonances in music, and a commiserating seventh is most likely the variety called a minor seventh. Being a somewhat less mournful interval than the lesser thirds and the diminished sixths, whether real or imaginary, yet not so final as 'those solutions' which seem to put an end to all uncertainty, and therefore to life, they arouse in the listeners to Galuppi's playing a hope that life may last, although in a sort of dissonantal, Wagnerian fashion. The 'commiserating sevenths' are closely connected with the 'dominant's persistence' in the next verse:—

> 'Hark! the dominant's persistence till it must be answered to:
> So an octave struck the answer.'

The dominant chord in music is the chord written on the fifth degree of the scale, and it almost always has a seventh added to it, and in a large percentage of cases is followed by the tonic, the chord on the first degree of the scale. Now, in fugue form a theme is repeated in the dominant key, the latter being called the answer. After further contrapuntal wanderings of the theme, the fugue comes to what is called an episode, after which the theme is presented first, in the dominant. 'Hark! the dominant's persistence' alludes to this musical fact; but, according to rule, this dominant must be answered in the tonic an octave above the first presentation of the theme; and 'so an octave struck the answer.' Thus the inexorable solution comes in after the dominant's persistence. Although life seemed possible with commiserating sevenths, the tonic, a resistless fate, strikes the answer that all must end—an answer which the frivolous people of Venice failed to perceive, and went on with their kissing. The notion of the tonic key as a relentless fate seems to suit well with the formal music of the days of Galuppi: while the more hopeful tonic key of Abt Vogler, the C major of this life, indicates that fate and the tonic key have both fallen more under man's control."—Miss Helen Ormerod's paper, read before the Browning Society, May 27th, 1887, throws additional light on some of the difficulties of this poem. "That the minor predominated in this quaint old piece (*Toccata*, by the way, means a *touch* piece, and probably was written to display the delicacy of the composer's touch) is evident from the mention of—

'Those lesser thirds so plaintive, sixths diminished, sigh on sigh,
Told them something? Those suspensions, those solutions,—'Must we die?'
Those commiserating sevenths—'Life might last! we can but try!'"

The interual of the third is one of the most important; the signature of a piece may mislead one, the same signature standing for a major key and its relative minor; but the third of the opening chord decides the question, a lesser 'plaintive' third (composed of a tone and a semitone) showing the key to be *minor*; the greater third (composed of two whole tones) showing the key to be *major*. Pauer tells us that 'the minor third gives the idea of tenderness, grief and romantic feeling.' Next come the 'diminished sixths': these are sixths possessing a semitone less than a minor sixth,—for instance, from C sharp to A flat: this interval in a different key would stand as a perfect fifth. 'Those suspensions, those solutions'—a suspension is the stoppage of one or more parts for a moment, while the others move on; this produces a dissonance, which is only resolved by the parts which produced it moving on to the position which would have been theirs had the parts moved simultaneously. We can understand that 'those suspensions, those solutions' might teach the Venetians, as they teach us, lessons of experience and hope; light after darkness, joy after sorrow, smiles after tears. 'Those commiserating sevenths,' of all dissonances, none is so pleasing to the ear, or so attractive to musicians, as that of minor and diminished sevenths, that of the major seventh being crude and harsh; in fact, the minor seventh is so charming in its discord as to suggest concord. Again, to quote from Pauer: 'It is the antithesis of discord and concord which fascinates and charms the ear; it is the necessary solution and return to unity which delights us.' After all this, the love-making begins again; but kisses are interrupted by the 'dominant's persistence till it must be answered to.' This seems to indicate the close of the piece, the dominant being answered by an octave which suggests the perfect authentic cadence, in which the chord of the dominant is followed by that of the tonic. The Toccata is ended, and the gay gathering dispersed. I cannot help the thought that this old music of Galuppi's was more of the head than the heart—more formal than fiery, suggestive rather of the chill of death than the heat of passion. The temporary silence into which the dancers were surprised by the playing of the Maestro is over, and the impressions caused by it are passed away, just as the silence of death was to follow the warmth and brightness of the glad Venetian life."

To Edward Fitzgerald. In the *Athenæum* of July 13th, 1889, appeared this sonnet:—

"TO EDWARD FITZGERALD.

"I chanced upon a new book yesterday;
I opened it, and, where my finger lay
'Twixt page and uncut page, these words I read—
Some six or seven at most—and learned thereby
That you, Fitzgerald, whom by ear and eye
She never knew, 'thanked God my wife was dead.'
Ay, dead! and were yourself alive, good Fitz,
How to return you thanks would task my wits.
Kicking you seems the common lot of curs—
While more appropriate greeting lends you grace,
Surely to spit there glorifies your face—
Spitting from lips once sanctified by hers.

"ROBERT BROWNING.

"*July 8th*, 1889."

The passage referred to is as follows: "Mrs. Browning's death is rather a relief to me, I must say: no more Aurora Leighs, thank God! A woman of real genius, I know; but what is the upshot of it all! She and her sex had better mind the kitchen and the children; and perhaps the poor. Except in such things as little novels, they only devote themselves to what men do much better, leaving that which men do worse or not at all." (*Life and Letters of Edward Fitzgerald.* Edited by Aldis Wright.)—*Browning Society Papers*, Notes, 229.

Tokay. See NATIONALITY IN DRINKS. (*Dramatic Lyrics*, III.)

Too Late. (*Dramatis Personæ*, 1864.) A man addressing a dead woman whom he has loved and lost, tells how he feels that she needs help in her grave and finds none; wants warmth from a heart which longs to send it. She married another who did not love her "nor any one else in the world." This great sorrow was the rock which stopped the even flow of his life current. Some devil must have hurled it into the stream, and so thwarted God, who had made these two souls for each other. Just a thread of water escaped from the obstacle, and that wandered "through the evening country" down to the great sea which absorbs all our life streams. He has hoped at times that some convulsion of nature might roll the stone from its place and let the stream flow undisturbed. But all is past hope now: Edith is dead that should have been his. What should he have done that he omitted? Had he not taken her "No" too readily? Men do more for trifling reasons than he had done for his life's whole peace. Perhaps he was proud—perhaps helpless as a man paralysed by a great blow; anyway, she was gone from his life, and he was desolate henceforth. She was not handsome,—nobody said that. She had features which no artist would select for a model; but she was his life, and even now that she is dead he will be her slave while his soul endures. The poem is full of concentrated emotion, and is the expression of a strong man's life passion for a woman's soul; a passion unalloyed by any gross affection; such a love of one soul for another congenial soul as proves that man is more than matter.

Transcendentalism: a Poem in Twelve Books. (*Men and Women*, 1855.) This poem is probably intended by Mr. Browning as an answer to his critics. It has been said of Mr. Browning's poetry by a hundred competent writers that he does not sing, but philosophises instead; that he gives the world his naked thoughts, his analyses of souls not draped in the beauty of the poet's art, but in the form of "stark-naked thought." There is no objection, says his interviewer, if he will but cast aside the harp which he does not play but only tunes and adjusts, and speak his prose to Europe through "the six-foot Swiss tube which helps the hunter's voice from Alp to Alp." The fault is, that he utters thoughts to men thinking they care little for form or melody, as boys do. It is quite otherwise he should interpret nature—which is full of mystery—to the soul of man: as Jacob Boehme heard the plants speak, and told men what they said; or as John of Halberstadt, the magician, who by his will-power could create the flowers Boehme thought about. The true poet is a poem himself, whatever be his utterance. Take back the harp again, and "pour heaven into this short home of life." Jacob Boehme (1575-1624) was a German mystical writer, who began life as a shoemaker and developed into a "seer" of the highest order. He was a follower of the school of Paracelsus, and professed to know all mysteries by actually beholding them. He saw the origin of love and sorrow, heaven and hell. Nature lay unveiled to him; he saw into the being of God, and into the heart of things. Mr. Browning refers to this in the line of the poem, "He noticed all at once that plants could speak." "William Law (1686-1761) was a follower of Boehme's system of philosophy. The Quakers have been much influenced by the Boehmenists. The old magicians thought they had discovered in the ashes of plants their primitive forms, which were again raised up by the force of heat. Nothing, they say, perishes in Nature; all is but a continuation or a revival. The germina of resurrection are concealed in extinct bodies, as in the blood of men; the ashes of roses will again revive into roses, though smaller and paler than if they had been planted. The process of the *Palingenesis*—this picture of immortality—is described. These philosophers, having burnt a flower by calcination, disengaged the salts from its ashes, and deposited them in a glass phial; a chemical mixture acted on it till in the fermentation they assumed a bluish and spectral hue. This dust, thus excited by heat, shoots upwards into its primitive form; by sympathy the parts unite, and while each is returning to its destined place we see distinctly the stalk, the leaves, and the flower arise; it is the pale spectre of a flower coming slowly forth from its ashes." (Disraeli's *Curiosities of Literature*, art. "Dreams at the Dawn of Philosophy.") John of Halberstadt was the magician who made the flowers on some such principles as is fabled above. He was an ecclesiastic, and had probably some knowledge of alchemy, often considered in those days as more or less a diabolical kind of learning. Transcendentalism is thus described by Webster: "Transcendental, Empirical.—These terms, with the corresponding nouns *transcendentalism* and *empiricism*, are of comparatively recent origin. *Empirical* refers to knowledge which is gained by the experience of actual phenomena, without reference to the principles or laws to which they are to be referred, or by which they are to be explained. *Transcendental* has reference to those beliefs or principles which are not derived from experience, and yet are absolutely necessary to make experience possible or useful. Such, in the better sense of the term, is the transcendental philosophy, or transcendentalism. The term has been applied to a kind of investigation, or a use of language which is vague, obscure, fantastic, or extravagant." The reference in the title of the poem is purely imaginary: there is no such work.

Tray. (*Dramatic Idyls*, 1879.) Three bards sing each a song of a hero; but the bard who sings of Olaf the Dane, and he who tells of the hero standing unflinching on the precipice, have not their song rewarded here: the place of honour is reserved by the poet for a dog story. Tray was the poet's hero of the three. A beggar child fell into the Seine in Paris. The bystanders prudently bethought themselves of their families ere risking their lives to save her. While the people were wondering how the child was to be extricated, "a mere instinctive dog" jumped over the balustrade and brought her to land. The people applauded the dog, who had no sooner deposited his burden on the shore than he was off again, apparently to save another child whom nobody had seen fall. The dog was so long under the water that he was thought to have been carried away by the current; but in a few minutes he was seen swimming to land with the child's doll in his mouth. The people began to pride themselves on man's possession of reason, and to vaunt the superiority of our race over that of the dog. Meanwhile Tray trotted off; till one of the crowd, with a larger share of "reason" than the rest, bade his servant go and catch the animal for him, that, by expenditure "of half an hour and eighteen-pence," he might vivisect it at the physiological laboratory and see "how brain secretes dog's soul." This was poor Tray's reward at the hands of humanity, endowed with the "reason" which had been denied to the brave and faithful little brain of the "lower animal." (See VIVISECTION.)

Twins, The. (Originally published in a little volume with a poem of Mrs. Browning's, on behalf of the Ragged Schools of London, 1854; then in *Men and Women*, 1855; *Romances*, 1863; *Dramatic Romances*, 1868.) In Martin Luther's *Table Talk* there is a story which is the foundation of this poem. In the talk "On Justification" (No. 316), he says: "Give, and it shall be given unto you: this is a fine maxim, and makes people poor and rich. . . There is in Austria a monastery which, in former times, was very rich, and remained rich so long as it was charitable to the poor; but when it ceased to give, then it became indigent, and is so to this day. Not long since, a poor man went there and solicited alms, which were denied him; he demanded the cause why they refused to give for God's sake? The porter of the monastery answered, 'We are become poor'; whereupon the mendicant said, 'The cause of your poverty is this: ye had formerly in this monastery two brethren—the one named *Date* (give), and the other *Dabitur* (it shall be given to you): the former ye thrust out, and the other went away of himself.' . . . Beloved, he that desires to have anything must also give: a liberal hand was never in want or empty.'" (Mr. Browning's poem is simply the above narrative in verse.)

Two Camels. (*Ferishtah's Fancies*, 8: "Self-mortification.") Is self-mortification necessary for the attainment of wisdom? Two camels started on a long journey with their loads of merchandise. One, desiring to please his master, refused to eat the food which was provided for him: he died of exhaustion on the road, and thieves secured his burden. The other ate his provender thankfully, and safely reached his destination with his load. Which beast pleased his master? We are here to do our day's work: help refused is hindrance sought. We are to desire joy and thank God for it. The Creator wills that we should recognise our creatureship and call upon Him in our need. As we are God's sons, He cannot be indifferent to our needs and sorrows. Neither work nor the spirit of self-dependence are antagonistic to prayer. The "ear, hungry for music," is a more intelligible phrase when we know that the organ of Corti in the human ear has three thousand arches, with keys ranged like those of a piano, marvellously adapted for the appreciation of every tone-shade. The "seven-stringed instrument" refers to light and the seven colours of the spectrum.—In the lyric, the chemical combination of two harmless substances produces an effect which either by itself would have been powerless to produce. How know we what God intends to work in us by the influences by which we are surrounded? We are not to reject the joys of earth, the bliss produced by slight and transient mental stimuli; they suffice to move the heart. There is earth-bliss which heaven itself cannot improve, but may make permanent: why despise it?

Two in the Campagna. (*Men and Women*, 1855; *Lyrics*, 1863; *Dramatic Lyrics*, 1868.) The Campagna di Roma is that portion of the area almost coinciding with the ancient Latium, which lies round the city of Rome. Gregorovius says we might mark its circumference "by a series of well-known points: Civita Vecchia, Tolfa, Ronciglione, Soracte, Tivoli, Palestrina, Albano, and Ostia." Anciently it was the seat of numerous cities, and is now dotted with ruins in its whole extent. In summer its vast expanse is little better than an arid steppe, and is very dangerous on account of the malaria almost everywhere prevalent. In winter and spring it is safer, and affords abundant pasture for sheep and cattle. There is a solemnity and beauty about the Campagna entirely its own. To the reflective mind, this ghost of old Rome is full of suggestion: its vast, almost limitless extent, as it seems to the traveller; its abundant herbage and floral wealth in early spring; its desolation, its crumbling monuments, and its evidences of a vanished civilisation, fill the mind with a sweet sadness, which readily awakens the longing for the infinite spoken of in the poem, the key-note of which is undoubtedly found in the lines—

> "Only I discern
> Infinite passion, and the pain
> Of finite hearts that yearn."

Says Pascal: "This desire and this weakness cry aloud to us that there was once in man a true happiness, of which there now remains to him but the mark and the empty trace, which he vainly tries to fill from all that surround him; seeking from things absent the succour he finds not in things present; and these are all inadequate, because this infinite void can only be filled by an infinite and immutable object—that is to say, only by God Himself." The speaker in the poem says to the woman, "I would that you were all to me." As pleasure, learning, wealth, have failed to satisfy the soul of man, so not even Love, the holiest passion of the soul, can satisfy the human heart, which can rest in God alone. Dr. Martineau says that "all finite loves are only *half-born*, wandering in a poor twilight, unknowing of their peace and power, till they lie within the encompassing and glorifying love of God." The restful music, the anodyne for the pain of yearning hearts, comes from no earth-born love, however pure.

Two Poets of Croisic, The. (1878, with *La Saisiaz.*) Le Croisic is an old town in Brittany, in the department of Loire Inférieure. Murray describes it as "a popular watering-place.

Croisic was formerly a place of some importance—was fortified, and had a castle, and reached its greatest prosperity in the sixteenth century, when it sent vessels to the cod-fishery, and had some six thousand inhabitants; but, like many other towns, was ruined by the revocation of the Edict of Nantes. There is a chapel of St. Gourtan to the west of the town, with a miraculous well near it. When there is a storm from the south the sailors' wives pray at St. Gourtan; when from the north, at the Chapel of the Crucifix, at the east of the town. About half a mile due north-west of the church is a menhir eight feet high, situated on a mound overlooking the sea. The rocky cliffs on the sea shore near it, for about a mile, have been worn by the waves and weather into the most extraordinary and fantastic shapes, and are well worth a visit." Croisic is one of the principal ports of the sardine fishery. Guérande and Batz, also referred to in the poem, are close to Le Croisic, the former being "a very curious old town, still surrounded," says Murray, "by the ditches and walls built by Duke John V. about 1431. On Sundays, the assemblage of Bretons from the north, peat-diggers from the east, and salt-makers from the west, is very striking. Soon after leaving Guérande the road descends into a wide plain covered with pits and salterns. This plain is of great extent, below the level of the sea, and protected by dykes. The water is admitted at high water, by channels or rivers, into reservoirs called *vasières*, from which it is passed into shallow, irregularly-formed receptacles called *fares*. In these a considerable portion of the water is evaporated, and the brine is allowed to run into square basins called *œillets*, where the sun finally evaporates the water and leaves a layer of salt. The salt is scraped off to square patches between the *œillets*, and is thence carried to a conical heap on the high ground, where it is left without protection from the rain until the autumn, when the heap is covered with wood, and so left until it can be sold. The men engaged in the work are called *paludiers*, and receive one-fourth of the salt, the owner of the salterns receiving the other three-fourths." Mr. Browning refers to such a process in *Sordello*, to illustrate his theory of the necessity of evil:—

"Where the salt marshes stagnate, crystals branch;
Blood dries to crimson; Evil's beautified
In every shape."

"The *paludiers*, and their assistants, called ***saulniers***, inhabit Batz, Pouliguen, Saillié, and other villages, and form a most peculiar class Their usual dress is an enormous black flapped hat, a long white frock or waistcoat, huge baggy white breeches, white gaiters and white shoes. The men of *Batz* are a magnificent race of large, stalwart, evident Saxons."—The opening stanzas of the poem are descriptive of a scene in winter, round a good log-fire of old shipwood. As the flames ascend, they are tinted with various brilliant colours, due to the chemicals with which the old timber is impregnated and the metals which are attached to it. Sodium salts from the sea brine account for the yellow and crimson flames; the greenish flame owes its tint to the copper; the flake brilliance is due to the zinc; and so forth. All this flame splendour suggests the flash of fame—brilliant for a few minutes, and then subsiding into darkness At the eleventh stanza begins a description of Croisic, Guérande, and Batz, and the salt industry as described above. An island opposite was the Druids' chosen chief of homes; where their women were employed, building a temple to the sun, destroying it and rebuilding it every May. Even at the present day women steal to the sole menhir standing and the rude stone pillars, with or without still ruder inscriptions, found in many parts of Brittany But Croisic has had its men of note: two poets must be remembered who lived there. René Gentilhomme, in the year 1610, flamed forth a liquid ruby; he was of noble birth, and page to the Prince of Condé, whom men called "the Duke." His cousin the King had no heir, so men began to call him "Next King," and he to expect the dignity. His page René was a poet, and had written many sonnets and madrigals. One day, when he sat a-rhyming, a storm came on; and, struck by lightning, a ducal crown, emblem of the Prince, was dashed to atoms. René ceased his sonnets, and, considering the destruction as an omen of the ruined hopes of the Duke, wrote forty lines, which he gave to the man, who asked how it came his ducal crown was wrecked—"Sir, God's word to you!" It happened as the poet foresaw: at the year's end was born the Dauphin, who wrecked the Prince's hopes. King Louis honoured René with the title "Royal Poet," inasmuch as he not only poetised, but prophesied. The other famous poet of Croisic, represented by the green flame, was a dapper gentleman, Paul Desforges Maillard, who lived in

Voltaire's time, and did something which made Voltaire ridiculous. He wrote a poem, which he submitted to the Academy, but which the Forty ignominiously rejected. When the poet's rage subsided, he made bold to offer his work to the Chevalier La Roque, editor of the *Paris Mercury*, who rejected it with the polite excuse that he could not offend the Forty. Flattered, though enraged at this excuse, the poet abused the editor till he explained that his poetry was execrable, but he had sought to conceal the truth in his rejection. Maillard had a sister, who determined to help him by strategy. Copying out some of her brother's verses, she sent them as the efforts of a young girl, who threw herself on the great editor's mercy, and begged his introduction to a literary career under the name of Malcrais. The editor fell into the trap, and published the poems from time to time till she grew famous. He even went so far as to fall in love with the authoress, and to offer her marriage. Voltaire moreover was deceived, and wrote "a stomach-moving tribute" in her honour. Naturally the brother, finding that his poetry had such value, was unwilling that he should be any longer deprived of the glory attaching to it; so he determined to go to Paris and confront the editor who had insulted him with the proofs of his incapability, by explaining who the real Malcrais was. This step was his ruin: the world does not like to be convicted of its foolishness. Voltaire was not the man to enjoy a jibe at his own expense. Maillard's literary career was over. Piron wrote a famous play on this subject, entitled *Métromanie.*

Up at a Villa—Down in the City. As distinguished by an Italian person of quality. (*Men and Women*, 1855; *Lyrics*, 1863; *Dramatic Lyrics*, 1868.) The speaker likes city life: it is expensive, he admits, but one has something for one's money there. The whole day long life is a perfect feast; but up in the villa on the mountain side the life is no better than a beast's. In the city you can watch the gossips and the passers-by; whereas up in the villa there is nothing to see but the oxen dragging the plough. Even in summer it is no better, and it is actually cooler in the city square with the fountain playing. He hates fireflies, bees, and cicalas, about which folks talk so much poetry: what he prefers is the blessed church-bells, the rattle of the diligence, the ever succeeding news, the quack doctor, the fun at the post office, the execution of "liberals," and the gay church procession in the streets on festivals, the drum, the fife, the noise and bustle. Of course it is dear; you cannot have all these luxuries without paying for them, and that is why he is compelled to live a country life; but oh, the pity of it,—the processions, the candles, the flags, the Duke's guard, the drum, the fife!—

"Oh, a day in the city-square, there is no such pleasure in life!"

NOTES.—Stanza ii., "*By Bacchus*": Per Bacco—Italians still swear by the wine-god. Stanza ix., "*with a pink gauze gown all spangles, and seven swords stuck in her heart!*" The "seven sorrows of Our Lady" are referred to here. They are (1) Her grief at the prophecy of Simeon; (2) Her affliction during the flight into Egypt; (3) Her distress at the loss of her Son before finding Him in the Temple; (4) Her sorrow when she met her Son bearing His cross; (5) Her martyrdom at the sight of His agony; (6) The wound to her heart when His was pierced; and (7) Her agony at His burial. The contrast of these sorrows with the pink gown, the spangles, and the smiles, is an exquisite satire on some peculiarities in Continental devotions, very distasteful to English people. Stanza x., "*Tax on salt*": salt is taxed in Italy; the salt monopoly, the lottery, the grist tax and an octroi are the more important items of Italy's immoral system of taxation. "*what oil pays passing the gate*": the *octroi* or town-dues have to be paid on all provisions entering the cities of Italy. *yellow candles:* these are used at funerals, and in penitential processions in the Roman Church.

Valence. (*Colombe's Birthday.*) The advocate of Cleves who marries Colombe.

"Verse-making was the least of my Virtues." (*Ferishtah's Fancies.*) The first line of the ninth lyric.

Villains. Browning's principal villains are the following:—Halbert and Hob; Ned Bratts; Count Guido Franceschini; the devil-like elder man of the *Inn Album*; Paolo and Girolamo in *The Ring and the Book*; Ottima and the Intendant of the Bishop, Uguccio, Stefano and Sebald, in *Pippa Passes* (Bluphocks, in the same poem, is rather a tool of others than a great villain on his own account); Louscha, the mother, in *Ivan Ivanovitch*; Chiappino in *A Soul's Tragedy.*

Vincent Parkes. (*Martin Relph.*) He was Rosamund Page's lover. The girl is accused of being a spy, and unless she can clear herself within a given time is to be shot. Parkes arrives at the place of execution with the proofs of the girl's innocence just as the fatal volley is fired.

Violante Comparini. (*The Ring and the Book.*) The supposed mother of Pompilia. She was the wife of Pietro, and by him had no children; she bought Pompilia of a courtesan, and brought the child up as her own, and was murdered, with her husband and Pompilia, by Count Guido.

Vivisection, or the cutting into living animals for scientific purposes. Mr. Browning was to the last a Vice-President of the Victoria Street Society for the Protection of Animals, and he always expressed the utmost abhorrence of the practices which it opposes. The following letter was written by Mr. Browning on the occasion of the presentation of the memorial to the Royal Society for the Prevention of Cruelty to Animals in 1875:—"19, Warwick Crescent, W., December 28th, 1874.—DEAR MISS COBBE,—I return the petition unsigned, for the one good reason—that I have just signed its fellow forwarded to me by Mrs. Leslie Stephen. You have heard, 'I take an equal interest with yourself in the effort to supress vivisection.' I dare not so honour my mere wishes and prayers as to put them for a moment beside your noble acts; but this I know: I would rather submit to the worst of the deaths, so far as pain goes, than have a single dog or cat tortured on the pretence of sparing me a twinge or two. I return the paper, because I shall be probably shut up here for the next week or more, and prevented from seeing my friends. Whoever would refuse to sign would certainly not be of the number.—Ever truly and gratefully yours, ROBERT BROWNING." —In two of his poems the poet has expressed his emphatic opinion upon Vivisection: in *Tray*, and in *Arcades Ambo.* See my chapter "Browning and Vivisection" in *Browning's Message to his Time.* In the recently published *Life and Letters of Robert Browning*, by Mrs. Sntherland Orr, there are many interesting incidents connected with the great poet's love for animals, which characterised him from infancy till death. Mrs. Orr says (p. 27) this fondness for animals was conspicuous in his earliest days. "His urgent demand for 'something to do' would constantly include 'something to be caught' for him: 'they were to catch him an eft ; 'they were to catch him a frog.'" He would refuse to take his medicine unless bribed by the gift of a speckled frog from among the strawberries: and the maternal parasol, hovering above the strawberry bed during the search for this object of his desires, remained a standing picture in his remembrance. But the love of the uncommon was already asserting itself; and one of his very juvenile projects was a collection of rare creatures, the first contribution to which was a couple of lady-birds, picked up one winter's day on a wall and immediately consigned to a box lined with cotton-wool, and labelled 'Animals found Surviving in the Depths of a Severe Winter.' Nor did curiosity in this case weaken the power of sympathy. His passion for beasts and birds was the counterpart of his father's love of children, only displaying itself before the age at which child-love naturally appears. His mother used to read *Croxall's Fables* to his little sister and him. The story contained in them of a lion who was kicked to death by an ass affected him so painfully that he could no longer endure the sight of the book; and as he dare not destroy it, he buried it between the stuffing and the woodwork of an old dining-room chair, where it stood for lost, at all events for the time being. When first he heard of the adventures of the parrot who insisted on leaving his cage, and who enjoyed himself for a little while and then died of hunger and cold, he—and his sister with him—cried so bitterly that it was found necessary to invent a different ending, according to which the parrot was rescued just in time and brought back to his cage to live peacefully in it ever after. As a boy he kept owls and monkeys, magpies and hedgehogs, an eagle, and even a couple of large snakes; constantly bringing home the more portable creatures in his pockets, and transferring them to his mother for immediate care. I have heard him speak admiringly of the skilful tenderness with which she took into her lap a lacerated cat, washed and sewed up its ghastly wound, and nursed it back to health. The great intimacy with the life and habits of animals which reveals itself in his works is readily explained by these facts."

Wall, A. The prologue to *Pacchiarotto* (*q.v.*) bears this title in the *Selections*, Series the Second (published in 1880).

Wanting is—what? (Prologue to *Jocoseria*, 1883.) In every phase of human life, and in every human action, there is imperfection—always something still to come. In the characters depicted and the incidents narrated in the volume called *Jocoseria* the poet asks us to say what is wanting to perfect them. His question "Wanting is—what?" governs the whole volume. In *Solomon and Balkis* what was wanting was not mere wisdom, but a sanctified nature. In *Christina and Monaldeschi* the woman was wanting in forgiveness. Here the love was not perfect. In *Mary Wollstonecraft and Fuseli* what was wanting was self-sacrifice. Had Mary really loved Fuseli, she would not have attempted to ruin his life by endeavouring to win him from his wife. In *Adam, Lilith, and Eve*, there was wanting, says Mr. Sharpe, "the union of perfect love with perfect holiness." In *Ixion* was wanting a just conception of the Fatherhood of God. God is not the tyrannical Master of the world, but the Loving All-Father. In *Jochanan Hakkadosh*, Mr. Sharpe says, in answer to the question, "Wanting is—what?" "One who shall combine perfect wisdom with the full experience of life, and the completeness of these intuitions of the Spirit." "Is not this the Christ?" In *Never the Time and the Place*, to completely develop our souls we need perfect conditions of existence. We shall not find them till we reach heaven. In *Pambo* the saint recognised that he could not perfectly fulfil the smallest of God's commandments, nor can we perfectly keep God's law. Wanting is the Atonement.

NOTE.—"*Come, then, complete incompletion, O Comer, Pant through the blueness*,"—*i.e.* descend from heaven. The Rev. J. Sharpe, M.A., thus explains the title "*O Comer*": "ὁ ἐρχόμενος, in the New Testament, is one of the titles of the Messiah—the Future One, He who shall come (Matt. xi. 3, xxi. 9; Luke vii. 19, 20; John xii. 13; also John vi. 14, xi. 27). So in the periphrase of the name Jehovah, ὁ ὢν καὶ ὁ ἦν καὶ ὁ ἐρχόμενος (Rev. i. 4, 8; iv. 8).—Robinson's *Greek Lexicon of the New Testament.* The title hints at the connection between this preface and the stories from the Talmud which follow. The Incarnation, the union of God and man, of Creator and creation, supplies the solution of the problem raised by the incompleteness and death all around us. The beauty is no longer without meaning, for it is a revelation of God; the huge mass of death is no longer revolting, for 'all things were created by Him, and for Him . . . and by Him all things consist,' and He will 'reunite all things . . .

whether they be things on earth or things in heaven.'" In the character of *Donald*, what was wanting was the development of "the latent moral faculty." He did not recognise the rights of the stag, which the commonest principles of justice, to say nothing of gratitude, should have made obvious to the sportsman.

Waring. Waring was the name given by the poet to his friend Mr. Alfred Domett, C.M.G., son of Mr. Nathaniel Domett, born at Camberwell, May 20th, 1811. He matriculated at Cambridge in 1829, as a member of St. John's College. In 1832 he published a volume of poems. He then travelled in America for two years, and after his return to London, about 1836-7, he contributed some verses to *Blackwood's Magazine*. Mr. Domett afterwards spent two years in Italy, Switzerland, and other continental countries. He was called to the bar in 1841. Having purchased some land of the New Zealand Company, he went as a settler to New Zealand in 1842. In 1851 he became Secretary for the whole of that country. He accepted posts as Commissioner of Crown Lands and Resident Magistrate at Hawke's Bay. Subsequently he was elected to represent the town of Nelson in the House of Representatives. In 1862 Mr. Domett was called upon to form a Government, which he did. Having held various important offices in the Legislature, and rendered great services to the country, he was created a Companion of the Order of St. Michael and St. George (1880) He returned to England and published several volumes of poems. His chief work is *Ranolf and Amohia*, full of descriptions of New Zealand scenery, and paying a warm tribute to Mr. Browning, whom he calls

"Subtlest assertor of the soul in song."

Mr. Domett suddenly disappeared from London life in the manner described in the poem. He shook off, by an overpowering impulse, the restraints of conventional life, and without a word to his dearest friends, vanished into the unknown. As the story is told in the poem, we see a man with large ideas, ambitious, full of great thoughts, inspired by a passion for great things, a man born to rule, and fretting against the restraints of the petty conventionalities of civilised life. Those about him cannot understand, and if they did could in no wise help him; he chafes and longs to break his bonds and live the freer life in which his energies can expand. The poem tells of the cold and unsympathetic criticism he received amongst his friends; and now that he has disappeared, the poet's spirit yearns for his society once more. He wonders where he has pitched his tent, and in fancy runs through the world to seek him. He has been heard of in a ghostly sort of way. A vision of him has been narrated by one who for a few moments caught sight of him and lost him again in the setting sun. The poet reflects that the stars which set here, rise in some distant heaven. The following obituary notice of Alfred Domett, by Dr. Furnivall, appeared in the *Pall Mall Gazette* of November 9th, 1887. It has had the advantage of being revised and corrected in a few small details by Mr. F. Young, "Waring's" cousin. See also an article in *Temple Bar*, Feb., 1896, p. 253, entitled "A Queen's Messenger."

"What's Become of Waring?"—IN MEMORIAM. (By a Member of the Browning Society.) "What's become of Waring?" is the first line of one of Mr. Browning's poems of 1842 (*Bells and Pomegranates*, Part II.), which, from its dealing with his life in London in early manhood, is a great favourite with his readers. Alas! the handsome and brilliant hero of the Browning set in the thirties died last Wednesday, at the house in St. Charles's Square, North Kensington, where he had for many years lived near his artist son. Alfred Domett was the son of one of Nelson's middies, a gallant seaman. He was called to the bar, and lived in the Temple with his friend 'Joe Arnold,' a man of great ability, afterwards Sir Joseph, Chief Justice of Bombay, who ultimately settled at Naples, where he died. Having an independency, Alfred Domett lingered in London society for a time,—one of the handsomest and most attractive men there,—till he was induced to emigrate to New Zealand, to join his cousin, William Young, the son of the London shipowner, George Frederick Young, who had bought a large tract of land in the islands. Alfred Domett landed to find his cousin drowned. He was himself soon after appointed to a magistracy with £700 a year. He had a successful career in New Zealand,—where Mr. Browning alludes to him in *The Guardian Angel*—became Premier, married a handsome English lady, and then returned to England. He first lived at Phillimore Place or Terrace, Kensington, and while there saw a good deal of his old friend Mr. Browning; but after he moved to St.

Charles's Square, the former companions seldom met. On the foundation of the Browning Society, Alfred Domett declined any post of honour, but became an interested member of the body. His grand white head was to be seen at all the Society's performances and at several of its meetings. He naturally preferred Mr. Browning's early works to the later ones. He could not be persuaded to write any account of his early London days, but said he would try to find the letters in which his friend 'Joe Arnold' reported to him in New Zealand the doings of their London set. Mr. Domett produced with pride his sea-stained copy of Browning's *Bells and Pomegranates*, now worth twenty or thirty times its original price. Before he left England, his poem on Venice was printed in *Blackwood*, and very highly praised by Christopher North. (The reprint is in the British Museum.) His longer and chief poem, *Ranolf and Amohia* (1872), full of New Zealand scenery, and paying a warm tribute to Mr. Browning, was reprinted by him in two volumes, revised and enlarged, some four or five years ago. A lucky accident to a leg, which permanently lamed him, soon after his arrival in New Zealand, saved his life; for it prevented his accepting the invitation of some treacherous native chiefs to a banquet at which all the English guests were killed. A sterling, manly, independent nature was Alfred Domett's. He impressed every one with whom he came in contact, and is deeply regretted by his remaining friends. We hope that Mr. Browning will in his next volume give a few lines to the memory of his early friend. Not many of the old set remain, possibly not one save the poet himself; and all his readers will rejoice to hear again of Waring, "Alfred, dear friend." The *Guardian Angel* question—

> "Where are you, dear old friend?"

needs other answer now than that of 1855—

> "How rolls the Wairoa at your world's far end?
> This is Ancona, yonder is the sea."

NOTES.—Canto iv., "*Monstr'—inform'—ingens—horren-dous*": from Vergil's *Æn.* iii. 657—"Monstrum horrendum, informe, ingens, cui lumen ademtum": a horrid monster, misshapen, huge, from whom sight had been taken away. vi., *Vishnu-land:* India, where Vishnu is worshipped; the second person of the modern Hindu Trinity. He is regarded as a member of the

Triad whose special function is to preserve. To do this he has nine times in succession become incarnate, and will do so once more. *Avatar:* the incarnation of a deity. The ten incarnations of Vishnu are—1. Matsya-Avatar, as a fish; 2. Kurm-Avatar, as a tortoise; 3. Varaha, as a boar; 4. Nara-Sing, as a man-lion, last animal stage; 5. Vamuna, as a dwarf, first step toward the human form; 6. Parasu-Rama, as a hero, but yet an imperfect man; 7. Rama-Chandra, as the hero of Ramayána, physically a perfect man, his next of kin, friend and ally Hamouma, the monkey-god, the monkey endowed with speech; 8. Christna-Avatar, the son of the virgin Devanaguy, one formed by God; 9. Gautama-Buddha, Siddhârtha, or Sakya-muni; 10. This avatar has not yet occurred. It is expected in the future; when Vishnu appears for the last time he will come as a "saviour." (Blavatzky, *Isis Unveiled*, vol. ii., p 274.) *Kremlin*, the citadel of Moscow, Russia. *serpentine:* a rock, often of a dull green colour, mantled and mottled with red and purple. *syenite:* a stone named from Syene, in Egypt, where it was first found. "*Dian's fame*": Diana was worshipped by the inhabitants of Taurica Chersonesus. *Taurica Chersonesus* is now the country called the Crimea. *Hellenic speech* = Greek. *Scythian strands:* Taurica is joined by an isthmus to Scythia, and is bounded by the Bosphorus, the Euxine Sea, and the Palus Mæotis. *Caldara Polidore da Caravaggio* (1495-1543): he was a celebrated painter of frieze, etc., at the Vatican. Raphael discovered his talents when he was a mere mortar carrier to the other artists. The "Andromeda" picture, of which Browning speaks in *Pauline*, was an engraving from a work of this artist. "*The heart of Hamlet's Mystery*": few characters in literature have been more discussed than that of Hamlet. Schlegel thought he exhausted the power of action by calculating consideration. Goethe thought he possessed a noble nature without the strength of nerve which forms a hero. Many say he was mad, others that he was the founder of the pessimistic school. *Junius:* the mystery of the authorship of the famous letters of Junius is referred to. *Chatterton, Thomas* (1752-70): the boy poet who deceived the credulous scholars of his day by pretending that he had discovered some ancient poems in the parish chest of Redcliffe Church, Bristol. *Rowley, Thomas:* the hypothetical priest of Bristol, said by Chatterton to have lived in the reigns of Henry VI. and Edward IV., and to have written the poems of which Chatterton himself was the author. ii. 2, *Triest:* the principal seaport of the Austro-Hungarian empire, situated very picturesquely at the north-east angle of the Adriatic Sea, in the Gulf of Trieste. *lateen sail:* a triangular sail commonly used in the Mediterranean. "*'long-shore thieves*": "along-shore men" are the low fellows who hang about quays and docks, generally of bad character.

'When I vexed you and you chid me." (*Ferishtah's Fancies.*) The first line of the seventh lyric.

Which? (*Asolando*, 1889.) Three court ladies make

> "Trial of all who judged best
> In esteeming the love of a man."

An abbé sits to decide the wager and say who was to be considered the best Cupid catcher. First, the Duchesse maintains that it is the man who holds none above his lady-love save his God and his king. The Marquise does not care for saint and loyalist, so much as a man of pure thoughts and fine deeds who can play the paladin. The Comtesse chooses any wretch, any poor outcast, who would look to her as his sole saviour, and stretch his arms to her as love's ultimate goal. The abbé had to reflect awhile. He took a pinch of snuff to clear his brain, and then, after deliberation, said—

> "The love which to one, and one only, has reference,
> Seems terribly like what perhaps gains God's preference."

White Witchcraft. (*Asolando*, 1889.) Magic is defined to be of two kinds—Divine and evil. Divine is white magic; black magic is of the devil. Amongst the ancients magic was considered a Divine science, which led to a participation in the attributes of Divinity itself. Philo-Judæus, *De Specialibus Legibus*, says: "It unveils the operations of Nature, and leads to the contemplation of celestial powers." When magic became degraded into sorcery it was naturally abhorred by all the world, and the evil reputation attaching to the word, even at the present day, must be attributed to the fact that white witchcraft had a singular affinity for the black arts. Perhaps what is now termed "science" expresses all that was originally intended by the term white magic. The men of science of the past were not unacquainted with black arts, according to their enemies. Hence Pietro d'Abano, John of Halberstadt, Cornelius Agrippa, and other learned men of the middle ages, incurred the hatred of the clergy. Paracelsus is made expressly by Browning to abjure "black arts" in his struggles for knowledge. Burton, in his *Anatomy of Melancholy*, speaks of white witches. He says (Part II., sec. i.): "Sorcerers are too common: cunning men, wizards, and white-witches, as they call them, in every village, which, if they be sought to, will help almost all infirmities of body and mind—*servatores*, in Latin; and they have commonly St. Catherine's wheel printed in the roof of their mouth, or in some part about them."

[THE POEM.] One says if he could play Jupiter for once, and had the power to turn his friend into an animal, he would decree that she should become a fox. The lady, if invested with the same power, would turn him into a toad. He bids Canidia say her worst about him when reduced to this condition. The Canidia referred to is the sorceress of Naples in *Horace*, who could bring the moon from heaven. The witch boasts of her power in this respect:—

> "Meæque terra cedit insolentiæ.
> (Ut ipse nosti curiosus) et Polo
> An quæ movere cereas imagines,
> Diripere Lunam."
>
> (HORAT., *Canid. Epod.*, xvii. 75, etc.)

Hudibras mentions this (Part II., 3);—

> "Your ancient conjurors were wont
> To make her (the moon) from her sphere dismount,
> And to their incantations stoop."

The *Zoophilist* for July 1891 gives the following, from Mrs. Orr's *Life of Browning*, as the origin of the reference to the toad in the poem: "About the year 1835, when Mr. Browning's parents removed to Hatcham, the young poet found a humble friend 'in the form of a toad, which became so much attached to him that it would follow him as he walked. He visited it daily, where it burrowed under a white rose tree, announcing himself by a pinch of gravel dropped into its hole; and the creature would crawl forth, allow its head to be gently tickled, and reward the act with that loving glance of the soft, full eyes which

Mr. Browning has recalled in one of the poems of *Asolando*." The lines are:—

> "He's loathsome, I allow;
> There may or may not lurk a pearl beneath his puckered brow;
> But see his eyes that follow mine—love lasts there, anyhow."

"Why from the World." The first words of the twelfth lyric in *Ferishtah's Fancies.*

Why I am a Liberal was a poem written for Cassell & Co. in 1885, who published a volume of replies by English men of letters, etc., to the question, "Why I am a Liberal?"

"Why I am a Liberal.

> "'Why?' Because all I haply can and do,
> All that I am now, all I hope to be,—
> Whence comes it save from future setting free
> Body and soul the purpose to pursue
> God traced for both? If fetters, not a few,
> Of prejudice, convention, fall from me,
> These shall I bid men—each in his degree,
> Also God-guided—bear, and gayly, too?
> But little do or can, the best of us:
> That little is achieved through Liberty.
> Who, then, dares hold, emancipated thus,
> His fellow shall continue bound? Not I,
> Who live, love, labour freely, nor discuss
> A brother's right to freedom. That is 'Why.'"

Will, The. (*Sordello.*) Mr. Browning uses the term "will" to express Sordello's effort to "realise all his aspirations in his inner consciousness, in his imagination, in his feeling that he is potentially all these things." See Professor Alexander's *Analysis of "Sordello,"* lvii., p. 406 (*Browning Society's Papers*); "The Body, the machine for acting Will" (*Sordello*, Book II., line 1014, and p. 477 of this work). Mr. Browning's early opinions were so largely formed by his occult and theosophical studies that it is necessary for the full understanding of his theory of the will and its power, to study the following axioms from the work of an occult writer, Eliphas Levi, as a good summary of the teaching so largely imbibed by the poet.

"THEORY OF WILL-POWER.

"*Axiom* 1. Nothing can resist the will of man when he knows what is true and wills what is good. *Axiom* 2. To will evil is to will death. A perverse will is the beginning of suicide. *Axiom* 3. To will what is good with violence is to will evil, for violence produces disorder and disorder produces evil. *Axiom* 4. We can and should accept evil as the means to good; but we must never practise it, otherwise we should demolish with one hand what we erect with the other. A good intention never justifies bad means; when it submits to them it corrects them, and condemns them while it makes use of them. *Axiom* 5. To earn the right to possess permanently we must will long and patiently. *Axiom* 6. To pass one's life in willing what it is impossible to retain for ever is to abdicate life and accept the eternity of death. *Axiom* 7. The more numerous the obstacles which are surmounted by the will, the stronger the will becomes. It is for this reason that Christ has exalted poverty and suffering. *Axiom* 8. When the will is devoted to what is absurd it is reprimanded by eternal reason. *Axiom* 9. The will of the just man is the will of God Himself, and it is the law of nature. *Axiom* 10. The understanding perceives through the medium of the will. If the will be healthy, the sight is accurate. God said, 'Let there be light!' and the light was. The will says: 'Let the world be such as I wish to behold it!' and the intelligence perceives it as the will has determined. This is the meaning of Amen, which confirms the acts of faith. *Axiom* 11. When we produce phantoms we give birth to vampires, and must nourish these children of nightmare with our own blood and life, with our own intelligence and reason, and still we shall never satiate them. *Axiom* 12. To affirm and will what ought to be is to create; to affirm and will what should not be is to destroy. *Axiom* 13. Light is an electric fire, which is placed by man at the disposition of the will; it illuminates those who know how to make use of it, and burns those who abuse it. *Axiom* 14. The empire of the world is the empire of light. *Axiom* 15. Great minds with wills badly equilibrated are like comets, which are abortive suns. *Axiom* 16. To do nothing is as fatal as to commit evil, and it is more cowardly. Sloth is the most unpardonable of the deadly sins. *Axiom* 17. To suffer is to labour.

A great misfortune properly endured is a progress accomplished. Those who suffer much live more truly than those who undergo no trials. *Axiom* 18. The voluntary death of self-devotion is not a suicide,—it is the apotheosis of free-will. *Axiom* 19. Fear is only indolence of will; and for this reason public opinion brands the coward. *Axiom* 20. An iron chain is less difficult to burst than a chain of flowers. *Axiom* 21. Succeed in not fearing the lion, and the lion will be afraid of you. Say to suffering, 'I will that thou shalt become a pleasure,' and it will prove such, and more even than a pleasure, for it will be a blessing. *Axiom* 22. Before deciding that a man is happy or otherwise seek to ascertain the bent of his will. Tiberius died daily at Caprea, while Jesus proved His immortality, and even His divinity, upon Calvary and the Cross."

"Wish no word unspoken." (*Ferishtah's Fancies.*) The first words of the lyric to the second poem.

Woman's Last Word, A. (*Men and Women*, 1855; *Lyrics*, 1863; *Dramatic Lyrics*, 1868.) In the presence of perfect love words are often superfluous, wild, and hurtful; words lead to debate, debate to contention, striving, weeping. Even truth becomes falseness; for if the heart is consecrated by a pure affection, love is the only truth; and the chill of logic and the precision of a definition can be no other than harmful; therefore hush the talking, pry not after the apples of the knowledge of good and evil, or Eden will surely be in peril. The only knowledge is the charm of love's protecting embrace, the only language is the speech of love, the only thought to think the loved one's thought—the absolute sacrifice of the whole self on the altar of love; but before the altar can be approached sorrow must be buried, a little weeping has to be done; the morrow shall see the offering presented,—"the might of love" will drown alike both hopes and fears.

Women and Roses. (*Men and Women*, 1855; *Lyrics*, 1863; *Dramatic Lyrics*, 1868.) The singer dreams of a red rose tree with three roses on its branches; one is a faded rose whose petals are about to fall,—the bees do not notice it as they pass; the second is a rose in its perfection, its cup "ruby-rimmed," its heart "nectar-brimmed,"—the bee revels in its nectar; the third is a baby rosebud. And in these flowers the poet sees types of the women of the ages,—the past, the present, and the future: the shadows of the noble and beautiful, or wicked women in history and poetry dance round the dead rose; round the perfect rose of the present dance the spirits of the women of to-day; round the bud troop the little feet of maidens yet unborn; and all dance to one cadence round the dreamer's tree. The dance will go on as before when the dreamer has departed, roses will bloom then for other beholders, and other dreamers will see and remember their loveliness; the creations of the poet even must join the dance. As the love of the past, so the love to come, must link hands and trip to the measure.

Women of Browning. The best are Pompilia, in *The Ring and the Book*, the lady in the *Inn Album*, and the heroine in *Colombe's Birthday*; the others, good and bad, are the wife in *Any Wife to any Husband*; James Lee's Wife, Michal, Pippa, Mildred, Gwendolen, Polixena, Colombe, Anael, Domizia, "The Queen," Constance; and the heroines of *The Laboratory*, *The Confessional*, *A Woman's Last Word*, *In a Year*, *A Light Woman*, and *A Forgiveness*.

Works of Robert Browning. The new and uniform edition of the works of Robert Browning is published in sixteen volumes, small crown 8vo. This edition contains three portraits of Mr. Browning, at different periods of life, and a few illustrations. Contents of the volumes:—

Vol. 1. *Pauline* and *Sordello*.
„ 2. *Paracelsus* and *Strafford*.
„ 3. *Pippa Passes*, *King Victor and King Charles*, *The Return of the Druses*, and *A Soul's Tragedy*; with a portrait of Mr. Browning.
„ 4. *A Blot in the 'Scutcheon*, *Colombe's Birthday*, and *Men and Women*.
„ 5. *Dramatic Romances*, and *Christmas Eve and Easter Day*.
„ 6. *Dramatic Lyrics*, and *Luria*.
„ 7. *In a Balcony*, and *Dramatis Personae*; with a portrait of Mr. Browning.
„ 8. *The Ring and the Book*: books i. to iv.; with two illustrations.
„ 9. *The Ring and the Book*: books v. to viii.
„ 10. *The Ring and the Book*: books ix. to xii.; with a portrait of Guido Franceschini.
„ 11. *Balaustion's Adventure*, *Prince Hohenstiel-Schwangau*, Saviour of Society, and *Fifine at the Fair*.

Vol. 12. *Red Cotton Nightcap Country*, and *The Inn Album.*
„ 13. *Aristophanes' Apology*, including a Transcript from Euripides, being the Last Adventure of Balaustion, and *The Agamemnon of Æschylus.*
„ 14. *Pacchiarotto*, and How he worked in Distemper; with other Poems; *La Saisiaz* and *The Two Poets of Croisic.*
„ 15. *Dramatic Idyls*, first series; *Dramatic Idyls*, second series, and *Jocoseria.*
„ 16. *Ferishtah's Fancies*, and *Parleyings with certain People of Importance in their Day*, with a portrait of Mr. Browning.

Also Mr. Browning's last volume, *Asolando, Fancies and Facts.*

Worst of it, The. (*Dramatis Personæ*, 1864.) A fleck on a swan is beauty spoiled; a speck on a mottled hide is nought. A man had angel fellowship with a young wife who proved false to him; he loves her still, and mourns that she ruined her soul in stooping to save his; he made her sin by fettering with a gold ring a soul which could not blend with his. He sorrows, not for his own loss, but that his swan must take the crow's rebuff. He desires her good, and hopes she may work out her penance, and reach heaven's purity at last. He will love on, but if they meet in Paradise, will pass nor turn his face.

Xanthus. (*A Death in the Desert.*) One of the disciples of St. John in attendance upon the dying apostle in the cave.

"You groped your way across my room." (*Ferishtah's Fancies.*) The first line of the third lyric.

"You'll love me yet." (*Pippa Passes.*) A song.

Youth and Art. (*Dramatis Personæ*, 1864.) A meditation on what might have been, had two young people who had the chance not missed it and lost it for ever. They lodged in the same street in Rome. The man was a sculptor who had dreams of demolishing Gibson some day, and putting up Smith to reign in his stead; the woman was a singer who hoped to trill bitterness into the cup of Grisi, and make her envious of Kate Brown. The warbler earned in those days as little by her voice as the chiseller by his work. They were poor, lived on a crust apiece, and for fun watched each other from their respective windows. She was evidently dying for an introduction to him; she fidgeted about with the window plants, and did her best to attract his attention in a quiet sort of way; she did not like his models always tripping up his stairs, which she could not ascend, and was glad to have the opportunity of showing off the foreign fellow who came to tune the piano. But life passed, he made no advances, and so in process of time she married a rich old lord, and he is a knight, R.A., and dines with the Prince. With all this show of success neither life is complete, neither soul has achieved the sole good of its earth wanderings. Their lives hang patchy and scrappy; they have not sighed, starved, feasted, despaired, and been happy. There was once the chance of these things; they were missed, and eternity cannot make good the loss. As for life "*Love*," as Browning is always telling us, "*is the sole good of it.*" This poem may be compared with the moral of *The Statue and the Bust.* In the one case reasons of prudence and the restrictions of religion and society prevented the duke and the lady from following the inclinations of their hearts; in the other case mere worldly motives operated to the same end—the missing of the union of the actors' souls. In both cases the lives were spoiled. In *Youth and Art* the woman's character cuts a very poor figure: love is subordinated to her art, and that to the mere worldly advantage of a rich marriage and the opportunity of becoming "queen at bals-parés." The man was cold, not because his art made him so, but because of his overwhelming prudence, which we may be sure did not make him a Gibson after all.

NOTE.—Verse ii., *Gibson, John* (1790-1866), the sculptor, best known to fame by his "Tinted Venus." He died at Rome. Verse iii., *Grisi, Giulietta* (born in Milan, 1812), one of the most distinguished singers of our time. She came to London in 1834, and at once took a leading position in the operatic world. Verse xv., *bals-parés* = dress-balls.

APPENDIX.

Charles Avison, Parleyings with. (Parleyings with Certain People of Importance in their Day; 1877, No. VII.)

[THE MAN.] Charles Avison was born at Newcastle-upon-Tyne in 1710, and died in 1770. He was organi t of St. Nicholas Church, Newcastle. Mr. Barnett Smith says that "very little is known of his life, but he had the reputation of being a man of great culture and polish, and for many years was the chief of a small circle of musical amateurs in the North of England who were devoted to his views."

He was the composer of the once popular air, "Sound the Loud Timbrel," and the "bold-stepping C major March."

His "Essay on Musical Expression," published in 1752, was highly esteemed in his day. His musical education was acquired in Italy, and he was the pupil of Geminiani on his return to England. He preferred French and Italian music to the German, and gave a higher position to Geminiani than to Handel.

[THE POEM.] This is one of the poet's great music poems; its subject is the *Grand March* by Avison, a manuscript copy of which belonged to Browning's father. The poet's aim is to prove that music interprets the soul as neither painting nor poetry can do. Painting is but reproduction, poetry can only tell what has taken place, but

> There is no truer truth obtainable
> By Man than comes of music.

Miss Helen Ormerod in her paper read at the Browning Society (27th May, 1887) on *Browning's Poems referring to Music*, says that "*Charles Avison* is speculative, almost analytical, of the Earth Earthy; while in *Abt Vogler* we gain admission to the Holiest of Holies. In *Charles Avison* we have the reasonings of an outsider, in *Abt Vogler* the white-heat enthusiasm of one of those favoured few 'whom God whispers in the ear.'"

NOTES.—(4) "*Great John Relfe*": a learned contrapuntist who was Browning's music-master. *Tonic:* the key note. *Dominant;* the fifth tone of the scale. *Pepusch:* a German organist at the Charter House. Died 1752. *Alexis:* one of six cantatas by Pepusch.

Great favourites in their day. (5) *Suite:* one of the old musical forms, consisting of a string or series of pieces all in the same key. *Fugue:* see my notes to "*Master Hugues of Saxe-Gotha*" (p. 267). (8) "*Radaminta*" and "*Rinaldo*," operas by Handel. (9) *C Major:* see notes to "*Abt Vogler*" (p. 7). (15) "*Little-Ease*": a form of punishment, as the stocks. "*Tyburn*": the historic place of execution in London. "*Larges and Longs and Breves*": "the long-drawn notes which were used in the early days of music" (Ormerod).

Epistle of Karshish. Dr. R. Garnett published the following note on this poem in the *Academy* of 10th October, 1896:—

"BRITISH MUSEUM,
"16*th Sept.*, 1896.

"Browning, in his 'Epistle of Karshish,' commits an oversight, as it seems to me, in making Lazarus fifty years of age at the eve of the siege of Jerusalem, *circa* 68 A.D. The miracle of which he was the subject is supposed to have been wrought about 33 A.D. He would consequently have been only about fifteen at the time, which is quite inconsistent with the general tenor of the narrative. According to tradition, Lazarus was thirty at the time, and lived thirty years longer, not surviving, therefore, to the date intimated in Browning's poem.

'A black lynx snarled and pricked a tufted ear.'

If I do not mistake, there is no such thing as a black lynx, except as a *lusus naturae*. It is easy to see how the generally accurate Browning fell into this error. The Syrian lynx, which he is describing, has black tufted ears—the whole outer surface of the ear is black—and the Turkish name by which it is commonly known, *cara-cal*, means 'black ear.' Browning, intent on the creature's special characteristic, has extended the blackness from the ear to the entire body."

Pietro of Abano. Verse 10.

"ALPHABET ON A MAN'S EYES.

"In Alonzo Lee, of Atlanta, Galveston, the Americans have found a singular phenomenon, nothing less than the alphabet marked quite plainly on the edge of the iris of each of his eyes similar to the figures on a watch. This wonder is said to have been caused by his mother, who was an illiterate woman, desiring to educate herself. In each eye the entire alphabet is plainly marked in capital letters, not, however in regular order. The 'W' is in the lower part of the iris and 'X' at the top. They appear to be made of white fibre wove cord, being connected at the top by another cord seemingly linked to the upper extremity of each letter. The eye itself is blue, with white lines radiating from the centre almost to the letters themselves: these letters do not slope exactly in the direction that the radials extend from the centre. Beginning at the bottom with 'W' and following the letters like the hands of a watch they can be more readily distinguished. So too, the irregularity is a striking feature, showing how the mother learned her letters in broken patches, as a child learns when beginning to read. Lee, who has been three times divorced, has a son whose eyes are similar to his father's."

Echo, 23rd March, 1896.

The Ring and the Book. Book I., l. 902. "*Caritellas*," evidently for "carretellas." "A kind of drosky with a single pony harnessed to the near side of the pole." See *The Romance of Isabel Lady Burton*, vol. ii., p. 538.

Book I. "*O Lyric Love*," etc. The following letter was sent to me as likely to be interesting on account of Mr. Browning's own explanation of his terms *Whiteness* and *Wanness*. My correspondent says: "I happen to have an original letter from R. Browning in which he says, 'The greater and lesser lights indicate the greater and less proximity of the person,'" etc. Wanness should be taken as meaning simply less bright than absolute whiteness, as Keats speaks of "wannish fire," etc.

Book VIII., l. 329. The torture referred to by De Archangelis as the *Vigiliarum*, is evidently identical with that called the "Vigilia" and which is described in Hare's *Walks in Rome*. "Upon a high joint-stool, the seat about a span large, and, instead of being flat, cut in the form of pointed diamonds, the victim was seated; the legs were fastened together and without support; the hands bound behind the back, and with a running knot attached to a cord descending from the ceiling; the body was loosley attached to the back of the chair, cut also into angular points. A wretch stood near pushing the victim from side to side; and now and then, by pulling the rope from the ceiling, gave the arms most painful jerks. In this horrible position the sufferer remained forty hours, the assistants being changed every fifth hour.

Book IX., l. 1109. "*The sole joke of Thucydides.*" Mr. F. C. Snow, writing from Oxford to the *Daily News*, says: "Browning was misled by a scholiast. The ancient critics said, 'Here the lion laughs,' with reference to the passage of Thucydides where the story of Cylon is told (I. 126, see also the Scholia). But they did not mean that the passage contained any joke, only that the narrative style was unusually genial. There are other passages of Thucydides where his grim humour comes much nearer to the modern idea of pleasantry."

"The lion, lo, hath laughed!" in the context, proves the correctness of Mr. Snow's explanation.

Sordello. Book III., l. 975. In the *Athenæum*, 12th December, 1896, Mr. Alfred Forman published a letter on this passage which is an important contribution to our commentary on *Sordello*.

"In a review of Dr. Berdoe's *Browning Cyclopædia*, I have seen it asked: 'In what form did Empedocles put up with Ætna for a stimulant?' In what form indeed! But I think a more pertinent question would have been: How can either Empedocles or, as is usually alleged, Landor have anything to do with the passage referred to? To me it has always appeared to be Æschylus whom Browning (vol. i., pp. 169-70, of the seventeen-volume edition, 1888-94, Smith, Elder & Co.) addresses as

'Yours, my patron-friend,
Whose great verse blares unintermittent on
Like your own trumpeter at Marathon,—
You who, Platæa and Salamis being scant,
Put up with Ætna for a stimulant.

I need not recall the legend of the Greek tragedian having fought at Marathon as well as at Salamis and Platæa (the 'stimulants' to his 'Persæ'), but his ancient biographer further says: 'Having arrived in Sicily, as Hiero was then engaged in founding the city of Ætna, he exhibited his "Women of Ætna" by way of predicting a prosperous life to those who contributed to colonise the city.' After a perusal of pp. 52-53, we may imagine that Æschylus was one of Browning's audience ('few living, many dead'), and not unlikely, as coming from the realm where Browning says he had 'many lovers' (p. 53), to be designated a 'patron-friend,' while the 'great verse' that 'blares unintermittent on,' etc., is surely identical (pp. 53-4) with

'The thunder-phrase of the Athenian, grown
Up out of memories of Marathon.

"I have not been able to discover any substantiating facts in the life, or passages in the works, of Landor; but possibly some correspondent of yours may be able to lay me under an obligation by pointing such out. A simple statement to the effect that 'Browning said so' could not, I think, in such a case as the one in question, be deemed satisfactory. Dr. Garnett writes to me on the matter as follows:—

"'Could the poet alluded to in *Sordello* possibly be R. H. Horne? Horne was, I think, an intimate friend of Browning's; he was more Æschylean than any other contemporary; he had served as soldier and sailor in the Mexican War; and, having given up arms for letters, might be said to have forsaken Marathon and Salamis for Ætna, although the introduction of Ætna would be quite incomprehensible but for the historical fact of Æschylus's secession thither. I do not feel convinced that the identification of Horne with Browning's "patron-friend" is the correct interpretation, but it seems to me to deserve attention.'

"While on the subject of *Sordello*, may I ask how (as I have seen it assumed in 'Browning' books) the 'child barefoot and rosy' of p. 288 can be Sordello himself? In the first place, are not the words he is singing taken from Sordello's own 'Goito lay' (cf. pp. 97, 249, 289), with which he vanquished Eglamor, long after he had ceased to be, if he ever was, a rosy and barefoot child? And, in the second place, is there any indication in the whole poem that Sordello was ever 'by sparkling Asolo,' where the aforesaid child is described as being?

"ALFRED FORMAN."

Book VI., l. 614:—

"*The old fable of the two eagles.*" They—

"Went two ways
About the world: where, in the midst, they met,
Though on a shifting waste of sand, men set
Jove's temple."

The story is referred to in Pindar's "Fourth Pythian Ode," where he speaks of "Jove's golden eagles." These were placed near the Delphic tripod, and probably gave rise to the story of the two birds sent by Jupiter, one from the east and the other from the west, and which met at Pytho or Delphi. Mr. Browning seems to be in error here. Delphi was not "on a shifting waste of sand," but on a mountain; and the temple was not that of Jove, but of Apollo. The poet appears to have sent the eagles to the oasis of Ammon, which was in the middle of a sandy desert and had a most famous oracle of Zeus.

755909

Printed in Great Britain by
Amazon.co.uk, Ltd.,
Marston Gate.